The Keys
to Power

Managing the Presidency

Shirley Anne Warshaw
Department of Political Science
Gettysburg College

LONGMAN

An imprint of Addison Wesley Longman, Inc.

New York • Reading, Massachusetts • Menlo Park, California • Harlow, England
Don Mills, Ontario • Sydney • Mexico City • Madrid • Amsterdam

Editor-in-Chief: Priscilla McGeehon
Acquisitions Editor: Eric Stano
Development Director: Lisa Pinto
Marketing Manager: Megan Galvin-Fak
Full Service Production Manager: Joseph Vella
Project Coordination, Text Design, and Electronic Page Makeup: York Production Services
Cover Design Manager: Nancy Danahy
Cover Designer: Ken Fredette
Cover Photo: © PhotoDisc, Inc.
Senior Print Buyer: Hugh Crawford
Printer and Binder: The Maple-Vail Book Manufacturing Group
Cover Printer: Coral Graphic Services, Inc.

Library of Congress Cataloging-in-Publication Data
  Warshaw, Shirley Anne, 1950-
      The keys to power : managing the presidency / by Shirley Anne Warshaw.
          p. cm.
      Includes bibliographical references and index.
      ISBN 0-321-07037-2
          1. Presidents—United States. 2. Presidents—United States—Decision making. 3.
  Political planning—United States. I. Title.

JK516. W374 1999
352.23'0973—dc21

                                                                            99-046656

Please visit our website at http://www.awlonline.com

ISBN 0-321-07037-2

12345678910—MA—02010099

Contents

Preface

The concept for *The Keys to Power: Managing the Presidency* emerged from several students who wanted to know why we skipped around during class from one textbook to another. My course on presidential decision-making utilized a number of different textbooks, in addition to the standard literature on the presidency, in order to ensure that we covered the wide range of material that I wanted to cover in class. I was particularly interested in analyzing the institutional resources available to the president for policy-making and policy implementation. These institutional resources included the vice president, the cabinet and the departments, the White House staff, and the Executive Office of the President. Few textbooks examine the role of these significant institutional resources in presidential decision-making.

The modern presidency is quite different, as this textbook makes eminently clear, from the presidencies of past generations. The modern presidency has enormous institutional resources available to it for national problem solving. At no point in American history has the presidency been as powerful as it is today, largely due to the breadth of financial, informational, and staffing resources available within the executive branch. The president guides the nation's policy agenda, serves as the nation's chief diplomat and commander in chief, and oversees a workforce of three million people and a budget that exceeds $1.7 trillion. The success of presidential leadership in each of these endeavors is largely due to the resources within the executive branch.

Another important aspect of presidential leadership presented in this textbook is the politics of personal relations. The media constantly refers to the politics of "the beltway," referring to the small group of people within the Washington, D.C., political community, and the politics "outside the beltway." I suggest that the media is quite right with this analysis, in that presidents must deal with two sets of variables in their political interactions. The first set of variables involves beltway politics. Legislative leaders within both parties must be courted to ensure that presidential initiatives are moved swiftly through the labyrinth of the legislative process. Presidents must astutely build adequate support on Capitol Hill and throughout the special interest groups to ensure such legislative success. Building personal relationships among the party leaders in Congress, for example, is critical to successful legislative agendas for the president.

The second set of variables involves a strategy to build support outside of the beltway. This strategy focuses on building public opinion in favor of presidential goals and objectives, which ultimately puts pressure on beltway politics. Presidents again must use the personal touch in developing the levels of public support they need for their policies and will employ such tactics as fireside chats on national television, a series of speeches across the country to reinforce the importance of a particular policy, and a constant process of goodwill activities, such as hosting the World Series champions or the Women's World Cup team at the White House. At no point does the president stop using the resources of the presidency to build public support for presidential policies, including determining what vacation site would present the best image of the president. In the summer of 1996, for example, President Clinton's political advisers recommended that the Clinton family vacation in the scenic mountains of Wyoming. The logic behind this recommendation was that most Americans identified with vacationing in outdoor settings, particularly in such beautiful, often rustic, areas. Political research had shown that many Americans felt little in common with a president who retreated to his own estate on the ocean, such as President Bush had in Kennebunkport, Maine, or as President Clinton had in visiting an estate on Martha's Vineyard.

The conclusion that this textbook reaches is that presidents can be successful if they effectively utilize the vast resources of the institutional presidency and effectively create a personal political strategy that reaches both within the beltway and outside of the beltway. It is a complex intersection of personal relations, agenda-setting, political strategy, and management expertise. Presidential leadership is in reality the effective management of the personal and institutional resources, the "keys to power," upon which the president can draw.

Acknowledgments

In preparing this book I am indebted to many people who worked tirelessly to help me complete the research, writing, and editing. I spent approximately three years writing this book, the first two years devoted to assembling the mountains of information that were needed and the last year devoted to crafting the final document. Research and editing assistance was provided by a number of outstanding Gettysburg College students, including Tim Peltier, Paul Redfern, Geoff Gosselin, Rachel Hanson, John Dunlap, John Nastasi, Dave Wiseman, Chris Warshaw, and Cammie Grant. In addition, Kim Tracy, who is currently studying at Tulane Law School, was instrumental in helping me with some of the earlier research for this book. I have to single out Chrissy Shott, however, who spent two years on the research and editing, plus oversaw creating the index. Jamee Conover and Karen Goldberg, who manage our Department of Political Science office, provided constant support in technical assistance. At Addison Wesley Longman, I am indebted to my editor, Eric Stano, who has been a dynamic influence on this work and who has constantly supported every phase of its development, and to Susan Free of York Production Services, who oversaw the many details in the production stages. I also appreciate the feedback I received on the manuscript from reviewers: Kevin Corder of Western Michigan University, Cary R. Covington of the University of Iowa, John R. Greene of Cazenovia College, and Robert Spitzer of SUNY-Cortland. Needless to say, the development of this book was a team effort, and I am deeply grateful to each and every one who worked so hard putting this manuscript together.

I also want to thank my wonderful family, who provide unlimited and unending support. This is my fifth book, so my family has been through the pain of my writing books several times before. But they have never complained and always cheerfully supported everything that I have done. I love them dearly and dedicate this to my very special husband, Allen, and three terrific children, Chris (19), Andy (16), and Bobby (10). I hope that now I can get to more soccer games and visit Chris in college in Massachusetts more often.

Shirley Anne Warshaw
Gettysburg College
Gettysburg, Pennsylvania
August 1999

INTRODUCTION

During the summer of 1787 when the framers of the Constitution were debating how to structure the national government, the primary debates focused on whether to reform the Articles of Confederation and Perpetual Union or to abandon the Articles of Confederation altogether and create a new national government. Once that debate had been resolved in favor of creating a new national government, the framers focused their attention on how to structure the legislative branch to ensure that both the small states and the large states were adequately represented. Only after these two key issues had been resolved did the framers turn to the issue of the executive branch. They concluded that the primary task of the president should be executing the laws and that the president should have relatively little power. In order to ensure that the president's power was indeed weak, one group at the constitutional convention argued for a plural executive rather than a singular executive. Under this plan, a group of people would oversee the executive branch rather than any one individual.

After a good deal of discussion on the merits of a plural executive, Alexander Hamilton convinced the members that the executive function must be held by a single individual rather than by a group of individuals. His argument rested on the necessity for quick and decisive action in time of war, which a process of collective decision making in a plural executive would render impossible. Once the key issue of plural versus singular executive had been resolved in favor of a singular executive, the debates moved to the issue of the powers of the president. Having only eleven years earlier shed the bonds of tyranny, the framers were not eager to create any form of government that gave significant power to the chief executive. Their intent in creating the presidency was to forge an office that was a combination of ceremonial head of state and manager of the executive branch. At no point in the deliberations on creating the new tripartite government did the framers intend for the president to operate independently of the Congress. Such independence in decision-making reminded many in 1787 of the abuses of King George III that had been so carefully chronicled by Thomas Jefferson in the Declaration of Independence. The framers intended for the president's powers to be muted in order to ensure that the president could not become a king or a tyrant.

The effect of this decision by the framers to mute presidential power was evidenced by the lengthy list of powers granted to Congress in Article I of the Constitution and the rather slim list of powers granted to the President in Article II. Throughout most of American history presidents have viewed this limited delineation of powers in Article II as an absence of power within the institution of the presidency. Most presidents in the 1700s and 1800s were unwilling to challenge Congress for power because they viewed Article II as providing little authority or opportunity. These presidents are referred to as strict constructionists, for they viewed the construction of the Constitution as limiting presidential authority. The authority to pass the laws and essentially run the country, constructionists would argue, laid with Congress not with the presidency.

Several presidents challenged this interpretation of the Constitution and expanded their power based on their own interpretations of Article II. Abraham Lincoln, Theodore Roosevelt, and Woodrow Wilson were among this genre of presidents, who challenged the conventional wisdom of Article II. But it was not until Franklin Delano Roosevelt that the president aggressively pushed to reinterpret Article II and sought to move the presidency into the forefront of the nation's agenda setting and national leadership. Roosevelt began asserting new powers of the presidency, often only vaguely addressed in Article II, and built an administrative apparatus called the Executive Office of the President to assist him in managing the new roles that the executive branch was addressing. Since Roosevelt's administration, the power of the presidency has constantly expanded as presidents have interpreted Article II to create new powers and as Congress has become increasingly hesitant to curb presidential powers. During the few times when Congress has sought to curb presidential power, they have been largely defeated. The Supreme Court often views congressional opposition to presidential power as politically motivated rather than constitutionally motivated and renders decisions that support presidential actions. Such was the case when President Carter in 1979 sought to terminate the mutual defense treaty with Taiwan. When Senator Barry Goldwater asked the Supreme Court to stop the President, the Court ruled that Goldwater did not represent the entire Congress but merely a small, politically motivated faction.[1]

We are now in an era of strong presidential leadership, an era in which the president, not the Congress, is viewed by the American people as the nation's chief agenda setter and as the nation's leader. The president is the dominant force today in the American political system, guiding the country through policy debates and forging coalitions of support for a presidential agenda. There is no equal to the power of the presidency in our current system of government.

This power in the presidency is the product of an electoral system that demands political compromises and produces leaders with agendas acceptable to the majority of citizens. *Moderation* has become the watchword of political leaders. In order to survive the demands of the election process, candidates must fashion platforms acceptable to the majority of voters. They cannot move too far to the political left or the political right and survive the rigors of the campaign. Once in office, presidents must continue to fashion agendas acceptable to the majority and to capture broad-based public support. The task of developing agendas acceptable to the political majority is strengthened by the institutional resources available to the president. The task of building broad-based public support for those agendas is enhanced by the public leadership role that the president plays as head of state, party leader, commander in chief, and legislative leader. At the heart of managing the presidency is the ability to use the keys of power that are available to the president.

Any discussion of presidential dominance of the national agenda or discussion of presidential management of the executive branch is reflective of contemporary times. This discussion would not have occurred a century ago and barely occurred half a century ago. Presidential government as we know it today is quite a change from congressional government in which Congress was the dominant player in our political and governmental structure. During the constitutional convention of 1787 the intent of the framers was to have Congress at the heart of the national government, with the president focused on executing the laws of the land and serving as the diplomatic head of state. The change in roles from congressional to presidential government has necessitated a change in management structures for the president, with more people involved and more management structures involved. These changes include the addition of numerous political advisers who now comprise the White House staff and include the expanded management structures housed within the Executive Office of the President and the executive departments.

The focus of this book, *The Keys to Power: Managing the Presidency*, is to examine the current advantages and constraints that presidents face in exercising leadership. The keys to power for the president lie in four essential areas: managing the presidential branch, leading Congress effectively, using prerogative powers within the parameters established by the Supreme Court, and using personal persuasion.

Perhaps the most important key to unlocking presidential power is the power of persuasion. Personality has long been the most important key to success for any president. How well presidents persuade the American people and persuade the members of Congress that the administration's policies are in everyone's best interest is a fundamental task of presidential leadership.[2] President Reagan, for example, was particularly adept at moving his policies forward through personal persuasion. Commentators during the Reagan era referred to President Reagan as the Great Communicator. Communicating the administration's goals and objectives in a clear and direct manner is essential for presidents to build public support for their programs. Presidents who fail to communicate well with the public often fail with their legislative agendas and often fail to gain a second term in office.

Yet the success of any presidency is not the product just of an effective communicator, but also of a president who understands the institutional apparatus that supports the presidency. Without a detailed understanding of the power of the executive branch in general and of the presidential apparatus in particular, presidents lose one of their keys to power. Effective management of the institutional apparatus of the presidency affords the president a significant edge in moving goals and objectives forward. A strong presidency is premised on presidents using the keys to open the door of the institutional parts of the presidency and using those institutional parts to the best advantage of the administration.

As the presidency has expanded its control over the decision-making and institutional apparatus of government in the post-Roosevelt era, it has reached a number of critical junctions. One of the first critical junctions came in the Eisenhower administration when President Eisenhower was faced with an expanding federal bureaucracy and little prospect of adequately managing that bureaucracy from the White House. The increased demands of an expanding federal government, the increased demands of Congress as new legislation built on the programs of the New Deal, and the increased demands of the television age forced President Eisenhower to expand the size of the White House staff and to create staff positions with specific functions. Without this larger, specialized staff, management of the expanded roles of the presidency would have been impossible.

The second critical junction occurred during the Johnson administration, when the White House staff, which had grown significantly in recent years, appeared to be shielding the president from information that was contradictory to his own views. White House press secretary George Reedy described this movement by the White House staff as leading to the "twilight of the presidency," for presidents were deprived of broader discussions of policy issues that might be at odds with the president's own viewpoints.[3] White House staff, according to Reedy, were too protective of the president and kept discussions of policy issues focused within very narrow parameters that met the test of presidential acceptance. Reedy argued that presidents would be unable to adequately gauge policy options without true assessments from White House staff. The future of the presidency, Reedy argued, was in jeopardy unless the president broadened his advisory structure and ensured that White House staff did not close the options available for decision making. Successive presidents heeded Reedy's advice by enlarging the decision structure through larger White House staffs and through increased reliance on the staffs in the Executive Office of the President and to some extent through increased reliance on the cabinet.

In each of these first two critical junctions, presidents were faced with decisions that required them to unlock a door that controlled power. In Eisenhower's case, the key that unlocked the door to power involved expanding the White House staff. Eisenhower used the key to open the door and add another tool to the repertoire of presidential power. For Johnson, the choice was more complex. The keys to power had opened the door to an authoritative and often commanding White House staff. Clearly the president needed a powerful White House staff, but he did not need a staff who closed the door to options in decision making. Although Johnson kept the door open, future presidents were forced to consider the shield that White House staff can drape around the Oval Office. The lesson learned is that informed decision-making requires presidents to consider multiple options from multiple sources. Although the political staff of the president are fundamental to the keys to power, they must be used judiciously.

The keys to power include managing not only the political appointees within the administration but also the career staff. Most federal employees are career staff, hired through the civil service process. They account for approximately ninety-nine percent of federal employees. For presidents to manage the executive branch successfully, the career staff must be included in the overall management design. Managing the federal bureaucracy has become somewhat of an art in recent administrations, as presidents have tried to increase the number of political employees, revamp the senior career structure, prioritize programs, revise legislative intent, and use executive orders and executive agreements to circumvent Congress. Throughout all of these machinations, presidents have had to convince the career staff and their allies within constituent groups that the primary purpose of the executive agencies is to move forward presidential goals and objectives.

President Nixon became particularly adept at transforming the departments into tools of presidential objective. Nixon moved his own staff into positions formerly held by career staff to ensure that policies were being addressed in accordance with White House goals. When Congress passed appropriations for programs that Nixon did not approve of, he ordered his departments to ignore the appropriations by impounding them. The money was not to be spent, Nixon ordered. With the federal government firmly under his control, Nixon began to view himself in somewhat monarchial terms. One of the more vivid indications of this monarchial tendency was when Nixon directed that the White House staff military aides be dressed in uniforms with bright red tops, black pants, and black pompadour hats and that they should raise their bugles when heads of state arrived. Nixon ignored Reedy's admonition against a closed White House staff and surrounded himself with a small, tightly knit group referred to as "the Prussian guards."

Many scholars think that Nixon dramatically misused the keys to power. Not only had his presidency misused power but it had also taken on imperial trappings. Arthur Schlesinger, Jr., accused Nixon of having an "imperial presidency."[4] The failings of the Nixon administration led Gerald Ford, Nixon's successor, to reassess the keys to power. For Ford, the keys had to be slowly and carefully turned to reestablish the power of the presidency. The doors within the executive branch, both within the White House and the executive departments, had to be opened to ensure honesty in decision-making. Nixon's Prussian guards had tightly closed the decision structure. The doors to Congress also needed to be opened to foster collaboration in the legislative process. Collaboration in the legislative process would allow presidential initiatives to move forward in Congress and would minimize roadblocks in implementation put up by the departments.

Unfortunately, neither Gerald Ford nor Jimmy Carter was able to use the keys to power to unlock all of the doors necessary to reestablish a strong presidency. Both failed to use the keys to open the doors to the institutional resources of the presidency. Reedy's admonition against a strong White House staff and Nixon's Prussian guards led both Ford and Carter to reduce the size of the White House staff and their role in managing policy development and oversight. The absence of a strong White House staff resulted in departments that often operated in their own spheres, without coordination with presidential goals and objectives. In some instances, cabinet officers during the Carter administration lobbied against presidential programs on the floor of Congress—reminiscent of Secretary of State Thomas Jefferson opposing George Washington's legislation for a federally chartered bank. Carter was also unable to use the keys to power to open the doors to Congress; he failed to coordinate legislation and failed to nurture the personal relationships necessary for a successful legislative agenda. Scholars often refer to this period of the Ford and Carter years as the "imperilled presidency," in which presidents watched their power slide away. The imperial presidency had become the imperilled presidency in only a few short years.

When Ronald Reagan moved into the Oval Office he faced a strong, Democratically controlled Congress. With recent presidents reluctant to use the institutional power of the presidency and unable to rally public support for presidential initiatives, the conventional wisdom of the time predicted that President Reagan would become a secondary player in the political system. Many thought that Congress would move to again reassert their dominance of the policy process. Reagan, however, was not to be so easily moved into the backwaters of decision-making and began to use the keys to power that had never moved from the president's desk.

The keys to power were aggressively and effectively used by President Reagan and have continued to be used by each successive president. Presidents Reagan,

Bush, and Clinton have been extremely proficient at using the keys to open the doors necessary to both manage the executive branch and move legislation through Congress. In an era dominated by divided government, in which the House and the Senate often were comprised of different parties and in which the Congress and the presidency were often comprised of different parties, successful presidential leadership has been dependent on building bridges to individual members of Congress. Presidents Reagan and Bush were perhaps more successful at building these bridges than President Clinton, who became the first president impeached since 1868. President Clinton, as had President Carter before him, often relied too heavily on the power of public persuasion and not enough on the power of personal relations.

Finally, it is important to discuss the importance of prerogative power. The absence of a long list of powers in Article II of the Constitution has not constrained strong presidents but rather has opened the door to endless powers. Strong presidents have viewed the absence of delineated powers as implied consent for all powers not constrained by the Constitution. Thus, while Article II requires the Senate to confirm cabinet appointees, it does not require the Senate to approve dismissals of cabinet appointees. Similarly, presidents have viewed the power to appoint ambassadors as the power to recognize or derecognize governments. President Kennedy chose no longer to recognize the government of Cuba after the missile crisis of 1962. In a similar interpretation of Article II, President Reagan chose to recognize the Vatican as an independent nation, to establish diplomatic relations, and to send an ambassador and complete staff to the newly recognized nation. Neither President Kennedy nor President Reagan discussed their decisions with Congress and neither sought congressional approval for their actions. They based their authority on inherent powers provided in Article II and reinforced by the Supreme Court.

How presidents use the keys to power determines the success of their administrations. If they wisely use the keys and carefully open the doors, presidents can successfully move their agendas forward. The institutional resources of the executive branch, the prerogative powers inherent in Article II, the ability of the president to capture national attention, and the fractured nature of Congress provide enormous opportunities for a president to be the nation's policy leader. The keys to power reside in how presidents open these doors.

Notes

1. *Goldwater v. Carter*. 444 U.S. 996 (1979).
2. Richard E. Neustadt. *Presidential Power and the Modern Presidents: The Politics of Leadership From Roosevelt to Reagan*. New York: Free Press, 1990.
3. George E. Reedy. *The Twilight of the Presidency*. New York: World Publishing, 1970.
4. Arthur M. Schlesinger, Jr. *The Imperial Presidency*. Boston: Houghton Mifflin, 1973, revised 1989.

Chapter 1

POWERS AND PERQUISITES
OF THE PRESIDENCY

Of the three branches of government in the United States, the executive branch is the most complicated and holds the most power. Neither the Congress nor the Supreme Court has the power to lead the country that the president, who heads the executive branch, has. The president has numerous advantages for exerting power within the national government, such as the power that ensues from having a national constituency and the power that ensues from having millions of people within the domain of the executive branch. Congress is limited by the constant confrontations within its membership of 535 individuals and by the often fractious relationship between the parties and between the houses, not to mention the comparatively small number of employees—30,000. The Supreme Court is limited by its mandate and by the overwhelming workload by which its nine members are annually besieged. The result is that Congress and the Supreme Court are both powerful institutions and essential within the structure of setting the course of public policy. Yet it is the president who plays the leadership role in the nation today of charting the course for the nation's public policy agenda and of moving that course toward fruition through the executive departments.

When we talk about the powers of the modern presidency, we are talking about both the constitutional powers bestowed on the president and the institutional advantages that the office of president has. The power of the presidency is a combination of the constitutional and institutional powers plus the enormous political power that the president has in the age of television and mass media. Only the president can command the attention of the media day in and day out. No member of Congress and no member of the Supreme Court holds the interest of the American people in the same way that the president does. Hardly a day goes by that the president is not on the front page of daily newspapers or in a lead story on the network evening news shows. Although Congress and the Supreme Court are essential to our system of balance of power and divided government, the president remains the dominant player in our structure of government. As the dominant player in this system of divided government, presidents must use the tools available to them in order to manage the executive branch. The keys to power are found in skillful use of the institutional, constitutional, and prerogative powers available to the president.

Qualifications for the Office of President

The **qualifications for the presidency** are fairly simple. One has to be a natural born citizen, at least 35 years of age, and a resident of the United States for at least fourteen years before taking office. There is nothing complicated about having the requisite qualifications for the presidency. There are no thresholds for educational levels, no tests for serving as an elected official in some other capacity, and no requirement for having worked in Washington, D.C. The framers of the Constitution wanted to ensure that everyone would have the opportunity to run for the presidency, regardless of their educational or economic background or their experience in government service. The first point, that one has to be a natural born citizen, had two purposes. On one hand, the framers did not want to take any chances that a loyalist to England and the monarchy would slip into the presidency and abandon many of the principles established in the Constitution. Although the Constitution would be in place, the framers were unsure that it could endure a president who could marshal public support for changing the nature of the presidency. On the other hand, the citizenship requirement mitigated any chance that the president would be from a foreign country and try to exercise control over foreign policy in a manner that was beneficial to the president's "home country" and detrimental to the United States. There is a caveat to the requirement that the president be a natural born citizen, which is that the president must be a "citizen of the United States at the time of the Adoption of this Constitution" if not a natural born citizen. This caveat was added to allow Alexander Hamilton, one of the original architects of the Constitution, to qualify for the presidency. Hamilton had been born in the Caribbean Islands rather than in the United States. The term "natural born citizen" does not mean, however, that the president must be born within the borders of the United States. We interpret the phrase "natural born citizen" to mean that anyone seeking the office of president must have been born either within the borders of the United States or on United States military or diplomatic ground. Persons born on military bases abroad or within the embassies are considered to be natural born citizens.

Finally, the Constitution required that the president be a resident of the United States for fourteen years, which ensures that anyone seeking the office of president must be knowledgeable about the nation and its people at the time. In the age of global television and international coverage in newspapers, this requirement would seem less important today than it had in 1787. The media age has allowed citizens living abroad to have constant access to issues within the United States.

The requirement that the president be 35 years of age follows the natural progression that was put in the Constitution for the elected officials of the new nation. Members of the House of Representatives, which was considered the least important member of the decision process, were required to be only 25 years old, members of the Senate had to be 30 years old, and the president had to be 35 years old. The president was seen by the framers as needing the most experience in decision-making and should be the most mature and the most experienced in such decisions (Figure 1.1).

1. 35 Years of Age
2. Resident of the United States for Fourteen Years before Taking Office
3. Natural Born Citizen

FIGURE 1.1   Qualifications for President.

Title

The title of the nation's chief executive was provided in the opening of Article II, Section I, with the simple phrase, "The executive Powers shall be vested in a President of the United States." But the succinctness of the language masked the highly charged deliberations that occurred during the constitutional convention. Throughout the discussions on the presidency on May 19, 1787, Charles Pinckney proposed that the "Executive power be vested in a 'President of the United States of America' and his title shall be 'His Excellency.'" As a result, when George Washington was elected president, the Congress, which had counted the votes of the electors, transmitted notification of his election with the phrase, "To his Excellency, George Washington, Esq." The letter read, "Sir: I have the honor to transmit to your Excellency the information of your unanimous election to the office of President of the United States."[1] Since the issue of **title** had not been resolved during the convention debates, the phrase that Pinckney used during the constitutional convention appeared to be the most logical. The issue did not arise again until the first Congress was officially convened under the new constitution on March 4, 1789. The Senate and the House established committees in April 1789 to study the issue of a formal title for the president. They agreed with Pinckney's proposal of the term "His Excellency." However, the full Senate disagreed with the phrase and convened another committee, which proposed the following language. "The Committee appointed to consider and report under what title it will be proper for the Senate to address the President of the United States of America reported that in the opinion of the Committee it will be proper thus to address him: 'His Highness, the President of the United States of America and Protector of their Liberties.'" The full Senate again killed this terminology and suggested that "the president be addressed 'To the President of the United States,'" without addition of title. The full Senate approved this language through a resolution. The House of Representatives never commented on the title of the president after its initial committee meetings in April 1789. Subsequently, the title "The President of the United States" is the title that the Senate has used by virtue of formal resolution and the House has used by virtue of tradition. The public has followed these precedents as part of its tradition of shedding the aristocratic traditions of the British governmental structure.

Tenure

The **tenure** of the president is four years in office, with the opportunity to run for office for another four-year term. When the framers designed the Constitution, they struggled with the length of time the president should hold office. Should it be four years, six years, or seven years? Should the president have an unlimited number of terms? After a series of debates on the length of the term and on the number of terms the president should serve, the decision was to have a four-year term in office with unlimited numbers of succeeding terms. There was a general sense in the constitutional convention that George Washington would be elected the nation's first president. The framers did not want to limit the number of terms that Washington could serve, because they were convinced that Washington would provide strong leadership for the fledgling nation. Washington was subsequently elected the nation's first president and served with overwhelming approval from the citizenry. But after two terms in office, although constitutionally eligible to run for a third term, Washington chose not to run again. As one biographer of Washington commented, "he would not have the hard office again."[2] Washington had thus effectively set in motion the two-term tradition.

Not a single president violated this precedent until 1944 when Franklin Delano Roosevelt was elected to a fourth term in office. Every president had continued the tradition that George Washington had fostered and voluntarily had limited their terms in office to eight years. With World War II dominating the national agenda, Roosevelt was easily elected to a third term in 1940 and then a fourth term in 1944. But there was some concern within Congress following Roosevelt's unparalleled four terms in office that the Constitution should be amended to limit the number of terms in office to two and to return to the tradition that George Washington had fostered. Ratified by the states in 1951 during Harry Truman's presidency, the twenty-second amendment to the Constitution limited the tenure in office for presidents to two terms. The amendment states that "no person shall be elected to the office of the President more than twice." While this seems to have settled the question, legal scholars are divided as to whether presidents are limited to two consecutive terms or to any two terms. If the amendment means only that the president is limited to two consecutive terms, then the door is open for a president to serve two terms and run for office after four years out of office. For example, President Clinton could under this interpretation run for office in 2004 and again serve two terms. This scenario has never been tested and probably will not be. Once presidents leave office they tend to move into a very productive life as senior statesmen and are quite content to be out of the public eye on a daily basis.

In addition to limiting presidential terms, the twenty-second amendment limited the term of vice presidents who succeed to the presidency. The amendment states that "no person who has held the office of President, or acted as President, for more than two years of a term to which some other person was elected President shall be elected to the office of the President more than once." This provided for vice presidents who were thrust into the presidency when the incumbent has resigned or died to have very clear direction on the length of time they could serve as president. Vice presidents who move into the presidency are constrained to serving only one more full term if they serve more than two full years of an unexpired term. The twenty-fifth amendment requires that if a vice president serves more than two full years of a president's unexpired term, he may serve only one full term as president and may not run for a second full term. For example, Gerald Ford was sworn into office as president on August 9, 1974, which was one year and seven months after President Nixon had begun his second term. Since Ford served more than half of President Nixon's term, he could not run for office for a full second term in 1980. He was only eligible to run in 1976.

The tenure of presidents is limited not only by the twenty-second amendment (1951), but also by the removal power granted to Congress under Article II of the Constitution. Article II, Section 4, states that the president can be removed by the Congress for "treason, bribery, or other high crimes and misdemeanors." The House of Representatives is empowered to impeach the president and the Senate is empowered to convict the president. Only two presidents, Andrew Johnson in 1868 and William Jefferson Clinton in 1998, have been impeached. Neither Johnson nor Clinton was convicted by the Senate and removed from office. Although many people believe Nixon was impeached before he resigned, he was not. The House of Representatives was in the process of conducting impeachment hearings when Nixon resigned. The Judiciary Committee in the House voted to approve a list of articles of impeachment, which would be deliberated individually within the full House. No vote was ever taken by the full House, but the vote would unquestionably have gone against Nixon. The Senate was poised to convict Nixon after an impeachment. He remained eligible for a presidential pardon, which later was given by President Ford. Pardons cannot be given if impeachment has occurred.

Perquisites of the Presidency

The president's **salary** is set by Congress and is currently set at $200,000 per year, although this could be raised or lowered by Congress. There are no regularly scheduled increases in the president's salary. Every increase in the president's salary is the result of a new bill in Congress. The framers debated the issue of compensation during the constitutional convention, with Benjamin Franklin arguing that money was at the root of political evil and the president should receive "no salary, stipend, fee or reward" except for expenses. This idea was rejected since it would keep anyone without substantial personal wealth from serving as president, an idea quite alien to the republican concepts of the Constitution. After some debate, the framers provided for an unspecified "compensation" for the president that was not to be "increased or diminished during the period for which he shall have been elected." This meant that the salary of the president could not be increased or decreased by Congress during the four-year term, although it could be changed during the second "period for which he shall have been elected." This ensured that decisions made by the president that were not popular with members of Congress would not lead to financial ruin for the president. It also provided that presidents would not be bribed for their decisions. As Alexander Hamilton describes the reasoning, the president would have "no pecuniary inducement to renounce or desert the independence intended for him by the Constitution."[3]

One of the first jobs of the Congress that met in 1789 after the ratification of the Constitution was to determine the pay of President Washington. But it was not until 1793 that they finally set the pay at $25,000 per year, a significant amount in those days. The $25,000 provided to George Washington included both salary and expenses, without a clear delineation of how much was specifically for salary.[4] The amount was fashioned to represent the importance the Congress placed on the responsibilities of the new president. Washington declined the salary. All subsequent presidents, except John F. Kennedy and Herbert Hoover, have taken their salaries. Both Kennedy and Hoover had substantial personal fortunes and chose not to accept their presidential salaries. The salary was not raised until 1873, when President Ulysses S. Grant was given an increase to $50,000. It was raised in 1949 to $100,000, in 1969 to $200,000, and in 2001 it will be $400,000. Although $200,000 is a significant amount, it remains less in inflation-indexed dollars than George Washington's original $25,000 salary (Figure 1.2).

The salary issue has been somewhat complicated by a small phrase in Article II, which adds that the president "shall not receive within that period any other emolument from the United States, or any of them." The framers intended that the president, the members of both houses of Congress, and the Supreme Court, be paid by the new national government rather than by the states they represented. This was symbolic of the change from a system of delegates from the states to a system of delegates for a national government. The delegates no longer represented only their state interests, as they had under the Articles of Confederation and Perpetual Union and during the two Continental Congresses, but represented the entire nation as national representatives. The salary of the president would be paid from the national coffers under the structure designed by the new Constitution. But the framers also wanted to ensure that the president did not receive additional funds from the states that they had come from, such as a pension from serving as governor or in the state legislature. Presumably, if the president were receiving additional money from a state, he might be prejudiced in favor of that state in policy decisions. Some presidents, such as Franklin Delano Roosevelt, Ronald Reagan, Jimmy Carter, and Bill Clinton were entitled to state pensions from their service as state governors. They could not accept these pensions until after they left the presidency. Other presidents have been entitled to federal pensions as a result of federal positions, such as John F. Kennedy and Lyndon Johnson as U.S. Senators and Richard Nixon and George Bush as vice presidents. The Constitution allows presidents to continue to receive federal pensions since they do not compromise their positions with regard to policy issues of individual states.

Presidents also receive a yearly travel expense account. In 1906 Congress provided $25,000 for the president; in 1949 this was raised to $50,000. This amount has remained the same every year, although now the $50,000 can be used for general expenses, rather than just for travel expenses. The president pays taxes on this expense account. In addition, the White House Office (not the president) receives an annual

Year	Salary
1793	$25,000
1873	$50,000
1949	$100,000
1969	$200,000
2001	$400,000

FIGURE 1.2   Salary of the President.

fund of $100,000 to cover presidential travel and other expenses and an entertainment allowance of $19,000. The entertainment allowance includes such costs as luncheons for the leadership of Congress, dinners for the U.S. Olympic teams, or musical groups for an event. All state dinners honoring foreign dignitaries are paid for by the State Department rather than by the White House entertainment budget.

Benefits to Ex-Presidents

Former presidents were historically not treated as well after leaving office as they had been while in office. They were not granted any pension or other financial assistance after leaving office. When the Trumans left the White House they paid their own train fare to their home in Missouri. Not until 1958 when Harry Truman sought Congressional help to remedy this problem did Congress act. In response, Congress created the **Former Presidents Act of 1958** to give ex-presidents "unless impeached and removed from office" a pension of $25,000 per year plus an allowance of $50,000 to hire staff and procure office space and furnishings; in addition, ex-presidents were given unlimited free postage for nonpolitical correspondence. The law required that the office space must be located in a federal office building as a means to cut down on costs and to protect against political chicanery. Ex-presidents could not rent office space, for example, from former political allies as a reward for their support. The law currently provides for an allowance of $150,000 for the first thirty months out of office and $96,000 per year after that. In addition, the law provides for a pension of $20,000 for the widows of ex-presidents. By 1989 Congress had raised the pensions for ex-presidents to $148,400 per year, which was equal to the salary of a cabinet officer. Under the law, secret service protection is provided throughout the lives of ex-presidents, to their widows, and to their children who are less than sixteen years of age. There is also funding of $1.5 million for the transition from public life to private life after presidents leave the White House. This allows them to hire additional staff during the transition period and to pay for moving expenses.

After leaving office presidents are also entitled to have the government build a presidential library to house their official papers. The libraries have been built with public funds since 1955 and administered by the National Archives. Eleven presidents (Hoover, Roosevelt, Truman, Eisenhower, Kennedy, Johnson, Nixon, Ford, Carter, Bush and Reagan) have presidential libraries. The libraries have always been constructed in the president's home state although there is no pattern to state location, such as the state capital or the birthplace of the president (Figure 1.3).

President Clinton, who spent most of his adult life in Little Rock, Arkansas, will begin construction of his presidential library in Little Rock once he leaves office. President Reagan built his atop a remote mountain in the Simi Valley, outside of Los Angeles and not far from his ranch in Santa Barbara, California. The opening of presidential libraries is always a public celebration, attended by every living president. When President Reagan opened his library on November 4, 1991, all five living presidents (Nixon, Ford, Carter, Reagan, and Bush) attended the ceremonies. The day is full of speeches, tours of the facilities, and promises of major events the library plans to host in the future. As one commentator noted, "the presidential libraries, therefore, have a significance that extends beyond their ostensible purposes.

Office of Presidential Libraries

http://www.nara.gov/nara/president/
    address.html
National Archives at College Park
8601 Adelphi Road
College Park, MD 20740-6001
Phone: 301-713-6050
Fax: 301-713-6045

Franklin D. Roosevelt Library

http://www.fdrlibrary.marist.edu
511 Albany Post Road
Hyde Park, NY 12538-1999
Phone: 914-229-8114
Fax: 914-229-0872
Email: library@roosevelt.nara.gov

Dwight D. Eisenhower Library

http://www.eisenhower.utexas.edu
200 SE 4th Street
Abilene, KS 67410-2900
Phone: 785-263-4751
Fax: 785-263-4218
Email: library@eisenhower.nara.gov

Lyndon B. Johnson Library

http://www.lbjlib.utexas.edu
2313 Red River Street
Austin, TX 78705-5702
Phone: 512-916-5137
Fax: 512-916-5171
Email: library@johnson.nara.gov

Jimmy Carter Library

http://carterlibrary.galileo.peachnet.edu/
441 Freedom Parkway
Atlanta, GA 30307-1498
Phone: 404-331-3942
Fax: 404-730-2215
Email: library@carter.nara.gov

George Bush Library

http://csdl.tamu.edu/bushlib/bushpage.html
1000 George Bush Drive West
College Station, TX 77845
Phone: 409-260-9554
Fax: 409-260-9557
Email: library@bush.nara.gov

Herbert Hoover Library

http://hoover.nara.gov
210 Parkside Drive
P.O. Box 488
West Branch, IA 52358-0488
Phone: 319-643-5301
Fax: 319-643-5825
Email: library@hoover.nara.gov

Harry S Truman Library

http://www.trumanlibrary.org
500 West U.S. Highway 24
Independence, MO 64050-1798
Phone: 816-833-1225
Fax: 816-833-4368
Email: library@truman.nara.gov

John F. Kennedy Library

http://www.cs.umb.edu/jfklibrary/
Columbia Point
Boston, MA 02125-3398
Phone: 617-929-4500
Fax: 617-929-4538
Email: library@kennedy.nara.gov

Nixon Presidential Materials Staff

http://sunsite.unc.edu/lia/president/nixon
    .html
8601 Adelphi Road
College Park, MD 20740-6001
Phone: 301-713-6950
Fax: 301-713-6916
Email: nixon@arch2.nara.gov

Gerald R. Ford Library

http://www.ford.utexas.edu
1000 Beal Avenue
Ann Arbor, MI 48109
Phone: 734-741-2218
Fax: 734-741-2341
Email: library@fordlib.nara.gov

Ronald Reagan Library

http://www.reagan.utexas.edu
40 Presidential Drive
Simi Valley, CA 93065-0600
Phone: 800-410-8354
Fax: 805-522-9621
Email: library@reagan.nara.gov

FIGURE 1.3   Presidential Libraries.

In many respects, they can be viewed as shrines constructed to commemorate the lives and achievements of the most recent heroes in the nation's collective memory"[5].

Presidential libraries usually have two components: the official library of presidential papers housed in a federal building, built by the General Services Administration and administered by the National Archives, and an adjoining private building, which is built using privately raised funds. The section administered by the National Archives houses the official papers of the president, while the adjoining private building houses personal items of the president and the president's family, usually has a replica of the Oval Office as the president had it, and chronicles the president's political career both before and during the presidency. Many mementoes are usually on display, such as gifts from heads of states and copies of major bills signed during the president's term in office.

In recent years, the presidential libraries have become an important part of the life of ex-presidents. Presidents spend a good deal of their time after leaving office raising money for the private components of their libraries and to fund programs there. President Bush's presidential library even includes an apartment for President and Mrs. Bush to use during their stay. Since they live in Houston and the library is at Texas A&M University in College Station, Texas, the inclusion of an apartment was reasonable to them.

Most presidents use the private part of their presidential libraries to host seminars or conferences on issues of importance to them. President Carter has worked closely with Emory University to create the Carter Center at his presidential library to deal with international issues, particularly agrarian issues in Africa and international mediation projects. President Ford regularly hosts small working groups of scholars with current and former government officials, such as Henry Kissinger, to discuss both national and international public policy issues.

Following the Watergate events of the Nixon administration, Congress passed the Presidential Records Act of 1978. The act gave the U.S. government ownership of all presidential papers, including all documents written by the president and the White House staff. Every single piece of paper, including notes, is saved during the president's term of office and then taken to the presidential library. The mandate that every piece of correspondence, both internal memos and letters generated for external use, will be opened to the public through the presidential libraries has tempered written communication in the White House. White House staffs are often reluctant to keep notes of meetings that may have involved controversial material for fear of being open to attack at a later time. Under the law, Ronald Reagan was the first president to be covered. Neither President Ford nor President Carter was required to turn all of their papers over to the presidential library, although both did.

The White House

One of the most visible perquisites of the presidency is residing in the **White House.** The White House has 132 rooms, is run by a staff of approximately one hundred full-time employees, and has such amenities as a heated swimming pool, a gymnasium, a tennis court, and a large library. The staff includes cooks, butlers, engineers, electricians, carpenters, painters, plumbers, and almost anyone you could think of that is necessary to keeping a large building operational. There is also a small personal staff for both the president and the first lady. The White House staff is composed of permanent employees both for security reasons, since each must pass a strict security clearance, and for logistical reasons, since the president and staff must be able to conduct business at all times.

The White House, located at 1600 Pennsylvania Avenue in the nation's capital, has served as the home to every United States president except George Washington. Washington worked closely with Pierre L'Enfant, the city planner for the new capital city, to choose a location for the president's house. Once the site was chosen, Washington appointed three commissioners to hold a contest to determine which architect should design the president's house. They chose James Hoban. Hoban designed the building we know today as the White House, although it had only a center structure without the east and west wings that currently are attached.

The cornerstone of the White House was laid on October 13, 1792, and it took almost ten years and $240,000 to build. In order to cut costs, Washington ordered Hoban to cut back and not include the third floor, to which Hoban agreed. The third floor was eventually added during remodeling in 1927. President and Mrs. John Adams became the first residents of the White House in 1800. Only six rooms were complete when they moved in, and water had to be carried from a park five blocks away. The semicircular portico with Ionic columns on the south side of the White House was not built until 1824. Running water was installed in 1833, and in 1891 the White House was wired for electricity. The most extensive renovations to the White House since its construction occurred during the administration of Theodore Roosevelt, when the west wing and the east wing were added. The interior of the White House was renovated by Jacqueline Kennedy in 1962 and by Nancy Reagan in 1981. Every presidential family, however, refurbishes the private residence on the second floor of the White House, bringing both their own furniture and redecorating with new furniture and other accouterments.

Another major renovation occurred during the Truman administration, but the renovations were primarily structural, to add new foundations, fireproofing, air conditioning, and other modern changes. President and Mrs. Truman moved across the street to **Blair House,** the official residence for visiting heads of state, and lived there from November 1948 to March 1952 during the renovations. Blair House was acquired by the government in 1942 for visiting heads of state because of its proximity to the White House. It has been used not only by heads of state, but also by vice presidents and by presidents during renovation projects.

While President Truman was living there in 1950, two Puerto Rican nationals attacked Blair House with automatic weapons hoping to kill the president. Truman survived the attack, but one secret service agent and one attacker were killed. Since that time, Blair House has been given enhanced security protection. It is currently part of the area surrounding the White House that is cordoned off by the secret service. An area immediately surrounding the White House has been restricted since the Reagan administration. Large concrete planters have been erected (as a security measure) to keep private cars from getting close to the White House. After a car bomb was used by terrorists to attack a military barracks in Lebanon during the Reagan administration, killing 283 marines, the secret service erected the barriers to minimize any chance of similar attacks on the White House. In 1995, during the Clinton administration, the barriers were moved further back to provide added protection.

Camp David

If the president wants to gain greater privacy, the government provides a retreat for the president in the Catoctin Mountains of Maryland, about fifty miles north of Washington, D.C. **Camp David,** as it is known today, was built in 1942 by Franklin Delano Roosevelt and named Shangri-La. It is situated on the highest point in Catoctin Mountain Park, just south of Gettysburg, Pennsylvania. The location was ideal for Roosevelt because of its high altitude and cool temperatures. During President Eisenhower's term the retreat was renamed Camp David, in honor of David Eisenhower, the president's grandson. Eisenhower hosted Soviet leader Nikita Khrushchev at Camp David in September 1959 to discuss the escalating problems in the Allied division of Berlin. Since Roosevelt's years, the retreat has been expanded to include a well-appointed lodge to house the president, guest lodges, a dining hall, sports facilities, heating swimming pool, bowling alley, archery and shooting ranges, riding stables, tennis courts, a small golf course, and a movie theater. Presidents do not generally conduct business at Camp David, as Eisenhower did, instead preferring to use it as a personal getaway. However, President Carter invited President Anwar Sadat of Egypt and Prime Minister Menachem Begin of Israel to Camp David to sign the Middle East peace accords. Those peace accords are now referred to as the Camp David Accords.

Presidential Transportation

In addition to the White House and Camp David, presidents for forty years during the twentieth century had the luxury of a presidential yacht, the *Sequoia*, which sailed along the Potomac River past Mount Vernon. The *Sequoia* was 105-feet long and was used for entertaining both friends and official guests of the president. Richard Nixon was particularly fond of using the *Sequoia* to entertain members of Congress and to relax with members of his staff. Nixon often used the *Sequoia* as a retreat to mull over the Vietnam War with Henry Kissinger.[6] Soon after taking office, however, President Carter sold the *Sequoia* for $286,000. For Carter, the *Sequoia* was an unnecessary trapping of the imperial presidency and had no real importance to the job of running the country. In large part, the sale of the *Sequoia* symbolized Carter's efforts to cut costs in government and to separate the style of his presidency from that of Nixon and the Watergate era.

Among the amenities provided to the president is protected travel on Air Force One and constant secret service protection. Air Force One is one of two jets available to the president for travel. Whichever jet the president is on becomes Air Force One. Each of the two jets can carry seventy passengers and is outfitted with a private bedroom and bathroom for the president, a conference room, medical facilities, and a kitchen. The communications systems are secure and are capable of handling any crisis, including nuclear war in which command of the nuclear forces would be necessary. President Franklin Delano Roosevelt was the first president to use an official plane in 1945, just before his death. President Truman continued to use an official plane, as has every succeeding president. One of the many benefits of flying on Air Force One is the availability of M&M's candies that have the presidential seal.

Presidential security, whether in the air on Air Force One or on the ground at any location, is provided by secret service agents. The secret service is a division of the Treasury Department and provides protective service to both the president and vice president and their families. **Secret service** protection for presidents did not exist until 1906 when Congress authorized it. The secret service had been a division of the Treasury Department responsible for the investigation of counterfeiting, a role it continues to handle. In 1908 Congress extended protection to the president-elect and in 1945 further extended protection to the vice president.

The issue of protecting the president is extremely important, since before secret service protection existed three presidents were assassinated: Abraham Lincoln in 1865, James Garfield in 1881, and William McKinley in 1901. However, the secret service cannot totally protect a president, as evidenced by the assassination of President Kennedy in 1963. President Ford was attacked by a would-be assassin while shaking hands along a street, but the secret service was able to stop the attack. President Reagan was not as fortunate on March 30, 1981, when a would-be assassin wounded the president and seriously injured the president's press secretary, James Brady, outside the Hilton Hotel in Washington, D.C. The assailant, John Hinckley, was apparently not trying to kill the president but wanted to draw attention to himself.

While the secret service cannot totally protect presidents, they are able to provide a significant degree of protection. Every foot of a trip that the president takes is examined by the secret service to ensure the greatest protection possible. Even when presidents go out to dinner in Washington, D.C., the restaurant is thoroughly examined by the secret service, including explosives-sniffing dogs. Every gift that the president receives must be opened before it is given to the president to ensure that it is not carrying a bomb or other explosive device. The secret service is so protective of the president that it will not allow the president to eat any "carry-out" food brought into the White House. During the budget negotiations in 1993, President Clinton met for fourteen hours in the Roosevelt Room with his staff. The staff ordered pizza brought in during the late-night session, but the secret service would not let President Clinton have any for fear of poisoning. In addition to the secret service protection, the Federal Bureau of Investigation (FBI) does a background check on everyone who meets with the president and everyone who works in the White House. Even when Chelsea Clinton had school friends visit the White House, each was required to undergo an FBI background check.

President Clinton has had several brushes with attackers, none of whom have come close to reaching him. During the fall of 1994, a man sprayed bullets at the White House from the White House gates. No one was injured, although bullet holes were clearly visible on the white facing of the White House. In May 1995 two people scaled the fence surrounding the White House but were quickly intercepted by White House guards. At another point in the Clinton presidency a light plane crash-landed on the White House grounds just below the president's private quarters. At no point was President Clinton in danger, but the threat was very apparent. As a result of the heightened risks to the president, in 1995 the secret service closed off the area around the White House with barriers to keep cars from entering. They also increased surveillance from the roof of the White

House, which has several agents constantly monitoring the White House grounds and, it is believed, has antiaircraft guns to protect the White House in the event of an air attack.

Health Crises

Although the secret service can offer protection from some crises, it cannot protect the presidents from their own health crises. Grover Cleveland had two cancer operations in 1893, Woodrow Wilson was unable to work from 1919 to 1920 after suffering a stroke, Franklin Delano Roosevelt's health deteriorated during his presidency from complications due to polio, and John F. Kennedy had constant back pain from Addison's disease. Kennedy was forced to wear special back braces to reduce the pain and Roosevelt was relegated to a wheelchair for most of his presidency. Dwight David Eisenhower also suffered several health setbacks, having a heart attack in 1955 and a stroke in 1957. Lyndon Johnson had gallbladder and hernia operations. In addition to the surgery following his assassination attempt, Ronald Reagan had operations for the removal of a malignant growth on his colon and on his face. George Bush was diagnosed with Graves' disease and had minor surgery to remove a cancerous growth on his skin, and Bill Clinton has regular allergy shots. In spite of the various maladies that presidents suffer, the presidency continues to operate smoothly with the help of the president's White House staff and the vice president. The twenty-fifth amendment, ratified in 1967 (see Chapter 3), provides further safeguards should the president be unable to carry out his duties because of health concerns.

The Presidency and the Constitution

The powers of the presidency are broadly drafted in Article II of the Constitution in four rather brief sections. In the opening section, the framers very carefully provided that the president would have "the executive power." In contrast to Article I, where the phrase "legislative power" is defined by a list of legislative responsibilities, the phrase executive power is given no further definition within Article II. For strong presidents such as Lincoln and the two Roosevelts, the absence of further definition for the term has provided ample opportunity for expansive interpretation. For weaker presidents such as Taft and Coolidge, the absence of further definition limits their powers and allows Congress to be the dominant player in the power relationship.

During the debates over the Constitution in the summer of 1787 in Philadelphia the issue of the presidency was one of the most hotly debated and most analyzed issues. The delegates to the convention wanted to ensure that the chief executive had limited powers and to preclude any possibility of a monarchy arising in the new government. Even prior to the opening of the convention in May, one of the delegates, Charles Pinckney of South Carolina, began discussions on the structure that the presidency would take. Would the president be required to have an official group of counselors, he asked? Pinckney's ideas were lost in the early debates of the convention, which focused on James Madison's Virginia Plan and the concept of a federal government with a tripartite structure. By June 1, 1787, the Madisonian principles had been adopted, with a federal government with executive, legislative, and judicial branches. The Virginia Plan called for a single executive, who was to be elected by the national legislature and would serve for a fixed term (which was not specified in the proposal). James Wilson of Pennsylvania immediately moved that the executive office should be composed of a single person rather than a council or cabinet of people. Wilson's proposal foreclosed any chance that the Virginia Plan would be expanded to include a plural executive, in which the presidency was focused within a council or group of people. John Rutledge of South Carolina reinforced this concept by arguing that the "executive magistrate" was simply an "agent" of the Congress, responsible for carrying out the laws, and was not to be feared as a powerful branch of government. The only major issue resolved on June 1 was that the executive power would be vested in a chief executive.

On June 2, the delegates returned to debating whether the executive would be singular or plural. John Rutledge moved, with Charles Pinckney seconding, that the executive should be one person rather than a group of people. There should be, they argued, a singular rather than a **plural executive.** Governor Edmund Randolph of Virginia, who had been the spokesman for the Virginia Plan, then rose to oppose Rutledge's proposal. Randolph believed that a **singular executive** would represent only the region of the country that he was from, leaving other regions without adequate representation in the executive branch. He proposed a council of three persons, "drawn from different portions of the Country." The country would be divided into three sections with an executive elected from each section. For the first time during the convention, the debate over a singular executive became intense.

Yet another proposal was thrown into the discussions of June 2 when Roger Sherman of Connecticut advanced the idea that the executive should work with a council of revision, similar to the earlier proposals of a plural executive. Rutledge and Wilson continued to support a single executive while Randolph wanted an executive with three members from three different sections of the country. With three distinct proposals on the table, the delegates had to decide which structure for the executive would serve the nation most appropriately.

Because June 3 fell on a Sunday, the delegates did not meet again until Monday, June 4. They returned to the debate on the chief executive. James Wilson led the debate, arguing that none of the states had plural executives. When the vote was taken later that day, the single executive was supported by all but three states: New York, Delaware, and Maryland. The motion was carried for a single executive with no council required to assist in decision making. This latter point would later prove important in the development of the president's cabinet, since the cabinet was purposely designed to be advisory and not a mandatory part of the president's decision process.[7]

In spite of the vote taken on June 4, the issue was later revisited during the ratification process. Opponents of the Constitution opposed ratification partly on the grounds that the single executive would centralize power within a single individual and that this individual could easily become a tyrant. The cabinet council system, or plural executive, would protect against such concentration of power, they argued. Alexander Hamilton became the principal champion of a single executive during the ratification process. He had championed the same argument during the debates from June 2 to 4, going against his own New York delegation to support the final vote on a singular executive on June 4. Writing in a series of letters to the editor to the *New York Packet* under the pseudonym "Publius," Hamilton argued that a collective decision-making process would seriously damage the presidency. Hamilton argued that the group could not meet quickly enough to make the necessary decisions in time of crisis and argued that the lack of accountability in group decision making went against democratic principles.[8] Hamilton's arguments were persuasive enough to blunt further criticism of a singular executive and contributed to the ratification of the Constitution.

By the end of June 1787, the fundamental questions concerning the new national government had been resolved. Many of the delegates returned to their home states, leaving a small group of convention delegates to discuss the operational details of the new national government. During the last days of July, they returned to how the presidency would work, specifically the issues of election, tenure, and qualifications for office. The most important issue involved the election of the executive. How would the nation elect its chief executive? Would there be a direct election process or a more limited electorate? The issue of election for the bicameral legislature had been relatively easily resolved, with the people electing the members of the House of Representatives and the State legislatures electing members of the Senate. The Connecticut Compromise had resolved the differences put forth by Madison and Randolph's Virginia Plan and Governor William Paterson's New Jersey Plan. The issue of election for the president would require still more discussion.

Most delegates wanted a limited election process, with either the Congress electing the president or a proportional system of electors with each state given a number of electors based on their populations. Smaller states opposed the electoral system, unless each state was given one elector with a single vote rather than a proportional process. The proposal finally accepted by the delegates was a compromise, in which a college of electors would meet in each state to vote on their choice for president. The number of electors would be based on the state's population. If no individual won a majority of electors, the Senate would make the final choice. Each state would have one vote in the Senate should this process become necessary. The convention agreed to this proposal, although it substituted the House for the Senate to choose the president. This structure for electing the president remains in effect today. State legislatures determine the process for choosing the electors, with the number equal to the number of Representatives and Senators. The elector system is a winner-take-all system, in which the presidential candidate who wins the popular vote in a state wins all of the electors rather than a proportion equal to the popular vote.

The issue of tenure was another problem with which the framers wrestled. What should the term of office be for the president? As early as June 18, 1787, the convention had discussed the issue of tenure, although not seriously. Alexander Hamilton delivered a six-hour speech to the delegates on how the new national government should operate. One of his proposals was for a strong national government with an executive "chosen by electors and granted lifetime tenure."[9] The delegates quickly discarded Hamilton's radical proposal and moved on to the more pressing issues surrounding the Virginia Plan and the New Jersey Plan. The Virginia Plan did not have a specific term of office for the president, which was defined as the "national executive," although it stipulated that the executive could not run for a second term. When the delegates pursued discussions on the tenure of office, other proposals included a three-year tenure with only one term, a seven-year tenure with only one term, and even a life term. After several debates on the term of office, no final decision was reached. The only common ground was that if the executive were to have the right to run for office again, the term of office should be shortened. When the convention could not agree on the length of the term, they moved on to other issues. Not until September did the issue arise again, when the Committee on Postponed Matters was forced to bring the issue to closure. The Committee suggested a four-year term with no limit on the number of terms that could be served and inserted this language into the final document, which was approved on September 17. The issue of tenure would surface again in the 1940s, after Franklin Delano Roosevelt's reelection to a fourth term. In 1951, the twenty-second amendment was ratified, which limited the president to two terms in office.

The constitutional convention had provided for the qualifications for office, election process, tenure in office, and the insurance for a singular executive. The basic issues for setting up the office had been established. But once the office had been established, the framers needed to at least outline the duties that the president was expected to fulfill. The list is relatively short, in contrast to the long list of responsibilities laid out in the Constitution for the Congress. Perhaps the most significant responsibility given to the president in the Constitution is to "faithfully execute the Office of President of the United States, and . . . to preserve, protect, and defend the Constitution of the United States." This simple phrase has provided presidents extraordinary powers, as they interpret these words to provide broad discretionary authority to "protect and defend" the nation from both internal and external forces.

More specifically, the Constitution provides that the president appoint the principal officers of the departments, ambassadors, judges of the Supreme Court (and lower federal courts), and other senior officials with the advice and consent of the Senate. The president also is required to give "to the congress information of the state of the union and recommend to their consideration such measure as he shall judge necessary and expedient." This has been the basis for the president's annual state of the union address to the Congress and the frequent suggestions to Congress for legislative action.

Yet another requirement in the Constitution is for the president to commission "all the officers of the United States." Every commissioned officer in the armed forces receives his or her commission from the president, which is one of the few documents that presidents sign personally today. Most documents are signed by a mechanized pen, known as the auto-pen, rather than by the president.

Presidential Roles

The powers provided for the president in the Constitution are far fewer than those provided for Congress. Yet the president has a number of specific roles that are inherent to the office. These presidential roles are that of head of state, chief executive, chief diplomat, commander in chief, legislative leader and party leader.

Head of State

No presidential role is more noticeable to the American people than the role of **head of state.** The president symbolizes the nation's strengths, its history, and its deep commitment to democracy and caring for its citizenry. As head of state, the president performs both symbolic and ceremonial functions, representing the nation in times of national celebration and crisis and serving as the nation's official representative with foreign leaders. As Arthur M. Schlesinger, Jr., describes the role of head of state, the president is "the central focus of political emotion, the ever more potent symbol of national community."[10]

The president leads the nation in mourning the deaths of soldiers killed in battle, such as President Reagan did in 1983 when the 283 Marines killed in a terrorist attack in Beirut, Lebanon, were returned home. President Reagan walked along the airfield saluting the caskets of the fallen soldiers as they were taken off the airplane from Beirut. The president also leads the nation in mourning the tragic deaths of ordinary citizens, such as President Clinton did when the nation grieved the deaths of passengers on a TWA airline flight that exploded in midair off the New York City coast in 1996. President Clinton met with all of the families on a Long Island beach near the sight of the wreckage in an emotional ceremony. When a gunman, Russell Weston, shot and killed two guards in the Capitol building during a rampage through the halls of the Capitol in the summer of 1998, President Clinton spoke on behalf of the American people at the memorial ceremony.

The president leads the nation in celebrations of holidays such as the Fourth of July, Memorial Day, and Thanksgiving or on the occasion of great events, such as Presidents Kennedy and then Johnson did when the first astronauts were launched into space. The president also hosts national heroes such as athletic champions at the state, college, and professional levels. The championship teams for the Super Bowl and the World Series usually are given warm welcomes at White House receptions. And to celebrate the nation's leading citizens, every year the president bestows the Presidential Medal of Freedom on a small group at a festive White House ceremony. Only the president can award the Medal of Freedom, which recognizes significant contributions to American life, the country's national security, or to world peace.[11]

More routine roles that the president plays as head of state are dedicating monuments across the country, hosting White House ceremonies to award medals for members of the armed forces, visiting schools and having children read and talk about their daily lives, and throwing out the first ball at the beginning of the baseball season. The American public expects the president to perform these roles, and presidents constantly seek to live up to those expectations. For presidents it is an important part of communicating strong leadership with the public and generally enhances their own popularity. There is nothing more important to a White House staff than a primetime news shot of the president smiling in the Rose Garden with U.S. Olympic gold medal winners or with the national spelling bee champion. However, many nonprofit organizations try to get on the president's schedule for a visit to the Oval Office. The president's staff must be vigilant as to which groups the president meets with, to ensure that their political goals are not at odds. It would be difficult for the president to host the National Rifle Association's target shooter of the year when the White House is aggressively pushing gun-control legislation opposed by the National Rifle Association. But the president might want to make the American Cancer Society a priority, such as President Clinton did following the death of his mother, Virginia Clinton, from cancer in 1994.

There may be instances in which the president is committed to using the White House to highlight an organization or a day of celebration, but is unable to be there. In these cases, the vice president is often called on to represent the president as the head of state. Since the vice president is second in line of succession to the president, this assignment is perfectly logical. Usually the vice president hosts the groups in his own office, with the requisite news groups taking pictures and preparing their stories. Traditionally only the president uses the White House for official ceremonies.

The role of head of state is not only one of leading the nation in times of sorrow and of celebration, but is also one of representative of the nation to other countries. When heads of state, both elected and ceremonial, visit the United States, the president hosts a state dinner at the White House. Whether the elected head of state, such as the Prime Minister of England, or the ceremonial head of state, such as the Queen of England, visits the United States, the president serves as the official representative on behalf of the nation. When traveling abroad, the president is the official representative of the United States and is accorded that status. In contrast to a parliamentary structure of government such as in Great Britain, Belgium, Denmark, or Spain, where a monarch serves as the head of state and the prime minister as the head of government, the American structure of government combines both roles in the presidency. To a large extent, the president performs many of the ceremonial roles that are reserved for the members of the royal families in other countries. In England, for example, the Queen opens and dissolves Parliament in a formal ceremony, approves all acts of Parliament before they can become law, and appoints all ministers and judges. The Queen also welcomes foreign dignitaries and hosts state dinners. In the United States, most of these roles are dealt with by the president as head of state.

Hosting foreign dignitaries is one of the more important parts of the president's job as head of state. Presidents have elaborate dinners for heads of states at the White House, inviting a wide range of the nation's leading citizens to join them. If the president of Poland visits, Polish-American leaders are included in the guest list, as are Italian-American leaders when the prime minister of Italy visits the president. Presidents use this opportunity with visiting heads of state to portray themselves as international leaders and statesmen and subsequently schedule many news events with the two leaders together. Similarly, the president uses his role as head of state to represent the United States in foreign countries and to reaffirm American foreign policy positions. President Clinton made a historic trip to China in June 1998 to symbolize a continuing effort by the United States to encourage democracy and to end human rights violations around the world. In 1963 President Kennedy traveled to Berlin to oppose the building of the infamous Berlin wall by the Soviet Union and to oppose Soviet expansionism.

The Constitution provides a strong basis for the president's role as head of state, both in representing the nation domestically and abroad. Although there is no specific reference to "chief of state" or "head of state" in the Constitution, the language indicates that the framers intended the president to serve as head of state. The most important constitutional provision for the president serving as head of state is in the oath of office, which requires the president to "the best of my Ability, preserve, protect, and defend the Constitution of the United States." The language requires the president to be the nation's leader, to ensure that the country is "preserved, protected, and defended." They are words that have been recited by every president since George Washington, providing continuity to our governmental structure.

The symbolism of every president repeating the same words for more than two hundred years offers a sense of security that our government is operating smoothly. After the president speaks these words at the inauguration, another tradition continues. The president gives an inaugural address, which every president has done. The inaugural address binds the nation together, solidifying the hopes and dreams for our future. Even after the bitter 1992 election, Bill Clinton included a peace offering to his defeated opponent, George Bush, in his inaugural address. "I salute my predecessor, President Bush, for his half century of service to America."[12] Every president has used the inaugural address to heal the wounds of an often divisive presidential election and to bring the nation together for common goals. Even after President Johnson was sworn into office aboard Air Force One in Dallas, Texas, he realized the importance of addressing the nation as a symbol of a peaceful transfer of power and later spoke on national television to begin a national healing process.

The inaugural ceremonies offer the president numerous opportunities to showcase his role as head of state. The official ceremony is carried on live television across the country and throughout the world, with the president sitting on the east portico of the Capitol with the Supreme Court, the Congress, the ambassadorial corps, and the members of the cabinet around him. Across the street the nation's press corps has set up offices atop buildings to have a clear view of the swearing-in ceremony. The nation is focused on only one person: the president of the United States. After the ceremony, the president's motorcade slowly progresses down Constitution Avenue toward the White House. Some presidents, such as Jimmy Carter and Bill Clinton, have chosen to walk the short distance as a symbol of their partnership with the American public. President Carter even wore a business suit rather than the more formal attire that other presidents have worn. At the White House, some presidents have opened the White House to the public. President and Mrs. Clinton stood at the door of the White House for hours welcoming the public to tour and enjoy their new home. In the evening following the inauguration, the president attends a multitude of inaugural balls held in various locations around Washington, D.C. These inaugural balls are generally not open to the public but are for supporters of the president who purchase tickets. The cost of the tickets is used to defray the costs of the inaugural balls and other inaugural celebrations. There are no public funds provided for the inaugural celebrations, which cost about $25 million for President Clinton's 1993 celebrations.

The inauguration of a president is a symbolic event highlighting the importance of the new president to the nation. But it is also an important constitutional event, for it signifies the election of a national leader and concurrently the head of state. Neither the Congress nor the Supreme Court is given the mandate to preserve, protect, and defend the nation by the Constitution, only the president. The president is the leader of the country, as the brief thirty-five word oath of office signifies. Since both the Congress and the Supreme Court are composed of many members, it would be difficult for either of those branches to represent the nation as the president does as head of state.

As the nation's head of state, the president represents the American people both within the nation and throughout the world. Although the president plays a deeply symbolic role in the American structure of government, often resembling the role of the monarch in other systems of government, the president must be constantly vigilant to ensure against any trappings that might exceed public standards. President Nixon went beyond these standards when he had his military aides dress in elaborate uniforms, complete with black high hats, red jackets, and trumpets, for certain events on the steps of the White House.[13] Historian Arthur Schlesinger, Jr., declared this Nixon ritual as rivaling the guards at Buckingham Palace and reflective of an "imperial" presidency.[14] Jimmy Carter's walk to the White House after the inauguration was his effort to reduce concerns about the imperial presidency that arose during the Nixon era. As Carter says in his memoirs, "I felt a simple walk would be a tangible indication of some reduction in the imperial status of the President and his family."[15] The symbols of the presidency that the role of head of state contributes to are essential in building and maintaining support for the president within the American electorate.

Chief Executive

As the nation's **chief executive,** the president is the formal head of government, charged with overseeing all of the executive branch and administering the laws passed by Congress. The first job of the president after taking the oath of office is to create an "administration" to administer the laws of the land. Today, the executive branch includes fourteen cabinet-level departments, numerous boards and commissions, independent agencies, and a total workforce of nearly three million federal employees, not including 1.8 million members of the armed forces. These numbers stand in stark contrast to the relatively small executive branch that George Washington presided over, which had only a few federal employees. By 1801, twelve years after Washington had first been sworn into office, the number of federal employees had risen only to three hundred. These three hundred federal employees administered a national government that represented a nation of four million people in thirteen states. By 1998 the nation had grown to a federal workforce of nearly three million serving 270 million people in fifty states.

The Constitution provides for the president to serve as the chief executive, or chief administrator, through a number of references. The source of the president's power as chief executive is found in Article II, Section 3, which provides for the president to see that all the laws are "faithfully executed," and in Article II, Section 2, which provides for the president to appoint, remove, and supervise all executive officers and to appoint all federal judges. The term "executive" refers directly to the president's power to execute the laws, which requires an administrative role. The Congress was empowered by the Constitution to create the laws and the president was empowered by the Constitution to execute or administer the laws. Through this constitutional assignment, presidents have created an administrative structure to meet this constitutional charge.

The administrative function of the president as the chief executive officer stems from the structure of government that operated under the Articles of Confederation and Perpetual Union following the nation's declaration of independence from England. Under the Articles of Confederation and Perpetual Union, the thirteen states formed an alliance in which the states retained their sovereignty. The national government had no authority over the states and operated primarily for purposes of national defense. The structure of the government that operated under the Articles of Confederation and Perpetual Union was a unicameral congress, which met in Federal Hall in New York City. Each state had one vote, although they had a varying number of delegates depending on the state's population. The unicameral congress elected a presiding officer, who became known as the president, and created four "departments" to manage the affairs of the government. When the Constitution superseded the Articles of Confederation and Perpetual Union with its ratification in 1789, the new Congress followed the path of the old unicameral congress and created executive departments. On July 27, 1789, one of the first acts of the Congress was to establish the first executive department, the Department of Foreign Affairs (State). This act was followed in the next few months by acts creating the Departments of War and Treasury, and an Attorney General (later renamed the Department of Justice). Since 1789, the cabinet has grown to fourteen executive departments. The executive departments are the foundation of the president's management capability for administering the laws of the country.

Oversight of the three million employees of the executive branch would be impossible for the president without substantial assistance. This assistance comes from several groups of people, including the president's cabinet, who manage the operations of the fourteen executive departments, the White House Staff, and the various units within the Executive Office of the President. Within each of the fourteen executive departments are both career staff (civil service employees) and political staff who work to implement the congressional mandates that the departments exist to fulfill.

Presidents use their **appointment power** for their political appointments. Most of the senior-level political appointments require Senate confirmations. Non-policy-making positions, such as a personal secretary or executive assistant, do not require Senate confirmation, even though they are political appointments. Which positions fall under the designation of "policy-making" and are subject to Senate confirmation are prescribed by statute. Presidents do not control which positions are subject to Senate confirmation and which positions are not.

The choice of individuals to fill the political positions, particularly the Senate-confirmed political positions, provide an important statement about how the administration will operate and what the president stands for. Dwight Eisenhower chose his cabinet and their senior staff from the boardrooms of corporate America, emphasizing his determination to bring effective fiscal management into government. Ronald Reagan emphasized political loyalty and conservative values in his nominees, to ensure that the Republican agenda was moved forward. Bill Clinton emphasized ethnic and gender diversity in his nominees, to ensure that governmental decisions represented the interests of all segments of society. One presidential scholar also points out that each presidential appointment should be carefully considered by the White House, since any high-level appointee who is accused of corrupt or improper activity can harm the president's reputation.[16] President Warren Harding's administration was forever tainted by the Teapot Dome scandal. Harding's Secretary of Interior, Albert B. Fall, was prosecuted and sent to jail for taking a secret $100,000 payment for arranging oil leases in the Teapot Dome oil reserve in Wyoming.[17]

A clear line of authority is developed within the executive agencies, with the president at the top and the cabinet secretaries, deputy and assistant secretaries, bureau directors, and division chiefs all reporting in a linear relationship. This line of authority is similar to the manner in which most businesses and industries structure their organizational relationships. The role of administrative head of the executive branch is the most important role that the president has, and it is the most difficult. The management of the thousands of laws already in existence plus the additions of new laws every year is a daunting task for any individual.

The job of managing the executive branch is complicated by the absence of clear language in many laws passed by Congress. The laws are purposely written vaguely by Congress because it is difficult to reach a consensus on the language within the 435-member House of Representatives and the 100-member Senate. Members of Congress often do not have the expertise to write more specific language. It is usually left to the executive departments responsible for implementing the laws to determine the specific language for the programs created by the laws. This discretion in managing the programs created by Congress gives the president the ability to craft language that moves the program in the direction that the administration wants. For example, the president uses his appointment power granted by Article II of the Constitution to appoint cabinet officers and other senior officials that will move programmatic language toward administrative goals. Since departmental staffs have a significant degree of authority in writing the regulations and other governing language for departmental programs, it is important that presidents maintain supervision. President Nixon appointed political appointees within the departments specifically to ensure that departmental programs were in line with the principles of the Nixon administration.[18] President Reagan required all political appointees to fill out a form before their appointment to verify their support of the Reagan political philosophy, particularly cutting federal spending and maintaining the conservative Republican philosophy.[19]

Execution of the laws is a complex process, which involves both the interpretation of the laws through regulations and the delivery of the services either directly to individuals or using state and local governments as conduits. The delivery of services involves thousands of departmental employees, many of whom are housed in Washington, D.C., within the federal complex and many of whom are housed around the country in regional offices.

Although the Constitution requires the president to execute the laws, Congress maintains a significant degree of oversight by reviewing how the laws are being implemented. **Congressional oversight** was mandated by the Legislative Reorganization Act of 1946, which required congressional committees to regularly examine how the agencies within their jurisdictions were applying the laws. The Legislative Reorganization Act of 1970 strengthened the role of Congress in oversight activities by providing funds for outside experts and additional committee staff to conduct financial and programmatic analysis. In recent years, the number of congressional oversight hearings has dramatically increased, due to the increase in the number of programs and due to the growing tension between the president and Congress. This tension is the product of both party differences, when the Congress is controlled by one political party and the presidency by another political party, and by institutional differences, in which both the president and Congress consider themselves the leader of public policy.

One of the most important parts of managing the executive branch is the budgeting power, which gives the president the authority to control who gets what, when, and how. The budget gives the president political power. As Richard Pious states, "to determine what goes into a budget . . . is to answer the key question of politics."[20] Using the Office of Management and Budget (OMB), the president establishes the budgets for each of the fourteen cabinet departments and a number of independent agencies, such as the National Aeronautics and Space Administration. Although Congress has its own budgeting agency, the Congressional Budget Office (CBO), the agenda established through the budgeting of the president's OMB is generally the course the budget follows. The very name of the president's budget, *The Budget of the United States Government*, establishes the president as the budget leader. Although the budget is actually a series of requests to Congress by the president for funding, the budget has become a tool of executive authority.

The role of the president as chief executive is a broad one. The duty incorporates the broad range of appointment powers, including all of the non-career federal employees, all federal judges, and all ambassadors, and the broad range of executive powers, including the administration of the entire executive branch and the execution of the nation's laws. Yet the president also has the power in his role as chief executive to issue executive orders and executive agreements in addition to proclamations and other directives. These do not require consultation with or approval by Congress. One of the most famous proclamations was in 1863, when Abraham Lincoln issued the Proclamation of Emancipation to free the slaves. President Roosevelt also used a proclamation when he issued his Limited National Emergency Proclamation on September 8, 1939, after the outbreak of World War II.

Executive orders are used by presidents to define specific ways that programs should operate across the administration, but they must remain within existing laws and cannot supersede a law. For example, in 1948 President Truman issued Executive Order 9981 to integrate the armed forces, and in 1963 President Kennedy issued an executive order to ban racial discrimination in all federally subsidized housing. In 1969, President Nixon ordered racial hiring quotas on federal construction projects, as outlined in the Philadelphia Plan. One of the more controversial uses of the executive order came during 1981 when President Reagan issued Executive Order 12333, which allowed greater use of electronic surveillance, or wiretaps, primarily by the Federal Bureau of Investigation (FBI). Executive orders are also used for administrative actions within the Executive Office of the President, such as creating or disbanding units. The Executive Office of the President itself was created by an executive order in 1939.

President Clinton relied heavily on executive orders, issuing 259 from the day he took office in 1993 through mid-1998.[21] In 1993, as one of his first official acts, President Clinton used an executive order to ban discrimination against homosexuals in the military. Clinton also used executive orders soon after taking office to lift the "gag rule" imposed by Presidents Reagan and Bush that prohibited anyone at federally funded family planning clinics except doctors from discussing abortions with patients. President Reagan used an executive order to ban medical research using tissue from fetuses derived from elective abortions. Other executive orders issued during the Clinton administration included applying a patients' bill of rights to all federal health plans (1998) and creating a national monument using 1.7 million acres in southern Utah (1997). Rahm Emanuel, a senior member of President Clinton's White House staff, explained why executive orders were so valuable to the administration. "Sometimes we use it [an executive order] in reaction to legislative delay or setbacks. Sometimes we do it to lead by example and force the legislative hand. . . . Obviously, you'd rather pass legislation that you can do X, but you're willing to make whatever progress you can on an agenda item."[22]

Executive agreements allow presidents to make treaties with other countries without subjecting the treaties to Senate approval, as required by the Constitution. Executive orders and executive agreements both allow presidents to change the course of policy without legislative action. The executive agreement power is widely used today for commercial treaties, particularly treaties in which large amounts of agricultural products are sold to foreign countries. The executive agreement was first used by Thomas Jefferson in 1803 when he arranged for the purchase of the Louisiana territory—what became known as the Louisiana Purchase. Throughout the nineteenth century, an average of only one executive agreement per year was made. But in more recent years, executive agreements have been regularly used for trade agreements, military commitments, and arms control pacts.[23] During the Kennedy administration, an executive agreement with Spain allowed the administration to put a Polaris submarine base there, and during the Nixon administration an executive agreement with Thailand allowed seven air bases to be built there.[24] In the post–World War II era, particularly during the cold-war era of nuclear proliferation, numerous executive agreements have been entered into for military commitments.

Although executive agreements allow presidents to circumvent the constitutional requirement that all treaties come before the Senate and receive a two thirds vote of approval, they are not technically considered treaties. In the modern presidency, executive agreements remain powerful tools for rapid execution of international agreements, whether military or commercial. As Congress becomes increasingly bogged down in its deliberative processes, forcing lengthy delays to presidential actions such as appointments and international agreements, the executive agreement has become a tool used more and more often by presidents. The Supreme Court allowed executive agreements to continue in a major court decision. The Supreme Court decided in the case of *United States v. Pink* in 1942 that an executive agreement is the legal equivalent of a treaty, despite the absence of Senate approval. Not to be totally left out of the treaty process, Congress passed the Case Act in 1972, which required that the president inform Congress of all executive agreements. The Case Act required all international agreements to be sent within sixty days to the Senate Committee on Foreign Relations and the House Committee on Foreign Affairs, although the law required only notification, not approval, of presidential actions.[25]

Chief Diplomat

The role as **chief diplomat** provides the president the authority to negotiate treaties, receive ambassadors, recognize foreign countries, and represent the nation with foreign leaders. Since the Congress, through the Senate, must approve all treaties and confirm all appointments of ambassadors, the role of managing the nation's foreign policy is to some degree a power shared with Congress. But as Edward S. Corwin notes, although the power for managing foreign policy is clearly divided between the president and Congress, the lion's share usually falls to the president.[26]

The reason that the framers placed foreign policy firmly within the hands of the president is that treaty negotiations require a great deal of secrecy and immediacy, neither of which can be handled by the large and rancorous Congress. Presidents are able to conduct treaty negotiations with a greater degree of secrecy and can move the negotiations along much faster than can Congress. In addition, the framers thought that the executive departments would be helpful to the president in gathering information for international discussions and treaty negotiations, information that would not easily be accessible to the members of Congress.

The treaty power is defined under Article II, Section 2, of the Constitution, which provides that the president "shall have the Power, by and with the Advice and Consent of the Senate, to make treaties, provided two-thirds of the Senators present concur." Presidents have interpreted this language to mean that the executive branch rather than the legislative branch handles all treaty negotiations, although the Constitution does not specifically state that there should not be collaboration with Congress in the treaty-negotiation process. Since Congress has not pressed for this collaborative relationship, presidents have understood the responsibility to be solely theirs.

Only once has the president tried to establish a collaborative relationship with Congress, and this attempt failed dismally. Soon after being sworn into office, George Washington and his Secretary of War, Henry Knox, went to the Senate to meet with members about a treaty with the Creek Indians. Washington and Knox met with the Senators on August 21, 1789, voicing their thoughts on how the treaty should be worded. The Senators were unable to agree and asked for time to meet alone. They called Washington and Knox back on August 24 to provide their thoughts on the treaty. Washington never sought the views of the Senate again, having determined it was too difficult to achieve a consensus in the larger body and to have any quick response.[27] Had Washington continued to seek Congressional collaboration in treaty negotiations, the precedent would have been set. However, he chose not to continue the collaboration and determined that the president should handle the negotiations totally within the executive branch. As one presidential scholar noted, "no president of the United States has since that day ever darkened the doors of the Senate for the purpose of personal consultation with it concerning the advisability of a desired negotiation."[28]

The role of the president as chief negotiator for international treaties has moved relatively smoothly since the days of George Washington. In general, Congress has acceded to the president as the nation's chief negotiator and made relatively few changes to treaties. There have been some notable exceptions, such as after World War I in 1919, when the isolationists in Congress opposed the Versailles Treaty because it included the participation of the United States in the League of Nations. During the Carter administration, Congress opposed the Strategic Arms Limitation Talks II (SALT II) treaty, which would have reduced the nation's nuclear arsenal. Jimmy Carter was furious at the Senate's opposition to the treaty: "Our failure to ratify the SALT II treaty and to secure even more far-reaching agreements on nuclear arms control was the most profound disappointment of my presidency."[29]

The role of the president as chief diplomat took another substantive turn during the administration of George Washington. Washington established the right of presidents to declare the United States as a neutral party between warring nations. During the war between France and England in 1793, Washington proclaimed the neutrality of the United States. On April 12, 1793, he issued a neutrality proclamation that the United States would be "friendly and impartial" with both England and France. Congress then endorsed the stand that Washington had taken with the Neutrality Act of 1794.

Thomas Jefferson, who resigned as Washington's Secretary of State, did not endorse the position that Washington had taken with regard to the president's authority to declare neutrality. For Jefferson, since the Constitution required Congress to declare war, it also intended Congress to keep us out of war or to maintain neutrality. This logic is often referred to as the theory of **parallel construction.** For Washington, the absence of any such language in the Constitution allowed him to use his executive powers to declare neutrality. The questions surrounding Washington's authority to declare neutrality were aired publicly in a series of letters to the editor in a variety of newspapers, similar to those letters written by Hamilton, Madison, and Jay (which became known as the *Federalist Papers*) in defense of the Constitution during the ratification process. Hamilton wrote a series of letters under the pseudonym "Pacificus," arguing that Washington had complete constitutional authority to declare neutrality in 1793. Jefferson, who was still a member of Washington's cabinet, enlisted the assistance of his fellow Virginian, James Madison, to argue against Hamilton. Writing under the pseudonym "Helvidius," Madison argued that the president was constrained by the executive role, which dominated the roles and responsibilities of the president in the Constitution. For Madison, the president was limited to executing the laws that Congress passed, including a declaration of war or a declaration of neutrality. The **Pacificus-Helvidius debates** focused on one of the problems that the president would deal with as chief diplomat but that had no specific constitutional guidelines.

Another issue that eventually caused significant problems between the president and Congress with regard to the president's role as chief diplomat involved the termination of treaties. Since the Constitution does not specify whether the president or Congress has the power to terminate treaties, presidents have taken responsibility for the process. As had George Washington with the concept of declaring neutrality, succeeding presidents viewed the process of declaring treaties to be terminated as a part of their executive responsibilities. One of the more charged cases came in 1979 when President Carter terminated the 1954 Mutual Defense Treaty with the Republic of China (Taiwan) in favor of establishing diplomatic relations with the People's Republic of China (mainland China). The civil war in China between the Nationalists, led by Chiang Kai-shek, and the Communists, led by Mao Tse-tung, during the 1940s had ended in the creation of two separate countries. Chiang Kai-shek and his followers fled to the small island of Taiwan off the coast of China, declaring themselves the true government of China as the Republic of China. Mao Tse-tung remained on mainland China establishing another entire governmental structure there known as the People's Republic of China.

Since the United States was avidly anticommunist during this period, the United States supported Chiang Kai-shek's government and refused to acknowledge Mao Tse-tung's government. Both Chinas viewed themselves as the only legitimate government of China, and the the United States was forced to choose between the two. The United States chose Chiang Kai-shek's Republic of China on Taiwan and formally signed the 1954 pact. This relationship remained firm throughout the 1950s and 1960s, until President Nixon began to pursue a reopening of relations with mainland China. In 1971 the United Nations voted membership for the People's Republic of China in place of Taiwan. The following year President Nixon traveled to China and met with Mao Tse-tung. At that time, the two signed the Shanghai Communique, which looked forward to the establishment of normal relations. Those normal relations, or formal diplomatic ties, which the Shanghai Communique sought were established in 1979 by President Carter. Carter terminated the treaty with Taiwan, which had designated the Republic of China as the sole representative of the Chinese people, and established diplomatic relations with the People's Republic of China on the mainland. Since Taiwan would not allow a policy in which both governments had diplomatic relations with the United States, President Carter chose to continue with mainland China. The Senate was not involved in the treaty termination process, although Senator Barry Goldwater brought a lawsuit in federal court against the president; it was ruled a political issue by the Supreme Court and dismissed.

Another area of the president's role as chief diplomat involves the formal recognition of new governments. This power was first used in 1793 when George Washington received Ambassador Edmond Genêt of the new French Republic following the French Revolution. This signaled the acceptance by the United States of the revolutionary government. The Genêt case also established the principle that the president could force a country to withdraw their ambassador. When Genêt tried to gain support for France in their war with England, even though Washington had declared the United States neutral in that war, Washington demanded that France recall Genêt. France recalled Genêt and sent another ambassador.

Several modern cases of presidents using their authority to establish diplomatic relations with other nations include Vietnam, China, Cuba, and the Vatican. When President Carter terminated the treaty with the Republic of China, he also established diplomatic relations with the People's Republic of China. In a similar vein, President Reagan recognized the Vatican as a country, rather than merely a part of Italy, and established diplomatic relations. Also, President Kennedy terminated diplomatic relations with Cuba after the Cuban missile crisis. Both the termination of diplomatic relations and the establishment of diplomatic relations have fallen within the province of the president's role as chief diplomat. Even though there is no specific authority in the Constitution for this power, it is rarely challenged by Congress. Most recently, President Clinton recognized the communist government of Vietnam and established formal diplomatic relations in 1995.

The role of the president as chief diplomat is most apparent when the president hosts summit meetings or travels abroad to summit meetings. **Summits** have become one of the overt symbols of presidential leadership in foreign policy. Since President Truman met in Potsdam in the summer of 1945 with Soviet and British leaders to partition Germany after World War II, the use of summits has solidified the president's command of the foreign policy apparatus and the president's role as the nation's chief diplomat. Summits have been routinely used since Potsdam, including President Eisenhower's Geneva Summit in 1955 to discuss the reunification of Germany with Soviet, French, and British leaders; President Nixon's 1972 Moscow Summit with Leonid Brezhnev to discuss the SALT I treaty; President Reagan's Reykjavik Summit in 1986 with Mikhail Gorbachev on arms control; and President Bush's Helsinki Summit in 1990, again with Gorbachev, on the Middle East crisis.

As international relationships have changed in the post-Soviet years, so too have the participants in summitry. On October 28 and 29, 1997, President Clinton hosted Chinese President Jiang Zemin for a two-day summit meeting in Washington, D.C. The two leaders addressed trade issues, including a $3 billion sale of U.S. airplanes to China and the sale of nuclear technology (the United States wanted to stop China's sale of nuclear technology to other countries, particularly to Iran). The summitry of the 1990s has focused on economic issues rather than on the nuclear disarmament and containment issues of the Cold War.

Many of the post–World War II summits were between the United States and the Soviet Union as arms control became a dominant theme. After the collapse of the Soviet Union, arms control summits gave way to economic summits. Economic summits have had a broader audience, with the leaders of the seven major industrialized nations meeting twice a year to discuss international economic issues. The Group of Seven (G-7) is made up of the United States, France, Japan, Great Britain, Germany, Italy, and Canada. Russia became a limited partner in the economic summits in 1997 after Russian President Boris Yeltsin actively sought to have his country included.

Commander in Chief

The role of **commander in chief** should be one of the most clearly defined roles in the Constitution that the president is given, but it is not. Article II, Section 2, of the Constitution states that "the President shall be Commander in Chief of the Army and Navy of the United States, and the Militia of the several States, when called into the actual Service of the United States." Although the president has control over the operations of the armed forces, the framers ensured in Article I of the Constitution that the president was checked on the use of the military. Congress was given the power of the purse. Presidents could not conduct a protracted war without funding from Congress, nor could presidents purchase military equipment without funding from Congress. Congress was also given the power to create new military services, such as it did with the creation of the Air Force.

The role of commander in chief centers around the president's ability to provide for the nation's defense. The framers deliberately divided the decision to go to war between the President and Congress. Congress has the power to declare war and fund the war while the President directs the military in times of war and peace. Yet this simple division of power is full of questions.

1. How is war defined?
2. Are there military missions short of war that the president can order without congressional authorization?

3. Can the president order an attack to preempt an attack from another nation?
4. Can the president order U.S. forces to invade the territory of a neutral nation in pursuit of enemy forces?
5. Can the president commit forces for the protection of American interests in another country without congressional approval?

Although these questions complicate the president's authority as commander in chief, some clear powers of the president are evident.

1. The president can order the military to stop fighting.
2. The president can order troops to withdraw from an area of conflict.
3. The president can negotiate an armistice.
4. The president can declare neutrality.

But these powers are further complicated because:

1. Congress must approve a treaty ending the war.
2. Congress can repeal its declaration of war.

The president's role as commander in chief is centered on the degree to which the president consults Congress in military actions involving foreign countries. As commander in chief, the president has the authority to determine the size, organization, and strength of the armed forces. These decisions, however, are constrained by funding provided by Congress. The president can also increase or decrease the size of the armed forces stationed at any military base around the world. And if the United States is attacked the president can order the military to respond to protect the nation. However, since only Congress has the power to declare war, how limited is the president in using the armed forces against foreign military forces?

The evolution of presidential war powers began when President Jefferson sent naval ships in 1801 to the Mediterranean Sea to protect U.S. ships from pirate attacks along the Barbary coast of Spain. Jefferson did not consult Congress on the use of force against the pirates since he viewed his role as commander in chief as justifying military action for defensive purposes. In 1861 President Lincoln ordered the navy to blockade Confederate ports after Confederate forces had attacked Fort Sumter. Lincoln viewed the blockade as a defensive action. During the 1800s presidents routinely sent troops to the western states to protect the settlers from Indian attacks, again never seeking congressional approval since the military action was for defensive purposes. In 1941 President Roosevelt ordered the navy to escort U.S. convoys across the Atlantic Ocean to protect them from attacks by the German navy. Roosevelt directed that the U.S. ships could fire on German ships on sight. Again, Roosevelt did not seek congressional approval since the military action was for defensive purposes. A clear trend had developed throughout the nation's history that presidents did not seek congressional approval for military actions of a defensive nature.

In more recent years, however, Congress has begun to question the president's use of war powers. In June 1950, using his power as commander in chief, President Truman sent troops to Korea under the authority of the United Nations resolution that authorized every United Nations member "to render every assistance to South Korea."

Congress was not consulted and did not try to force a return of the troops. The President's use of the war power was scrutinized in 1951 when Congress examined Truman's decision to send four more divisions to Europe to bolster Allied defenses against the growing Soviet troop level in Eastern Europe. Congress also reopened Truman's authority to send troops to Korea during this wide-ranging debate, which became known as the "Great Debate." In the end, the Senate approved Truman's decision to send new troops to Europe and said it was the sense of Congress that any further deployment of U.S. troops to Europe should be approved by Congress. In essence, Congress had not challenged the president's primacy in national security or military deployments, but had begun to question some aspects of presidential war powers.

After the Korean War, Congress continued to question war powers decisions by the president, but overwhelmingly supported presidential actions. Congress gave almost blanket authority for presidents to use military force without further consultation with Congress. In 1955 Congress passed the Formosa Resolution to protect Formosa from mainland China's aggression. In 1957 the Middle East Resolution gave the president authority to protect Israel from invasions, the Cuban Resolution of 1962 authorized the president to defend Latin America against Cuban aggression, and the Berlin Resolution of 1962 authorized the president to defend West Berlin against further Soviet encroachment or attack. The Gulf of Tonkin Resolution in 1964 authorized President Johnson to use military force and to "take all necessary measures to repel any armed attack against United States Forces" and "to prevent further communist aggression" in Southeast Asia. When some members of Congress complained about the escalation of the Vietnam War, both Presidents Johnson and Nixon cited the broad authority that they had been given in the Gulf of Tonkin Resolution.

However, by the early 1970s an activist Congress sought to reestablish a role in using military force abroad. Most members of Congress prior to the 1970s believed that the president had the authority to use military force for defensive actions to protect American citizens in foreign countries and to protect the armed forces. The Vietnam War brought new scrutiny to this standard since many members of Congress felt that the president had gone beyond the mandate of the Gulf of Tonkin Resolution and was actively waging war, which Congress had to authorize. As a result, Congress passed the War Powers Resolution of 1973, which required the president to consult with Congress "whenever possible" before committing U.S. troops to any area of "hostilities." The law declared that its purpose was "to fulfill the intent of the framers of the Constitution of the United States and to insure that the collective judgement of both the Congress and the President will apply to the introduction of U.S. armed forces into hostilities." President Nixon did not support this interpretation that the collective judgment of Congress and the president was necessary for military action. Nixon subsequently vetoed the bill, but the veto was overridden.

The War Powers Resolution of 1973 has had little effect on the conduct of presidents as they exercise their commander in chief role. In 1975 when President Ford conducted a series of rescue missions from Danang and Saigon in South Vietnam as the United States pulled its forces out at the end of the war, he did not consult Congress as the War Powers Resolution required. Ford maintained that he had authority as commander in chief to use U.S. troops to rescue U.S. citizens. Later that year President Ford sent the marines to rescue the *Mayaguez*, a U.S. merchant ship that had been seized by Cambodian naval forces in international waters in the Gulf of Thailand. The ship's crew of thirty-nine was rescued, but eighteen marines were killed during the rescue mission. Again, Ford did not consult with Congress on the rescue mission and defended his position by stating that, "When a crisis breaks out, it is impossible to draw the Congress in with the decision-making process in an effective way." Ford continued by stating that the War Powers Resolution "was a very serious intrusion on the responsibilities of the President as Commander in Chief and the person who formulates and ought to execute foreign policy."[30]

In 1980 President Carter similarly conducted a rescue mission for the 49 hostages held in the American embassy in Tehran, Iran. The rescue mission failed when one of the helicopters crashed on the desert in Iran; eight marines were killed. President Carter had not consulted with Congress prior to committing the troops for the rescue mission. President Reagan also chose not to consult with Congress four times before he ordered U.S. troops into combat situations. In 1983 he stationed troops in Beirut, Lebanon, to combat terrorist attacks on Israel; in 1983 he ordered nineteen hundred marine and army troops to Grenada to pull out a group of medical students who had been stranded during a government coup; in 1986 he ordered the bombing of key centers in Libya in retaliation for Libyan terrorist attacks on military personnel stationed in Europe; and in 1986 he diverted profits from the sale of arms to Iran to finance the contra rebels in Nicaragua. Nor did President Bush seek congressional authorization for the 1991 invasion of Kuwait to push out the Iraqi army. President Clinton also ignored the War Powers Resolution when he sent troops to Haiti in 1993 and when he sent twenty-three Tomahawk cruise missiles against Iraqi intelligence headquarters on the evening of June 26, 1993. In 1998 President Clinton ordered the bombing of Afghanistan and Sudan in an attempt to curb suspected terrorist groups in those areas. In perhaps the most dramatic moments of the Clinton presidency, he ordered bombing raids of Iraq the night before the impeachment vote in December 1998. Although his future rested in the hands of Congress, Clinton did not consult with Congress about the bombing raids.

The War Powers Resolution has not hindered the president's role as commander in chief and perhaps has even strengthened it. Since Congress did not try to gain greater involvement in the deployment of troops for any of these actions since the passage of the War Powers Resolution in 1973, they appear to have authorized broad discretion for the president to use in the commitment of military forces. In 1995 Congress debated repealing the War Powers Resolution, but members of the Senate blocked any further action.

The president has strong historical authority to use the commander in chief role to defend U.S. citizens and military personnel around the world. Public support has been firmly behind the president every time military force has been used, including the commitment of 500,000 troops during the Persian Gulf War in 1991. Although not a declared war, President Bush committed troops to a scenario called the Persian Gulf "War." For Congress to effectively become a partner in the command activities of American troops, it will have to rely on its power of the purse to limit presidential decisions. In short military incursions, such as Grenada and the rescue of the *Mayaguez,* Congress had little power, since funding does not become an issue. However, in protracted military engagements, such as Vietnam or President Clinton's commitment of troops to Bosnia or Kosovo, the power of the purse can be a powerful tool.

Legislative Leader

As the leader of the nation, the president is seen as the nation's chief policy-maker and **legislative leader.** He presents an annual legislative program to Congress and regularly meets with members of Congress in support of the legislative package. When presidents are campaigning for the presidency, they present the electorate with a package of legislative proposals (although not necessarily clearly developed proposals) that will achieve their policy agenda. These proposals are refined after the election and specified in the annual State of the Union address. The State of the Union address allows the president to prioritize the legislative goals for the administration and to give more information on those goals than the campaign process had allowed. Every January the president stands before a joint session of Congress and in a speech that lasts approximately one hour presents a list of legislation that the president would like Congress to more forward on.

The leadership role that the president plays in setting the nation's legislative agenda is a product of the twentieth century, as we have moved from an era of congressional government to an era of presidential government. As Woodrow Wilson noted in his famous 1885 study *Congressional Government*, Congress was the dominant player in the development of the nation's legislative agenda. According to Wilson,

> That high office [of president] has fallen from its first estate of dignity because its power has waned, and its power has waned because the power of Congress has become predominant. . . . It does not domineer over the President himself but it makes the Secretaries the humble servants.[31]

But by the time Wilson became president, the tide was turning away from congressional government to an era of presidential government. Presidents have tried during this era of presidential government to lead Congress by using the State of the Union Address to describe their legislative agenda. During the twentieth century, the president's legislative agenda has been given a series of labels: Wilson's New Freedom, Roosevelt's New Deal, Truman's Fair Deal, Kennedy's New Frontier, Johnson's Great Society, Nixon's New Federalism, Reagan's Conservative Revolution, and Clinton's Bridge to the Twenty-First Century.

The difficulty that presidents face in moving their legislative programs through Congress is heightened by divided government, in which one or both houses of Congress are controlled by the political party opposite to that of the president, and by institutional rivalries between the executive and legislative branches. Political rivalries between the branches have always caused difficulty in moving the president's legislative package forward, but the post–Vietnam War era has heightened the institutional rivalries between the branches. President Johnson was able to move his Great Society legislation through Congress since the Democrats controlled both Houses and there was minimal institutional rivalry. However, when both Democrats Jimmy Carter and Bill Clinton controlled the executive branch, Democratic Congresses opposed many of their initiatives. Bill Clinton faced almost hostile opposition from the Democratic Congress in 1993 and 1994 in his efforts for health care and welfare reform. Both divided government and institutional rivalries have seriously hampered the president's ability to gain support in Congress.

The advent of television and other mass media has played an important part in the enhanced role of the president as the legislative leader. Presidents have the opportunity to regularly reinforce their programs through speeches and other events that are covered by the national press. Because the press covers the president far more than any other national leader, such as members of Congress, the president's legislative agenda remains at the forefront of the national discussion. With 435 members in the House of Representatives and 100 members in the Senate, achieving a consensus on programs is difficult. As party leadership in Congress has declined and the committees have become increasingly dominant in determining legislative direction, the process has become even more divisive.

Party Leader

The role of the president as **party leader** goes hand in hand with the president's role as legislative leader. The president's party can generally, although not always, be counted on to support the president's legislative package. When the president is more liberal or more conservative than party members in Congress, the support for presidential legislative initiatives is weakened. Presidents Reagan and Carter were noteworthy in their uncomfortable relations with members of their own parties in Congress. Reagan was more conservative than most Republicans in Congress and Carter was more conservative than most Democrats in Congress. As presidential scholar George Edwards noted, the political philosophies of Reagan and Carter "gave the presidents very different relations with their respective parties. Carter was not the natural leader of the Democratic party. His views ran against the tide of his party and its historic practices, rhetoric, and ideology."[32] This difference in political philosophy with members of their own party has been costly to presidents, as Bill Clinton found out when he tried to push through the health care and welfare reform packages in 1993 and 1994 while he had Democratic majorities in both the House and the Senate. Democrats were as opposed to the package as were the Republicans, who viewed the proposals as increases in big government.

Another role that the president plays as party leader is to name the chairperson of the party after the presidential election. Tradition calls for the newly elected president to name a new chairperson for the party, typically a key supporter during the campaign. President Clinton named Senator Christopher Dodd (D-Conn.) to head the party after the 1996 election. Senator Dodd had been an outspoken supporter of the president's during the first term. In contrast, when an incumbent president loses an election, such as President Bush did in 1992, the president's relationship with the party ends. The party chooses its own chairperson without consulting with the vanquished president. In elections in which both parties have nonincumbents running for office, the party chooses both chairpersons.

The president has numerous responsibilities as the nation's leader, wearing many hats and serving in many different roles. The job of president has relatively few specifications in the Constitution. Strong presidents have expanded their job description as given in the Constitution and used their power to augment their authority through their own leadership techniques. They have dominated the policy process and have been viewed by the public as the nation's leader. Weak presidents have allowed Congress to dominate the policy process and have failed to move past the strict delineation of powers defined in the Constitution. Without fail, however, every president since Franklin Delano Roosevelt in the era known as the modern presidency has given an expansive interpretation to constitutional powers.

Key Words

appointment power
Blair House
Camp David
chief diplomat
chief executive
commander in chief
congressional oversight
executive agreements
executive orders
Former Presidents Act of 1958
head of state
legislative leader

Pacificus-Helvidius debates
parallel construction
party leader
plural executive
qualifications for the presidency
salary
secret service
singular executive
summits
tenure
title
White House

Notes

1. Malcolm Townsend. *Handbook of United States Political History*. rev. ed. Boston: Lothrop, Lee and Shepard, 1905, revised 1910, p. 269.
2. Woodrow Wilson. *George Washington*. New York: Schocken, 1969 (first published in 1896), p. 308.
3. Alexander Hamilton, James Madison, and John Jay. *The Federalist Papers*. Number 73. New York: Bantam, 1982, p. 372.
4. John Hart. *The Presidential Branch: From Washington to Clinton*. 2nd ed. Chatham, NJ: Chatham House, 1995, p. 14.
5. Norman C. Thomas and Joseph A. Pika. *The Politics of the Presidency*. 4th rev. ed. Washington, DC: Congressional Quarterly, 1997, p. 99–100.
6. Stephen E. Ambrose. *Nixon, The Triumph of a Politician 1962–1972*. New York: Simon & Schuster, 1989, pp. 348–349.
7. Shirley Anne Warshaw. *Powersharing: White House–Cabinet Relations in the Modern Presidency*. Albany, NY: State University of New York Press, 1996, p. 13.
8. Alexander Hamilton, James Madison, and John Jay. *The Federalist Papers*. Number 70.
9. Michael Nelson, ed. *Guide to the Presidency*. 2nd ed. Washington, DC: Congressional Quarterly, 1996, p. 17.
10. Arthur M. Schlesinger, Jr. *The Imperial Presidency*. Boston: Houghton Mifflin, 1973, p. 210.
11. Bruce Wetterau. *The Presidential Medal of Freedom: Winners and Their Accomplishments*. Washington, DC: Congressional Quarterly, 1996.
12. *Public Papers of the Presidents of the United States: William Clinton, 1993*. Washington, DC: Government Printing Office, 1994, p. 75.
13. Arthur M. Schlesinger, Jr. *The Imperial Presidency*. Boston: Houghton Mifflin, 1989, p. 218.
14. Ibid., p. 218.
15. Jimmy Carter. *Keeping Faith*. New York: Bantam, 1982, pp. 17–18.
16. Judith E. Michaels. *The President's Call: Executive Leadership from FDR to George Bush*. Pittsburgh, PA: University of Pittsburgh Press, 1997, p. 1.
17. Michael Nelson, ed. *The Presidency from A to Z*. rev. ed. Washington, DC: Congressional Quarterly, 1994, p. 412.
18. Richard P. Nathan. *The Administrative Presidency*. New York: Wiley, 1983, p. 44.
19. Lou Cannon. *President Reagan: The Role of a Lifetime*. New York: Simon & Schuster, 1991.
20. Richard Pious. *The Presidency*. Boston: Allyn & Bacon, 1996, p. 338.
21. Alexis Simendiger. "The Paper Wars." *National Journal*, July 25, 1998, p. 1736.
22. Ibid., p. 1737.
23. Nelson. *The Presidency from A to Z*, pp. 97–98.
24. Schlesinger. *The Imperial Presidency*, pp. 203–204.

25. Louis Fisher. *Constitutional Conflicts Between Congress and the President*. 4th ed. rev. Lawrence, KS: University Press of Kansas, 1997, p. 253.
26. Edward S. Corwin. *The President: Office and Powers 1787–1984*. 5th rev. ed. New York: New York University Press, 1984, p. 201.
27. Stephen H. Wirls and Daniel C. Diller. "Chief Diplomat." *Powers of the Presidency*, 2nd ed. Washington, DC: Congressional Quarterly, 1997, p. 136.
28. Corwin. *The President: Office and Powers 1787–1984*, p. 240.
29. Carter. *Keeping Faith*, p. 265.
30. Larry Berman. *The New American Presidency*. Boston: Little, Brown, 1987, p. 75.
31. Woodrow Wilson. *Congressional Government*. Baltimore: Johns Hopkins University Press, 1981 (first published in 1885), pp. 48–49.
32. George Edwards III. *At the Margins*. New Haven, CT: Yale University Press, 1989, p. 214.

Chapter 2

PRESIDENTIAL ELECTIONS

The election of a president is one of the world's great transitions of power. There is no blood shed in the process and the citizenry has a choice about whom they want to lead the nation. Military force does not determine who will be president, nor does one party name the next leader of the country. In the United States, the election of the president is handled according to precepts established by both state laws and the Constitution. It is a process that allows a multitude of people to enter the race and that winnows the number down to one each from the Democratic and Republican Parties and from a plethora of third parties. The process, although not perfect, is a process that works in this country.

Getting elected president, however, is an arduous and lengthy proposition, which requires raising millions of dollars and building bridges to the party in order to win the primaries. Winning the primary elections and gaining the party nomination is the most difficult part of securing the keys to the Oval Office. One to two years, or more, before the quadrennial election, most candidates begin meeting with leading members of their party in states with early primary elections and in states with large electoral votes. Candidates begin to attend fund-raising events for other people running for office or for entrenched elected officials as a way of building alliances for the presidential election. Many presidential candidates establish political action committees (PACs) that raise money to give to candidates running for other state and federal offices so that they will lend their support to the presidential candidate at a later time. Deciding to run for the presidency is a decision that must be made far in advance of the first primary. Between raising money and building bridges to state party organizations, candidates have a significant job before they declare their candidacy for president.

The rules that govern fund-raising for presidential elections have changed dramatically since the Federal Election Campaign Act of 1972 was originally passed. The law has gone through three major amendments, first in 1974, then in 1976, and again in 1979, but the law remains the governing legislation for how candidates for the presidency can raise and expend funds. The purpose of the Federal Election

Campaign Act is to limit the amount of money that candidates can receive from any individual, corporation, or other group to ensure that the presidency is not "bought." The law entered the public spotlight when Ross Perot used millions of dollars of his own money in the 1992 election and in 1996 when Steven Forbes used millions of dollars of his own money. The law allows individuals to spend unlimited amounts on their own personal campaigns, but limits the amount of money that others can spend on a candidate's campaign. This raised the specter of elections again being bought, but the Supreme Court ruled in *Buckley v. Valeo* in 1976 that the first amendment guaranteed an individual's freedom of speech, which included the freedom to support one's own campaign financially.

In order to gain a sounder understanding of the election process, an understanding of the electoral college and earlier elections in American history is important. Today's election process is somewhat different from the one that evolved out of the constitutional convention, but it retains the basic principles that were forged during the convention. The process retains both state and federal parts, as the framers intended, thus ensuring the essentially federal (or dual nature) of the election structure. Yet today it is a process that allows direct participation of the entire citizenry of voting age to participate. The architects of the Constitution were hesitant to allow everyone to participate in the election of the president, fearing that most of the nation's citizens would not be able to judge the most capable person or to keep emotion from clouding their judgment. The electoral college was molded from this fear of public participation in the election process.

The larger nine states, known as the battleground states, control 243 of the 270 electoral votes needed to win. These battleground states are California, New York, Illinois, Pennsylvania, Ohio, Michigan, New Jersey, Texas, and Florida. Under the rules of the electoral college, the candidate who wins a plurality of votes in each state wins all of the electoral votes. The electors are not apportioned in this winner-take-all system. The goal of a presidential candidate is to win a majority (270) of the electoral votes. A presidential campaign needs to carry state electoral votes, not the popular national vote.[1]

In modern elections, the electoral vote count has been central to how candidates design their campaign schedules and campaign advertising. States with large electoral votes, such as California, Texas, and New York, receive far more attention during the presidential campaign than states with few electoral votes, such as Delaware, Montana, and Wyoming. Candidates will visit California repeatedly during the campaign, trying to shore up the sizable number of electoral votes that the state controls. In contrast, candidates will rarely if ever visit Montana, given the scant number of electoral votes held there.

Presidential campaign managers carefully map out the trips that a candidate takes and the advertising that is purchased to target the states with the larger electoral vote counts. Campaign managers will also develop trip schedules for the candidate that combine neighboring states with large electoral counts. For example, candidates will make "swings" into Pennsylvania and New York for one day, or New Jersey and Pennsylvania for one day, because these neighboring states are both important to win. The only time that this strategy is not put into play occurs when a state with a large electoral count will clearly go to the candidate of the other party. Time and money are too precious to throw away when the polls indicate little or no chance of winning the state.

The Electoral College

The electoral college is a process often misunderstood by the public, yet it is a process that is critical to winning a presidential election. It involves the decision of 538 electors who determine the election of a president. Although there have been regular calls during the quadrennial elections for abolishing the electoral college and for allowing direct election by the public, no serious attempts have been made to amend the Constitution to provide for this change. After more than two hundred years in service, the electoral college remains one of the most important keys to the Oval Office.

While millions of individuals across the country vote for president, only the 538 individuals who are **presidential electors** actually cast the official votes for president. Until the electors have cast their votes and they have been duly certified by both their state officials and by the Congress of the United States, the presidential election is not finalized. The number of presidential electors is the total of the entire membership in the House of Representatives, which is 435, plus the entire membership in the Senate, which is 100, plus three for the District of Columbia, for a total of 538. The candidate must win a majority of the electors in order to win the electoral vote. Since 269 is one half of the **electoral college,** the winner must gain 270 electoral votes to gain a majority. Thus, in order to win the presidency, a candidate must obtain 270 or more electoral votes. This number would increase should additional states, such as Puerto Rico, be added to the union.

The number of electors assigned to each state is derived directly from the Constitution. According to Article II of the Constitution, every state is given electors equal to the number of that state's delegation in the House of Representatives plus the state's two Senators. For example, if a state has four members in its delegation to the House of Representatives and two Senators, its number of electors will be six. Similarly, if a state has twenty-six members in its delegation to the House and two Senators, its number of electors will be twenty-eight. The twenty-third amendment (1961) to the Constitution made a slight adjustment to this procedure by giving the District of Columbia, which had essentially become disenfranchised, three electoral votes. The number three was determined by assigning the District the same number of votes as the smallest state would be given. The smallest state has three electoral votes since it has only one delegate to the House of Representatives and two Senators. Delaware, for example, has only three electors (Figure 2.1).

Article II of the Constitution originally provided for an unlimited number of electors to be in the electoral college. However, since the number of electors is directly tied to the size of the Senate and the size of the House of Representatives, which was capped at 435 in 1913, it slowed any significant growth in the size of the electoral college. Today, the only way the electoral college can increase in size is through a constitutional amendment, such as the **twenty-third amendment,** which provided electors for the District of Columbia, or by states' being added to the union. Should another state be added to the union, the number of electors would increase only by two, which would represent the number of Senators added. The number of Representatives is not added to the electors anymore. It is important to remember, however, that when new states

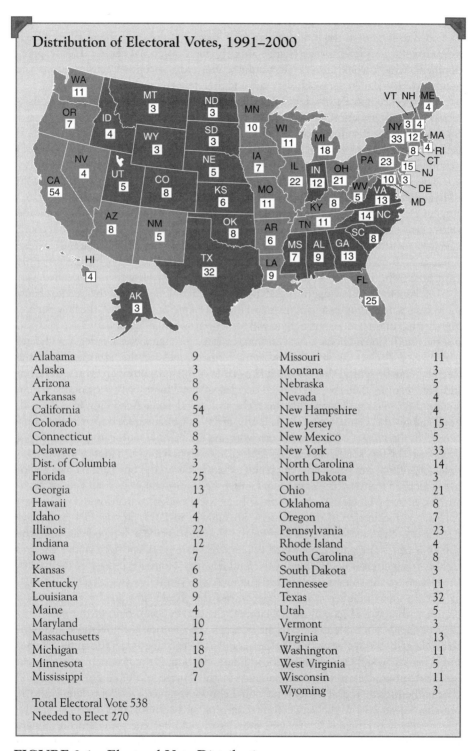

Distribution of Electoral Votes, 1991–2000

State		State	
Alabama	9	Missouri	11
Alaska	3	Montana	3
Arizona	8	Nebraska	5
Arkansas	6	Nevada	4
California	54	New Hampshire	4
Colorado	8	New Jersey	15
Connecticut	8	New Mexico	5
Delaware	3	New York	33
Dist. of Columbia	3	North Carolina	14
Florida	25	North Dakota	3
Georgia	13	Ohio	21
Hawaii	4	Oklahoma	8
Idaho	4	Oregon	7
Illinois	22	Pennsylvania	23
Indiana	12	Rhode Island	4
Iowa	7	South Carolina	8
Kansas	6	South Dakota	3
Kentucky	8	Tennessee	11
Louisiana	9	Texas	32
Maine	4	Utah	5
Maryland	10	Vermont	3
Massachusetts	12	Virginia	13
Michigan	18	Washington	11
Minnesota	10	West Virginia	5
Mississippi	7	Wisconsin	11
		Wyoming	3

Total Electoral Vote 538
Needed to Elect 270

FIGURE 2.1   Electoral Vote Distribution.

are added to the union the total population changes and therefore the number of Representatives for each state may change after the next decennial census. This reapportionment, which would also occur naturally after each decennial census, affects the number of House members each state has and therefore the number of electors.

Electors are chosen by each state from state residents. According to the Constitution, electors are chosen "in such Manner as the Legislature thereof may direct." State legislatures develop their own rules for choosing electors. Some states, such as Pennsylvania, have popular elections, but the majority of states allow the legislatures to choose the electors.

The electors meet in their state capitols in a location designated by state law in early December and cast their votes. The candidate who wins the majority of a state's popular election wins all the electoral votes in a winner-take-all system. Once the votes of the electors are certified by the state authorities, the state's official vote count is sent by registered mail to the President of the Senate of the United States Congress. There is no meeting of the "electoral college" as is commonly thought. Electors only meet in their home states and no larger gathering of all the electors is ever called.

On January 6, following the presidential election the President of the Senate counts the votes before a joint session of the new House of Representatives and the new Senate. Membership of the House and Senate will have been sworn in on January 3 according to the **twentieth amendment.** The votes are counted in alphabetical order. Candidates must have 270 electoral votes before being formally declared the winner. Should the electoral vote be split so that no candidate achieves the mandatory 270 votes, the Constitution requires that the election be decided in the House of Representatives from among the three candidates with the highest electoral vote. According to Article II, Section I, of the Constitution, "a majority of the states is required to win the presidency." In the House, each state has one vote and a candidate must garner a majority of votes from the fifty states, or twenty-six votes, in order to win. The House will take multiple votes if one candidate does not emerge the winner on the first ballot. Once a winner is declared for the office of president, either by counting the electoral vote on January 6 or after the House has chosen the winner, the president is inaugurated on January 20. Prior to ratification of the twentieth amendment in 1933, presidents were inaugurated in March to allow enough time for the House to decide a disputed election. The Senate is constitutionally empowered to name the vice president from among the two highest vote getters if no one has an electoral majority. However, passage of the twelfth amendment to the Constitution in 1804 removed this possibility (see Figure 2.2).

There are a number of other possibilities that could arise in the election of a president that would jeopardize the normal election process. First, if the president-elect or the vice president were to die between the election in November and mid-December when the electoral ballots are counted by the electors in the states, the political parties would choose another candidate. Second, if the president-elect should die between mid-December and January 6, the House of Representatives would choose the president and the Senate would choose the vice president. Finally, if the president-elect were to die between the counting of the ballots on January 6 and the inauguration on January 20, the vice president would become president on January 20 according to the twentieth amendment.[2] The **twenty-fifth amendment** would

Amendment XII

(Ratified in 1804)

The Electors shall meet in their respective states and vote by ballot for President and Vice President, one of whom, at least, shall not be an inhabitant of the same state with themselves; they shall name in their ballots the person voted for as President, and in distinct ballots the person voted for as Vice President, and they shall make distinct lists of all persons voted for as President, and of all persons voted for as Vice President, and of the number of votes for each, which lists they shall sign and certify, and transmit sealed to the seat of government of the United States, directed to the President of the Senate;— The President of the Senate shall, in the presence of the Senate and House of Representatives, open all the certificates and the votes shall then be counted;—The person having the greatest number of votes for President, shall be the President, if such number be a majority of the whole number of Electors appointed; and if no person have such majority, then from the persons having the highest numbers not exceeding three on the list of those voted for as President, the House of Representatives shall choose immediately, by ballot, the President. But in choosing the President, the votes shall be taken by states, the representation from each state having one vote; a quorum for this purpose shall consist of a member or members from two-thirds of the states and a majority of all the states shall be necessary to a choice. *And if the House of Representatives shall not choose a President whenever the right of choice shall devolve upon them, before the fourth day of March next following, then the Vice President shall act as President, as in the case of the death or other constitutional disability of the President.*—The person having the greatest number of votes as Vice President, shall be the Vice President, if such number be a majority of the whole number of Electors appointed, and if no person have a majority, then from the two highest numbers on the list, the Senate shall choose the Vice President; a quorum for the purpose shall consist of two-thirds of the whole number of Senators, and a majority of the whole number shall be necessary to a choice. But no person constitutionally ineligible to the office of President shall be eligible to that of Vice President of the United States.

FIGURE 2.2   The Twelfth Amendment.

then provide for the president to choose a vice president. If both the president-elect and the vice president-elect were to die or not to qualify for office, the **Succession Act of 1947** would be set in motion. The Speaker of the House would be next in line for the presidency, followed by the President Pro Tempore of the Senate, and then the cabinet officers according to the date their departments were created (from State down to Veterans Affairs).

The process for establishing how the electors are chosen and for counting the votes of the electors is a very orderly one. States are the unit of government that handle this part of the process. There is little left to chance, since every state has a prescribed method for handling the electors based on state enabling legislation. Once the electors have elected a president in mid-December, the process becomes a national one governed by the Constitution and federal statutes. It is a remarkable system based on James Madison's goal that the new government would be both state and federal in nature. Clearly the electoral process meets his requirements. It is also quite remarkable, since the system was completely conceived by the architects of the Constitution and had no basis in other governing structures. The framers of the Constitution were "inventing America," or creating a system that often (such as with the electoral system) had no model.[3]

Four Controversial Elections

Throughout the nation's history only four elections, all in the 1800s, have been controversial when the votes were counted. All other elections have produced clear winners. The first two controversial elections (1800 and 1824) failed to produce a winner who had a majority of electoral votes. The problem was the result of multiple candidates on the ballot, each with substantial popular support, who split the electoral vote. In these two elections the House of Representatives was required to choose the president. In the third and fourth controversial elections (1876 and 1888), the winner of the electoral vote was not the winner of the popular vote.

The first controversial election was the election of 1800, in which neither of the two leading candidates, incumbent John Adams nor challenger Thomas Jefferson, received a majority of votes. The tie, however, was not between Adams and Jefferson but between Jefferson and his vice presidential candidate, Aaron Burr. The vote count ended with Jefferson and Burr tied with seventy-three votes, Adams with sixty-five votes, and Adams's running mate Charles Pinckney of South Carolina with sixty-four votes. After thirty-five ballots with no candidate receiving a majority, Alexander Hamilton intervened and lobbied on behalf of Thomas Jefferson. On the thirty-sixth ballot, Jefferson was elected president and Burr was elected vice president. Aaron Burr's animosity for Hamilton grew over the next few years, finally leading to the famous 1804 duel in New Jersey which cost Hamilton his life. On the morning of July 11, 1804, Alexander Hamilton met Aaron Burr in Weehawken, New Jersey, for a duel. Burr shot Hamilton in the right side and he died thirty-six hours later.[4]

The contentious election of 1800 led to the passage of the **twelfth amendment** to the Constitution, which provided for the president and vice president to run as a single ticket. This precluded the possibility of the presidential candidate and the vice presidential candidate competing for the presidency in the House of Representatives, as happened in 1800 with Jefferson and Burr. The amendment also precluded the president and vice president from being elected from different parties, as happened in 1796 with Adams (a Federalist) and Jefferson (a Republican) (Figure 2.3).

The second election to be determined by the House of Representatives occurred in 1824, when Andrew Jackson made his first run for the presidency. Once the votes

Year	Winner	Loser
1800	Thomas Jefferson	Aaron Burr
1824	John Quincy Adams	Andrew Jackson
1876	Rutherford B. Hayes	Samuel Tilden
1888	Benjamin Harrison	Grover Cleveland

FIGURE 2.3   Four Controversial Elections.

were counted, Jackson had received ninety-nine electoral votes, John Quincy Adams had received eighty-four electoral votes, and William Crawford of Georgia had received forty-one electoral votes. Henry Clay, the Speaker of the House, received only three electoral votes, much to his dismay. John C. Calhoun had withdrawn from the election when both Adams and Jackson promised him the vice presidency. Secretary of the Treasury William Crawford, a popular candidate, suffered a paralyzing stroke in the fall of 1823 and was not able to campaign.[5] Prior to his stroke, he had been considered a major candidate.

Although Jackson received the most electoral votes in 1824, he did not receive a majority, which again forced the House of Representatives to decide an election. Once the House was faced with deciding the election, Henry Clay became the dominant player, or king maker, and each of the three top candidates courted his support. John Quincy Adams successfully brought Clay and the other requisite delegates to his side in order to win the majority of votes in the House. After John Quincy Adams was inaugurated, he appointed Clay his secretary of state. Four years later, Jackson ran against John Quincy Adams again, but this time, won by a landslide.

The third election to be determined outside of the normal electoral process occurred in 1876, one hundred years after the nation first declared its independence from Great Britain. Unlike the elections of 1800 and 1824, the election of 1876 was resolved by a special Electoral Commission rather than by the House of Representatives. The Republican candidate for president was Ohio Governor Rutherford B. Hayes, well known for opposing the Jacksonian spoils system. The Democratic candidate was New York Governor Samuel J. Tilden, an equally well known reformer who had reduced the influence of Tammany Hall's machine politics in New York. Both candidates had similar views on issues of the day and had gained reputations as political reformers. The presidential campaign turned more on personality than on issues, leading to a very bitter campaign, with personal attacks hurled at regular intervals.

When the votes were counted it appeared that Tilden had bested Hayes by 264,000 popular votes and had nearly won the electoral vote by 184 to Hayes's 165, with 185 electoral votes needed to win. Twenty electoral votes had not been counted since the popular vote had not been finalized, although Hayes believed he had unquestionably lost the election to Tilden. When the final votes were tabulated from South Carolina, Florida, and Louisiana, and also Oregon, it appeared that all went for Hayes, giving him the necessary votes. But there was substantial evidence of voter fraud through bribery, forgery, and ballot box stuffing on both the Democratic and Republican sides in the three Southern states. Congress was politically divided, with the Democrats controlling the House and the Republicans controlling the Senate.

The Democratic House would not allow the Republican President of the Senate to control the counting of the votes, as the Constitution required, nor would the Republican Senate let the Democratic House operate alone.

Congress subsequently created a bipartisan Electoral Commission, which had five senators, five representatives, and five Supreme Court Justices, to decide who would review the electoral votes. There were seven Democrats and seven Republicans, with the tie-breaking vote to be cast by a Supreme Court justice who was known as an independent. The Electoral Commission voted eight to seven for Hayes after all the votes were cast. This decision was largely the result of a backroom deal. The Democrats agreed to allow Hayes to become president in exchange for an end to Reconstruction and the military occupation of the South. Tilden's supporters erupted in disapproval, with rioting across the country. Tilden's supporters believed that Tilden had been unduly stripped of the presidency. Hayes was shot at in his home while he was eating dinner, although the bullet missed him and lodged in the wall. In the end, Hayes was sworn into office and Tilden, although angry at the decision, did not further contest it. Ten years later Congress passed a law to reduce the chances of such violence occurring and to establish firm rules for challenges to electors. According to the Electoral Count Act of 1887, the states must determine for themselves whether electors are valid. Any challenges must occur at the state level so that the House of Representatives can manage the resolution of elections in a straightforward manner as the Constitution provided for. No one wanted an election that resulted in such violence or animosity between the parties as had occurred in 1876.

The fourth controversial election in the nation's history occurred in 1888 when the winner of the popular vote did not gain the electoral votes to win the presidency. When Democrat Grover Cleveland sought a second term of office in 1888, he won the election with over 95,000 more votes than his opponent, Republican Benjamin Harrison. But Harrison had received 233 electoral votes to Cleveland's 168 electoral votes, giving Harrison the presidency. Cleveland's popular victory did not produce an electoral victory, and thus Harrison became president. However, Cleveland did not completely give up on his quest for the presidency. In a rematch in 1892, Cleveland regained the keys to the White House.

These four elections provide important case studies on the resolution process for controversial elections. In addition, they are testaments to the careful crafting of our electoral process, for it is a system that works even under significant duress, as occurred in 1876. The marvel of the U.S. electoral process is that it works even under stress. The transition of power from one administration to another is done without force and with the consent of the people, even when that consent is marginal.

Nominating Procedures for President

When the architects of the Constitution framed the election process, most of their efforts were devoted to crafting the electoral college. Other aspects of the election process, such as how candidates would be nominated and what process would be used to winnow the number of candidates, were left to others to determine at a later date. When the first Congress met after the ninth state, New Hampshire, had ratified the

Constitution, they began to debate the location of a capital city. They soon moved the debate to the election of a president, focusing on when the states should hold an election of presidential electors. Congress authorized an election to be held in January 1789, but realized that some states might not be able to meet this date because of problems of transportation and communication. During the winter months state legislatures established procedures for the election of electors, but only ten of the states succeeded in having elections. New York, Rhode Island, and North Carolina did not send election results, for varying reasons. The final tabulation on February 4, 1789, was from ten states with sixty-nine electors, rather than the full thirteen states with ninety-one electors.[6] On April 6 the electoral votes were officially counted in the Senate. The votes gave George Washington the presidency with all sixty-nine electors and John Adams the vice presidency with the second highest vote count of thirty-four electors. In a ceremony held on April 30 on the balcony of Federal Hall at the corner of Wall Street and Broad Street in New York City, the first president and vice president of the United States were sworn into office. President Washington then delivered his inaugural address in the Senate chamber of Federal Hall.[7]

In spite of the fact that the states had no way of formally nominating candidates for the presidency, George Washington was named by every delegate. All sixty-nine electors voted for Washington for president, making him the unanimous choice of the states. But the election of 1789 was not a normal election and a system needed to be developed for candidates to be nominated and formally moved through the state election process. By the next election in 1792, the process had not moved very far and George Washington again easily won the presidency. The first major test of the elections process for the presidency occurred in 1796 when Washington declined to serve a third term, leaving the office open.

King Caucus

John Adams, who had served as Washington's vice president for two terms, aggressively sought the presidency, as did Thomas Jefferson, Washington's secretary of state in his first administration. The major change that had occurred in the period from 1789 to 1796 was that political parties emerged as a significant factor in the nation's political life. Adams, a Federalist, had strong backing among the Federalists and Jefferson had an equally strong base among Republicans. The result was that the Federalist and Republican Parties in the Congress named Adams and Jefferson, respectively, as their candidates. Parties had quickly surfaced as the means of gaining a position on the ballot for president, and the parties in the Congressional Caucus, or **King Caucus** as it became known, were the path to nomination. The nomination process for president was managed in Congress by the leaders of the two political parties. But the Federalist Party essentially ceased to exist during the early 1800s, and the Republican Party dominated the presidential selection process. Jefferson was re-elected to the presidency with virtually no opposition. When James Madison was nominated for president in 1808, he also had virtually no opposition. Madison and his running mate, Senator George Clinton of New York, had little opposition in their two runs for the presidency and easily won both. When James Monroe sought the office in 1816, he won sixteen of nineteen states and was reelected without opposition in 1820. The two-party system had effectively disappeared, and nomination by the dominant new Democratic-Republican party in Congress ensured victory in the presidential contest.

Not until the election of 1824 was King Caucus challenged as the mechanism for choosing presidential candidates. The election of 1824 created a split in the **one-party system** that had become the Democratic-Republican Party, the party once dominated by Thomas Jefferson. The supporters of John Quincy Adams became the National Republicans while the supporters of Andrew Jackson became the Democrats, creating what became known as the second party system. The first party system, comprised of the Federalist and Republican Parties, had all but disappeared in the early 1800s. After Jackson lost the election in 1824, his supporters worked to build the Democratic base at the local level rather than in Congress. This strategy produced not only the victory for Jackson in 1828 but also a change in the nominating procedures for the parties. The decision of the Congressional Caucus to support William Crawford over Jackson destroyed the credibility of the existing nominating structure. The Congressional Caucus was never resumed and was replaced by nominating conventions in 1831. To have members of Congress choosing the presidential nominees, and essentially making them beholden to the Congress, clearly violated the concept of separation of powers. Nominating conventions avoided this collision between the two branches of government.

Nominating Convention

The first national **nominating convention** was held in 1831 by the Anti-Masons, which was a small third party that had no members serving in Congress. The nominating convention soon replaced the Congressional Caucus system and allowed parties with no congressional delegation to finally have their own presidential nominee. The structure of the prior nominating process under the Congressional Caucus would never have allowed the Anti-Mason's who had no delegates in Congress to nominate a presidential candidate. Later that same year, the National Republicans, or Whigs as they soon were referred to, met in a national convention to choose their own presidential nominee. The Democratic Republicans followed suit and met in Baltimore the next year. The practice of national meetings to nominate the party's presidential candidate had now replaced King Caucus.

Throughout the middle and late 1800s the nominating conventions grew in size, with representatives from the state parties becoming the primary delegates. In large part these delegates were the urban political bosses and the state party leaders (such as mayors and governors). Political bosses and state party leaders soon dominated the national convention. As Stephen Wayne describes the nomination process at these party-boss dominated conventions, "Much of the bartering was conducted behind closed doors. Actions on the convention floor often had little to do with the wheeling and dealing that occurred in the smoke-filled smaller rooms."[8] As a result of the wheeling and dealing among the party leaders, nominees for president during this period often came from the ranks of governors rather than members of Congress or of the cabinet. Party conventions during this era often were brokered by the large state delegations. Power brokers within state delegations traded their votes in return for their candidate or party leader receiving a cabinet post, the vice presidency, or some other favor. **Brokered conventions** (a name that came from the power brokers in the convention) endured until the primary process took nominations out of the smoke-filled rooms and into the ballot boxes.[9]

Primary Elections

With the emergence of machine politics in presidential nominating conventions, re-formers began to seek broader representation in the choice of presidential candidates. The **Progressive Era** marked the next major step in the evolution of the nominating process. With Senator Robert LaFollette of Wisconsin leading the calls for reform in the early 1900s, the Progressives began to lobby the parties for open participation and popular election of convention delegates. In 1904, Florida passed legislation al-lowing the parties to hold popular elections for convention delegates. Wisconsin fol-lowed in 1905, as did Pennsylvania in 1906. Other states soon followed Florida's lead. By 1912, fifteen states had developed an open election process, called **primary elec-tions,** in which the state's voters decided on the delegates to the national political conventions. The nominating conventions that exist today are the product of the Progressive movement's drive to wrest the process from the party bosses. This was part of the broader Progressive movement, which sought to increase the democratic nature of our electoral process. Such proposals as referendums and recall votes, direct election of U.S. senators, and voter initiatives all emerged during this era in addition to the primary election system for presidential candidates.

The primary system has created a structure, although not a perfect one because of the continued influence of party leaders, that is largely controlled by the elec-torate. The problem that has recently developed within the primary system is that only a limited number of party members vote in the primary election, averaging nineteen to twenty percent of the total. These few party activists who vote in the pri-maries can now determine the party's nominee, in the same way that the party bosses did a century ago.

Throughout the twentieth century the number of primary states has continued to increase. Today, the number of states with primary elections ensures that the majority of delegates for both the Democratic and Republican Party are chosen by the elec-torate rather than by party bosses in state caucuses. The present system, which mini-mizes the influence of party bosses, has only been in effect since 1972 (Figure 2.4).

During the 1968 election, the nominee for the Democratic Party, Vice President Hubert Humphrey, did not enter a single primary yet still won the party's nomina-tion. Humphrey had been challenged by both Senator Robert F. Kennedy and Sena-tor Eugene McCarthy, who were opposed to President Lyndon Johnson's position on the Vietnam War. Johnson had escalated the war in January 1968 when he sent thou-sands of new troops to stop the Tet offensive from North Vietnam against South Vietnam. While Humphrey did not fully support Johnson's stand on the war himself, he could not completely distance himself from Johnson's policies. Humphrey built strong relations with the party leaders, especially mayors such as Richard Daley of Chicago, who still controlled the urban political machines. The bridges that Humphrey built with the party leaders in the states that did not have primary elec-

Year	Number of Primaries (Democrats)	Percentage of Delegates from Primary States (Democrats)	Number of Primaries (Republicans)	Percentage of Delegates from Primary States (Republicans)
1912	12	32.9	13	41.7
1916	20	53.5	20	58.9
1920	16	44.6	20	57.8
1924	14	35.5	17	45.3
1928	17	42.2	16	44.9
1932	16	40.0	14	37.7
1936	14	36.5	12	37.5
1940	13	35.8	13	38.8
1944	14	36.7	13	38.7
1948	14	36.3	12	36.0
1952	16	39.2	13	39.0
1956	19	41.3	19	43.5
1960	16	38.4	15	38.6
1964	16	41.4	17	45.6
1968	17	48.7	17	47.0
1972	23	66.5	22	58.2
1976	30	76.1	29	70.4
1980	35	81.1	36	78.0
1984	30	67.1	29	66.6
1988	37	81.4	38	80.7
1992	40	88.0	39	85.4
1996	35	70.9	43	85.9

Source: Michael Nelson. *Guide to the Presidency*. 2nd ed. Washington, DC: Congressional Quarterly Press, 1996, p. 201.

FIGURE 2.4   Presidential Primaries 1912–1996.

tions were strong enough to assure him of their votes in the nominating convention in Chicago in 1968. Although Robert Kennedy had secured the majority of votes in the primary elections, including California the night he was slain, the number of votes that were controlled by the primary states was not enough to offset the number of votes controlled in nonprimary states. In 1968 only 48 percent of the Democratic Convention delegates were selected by primaries. Nearly 52 percent of the delegates were selected by state party leaders, which gave Humphrey the ability to manipulate the convention without entering the primaries.

Not surprisingly, supporters of both Kennedy and McCarthy were furious at Humphrey's selection by the party. Many delegates and other supporters at the convention joined forces with antiwar demonstrators, rioting that night in Chicago, and causing significant damage to both private and public property. Mayor Richard Daley called in the riot police to quell the chaos.

In the four years before the next presidential election, members of the Democratic Party heavily lobbied state legislatures to create primary elections within their states. They successfully argued that the nomination of Hubert Humphrey was controlled by a small group of back-room deals rather than by the broader membership of the Democratic Party. Had Robert Kennedy been the nominee, as the primaries indicated he should have been, perhaps Richard Nixon would not have been elected president, they further argued. State legislatures responded to their pleas and most changed their election laws prior to the 1972 election to provide for primary elections.

Although all states do not have primary elections today, most do. Voting traditionally has been controlled by the states, as part of the federal system created by the architects of the Constitution. The only time that the federal government has interposed itself in state voting laws has been with regard to eliminating the exclusion of certain classes of voters, such as women and minorities. The federal government has also moved to end any discrimination in voting, such as the requirement to pay a poll tax or to write one's name according to certain prescribed rules.

Costs in Early Presidential Campaigns

In modern elections, money has become the most important asset that a candidate can have. Without money, candidates cannot afford to have major campaign organizations at either a national or a state level, nor can they purchase the necessary advertising needed in every major media market across the country. Money, lots of it, is essential to any presidential campaign.

The extensive role that money plays in modern-day campaigns is not a role unfamiliar in the presidential election process. As early as 1828, when Andrew Jackson was seeking the presidency, money had become a vital part of gaining the nomination. Whether to support newspapers that advocated a candidacy or to hand out "street money," presidential candidates needed money to run their campaigns. By 1860, Abraham Lincoln needed the princely sum of $100,000 for his campaign.[10] Lincoln's campaigns received a number of large donations, including $1,000 from financier Jay Cooke in the 1864 race.

During the latter half of the nineteenth century, wealthy industrialists such as Cornelius Vanderbilt, John Astor, and Henry Hilton were regular financial supporters of the presidential candidates of both parties, although predominantly the Republican Party. In the 1868 election, Ulysses S. Grant was a major benefactor of funding from wealthy industrialists, particularly Jay Cooke. By 1896, the costs of running the presidential campaign for William McKinley's winning effort had grown to $16 million, mostly from the costs of travel and advertising.[11] McKinley, a former governor and congressman from Ohio, had long known the value of having significant financial backing in campaigns. McKinley's primary benefactor was Cleveland millionaire Marcus Hanna, who was also a member of the Republican National Committee. In Hanna's push to support McKinley's various electoral endeavors, he regularly tapped wealthy individuals and corporations both inside and outside the state of Ohio.[12] Hanna sought and received a $250,000 contribution from Standard Oil in both 1896 and 1900.[13] During the 1904 presidential campaign, Theodore Roosevelt's costs continued to escalate, and he too accepted large sums of money from wealthy contributors. Writing in his memoirs about the power of money, Roosevelt describes his concern that many Wall Street financial bankers opposed his candidacy, "As the time for the Presidential nomination of 1904 drew near, it became evident that I was strong with the rank and file of the party," Roosevelt said, "but that there was much opposition to me among many of the big political leaders, and especially among many of the Wall Street men."[14] Money has become an essential tool for opening the doors in the race to the White House.

Campaign Finance Reform

During the period of the Progressive Party's drive to reform government, Congress passed the **Tillman Act of 1907,** which banned bank and corporate gifts to candidates seeking federal office.[15] The law was passed to curb large corporate donations to presidential and congressional candidates. It was in direct response to Marcus Hanna's successful attempts to raise large sums of money from corporations for his friend and future president William McKinley and other candidates. Unfortunately, the Tillman Act proved ineffective without any sanctions for violations. Corporations were able to circumvent the law by giving bonuses to their executives who in turn gave money to political campaigns. The Progressive Era produced another attempt to deal with campaign financing. In 1925, the **Federal Corrupt Practices Act** set disclosure requirements on candidates running for the House and Senate. Candidates were required to disclose all campaign receipts and expenditures. The law, however, had no penalties for violating the law, making it effectively null and void. More importantly to presidential elections, the law dealt only with House and Senate campaigns and was silent on candidates seeking the presidency and vice presidency. The efforts by the Progressives were the first major steps toward campaign finance reform.

Throughout the early twentieth century, the cost of presidential campaigns continued to escalate. Media costs became one of the largest parts of a campaign budget. As newspapers and radio programs began to have advertisements for presidential candidates, the cost of advertising grew rapidly. When television became a serious part of the mass media in the 1950s, the cost of advertising further increased. In 1952, Dwight Eisenhower was the first presidential candidate to use television advertising, spending $800,000 on television advertising alone.[16] Campaign spending included not only advertising, but significant costs for professional campaign consultants, polling, and large staffs at national headquarters. The heights that political spending had reached were evident in 1952 during Dwight Eisenhower's run for the presidency when his running mate, Richard Nixon, was accused of having a political slush fund and using it for personal profit. Nixon went on national television to assure the public that he had not profited from the fund, although he admitted to having one. In the now famous **Checkers speech,** he told the nation that no money in the fund went for his personal use and no favors were granted in return for contributions to the fund. Nixon recited his family history, growing up as a poor boy and then working his way through college, going off to war, practicing law, and then running for Congress. The only gift he said he had ever taken for personal use was a cocker spaniel named Checkers.[17] The high cost of advertising and of hiring political consultants was chronicled in Joe McGinniss' *The Selling of the President 1968,* describing Nixon's 1968 presidential campaign.[18] Lyndon Johnson had also sought large gifts from contributors, and in the 1964 presidential election against Republican nominee Barry

Goldwater, Johnson collected more than $2 million in contributions of $10,000 or more.[19]

Changing the Campaign Finance Structure: The Federal Election Campaign Act

As the cost of campaigns skyrocketed, the efforts to reform the system increased. In 1984, the major candidates raised $137 million in their quest for the presidency.[20] In just twelve years the cost of running a presidential election grew dramatically. The seventeen major candidates who ran for the presidency in the 1996 election raised a total of $244 million, in addition to the $61.8 million given to each of the two major political parties.[21] Campaigns in the modern era cost millions of dollars to finance and these costs have already limited the pool of nominees.

The first major effort to reform the campaign finance laws governing presidential candidates came during the Kennedy administration. Concerned that officeholders were becoming overly beholden to contributors, President John F. Kennedy established the bipartisan President's Commission on Campaign Costs, which lasted from 1961 to 1962. The Commission was charged with examining ways to reduce the costs of presidential campaigns and to find ways to finance those costs, if possible. Although the Commission proposed some ways to change the system, it received tepid support in both the White House and in Congress. According to one Commission member, Kennedy never had any serious interest in changing the campaign finance process for he believed that the system "was always fluid and changing. . . . And there was nothing final that could be done to it."[22] In reality, nothing came of the Commission's recommendations, and campaign finance laws remained unchanged, as Kennedy actually seemed to want. A decade later, however, significant change did come to campaign finance laws.

Federal Election Campaign Act

The most significant change to campaign finance legislation came in 1971 with passage of the **Federal Election Campaign Act (FECA).** The bill, which passed the Democratically controlled Congress in 1970, was originally vetoed by President Nixon but when Congress amended the law to take effect only after the 1972 election, Nixon signed it. Signed by Nixon on February 14, 1972, the law went into effect sixty days later. During this sixty day period both parties attempted to raise large sums of money before the law went into effect, with the Republicans raising more than $20 million for Nixon's campaign.

The Federal Election Campaign Act of 1972 attempted to deal with several problems in the campaign process. First, it limited the amount of money that candidates for federal office could spend on their own elections. This included not only candidates but their families as well. Second, the law required the disclosure of receipts and expenditures used during the campaign. Third, it limited advertising expenditures. The law had been passed by an activist Congress attempting to bring some controls to what they perceived as an out-of-control campaign finance system.

The primary purpose of the law for congressional Democrats was to balance the political landscape. Republicans had for years been more successful at generating large sums of money from individuals. During the 1968 campaign, Richard Nixon had received large amounts of cash from wealthy contributors, particularly W. Clement Stone, an insurance company executive from Chicago. In order to energize large contributors, Nixon's campaign manager, Maurice Stans, established the Century Club for individuals who gave $100,000 or more. As an indication of how many contributors gave at this level, the Century Club had twenty-six members; there were also numerous members who gave $1,000 or more who were given a gold lapel pin that read "RN Associates."[23] The Federal Election Campaign Act of 1972 was an attempt by the Democrats, who controlled both houses of Congress, to reduce the large contributions that flowed into the Republican coffers by placing caps on both individual and corporate contributions. The Democratic Congress hoped to reduce the inequity in campaign financing that had tilted the balance in favor of the Republicans.

Another major piece of campaign finance reform legislation was the Revenue Act of 1971. This law encouraged individuals to make small contributions to political campaigns and then provided a tax deduction for certain contributions. In addition, the **Revenue Act of 1971** provided for individuals to contribute money directly to future presidential campaigns through the Presidential Campaign Fund. When filing tax returns, individuals could check off a box that allowed them to donate $1.00 to the fund. Approximately twenty-five percent of taxpayers have used the check-off for presidential campaigns since the law was first enacted.

Buckley v. Valeo

The Federal Election Campaign Act had little impact on the 1972 election. As a result, Congress amended the act in 1974 to tighten the rules and to provide an oversight mechanism. In addition, a Federal Election Commission was created to oversee compliance with the law. In spite of the changes in the law, critics continued to attack it and to file lawsuits against it. One landmark case, moved forward by New York Senator James L. Buckley, was **Buckley v. Valeo** (1976) in which the Supreme Court supported most of the provisions of the law, including Congress's right to control the financing of federal elections.[24] In its decision, which ran almost 300 pages, the Court reviewed at length the constitutionality of the Federal Election Campaign Act of 1972, as amended in 1974. The Court disallowed the provisions of the statute that put a $50,000 limit on the use of personal funds, stating that this infringed on the first amendment right of freedom of speech. In its opinion the Court said that, "The first amendment requires the invalidation of the Act's independent expenditure ceiling, its limitation on a candidate's expenditures from his own personal funds, and its ceilings on overall campaign expenditures, since those provisions place substantial and direct restrictions on the ability of candidates, citizens, and associations to engage in protected political expression, restrictions that the first amendment cannot tolerate."[25]

The Court did allow the requirement that individuals were limited in giving $1,000 per election ($1,000 for the primary and $1,000 for the general election) and groups were limited to giving $5,000 per election. In addition, the Court upheld the right of independent political action committees (PACs) to spending unrestricted amounts of money on behalf of a candidate as long as the candidate did not work with the PAC on the advertising. In its decision in *Buckley v. Valeo*, the Supreme Court also ruled that the composition of the Federal Election Commission was unconstitutional, since four of the six members of the Commission were to be appointed by Congress and two to be appointed by the president. The Court said that all members of the Commission had to be appointed by the President, as were all independent regulatory bodies. Perhaps the most controversial part of the Federal Election Campaign Act was the provision for public financing of presidential elections. The Court allowed these provisions, which set limits on revenues and expenditures for presidential elections.

After the *Buckley v. Valeo* decision in 1976, Congress was again forced to amend the Federal Election Campaign Act. The revised legislation became officially known as the Federal Election Campaign Act, as amended in 1976.

One of the most significant products of the earlier 1974 amendments to the Federal Election Campaign Act was the sanctioning of "political committees," known today as **political action committees (PACs).** The PACs have provided a significant portion of the funding in national presidential elections, although the majority of PAC money is given to elections for House and Senate incumbents. Individual contributions to PACs are limited to $5,000 per PAC to a maximum of $25,000 per year. The Federal Election Campaign Act, as amended in 1976, provides for the following:

All Federal Campaigns

- Public Disclosure: Contributions of $200 or more and expenditures of $200 or more must be disclosed in regular reports to the Federal Election Commission.
- Contribution Limits: Contributions are limited to $1,000 per election (primary and general elections each) from each individual. The total contribution from any individual cannot exceed $25,000 per year, which can include contributions of $20,000 to a national political party committee and $5,000 to other political action committees.

Only Presidential Campaigns

- Public Financing: Presidential candidates who want to supplement their own fund-raising can qualify for federal funding of the campaign for both their primary expenses and their general election expenses. To qualify, candidates must demonstrate that they are viable candidates. Qualifying requires candidates to raise at least $5,000 in contributions of $250 or less in at least twenty states, for a total of $100,000. Once eligible, public funds are given to the candidate during the primary election period on a dollar-for-dollar matching basis. For every dollar received from an individual to a maximum of $250, the federal government will provide an equal amount of money per year. These are called **matching funds.**
- Spending Limits in the Nomination Process: Presidential candidates who accept public financing are limited in their spending to $10 million in pursuit of the party's nomination. These numbers are based on 1974 dollars and are indexed for inflation. In addition, the law provided for an additional 20 percent for fund-raising expenses and unlimited legal and accounting expenditures. In 1996 this

amount had risen to $30.9 million, plus $6.2 million for fund-raising and other expenses. In 1988 the indexed allowance was $22.3 million plus $4.7 million for other expenses.

- State Spending Limits in the Nomination Process: Presidential candidates who accept public financing are limited in spending in each state during the nomination period. These limits are based on the size of the voting-age population in each state. The larger the state, the more money is allowed to be spent. In 1996, the smallest state (Delaware) was allowed $618,200 during the nomination period and the largest state (California) was allowed $11.3 million. These amounts are indexed each year.

- Campaign Financing in the General Election: Presidential candidates who accept public funding in the general election are limited to spending $20 million during the general election. These numbers are based on 1974 dollars and are indexed for inflation. By 1996, the amount of the public subsidy for the general election had risen to $61.8 million for each of the two major parties, since presidential candidates accepted public financing. This was a significant increase from the $40.4 million for each party in the 1984 election and the $45 million in the 1988 election.

The Federal Election Campaign Act was amended again in 1979 to increase the minimum contributions and expenditures that had to be reported. The 1979 amendments also allowed state and local party committees to purchase an unlimited amount of advertising on behalf of a candidate, as long as the candidate did not collude or work with the committee. The advertising must be developed independently of the presidential campaign. This type of uncoordinated advertising on behalf of presidential candidates is known as **soft money.** The Federal Election Campaign Act wanted these funds to be used by the political party for party-building activities, which would benefit the parties in general rather than specific candidates. The funding is to be used for state and local political activities, such as voter registration, get-out-the-vote drives, and generic party-building advertising supporting the broad platforms of the parties but not particular candidates.

During the 1992 presidential campaign the national Democratic Party raised an estimated $34 million and the national Republican Party raised an estimated $48 million in soft-money contributions. Soft money is critical to presidential campaigns because it is not subject to contribution limits. Since individual contributors are limited to giving $25,000 in any year to political campaigns under the Federal Election Campaign Act, wealthy individuals often use soft money through the national committees as a means to funnel additional monies to the campaigns. During the 1988 campaign, the Republicans even organized a formal group of contributors, called Team 100, made up of contributors who gave $100,000 or more. For the 1996 presidential election cycle, which officially began on January 1, 1995, the Federal Election Commission reported that the national committee of the Republican Party raised $121 million in soft money and the national committee of the Democratic Party raised $106 million, three times more than their 1991–1992 receipts. Soft money has become a significant and almost crucial part of the financing structure for presidential campaigns.

While the lure of federal matching funds is tantalizing to presidential candidates, and both the Democratic and Republican Party candidates have consistently accepted the funds, there are drawbacks. The most significant drawback is that if candidates accept matching funds they are limited in their expenditures, both in national expenditures during the primaries and in individual state expenditures. Since two small states, New Hampshire and Iowa, are early primary states, candidates have had to carefully limit their expenditures. One way that candidates have circumvented the rules is to charge as much as possible to the expenditure limits in neighboring states. For example, during the New Hampshire primary as many costs as possible will be charged to adjacent states, including television advertising through the Boston television stations, which reach the New Hampshire audience.

The costs of running the national conventions have also soared in recent years, although a significant part of the funding is now supplied by the federal government as part of the process created by the Federal Election Campaign Act. During 1992, the Democrats spent $38.6 million on their New York City convention—a dramatic increase from the $22.5 million spent on their convention in Atlanta four years earlier. The 1992 total for the Democrats included $11 million in federal funds plus an additional $21.1 million spent by the host city of New York. The Republicans spent $21 million at their Houston Convention in 1992, up from $18 million spent in New Orleans four years earlier. Houston gave the Republicans $5.7 million in addition to the $12 million in federal funding.[26] The remaining funds for the convention primarily came from corporations renting space at the convention headquarters. In 1996, for example, major corporations spent up to $50,000 a piece for elegant skybox suites at the Republican National Convention in San Diego.[27]

Third-Party Candidates

While the Federal Election Campaign Act has been very important for financing the campaigns of the major party candidates, it has hindered **third-party candidates.** The visibility that candidates receive during the primary process is essential to gaining broad-based public support. Since only the two major parties, the Democrats and the Republicans, hold primaries, the matching funds provided through public financing reward the major parties. The culmination of the primaries is the nominating convention held by each party, in which free air time is given to the two major parties. Approximately 18 million people watched the 1996 Democratic Convention and 16.6 million people watched the 1996 Republican Convention.[28] The only equivalent visibility that third-party candidates have has been national talk shows, which Ross Perot became an expert at using in both 1992 and 1996. Perot was a regular guest on CNN's *Larry King Live* and numerous other talk and news shows.

Another important reason that public financing benefits the two major parties more than third parties is that the law will not provide funding for third-party candidates unless they receive a minimum of five percent of the general election vote. They cannot qualify for funding until after the election, while the two major party candidates receive their funding from the outset of the general election. Thus, a third-party candidate can apply for funds only retroactively, and only if he or she receive at least five percent of the vote in November.

The law does allow for public funding during the next presidential election if a third-party candidate achieves the five percent threshold. In 1980, independent candidate John Anderson qualified for matching funds, receiving $4.2 million based on his 6.6 percent of the popular vote (5,720,000). Had he run for president again in 1984, he would have qualified for matching funds automatically. Anderson, a Republican congressman from Illinois, began running for the 1980 Republican nomination during 1979. When he lost in the Illinois Republican primary in March 1980 with thirty-seven percent of the vote, as compared with Ronald Reagan's forty-eight percent, and then in April again lost to Reagan in Wisconsin, he decided to run outside of the Republican Party. On April 20, 1980, Anderson announced that he would run for president as an independent on the National Unity ticket.[29] In an interview several years after the election, Anderson explained how he thought the Federal Election Campaign Act seriously hampered third party candidates. "It's not fair," Anderson said of the law. "There isn't any question about that, when each of the older parties, the Democrats and the Republicans, starts out with $29.4 million plus $4.3 million in federal funding for each of their conventions, while the most an independent or third party candidate can expect is retroactive funding after the election is over if he gets at least five percent of the total vote. Obviously we are at a severe disadvantage."[30]

The Perot Candidacy

George Wallace's candidacy with the American Independent Party in the 1968 election occurred prior to the passage of campaign finance reform. (It should be noted, however, that Anderson did not create a separate political party but ran as an independent candidate. He did not have a formal political party behind him as Wallace did.) John Anderson's candidacy was the only candidacy outside of the Democratic and Republican Parties during the 1970s or 1980s that qualified for federal matching funding. Not until 1992, when Ross Perot sought the presidency did the issue surface again. On February 20, 1992, Texas billionaire Ross Perot announced during a television appearance on CNN's *Larry King Live* that he was going to run for president as an independent candidate. He had no party relationship, would not use public financing, and would spend up to $100 million of his personal fortune on the campaign. At that point in time, Perot's personal fortune was estimated to be $3.3 billion.[31] Perot's fortune had been largely made in the computer industry, following the sale of his Electronic Data Services to General Motors in 1984 for $2.5 billion, of which he had a personal stake of $1.4 billion. He later went on to a very successful career in real estate investing. By the end of the presidential campaign, Perot had garnered 18.9 percent of the vote in the November election without accepting any funding from public financing. According to one study, Perot spent $68.4 million in his race for the presidency in 1992.[32]

In 1996 Perot ran again; but this time he worked through his newly formed political party, the Reform Party. Perot did give $8.2 million in soft money to the Reform Party for party building and to qualify himself on state ballots.[33] As a candidate who received more than five percent of the national vote in the last presidential election, Perot received $29.1 million from the Federal Election Commission for the general election campaign.[34] This compared to the $61.8 million that President Clinton and his challenger, Senator Robert Dole, each received for their campaigns from the Federal Election Commission. Although Perot won more than 19 million votes in 1992 and almost 8 million votes in 1996, he received no electoral votes in either election. George Wallace received a small number of electoral votes in the 1968 election, but John Anderson received no votes in the 1980 election. One argument against giving third-party candidates federal funding is that they rarely receive electoral votes and are therefore not viable presidential candidates. The Wallace campaign of 1968, the Anderson campaign of 1980, and the Perot campaigns of 1992 and 1996 had all failed to provide significant challenges to the Democratic and Republican Parties in the presidential election.

Reforming the Campaign Finance Laws

The 1996 election also saw the emergence of Malcolm Forbes, Jr., better known as Steve Forbes, who ran within the Republican Party but refused to accept federal matching funds during the primaries. As Ross Perot had done in 1992, Forbes chose to use his own personal fortune for his campaign, a fortune amassed from ownership of the business magazine with the family name—*Forbes*. Forbes lent his campaign the rather significant sum of $37.5 million. During the 1996 election another wealthy Republican, Maurice Taylor, joined the primaries. Taylor had made his fortune as a manufacturer of tires and tire rims and invested $6.5 million of his $30 million fortune in his campaign.[35]

After the 1996 presidential election, numerous calls for campaign finance reform were heard in Congress. In 1997, Senators Russell Feingold (D-Wis.) and John McCain (R-Ariz.) supported a bipartisan effort to curb campaign spending and to eliminate soft money. Their bill reduced the amount that could be given to PACs from $5,000 to $2,500 and limited PAC contributions to a total of twenty-five percent of the $25,000 total contribution. The bill also aimed at significant changes to the soft-money provisions in the Federal Election Campaign Act, banning advertising directed at a specific candidate within thirty days of a primary or sixty days of the general election. Former Senator Nancy Kassebaum and former Vice President Walter Mondale joined forces during the debates on the McCain–Feingold legislation to urge support for the reform legislation. In a letter published in the *Washington Post*, they wrote that "Congress should promptly ban 'soft money,' the huge uncontrolled contributions to national parties and their campaign organizations that have so dismayed the public. This prohibition would do much to slow the flood of campaign money and enable the nation to adhere to the justified premise of earlier reforms that massive amounts of money from powerful sources distort elections and government."[36] In spite of broad support for the bill, it failed to gain passage and died in Congress.

Campaigning for President

The campaign for president is a long, time-consuming, and expensive endeavor that begins years before the candidacy is even declared. While there is no direct path to the presidency, there are some fairly clear roads that candidates need to take. The campaign process involves securing a strong national staff, building equally strong staff in every state, gaining national media coverage, securing financial support in order to gain federal matching funds for the primaries, winning enough delegates during the primaries to win the party nomination, and finally winning the general election. The primaries, which begin in January or February of the election year, are the culmination of months or years of developing a campaign organization that will be viable throughout the following months until November.

Qualities of Presidents: General Assessments

In taking the first steps on the road to the White House, candidates should assess their position in relation to the qualities of past presidents. The Constitution, which is the most important determinant of who can and cannot run, requires individuals to be 35 years of age, a natural born citizen, and a resident of the United States for 14 years. The age requirement was intended to ensure that the president had a certain level of maturity and the citizenship requirement was intended to ensure total loyalty to the United States. Many current citizens of the United States who may have political aspirations, such as former Secretary of State Henry Kissinger and former National Security Adviser Zbigniew Brezinzski, are not eligible to serve as president since they were not born in the United States.

The next test for eligibility is based less on formal rules than on historical precedent. All of the presidents of the United States have been white, male, and generally Protestant. The only non-Protestant to serve as president was John F. Kennedy, a Roman Catholic, who was routinely criticized during the campaign for his religion. Both Democrats and Republicans argued in the 1960 election that his allegiance would be to the Pope in Rome rather than to the American people. Alfred Smith, also a Roman Catholic, was nominated by the Democrats in 1928 but did not win in the general election. Jimmy Carter, a born-again Christian, suffered similar barbs during the 1976 campaign with regard to choices he would have to make regarding his religion. Ethnic background has also been a fairly consistent test of presidents. All of the presidents have come from a European family background, mostly northern European. There have been no African-American presidents and no female presidents, although Geraldine Ferraro of New York was on the Democratic ticket in 1984 as a candidate for vice president. The American public has also preferred to have their presidents married, and preferably married only once. An exception was Ronald Reagan who had been married to Jane Wyman before he married Nancy Davis. There were subtle remarks in the 1980 campaign about Reagan's view of family values in light of his own divorce and remarriage.

Presidents have tended to be wealthy. Lyndon Johnson, Richard Nixon, Jimmy Carter, Ronald Reagan, and George Bush all entered the White House as millionaires. Since World War II, only Harry Truman, Dwight Eisenhower, and Bill Clinton have not had substantial personal wealth. Another common bond that presidents have shared in the past is their political experience. Nearly all presidents have served in an elected capacity at the state level or have served in the House of Representatives or the Senate. This political experience provides the framework to manage the presidency, our nation's highest political office. Many presidents have served as governors—Franklin Delano Roosevelt, Ronald Reagan, Jimmy Carter, and Bill Clinton—a position that gave them a strong background to run the billion-dollar enterprise of the U.S. government. They had served as chief executive officers of their states and had dealt with legislatures, courts, and disparate public opinion.

Many presidents have also moved from the Congress into the presidency, such as John F. Kennedy, Lyndon Johnson, and Gerald Ford. Kennedy and Johnson moved directly from the Senate and Ford from the House. Their skills at dealing with national problems and their knowledge of the demands on the presidency helped prepare them for the Oval Office. Three recent presidents, Harry Truman, Richard Nixon, and George Bush, observed the operation of the presidency directly while serving as vice president. All three had also served in Congress. One political scientist, Bruce Buchanan, commented that serving in an elected position prior to running for president solidifies the electability of a candidate. "Anyone who has held high state or national public office and performed adequately can, by this standard, plausibly claim a reasonable chance to do the same as presidents."[37] In recent administrations only Dwight D. Eisenhower had not risen through the political ranks.

The choice by the public of established politicians for the presidency can be explained by several factors. First, established politicians are knowledgable about the election process and how to create a campaign structure. When a candidate is running for the presidency, there is no time to learn the process. Having run in campaigns in the past is a benefit for any presidential candidate. Second, established politicians deal well with the general public. They are affable, always willing to talk to supporters, and are very careful in what they do and say. This skill may look easy for the candidates, but it is a skill that is honed over a long period. Third, established politicians have a sense of what issues to support and what issues to avoid. They know how to build their agendas around consensus issues, such as a cleaner environment and better education for the nation's children. Politicians with track records in campaigning focus around proposals that have wide support and shy away from any issues that are divisive and might lose voter support.

Perhaps the most important quality a candidate can have during the election process is the image of good health. Americans want their presidents to be vigorous and energetic, essential criteria to managing the often overwhelming responsibilities of the presidency. When Senator Robert Dole challenged President Clinton in the 1996 election, he was sharply criticized for not having the necessary stamina to handle the office because of his age. At 73, Dole was the oldest person to run for president on one of the major party tickets. Both Presidents George Bush and Bill Clinton were regularly seen jogging during their campaigns to emphasize their good health. While their physical health clearly benefited from these jogging outings, their political health also benefited as the nation saw that they were physically capable of handling the stress of the Oval Office. The rigors of the election probably killed one president, William Henry Harrison, who died soon after he was inaugurated. Weak from the campaign, Harrison caught pneumonia during the rain-soaked inauguration in 1841. Harrison became the first president to die in office and also had the distinction of serving in office for the shortest time.

Running a Campaign

Once an individual has decided that a candidacy is worth pursuing, a campaign staff needs to be built and money raised. The **campaign staff** first needs a campaign manager who has already handled a number of national campaigns—running a presidential campaign is no place for hands-on learning. Preferably, campaign managers have run other presidential campaigns, but at the very least they should have run major state campaigns, such as for governor or U.S. Senate. Managing a race for the House of Representatives or for a state legislature is far less intense and demands less expertise than a national or statewide election. Good campaign managers are expensive to hire and candidates need to be prepared to pay whatever the market bears.

The campaign then needs a campaign headquarters in Washington, D.C., complete with impressive office furniture, computers, telephones, and numerous paid staff and volunteers. Major primary states also need to have campaign offices, and if the candidate wins the party nomination, offices need to be established in every state. Grass-roots organizers are needed; it is they who work throughout the early primary and caucus states to get out the vote, a process that will need to be expanded for the general election. At every stage in the campaign, the candidate needs fund-raisers, pollsters, advertising consultants, legal staff, accountants, advance staff, and a host of others. Media consultants are critical to every campaign; they also rank among the highest costs to the campaign. In 1996, President Clinton's reelection campaign paid $2.4 million to Squier Knapp Ochs, a Washington-based media consulting firm, and the Democratic National Committee paid the firm $1.5 million. Robert Dole's presidential campaign paid $1.5 million to Multi Media Services Corp., and during the primaries Republican Lamar Alexander paid more than $2.2 million to Murphy, Pintak & Gautier for media consulting. One of the largest amounts paid to a consulting firm during the 1996 elections was by Steve Forbes, who paid $25 million of his own money to pollsters and other professional consultants.[38] Candidates also hire personal groomers, who make sure that the candidate dresses correctly and is groomed most effectively. Dressing correctly is critical to success, both in what clothes are worn to each different type of event and how well those clothes look. Nothing in a presidential campaign is left to chance; every item is thoroughly choreographed by the campaign staff.

The Primaries

Candidates for the Democratic and Republican parties are required to spend the first six months of the year, approximately January through June, running in state primaries. Each state has different rules for gaining access to the primary ballot, but generally candidates can gain access by paying a filing fee and having signed petitions. In Pennsylvania, for example, presidential candidates who want to be placed on the state Democratic primary ballot have to pay a filing fee of $200 and secure petitions with 20,000 signatures of registered voters who are enrolled members of the Democratic Party of Pennsylvania.[39]

The candidate who wins the most delegates in the primaries and state caucuses becomes the party's endorsed candidate at the summer's nominating convention. Most observers of presidential campaigns view the primaries as the most arduous part of the election since so many people are seeking the nomination. During the 1996 primary season, eleven Republican candidates were seeking to carry the party's mantle against the incumbent president, Bill Clinton. Candidates are required to meet nearly impossible timetables as they comb the key primary states for votes, often moving from early morning breakfasts in the northern part of a state to late evening sessions in the southern part of that state. In many cases, each campaign stop requires a different speech and requires addressing a different set of issues.

The primary process is the culmination of months (more likely years) of subtle campaigning and meetings in key primary and caucus states. The two earliest states, Iowa (a caucus state) and New Hampshire (a primary state), are bellwether early elections. Candidates who win these two states are perceived as front-runners and often turn perceptions into realities in later primary states. As a result of the importance of Iowa and New Hampshire, most serious candidates for the presidency spend at least a year making regular trips to these two states for both public and private appearances. Candidates also spend at least the year before the primaries building support among powerful electoral blocs, such as the Christian Coalition, National Association for the Advancement of Colored People (NAACP), labor unions, the American Association of Retired Persons (AARP), and a wide assortment of other groups, in anticipation of winning the party's nomination. In the general election, these electoral blocs can provide major funding support, volunteers, and votes. Candidates spend a good deal of their time meeting with party activists in each state, since only about nineteen to twenty percent of registered voters vote in the primaries. Those who vote are active in party affairs and tend to have strong opinions on issues that the candidates need to address.

Candidates try to gain as much free television exposure as possible, given the high cost of advertising. Media buys are the largest single cost of an election. Whenever possible, candidates try to have large outdoor events where local and national television cameras can capture them at no cost to the campaign. They also attempt to be seen on as many local and national television programs as possible. During the 1992 presidential campaign, Bill Clinton, a relatively unknown Arkansas governor, maximized his free television time by accepting nearly every television invitation that he was offered, including cable news shows, morning news shows, and talk shows. These television shows were not only free, they also offered a format that was nonconfrontational.[40] Candidates were more likely to get their message across with talk show hosts than with more confrontational news journalists. Talk shows also had other advantages to the candidates, such as during the 1992 Democratic primaries when former California governor Brown frequently used the talk shows to publicize his toll-free telephone number to donate money to his campaign. It would be difficult to publicize the telephone number in a routine press conference or other interview scenario.

Third-party candidates do not participate in the primary campaign process, since it is a function only of the Republican and Democratic Parties. Third parties have national conventions and choose their candidates at the conventions. For third parties the battles over who will become the national candidate are fought out of the public eye. Smaller third parties have conventions and tend to choose their candidates in a very orderly fashion. These candidates represent a political philosophy, such as in the Libertarian Party or the Green Party, and the candidates are less important than the message. The candidate is the product of the party. In contrast, the larger third parties of recent years, such as that of George Wallace in 1968 and Ross Perot in 1996, were born totally out of the candidate's drive to the presidency. These parties were products of the candidate rather than the candidate being the product of the party.

The Nominating Convention

For the Democratic and Republican Parties, the nominating conventions are a public crowning of the victor in the primary process. It is an opportunity, most of all, for the party to pull together in front of the entire country under one banner. With primaries causing significant divisions within a party, the nominating convention offers a very important chance for the losers to offer their support to the winner. The nominating convention also allows the losers to withdraw gracefully, for the party platform usually incorporates agenda items from all of the party's candidates. Although they lost the nomination, candidates who lost in the primaries can derive some comfort that the goals they fought for were not lost to the party. Incorporation into the party platform is a testament to the value of their ideas and of their campaign.

Nominating conventions for the Democratic and Republican parties are held in different cities each year, with the party out of power holding their convention in July and the party in power (controlling the White House) holding theirs in August. The location of the convention is always a major city, since thousands of delegates, their families, and the media descend on the city and require adequate hotel space and transit facilities. Host cities by tradition have numerous tourist and sightseeing opportunities, since most delegates spend their own funds to attend the conventions and want the week to be both personally and politically rewarding. Typical convention cities are Los Angeles, New York, Philadelphia, New Orleans, Miami, San Francisco, San Diego, and Chicago. A rule of thumb holds that conventions are moved from one geographic region of the country to another, so that a convention in Philadelphia would be followed by a convention in Los Angeles or New Orleans rather than in Baltimore or Boston. City officials avidly court representatives from the nominating conventions, promising to contribute millions of dollars to the convention in return for choosing their city.

The national conventions usually last one week, with the first part of the week devoted to discussions and voting on the party platform and to a series of speeches by party officials. The last night of the convention is devoted to the formal nomination of the presidential candidate. The only mystery that surrounds the convention is the choice of the vice president. Most, but certainly not all, presidential candidates do not reveal their vice presidential candidates until the last night of the convention. During the era of brokered conventions, vice presidents were part of the spoils system and delegate bartering. Today, the choice of the vice president is made by the party nominee alone or in concert with a small group of close advisers. Some choices are very carefully planned, such as President Clinton's choice of Senator Al Gore. Some choices appear to have been made with less deliberation, such as President Bush's choice of Senator Dan Quayle.

The General Election

The primary elections succeed in winnowing the numerous candidates down to one acceptable candidate for the Democrats and one acceptable candidate for the Republicans. Each party produces a candidate who is acceptable to more members of the party than any other candidate. While the process has been grueling for the candidates, it has ensured that the party's nominee is one who is within the mainstream of the party. Candidates who are either too conservative or too liberal for the majority of party members to accept slowly drop out during the primaries. By the time the final votes are tabulated, each party has chosen the candidate who has the strongest support among those who campaigned. Since these candidates are generally in the mainstream of the party and hold centrist views, they are able to attract voters from the other party in the general election. Most recent elections have been relatively close in the popular vote, since both parties have produced centrist candidates.

After the nominating conventions, the presidential candidates usually take several weeks off to vacation and to plan strategies for the upcoming general election. August is a slow political month in the presidential campaign. By tradition, the general election campaign officially begins Labor Day weekend and runs through election day in November. For the three months from Labor Day to election day, candidates work seven days a week and eighteen hours a day. They take very little time off during this grueling period, if any. They are given secret service protection, since one will inevitably become the next president of the United States. The summer break is also an opportunity for one or both candidates, if there is no incumbent, to attend briefing sessions on military and foreign policy issues. Since Franklin Delano Roosevelt set the precedent in 1944 by having White House staff and others brief Governor Tom Dewey, the Republican challenger, presidents have offered their opponents briefings after the nominating conventions. The briefings are designed to ensure that erroneous statements, or even damaging information, are not put on the record by the challenger. As one observer described the briefings process, they "may or may not prevent ill-advised campaign statements and protect the current conduct of foreign policy, but they at least signify basic American unity to the outside world and open lines of communication between the President and his potential successors that may be useful later."[41]

The goal during the general election is to devise a strategy that captures 270 or more electoral votes. This strategy involves channeling the financial and staffing resources of the campaign to states that have large electoral counts and that are leaning toward the candidate. If polls indicate that the voters in a certain state strongly support the candidate of the other party, there is little reason to spend limited resources campaigning there. For example, Bill Clinton did not campaign in Kansas and Bob Dole did not campaign in Arkansas in 1996, deferring to the home-state advantage of the opposition. Both Clinton and Dole fought aggressively for Texas, Florida, and California, which were seen as tossup states but had very large populations and electoral counts. Strategy is critical in the general election, since the candidate has to win the electoral college.

The campaign is usually won or lost in about ten key states with large electoral counts. Texas (32), Florida (25), and California (54) account for 111 electoral votes after the 1990 decennial census. These numbers are likely to go even higher after the year 2000 decennial census, due to population shifts, adding to their importance in the presidential elections. Seven industrial states control another 144 electoral votes, New Jersey (15), New York (33), and Pennsylvania (23) in the east, and Ohio (21), Illinois (22), Michigan (18), and Indiana (12) in the midwest. These ten states control 255 of the 270 electoral votes needed to win the election. As a result, most of the general election campaign is fought in these ten battlegrounds. States that are regarded as safe states for the candidate are visited once or twice to shore up support. States regarded as hostile are probably ignored during the campaign.

Presidential Debates

As the political parties increasingly choose centrist candidates, their positions on issues tend to be similar and often difficult for the American public to separate. There are, however, some issues on which the candidates disagree and to which they have very different solutions. One of the techniques that has emerged in recent years to allow the American public to gain a clearer understanding of the positions each candidate has taken is the **presidential debate.** Candidates are given free air time by the national television stations for a question-and-answer period, usually lasting two hours. This enables the voting public not only to sharpen their own understanding of where candidates stand on issues, but also to contrast the candidates in their mastery of the facts and their control of the event. Both are considered important leadership qualities for presidents and can often be more important to voters than the actual position taken.

Televised presidential debates are a relatively modern occurrence, first used during the Kennedy–Nixon election in 1960. Radio and television stations had purposely not hosted such debates due to Section 315 of the Communications Act of 1934, which required all radio and television licensees to afford "equal opportunities" to all "legally qualified candidates."[42] The **equal time rule,** as it became known, was an attempt by Congress to ensure that all candidates had equal access to the airwaves. Section 315 of the act was strictly enforced until 1960 when the Federal Communications Commission waived the rule for the Kennedy–Nixon debate.

Television stations requested the waiver for purely financial reasons. The print media and radio had historically dominated the presidential campaign coverage. The public in particular turned to newspapers to learn the events of the primary and general elections. In order to gain a foothold in the market share of campaign coverage, the networks conceived the debate idea. The networks hoped that this would enlarge their market share and convince the public that television was the centerpiece for elections coverage.

The Federal Communications Commission agreed to the network request and allowed a waiver for the 1960 debates, but refused to allow waivers of the equal time rule in successive elections. The 1960 debate was the exception, not the rule. A thaw in the Federal Communications Commission's view of presidential debates did not occur until 1972 during the primary elections. All three major networks (ABC, NBC, and CBS) broadcast interviews with the two leading Democratic candidates, George McGovern and Hubert Humphrey. The two minor candidates, Congresswoman Shirley Chisholm and former Los Angeles mayor Sam Yorty, were not interviewed. Chisholm and Yorty challenged the networks for violating the equal time rule and sought a ruling from the Federal Communications Commission. The ruling came down in favor of the networks, with the argument that the interviews were simply "newsworthy events" and did not violate the equal time rule. Again in 1975 the issue surfaced when the Aspen Institute Program on Communications asked the Federal Communications Commission to declare political debates to be "on the spot coverage of bona fide news events."[43] The

Commission ruled that debates by legally qualified candidates, appearing in a bona fide news event, initiated by nonbroadcast entities, and covered live and in its entirety did not violate the equal time rule. In other words, a media organization such as the networks could not host the debates but almost any nonbroadcast entity could.

As a result of the ruling, the League of Women Voters, a nonpartisan organization that exists to encourage voting, sponsored the 1976 debates and repeated that sponsorship for the next two presidential elections.[44] In the fall of 1980, the League of Women Voters allowed third-party candidate John Anderson into the debates with Jimmy Carter and Ronald Reagan. Jimmy Carter refused to attend. The debate went on as planned with Reagan, Anderson, and an empty chair for Carter. Later in the election Carter and Reagan debated without Anderson, to ensure that Carter and Reagan did debate.

After hosting three presidential debates (in 1976, 1980, 1984), the League of Women Voters withdrew, citing the high costs of lawsuits from minor candidates who wanted to be included. The League successfully met the court challenges based on the Federal Communications Commission's earlier rulings, but spent an inordinate amount of money defending themselves. The void was quickly filled in time for the 1988 presidential debates by the Republican and Democratic parties. They created a nonprofit organization called the Commission on Presidential Debates, headquartered in Washington, D.C. Board membership on the Commission on Presidential Debates was split equally between with Democrats and Republicans and was co-chaired by the chairs of the two parties. Funding came from private sources, such as AT&T and Phillip Morris, and from a flat payment of five hundred thousand dollars from the host city paid directly to the Commission on Presidential Debates.

The Commission seeks bids from cities who are willing to host the debates, but the dates and the format are established by the Commission. In 1988, 1992, and 1996, two debates were held between the presidential candidates and one debate was held between the vice-presidential candidates. Ross Perot was included in the 1992 debates but not in the 1996 debates. The commission had established a threshold level of fifteen percent support in the polls in order to include third-party candidates. Perot achieved that in 1992 but not in 1996. Perot sued in 1996, but the Supreme Court ruled that the Commission could establish its own threshold requirements for third-party candidates. The debates continue to be an important part of the election process, although polls indicate that few voters actually base their decisions on the performance of the candidates during the debates. The general rule is that candidates do not need to do well, but they cannot do badly, such as by misstating facts or becoming flustered.

Transitions

On the first Tuesday in November the electorate cast their votes for the next president of the United States. Very soon after the polls close, the national media have tallied the state-by-state vote count and projected a winner. The morning's newspapers blare with banner headlines declaring the winner, although not until the electors are counted on January 3 by the new Congress is the winner formally announced.

From the moment the final tallies are in until the inauguration day, the winner becomes the president-elect and is accorded certain privileges. Secret service protection continues for the president-elect as he begins to meet with leaders of Congress and with heads of state in preparation for the transition of power. When an incumbent president wins the election, few changes occur, and business continues as usual in the White House. Some cabinet members or White House staff may leave or change positions within the administration, but the transition period is not a major period of change as it is for new administrations. When a challenger wins or the office is open, the transition is critical to forming the new government.

The Presidential Transition Act of 1963 authorizes funding for government office space, transportation, communications, and other facilities for the president-elect and the vice president-elect during the period between the election and the inauguration. The General Services Administration is responsible for finding office space in a federal building in Washington, D.C., for the offices. The 1963 Act appropriated a sum of $900,000 to cover the expenses of the administration during the transition and also to assist the ex-president and the ex-vice president during the first six months out of office. The funding was not used until the 1968–1969 transition. For whatever reason, the law did not divide the funding among the four individuals, so President Johnson determined that the incoming and outgoing vice presidents would each have $75,000, with the balance of $75,000 split evenly between President Johnson and the newly elected Richard Nixon. Nixon also raised another $1 million in private funds for the transition. In 1952 Dwight Eisenhower had handled his transition with only $400,000, all of it raised from private sources.[45] The sum has grown considerably since the 1968–1969 transition year as Congress has appropriated increased sums of money. George Bush received $3.5 million from Congress for the 1988 transition. During the 1992–1993 transition, Bill Clinton was also appropriated a $3.5 million budget from Congress but he raised an additional $4.8 million in private funding.

The transition period is usually cordial from one administration to the next. Only six days after Richard Nixon was elected in 1968, President and Mrs. Johnson invited the Nixons to the White House for a luncheon. Nixon met later in the day with Johnson for a briefing session on the Vietnam War. When President Bush lost the election to Bill Clinton, the Bushes also held a luncheon for the Clintons and showed them though the private quarters of the White House. There are no legislative mandates on the orderly transition of power, and each administration handles it differently. Most presidents do not meet often with their successors during the transition and rely on their staffs to handle the process. Every administration has a person designated as the liaison officer for the transition. In addition, the president usually sends a memo to the cabinet officers urging their cooperation with the task forces and other advisers for the new administration. As a rule of thumb, transitions to presidents of different parties are more difficult than to presidents of the same party. Political appointees are far less interested in helping the new administration if they are from different parties.

The period from the election to the inauguration was not originally intended for presidents to form their administrations. It was originally intended to provide adequate time for the electors to meet in their states and for the votes to be counted, duly authorized by the state officials, and transmitted to the Congress. Problems of transportation and communication were the primary reason for the lengthy time period. In modern times, the three-month interval has become a transition period from one administration to another. The president is responsible for appointing fourteen cabinet officers, White House staff, and 5200 political appointees as soon as possible after the inauguration. In addition to appointments, the president needs to have a full understanding of the legislative mandates on the fourteen executive departments and the way in which the federal budget is allocated. By the end of January, the new president has to deliver a State of the Union message to Congress which explains what programs will be prioritized and what budget constraints will be imposed.

The transition period is often set in motion months before a candidate is elected in November. Jimmy Carter had Jack Watson and a small team within the campaign begin in 1976 to develop a list of names of individuals for cabinet and subcabinet appointments in what was formally called the Talent Inventory Program (TIP). This list of names was given to Carter at the end of October in anticipation of an election victory. Carter planned to "hit the ground running" as the transition began.[46] When Ronald Reagan was running for the presidency in 1980, E. Pendleton James assembled a small outside group of advisers to assess possible cabinet and subcabinet appointees.[47] Watson and James both had been senior advisers during the presidential campaign and both moved into senior positions on the White House staff. The transition of George Bush in 1988, however, had far less planning than either Carter's or Reagan's transitions. Bush did not allow his campaign staff to develop personnel lists for the new administration until late in the campaign. As James Pfiffner describes the transition, Bush forbade his campaign staff to take any steps to assemble the beginnings of a personnel operation. As a result, many serious administration positions went unfilled in the weeks and months after the inauguration.[48]

The transition process varies from administration to administration. Each incoming president establishes a different relationship with the outgoing president, and the transition reflects that relationship. As noted in the opening sentence of this chapter, the election of a president is one of the world's great transitions of power. The transition period is cordial and informational and the first step in the next chapter in the nation's history.

Key Words

brokered conventions
Buckley v. Valeo (1976)
campaign staff
Checkers speech
electoral college
equal time rule
Federal Corrupt Practices Act
Federal Election Campaign Act
    (FECA)
King Caucus
matching funds
nominating convention
one-party system
political action committees (PACs)

presidential debate
presidential electors
primary elections
Progressive Era
Revenue Act of 1971
soft money
Succession Act of 1947
third-party candidates
Tillman Act of 1907
twelfth amendment
twentieth amendment
twenty-fifth amendment
twenty-third amendment

Notes

1. James W. Davis. *The American Presidency*. 2nd ed. Westport, CT: Greenwood Press, 1995, p. 80.
2. Walter Berns, ed. *After the People Vote: A Guide to the Electoral College*. Washington, DC: AEI Press, 1992, pp. 3–31.
3. Garry Wills. *Inventing America: Jefferson's Declaration of Independence*. Garden City, NJ: Doubleday, 1978.
4. Forrest McDonald. *Alexander Hamilton: A Biography*. New York: Norton, 1979, p. 361.
5. L. Sandy Maisel. *Parties and Elections in America: The Electoral Process*. New York: Random House, 1987, p. 32.
6. Rexford G. Tugwell. *How They Became President*. New York: Simon & Schuster, 1964, p. 28.
7. Richard B. Morris, ed. *Encyclopedia of American History*. New York: Harper, 1953, p. 121.
8. Stephen J. Wayne. *The Road to the White House: The Politics of Presidential Elections*. 3rd ed. New York: St. Martin's, 1988, p. 11.
9. Norman C. Thomas and Joseph A. Pika. *The Politics of the Presidency*. 4th rev. ed. Washington, DC: Congressional Quarterly, 1997, p. 47.
10. Charles C. Euchner and John Anthony Maltese. "The Electoral Process." In: Michael Nelson, ed. *Guide to the Presidency*. Washington, DC: Congressional Quarterly, 1996, p. 221.
11. Ibid., p. 223.
12. Margaret Leech. *In the Days of McKinley*. New York: Harper, 1959, pp. 50–51.
13. Wayne. *The Road to the White House*, p. 35.
14. Theodore Roosevelt. *An Autobiography*. New York: MacMillan, 1913, p. 421.
15. The Tillman Act was named after Senator Ben Tillman, the Democratic Senator from South Carolina who had been a leader of the Progressive movement with Robert LaFollette.
16. Samuel Kernell. *Going Public: New Strategies of Presidential Leadership*. 3rd ed. Washington, DC: Congressional Quarterly, 1997, p. 126.
17. Marvin R. Weisbord. *Campaigning for President*. New York: Washington Square Press, 1966, pp. 181–182.
18. Joe McGinniss. *The Selling of the President 1968*. New York: Pocket Books, 1969, p. 107.
19. Wayne. *The Road to the White House*, p. 36.
20. Wayne. *The Road to the White House*, p. 27.
21. Anthony Corrado. "Financing the 1996 Elections." In: Gerald M. Pomper, ed. *The Election of 1996*. Chatham, NJ: Chatham House, 1997, pp. 137, 150.
22. Thomas R. Wolanin. *Presidential Advisory Commissions: Truman to Nixon*. Madison: University of Wisconsin Press, 1975, p. 165.
23. Stephen Ambrose. *Nixon: The Triumph of a Politician 1962–1972*. New York: Simon & Schuster, 1989, p. 140.
24. *Buckley v. Valeo*. 424 U.S. 1 (1976).
25. Ibid.
26. Herbert E. Alexander and Anthony Corrado. *Financing the 1992 Election*. Armonk, NY: ME Sharpe, 1995.
27. James A. Barnes and Peter H. Stone. "Shameless in San Diego." *National Journal Convention Special*, August 17, 1996, p. 1756.
28. James A. Barnes. "Clinton's Big Bounce." *National Journal*, September 7, 1996, p. 1898.
29. Frank Smallwood. *The Other Candidates: Third Parties in Presidential Elections*. Hanover, NH: published for Dartmouth College by the University Press of New England, 1983, p. 226.
30. Ibid, p. 238.
31. Robert D. Loevy. *The Flawed Path to the Presidency 1992: Unfairness and Inequality in the Presidential Selection Process*. Albany: State University of New York Press, 1995, p. 125.
32. Alexander and Corrado. *Financing the 1992 Election*.
33. Corrado. "Financing the 1996 Elections," p. 140.
34. For a discussion of the Perot campaign, see the transcript of a broadcast on public television, August 19, 1996, entitled *The Third Dimension*. From the Corporation for Public Broadcasting.
35. Anthony Corrado. "Financing the 1996 Elections," *The Elections of 1996*. Gerald Pomper, ed., pp. 137–140.

36. Nancy Kassebaum Baker and Walter F. Mondale. "Campaign Finance: Fix It." *Washington Post,* July 18, 1997, p. A21.
37. Bruce Buchanan. "The Presidency and the Nominating Process." In: Michael Nelson, ed. *The Presidency and the Political System.* 4th ed. Washington, DC: Congressional Quarterly, 1995, pp. 236–237.
38. John Marks. "Meet the Puppetmasters." *U.S. News & World Report,* March 11, 1996, pp. 28–30.
39. The Pennsylvania Delegate Selection Plan for the 1992 Democratic National Convention, as filed with the Pennsylvania Department of State, Bureau of Elections, Harrisburg, Pennsylvania.
40. Bruce Buchanan, "The Presidency and the Nominating Process." In: Michael Nelson, ed. *The Presidency and the Political System.* 4th ed. Washington, DC: Congressional Quarterly, 1995, p. 235.
41. Laurin L. Henry. "Presidential Transitions: The 1968–69 Experience." *Public Administration Review,* September/October 1969, p. 472.
42. Charles Firestone. "Legal Issues Surrounding Televised Presidential Debates." In: Joel L. Swerdlow, ed. *Presidential Debates 1988 and Beyond.* Washington, DC: Congressional Quarterly, 1987, p. 18.
43. Ibid., p. 19.
44. For a detailed discussion of the presidential debates, see Kathleen H. Jamieson and David S. Birdsell. *Presidential Debates.* New York: Oxford University Press, 1988.
45. Michael Nelson. *The Presidency from A to Z.* rev. ed. Washington, DC: Congressional Quarterly, 1994, p. 426.
46. Burton I. Kaufman. *The Presidency of James Earl Carter.* Lawrence, KS: University Press of Kansas, 1993, p. 25.
47. Shirley Anne Warshaw. *Powersharing: White House–Cabinet Relations in the Modern Presidency.* Albany, NY: State University of New York Press, 1996, p. 107.
48. James P. Pfiffner. "Establishing the Bush Presidency." *Public Administration Review,* January/February 1990, p. 65.

Chapter 3

The Vice President

Unlike the president, for whom the Constitution lists many responsibilities, the vice president is given very few responsibilities under the Constitution. The primary job of the vice president is to wait until he is needed to fill in for the president if he is incapacitated or should die in office. The vice presidency has historically not been a very exciting life. In fact, most vice presidents have looked back on their tenure as a rather boring existence. John Adams, vice president to George Washington, said of his job, "My country has in its wisdom contrived for me the most insignificant office that ever the invention of man contrived or his imagination conceived."[1] Little had changed by the 1940s, for Harry Truman met with President Roosevelt only twice during his two and a half months as vice president.[2] As late as 1960 the job of the vice president had not improved. In 1960 Clinton Rossiter wrote in his epic *The American Presidency* that "the vice presidency is a hollow shell of an office— it is a disappointment in the American constitutional system."[3]

More recently, however, vice presidents have been given added responsibilities by the president, such as Vice President Quayle, who managed President Bush's mandate to reduce federal regulations, and Vice President Gore, who oversaw the National Performance Review endeavor to operate government more efficiently. Gore also served as a presidential adviser, meeting once a week with President Clinton to discuss policy and political issues. However, the role that Gore played was not typical of the role of most vice presidents. Vice presidents generally serve as stand-ins for the president at political party events and campaign rallies, meet with representatives from various groups who are unable to meet with the president, represent the president at state functions that the president cannot attend, and serve as the spokesperson for administration programs. The only significant role that the vice president plays that is not as a representative of the president is the constitutional role of serving as president of the Senate and casting a vote in case of a tie.

The job of vice president has its perquisites. The salary of the vice president since 1974 has been set by Congress at $171,500, plus a taxable expense account of $10,000. In 2000 the salary will rise to $181,400. The salary was relatively low throughout the tenure of most vice presidents, though. When George Washington was president, Congress appropriated $25,000 for the president's salary but only $5,000 for John Adams's salary as vice president. In 1873, nearly one hundred years later, Congress finally doubled the president and the vice president's salaries. In 1906, the vice president received an additional raise to $12,000, but the salary was still substantially less than the president's salary of $50,000. Following World War II, Congress again reexamined the vice president's salary and raised it to $20,000 in 1946, to $30,000 in 1949, to $35,000 and then $43,000 during the Kennedy and Johnson years, and finally to $62,500 in 1969. The jump from $62,500 to $171,500 in 1974 was an indication of the increased responsibilities that vice presidents have had in modern administrations as the role of the federal government burgeoned in the post-war years.

In addition to a relatively high salary and an expense account, an official residence is provided for the vice president on the grounds of the Naval Observatory on Massachusetts Avenue in Washington, D.C. The home and grounds at the Naval Observatory were transferred from the navy to the vice president by Congress in 1974. The home, which was built in 1893, underwent a major $1.6 million structural renovation during the early part of the Clinton administration. Entirely new heating, air conditioning, and ventilation systems were installed during the renovation, to replace systems that had been in place for as long as eighty years. The residence is quite large, with a dining room that will hold thirty guests and 12,000 square feet of living space, and is situated on twelve landscaped acres. The house had served as the official residence for the superintendent of the Naval Observatory until 1928 and then as the home of the chief of naval operations until 1974. Admiral Elmo R. Zumwalt was the last military resident of the home before the vice president moved in. When Vice President and Mrs. Quayle lived in the house during the Bush administration, they added a putting green, a swimming pool, hot tub, and pool house, using private funds for each project.

The official office of the vice president is in the Old Executive Office Building, next door to the White House. The office has a large formal ceremonial room, complete with fireplace and mahogany wall paneling, plus a large personal office for the vice president. There are also offices nearby for the vice president's staff. It is in the Old Executive Office Building that the vice president does most of his work, both public and private. There are also two other offices available to the vice president, one in the West Wing of the White House near the president and one in the Senate. Although vice presidents use both the offices in the White House and in the Senate, they spend most of their time in the Old Executive Office Building because the office is far larger and more stately and because their staff, currently more than ninety, are located there (Figure 3.1).

Constitutional Framework and Original Intent

The **constitutional role of the vice president** is limited to serving as acting president should the president become incapacitated or to taking over the presidency if the president should die in office. The United States is unique in this respect, for it is the only nation in the world with an elected official whose primary job is to fill the unexpired term of the leader of government. In addition, the vice president is president of the Senate and is empowered to cast only tie-breaking votes. The framers gave little thought to

President	Term	Vice President
George Washington	1789–1793	John Adams
George Washington	1793–1797	John Adams
John Adams	1797–1801	Thomas Jefferson
Thomas Jefferson	1801–1805	Aaron Burr
Thomas Jefferson	1805–1809	George Clinton
James Madison	1809–1813	George Clinton*
James Madison	1813–1817	Elbridge Gerry*
James Monroe	1817–1821	Daniel D. Tompkins
James Monroe	1821–1825	Daniel D. Tompkins
John Q. Adams	1825–1829	John C. Calhoun
Andrew Jackson	1829–1833	John C. Calhoun†
Andrew Jackson	1833–1837	Martin Van Buren
Martin Van Buren	1837–1841	Richard M. Johnson
W. H. Harrison*	1841–1841	John Tyler
John Tyler	1841–1845	(none)
James K. Polk	1845–1849	George M. Dallas
Zachary Taylor*	1849–1850	Millard Fillmore
Millard Fillmore	1850–1853	(none)
Franklin Pierce	1853–1857	William R. King*
James Buchanan	1857–1861	John C. Breckinridge
Abraham Lincoln	1861–1865	Hannibal Harrfan
Abraham Lincoln*	1865–1865	Andrew Johnson
Andrew Johnson	1865–1869	(none)
Ulysses S. Grant	1869–1873	Schuyler Colfax
Ulysses S. Grant	1873–1877	Henry Wilson*
Rutherford B Hayes	1877–1881	William Wheeler
James A. Garfield*	1881–1881	Chester A. Arthur
Chester A. Arthur	1881–1885	(none)
Grover Cleveland	1885–1889	Thomas A. Hendricks*
Benjamin Harrison	1889–1893	Levi P. Morton
Grover Cleveland	1893–1897	Adlai E. Steveson
William McKinley	1897–1901	Garret A. Hobart*
William McKinley*	1901–1901	Theodore Roosevelt
Theodore Roosevelt	1901–1905	(none)
Theodore Roosevelt	1905–1909	Charles W. Fairbanks
William H. Taft	1909–1913	James S. Sherman*
Woodrow Wilson	1913–1917	Thomas R. Marshall
Woodrow Wilson	1917–1921	Thomas R. Marshall
Warren G. Harding*	1921–1923	Calvin Coolidge
Calvin Coolidge	1923–1925	(none)
Calvin Coolidge	1925–1929	Charles G. Dawes
Herbert Hoover	1929–1933	Charles Curtis
Franklin D. Roosevelt	1933–1937	John N. Garner
Franklin D. Roosevelt	1937–1941	John N. Garner
Franklin D. Roosevelt	1941–1945	Herry A. Wallace
Franklin D. Roosevelt*	1945–1945	Harry S Truman
Harry S Truman	1945–1949	(none)
Harry S Truman	1949–1953	Alben W. Barkley
Dwight D. Eisenhower	1953–1957	Richard Nixon
Dwight D. Eisenhower	1957–1961	Richard Nixon
John F. Kennedy*	1961–1963	Lyndon B. Johnson

FIGURE 3.1   U.S. Presidents and Vice Presidents.

Lyndon B. Johnson	1963–1965	(none)
Lyndon B. Johnson	1965–1969	Hubert H. Humphrey
Richard Nixon	1969–1973	Spiro T. Agnew
Richard Nixon[†]	1973–1974	Spiro T. Agnew[†]
Gerald Ford	1974–1977	Nelson Rockefeller
Jimmy Carter	1977–1981	Walter F. Mondale
Ronald Reagan	1981–1985	George Bush
Ronald Reagan	1985–1989	George Bush
George Bush	1989–1993	Dan Quayle
William J. Clinton	1993–1997	Albert Gore
William J. Clinton	1997–2001	Albert Gore

[*]Died in office
[†]Resigned

Source: Michael Nelson, ed. *The Presidency A to Z*. Washington, DC: Congressional Quarterly Press, 1994.

FIGURE 3.1 *Continued*

the role of the vice president, focusing all their attentions on that of the president. They saw the vice president as necessary should anything befall the president, but provided no other job for the vice president except for the role in the Senate. One of the few discussions on the vice presidency during the constitutional convention occurred in a general debate on the presidency in June 1787 in which Alexander Hamilton noted that "On the death, resignation or removal of the governor [the term given the executive before the term *president* was inserted] his authorities are to be exercised by the president of the Senate till a successor be appointed."[4] The issue of a vice president was considered so secondary to the discussion of the presidency that Hamilton did not pursue it, nor did anyone else, until the final session of the convention in September.

Only when the framers realized that a mechanism needed to be devised to ensure an orderly transition of government should anything happen to the president was there serious discussion of the vice presidency. The office of the vice president was created to ensure that orderly transition. When the Committee of Style was given the task at the end of the constitutional convention with formulating a written document that addressed all of the pertinent issues of the convention, they were given two somewhat different resolutions regarding the vice presidency. The first resolution was prepared by the Committee of Eleven, representing one delegate from each of the states remaining at the convention, and submitted on September 4. The resolution stated that, "In case of his [the president's] removal is aforesaid, death, absence, resignation, or inability to discharge the powers or duties of his office the Vice President shall exercise those powers and duties until another President be chosen, or until the inability of the President be removed." This resolution dealt only with the issue of succession from the vice president to the president. Three days later another resolution was put forward by Governor Edmund Randolph of Virginia. Randolph's resolution was slightly different, for it was intended to supplement the September 4 resolution by providing for an election for the president while the vice president was serving as *acting* president. He also provided for Congress to name an acting president should both the president and vice president be unable to serve, for whatever reasons. Randolph proposed that "The Legislature may declare by law what officer of the United

States shall act as president in the case of death, resignation, or disability of the President and Vice President, and such Officer shall act accordingly, until such disability be removed, or a President shall be elected." For both the September 4 and September 7 resolutions, the intent was for the vice president to serve as acting president until an election could be called to elect a new president. There was no intent for the vice president to actually fill out the president's term until the next scheduled election.[5]

When the Committee of Style met to merge these two resolutions, the result was a somewhat blurred version. Paragraph 6 of Article II, Section 2, of the Constitution reads:

> In case of the Removal of the President from the Office, of or his Death, Resignation, or Inability to discharge the Powers and Duties of said Office, the Same shall devolve on the Vice President, and the Congress may by law provide for the Case of Removal, Death, Resignation, or Inability, both of the President and Vice President, declaring what Officer shall then act as President, and such officer shall act accordingly, until the Disability be removed, or a President shall be elected.

The final version in the Constitution inadvertently blurred two points made clearly in the September 4 and September 7 resolutions. The first point that became obscured involved the words "the same" when referring to "of said office." The original resolution meant that the vice president would act as president, discharging the powers and duties of the president until a president was soon elected. In the final version there is enough ambiguity with the words "the same" to allow an interpretation by vice presidents that the office of president will devolve on the vice president and he will become president.

The second critical ambiguity in the final version involves the words "or a President shall be elected." The Randolph resolution provided for the vice president to serve as acting president until "a President shall be elected." James Madison had specifically amended Randolph's resolution with this phrase in order to permit "a supply of vacancy by an intermediate election of the President."[6] The intent of Madison's amendment was to ensure that the vice president would serve only until an election was held for the presidency. One of the keystones of the new Constitution was that the president would be elected by the people, and Madison wanted to ensure that this principle was consistent throughout the Constitution. The job of the vice president, according to original intent, was to serve only until an election could be held, not until the term of the president was over. However, the language of paragraph 6 of the Constitution did not spell this out. Vice presidents who have succeeded to the presidency have always interpreted paragraph 6 to mean that they would hold office until the end of the president's elected term of office. Neither the public nor Congress has ever challenged this interpretation, and now tradition holds that vice presidents serve out the term. The issue did not arise until 1841, when President William Henry Harrison died of pneumonia shortly after the inauguration. Vice President John Tyler saw his new role not as acting president but as president. Tyler was sworn into office, gave an inaugural address, moved into the White House, and began to operate as president. Congress did not fully accept his move to serve as president rather than as acting president and addressed him in correspondence as "Vice President, on whom, by the death of the late President, the powers and duties of the office of President have devolved."[7] Tyler ignored this slight by Congress and continued to run the office of president as president rather than as acting president. Tyler set a precedent that every vice president has continued with regard to succession to office and carrying out the balance of the term. Not until the twenty-fifth amendment was ratified in 1967 did the Constitution specifically provide that the vice president become the president when a vacancy occurred.

Another thorny issue concerning the vice president that arose during the constitutional convention was selection. How was the vice president to be selected? As in the issue of succession, the issue of selection was discussed during the proceedings and a number of options were offered. It was left to the **Committee of Eleven** at the end of the convention to develop the final proposal from these options. They forged a proposal called the "electoral college," which provided for the election of both the president and the vice president. The Committee of Eleven developed the electoral college to allow states to control the election of the president, in deference to the Republicans who did not want to wholly dissolve the Articles of Confederation and lose all state power to the national government. Each elector was allowed to cast two votes for two different candidates, but was not allowed to state which vote was for president and which vote was for vice president. The process provided that the person who received the most electoral votes (with each state having two) would be president and the person who received the second most electoral votes would be vice president. To the framers of the Constitution, this process allowed for the two individuals with the most state support to secure the number one and number two posts in the country. The vice presidency became a consolation prize to the person who finished second in the balloting.

Although the vice presidency was largely a consolation prize, it did solve two problems for the framers. The first problem was succession and the second was a problem in the Senate. Since the leader of the Senate had no vote in voting matters, the framers reasoned that by choosing a member of the Senate as the chamber's leader, one state would effectively be denied half its vote. The remedy they decided on was for the vice president to serve as president of the Senate but to vote only if a tie occurred. Roger Sherman of Connecticut said of this solution that without his role in the Senate, the vice president "would have no other role." This put the vice president in the singular position of having both a constitutional legislative and a constitutional executive role.

During the first ballot of the electoral college, all 69 members cast one of their two ballots for George Washington. The ballots for their second choice were divided among John Adams, with thirty-four votes, and ten other individuals. Adams became an active vice president, often meeting with the cabinet when Washington was out of town and regularly serving as president of the Senate. Since the Senate membership was small, with only twenty-six members from the thirteen states, Adams was often called on to break ties. During his two terms in office as vice president, he was called on to break twenty-nine ties, a record that still stands. One of the more important votes he cast upheld the right of the president to remove appointees without the consent of the Senate. In the beginning of his term, Adams even tried to debate issues on the Senate floor, but soon pulled back from that role and simply listened to the debates from his seat in the front of the Senate.

The first test of the electoral college had worked well, with the electors' first and second choices being elected president and vice president. The second test of the electoral college showed its flaws and created a divided executive branch. In the **election of 1796,** John Adams, a Federalist, was elected president and Thomas Jefferson, a Republican, was elected vice president. The politically divided executive that emerged in 1796 was the result of Alexander Hamilton's lobbying against John

Adams during the election process. Hamilton urged the Federalist electors to support Thomas Pinckney of South Carolina rather than Adams. Hamilton believed that this strategy would lead to Pinckney's election, since the Federalists had the most electors, and election of a favorite-son candidate as vice president. Pinckney would then turn to Hamilton as his senior advisor. But the strategy failed when Adams learned of the scheme and urged the New England Federalists (Adams was from Massachusetts) to cast their second vote to a candidate other than Pinckney. So many different candidates received the second votes that the Federalists effectively lost the vice presidency to the Republicans, who remained united behind Thomas Jefferson. Adams, a Federalist, received the highest number of votes in the electoral college and Jefferson, a Republican, the second highest number.

Adams realized the gravity of having a president and vice president of very different political philosophies. Soon after the inauguration Adams sought to minimize the damage by urging Jefferson to take on a diplomatic mission in France as part of his vice-presidential responsibilities. Adams saw this is an important role for Jefferson since relations with France had been deteriorating following the Jay Treaty. This was a logical solution to Adams, since Jefferson had served as Ambassador to France under the Articles of Confederation. Jefferson refused, arguing that such a role lay outside his constitutional responsibilities. During his tenure as vice president, Jefferson emerged as the chief Republican Party leader, a role that had been held by James Madison. Jefferson actively opposed many of Adams's policies, leading Republican opposition in Congress and often meeting with Republican leaders in the Senate to form opposition strategies to Adams's proposals. One of Jefferson's most daring acts of opposition to Adams was his drafting of the Kentucky Resolutions in 1798, which labeled the Federalist-supported Alien and Sedition Acts as unconstitutional. The Kentucky Resolutions also asserted that states had the right to declare null and void any law that they viewed as violating constitutional guarantees for the states.

After one term as vice president, Jefferson challenged Adams for the presidency in the **election of 1800**. Adams, who had sixty-five electoral votes, lost to Jefferson, who had seventy-three. But another problem with the electoral college ensued. Both Jefferson and Aaron Burr, a Republican and the vice-presidential nominee, received seventy-three votes and forced the House of Representatives to determine the outcome of the election. After thirty-six ballots, Jefferson prevailed in the House, but only after Alexander Hamilton campaigned among the Federalist states on behalf of Jefferson. Jefferson believed that Burr had conspired with state delegations of both parties to win the presidency away from Jefferson and therefore never trusted Burr. Burr then took an active role as the Senate president and even broke a tie vote to oppose a judiciary bill that Jefferson supported.[8]

The problems of both the Adams–Jefferson administration and the Jefferson–Burr administration forced Congress to reconsider the voting structure of the electoral college. Congress subsequently passed the **twelfth amendment** to the Constitution, ratified by the states in 1804, which provided for the president and vice president to be elected as part of the same ticket by a political party. This ended the disagreements between the president and vice president when they had come from different political parties and created the unified ticket under which we operate today. But the new system also created an election process quite different from what the framers had intended in 1787. When the original system was crafted, the intent was to elect for the offices of president and vice president the two most distinguished candidates available. The president and vice president would be individuals with broad support within the electoral college. When the system was changed by the twelfth amendment, the president and vice president were no longer individuals of equal stature. The president became the dominant individual, with the vice president often much lesser known and with less impressive credentials than the president.

Vice presidents were often brought to the ticket for purely political reasons, and their relationship with the president had little substance. Governor George Clinton of New York was added to the presidential ticket of James Madison of Virginia in order to garner the New York state electoral votes and to bring geographic balance to the ticket. Clinton had not supported Madison and chose not to attend the inauguration, although he did serve out his term. As vice president John C. Calhoun, Andrew Jackson's vice president, openly opposed Jackson's policies. Chester Arthur, James Garfield's vice president, also openly opposed presidential policies. Some vice presidents simply ignored their jobs, such as Richard Johnson who operated a tavern while he served as Martin Van Buren's vice president. Throughout most of the nineteenth century and part of the twentieth, partisan disagreements and disinterest in the job often strained the relationship between the president and vice president. Few men of stature were interested in the job of vice president, and almost no one viewed it as a stepping stone to the presidency. Many of those who did take the job were in ill health, and several died while in office. Only four vice presidents have ever succeeded directly to the presidency through election: John Adams, Thomas Jefferson, Martin Van Buren, and George Bush, although Richard Nixon succeeded to the presidency after an eight-year interval. In 1989, George Bush became the first vice president since Martin Van Buren in 1837 to move directly from the vice presidency to the presidency.

Since the Constitution provided relatively little responsibility for the vice president within the executive branch except to wait to either serve as president or as acting president, they often turned to the legislative branch to occupy their time. As the president of the Senate, all vice presidents have been given an elegant office immediately off the Senate floor. For many vice presidents this office became their refuge, particularly when the size of the Senate was relatively small. Throughout most of the nation's history, the only office available to vice presidents was their Senate office. Not until the Kennedy administration was Vice President Lyndon Johnson given an office in the Old Executive Office Building. Doris Kearns, a former White House fellow who worked in the Johnson White House, describes Johnson as happy to have his new office but concerned that the existence of an office did not guarantee a role in the administration. He subsequently drafted a memo for an executive order for President Kennedy to sign that gave the vice president greater policy responsibility and that directed the executive departments to send Johnson all the reports being sent to the president. Kennedy was not about to bring Johnson, his political opponent in the Senate, into the inner circle. The memos were diplomatically shelved, never to see the light of day.[9] Kennedy had no intention of giving Johnson such authority.

During the early presidencies, vice presidents regularly used their Senate office. For some vice presidents, the office provided a place to lobby for (or in some cases against) the president's agenda and to meet with friendly Senators and develop strategies for winning votes. For other vice presidents the office provided a retreat away from the president and to be with sympathetic friends. When the size of the Senate allowed for closer votes and often produced tie votes, vice presidents regularly used their Senate office. However, as the size of the Senate has grown, there have been fewer and fewer tie votes. John Adams cast twenty-nine tie breakers, John C. Calhoun cast twenty-eight, but more recent vice presidents have cast very few tie breakers. Lyndon Johnson cast no tie breaking votes, Spiro Agnew cast two, Walter Mondale cast one, George Bush cast eight, and Dan Quayle cast no tie breaking votes.

Statutory Roles

In addition to the two roles provided by the Constitution of waiting to be president and of casting tie-breaking votes in the Senate, the vice president has several **statutory roles.** The most important of these statutory roles is provided by the 1947 National Security Act, which made the vice president an *ex officio* member of the National Security Council. Although the original act did not include the vice president on the National Security Council, at the request of President Truman, Congress amended the act in 1949 to include the vice president as a statutory member. The vice president also is a statutory member of the Board of Regents of the Smithsonian Institution. For one vice president, Thomas Marshall, who served with Woodrow Wilson, the role at the Smithsonian Institution was symbolic of his entire job. Marshall noted that his membership on the Smithsonian's Board of Regents allowed him "the opportunity to compare his fossilized life with fossils of all ages."

The vice president has the additional statutory role of nominating four Senators to the Board of Visitors of the Naval Academy and nominating two cadets to the U.S. Military Academy, as do members of Congress. This latter role stems from the vice president's constitutional role as president of the Senate. Finally, the vice president signs enrolled bills and joint resolutions before they are sent to the president in his capacity as president of the Senate. The list of statutory roles for the vice president is very limited, as are the constitutional roles, which further illustrates how dependent the vice president is on the president for a part to play in the administration. Unless the president creates specific job assignments for the vice president, the vice president will have little to do in government.

Succession

Of the forty-one men who have been elected president from George Washington to Bill Clinton, eight died in office and one resigned. In every case, the vice president took over the reins of power in a rapid and smooth transition. These nine transitions included:

- John Tyler, who succeeded William Henry Harrison in 1841 after Harrison died from pneumonia contracted during exposure to cold rains and wind during the inauguration.
- Millard Fillmore, who succeeded Zachary Taylor in 1850 when Taylor died of natural causes during his second term.
- Andrew Johnson, who succeeded Abraham Lincoln in 1865 following the assassination of Lincoln barely six weeks into his second term.

- Chester A. Arthur, who succeeded James A. Garfield in 1881 after Garfield was assassinated early in his term.
- Theodore Roosevelt, who succeeded William McKinley in 1901 after McKinley was killed by an assassin halfway through his first year in office.
- Calvin Coolidge, who succeeded Warren G. Harding after his death in 1923.
- Harry Truman, who succeeded Franklin Delano Roosevelt after his death in 1945, three months into his fourth term in office.
- Lyndon Johnson, who succeeded John F. Kennedy after his 1963 assassination in Dallas.
- Gerald Ford, who succeeded Richard Nixon when Nixon resigned before impeachment articles were formally deliberated and voted on in the House of Representatives.

The chance of moving up to the presidency from the vice presidency is nearly twenty-five percent, since nine of forty-one have become **accidental presidents.** But the success of these accidental presidents in making a mark on history is not particularly good. Historian Arthur M. Schlesinger, Jr., asked historians around the country in 1996 to rank all of the presidents in one of five categories: great, near great, average, below average, and failure.[10] Harrison and Garfield were not included in any group because they died so soon after taking office. Schlesinger's survey replicated one done in 1948 by his father, Arthur M. Schlesinger of Harvard University. Both surveys drew nearly identical conclusions, although the latter one had fifty more years of data to include. Of the nine accidental presidents, none were deemed great, two were deemed near great (Theodore Roosevelt and Harry Truman), one was judged high average (Lyndon Johnson), two were judged low average (Chester Arthur and Gerald Ford), three were judged below average (John Tyler, Calvin Coolidge, and Millard Fillmore), and one was judged a failure (Andrew Johnson). The assessment by the historians of the accidental presidents was that six of nine, or two thirds, were low average, below average, or failures (Figure 3.2).

Accidental presidencies have nearly always occurred because the president died in office; the one exception is when President Richard Nixon resigned his office during

Near Great	Theodore Roosevelt, Harry Truman
High Average	Lyndon Johnson
Average	Martin Van Buren, Gerald Ford
Low Average	Chester Arthur, Calvin Coolidge, George Bush
Below Average	John Tyler, Millard Fillmore
Failure	Andrew Johnson

Source: Arthur M. Schlesinger, Jr. "The Ultimate Approval Rating." *The New York Times Magazine,* December 15, 1996: pp. 44–51.

FIGURE 3.2   1996 Schlesinger Poll: Ratings of Vice Presidents Who Became Presidents.

the Watergate investigation. Vice presidents have never moved into the presidency because the president has been removed from office through impeachment and conviction under Article II of the Constitution for "treason, bribery, or other high crimes and misdemeanors." Only two presidents have been impeached by the House of Representatives, Andrew Johnson and William Jefferson Clinton, but the Senate failed to convict either man.

Johnson was impeached by the House of Representatives for refusing to obey the recently passed Tenure in Office Act, and thus accused Johnson of a "high crime." The **Tenure in Office Act of 1867,** passed after Lincoln's death, required the president to seek Congressional approval for dismissing any cabinet officer, under the logic that if the Senate has to confirm cabinet appointments it also has to approve cabinet dismissals. Johnson argued that the law violated the Constitution, which only required cabinet officers to be confirmed by the Senate and did not address dismissal.

Without regard to the law, Johnson fired Secretary of War Edwin M. Stanton. Stanton was working with Republican members of Congress to create laws that punished Southern states for secession. He barricaded himself in his office and refused to relinquish his job. Tensions mounted throughout the country, with newspaper headlines screaming both for and against Johnson, generally depending on the city in which the newspaper was located. During the Senate trial in May 1868, Johnson never attended any of the hearings. When the vote was finally cast and Johnson acquitted of the charges, tensions died down and Stanton gave up his office. Johnson continued to run the country, and after he left office he was so popular that he was elected to the Senate from Tennessee. John F. Kennedy chronicled the Johnson impeachment and conviction hearings in his Pulitzer Prize winning book, *Profiles in Courage*[11] (Figure 3.3).

In addition to the nine accidental presidents, five vice presidents have become president through election. These were John Adams, Thomas Jefferson, Martin Van Buren, Richard Nixon, and George Bush. In total, fourteen vice presidents have become president. The 1996 survey by historian Arthur Schlesinger, Jr., gave higher

Vice President	Years Served as President	Former President
John Adams	1797–1801	George Washington
Thomas Jefferson	1801–1805 & 1805–1809	John Adams
Martin Van Buren	1837–1841	Andrew Jackson
Theodore Roosevelt	1901–1905*	William McKinley
Calvin Coolidge	1925–1929*	Warren G. Harding
Harry S Truman	1949–1953*	Franklin D. Roosevelt
Lyndon B. Johnson	1965–1969*	John F. Kennedy
George Bush	1989–1993	Ronald Reagan

* served partial term prior to election to full term

Source: Michael Nelson. *Congressional Quarterly's Guide to the Presidency.* 2nd ed. Washington, DC: Congressional Quarterly Press, 1996.

FIGURE 3.3   Vice Presidents Elected President Immediately Following Service as Vice President.

marks to the elected vice presidents, with three of the five receiving marks of average (Van Buren), high average (Adams), and near great (Jefferson). Only two received lower marks, Nixon (failure) and Bush (low average) (Figure 3.4).

Rating	Schlesinger Poll 1948	Rating	Schlesinger Poll 1996
1	Lincoln (G)	1	Lincoln (G)
2	Washington (G)	2	F. Roosevelt (G)
3	F. Roosevelt (G)	3	Washington (G)
4	Wilson (G)	4	Jefferson (NG)
5	Jefferson (G)	5	Wilson/Jackson (NG)
6	Jackson (G)	6	T. Roosevelt (NG)
7	T. Roosevelt (NG)	7	Truman (NG)
8	Cleveland (NG)	8	Polk (NG)
9	J. Adams (NG)	9	Eisenhower (HA)
10	Polk (NG)	10	J. Adams (HA)
11	J.Q. Adams (NG)	11	Kennedy (HA)
12	Monroe (A)	12	L. Johnson (HA)
13	Hayes (A)	13	Cleveland (HA)
14	Madison (A)	14	McKinley (HA)
15	Van Buren (A)	15	Monroe (HA)
16	Taft (A)	16	Madison (LA)
17	Arthur (A)	17	J.Q. Adams (LA)
18	McKinley (A)	18	Clinton (LA)
19	A. Johnson (A)	19	Reagan (LA)
20	Hoover (A)	20	B. Harrison (LA)
21	B. Harrison (A)	21	Van Buren (LA)
22	Tyler (BA)	22	Taft (LA)
23	Coolidge (BA)	23	Hayes (LA)
24	Fillmore (BA)	24	Bush (LA)
25	Taylor (BA)	25	Carter (LA)
26	Buchanan (BA)	26	Arthur (LA)
27	Pierce (BA)	27	Ford (LA)
28	Grant (F)	28	Coolidge (BA)
29	Harding (F)	29	Taylor (BA)
		30	Tyler (BA)
		31	Fillmore (BA)
		32	Hoover (F)
		33	Nixon (F)
		34	Pierce (F)
		35	A. Johnson (F)
		36	Grant (F)
		37	Buchanan (F)
		38	Harding (F)

G = great; NG = near great; HA = high average; A = average; LA = low average; BA = below average; F = failure.

Sources: Arthur M. Schlesinger. "Historians Rate U.S. Presidents." *Life Magazine,* vol 25. November 1, 1948: p. 65.

Arthur M. Schlesinger, Jr. "The Ultimate Approval Rating." *The New York Times Magazine,* December 15, 1996: pp. 44–51.

FIGURE 3.4   How Scholars Have Ranked the Presidents.

Disability

In each of the fourteen cases, the vice president became president only after the death of the president. The Constitution also considered what would happen should the president become disabled. Paragraph 6 of Article II, Section 1, of the Constitution said that "in the case of . . . Inability (of the president) to discharge the Powers and Duties of the said Office, the Same shall devolve on the Vice President . . . until the Disability be removed or a President shall be elected." The lack of definition of the word "disability" was raised during the constitutional convention by John Dickinson of Pennsylvania, who said on August 20, 1787, "What is the extent of the term 'disability' and who is to be the judge of it?"[12] But no one answered him and the convention left the language as written.

The first question of presidential disability came when sixty-two-year-old President James Madison was suffering from a case of "bilious fever." Rumors began that his health was seriously deteriorating and that he could not handle the responsibilities of office. Senator Daniel Webster reported that he had found the president too ill to read a congressional resolution that needed a presidential answer. In spite of the rampant reports of the president's ill health and inability to discharge his official duties, neither the vice president nor Congress made any attempt to unseat Madison. He eventually recovered and served out his term.

One of the earliest debates over succession occurred during the Garfield administration. President Garfield was shot by an assassin in 1881 and hovered near death for eighty days. The cabinet, including the attorney general, did not want to give power to the vice president during those eighty days for fear that Garfield would recover and be unable to retake the presidency from the vice president. In 1841 when John Tyler assumed the presidency after the death of William Henry Harrison, he declared himself president rather than acting president. Garfield's cabinet was fearful that a precedent had been set by Tyler, which did not provide for an acting president at any time. When Garfield died, the crisis was resolved when Chester Arthur moved into the presidency.

Fearful of the possibility that he might be removed from office during an operation, President Grover Cleveland secretly underwent surgery for the removal of a cancerous growth on the roof of his mouth. During his second term in 1893, Cleveland leaked the story that he was going on a pleasure cruise on a private yacht on Long Island Sound. Once on board, a surgeon removed a major part of his upper jaw. He recovered at his summer home in Massachusetts and was fitted with an artificial jaw. No public announcement was made, nor did the cabinet or vice president know of the surgery.

A second quite public question on presidential disability arose when Woodrow Wilson was felled by a stroke and unable to discharge his duties seventeen months before the end of his second term. Fearful of any attempt to remove Wilson, the White House hid many of the medical facts from Congress and from the public. When the reality of the situation did become public, Wilson's cabinet was interested in giving Vice President Thomas R. Marshall the role of acting president. But as Garfield's cabinet had been, Wilson's cabinet was unsure of the constitutionality of such a transfer of power. The issue never moved passed the discussion stage because Wilson's White House staff refused to allow any discussion on the subject, saying power could not be transferred from the president under any circumstances. President Wilson's private secretary noted to Secretary of State Robert Lansing that "You may rest assured that while Woodrow Wilson is lying in the White House on the broad of his back I will not be a part to ousting him."[13] Mrs. Wilson and the White House staff essentially carried out the duties of the president until the end of his term. The White House staff was equally protective of Franklin Roosevelt toward the end of his administration. In 1944, Roosevelt's physicians diagnosed his health as seriously deteriorating due to hypertensive heart disease, hardening of the arteries, and acute bronchitis. This information was never made public nor shared with his vice president or cabinet during the 1944 election. Roosevelt won the election, but died three months into his fourth term.

Not until the Eisenhower administration did the issue become of serious concern following Eisenhower's heart attack in 1955, an ileitis operation in 1956, and a stroke in 1957. After Eisenhower's heart attack, Vice President Nixon worked closely with the cabinet and the White House staff to handle routine issues. The White House press secretary, James Hagerty, provided the public full disclosure of Eisenhower's medical condition. Since everyone assumed that Eisenhower would recover, based on a constant series of positive health reports from Hagerty, there were no public or congressional calls for the vice president to take over the presidency. The issue of presidential succession or **disability** did not publicly surface, but Eisenhower was acutely sensitive to it.

Eisenhower then asked his Attorney General, Herbert Brownell, to explore what the Constitution meant by "disability," who declared the president disabled, who declared the president able to resume official duties, and whether the vice president served as acting president should the president become disabled.[14] Brownell created a study group of constitutional scholars to advise him on these questions. They agreed that should the president become disabled, the vice president would assume the powers of the presidency as acting president for the duration of the disability. The question about whether a disability existed, they said, should be made by the president himself. But they argued that their findings were merely their interpretation of the Constitution and should be formally written into the Constitution through an amendment. Brownell drafted a constitutional amendment and presented the draft to the House and Senate leaders, Speaker Sam Rayburn and Senator Lyndon Johnson. The leadership rejected the plan, arguing that the public would view the amendment as indicating that Eisenhower had a more serious health problem than they were led to believe. This, they argued, would lead to broad concern and perhaps even panic. In spite of Johnson and Rayburn's opposition, the House Judiciary Committee proceeded with hearings. Eventually the plan died due to lack of support from the Democratically controlled Congress.

Nearly a decade later, the plan was resurrected following the assassination of President Kennedy. Now serving as president rather than Senate majority leader, Lyndon Johnson supported passage of the disability amendment that Eisenhower had sponsored. Former President Eisenhower testified in favor of the amendment as did leading members of the American Bar Association. The amendment was broadly supported now, although it had an additional section at the urging of President Johnson—a section on filling the vacancy in the vice presidency should the vice president move up to the presidency. The Constitution was silent on this, and as a result every vice president who moved to the presidency had no vice president until the next election. When Kennedy was assassinated and Johnson became president in 1963, he did not have a vice president until after the 1964 election, when Hubert Humphrey was sworn in. Congress passed the twenty-fifth amendment in 1965, and it was ratified by the states in 1967.

The **twenty-fifth amendment** to the Constitution as originally written by Attorney General Brownell provided for two basic provisions: (1) Whenever the president determines that he is, or is about to be, unable to discharge the powers and duties of his office, and until such time as he decides to resume them, the powers and duties of the presidency shall be discharged by the vice president as acting president, and (2) Whenever the vice president and a majority of the cabinet shall decide that the president is unable to discharge the powers and duties of his office, the vice president shall immediately assume the office as acting president. Congress was also given authority to designate "another body" to determine if the president was disabled should the cabinet be unable to decide. These two provisions resolved the question that Roger Sherman had raised during the constitutional convention of who determines disability and the later question of whether the vice president would become president or only serve as acting president. Lyndon Johnson successfully added the section providing for the office of vice president to be filled when the vice president moved into the presidency (Figure 3.5).

Although the twenty-fifth amendment appeared to solve a number of succession and disability problems, it opened the door to further dilemmas. For example, the twenty-fifth amendment allows for the president to declare the disability and to declare that the disability is over. There is no provision for the vice president and cabinet or other body to object to the president declaring the disability over. This would force the vice president and cabinet to declare that the president is in fact unable to handle the job. Another problem with the disability section is that the cabinet, if totally loyal to the president, would be very cautious in declaring a president disabled and vesting even the position of acting president with the vice president. Cabinet officers, who tend to be loyal to the president rather than to the vice president, would be reluctant to pass power to the vice president.

The White House staff is also very protective of the president and would urge the cabinet officers not to move to declare the president disabled. When Ronald Reagan was shot by John Hinkley at the Washington, D.C., Hilton Hotel on March 30, 1981, he was rushed to surgery to remove the bullet and was thus clearly disabled. But the White House staff and Mrs. Reagan refused to invoke the twenty-fifth amendment and have Vice President Bush serve as acting president. Vice President Bush was not a political ally and had run against President Reagan during the 1980 Republican primaries. He was put on the Republican ticket for reasons of political and electoral balance rather than for his personal connections to Reagan. The Reagan White House staff did not want to transfer power to someone they had campaigned against just over a year earlier. Several years later, however, after some of the hard feelings of the 1980 primaries had relaxed and Bush had proven to be a loyal member of the Reagan team, Reagan did allow the twenty-fifth amendment to be used during another surgery. In July 1985 Reagan underwent surgery to remove a cancerous part of his colon. During the eight-hour period in which Reagan was under anesthesia, he signed over authority to Bush under the twenty-fifth amendment. As

Amendment XXV

(Ratified in 1967)

Section 1: In case of the removal of the President from office or of his death or resignation, the Vice President shall become President.

Section 2: Whenever there is a vacancy in the office of the Vice President, the President shall nominate a Vice President who shall take office upon confirmation by a majority vote of both Houses of Congress.

Section 3: Whenever the President transmits to the President pro tempore of the Senate and the Speaker of the House of Representatives his written declaration that he is unable to discharge the powers and duties of his office, and until he transmits to them a written declaration to the contrary, such powers and duties shall be discharged by the Vice President as Acting President.

Section 4: Whenever the Vice President and a majority of either the principal officers of the executive departments or of such other body as Congress may by law provide, transmit to the President pro tempore of the Senate and the Speaker of the House of Representatives their written declaration that the President is unable to discharge the powers and duties of his office, the Vice President shall immediately assume the powers and duties of the office as Acting President.

Thereafter, when the President transmits to the President pro tempore of the Senate and the Speaker of the House of Representatives his written declaration that no inability exists, he shall resume the powers and duties of his office unless the Vice President and a majority of either the principal officers of the executive departments or of such other body as Congress may by law provide, transmit within four days to the President pro tempore of the Senate and the Speaker of the House of Representatives their written declaration that the President is unable to discharge the powers and duties of his office. Thereupon Congress shall decide the issue, assembling within forty-eight hours for that purpose if not in session. If the Congress, within twenty-one days after the receipt of the latter written declaration, or, if Congress is not in session within twenty-one days after Congress is required to assemble, determines by two-thirds vote of both Houses that the President is unable to discharge the powers and duties of his office, the Vice President shall continue to discharge the same as Acting President, otherwise, the President shall resume the powers and duties of his office.

FIGURE 3.5   The Twenty-Fifth Amendment.

soon as Reagan was out of the recovery room, Bush's authority was withdrawn. The limited amount of time that Bush did serve as acting president, eight hours, under the twenty-fifth amendment was an indication of how reluctant the president and the White House staff can be in assigning the vice president the role of acting president. This is the only time that the twenty-fifth amendment has been used.

There have been a number of recommendations to have a prescribed transfer of power should the president become disabled. In 1988 the Twentieth Century Fund Task Force on the Vice Presidency recommended that "presidents should be encouraged to invoke the amendment routinely, whenever medical procedures take them out of commission for even an hour or two. If they do so, they will educate and accustom the nation to disability, and perhaps win political credit for acting prudently."[15] Both Presidents Bush and Clinton accepted this recommendation and have arranged with their vice presidents to invoke the twenty-fifth amendment when possible during medical procedures or other disabilities. It was not used by either President Bush or President Clinton and the concept is not yet institutionalized. It remains to be seen whether future presidents will follow this procedure.

The twenty-fifth amendment was created primarily to deal with presidential disability, such as Eisenhower's heart attack and Wilson's stroke. It would allow the vice president to handle the duties of the presidency until the president recovered. The amendment did not deal with a double vacancy in the presidency and vice presidency. The Succession Act of 1947 continues to be the controlling statute since double vacancies were not included in the amendment. The **Succession Act of 1947** requires that in the case of a double vacancy the Speaker of the House, then the President Pro Tempore of the Senate, and finally the cabinet in the order in which their departments were statutorily created move into the presidency. When the president delivers the State of the Union address in front of the joint session of Congress each January, all but one member of the cabinet is present. One member of the cabinet always goes to an undisclosed destination to ensure there is a constitutionally empowered person to run the country should a bomb or some other device destroy the Capitol Building during the State of the Union address (Figure 3.6).

Prior to the Succession Act of 1947, two succession acts had been passed by Congress: the Succession Act of 1792 and the Succession Act of 1886. Under the Succession Act of 1792, if a double vacancy occurred the President Pro Tempore of the Senate would become acting president until a special election was held. When the Succession Act of 1896 replaced this act, the Congress was completely ignored, and a member of the cabinet, in the order in which their departments were statuto-

1. President
2. Vice President
3. Speaker of the House
4. President Pro Tempore of the Senate
5. Secretary of State
6. Secretary of Defense
7. Secretary of the Treasury
8. Attorney General
9. Secretary of Interior
10. Secretary of Agriculture
11. Secretary of Commerce
12. Secretary of Labor
13. Secretary of Health and Human Services
14. Secretary of Transportation
15. Secretary of Housing and Urban Development
16. Secretary of Energy
17. Secretary of Education
18. Secretary of Veterans Affairs

FIGURE 3.6   Succession Act of 1947.

rily created (the Secretary of State would be first), would become president. Another change in the two laws was the replacement of the term *acting president* in 1792 with the term *president* in 1896. The deletion of the term of *acting president* was largely due to the precedent set by John Tyler in 1841, who declared himself president rather than acting president following the death of William Henry Harrison. Although the Succession Act of 1947 remains in effect, it has one basic flaw. If there were a double vacancy, the Speaker of the House would become president. But, if the President and Vice President were Republicans and the Speaker of the House were a Democrat, the executive branch would move under the control of the Democrats. Electoral accountability would be lost in this scenario.

Choosing a Vice President

How presidents choose their vice president depends largely on the president. Since the passage of the twelfth amendment in 1804, presidents and vice presidents have been chosen as one ticket. Prior to 1804, the vice president was the second highest vote getter in the balloting of the electoral college. Since 1804, the vice president has been selected by the president, a prerogative given to the senior member of the party's presidential ticket. The general selection criterion for choosing the vice president has focused on three guiding principles: providing geographic balance, enhancing the electoral count, and building bridges within the party to repair damage done during the primary elections.

Providing geographic balance is an effort to reassure other parts of the country that the president will not prioritize his home state and will protect the needs of all the states. The process of balancing the ticket geographically is a symbolic gesture to the nation that presidents represent the nation, not any individual state. The presiding officer of Congress during the Articles of Confederation, called the president of the Congress, remained a representative of his state. When the architects of the Constitution framed the presidency, they crafted a position that represented the entire nation rather than a particular state. Article II, Section 1, Paragraph 7, of the Constitution purposely provides a salary for the president paid by the national treasury rather than by the states and prohibits the president from receiving any form of salary or emolument from a state. Using geographic balance to ensure broad political support around the country is also part of the cabinet selection process. Presidents never choose their vice presidents from their own state and usually choose their vice presidents from a state distant from their own. President Kennedy, for example, who was from Massachusetts, chose Lyndon Johnson from Texas; President Nixon, who was from California, chose Spiro Agnew from Maryland; President Carter, who was from Georgia, chose Walter Mondale from Minnesota. The pattern of geographic distribution is rarely broken, although President Clinton, who was from Arkansas, chose a fellow southerner, Albert Gore from Tennessee, as his vice president.

Enhancing the electoral count is another tool in vice-presidential selection. Vice presidents may be able to deliver the electoral votes of states that are not absolutely in the president's corner. Ronald Reagan, from California, chose George Bush, from Texas, for the ticket partly to win the Texas electoral vote, the second largest electoral vote in the country. Similarly, John F. Kennedy chose Lyndon Johnson to gain the Texas electoral vote and Dwight Eisenhower of Kansas chose Richard Nixon of California for the electoral vote.

Yet another tool used in **vice-presidential selection** is building bridges within the party to repair damage done during the primary fights. Presidents from the conservative wing of the party often choose their vice presidents from the moderate or liberal wing of the party. Gerald Ford, a moderate, chose the more conservative Bob Dole as his vice presidential running mate in the 1976 election. Ford chose to replace Vice President Nelson Rockefeller with Dole on the 1976 ticket in anticipation of a primary challenge from Ronald Reagan. Dole was considered by the Ford campaign director, Howard H. "Bo" Calloway, less threatening to conservative voters than Rockefeller.[16] Ronald Reagan, a conservative, chose the more moderate George Bush as his vice-presidential running mate in the 1980 election, and George Bush chose the more conservative Dan Quayle as his running mate in the 1988 election. On the Democratic side, John F. Kennedy, a liberal, chose the more conservative Lyndon Johnson as his running mate in the 1960 election, Lyndon Johnson chose the more liberal Hubert Humphrey as his running mate in the 1964 election, and Jimmy Carter, a moderate, chose the more liberal Walter Mondale as his running mate in the 1976 election.

These three guiding principles lead presidents in their choice of vice presidential candidates, although other considerations have also come into play. Often presidents choose vice presidents because they represent a different generation and can draw votes from a different demographic group. Eisenhower chose Nixon, Kennedy chose Johnson, and Bush chose Quayle partly because the two candidates appealed to different generations of voters. Some presidents choose vice presidents within their own age group because they feel more comfortable working with them. This can be an indication that the relationship between the president and the vice president will be relatively strong. Jimmy Carter and Walter Mondale were close in age, and they had a very strong working relationship while in office. Bill Clinton and Al Gore are close in age and have a strong working relationship.

Choosing the vice president from the ranks of the Senate has also become more popular in recent years. This strategy brings someone with campaign skills, political skills, and a fund-raising base to the presidential campaign. Senators are used to the rigors of campaigns and are able to move quickly into the very strenuous demands of the general election. They have also been heavily scrutinized by the media and opposition campaigns during their own Senate campaigns. This prior scrutiny minimizes the chances of negative information surfacing during the general election. This is critically important to the president, for any scandal or embarrassing material about the vice president that emerged during the campaign could erode the chances of winning the election. During the 1972 election, the press discovered that George McGovern's running mate, Thomas Eagleton, had undergone shock treatment for psychiatric problems several years earlier. McGovern was forced to drop Eagleton from the ticket and replace him with Sargent Shriver. McGovern lost the election to Richard Nixon (Figure 3.7).

Another benefit to choosing a running mate from the Senate is the broad understanding that Senators have of national issues. This broad understanding allows them to move quickly into the national campaign, with minimal time needed to learn im-

Term	Vice President	Past Political Office
1993–1997, 1997–2001	Albert Gore	U.S. Senator (TN)
1989–1993	Daniel Quayle	U.S. Senator (IN)
1981–1985, 1985–1989	George Bush	Washington Political Insider
1977–1981	Walter F. Mondale	U.S. Senator (MN)
1974–1977	Nelson A. Rockefeller	Governor (NY)
1973–1974	Gerald R. Ford	U.S. House (MI)
1969–1973	Spiro Agnew	State Elected Official (MD)
1965–1969	Hubert H. Humphrey	U.S. Senator (MN)
1961–1963	Lyndon B. Johnson	U.S. Senator (TX)
1953–1957, 1957–1961	Richard Nixon	U.S. Senator (CA)
1949–1953	Alben W. Barkley	U.S. Senator (KY)
1945–1945	Harry S Truman	U.S. Senator (KS)
1941–1945	Henry A. Wallace	Secretary of Agriculture
1933–1937, 1937–1941	John N. Garner	House Speaker (TX)

Source: Michael Nelson. *Congressional Quarterly's Guide to the Presidency.* Washington, DC: Congressional Quarterly Press, 1996.

FIGURE 3.7   Background of World War Two and Post–World War Two Vice Presidents.

portant details. They often have more knowledge of issues than the presidential candidate and can provide critical material to the president's campaign staff. Perhaps the most important reason for choosing a member of the Senate for the vice presidency is the knowledge of legislative affairs brought to the administration once in office. Although choosing a member of the Senate for the ticket is valuable to the election process, the more important reason that a Senator is chosen has to do with governance rather than elections. The choice of a member of the Senate enhances the president's ability to govern the country, since the vice president is a member of the Washington establishment, is a vital link to Congress, and can move the administration's legislative agenda forward. Not only will the vice president have immediate contacts in the Senate, which the president generally will not, but he or she will be able to advise the president on the most appropriate strategies for moving bills through the legislative labyrinth.

Yet another consideration in choosing a vice president in more recent elections has been to balance religious affiliation. John F. Kennedy was extremely concerned in the 1960 election that his Roman Catholic religion would alienate many southerners, particularly southern Baptists, who were concerned that papal decrees might influence presidential decisions. In order to blunt that criticism and any criticism that his religion would influence his decisions as president, Kennedy chose a non-Catholic, Lyndon Johnson, to shore up Protestant support for the Democratic ticket. Religion also became a factor in the 1976 election, when Jimmy Carter was concerned that his Baptist, born-again Christian faith would hamper his chances for winning the presidency. Carter chose Walter Mondale, who was Protestant but not a born-again Christian, to balance the ticket.

Most presidents have tried to blend all of these points into their selection of a vice president. Jimmy Carter's choice of Walter Mondale was typical of the blend of factors. Carter's campaign manager, Hamilton Jordan, described the decision process for a vice president as follows,

> Despite the anti-establishment rhetoric of the primary campaign, I knew, and Jimmy Carter knew, that we needed an experienced Senator as his running mate and as his Vice President. Mondale was chosen to run precisely because he was a product of the Washington establishment, was from a different area of the country, and represented the other wing of the Democratic Party.[17]

While the selection process for vice presidents has followed these general themes, two recent selections have been somewhat outside of the traditional model. The first of these was the 1974 selection process used by Gerald Ford for a vice president after Richard Nixon resigned. This process remained close to the model for vice-presidential selection, although it had a few modifications. When Gerald Ford was suddenly thrust into the presidency he had to choose a vice president. Ford, as the minority leader of the House of Representatives before he was tapped for the vice presidency, did not need a member of Congress for his vice president. In general, however, the other criteria held. Nelson Rockefeller was chosen by Ford for the vice presidency because Rockefeller represented the more liberal wing of the Republican party than Ford, provided geographic balance to the ticket (Rockefeller was from New York while Ford was from Michigan), and would be helpful in the 1976 election with the New York electoral vote. The second variation on the traditional model involved the 1992 election of Bill Clinton and Al Gore. Both Clinton and Gore were southerners, both came from the moderate wing of the Democratic Party, Gore's home state of Tennessee did not offer a major bloc of electoral votes, and both were the same age. Gore did bring valuable balance to the ticket by being a member of the Senate and a member of the Washington establishment, both factors needed by Clinton in order to successively move his legislative agenda through Congress.

In more recent years there has been some consideration of gender and race in choosing a vice-presidential nominee, but only once has that translated into the nominee being brought onto the ticket. There has never been an African-American or Hispanic American chosen to run for vice president on the Democratic or Republican tickets and only once was a woman chosen. Walter Mondale brought Congresswoman Geraldine Ferraro onto the ticket in 1984 as his running mate. During the 1996 election there was speculation that General Colin Powell, an African-American, might be a candidate for either president or vice president on the Republican ticket, but he chose not to run. Elizabeth Dole was often mentioned as a candidate for the Republican nomination for president or vice president in 1996, but Senator Robert Dole, her husband, became the Republican standard bearer for president. Elizabeth Dole is a candidate for the year 2000 Republican nomination for the presidency.

Recently the Miller Center of Public Affairs at the University of Virginia convened a panel of former vice presidents, political party chairs, scholars, former presidential staff, members of the media, and political activists to discuss the vice presidency. In their discussions on the selection criteria, they developed a number of general proposals.[18] The first proposal was to "give early and full attention to the qualifications of any vice presidential nominees for accession to the presidency." The commission felt that too much attention was given to the political weight that a vice-presidential candidate brought to the ticket rather than to the criteria they called "suitability for the presidency." The commission wanted to ensure that all vice presidents could easily step into the presidency, since there was a one-in-four chance that the vice president would succeed to the presidency. The second and third recommendations involved the actual selection process. The commission criticized the selection process for allowing a very quick decision by the president on the nomination of a vice president. The process, they reasoned, should be very carefully and methodically undertaken. Their second recommendation was that at least four weeks prior to the nominating convention the presidential candidate should begin to interview vice-presidential candidates. Their third recommendation was that the party nominating conventions be changed to have forty-eight hours between the nomination of the president and the nomination of the vice president. This would allow the presidential candidate more time to narrow the choice for vice president and review their compatibility on agenda issues. Unfortunately, the commission's recommendations have not been seriously considered by presidential contenders.

Roles of the Vice President

The modern vice president has served in a number of roles, depending on the needs of the president. Since there is no constitutional role for the vice president in the executive branch, every role that the vice president plays is a role developed or encouraged by the president. For presidents and vice presidents with strong political and personal ties, the vice president has played a role as a policy adviser, such as Vice Presidents Mondale and Gore. For most vice presidents, their role is limited to ceremonial functions, political assignments, and serving on various task forces and commissions. In cases in which there was minimal personal rapport between the president and vice president, such as between Eisenhower and Nixon or between Reagan and Bush, the vice president was generally relegated to attending state funerals and was regularly sent out of the country on fact-finding missions. Although this was somewhat of a banishment during their tenure as vice president, the international travels of both Nixon and Bush during their vice presidencies allowed them to present themselves during their own presidential campaigns as foreign policy experts.

The common thread for all vice presidents is their role as campaigner. Vice presidents serve as tireless stand-ins for the president during the midterm elections and during political events throughout the entire term. Both incumbents and challengers for congressional seats entreat the president and vice president to come to campaign events. In most cases, it is the vice president who represents the administration at these events, given the pressures on the president's schedule. In more recent years, the vice president has also become a central part of the presidential election and re-election fund-raising effort. Vice President Gore was constantly attending small and large fund-raisers both for the Clinton–Gore campaign and for the Democratic National Committee in 1992 and again in 1996.

Another common thread for all vice presidents is their role as presidential spokespersons, traveling around the country in support of presidential policies and programs. During the Bush administration, Vice President Quayle often met with business and industry groups and state and local government associations to explain the programs being supported by President Bush. Quayle was also a spokesperson for the administration on the Strategic Defense Initiative in an effort to continue public support for the costly defense program. When a major proposal is before Congress, the vice president takes on a major speaking tour to laud the benefits of the program, such as Vice President Gore did during the North American Free Trade Agreement (NAFTA) treaty debates and during the tobacco legislation debates. One cardinal rule of serving as vice president is always to support the president and never to oppose him. This rule was broken by Vice President Hubert Humphrey, who publicly disagreed with President Johnson's handling of the Vietnam War, particularly the bombing of North Vietnam. Humphrey became a persona non grata in the White House and was rarely assigned speaking assignments by the president. Johnson was so angry at his staff for opposing his Vietnam policies that he did not convene the National Security Council in order to keep them, and especially to keep Humphrey, from attending national security briefings.

In at least one administration the vice president has gone beyond simply lauding the benefits of the program and has aggressively attacked opponents. Vice President Spiro Agnew, Nixon's first vice president, was frequently on the attack against the Democrats, against the media, and against liberal government in general. He became known more for his attacks against people than for his support of presidential programs. Agnew was forced to resign the vice presidency in 1973 when accusations arose that he accepted kickbacks during his tenure as an elected official in Maryland. Agnew pleaded nolo contendere to a federal charge of tax evasion; he was fined $10,000 and placed on three years unsupervised probation following his resignation. Few mourned his resignation, including most members of the Nixon administration and most Republicans. There is some evidence that Nixon was ready to replace Agnew because he had become too divisive. Nixon apparently was considering John Connally to replace Agnew for the 1972 reelection campaign, but for whatever reasons did not. Once Agnew resigned after the nolo contendere plea, he was replaced by Gerald Ford in the first transition in the office of vice president under the twenty-fifth amendment.[19]

Several vice presidents were given moderate advisory roles by the president. Lyndon Johnson was made the chair of the National Aeronautics and Space Council (created by the Space Act of 1958), the Peace Corps Advisory Committee, and the Presidential Committee on Equal Opportunity. With few other responsibilities, Johnson became very involved in both the Space Council and the Equal Opportunity Committee, with particular interest in the Space Council. During Johnson's leadership of the Space Council, proposals were developed for the moon-landing program and for communications satellites. Kennedy, who rarely sought Johnson's political or policy advice, did turn to Johnson for technical advice on the space program. Vice President Dan Quayle, who was not a close adviser to President Bush, also served as chair of the (renamed) National Space Council and as chair of the high-profile Council on Competitiveness, which was created by President Bush in response to the business community, who argued that federal regulatory mandates discouraged a competitive business environment. Quayle and his staff reviewed every existing and proposed set of federal regulations in an effort to refine the original language or to simply discontinue the regulation. President Reagan gave his vice president, George Bush, the assignment of heading the crisis-management team to oversee national disasters and national security crises and the Special Situation Group to handle the administration's response to the emerging democracy in Poland.

In both the Johnson and Quayle examples, their roles were created because the president needed a role for the vice president that had little input into the mainstream of presidential policy decisions and that would occupy a significant amount of the vice president's time. In Bush's case, the role of heading the crisis-management team was created so that President Reagan would not have to name either the Secretary of State or the Secretary of Defense as the chair, since there was a bitter rivalry between them and Reagan did not want to further the animosity. Vice President Nixon was given almost no domestic role during Eisenhower's first term and spent significant time on trips abroad, including one in 1953 that lasted sixty-nine days. As a result, Eisenhower tried to ease Nixon off the ticket for the 1956 reelection campaign and move him to the cabinet as secretary of commerce.[20] This scenario was never advanced, however, since Nixon did not want to vacate his position as vice president and Eisenhower did not want to force him off the ticket. At a press conference in 1960 Eisenhower was asked "What major decisions of your administration has the vice president participated in?" After a moment Eisenhower replied, "If you give me a week, I might think of one. I don't remember."[21]

One of the most significant roles given to vice presidents in the modern presidency has been to attend cabinet meetings and to participate in policy discussions during these meetings. Franklin Delano Roosevelt fostered the tradition during his first term when he invited Vice President John Nance Garner to actively participate in cabinet meetings. When Dwight Eisenhower was felled by a heart attack in 1955, Richard Nixon, who had regularly attended cabinet meetings, presided over the cabinet meetings during Eisenhower's recuperation. Nixon set a record for this by presiding over cabinet meetings nineteen times during Eisenhower's various illnesses. Lyndon Johnson regularly sat in on cabinet meetings, although he rarely spoke. Johnson's poor relationship with Robert Kennedy, the Attorney General, did not engender discussion during cabinet meetings. Not surprisingly, during the Cuban Missile Crisis in 1962, Johnson was kept out of the inner circle and was not a member of the Executive Committee, or ExCom. The ExCom was run by the Attorney General. Every vice president since John Nance Garner in 1933 has continued to attend cabinet meetings, with some vice presidents more active participants than others.

Perhaps the least important role of the vice president is serving as **president of the Senate.** Since members of the Senate view the vice president as a member of the executive branch and not a member of the Senate, they do not warmly welcome the vice president into their midst today. Although vice presidents do spend time seeking congressional votes on behalf of the president's legislative programs, they spend relatively little time serving as president of the Senate. Vice presidents are more comfortable today representing the executive branch than the legislative branch.

Walter Mondale spent only nineteen days presiding over the Senate for a total of eighteen hours during 1977, a statistic very similar for other years and other modern administrations.

The Policy Adviser Role:
Rockefeller, Mondale, and Gore

Three vice presidents have played a significant role as policy advisers to the president: Nelson Rockefeller for Gerald Ford, Walter Mondale for Jimmy Carter, and Albert Gore for Bill Clinton. Each of these three vice presidents accepted the position only with the understanding that they would have a major policy advisory role and not be relegated to a board or commission as their primary duty. In Rockefeller's case he sought and received not only an advisory role but a policy role. Rockefeller wanted to manage the domestic agenda for the White House, a role which had been played by White House staff since the Roosevelt administration. The advisory role of vice presidents is rare, since presidents regularly turn to their White House staffs and kitchen cabinets (personal friends) for both political and policy advice.

Nelson Rockefeller

Nelson Rockefeller became the first vice president to become a presidential adviser within a major policy area. But he was constantly at odds with the Ford White House staff, and after eighteen months of battles with them, he removed himself from all policy activities. Not surprisingly, Rockefeller was taken off the 1976 presidential ticket and replaced by Senator Robert Dole. Despite the problems that Rockefeller had in finding a policy role, he set in motion a model for a stronger relationship between the president and vice president that was often followed in later presidencies. The lessons learned from the Rockefeller experience allowed future vice presidents to approach their job in a manner that was less threatening to White House staff than Rockefeller's approach had been.

Rockefeller was nominated by Ford soon after assuming the presidency. Ford's first choices for vice president were George Bush, Chairman of the Republican National Committee, and Nixon cabinet member and former Wisconsin congressman Melvin Laird. For Bush, the timing was bad since he was being linked to a Nixon "slush fund," and Laird flatly refused the job. Ford then turned to Rockefeller, who was hesitant to take the job since he had so often sought the presidency itself. Rockefeller eventually accepted the appointment, convinced that he would be able to work toward major domestic policy changes that would be directed at the nation's poor. During their discussions of the vice presidency during August 1974, Ford agreed to Rockefeller's request for a substantive role in domestic policy, noting that "I want you on the domestic, and Henry (Kissinger) on the foreign, and then we can move these things."[22]

With Ford's approval, Rockefeller became the president's manager of domestic policy. At first Rockefeller wanted to be executive director of the Domestic Council, as John Ehrlichman had been under Nixon. But this idea never reached fruition. Philip Buchen, Ford's legal counsel, determined that the vice president was the vice chair of the Domestic Council according to the original executive order and not eligible to also serve as executive director. Rockefeller subsequently chose a close associate, James Cannon, as executive director and moved other staff from New York into the Domestic Council.

Rockefeller immediately began to ruffle feathers within the White House staff. Not only had Rockefeller brought his own staff into the White House, breaking a long-standing tradition that the members of the White House senior staff are presidential (not vice-presidential) loyalists, but he had tried to circumvent the chief of staff. Donald Rumsfeld, the president's chief of staff (with the title staff coordinator), immediately objected to Rockefeller being given direct access to the president. Rumsfeld wanted all paper flow to go across his desk, including material on domestic policies that Rockefeller was working on. Rockefeller did not want to deal with Rumsfeld and worked directly with Ford, circumventing any dealings with Rumsfeld. Rumsfeld, and his successor Dick Cheney, never reached an accord with Rockefeller, and the tension continued to mount during Rockefeller's brief oversight of the domestic agenda.

In January 1975, soon after his confirmation hearings had been completed, Rockefeller proposed to Ford that the Domestic Council prepare a comprehensive domestic agenda and develop options that could be completed before the 1976 election was underway. The largest review undertaken by the Rockefeller task forces was that of federal social programs. As governor of New York, Rockefeller had seen the proliferation of welfare and other social programs and now wanted a review of the objectives, costs, and delivery systems of those programs. In Rockefeller's view, if Ford could redesign the welfare program or other major social programs before the 1976 election, he would have a major election standard to carry. Rockefeller felt strongly that Ford needed a program that would carry him through the election that was separate and distinct from the Nixon agenda. Ford agreed and Rockefeller moved forward with his review of major social programs.

Rockefeller began to develop a series of programs for Ford, as promised, meeting regularly with cabinet officers and their staffs. He also created his own study group that was operating somewhat independently of the Domestic Council staff. The constant interaction with cabinet officers and the manner in which Rockefeller operated did not encourage warm relations with the White House staff, particularly the senior staff. After Rumsfeld departed to head the Defense Department, Cheney began to discourage Rockefeller from proposing any programs that would add to the federal budget. Cheney wanted to cut programs, not create new ones. This led to growing tension between Rockefeller and Cheney. Eventually Cheney prevailed and convinced Ford not to support some of the programs proposed by Rockefeller that would add to the budget. Rockefeller pulled back from his domestic initiatives and withdrew from the Domestic Council.

Although Rockefeller had not been successful at moving into the inner circles of the White House and becoming a presidential adviser, future vice presidents learned from the Rockefeller experience. Rockefeller's first mistake was to move into a role reserved for White House staff: advising the president. The White House staff is a small group of presidential loyalists; they clearly saw the vice president as an interloper in their territory. Rockefeller threatened their relationship with the president and their role in the president's advisory system. In large part, the White House staff refused to allow Rockefeller to enter their domain of presidential assistants and presidential confidantes.

Rockefeller's second mistake was to challenge the senior White House staff, such as Rumsfeld and Cheney, for a role in decision-making. Senior White House staff are very protective of their relationship with the president and their advisory role. Rockefeller threatened that relationship and threatened their power. Perhaps this would have been less of a problem had Rockefeller been part of the original group in the White House in August 1974. Many policy roles were already in place when Rockefeller became part of the administration. Had Rockefeller entered the Ford presidency in August, when most of the staff did, rather than in December, the White House staff might have felt less threatened.

Rockefeller's third mistake was to fail to understand a major priority in the administration, which was to cut costs and reduce the budget. By pushing for increased spending on social programs, Rockefeller lost credibility with Ford and gave Cheney the leverage he needed to discredit Rockefeller. Rockefeller's final mistake was using his own political capital to move ideas forward. He drew on past relationships at both the national and state level to gather data and assess ideas on restructuring social programs. Again, this threatened the White House staff, who did not want Rockefeller pursuing his own agenda, although he clearly had the political connections to do so.

Although Nelson Rockefeller did not succeed at reframing the role of the vice president from a passive to an active member of the president's advisory team, he did make measurable changes in the job. Rockefeller, irritated that the vice presidency had so little power or status, used his own money to refurbish the vice president's official office in the Old Executive Office Building. He first demanded that the **vice-presidential seal** be reviewed. The seal had rarely been used by vice presidents, and after examining the seal Rockefeller and Ford decided it should be replaced. Rockefeller, using his own funds, had the seal redesigned and then woven into a wool rug for his office in the Old Executive Office Building. Rockefeller reestablished the grandeur of the office in the Old Executive Office Building, changing it from a routine staff office to an office elegant enough to host heads of state.

In later administrations, as vice presidents have had closer working relationships with the president, they have been mindful of the Rockefeller experience. None have tried to usurp the traditional White House staff roles, such as Rockefeller did with the Domestic Council. Walter Mondale was very careful to stay away from a line assignment, which he noted only put the vice president in the forefront of bureaucratic infighting and political hammering. Instead, vice presidents have tried to carve out new roles for themselves, such as Albert Gore did with environmental policy and with technology policy. To some extent, Gore followed the model created by Lyndon Johnson through his role on the Space Council. Both Gore and Johnson became policy experts who advised the president on issues for which the president had few immediate staffers with that expertise. Gore and Johnson were able to supplement the policy information given to the president, rather than replace policy information already available through the White House staff. Rockefeller replaced the Domestic Council staff, but Gore and Johnson merely supplemented the staff with their own area of expertise.

Walter Mondale

When Walter Mondale joined Jimmy Carter on the Democratic ticket in 1976, he was careful to discuss the role of the vice president with Carter and to reach accords on what the position would entail. Carter was also sensitive to the problems with the Ford–Rockefeller relationship and promised to give Mondale a substantive role and to make him a key presidential adviser. Carter said during the campaign that he was "determined to make the Vice Presidency a substantive position. . . . [T]he Vice President would share with me all the purposes of the administration in an easy and unrestrained way."[23] Mondale, conscious of the problems that Rockefeller had faced, wanted to work closely with Carter but not in a specific position that would rival White House staff. Mondale described his role as vice president as a general adviser and troubleshooter for the president.

As soon as Carter asked him to be his vice president, Mondale moved his campaign staff to Georgia in order to work directly with the Carter staff. The Mondale staff showed the Carter staff that they were competent, hard working, and totally understanding of the senior role that the Carter staff played. The close ties forged during the campaign enhanced the strong working relationship between the Carter and Mondale staffs during the Carter presidency, and paved the way for Mondale staff to work within the White House.

Once in office, Mondale made himself available to Carter to serve as a general adviser, meeting weekly with Carter for private lunches and attending a wide variety of meetings that Carter had with cabinet officers and staff. Mondale had an open invitation to attend any meeting on Carter's schedule, but chose to attend only those that he felt he could contribute to. Although Carter did not always agree with Mondale's advice, he always listened to and welcomed it. Carter directed that all presidential briefing papers be routed through the vice president and that the vice president be included on the routine tracking sheet for general White House memoranda. Mondale had finally achieved what Lyndon Johnson had sought fifteen years earlier.

Mondale's schedule also included weekly congressional leadership sessions with the president; twice-weekly intelligence briefings with Hamilton Jordan, White House chief of staff, National Security Adviser Zbigniew Brzezinski, and CIA director Stansfield Turner; and Friday foreign policy breakfasts with Brzezinski, the chief of staff, and the Secretary of State.

One of the strengths of the relationship between Carter and Mondale was that Carter entered office with a very experienced campaign staff but a not very experienced Washington-insider staff. Mondale, an experienced Washington insider, brought a strong staff to the White House with an insider's knowledge of politics in the nation's capital. As one Mondale staffer noted, "We liked the Carter people very much. Most of them were down-to-earth and easy to work with. It was no secret, however, that they weren't well prepared for the administration. Very few of the top people had much understanding of how the federal government worked. That's where we fit in so well."[24]

Carter merged some of Mondale's Senate staff into the White House staff, providing Mondale a stronger base within the White House staff. David Aaron, Mondale's foreign policy adviser in the Senate, became the deputy national security adviser and Bert Carp, also a Mondale staffer, became the deputy domestic policy adviser. In the Ford White House staff, which was already feuding as a result of the Nixon holdovers believing they knew more than the new Ford staff, the Rockefeller staff members were viewed as interlopers when they came on the scene in December 1974 and January 1975. The Ford staff had already fended off the Nixon staff and saw the Rockefeller staff as a further problem. One of the problems with the Ford experience was that Ford did not work at integrating the staffs.

In contrast to the Ford–Rockefeller working relationship, Carter welcomed the experience that the Mondale Senate staff brought to the White House and encouraged their full participation in presidential issues. Carter was so eager to include the Mondale people on the White House staff that at one point he asked Mondale to be his chief of staff, which Mondale wisely refused. Although Mondale had few specific assignments, he worked closely with some of the more liberal parts of the Democratic Party in order to forge a governing coalition. In particular, Mondale met regularly with representatives from organized labor, civil rights groups, and party activists. Since Carter had entered the national dialogue for the Democrats as a conservative, having Mondale continue to work with the liberal wing of the party was essential to the administration.

Mondale consistently represented many of these groups in legislative discussions with Carter, such as pushing for a raise in the minimum wage and urging a tax rebate. Carter, who was a fiscal conservative, often listened to Mondale but did not always agree with his positions. Paul Light, in his study of the Rockefeller and Mondale vice presidencies, lists six reasons why Mondale succeeded as vice president: (1) the merging of the Carter and Mondale campaign staffs, (2) Mondale's refusal of line assignments, (3) the rise of strong allies, (4) Mondale's personal style, (5) the political context outside the Carter White House, and (6) Carter's own management style and policy goals.[25]

Mondale contributed in other ways to the role of the vice president as a presidential adviser. He was the first vice president to have an office both in the Old Executive Office Building and in the West Wing of the White House and he was the first vice president to have a large, independent staff. Mondale had a staff that paralleled the same positions that existed in the White House, although to a lesser degree. He had a scheduler, an advance team, a foreign policy adviser, a domestic policy adviser, a chief of staff, a congressional liaison staff, an administrative staff, and others. The primary difference between Mondale's seventy-person staff and the three-hundred-fifty-member staff of the White House was that Mondale had no large staffing units under his staff. Just as importantly, the Mondale staff was independent of the

White House staff and was chosen solely by Mondale. The vice presidency was not a patronage ground for Carter administration job-seekers. This allowed Mondale to carry on his responsibilities independently of the White House staff.

Albert Gore

The third policy vice president in the post-Roosevelt era is Albert Gore, who has served as vice president during the two Clinton administrations. Unlike either Nelson Rockefeller or Walter Mondale, Al Gore built a strong relationship with Bill Clinton prior to the presidential campaign. Both Clinton and Gore had been founding members of the Democratic Leadership Council, created in the mid-1980s by moderate leaders in the Democratic Party. Their goal was to refocus the Democratic Party away from the traditionally liberal values that the party eschewed, toward more moderate positions, particularly in the area of spending for federal social programs. Both Clinton and Gore believed they represented the mainstream of the Democratic Party and wanted to actively move the party toward centrist positions on policy issues.

Clinton, as the governor of a southern state, and Gore, as the senior Senator from a southern state, had similar views on the role of the party both nationally and within the South. As they worked together through the Democratic Leadership Council over the years, they became both personal and political allies. When Clinton ran for president in 1992, his choice for vice president immediately centered on his friend Al Gore. Although the choice of Gore broke many of the traditional geographic and political balancing protocols that the ticket usually requires, Clinton forged ahead with bringing Gore onto the ticket.

Gore, who had once entered the Democratic fray as a candidate for president, saw the vice presidency as a possible stepping stone to the presidency. He eagerly accepted the invitation to join the ticket extended by Clinton. While both Rockefeller and Mondale had long conversations with Ford and Carter about their role as vice president, there is little evidence that this occurred for Gore during the campaign. The Clinton campaign was focused on winning the election not on issues of governance, such as who would serve as vice president or in the cabinet. Clinton apparently chose Gore to join the ticket because they shared the same political goals, were both "baby boomers" and offered a new generation of leaders, and had already developed strong personal rapport. Gore also offered the same Washington insider knowledge that Mondale had brought to the ticket.

Once elected, both Gore and Mondale were able to bring a keen sense of Washington politics to the outsiders who had been elected president. Both Gore and Mondale were respected members of the Senate, with strong working relationships on both the Democratic and Republican sides of the aisle. For Washington outsiders such as Carter and Clinton, it was important to have immediate access to the power structures of the beltway and to have access to an institutional memory of legislative history.

Gore accepted the job of vice president having done his homework on the Rockefeller and Mondale experiences as policy vice presidents. Gore agreed to accept the vice presidency if he could become a working partner of Clinton, rather than an outsider only called into the White House for photo opportunities. Clinton and Gore agreed that Gore would have a role somewhere in between the Rockefeller and Mondale experiences. The Rockefeller experience had been one of direct oversight of White House staff for a major policy area, the domestic agenda. The Mondale experience had been one of regular participation in Oval Office meetings and policy discussions, but no direct involvement in policy development. Mondale provided his thoughts to Carter's advisers but never sought to become more involved than that. Gore wanted a role somewhere in between these two experiences and settled on one in which he oversaw a major review of government programs, called the National Performance Review, and worked as a policy adviser to Clinton in the areas of the environment and technology.

The National Performance Review, which became popularly known as the reinventing government program, gave Gore high enough visibility to keep his chances alive for seeking the year 2000 Democratic presidential nomination but did not conflict with or threaten the existing roles of the White House staff. Rockefeller had been fatally damaged by the secret war against him by White House staff who felt that their territory had been invaded by an outsider. Gore avoided this problem by finding a role outside the policy development structure of the White House. The reinventing government endeavor was part of Clinton's campaign pledge to find ways to reduce the size of government and operate it more efficiently without affecting the delivery of services. Gore and his team reviewed each one of the fourteen executive departments, examining how the department conducted routine operations, including purchasing, dealing with regional offices, and managing programs. Their goal was to find ways to operate more effectively and efficiently, with less staff, but without reducing services. Gore had successfully carried out this program without alienating any member of the White House staff and had regularly given Clinton the credit for fulfilling his campaign promise of improving government operations. For Gore, this had been a win–win situation. He not only kept his political visibility high, but he was able to build a large staff to carry out the reinventing government responsibilities and to stay in favor with the president.

Gore became a frequent participant in White House policy discussions and, as Mondale had, Gore offered his opinions. He met regularly for lunch with Clinton, often discussing how Congress was handling administration-sponsored legislation and discussing political issues. Throughout most of the first term, both Clinton and Gore worked with the Democratic National Committee to raise funds for the midterm congressional elections and then for the 1996 reelection campaign. Although Clinton had several political advisers on the White House staff, he frequently sought Gore's advice on a wide range of political issues.

Throughout Gore's tenure in office he also spoke frequently on issues relating to the environment and on issues relating to technology and the "information highway." Clinton supported Gore's speeches on these subjects and allowed Gore to become the administration's spokesperson for the information highway and, to a lesser degree, on environmental issues. Gore had to moderate some of his positions on the environment to ensure that they did not conflict with positions of the Environmental Protection Agency or other agencies with environmental regulations. But Gore realized that his primary service to the administration was to focus national attention on environmental issues already flushed out by the executive agencies. For some un-

popular policies he could serve as a lightning rod for the president, deflecting opposition away from the president; for more popular policies he could encourage stronger
public support. Gore carefully developed his role in environmental and technology
policies so as not to threaten the policy-making role of the White House staff or to
take the limelight from the president.

Gore's success as a strong vice president came from his understanding of the pit-
falls, both with the president himself and with the president's staff. He also had the
good fortune of a strong personal chemistry with Clinton, the same type of personal
chemistry that Mondale had with Carter. Neither Reagan and Bush nor Bush and
Quayle had the personal chemistry that Clinton and Gore enjoyed. This contributed
to the weaker role of Bush and Quayle as vice presidents.

One of the ways that Mondale had been able to work so closely with Carter was
by placing several of his key staff within the White House. This facilitated greater
communication between the president and vice president's office and ensured that
Mondale would be kept apprised of major, political and policy issues. When Gore entered the vice presidency, he emulated the Mondale model of having his own staff
move into the White House. The most important of these various staff members was
the appointment of Roy M. Neal, Gore's chief of staff, to serve as deputy chief of staff
for Thomas "Mack" McLarty. Neal joined Mark Gearan, also with the title of deputy
chief of staff, who had worked on Gore's campaign and had worked with Clinton as
executive director of the National Governor's Conference.

The Modern Vice President

Since Franklin Delano Roosevelt demanded that he be given the right to choose his
own vice president during the 1940 Democratic convention, rather than relying on
the choice of the party bosses who traditionally chose the vice president, the vice
president has had greater opportunity to serve as a presidential adviser. When vice
presidents were chosen by the party bosses for political benefits to the ticket and for
political payoffs, there was little chance of camaraderie or trust between the president and vice president.

While the opportunity was greatly enhanced for a closer working relationship between the president and vice president as a result of Roosevelt's involvement in choosing his running mate, it was not guaranteed. In successive elections, the choice of a
vice president was usually left to the president's campaign staff. Their decision was
based on the electability of the vice president and how much balance the vice president brought to the ticket. The Kennedy campaign staff chose Johnson for religious,
political, electoral, and geographic balance. There was never any question whether
Kennedy and Johnson would work closely together if elected, since they had never got-
ten along particularly well in the Senate. Johnson was added solely for the strengths he
brought to the ticket and without any consideration of how well he would work with
Kennedy as an adviser once in office. Similarly, Ronald Reagan's campaign staff chose
George Bush. Fearing that Reagan was too conservative for much of the Republican
Party, they brought Bush onto the ticket to garner the moderate Republican vote.
Bush, from Texas, also represented a significant electoral vote if he could deliver it.

Richard Nixon did choose his own vice president, but never considered Spiro Agnew to be part of the inner circle. Agnew, who had been a prominent sponsor of the National Draft Rockefeller Committee in 1968, was brought onto the ticket for purely political reasons. As Nixon describes in his memoirs,

> From a strictly political standpoint, Agnew fit perfectly with the strategy we had devised for the November election. With George Wallace in the race, I could not hope to sweep the South. It was absolutely necessary, therefore, to win the entire rimland of the South—the border states—as well as the major states of the Midwest and West. Agnew fit the bill geographically and, as a political moderate, he fit philosophically.[26]

Nixon eschewed choosing a vice president for anything other than political reasons.

George Bush also chose his own vice president and also for political reasons. The choice of Senator Dan Quayle of Indiana appears to have been made to balance the ticket geographically, since Quayle represented a northern industrial state, and politically, since Quayle had the backing of the conservative wing of the party. The most interesting reasoning that Bush used was that Quayle represented a younger political audience, from a different generation. Bush believed that Quayle could deliver a large segment of the baby-boomer vote.

In only two recent cases did the president choose the vice president for reasons of personal compatibility. Both Jimmy Carter and Bill Clinton chose their vice presidents partly because they genuinely liked their vice presidents. Not surprisingly, both Carter and Clinton wanted to build a closer working relationship with their vice presidents than had traditionally been held. Both Carter and Clinton knew that if the vice president was to become an adviser and working partner to the president, they had to have personal rapport. Bill Clinton was so intent on choosing Al Gore for his vice president that he overlooked how little Gore brought to the ticket within the general rules for ticket balancing.

While there is little evidence that all of the careful consideration that presidents put into ticket balancing has actually helped the ticket win, most presidential candidates continue to seek a wide range of balance (political, geographic, religious, etc.) when selecting the vice president. Bill Clinton broke the mold by not relying on ticket balancing when he chose Al Gore as his vice-presidential nominee. For Clinton, having a strong working relationship with the vice president was critical to a Clinton presidency, and Al Gore was the right person for the job. Whether future presidents will emulate the Clinton model for choosing a vice president and using the vice president as an inner circle adviser is problematic. Every president will approach the vice presidency in a different manner. But as the responsibilities of the president continue to grow nationally and internationally, it is reasonable to assume that the vice president should also continue to have expanded responsibilities and work closely with the president. The vice president will have to have the full confidence of the president, such as Walter Mondale and Al Gore have had, however, in order to keep the White House staff from gaining even more power and shutting the vice president out of the inner circle.

Key Words

accidental presidents
Committee of Eleven
constitutional role of the vice president
disability
election of 1796
election of 1800
President of the Senate

statutory roles
Succession Act of 1947
Tenure in Office Act of 1867
twelfth amendment
twenty-fifth amendment
vice-presidential seal
vice-presidential selection

Notes

1. Emmet John Hughes. *The Living Presidency*. New York: Coward, McGann, and Geohegan, 1972, p. 123.
2. Ibid.
3. Quoted in Clinton Rossiter. *The American Presidency*. 2nd ed. New York: Time, 1960, p. 143.
4. Quoted in Michael Turner. *The Vice President as Policy Maker*. Westport, CT: Greenwood Press, 1982, p. 4.
5. Twentieth Century Fund Task Force on the Vice Presidency. *A Heartbeat Away: Report of the Twentieth Century Fund Task Force on the Vice Presidency*. New York: Priority, 1988, p. 80.
6. Ibid., p. 81.
7. Ibid., p. 81.
8. Donald Young. *American Roulette: The History and Dilemma of the Vice Presidency*. New York: Holt, Rinehart and Winston, 1965, p. 14.
9. Doris Kearns. *Lyndon Johnson and the American Dream*. New York: Harper & Row, 1976, p. 165.
10. Arthur M. Schlesinger, Jr. "The Ultimate Approval Rating." *The New York Times Magazine*, December 15, 1996, pp. 44–51.
11. John F. Kennedy. *Profiles in Courage*. New York: Pocket Books, 1955, p. 121.
12. Max Farrand. *The Records of the Federal Convention of 1787*. vol. 2. New Haven, CT: Yale University Press, 1966, p. 427.
13. John D. Feerick. *The Twenty-Fifth Amendment: Its Complete History and Early Applications*. New York: Fordham University Press, 1976, p. 13.
14. Herbert Brownell and John Burke. *Advising Ike: The Memoirs of Attorney General Herbert Brownell*. Lawrence, KS: University Press of Kansas, 1993, p. 277.
15. Twentieth Century Task Force on the Vice Presidency, p. 99.
16. John Robert Greene. *The Presidency of Gerald R. Ford*. Lawrence, KS: University Press of Kansas, 1995, pp. 158–160.
17. Hamilton Jordan. "Can the Whole Be More Than the Sum of Its Parts? Mondale's Choice." *New Republic*, June 6, 1983.
18. Kenneth Thompson. *Choosing and Using Vice Presidents: A Report of the Sixth Miller Center Commission*, chaired by Senator Edmund S. Muskie and Senator Charles Mathias, Jr. No date listed.
19. John Robert Greene. "Spiro T. Agnew." In: Edward Purcell, ed. *The Vice Presidents*. New York: Facts on File, 1998, p. 354.
20. Stephen E. Ambrose. *Eisenhower: The President*. vol. 2. New York: Simon & Schuster, 1984, p. 292.
21. Richard Nixon. *Six Crises*. Garden City, NY: Doubleday, 1962, p. 339.
22. Michael Turner. *The Vice President as Policy Maker*. Westport, CT: Greenwood Press, 1982, p. 52.
23. Frank Kessler. "Walter F. Mondale." In: Edward Purcell, ed., *The Vice Presidents*. New York: Facts on File, 1998, p. 380.
24. Paul C. Light. *Vice Presidential Power*. Baltimore: Johns Hopkins University Press, 1984, p. 202.
25. Ibid., p. 203.
26. Richard M. Nixon. *RN: The Memoirs of Richard Nixon*. New York: Grosset and Dunlap, 1978, p. 312.

Chapter 4

THE PRESIDENT'S CABINET

Of all the parts of the president's advisory system, the cabinet is clearly the most visible and generally the most understood. Unlike the White House staff and the assorted parts of the Executive Office of the President, the **president's cabinet** is frequently in the public eye. As a result, the public knows who the members of the cabinet are and understands the role that members of the cabinet play. When asked who the Secretary of Defense is, many people can identify the Secretary of Defense by name and can give a fairly solid overview of the responsibilities of the job. Similarly, when asked who the Attorney General is and what the responsibilities of the job are, a majority of people would have a very good idea. In contrast, if you ask the average person who the president's chief of staff is or who the director of the Office of Management and Budget is, relatively few people would know.

The president's cabinet is unquestionably the part of the presidential advisory structure most understood and most recognized by the public. Even the vice president is less understood than the cabinet, since the vice president has few defined roles. Few people could identify exactly what the vice president does except wait to be president. Yet this is not true of the president's cabinet. Not only do cabinet officers have very defined roles as department officers, but the public understands these roles and views the cabinet members as the president's most important advisors by virtue of the information they control coming out of their departments.

How Departments Are Created

Today the president has fourteen cabinet officers, each of whom oversees one of the fourteen executive departments. All of the fourteen departments were created by Congress through **enabling legislation.** The legislation defined the mission of the department and provided for the appointment of a principal officer by the president. In Article II the Constitution requires that the principal officers of the executive departments be confirmed by the Senate. This is part of the broad checks-and-balances system established by the framers of the Constitution, who sought to mitigate through the Senate confirmation process unqualified appointments. The Senate confirmation process affects cabinet officers only once. If presidents are reelected, there is no constitutional requirement that cabinet members' names be resubmitted to Congress for approval. Most appointments have been handled routinely by the Senate. Once the president nominates a cabinet officer, rarely is the nominee rejected; but it does happen. President Bush's nominee to head the Defense Department, former Senator John Tower (R-Tex.), was rejected by the Senate because a number of Senators thought that his defense-oriented lobbying business would not allow him to make impartial decisions on defense contracts. Cabinet members who change departments, however, must be reconfirmed by the Senate for their new position (Figure 4.1).

The fourteen executive departments are distinct from the assorted **independent agencies** and commissions that Congress has created to deal with very specific issues. Agencies such as the Environmental Protection Agency and the National Aeronautics and Space Administration are entities created by Congress with very narrow missions, but missions that Congress did not want to see consumed by the larger mission of an executive department. The independent agencies have department heads, usually called directors, who are nominated by the president and confirmed by the Senate. Although these independent agencies are not executive departments by virtue of their relatively small size and narrow missions, they are quite similar to the executive departments. They are statutorily created by Congress, have mission statements, have congressionally authorized budgets through the president's budget, and have presidentially appointed heads confirmed by the Senate (Figure 4.2).

Since the first executive departments were created in 1789, Congress has routinely added to the original four departments. Every additional department since 1789 was created as the federal government increased its role in national activities.

Nominee	Position	President	Date	Vote
Roger B. Taney	Secretary of Treasury	Jackson	6/23/1834	18–28
Caleb Cushing	Secretary of Treasury	Tyler	3/3/1844	19–27
Caleb Cushing	Secretary of Treasury	Tyler	3/3/1844	10–27
Caleb Cushing	Secretary of Treasury	Tyler	3/3/1844	2–29
David Henshaw	Secretary of Navy	Tyler	1/15/1844	6–34
James M. Porter	Secretary of War	Tyler	1/30/1844	3–38
James S. Green	Secretary of Treasury	Tyler	6/15/1844	not recorded
Henry Stanbery	Attorney General	A. Johnson	6/2/1868	11–29
Charles B. Warren	Attorney General	Coolidge	3/10/1925	39–41
Charles B. Warren	Attorney General	Coolidge	3/16/1925	39–46
Lewis L. Strauss	Secretary of Commerce	Eisenhower	6/19/1959	46–49
John Tower	Secretary of Defense	Bush	3/9/1989	47–53

Source: Harold W. Stanley, and Richard G. Niemei. *Vital Statistics in American Politics.* 4th ed. Washington, DC: Congressional Quarterly Press, 1994.

FIGURE 4.1   **History of Senate Rejections of Cabinet Nominations.**

Presidential Agencies

Action
Arms Control and Disarmament Agency
Commission on Civil Rights
Energy Research and Development Agency
Environmental Protection Agency
Federal Mediation and Conciliation Service
General Services Administration
National Aeronautics and Space Administration
Postal Service
Small Business Administration
All Executive Departments
Executive Office of the President

FIGURE 4.2   Presidential Agencies.

In 1849 the Department of Interior was created to create a national park system in the Western states as a means of protecting the land from exploitation by loggers, ranchers, and others. Forty years later, in 1889, the Department of Agriculture was created to ensure stable markets for farmers, paving the way for the price supports that remain a central role of the department's activities.

As the nation moved from an agrarian to an industrial economy in the latter half of the nineteenth century, an immigration wave swept the urban areas. The federal government was called on to oversee labor-management issues. The Department of Commerce and Labor was created in 1903, but was separated in 1913 when it became clear one department could not represent both labor and management. After World War I and World War II, the nation returned to examining what role the federal government could play in the nation's social and economic health. The result was the creation during the Eisenhower administration in 1953 of the first executive department devoted solely to social issues: the Department of Health, Education, and Welfare (HEW). Eisenhower, who opposed the expansion of the federal government as a general principle, supported the creation of HEW. One of the primary goals of the HEW was to carry out federal legislation that required every child in the nation to have the newly developed polio vaccine before entering first grade. This was one of the primary reasons the department tied education and health into one umbrella organization. Through this program, polio, which had crippled Franklin Delano Roosevelt, had the potential of being eradicated within the United States.

The civil rights movement of the early 1960s was a major force in the creation of the next department in 1965—the Department of Housing and Urban Development (HUD). It was supported by President Lyndon Johnson as a means of improving the blighted conditions of the inner city, conditions that were being spotlighted in race riots in the urban areas. Eager to reduce racial tensions, Johnson saw the Department of Housing and Urban Development as a major tool to fund improvements in housing conditions and in upgrading neighborhoods in badly deteriorating inner cities. The social consciousness of the nation had been awakened both by the civil rights movement and by the television cameras that graphically detailed the squalid conditions in which many inner city poor people lived. The Department of Housing and Urban Development was widely seen as an important first step in bridging the gap between the nation's rich and poor, black and white.

In 1966, Congress, in one of its more activist eras, created yet another major department, the Department of Transportation. The Department of Transportation was charged with completing the interstate highway system, inaugurated under the Eisenhower administration as an amendment. The amendment to a defense appropriation propose that the federal government facilitate a modern inner city transportation network and oversee all other transportation systems, such as the railroad, airlines, and interstate waterways. This was particularly important because the airline industry was becoming a major force in travel for all citizens, and not simply for the wealthy.

As the Vietnam War and Watergate consumed the national interest, no new executive departments were created during the late 1960s and early 1970s. In 1977 President Carter urged Congress to create a department whose sole interest was to manage the nation's energy issues and to focus on developing sources of energy that did not rely on oil. This call to action came when the nation was in the depth of an energy crisis, with skyrocketing oil prices causing lines at gas pumps and precipitating a presidential order to conserve fuel. President Carter ordered the temperature in the White House turned down to sixty-eight degrees, wore a sweater whenever he spoke on television from the White House, and urged households around the country to follow his lead. Congress subsequently created the Department of Energy that year. Two years later Carter returned to Congress to create yet another executive department, the Department of Education. During his 1976 election campaign Carter had promised the teachers' unions that he would support a separate agency for educational issues in return for their support. The teachers' unions believed that the welfare programs in the Department of Health, Education, and Welfare had consumed the department, which left little attention for educational issues. Congress supported Carter's request, and the Department of Education was created in 1979.

Finally, in a move similar to that of President Carter, President Reagan asked for and received in 1989 congressional approval for the creation of the Department of Veterans Affairs. Reagan wooed the veterans' vote during the 1980 election. In return for their vote he promised that he would seek to expand the Veterans Administration to a cabinet-level department, which veterans believed would provide more funding for their causes. With the 1989 legislation, the Veterans Administration was collapsed into the newly created Department of Veterans Affairs. The subsequent federal budgets reflected significant veterans' benefits as a result of the creation of the Department of Veterans Affairs (Figure 4.3).

The twentieth century has seen an explosion in the number of executive departments. Eight of the fourteen executive departments have been created in the twenti-

Veteran's Benefits

1988	1990	1996
$29,386	$28,998	$36,985

Source: U.S. Bureau of the Census. *Statistical Abstract of the United States: 1997.* Washington, DC: Government Printing Office, 1997.

FIGURE 4.3   Federal Budget Outlays for Veterans' Benefits (in millions of dollars).

eth century and six of the eight since 1950. What is noteworthy about the evolution of the executive departments is that the last two departments, Education and Veterans Affairs, were supported by the president in order to gain political support in an election. A key question about the future is whether this is a trend or simply an anomaly in the expansion of the president's cabinet.

Evolution of the President's Cabinet: The Constitutional Debates

Since the first four cabinet officers were appointed by President George Washington, the cabinet has served as the president's first line of operational and advisory responsibilities. Operationally, the cabinet officers manage large departments, overseeing thousands of employees and billions of dollars in programmatic funding. As the nation's chief executive officer, the President relies heavily on the cabinet to ensure that the executive branch is well managed and implements the programs that Congress authorizes. In addition, cabinet members are responsible for providing the President sound political and policy advice on the programs within their jurisdiction. The president's policy agenda is largely fashioned with the information provided by the cabinet officers and their departments.

The concept of a cabinet for the President is deeply rooted in our British heritage. Although Thomas Jefferson endeavored to remove the shackles of British tyranny through the Declaration of Independence, the core of British governing principles remains firmly woven into our governmental structure. The president's cabinet is one of many such governing structures that is derived from our British heritage.

The president's cabinet is directly related to the King's cabinet in Great Britain, which was conceived as an advisory group to provide advice on matters of state. Until the fourteenth century, these counselors, drawn from the nobility, had neither title nor official duties. They were referred to simply as the King's counselors rather than as the King's cabinet. The terminology for the King's advisers changed, however, in the fourteenth century when these aristocratic counselors were given the formal title of the King's Council. During the next one hundred years the term for these advisers changed again as they became known as the Privy Council, a term more appropriate for those *privy* to the King's decision making. Members of the Privy Council emerged during this period as not only advisers and counselors, but as managers of the King's executive departments.

Under Charles II in 1660, the Privy Council was enlarged to forty members, including some members of Parliament. The larger unit not surprisingly proved difficult for Charles II to work with. He complained that "the great number of the council make it unfit of the secrecy and dispatch that are necessary in many great affairs of state." He subsequently created a subunit of the Privy Council for the great affairs of state, which he called his cabinet council. As was to be expected, during the reign of Charles II, the cabinet council became the principal source of managerial advice and political decision making.

The concept of a cabinet advising the President, indeed the term itself, is therefore a direct descendant of our British heritage. We began to use the term *cabinet* early in our political lexicon as a result of this heritage. Following our declaration of independence from Britain in 1776, the thirteen former colonies needed to establish a governing structure. They chose a loose confederation of states (they now referred to themselves as states rather than colonies), which provided a weak national government and strong state governments through a document referred to as the Articles of Confederation and Perpetual Union. The Articles of Confederation and Perpetual Union, which were finally ratified in 1781, provided for a unicameral congress that handled both the executive and legislative functions of the new national government. In order to oversee the executive functions of the new government, the unicameral congress created an administrative structure of executive departments that were run by professional administrators, not by members of the congress. During this period the term **cabinet secretary** emerged to describe the departmental administrators, a term that remains in effect today. This administrative structure freed members of congress to focus on deliberative rather than administrative matters. The framework created by this administrative structure became the foundation of the executive departments established under the new government created by the Constitution in 1789.

When the Articles of Confederation appeared to be clearly failing the fledgling nation, delegates to the unicameral congress approved the convening of a convention in Philadelphia. The convention would be convened in May 1787 to revise and amend the Articles of Confederation in order to create a document that would be more serviceable to the member states. Soon after the convention was underway, however, the delegates chose to scrap the Articles and the unicameral congress that managed the nation's affairs and to create a new governing structure with a strong national government. A new Constitution would replace the Articles and a tripartite structure of government would replace the unicameral congress.

One of the major debates on the structure of government during the constitutional convention focused on the presidency and the president's advisory structure. Once the debate over abandoning the Articles of Confederation and adopting a constitution had subsided, the major debate became the role of the chief executive, the president. The delegates sought to limit presidential power in order to ensure against tyranny and the concentration of power within one branch of government. The system of checks and balances and divided government was a reaction against executive domination of the national government. Such domination by King George of England remained riveted in the minds of the delegates during the deliberations.

Pressure to limit presidential power and to limit the chief executive to executing the laws led to numerous debates within the Philadelphia convention on ways to control presidential power. Yet, as the framers debated ways to limit presidential power, they also debated ways to ensure that the president had a strong advisory system. This advisory system would, among other responsibilities, assist him in managing the executive departments. Taking a page from the workings of the government under the Articles of Confederation, proposals were put forth for the president to have a "council," who would serve in the dual roles of presidential advisers and heads of the administrative departments. Charles Pinckney of South Carolina ardently supported this position and argued for inclusion of a mandatory advisory council in the Constitution.

In essence, the advisory council concept provided for a plural executive, from which the president was required to seek the advice of the council before executive decisions were made. The plural executive would require a **collective decision-making process** between the president and the advisory council. As the debates wore on over the plural executive, John Rutledge, another of South Carolina's four delegates, proposed that a singular executive be adopted. He argued that the "executive magistrate" was simply an agent of the Congress, executing the laws of the land and did not require a formal advisory structure. Rutledge further argued that by enlarging the mandatory advisory structure, the power of the president was enhanced. A singular executive, he argued, was less of a threat than was a plural executive.

Alexander Hamilton, who had been the champion of executive power during the constitutional debates, joined Rutledge in support of the singular executive. Hamilton argued that the plural executive was administratively unworkable, since many presidential decisions required speed and gathering the council could not be handled with appropriate speed. Hamilton further argued that the plural executive broached democratic principles since the nature of collective decision making reduced accountability of the executive. If the public should oppose a presidential decision, the nature of collective decision making by the council allowed the president to deflect accountability. He also argued that the collective process could create a system in which the president was "overruled by my Council," a point particularly articulated in *The Federalist Papers*, Number 70.[1]

The debates over the plural or singular nature of the chief executive led to some concern within the convention that if the term *council* or *cabinet* were inserted into the constitution that a collective decision-making process could emerge. As a hedge against that prospect, the framers purposely deleted any reference to the council or cabinet to protect the nature of the singular executive. Hamilton's call for a singular executive was heeded by the framers. Article II of the Constitution has no mention of a council or a cabinet, and refers only to the "heads of the departments" in one phrase. At no point in the Constitution is the word *council* or *cabinet* found. Even the twenty-fifth amendment, ratified nearly two hundred years later, does not use the word *cabinet*. The twenty-fifth amendment defines the cabinet using the phrase "the principal officers of the executive departments."

In the absence of a constitutional framework from which to build an advisory structure, the task was left to George Washington as the nation's first president. Soon after the new government was formed in 1789, following the ratification of the Constitution, Congress created three executive departments to oversee foreign affairs, military affairs, and fiscal affairs. But the task of determining the role that the department heads would play as presidential counselors was still unfolding. The legislation that created the executive departments discussed only the jurisdiction of the departments, not the role of the department head. Determining the role of the department head was left to President Washington (Figure 4.4).

The Constitution had mandated in Article II that the president "may require the opinion in writing of the principal officer in each of the executive departments." This language purposely excluded any requirement of either private meetings or collective meetings with the cabinet officers in order to preclude the development of a plural executive. Washington proceeded cautiously, quite conscious that his administration was establishing precedents for the operation of the presidential advisory structure. At the urging of his former aide de camp and now his Treasury Secretary, Alexander Hamilton, Washington pursued a course in which the cabinet officers were consulted on a regular basis, both as a group in cabinet meetings and indirectly on issues directly affecting their departments. During the first two years of the administration, Washington traveled extensively to convince the citizenry that the new national government would prove to be a more stable governmental system than had operated under the Articles of Confederation. While he was away from Washington, he depended heavily on the advice of his cabinet officers to oversee the government. Once he returned, he continued this close working relationship with his cabinet. In fact, it was during Washington's travels during these first two years that James Madison referred to the "cabinet conferences" that were being held in Washington's absence to run the country. Madison's phrase held and the term cabinet became widely used to describe the heads of the executive departments. But, as presidential scholar Gordon Hoxie notes, "the president was bound neither to consult nor to accept the advice received" from the cabinet[2].

The model established by Washington for using the cabinet for management of the departments, for group discussions over policy matters, and for individual cabinet advice continues today. Washington created the model that solidified the American cabinet as a key player within the president's advisory structure. Had

Department	Cabinet Secretary
Foreign Affairs (State)	Thomas Jefferson
Treasury	Alexander Hamilton
War	Henry Knox
Attorney General	Edmund Randolph

FIGURE 4.4   Cabinet of George Washington, 1789.

Washington discarded the cabinet as policy advisers and sought outside players for policy advice, the role of the cabinet could easily have deteriorated into a purely operational one. The dual role of the cabinet as both an operational unit and a policy advisory unit is directly linked to George Washington and his concept of how the cabinet should be used.

Cabinet Meetings

With the decision by Washington to use his cabinet officers as advisers on the operation of government, rather than using a cadre of congressional leaders, personal friends, or local politicians, a regular process of meetings with the cabinet officers had to be initiated. These meetings became commonly referred to as cabinet meetings and have retained that description today. While the early cabinet met variously in Washington's home and office, the modern cabinet meets in the cabinet Room of the White House.

The cabinet table is an oblong table, surrounded by sixteen high-backed deep burgundy leather chairs. All fourteen members of the cabinet have a chair, as do the president and vice president. Around the outside walls of the Cabinet Room are a number of simpler chairs, in which the president's chief of staff and other presidential assistants sit. Each member of the cabinet is fitted for a leather chair when he or she enters the administration. On the back of each chair is a brass plate with the cabinet member's name engraved on it. When the cabinet member leaves the administration, he or she takes the chair. A new chair is made for the next cabinet member.

The order of seating assignment around the cabinet room table is dictated by tradition. The president sits in the middle of the table nearest the doors. The vice president sits at his left and the secretary of state at his right. Then, moving from right to left around the table, cabinet members sit in the order in which their departments were created. Since the Department of State was the first department created, the Secretary of State sits directly to the right of the president. To the left of the vice president is the Secretary of Treasury and so on. As the number of cabinet officers increase, the order simply continues moving from right to left. The cabinet officer representing the department last created will always be sitting directly in front of the president because of the left–right rule.

The frequency of **cabinet meetings** is not subject to tradition like the cabinet seating order. Presidents call cabinet meetings at their discretion, and the frequency varies tremendously from president to president and from year to year within the administration. All presidents begin their term eager to meet regularly with their cabinets; however, this eagerness quickly dissipates as they find cabinet meetings to be primarily show-and-tell hours. Since the president generally already knows the information, he finds that his time could be better spent on more pressing issues. President Kennedy quickly tired of the show-and-tell nature of the cabinet meetings, remarking to a friend, "Cabinet meetings are simply useless. Why would the Postmaster General sit and listen to a discussion of the problems of Laos?"[3] Kennedy wanted short, carefully focused cabinet meetings without the show and tell.

Another problem with cabinet meetings is that the president can be cornered by cabinet officers who have been unable to secure a private appointment and want to resolve an issue. This catches the president off guard and can result in a difficult moment for the president, especially if he lacks any information on the issue.

Most modern presidents have tried to keep the show-and-tell nature of the cabinet meetings to a minimum, preferring to use the opportunity to discuss key presidential initiatives, political problems, congressional activities, or national emergencies that require broad departmental coordination. Since Dwight Eisenhower created the position of the Cabinet Secretariat in the fall of 1954,[4] presidents have had a White House staff member within the cabinet meeting recording the minutes of the meetings and recording presidential directives to cabinet officers. This process has ensured not only a written record of the cabinet meetings, but ensures that the White House staff know what issues the president has directed each cabinet officer to specifically address. The **Cabinet Secretariat** of Eisenhower, renamed in recent presidencies as the Cabinet Secretary, has also played the more important role of setting the agenda. The Cabinet Secretary asks every cabinet officer to send a memo of issues that would be important for the cabinet to discuss for the next meeting. Once all the memos are reviewed, the Cabinet Secretary meets with the president's chief of staff to determine which issues would be important for the president to discuss with the cabinet as a whole at the cabinet meeting.

During the early months of the administration, the cabinet meetings serve as an important tool for reducing tension between cabinet officers who hardly know each other. The meetings allow the cabinet members to get to know each other and to get to know the president (as political scientist Hugh Heclo so aptly noted, the president has "a government of strangers"[5]). Since the cabinet officers often have never met one another prior to the transition period, and many have little relationship to the president, the cabinet meetings are a valuable tool for building the personal relationships that are key to running any organization. Cabinet meetings provide a regular means of building the relationships between cabinet members, and they reduce the problems of strangers running government.

One cabinet member in the Reagan administration, James Watt who headed the Interior Department, reflected that the cabinet meetings afforded him an opportunity to get together with his fellow cabinet officers to discuss interdepartmental issues. He noted that he often discussed issues over a cup of coffee outside of the Cabinet Room as they waited to go in. For Watt, this was an invaluable opportunity to address a thorny problem with another cabinet member in a very informal setting.[6] The value of cabinet meetings in forging this type of interpersonal relationship between cabinet officers is of particular value in the early months of the administration. By the end of the first year, these relationships have been forged. But the cabinet meetings remain a place to sort out important issues, albeit quickly, that have not been resolved at the departmental staff level.

During the first year of the administration, the cabinet meetings serve to familiarize the members of the cabinet with each other, to provide discussions of departmental issues as a learning tool for all of the members, and to provide the president time to discuss key priorities and politically sensitive issues. After about a year, the regularity of cabinet meetings diminishes. Cabinet members know each other and do not need the cabinet meetings for the introductions they earlier served. They are familiar with the broad goals of other departments and they are fairly knowledgeable about administration priorities. In addition, the president's time has become occupied with other matters, and his schedule does not have the flexibility it may have had earlier. The result is that as the administration moves past its first year, the number of cabinet meetings drops. By the fourth year of the administration, the meetings are less frequent than at any other point in the term. If presidents gain a second term, they begin the cycle again because many cabinet officers are new. As in the first term, the frequency drops rapidly as each year passes. President Clinton met formally with his cabinet only eighteen times during his first term as president, however, he met with individual cabinet members many times.

Presidents tend to call cabinet meetings during the latter part of their terms for two reasons. The first is to discuss a national emergency such as a snowstorm, a flood, or a drought. The cabinet is convened in order to develop a coordinated scheme for assisting the states and the individuals in need of federal assistance. A national emergency could also involve major commitments of U.S. armed forces, such as in the Persian Gulf War or the Bosnian peacekeeping efforts, or a military alert in which another country has detonated nuclear weapons. Presidents use their cabinet meetings in this case primarily for informational reasons.

The second reason cabinet meetings are called is political. During the midterm congressional elections and during the president's reelection campaign, cabinet officers are brought together and given assignments regarding where to travel and what to discuss. Cabinet officers are routinely briefed in the cabinet meetings on key congressional races for the midterm elections and key electoral states in the presidential elections. In addition, they are briefed about the issues on which the president's election campaign wants to focus and on which issues to stay away from. Jimmy Carter often used his cabinet meetings to review what cabinet officers were saying on the Sunday morning news shows and how they were quoted in the national press. Carter's cabinet officers came to the cabinet meetings armed with editorials about departmental policies and favorable quotes in major newspapers. The minutes of one particular cabinet meeting reflected that Secretary of Defense Harold Brown, "reiterated his position on SALT in an appearance on *Issues and Answers* which, because of a technical error, was not to be shown by the Washington, D.C. network affiliate until after midnight on Monday night. The President expressed interest in obtaining a transcript."[7]

The value of cabinet meetings changes over the course of the administration, from one of team building to one of information gathering to one of information dissemination. In spite of their changing nature, cabinet meetings remain an essential tool for the president to manage the executive branch. They are not a tool for collectively reviewing presidential policies and making collective decisions about these policies. One of the more famous instances in which the cabinet tried to govern collectively occurred in 1919 when President Woodrow Wilson had suffered a stroke and was unable to handle daily policy briefings. Robert Lansing, secretary of state, learned that an American official of the State Department had been abducted in Mexico by bandits who were demanding a $150,000 ransom. Lansing called together the cabinet to deliberate what the official response should be. The collective cabinet decided that Lansing should send a note demanding the immediate release of the American. Several months later, Wilson found out about Lansing's actions and sent him a letter:

> Is it true, as I have been told, that during my illness you have frequently called the heads of the executive departments of the government into conference? Under our constitutional law and practice, as developed hitherto, no one but the president has the right to summon the heads of the departments into conference.[8]

For Wilson, any activity by the cabinet as a collective decision-making body, with or without presidential consent, was unacceptable.

While the president may solicit the advice of the cabinet on a policy issue during the cabinet meetings, their views remain merely advisory, with no formal weight in the decision-making process. Cabinet officers often disagree with the president, but their views do not necessarily change the president's mind. One of the more famous presidential-cabinet debates occurred during the Lincoln administration when he sought the advice of his cabinet about issuing the Emancipation Proclamation. The cabinet was unanimously against issuing the proclamation. As he counted the votes there were five nays and only his aye, with his vote being the only aye. He then re-marked that "the ayes have it." For presidents, the opinion of the cabinet carries no weight in the final decision. They can only provide advice, which may or may not be taken by the president. But Lincoln's cabinet meeting did allow an open debate on the Emancipation Proclamation and fostered a sense of inclusion by the cabinet offi-cers in presidential decision making. Although Lincoln failed to take their advice, the cabinet members were afforded an opportunity to provide their advice and to dis-cuss why the president was moving in a different direction. This is one of the many critical roles that cabinet meetings provide for the president as he works with his cab-inet officers in managing the executive branch.

Cabinet-Building Strategies

With the establishment of the cabinet in the role of unofficial presidential coun-selor, George Washington opened the door for jockeying by cabinet members for a preeminent role in policy advice. One of the earliest conflicts within the cabinet in-volved the conflicting advice being given to Washington by his secretary of state, Thomas Jefferson, and his secretary of the treasury, Alexander Hamilton. Jefferson and Hamilton provided Washington different perspectives on the value of such is-sues as federal subsidies to states and the establishment of a national bank. To a large degree the differences in their advice stemmed from differences in their political philosophies. Jefferson, a Republican, sought a minimal role for the national govern-ment, while Hamilton, a Federalist, sought a more involved role for the national government. Washington, also a Federalist, tended to side with Hamilton and grew disenchanted with Jefferson's lobbying members of Congress to oppose presidential positions.

The choice of cabinet officers from the two opposing political parties had been done quite deliberately by Washington in an effort to maximize political support for the administration's policy agenda. Washington designed his cabinet to enhance political support in Congress and to put forth an image of bipartisan support within the administration for presidential proposals. By 1794 it was clear that Jefferson could no longer remain in the cabinet given his opposition to Washington's agenda. He resigned and was immediately replaced by a Federalist, Edmund Randolph. In 1801 when Jefferson took over the reins of office, he nominated only Republicans to his cabinet. Since this early conflict in political philosophy within the cabinet, Presidents have followed Jefferson's lead and turned to members of their own party for cabinet nominees.

There have been exceptions to having political harmony in the cabinet, but they are few and far between. In 1961, John F. Kennedy chose the president of Ford Motor Company, Robert McNamara, a Republican, as his secretary of defense. Lyndon Johnson followed Kennedy's lead and appointed John W. Gardner as Secretary of Health, Education, and Welfare (although Johnson boasted that he didn't know Gardner was a Republican). At the beginning of his second term in 1997, President Bill Clinton followed Kennedy's lead and chose William Cohen, a Republican Senator from Maine, to head the Defense Department. Richard Nixon tried to appoint a Democrat to his cabinet, but none would accept. With few exceptions, presidents have brought members of their own party into the cabinet to minimize the chance the cabinet officer would oppose presidential proposals. While cabinet officers have been known to lead just such opposition, the primary reason has been cooption by the bureaucracy rather than inherent political differences.

While Washington ultimately failed at his attempt to bring a **bipartisan cabinet** into the administration, he succeeded at bringing **geographic diversity** to the cabinet. Washington chose members of his cabinet from both the north (Alexander Hamilton of New York and Henry Knox of Massachusetts) and the south (Thomas Jefferson and Edmund Randolph, both of Virginia). His logic was to prevent the government from "being unduly influenced by men from another area, for the bonds of loyalty were slim enough to be strained by such confidences."[9] This tradition of geographic diversity has remained consistent from administration to administration. As the nation moved westward past the Mississippi River, the configuration of diversity for the north and the south was expanded to include the east and the west. The nation was divided into quarters essentially, with the Mississippi River dividing the east and the west and the Mason-Dixon line dividing the north and the south. The cabinet had to include representatives from each of the four geographic sections.

This principle of geographic diversity was modified over time to provide for certain cabinet positions to be assigned certain geographic areas. The secretary of agriculture, for example, has generally been from the midwest, the secretary of interior from the west, and the secretary of the treasury from the northeast. Modern presidents have been particulary adept at choosing cabinet officers from appropriate geographic venues. The Department of Agriculture serves to illustrate this principle: President Richard Nixon chose Dr. George Shultz of the University of Nebraska, President Jimmy Carter chose Representative Bob Bergland of Minnesota, and President Ronald Reagan chose John Block, an Illinois farmer. Similarly, the secretary of interior is usually from the west, a point illustrated by President Reagan who chose James Watt, a rancher from Wyoming, and President Clinton who chose Bruce Babbitt, the former governor of New Mexico and an environmental activist. The secretary of interior is almost always a western activist who seeks to protect (and usually expand) the nation's national park system, most of which lies in the western United States.

Another principle of cabinet representation that has emerged since Washington's first administration is the principle of **party bridge building.** As the political parties have become increasingly factionalized with liberal, moderate, and conservative wings, presidents have used their cabinets to build bridges within the party. After the advent of primaries in the early twentieth century and the increasing factionalism of the parties, presidents have turned to their cabinets as a tool to repair political damage caused by bitter primary fights. Although Dwight Eisenhower had a bitter primary fight with Robert Taft in 1952, he included four men from the Taft wing of the party (Weeks, Humphrey, Benson, and Summerfield) in his cabinet. Richard Nixon turned to George Romney, a liberal Republican who had actively opposed Richard Nixon in the primaries, to head the Department of Housing and Urban Development. Even Nixon's vice president, Spiro Agnew, was a concession to party bridge building to the conservative wing of the party. Jimmy Carter, who represented the conservative wing of the Democratic Party, brought Joseph Califano, Jr., into the administration to head the Department of Health, Education, and Welfare. Califano was considered a liberal Democrat through his work in the Johnson White House and his involvement with the Great Society legislation. Bill Clinton, a moderate Democrat, reached out to the liberal wing of the Democratic party by his appointment of Donna Shalala, a liberal, to head the Department of Health and Human Services. Building political bridges within the president's own party has become one of the basic tools of cabinet building.

Perhaps the most important cabinet-building tool in recent years has been the inclusion of **gender and ethnic diversity** in the cabinet. Not unexpectedly, throughout the nineteenth century presidents chose white males for their cabinets. Women and minorities often did not have the right to vote and even when given the right, they often did not vote. White males were the dominant voting bloc. In addition, white males dominated the political and economic landscape and were the logical choice for the president's cabinet. With little political power, little managerial skill, and little access to corporate boardrooms, women and minorities were not considered cabinet material. This changed under Franklin Delano Roosevelt with the appointment of the first female cabinet officer, Frances Perkins, to head the Department of Labor. Perkins' appointment represented the increasing political power of women by the 1940s. But the appointment of women to the cabinet was not institutionalized. Presidents Eisenhower, Kennedy, Johnson, and Nixon failed to appoint any women to their cabinets. Not until the Ford administration was a woman again included in the cabinet (with the appointment of Carla Hills as Secretary of Housing and Urban Development in 1975). Ford began a trend that every president has since followed. President Clinton broke another gender barrier by appointing women for two positions traditionally held by men, Attorney General and Secretary of State.

The racial barrier in the cabinet was broken in 1966 by President Lyndon Baines Johnson, who appointed the first minority member of the cabinet, Robert C. Weaver, to head the Department of Housing and Urban Development. Although Richard

Nixon was unable to convince an African-American to join his cabinet, every president since Ford has been able to. It is now an accepted proposition that the cabinet will include women and minorities, although most presidents have had only one woman and one minority as a token representative. The inclusion of Hispanics has been another major step in the diversification of the cabinet, a reflection of the increasing political power of the Hispanic population. President Reagan brought in the first Hispanic cabinet member, Lauro F. Cavazos, a trend that has been continued in every presidential cabinet since.

The diversification of the cabinet has become an integral part of the cabinet selection process in recent administrations, although the Clinton administration took the process to another level. During the 1992 election, candidate Clinton promised that if elected he would build a cabinet that "looked like America." His promise was to create a cabinet with more than a mere token woman, African-American, and Hispanic. He would create a cabinet with broad gender and ethnic diversification. The cabinet, he pledged, would no longer be the bastion of white males. Once elected, Clinton kept his promise and built a cabinet with more women and more minorities than any cabinet in history. As he built diversity in his cabinet, he continued to include geographic distribution and party building as key components of his strategy, yet gender and ethnic diversity had become an additional building block of cabinet composition. Thus, as the new millennium dawns, the cabinet building strategy has become a strategy with three central themes: geographic distribution, party building, and gender and ethnic diversity. Although the Democrats have forged the lead in all three of these themes, the Republicans have followed their lead without hesitation. Cabinet building strategies have basic themes without regard to party affiliation.

As discussed above, the three central themes of cabinet building remain intact without regard to party affiliation, but several other considerations come into play with each president. These considerations involve the degree to which managerial experience, expertise within the department's field, personal loyalty to the president, personal loyalty to the party, and personal loyalty to the ideology of the president are involved in cabinet selection. For some presidents, managerial experience has been a dominant factor. Dwight Eisenhower viewed the position of department head primarily as management, requiring strong managerial skills for the job. Richard Nixon similarly viewed the role as primarily managerial, although he injected a dose of ideological consistency with his cabinet selections. Jimmy Carter saw technical expertise as the driving factor in his cabinet and demanded competency in the areas that the cabinet officers oversaw. This level of technical expertise in the Carter cabinet resulted in the highest number of Ph.D.s that the cabinet had ever incorporated. For Carter, technical expertise was combined with another factor: fresh faces in Washington. Carter believed that by bringing people with little background in government into the administration, he would bring fresh ideas and new ways of doing business into government. As Carter adviser Hamilton Jordan declared during the transition process in the fall of 1976, "You're going to see new faces, new ideas. The government is going to be run by people you have never heard of."[10]

Lyndon Johnson was an exception in his cabinet-building strategy, caught as he was between maintaining his martyred predecessor's cabinet and choosing his own.

He chose to maintain Kennedy's cabinet until after the 1964 election. But, as he began to seek his own cabinet in 1965 and 1966, the nation had become seriously divided by the Vietnam War. Johnson was unable to bring to government Democrats with his same conviction about the war. Subsequently, he moved most of his cabinet officers into their positions from lower ranks in the bureaucracy. Of the fifteen cabinet members whom Johnson appointed during his tenure, all but four were promoted from within the federal government. The result of this cabinet building strategy was to build a cabinet with few personal or political ties to Johnson but with strong ties to the departments they oversaw. Given the activist nature of the Johnson presidency and the aggressive Great Society legislation, which enhanced bureaucratic responsibilities, Johnson's strategy did not hurt his advisory structure. There is actually an argument to be made that Johnson's strategy helped his administration, since none of the cabinet officers had independent political constituencies to threaten presidential positions.

For Ronald Reagan, the combination of personal loyalty, ideological consistency, and party involvement were factors critical to the cabinet-selection process. Of this combination, ideological consistency was the most critical. The political philosophy of each of the cabinet members was identical to Reagan's: cut the federal bureaucracy, increase defense spending, reduce taxes, and cut the federal deficit. It was a short list, but one that demanded absolute concurrence by the cabinet members. Reagan was so committed to the principle of ideological consistency that he rejected numerous cabinet possibilities who did meet his stiff ideological tests. The result was a cabinet of white men, with the exception of Jeane Kirkpatrick, who was named as United Nations ambassador (and not technically a member of the President's cabinet), and Samuel Pierce, an African-American, named to head the Department of Housing and Urban Development. There was a standing joke throughout the Reagan administration, however, that Reagan once thought Pierce, who had been a prominent New York lawyer, was the janitor and Pierce had to inform Reagan that he was a cabinet secretary. This problem stemmed from Reagan's failure to find any conservative African-Americans willing to join his cabinet. When Pierce was identified by the vetting team, Reagan approved Pierce without meeting him.

The Reagan administration was so committed to the ideological commitment, that it required subcabinet officials to fill out a form that indicated their commitment. The form, prepared by White House staffer Lyn Nofziger, asked:

1. Are you a Carter appointee? If so, you're rejected.
2. Are you a Democrat who didn't work for Ronald Reagan? If so, you're rejected.
3. Are you a Republican? Are you the best Republican for the job?
4. Are you a Ronald Reagan–George Bush supporter?
5. Did you work in the Reagan–Bush campaign? How early before the convention?
6. Are you the best qualified person for the job? But that's only number 6.[11]

Perhaps the most interesting point in this list is in number six, in which Nofziger states that being the most qualified person for the job is a relatively unimportant part of getting the job. The most important part of getting a senior post in the Reagan administration was loyalty to Reagan, loyalty to the Reagan–Bush ticket, and loyalty to the Reagan–Bush principles of government.

For George Bush, quite another qualification was important: connections to the Bush family. George Bush saw loyalty and family connections as a critical part of cabinet building and subcabinet building. The Bush cabinet was peppered with longtime associates whom he knew and trusted. Personal relationships, particularly personal relationships of long standing, were important tests of entrance into the Bush cabinet. Yet unlike Ronald Reagan, George Bush remained moderately committed to diversity and included in his administration two Hispanics, Manuel Lujan at the Interior Department and Lauro F. Cavazos at the Education Department, one African-American, Louis Sullivan at Health and Human Services, and in the second round of cabinet appointments a woman, Barbara Franklin, at the Commerce Department. Of nineteen cabinet appointees during his four years in office, three were nonwhite males and one was a woman.

While ideology and loyalty dominated the Reagan cabinet building strategy and personal relationships dominated the Bush administration, the Clinton administration was driven by gender and ethnic diversification. Of the fourteen original cabinet officers, three were women (Donna Shalala, Janet Reno, and Hazel O'Leary), three were African-American (Mike Espy, Jesse Brown, and Ron Brown), and two were Hispanic (Henry Cisneros and Federico Peña). The Clinton cabinet had broader gender and ethnic diversity than any cabinet in history. Over fifty percent were non-white males, in stark contrast to the zero percent of the Nixon cabinet only twenty-four years earlier. The Clinton vetting team, although driven by gender and ethnic diversity, sought a cabinet with a clear commitment to the goals of the New Democrats, the moderate wing of the Democratic Party. The cabinet was not required to have been involved with the campaign or even committed to Bill Clinton prior to the election, but they did have to be committed to the political goals of the administration.

Again, this was quite distinct from either the Reagan or Bush cabinet building strategies but reflected the basic premise of the Carter cabinet building strategy. There was one prominent exception to this strategy—Attorney General Janet Reno. Clinton had repeatedly promised to bring a woman into the position of Attorney General, a position that had never been given to a woman. He chose two different women, both of whom had solid reputations with the moderate wing of the Democratic Party. Although not party activists, they were known to key members of the New Democratic leadership. When both women admitted that they had failed to pay Social Security taxes on their household workers, Clinton withdrew their names for fear of public disapproval and subsequent problems in the Senate Judiciary Committee. His third choice for Attorney General was a little-known Florida prosecutor named Janet Reno, whom Clinton neither knew nor had ever heard of. But she did not have a "nanny tax" problem and had a solid reputation as a prosecutor. Clinton needed to fill the position and supported Reno in spite of knowing little about her. This decision paralleled Reagan's appointment of Samuel Pierce, whom he neither knew nor had heard of. Yet both Reno and Pierce met the test of diversification that was so necessary at the outset of the administration. Not surprisingly, both Reno and

Pierce proved to be thorns in the administration. Pierce was brought before an independent counsel under the Ethics in Government Act of 1978 for allegedly allowing paybacks for federal contracts among his senior staff. Reno approved seven independent counsels during the Clinton administration, including Kenneth Starr, who pursued the Whitewater and Monica Lewinsky investigations.

The cabinet selection process continues to be based on traditional cabinet building strategies. But these traditional strategies have recently been broadened to include ethnic and gender diversity and a certain level of ideological commitment. The Clinton cabinet is likely to become a model for future cabinets, blending the new political coalition into the cabinet and ensuring that cabinet officers share the president's political agenda.

Managing the Executive Departments

Members of the modern cabinet have a number of managerial and political responsibilities. They manage their departments, they provide policy advice to the president, they work with the White House staff on formulating legislative initiatives, they serve as public spokespersons on administration issues, and they serve as lightening rods to deflect negative attention away from the president.

Of all the roles that the members of the modern cabinet play, the role of **departmental manager** is the most important. Cabinet members are responsible for ensuring that the mandates imposed by Congress on their departments are fulfilled. Legislation is broadly written by members of Congress and requires that the departments write the specific guidelines for running the programs. This entails ensuring that the department has the requisite specialists in the field to develop the guidelines for running the program and developing means of working with state and local governments to implement the program. For example, Congress can pass legislation that requires the Department of Energy to reduce the nation's energy dependence on oil. In order to implement this legislation, the Department of Energy would have to determine what programs were in place that were already addressing this issue and what programs would need to be developed. Specialists in hydroelectric power, wind-driven power, and solar power would be among the staff added to the department. In addition, budget analysts would need to be hired to determine the costs of the projects developed by the staff, and congressional liaisons would need to be hired to ensure that Congress appropriated the money needed to move the projects forward. If projects were going to be jointly managed with private enterprises, experts in public–private cooperative agreements would need to be included in the department's staff. If state and local governments were to be key players, experts in intergovernmental relations would need to be included. And for all of the specialists hired, support staff and additional personnel officers would need to be hired, additional building space acquired, and additional accountants hired to review expenditures. Not to mention the additional staff that would be necessary to respond to congressional oversight committees who are seeking assurances that the legislative mandate is being properly dealt with, within both the letter and the spirit of the law. The list is endless with possibilities, but the example is clear. Departments need large staffs to move forward on programs that Congress hands them. And the more programs that Congress hands to a department, the larger the departmental staff becomes and thus the more responsibility the cabinet secretary accrues.

The managerial responsibility of the cabinet officer is enormous, as he or she strives to understand the myriad programs that the Congress has handed to the department and the programs that have simply spun off from existing ones. Once the cabinet officer has some understanding of these programs, he or she needs to ensure what discretion is available within the administration of these programs. Discretion is key to departmental management because Congress generally provides vague guidelines for the departments in the construction of mandated programs. Conservative presidents will instruct their cabinet officers to move very differently than will more liberal presidents with regard to administrative discretion within programs. This leverage is essential to presidents in moving the federal government in their political direction without legislative approval. Richard Nathan has termed this strategy the "administrative presidency," a term that is meant to contrast with the "legislative strategies" to which the public is most attuned.[12]

Not surprisingly, managing the budget of the executive departments remains a significant part of the cabinet secretary's job. With a budget larger than that of most countries in the world, the cabinet secretary is constantly policing the current fiscal year's expenditures to prevent overruns, reporting to Congress's and the Office of Management and Budget's requests for budget information, and developing the next fiscal year's budget. With billions of dollars at stake in every department, budget management is a critical part of the cabinet officer's job.

Another perhaps mundane but extremely time-consuming part of the job is personnel selection. Cabinet officers have a number of political appointees available to them, a small portion of whom require Senate confirmation. The positions that require Senate confirmation are the most senior members of the department, such as the Assistant and Deputy Secretaries. The personal staff of the cabinet officer, such as private secretaries, a chief of staff, a press or communications officer, and a legislative officer are also political appointees but do not require Senate confirmation. Choosing the right staff has become a very important part of the job, and one that cabinet officers have often taken too lightly. Given the demands on their time, having the right deputies allows the cabinet officer time to work on pet projects and to deal directly with constituency groups, members of Congress, and the White House staff. Competent senior staff will ensure that the cabinet officer is constantly fed the necessary information to run the department and is never blindsided by the press, Congress, or the White House about an issue. Nothing is more damaging to a cabinet officer than being called about an issue for which he or she knows little or nothing.

Selection of the deputies, or subcabinet as they are called, has become a political football in recent administrations. Until relatively recently, cabinet officers were given full authority to choose their own staff. But Richard Nixon changed this process, although he had initially promised to "let the cabinet run their own shows."[13] Nixon became increasingly concerned throughout his first term that the cabinet officers had, as John Ehrlichman noted, "married the natives." Nixon blamed

Department	Employees	Budget*
Agriculture	109,586	54,344
Commerce	35,156	3,702
Defense	795,813	285,789
Education	4,721	29,727
Energy	18,237	16,203
Health and Human Services	58,491	319,803
Housing and Urban Development	11,462	25,508
Interior	71,028	6,725
Justice	109,794	11,954
Labor	15,230	32,492
State	24,489	4,951
Transportation	63,309	38,780
Treasury	146,137	364,629
Veterans Affairs	250,899	36,920

* in millions of dollars

Source: U.S. Bureau of the Census. *Statistical Abstract of the United States: 1997*. Washington, DC: Government Printing Office, 1997.

FIGURE 4.5   Executive Departments: Employee and Budget Totals 1996.

the subcabinet officials for allowing programs to be developed that were more liberal than he wanted. Proposals that Nixon wanted to pursue were, in his eyes, being undermined within the departments with the consent if not the full assistance of the cabinet officers. In order to restore some control over departmental decision-making, Nixon began to install his own appointees in the subcabinet positions (Figure 4.5).

After Carter was elected president, he promised to allow members of his cabinet to bring to the senior staff anyone they wanted. But after policies began to emerge in the departments that Carter disapproved of, he, too, began to install his own appointees in the subcabinet positions. Hamilton Jordan, named Carter's chief of staff in mid-1979, was given authority to clear all subcabinet appointees. Cabinet members who had accepted their positions in 1976 with the clear understanding that they could appoint their own staff were outraged at the President's change of heart. But they had no choice but to accept the new White House clearance process.

Three recent presidents (Reagan, Bush, and Clinton) have insisted that the White House oversee subcabinet personnel hiring. Subcabinet officials could not be hired merely because of technical expertise, as Carter had done, or because of personal relationships with the cabinet officer, as Nixon had done. They had to be hired as a means of ensuring that the president's agenda remained at the forefront of departmental decision making and was not compromised by bureaucratic politics. The result has been the creation of the President's Personnel Office within the White House. The director of the President's Personnel Office is a member of the President's senior staff and is part of senior staff meetings. All subcabinet personnel are now cleared by the President's Personnel Office.

Roles and Responsibilities of the Cabinet Officers

The managerial roles of the president's cabinet include managing the departments they head, ensuring that programs are implemented in accordance with congressional mandates, and providing accountability for their expenditures. Management is perhaps the most essential role that the cabinet officers play, overseeing thousands of employees who are often scattered around the country in regional offices overseeing a variety of complex and interlocking programs. The management aspect of the cabinet officer's responsibilities entails oversight of every departmental program so that the funds spent are spent in absolute accordance with the programmatic regulations. Given the billions of dollars at stake, errors cannot be tolerated.

Financial management of departmental expenditures is perhaps the most important official part of managing a department, but it requires constant discussion with members of Congress, with members of the White House staff, and with members of the Office of Management and Budget. Money, of course, is the reason that cabinet officers are also deluged with visits from interested constituents, particularly representatives of the largest constituent groups. Individual citizens rarely are able to wrangle a visit with a cabinet officer, but large constituent groups often do. When the Department of Housing and Urban Development was deciding whether to continue the "Model Cities" program during the Nixon administration, George Romney, the cabinet secretary, was regularly visited by representatives of the League of Cities. When the Social Security Administration was considering revamping Social Security during the Clinton administration, Donna Shalala, Secretary of Health and Human Services, was regularly visited by representatives from the American Association of Retired Persons (AARP). And when Ronald Reagan was considering increasing the defense budget, Secretary of Defense Caspar Weinberger was regularly visited by representatives from Boeing, Martin-Marrietta, and Lockheed Corporations.

While the cabinet officer may appear to be at odds with these lobbyists, cabinet officers and constituent lobbyists have become quite aligned throughout the years. This is due to a process that former White House staffer and presidential scholar Bradley Patterson has labeled the "centrifugal force" effect of the departments in relation to the White House. Department officers are pulled outward, away from the president and the White House, toward their own constituencies and Congress throughout the administration. Cabinet officers begin their tenure in office committed to implementing the president's goals and objectives; yet fairly early into their terms they find that their own constituencies and often their own staff are at odds with presidential goals. During the Carter administration, Agriculture Secretary Bob Bergland actually testified against the president in congressional hearings in regard to price supports. Bergland wanted the price supports increased and Carter wanted price supports decreased. Bergland supported the farmers' interests, who were the department's primary clientele, over the interests of the president. In this particular case, Carter had demanded, as a means of decreasing the federal budget, that his cabinet officers not support increases in their departmental budgets.[14] Bergland felt it was more important to support his department's clientele than the president's promise of a reduced federal budget.

Similarly, in early 1979 Secretary of Health, Education, and Welfare Joseph Califano, Jr., wanted the federal government to implement antismoking programs in spite of President Carter's concern about a southern tobacco backlash in the 1980 election. Califano supported the clientele interests from health groups who convinced him that smoking was a serious national problem that the federal government should take a lead role in alleviating, if not seriously reducing. Carter objected, and Califano was eventually fired later that year. The influence of clientele groups over their departments has led to a serious erosion of the influence that cabinet officers have within the inner circles of presidential decision making.[15]

Another cause of this erosion of cabinet influence in presidential decision-making has been the tendency of cabinet officers to support their own staff, primarily the career bureaucracy, when the bureaucracy support creation of new programs. These programs may be at odds with the president's objectives for the administration, for they may not be in the president's budget or have already been redlined by the Office of Management and Budget. Often the career bureaucracy will convince the cabinet officer that new programs need to be created in order to move the department's mission forward. All departments have statutory missions outlined in their enabling legislation. When the career bureaucracy believes that new programs need to be pushed forward as part of this legislative mandate, they will urge the cabinet officer to push the president to incorporate the programs in the administration's budget.

The process by which the cabinet officer begins to support the departmental staff in policies that conflict with the president's objectives, either because of policy goals or simple budgetary priorities, has led the White House to label cabinet officers as "coopted." Political scientist Richard Fenno, in his seminal work *The President's Cabinet,* maintained that "the President's influence over a cabinet member becomes splintered and eroded as the member responds to political forces not presidential in origin and direction."[16] The phrase "coopted by the bureaucracy," or often referred to as "captured by the bureaucracy," means that the cabinet officer has chosen to support the departmental staff rather than the president when policy or budgetary conflicts arise. John Ehrlichman, President Nixon's domestic policy adviser, referred to this process as the cabinet officers **"marrying the natives."**[17] While this seems to be an unlikely scenario, since the cabinet officers are chosen by the president and are supposed to be loyal to the president, cooption regularly occurs. Richard Neustadt noted in *Presidential Power* that, "Their [cabinet secretaries] personal attachment to the President is all too often overwhelmed by their duty to other masters."[18]

Cabinet officers are physically located in the department, meet regularly with departmental staff, and quickly become part of the department. Although all presidents view their cabinet officers as representatives of the president to the department at the beginning of the administration, very soon after taking their job cabinet officers become representatives of the department to the president. This is particularly true of the clientele departments, such as the Departments of Agriculture, Commerce, Labor, and Veterans Affairs. These departments have very strong clientele, or constituent, representation. They demand services from the department, services that are often quite expensive. If the president fails to include the services and programs demanded by the clientele groups in the administration's annual budget, the clientele groups push additional appropriations through Congress or succeed in having Congress increase the president's budget request to meet their demands.

Clientele and Nonclientele Departments

The concept of clientele departments has been described by political scientist Thomas Cronin as a problem of two very different types of departments: **clientele** and **nonclientele.** Cronin divides the president's cabinet into the "inner cabinet," which are the four nonclientele departments, and the "outer cabinet," which are the remaining ten clientele departments (Figure 4.6).

The outer cabinet serves large and varied clientele groups. The mission of the departments is to implement programs that serve very specialized groups. For example, the Department of Transportation serves state and local governments and is thus heavily involved with clientele groups from state and local governments in addition to myriad contractors. State and local government clientele groups include the National Association of Legislatures, the National Governor's Association, and the County Commissioners Association. In addition, because the Department of Transportation oversees railroad issues, interstate-waterway issues, highway safety issues, inner-city transportation networks, and interstate highway construction, among many other issues, the department is heavily involved with contractors seeking to guarantee funding to state and local governments.

The relationship between the clientele departments and their clientele is extremely important. The clientele groups lobby both the departmental staff and members of Congress to provide adequate funding for their programs. The reward for the clientele groups is funding for their programs. However, the departments also receive a reward in that departmental staff have job security since they have programs to run. Without the programs to run, their jobs are in jeopardy. And the larger the program, the larger the staff and the more mobility staff have in gaining promotions to manage the larger staff.

Cabinet officers from the clientele agencies become drawn into the web of power that the clientele groups and the bureaucracy are constantly pushing. The more programs the department has, the more funding from Congress it will receive, and the more power the department eventually gains in the federal scheme. In essence, the external relationships of the clientele departments provide the cabinet

Clientele Departments	Nonclientele Departments
Agriculture	State
Interior	Defense
Commerce	Justice
Labor	Treasury
Transportation	
Housing and Urban Development	
Health and Human Services	
Education	
Energy	
Veterans Affairs	

FIGURE 4.6   Cabinet Departments.

secretaries an independent power base in negotiating with the president and with the president's budget staff in the Office of Management and Budget with regard to departmental funding for programs.

In contrast to the ten clientele or outer departments who have independent political bases from the constituent groups they serve, the four nonclientele or inner departments serve no clientele groups. The president is the clientele they serve. The Departments of State, Defense, Justice, and Treasury have the nation's full interest at stake, rather than a particular clientele. They serve the president and represent the national interest as he directs. It should be noted, however, that the nonclientele departments are just as willing as the clientele departments to wield independent political power when their budgets are in jeopardy. For example, when David Stockman, President Reagan's director of the Office of Management and Budget, sought to reduce the annual growth rate of the Defense Department's budget from nine percent to five percent, Secretary of Defense Caspar Weinberger brought to bear the "leadership of the national security community" to defend the existing budget.[19] Weinberger succeeded in protecting his budget.

Not surprisingly, as presidents choose their cabinet officers, they tend to choose closer personal associates for the inner cabinet positions. Richard Nixon chose his 1972 campaign manager, John Mitchell, as his Attorney General and his former law partner, William Rogers, as his Secretary of State. Jimmy Carter chose his personal attorney, Griffin Bell, as his Attorney General and Michael Blumenthal, a Wall Street banker and 1976 senior campaign staffer, as his Treasury Secretary. Ronald Reagan chose Caspar Weinberger, who had worked in the Reagan cabinet in California, as his Defense Secretary, and chose his personal lawyer, William French Smith, as Attorney General. Similarly, George Bush chose his close friend and 1980 campaign manager, James A. Baker III, to head the State Department and Nicholas Brady, another close friend, to head the Treasury Department. Bill Clinton chose campaign supporters Lloyd Bentsen for Treasury and Warren Christopher for State. The pattern is clear that of all the cabinet positions, the inner cabinet generally contains the people who are personally closest to the president.

The Two Presidencies Theory

As presidents have learned, pushing through a domestic agenda is difficult. Congress, particularly in a system of divided government, often opposes presidential initiatives in domestic policy. Clientele groups are also very successful at opposing cuts in programs that the president has proposed and are equally successful at moving forward programs that the president does not want in the budget. As presidents become increasingly frustrated at the difficulties of moving their domestic programs forward, they turn to foreign policy as a key part of their presidential legacy. Presidential scholar Aaron Wildavsky has referred to this as the **two presidencies theory:** the domestic presidency and the foreign policy presidency.[20] He notes that presidents generally begin their terms supporting major domestic initiatives and seeking major domestic legislative packages. A second point made in the two presidencies theory is that foreign policy initiatives involve both shared power and power in which the president is dominant. Foreign policy tends to be solely in the realm of the president. Foreign aid packages and other programs requiring appropriations require far more consultation with Congress. Since the publication of Wildavsky's original work in 1966, presidents have significantly increased their domination in foreign policy, particularly through the use of executive agreements to circumvent the treaty process.[21]

Modern presidents have particularly used their domestic policy initiatives to build their presidential track record. Richard Nixon supported a reduction in the Great Society expenditures and a restructuring of federal–state grant programs in his New Federalism. When Congress failed to aggressively tackle these issues, Nixon turned his attentions to detente with the Soviet Union and opening relations with mainland China. When Jimmy Carter was beset with rising inflation and unemployment and a national energy crisis, he turned to foreign policy issues in the Middle East with the Camp David Accords and in negotiating a new Panama Canal treaty that returned control of the Panama Canal to Panama. The Reagan administration used Grenada, Libya, and to some extent the Star Wars initiative as tools to enhance the administration's overall record in an era of a rapidly increasing national debt, recession, and confrontation with Congress on the domestic front. Bill Clinton sought to deflect his problems with a conservative Republican Congress through his peace initiatives in Ireland and the Middle East. Thus, as presidents see their domestic agendas being eroded by departments captured by their clientele interests and a Congress hostile to presidential initiatives, they turn to foreign policy as a safe haven.

Keeping the Cabinet in the Presidential Orbit

As the federal budget has increased, so too has the power of the departments. Cabinet secretaries oversee billions of dollars in federal program funding every year. The result of the escalating federal budget has been a parallel increase in the power of the departments as they manage these programs.

The federal budget has particularly increased since the late 1960s, when Congress passed vast legislative programs that provided safety net programs for America's poor. These programs included housing programs, medical assistance programs, welfare support programs, and work training programs. In addition, the Medicare system was inaugurated, which provided that all citizens over 65 years of age were guaranteed medical care funded by the federal government (Figure 4.7).

As the departments grew in size and scope of programmatic responsibilities, their relationship to clientele groups increased. Their power was thus significantly increased to support programs that were in the department's interest although not necessarily in the president's interest. During the Bush administration, for example, Secretary of Housing and Urban Development Jack Kemp opposed the White House proposal to cut his departmental budget. Kemp wanted to completely revamp the subsidized housing program, referred to as Section 8 housing, to keep people out of large high-rise buildings where crime and drugs were a dominant concern. Bush did not want to in-

Year	Receipts	Outlays	Surplus or Deficit
1932	1,924	4,659	−2,735
1936	3,923	8,228	−4,304
1940	6,548	9,468	−2,920
1944	43,747	91,304	−47,557
1948	41,560	29,764	11,796
1952	66,167	67,686	−1,519
1956	74,587	70,640	3,947
1960	92,492	92,191	301
1964	112,613	118,528	−5,915
1968	152,973	178,134	−25,161
1972	207,309	230,681	−23,373
1976	298,060	371,792	−73,732
1980	517,112	590,947	−73,835
1984	666,499	851,888	−185,388
1988	909,303	1,064,489	−155,187
1992	1,091,279	1,381,681	−290,402
1996	1,453,062	1,560,330	−107,268

Source: Executive Office of the President, Office of Management and Budget. *Budget of the U.S. Government.* Washington; DC: Government Printing Office, 1998.

FIGURE 4.7   **Federal Budget Totals of Receipts, Outlays, and Surpluses or Deficits in Presidential Election Years: 1932–1996 (in millions of dollars).**

crease departmental expenditures because it would affect his effort to reduce the federal budget. Kemp eventually won after a major lobbying effort by his staff and his clientele groups aimed at both congressional committees and the White House.

While this example shows the power of the cabinet secretaries in affecting the department's programs, even though the programs are opposed by the White House, it also shows how difficult it has been for the White House to contain the departments. Cabinet officers know that departmental staff and clientele groups are a powerful lobbying tool. In addition, cabinet officers go public and provide interviews in the national media to support their causes. This leaves the president at a definite disadvantage in these high-stakes games. When Jack Kemp publicly argued that the Department of Housing and Urban Development should raze rat-infested and crime-ridden federal housing projects in Chicago, it was politically difficult for the president to argue against it simply because it would mean increasing a line item in the department's budget. Kemp, a former congressman from Buffalo, New York, was a master politician and realized the box that he had put Bush into. Bush relented and was forced for political reasons to support Kemp's proposal.

The White House has become increasingly concerned that cabinet officers are moving away from the presidential orbit into the departmental orbit. Although the nature of the clientele departments makes it difficult for the cabinet officers not to move into the departmental orbit, the White House has tried to develop mechanisms that will try to keep them in the **presidential orbit.** These mechanisms have become increasingly popular as the departments have gained in size and budget since the Johnson era.

Richard Nixon was the first president to formally initiate a process designed to bring the cabinet officers closer to the White House on a regular, sustained basis. Although all presidents have tried to keep cabinet officers in the presidential orbit through social mechanisms such as invitations to state dinners, to use the White House tennis courts, to visit Camp David, to travel with the President, or to use the presidential box at the Kennedy Center, Nixon realized that more aggressive tactics were needed.

Nixon relied on his domestic policy adviser, John Ehrlichman, to devise a means for the White House to have greater interaction with the cabinet, interaction which they hoped would lead to greater control over departmental policies. The only routine interaction that Nixon had had with his cabinet was in the form of cabinet meetings, which rapidly decreased in regularity as the president became involved in the military operations of the Vietnam War. Ehrlichman began to see the cabinet members being "captured" by their departments and moving in directions quite different from the objectives established in the 1968 campaign for the administration. The challenge that this created for Ehrlichman was to find a mechanism that kept the cabinet in the presidential orbit and linked to the White House. Ehrlichman wanted cabinet officers to believe that they represented the president to the departments rather than the departments to the president.

The Cabinet Council Structure

The tool that Ehrlichman created was an interagency task force that met frequently, as often as once per week, with members of the White House staff. These task forces were formally designated as cabinet councils. For Nixon, the cabinet councils were a means for bringing the cabinet officers together in small groups in a very routine way to meet with the White House staff. The cabinet councils were built around large themes, such as transportation or human services. To some degree the concept of cabinet councils had been honed as early as 1944, when Professor Arthur W. MacMahon of Columbia University explored ways to make the larger cabinet more responsive to presidential needs. MacMahon proposed that smaller cabinet groups could have more frequent meetings and discussion and could "serve as committees on matters of particular interest to various departments."[22] While MacMahon did not envision the oversight role that the White House staff would play with these smaller cabinet meetings, he did envision stronger communication within the cabinet to move policies forward.

Ehrlichman's **cabinet council** strategy was a well-crafted device for cabinet officers to reenter the president's team. When cabinet officers are interviewed by the president during the transition period, they are made to feel that they will be major players in policy development. The inference during this interview and in later conversations with the president is that they will be meeting regularly with the president to discuss key issues that affect their departments and that affect the president's overall agenda. However, very quickly, cabinet officers discover that the White House staff are the senior players in the policy-development process. The White House staff have regular access to the president, senior staff meet daily with the president, and they have the president's ear. In contrast, cabinet officers become quickly consumed by the predictable management activities of running a large department, dealing with constituent issues, working with congressional staff, and working around the nation with departmental programs. As a result, cabinet officers rarely see the president and grow distant from the president and presidential priorities.

The cabinet council structure provided a mechanism for the cabinet officers to meet regularly with the White House staff and, when the president was available, with the president himself. This cabinet council structure renewed the sense of inclusion in presidential decision making that cabinet officers often complain about. Cabinet officers were brought back into the presidential orbit. They appreciated being consulted on presidential policies and establishing stronger ties to White House staff. Cabinet officers themselves gained greater prestige within their departments, as departmental staff saw their department heads regularly going to the White House for meetings.

For departmental staff, the regular visits of their cabinet officers to the White House also meant that departmental policies were being more seriously considered by the president than if they were simply sent in memo form. Departmental staff knew that their policy proposals were being given a forum for discussion, rather than simply filed with some unknown White House staffer's pile of papers. What is interesting about this scenario is that if the departmental proposal was rejected by the White House after the cabinet officer had argued on its behalf, departmental staff were far less likely to mount a battle to reverse the decision. The very process of having a spokesperson in the White House decision-making process appeared to alleviate numerous White House departmental battles. Departmental staff believed that they had been heard in the White House and were willing to accept the White House position, knowing that their position had been given a hearing.

The use of cabinet councils has varied from administration to administration since Richard Nixon's presidency, but every president has employed the technique in one form or another. Gerald Ford continued the Nixon model of having cabinet groups meet around broad themes.[23] Cabinet officers would regularly meet in the White House to discuss the many issues with the broad theme of their council. Jimmy Carter and Bill Clinton established another model in which cabinet officers were brought together in smaller groups around specific policy issues. They were referred to as "ad hoc" cabinet group discussions.[24] The ad hoc groups did not have a regular membership list, as did the Nixon and Ford cabinet councils, but were drawn from cabinet officers specifically affected by the policy discussion.[25] In his first term Ronald Reagan followed the Nixon–Ford model of having several large cabinet councils organized around large themes. But during the second term of the Reagan administration and continued throughout the Bush administration yet another model developed. Reagan and Bush built only two cabinet councils, one for domestic policy and one for economic policy. The larger councils met on a semiregular basis, although smaller working groups of the larger councils were more regularly convened by the White House.

Regardless of which model the White House established, the cabinet officers were brought into the policy-making process in a more routine way than they ever had been. The primary purpose of this process was to keep the cabinet officers from being captured by their own departments and from supporting departmental policies that were unacceptable to the White House. The system has not always worked, for cabinet officers have continued to support departmental policies over presidential objectives at times. But the cabinet council system has mitigated the problem. The more often cabinet officers or their deputies can be brought on a regular basis to the White House for consultation, the less chance that cooption will occur. While cabinet officers will always be defenders of their departments, regular White House interaction is one tool to keep cabinet officers from becoming blind to presidential goals and objectives.

Conclusion

The president's cabinet officers play a critical role in the president's advisory structure. They assist the president in the management of the executive branch and they provide essential information to the White House staff for policy development. It is, after all, the president's constitutional responsibility to execute the laws that Congress writes. Without an able cabinet, the president cannot carry out his constitutional responsibilities. Presidents need strong cabinet officers who can manage large departments with budgets in the billions of dollars, and yet who can provide policy advice that meets the president's political needs. This is a tall order. It is difficult for presidents to find both politically savvy and managerially strong department heads, and this is the great challenge to presidents as they pick their cabinet officers.

Cabinet-building has become one of the most important parts of the transition period, as presidents try to put together fourteen individuals to run the departments who are skilled managers yet are also loyal to presidential goals and objectives. These two criteria are in themselves difficult to accomplish, but in the past twenty years the difficulties have been exacerbated by the additional criteria of gender and ethnic diversity. Recent presidents, particularly President Clinton, have sought not only managerial and political skills in their cabinet officers, but a cabinet with gender and ethnic diversity.

The result has been that department heads generally have all the requisite skills and diversity, but may lack a personal relationship with the president. As Bill Moyers, a White House staffer in both the Kennedy and Johnson administrations, observed,

> Since power is his [the President's] greatest resource, . . . it is not something he is likely to invest in people whose first allegiance is not to him. He is not likely to share what is his most precious resource with people whom he does not know well. Many Cabinet officers are not personally well known to the President. They also become individvals with ties to their own departments, to the bureaucracy, to Congressional committees, rather than exclusively to the President, as is the case with White House assistants.[26]

Therefore, the loyalty of cabinet officers to presidential objectives may have been compromised in the search for the other credentials.

Presidents have sought other ways to build bridges to their cabinet officers through regular meetings with White House staff. These meetings have become known as the cabinet council meetings, and are designed to keep the cabinet officers from being captured by their departments. By having regular meetings in the White House through the cabinet council process, cabinet officers were less likely to feel threatened by the White House staff or feel that their policy proposals are being unceremoniously rejected. The recent efforts by the White House to nurture the cabinet officers helped to break down the walls that often were erected between the departments and the White House. Yet the members of the cabinet remain the president's chief deputies. They run the departments, they represent the president to the public, they justify the president's programs to Congress, and they provide the information necessary to develop the president's policy agenda. The president's cabinet remains at the center of the nation's policy-making apparatus and keeps the machinery of government working smoothly.

The relationship between the president's cabinet and the White House staff remains riddled with tension as each seeks to have the president's ear in the final policy decision. White House staff constantly try to protect the president from departmental advice they believe fails to incorporate the broad national interest or the president's political agenda. Senior White House staff firmly believe that departments have narrow interests and often fail to see the full implication of policy recommendations. This cabinet–White House tension has increased as the power of the departments has increased by virtue of their burgeoning budgets and staff, and concomitantly the White House staff has added to its own budget and staff. Reagan's Secretary of State, Alexander Haig, resigned eighteen months after taking the job. National Security Adviser, Richard Allen, convinced Reagan that Haig's position in the United Nations regarding sanctions on Israel were not in the best interest of the United States. Haig, who had been repeatedly told by Reagan that he was in charge of (or as he referred to the role "as the vicar of") foreign policy, believed that Allen and the National Security Council staff had preempted the decision-making authority of the Secretary of State. For Haig, this was an unacceptable role for the White House staff and he subsequently resigned.[27]

Finding a balance between the cabinet and the White House staff in policy making is an essential role for presidents as they manage the executive branch. On one hand is the fear, as Johnson staffer Jack Valenti noted, that the White House staff will become "courtiers" and shield the president from unpleasant information and difficult decisions. On the other hand is the fear that cabinet officers will become coopted by their departments and provide narrow, uncoordinated policy proposals to the president. There is obviously no easy answer to this dilemma, and presidents need to find their own management style that strikes the right balance for utilizing the advisory talents of both the cabinet officers and the White House staff.

Key Words

bipartisan cabinet	collective decision-making process
cabinet councils	departmental manager
cabinet meetings	enabling legislation
Cabinet Secretariat	gender and ethnic diversity
Cabinet Secretary	geographic diversity
clientele departments	independent agencies

marrying the natives (cooption)
nonclientele departments
party bridge building

presidential orbit
president's cabinet
two-presidencies theory

Notes

1. Alexander Hamilton, John Jay, and James Madison. *The Federalist Papers*. Number 70. New York: Bantam, 1982, p. 354.
2. R. Gordon Hoxie. "Cabinet." In: Jack P. Greene, ed. *Encyclopedia of American Political History: Studies of the Principal Movements and Ideas*. New York: Scribner, 1984, 1:149.
3. Richard Tanner Johnson. *Managing the White House: An Intimate Study of the Presidency*. New York: Harper & Row, 1974, p. 134.
4. Bradley H. Patterson, Jr. *The Ring of Power: The White House Staff and Its Expanding Role in Government*. New York: Basic, 1988, p. 29.
5. Hugh Heclo. *A Government of Strangers: Executive Politics in Washington*. Washington, DC: Brookings Institution, 1977.
6. Author interview with James Watt, Secretary of Interior.
7. Robert Sherrill, "Cabinet Eavesdropping: Message of the Leaked Minutes." *The Nation*, September 30, 1978, p. 206.
8. Jospehus Daniels. *The Life of Woodrow Wilson 1856–1924*. City unknown: Will H. Johnson, 1924, p. 151.
9. Robert Jones. "George Washington and the Establishment of a Tradition." In: eds. Philip C. Dolce and George H. Skau, *Power and the Presidency*. New York: Scribner's, 1976, p. 15.
10. Dom Bonafede. "Cabinet Government." *National Journal*, December 11, 1976, p. 1784.
11. Lou Cannon. *Reagan*. New York: Putnam, 1982, p. 317.
12. Richard P. Nathan. *The Administrative Presidency*. New York: Wiley, 1983.
13. Theodore H. White. *The Making of the President 1968*. New York: Atheneum, 1969, p. 432.
14. "1977 Farm Bill Raises Crop Price Supports," *1977 Congressional Quarterly Almanac*, vol. 33, p. 417. See also a memo that Carter sent to Bergland demanding that he not oppose the president's legislative agenda in "Memorandum for the Heads of Executive Departments and Agencies from the President," September 30, 1977, Box FG 96, Jimmy Carter Presidential Library, Atlanta, Georgia.
15. Joseph A. Califano, Jr. *Governing America*. New York: Simon & Schuster, 1981, p. 188.
16. Richard F. Fenno, Jr. *The President's Cabinet*. New York: Vintage, 1959, p. 248.
17. John Ehrlichman. *Witness to Power: The Nixon Years*. New York: Simon & Schuster, 1982.
18. Richard E. Neustadt. *Presidential Power and the Modern Presidents: The Politics of Leadership from Roosevolt to Reagan*. New York: Free Press, 1990.
19. Richard Darman. *Who's in Control? Polar Politics and the Sensible Center*. New York: Simon & Schuster, 1996, p. 86.
20. Aaron Wildavsky. "The Two Presidencies." In: Steven A. Shull, ed. *The Two Presidencies: A Quarter Century Assessment*. Chicago: Nelson-Hall, 1991, pp. 11–25.
21. The original two presidencies theory appeared in *Trans-Action*, December 1966, pp. 7–14.
22. Arthur W. MacMahon. "The Future Organizational Pattern of the Executive Branch." *American Political Science Review*, vol. 38, December 1944, p. 1187.
23. For an overview of Ford's strategy for the cabinet councils, see Michael Turner, *The Vice President as Policy Maker*. Westport, CT: Greenwood Press, 1982, p. 82+. See also John Robert Greene. *The Presidency of Gerald R. Ford*. Lawrence, KS: University Press of Kansas, 1995, p. 84.
24. Shirley Anne Warshaw. *The Domestic Presidency: Policy Making in the White House*. Needham Heights, MA: Allyn and Bacon, 1997, p. 90+.
25. Gerald M. Boyd, "Reagan Renaming Cabinet Councils: 2 Key Aides Named." *New York Times*, April 12, 1985, p. A1. See also White House fact sheet, "Fact Sheet: Economic Policy Council; Domestic Policy Council," April 11, 1985.
26. Bill Moyers, "The White House Staff vs. The Cabinet." *The Washington Monthly*, vol. 1, February 1967, p. 2.
27. Alexander M. Haig, Jr. *Caveat*. New York: MacMillan, 1984, p. 347.

Chapter 5

THE WHITE HOUSE STAFF

While the cabinet is the part of the president's advisory structure that is more visible to the public, the White House staff is more powerful. Clearly the president needs the management skills of the cabinet and the information that the cabinet officers provide, but it is the White House staff who are in daily contact with the president and are the principal architects of policy development and strategy. The White House staff members are the president's confidantes. They meet daily with the president to discuss what policies should be initiated to fulfill the campaign agenda. They assess the political realities of friends and enemies and Congress. They examine public opinion polls to assess the mood of the country and the support for presidential programs.

Unlike members of the cabinet, the White House staff has only one master: the president. In the early months of the Nixon administration, Daniel Patrick Moynihan, who had been tapped to oversee the president's domestic agenda, lectured to his fellow White House staffers, "Remember this, we are the only people in Washington who work only for the president."[1] The White House staff need not please constituent groups, congressional staffers, or career staffers who demand responsiveness. The White House staff serve only the president, constantly working to develop policies that serve the president's agenda priorities. As political scientist Louis Koenig notes, the White House Staff is part of "the invisible presidency."[2]

The criterion for White House staff selection is quite different from that for the cabinet. White House staff members do not need to meet the geographic, gender, and ethnic distribution tests that cabinet members do. They do not need to have the managerial skills to run a vast department. And they are not burdened with developing budgets, overseeing personnel selection, dealing with congressional committees, or traveling around the country to meet with constituent groups. The only responsibility of members of the White House staff is to focus all of their energies on shaping the administration's agenda and keeping programs concentrated within the scope of that agenda.

Their ranks are usually taken from the president's election campaign and from a pool of friends of long standing. The Ford White House was peppered with Ford's staff from the House of Representatives and old friends from Michigan. Similarly, Reagan's White House staff had many members who served with him in California during his eight-year tenure as governor. Carter's staff was taken primarily from his staff while Governor of Georgia, most of whom had worked full-time on the presidential campaign. Most of the Clinton White House staff had worked on the election campaign or had worked with Clinton in various capacities of the Democratic Leadership Conference.

With few exceptions (such as Henry Kissinger and Daniel Patrick Moynihan in the Nixon administration), senior White House staff members have had close personal relationships with the president. Many have been through difficult prior elections with the president, such as Bob Haldeman and John Ehrlichman with Nixon, or were key advisers to the president during the last election, such as Hamilton Jordan and Jody Powell with Carter, and Edwin Meese and Michael Deaver with Reagan. Some had worked for many years with the president, such as Ted Sorensen, who had worked for John F. Kennedy in his Senate office since 1953.

Power in the White House

White House staff loyalty to the president is rewarded by power. White House staffers are given enormous power to control the information that the president receives and the people with whom the president deals. But not surprisingly, this power leads to conflicts between the White House staff and cabinet officers. Cabinet officers often perceive the White House staff as hostile to their departments and their proposals. As one cabinet secretary complained about the White House staff, "They appeared to regard themselves as managers of the presidency, deciding through control of the schedule who the president would see, deciding through control of the flow of paper what documents the president would read and sign, and deciding through manipulation of the press which policies and which servants of the president should be advanced and which defeated."[3]

Most White House staffers enter the administration believing that of all the various components of the president's advisory structure, they are the ones most likely to protect the president's interests. While cabinet officers purport to be loyal to the president, White House staff members widely believe that department heads quickly become political opponents of the president.[4] They are considered by the White House staff to be clientele-based, representing the departments to the president rather than the president to the departments. James MacGregor Burns supported this view by arguing that, "The 'clientele' departments such as Commerce, Agriculture, Labor and Interior continue to speak for their interest groups through their department heads."[5] As early as 1948, Princeton University professor Edward S. Corwin complained that the cabinet was "composed of men whose principal business is that of [departmental] administration,"[6] rather than serving the president and the presidency. Thus, there was ample reason for White House staff to worry about the loyalty of cabinet officers. The White House staff, not surprisingly, saw themselves as absolute loyalists whose only responsibility was to serve the president.

Creation of the White House Staff

The president's White House staff as we know it today is a relatively modern development. In fact, the president has only had an official White House staff since 1939. Before 1939, presidents relied on a small cadre of volunteers and clerical staff to assist them in their official duties. Some presidents borrowed staff, known as detailees, from the cabinet departments to bolster their own staff. Staff from the State and War Departments were relatively frequently detailed to the White House to assist the president in foreign policy deliberations. Before the National Security Council was created in 1947, the principle way for the president to gather foreign policy information was through the detailees from these two departments.

Most domestic advisers to the president, however, were either friends or cabinet officers recommending policy proposals. Presidents often preferred to use their friends, better known as their **kitchen cabinets,** rather than their cabinet officers for advice as the cabinet became increasingly politicized during the nineteenth century. Beginning with Andrew Jackson's administration in 1829, cabinet seats were often given to political supporters as a reward for their work in the presidential campaign. Not surprisingly, presidents frequently distrusted their own cabinet officers, since there was almost no personal relationship between the president and the cabinet prior to the election.

The White House staff began in 1789 with only one person to assist the president. George Washington ran the country with only the services of young Tobias Lear, who served as his personal secretary from 1786 to 1793 and again from 1798 until Washington's death in 1799. As the volume of mail to Washington grew, he enlisted the support of two brothers, Robert and Howell Lewis, Washington's nephews, who were hired in 1792 to assist in answering correspondence.[7] Washington paid for all three assistants, since Congress had not appropriated funds for a staff. Thomas Jefferson served in office with only one messenger and one secretary.[8] During this early period, presidents often hired family members and other relatives to serve as their secretaries. John Quincy Adams hired his son, Andrew Jackson hired his wife's nephew, and James Monroe hired his brother.

Congress first funded a full-time staff member for the president in 1833 when it authorized a secretary to the president whose sole purpose was to sign land patents on the president's behalf. President Monroe had written Congress in 1825 that too much of his time was spent "on the mere signature of patents," but it took eight years for Congress to respond with even the small funding that it did provide.[9] Not until 1857 did Congress specifically appropriate funds for a small White House staff, when it authorized $2,500 for a presidential secretary, $1,200 for a steward to oversee the executive mansion, $900 for a messenger, and $750 for a contingency fund. By 1900 the White House staff had grown to a personal secretary to the president, two assistant secretaries, two executive clerks, a stenographer, three clerks, four general office personnel, and other staff, for a total of thirty with a budget of $48,540. Under Warren Harding the office grew even larger. Harding had a staff of twenty-one clerks, two stenographers, a records clerk, an appointments clerk, a chief clerk, an executive clerk, a secretary to the president, and assorted other staff.[10] Herbert Hoover further increased the staff by adding two more secretaries and additional typists and messengers. The White House staff, although growing, remained populated by clerical rather than advisory staff. This began to change in the 1930s during Franklin Roosevelt's second term with the creation of a White House staff that would have a role in substantive policy decisions.

Franklin Delano Roosevelt

Franklin Delano Roosevelt's drive to establish a policy-oriented White House structure emanated from his own presidential activism, particularly as he strove to deal with the economic crises of the Depression. The White House deliberations on the New Deal programs with his kitchen cabinet convinced Roosevelt that the president needed a formal staff to provide systematic advice on national issues. In 1936 Roosevelt created the **Committee on Administrative Management,** to design a plan for enhancing the president's oversight of the executive branch. Roosevelt selected Columbia University professor Louis Brownlow to chair the three-member committee, which became known more popularly as the **Brownlow Committee.**

The Brownlow Committee's deliberations took only months, and in 1937 the committee issued its famous recommendation that "the president needs help." Their solution was to create a formal White House staff with six assistants "possessed of high competence, great vigor, and a passion for anonymity." They argued that the president needed staffing help in the White House in the oversight of the executive branch, particularly in carrying out its legislative mandates, and in the creation of new policy initiatives. Congress supported the recommendations of the Brownlow Committee and in 1939 passed the **Reorganization Act of 1939,** providing the president authority to reorganize the executive branch. The reorganization resulted in the creation of the **Executive Office of the President,** which included the newly created White House Office (WHO) and merged the Bureau of the Budget, the Central Statistical Board, and the National Resources Planning Committee into it.[11] In 1939 the White House staff consisted of three secretaries to the president, four administrative assistants, a personal secretary, and an executive clerk. By 1945 that number had increased to a White House Office of fifty-one, including both policy and clerical staff.

Since the creation of the Executive Office of the President, presidents have grown increasingly reliant on their White House staff. The staff has grown from fifty-one in 1945 to nearly 450 today, which does not include staff in the larger units such as the Office of Management and Budget, National Security Council, or Council of Economic Advisers. During the Nixon–Ford years the White House staff grew to an even larger size of 600, which every subsequent president has endeavored to reduce (Figure 5.1).

The cost for this growing White House staff has increased from $473,000 at the end of the last Roosevelt administration to the 1995 budget allocation of $40,497,000.[12] The White House staff has grown so large that it is now housed not only within the White House, but within the Old Executive Office Building next door to the White House and the new Executive Office Building on the north side of Pennsylvania Avenue.

Year	President	Staff Size
1937	Roosevelt	45
1945	Truman	61
1995	Eisenhower	290
1963	Kennedy	388
1968	Johnson	273
1974	Nixon	583
1975	Ford	625
1985	Reagan	362
1990	Bush	374
1995	Clinton	400

Source: Lyn Ragsdale. Vital Statistics on the Presidency: Washington to Clinton. Washington, DC: Congressional Quarterly, 1996.

FIGURE 5.1   Size of White House Staff: 1937–1995.

Growth of the White House Staff: 1939 to the Present

The growth in the White House staff is directly related to the growth in the size of the federal government. As executive departments have grown in response to increased legislative mandates, the White House staff has grown to ensure that the departments implement those mandates without duplication or overlapping programs and within budgetary constraints. But just as important as their oversight role is that the White House staff have also become policy innovators. As Congress has become bogged down in partisan and jurisdictional conflicts, the task of framing the national agenda and developing policies for that agenda has fallen to the president. The majority of the president's staff today are involved with developing policy proposals, ensuring that those policy proposals have the requisite political support, and shepherding those proposals through Congress. The staff of the modern president is a policy staff rather than an administrative or clerical staff, as it was prior to the mid-1940s (Figure 5.2).

Although the president maintains a large administrative and clerical staff, including such positions as staff secretary, scheduling, advance, management and administration, and personnel, the majority of staff are policy oriented. This discussion of policy staff, however, should be referenced within a broader context. The term *policy staff* refers to the members of the White House staff involved both in the formulation of policy and the dissemination of policy. Staff involved in the direct formulation of policy include the chief of staff, the domestic policy adviser, the economic policy adviser (when separate from the domestic policy staff), and the national security adviser. Those with an indirect impact on policy decisions within the White House are the counselor(s) to the president, special adviser to the president, political affairs, intergovernmental affairs, public liaison, special projects, intergovernmental affairs, cabinet affairs, and legislative affairs. Even the president's counsel has become involved in policy is-

Chief of Staff	Thomas McLarty III
Senior Policy Adviser	George Stephanopoulos
Counselor to the President	David Gergen
Assistant to the President/	
Deputy Chief of Staff	Roy Neel
Assistant to the President/	
Deputy Chief of Staff	Ricki Seidman
Intergovernmental Affairs	Regina Montoya
Legislative Affairs	Howard Paster
Communications	Mark Gearen
Assistant to the President/	
Deputy Directory of Communications	Rahm Emanuel
Assistant to the President/Senior Adviser	Bruce Lindsey
Public Liaison	Alexis Herman
Scheduling and Advance	Marcia Hale
Office of National Service	Eli Segal
Staff Secretary	John Podesta
Management and Administration	David Watkins
Chief of Staff to First Lady	Margaret Williams
Assistant to the President/	
Deputy Directory of Political Affairs	Joan Baggett
Domestic Policy	Carol Rasco
Economic Policy	Robert Rubin
National Security Affairs	Anthony Lake
Science and Technology	John Gibbons
Counsel	Bernard Nussbaum

Source: Office of the Federal Register/National Archives and Records Administration. *The United States Government Manual 1993*. Washington, DC: Government Printing Office, 1993.

FIGURE 5.2   1993 Senior White House Staff.

sues, recommending whether the president should veto certain pieces of legislation. The titles of some staff and staffing units may vary from administration to administration, but most units have remained stable in function since the Nixon administration.

The growth of the White House staff has evolved through four distinct stages: (1) the early growth stage, characterized by the Roosevelt and Truman administrations, (2) the shift toward larger staffs with functional responsibilities in the Eisenhower, Kennedy, and Johnson administrations, (3) the institutionalization of domestic and economic policy staffs in the Nixon and Ford administrations, and the expansion of that staff in the Carter, Reagan, and Bush administrations, and finally (4) the increased use of political staff in the Clinton administration. Each of these four stages has led to added layers of staff and has increased the number of players in the advisory structure.

The Roosevelt Years: 1939–1945

The first stage in the evolution of the White House staff is characterized by the relatively small size of the senior staff during the Roosevelt administration following passage of the Reorganization Act of 1939. This group consisted of eight staff in 1939, of which six were professional and two were clerical[13]:

- Secretary to the President, Stephen Early
- Secretary to the President, Brigadier General Edwin M. Watson
- Secretary to the President, Marvin H. McIntyre
- Administrative Assistant, William H. McReynolds
- Administrative Assistant, James H. Rowe, Jr.
- Administrative Assistant, Lauchlin Currie
- Personal Secretary, Marguerite LeHand
- Executive Clerk, Rudolph Forster

The six professional members of the White House staff had few specific functions. Most worked on presidential speeches, bill drafting, and general coordination activities with the departments. There were no formal staff meetings, and each member of the staff had direct access to the president. Roosevelt was the first president to employ the "spokes of the wheel" process of staffing, in which the president served as the hub of the wheel with each of the staff serving as spokes. Each staff member was equal in importance and in relationship to the president. The White House staff structure had little definition and bore no similarity to the well-defined staff structures of later administrations. Roosevelt met frequently with each member of the staff and often encouraged competing advice and analysis from the staff.[14]

One of the key functions of the six professional staffers was to serve as radar, picking up pieces of information and transmitting that information to the president. Bradley Patterson, a former White House staffer, describes a conversation between Roosevelt and James Rowe, Jr., in which Roosevelt says simply, "Your job is to be a bird dog. . . . Just run around town and find out what's happening."[15] Unlike the White House staff of the 1990s, the White House staff of the 1940s had ever-changing roles and responsibilities and had no subordinate staff. Senior staff in the White House of the 1990s all have their own staffs, including both clerical and professional staff.

The Roosevelt staff began to grow in both size and functional responsibility during the mid-1940s, as Roosevelt's health began to fail and as the war dominated his attention. White House staff played an increasing role in domestic and economic policy issues. Roosevelt added three new advisers: Harry Hopkins, who served as an intermediary with the State Department and often met with representatives of foreign governments; Admiral William Leahy, who kept Roosevelt abreast of military affairs; and Samuel Rosenman, who oversaw the span of domestic issues. After American troops entered the European theater, Roosevelt assigned Rosenman greater responsibility for domestic policy, requiring additional aides assigned to him. Although a White House staffing unit was not officially created until 1970 for managing domestic affairs, the foundation for such management was laid by Rosenman, who built the first in-house domestic policy system.

Roosevelt's major contribution to the organizational development of the White House advisory structure was the creation of **in-house policy advisers.** The president no longer needed to rely on the cabinet, the kitchen cabinet, or a host of outside networks to devise policy options for the administration. The policy advisers within the

White House provided the president both in-house policy options and policy recommendations for action prepared by the departments.

Every succeeding president continued to build on Roosevelt's plan for an in-house advisory structure. Harry Truman, who succeeded Roosevelt in the Oval Office, initially sought to continue Roosevelt's original plan for generalists in the White House. Truman saw little need for the functionally oriented roles that Hopkins, Leahy, and Rosenman had played during the latter Roosevelt years.[16] But as World War II continued and the agonizing decisions of atomic warfare overshadowed other domestic and international issues, Truman turned to White House staff to handle specific assignments. Added to the initial White House staff of generalists were John Steelman as Assistant to the President, responsible primarily for labor-management issues; Clark Clifford as Special Counsel, responsible for broad domestic policy formulation; Charles Murphy as Administrative Assistant to the President, responsible for congressional relations; Donald Dawson as Administrative Assistant to the President, responsible for personnel and patronage; and David Niles as Administrative Assistant to the President, responsible for liaison with minority groups.[17] The title of Administrative Assistant became the title designated for the president's senior staff.

In more recent administrations, the title for the senior staff has been simply Assistant to the President. However, as the White House staff grew in size, the Assistants to the President became so numerous that all Assistants to the President also had a descriptive title. For example, the chief of staff became the Assistant to the President and Chief of Staff. Similarly, the press secretary became the Assistant to the President and Press Secretary. The title Assistant to the President has today become a coveted title on the White House staff, for it is the designation for only the most senior staff.

The Truman Years: 1945–1953

President Truman followed Roosevelt's lead in using the White House staff as policy advisers. Truman could easily have returned to the kitchen cabinet concept of policy making or relied more heavily on his cabinet. But the decision by Truman not only to use but to expand the White House policy staff marked a turning point in the evolution of presidential decision making. Truman realized the value of an in-house policy advisory staff and, as a result, expanded the size of the White House staff. Although Truman originally envisioned his cabinet as significant policy advisers, and even referred to them early in his administration as his board of directors, he soon turned to his White House staff for policy advice.[18]

Truman continued the generalists positions and even added a number of the policy positions. But throughout Truman's tenure in office, he gradually moved from the generalist positions that Roosevelt had created to far more functional responsibilities for the White House staff. Although the senior staff had the broad title Administrative Assistant, each had a specific role. For example, Charles Murphy focused on congressional liaison work and Donald Dawson focused on personnel and patronage issues. Among the functional positions initiated in the Truman White House were staff dealing with press relations, correspondence, and appointments. Clark Clifford was given a somewhat different title, Special Counsel to the President, although his responsibilities focused on domestic policy rather than legal affairs as the name implies. Clifford also advised the president in some areas of foreign policy, based on his naval background.

As the White House staff grew throughout the Roosevelt and Truman years, the organizational relationship of the staff to the president changed slightly. In both administrations, the White House staff reported directly to the president in an organizational process known as a collegial or **spokes-of-the-wheel structure.** The White House staff was a collegial group and all members had equal access to the president. No member of the staff had seniority over another member and everyone could meet directly with the president. There was no gatekeeper to stop a staff member from meeting with the president, nor was there any attempt to limit the time White House staff spent with the president. As one former staff member described the Truman organization, "Harry Truman would never have felt comfortable if access to him was controlled by a single person."[19] The term *spokes of the wheel* emerged to describe this organizational structure, for the president was the hub of the wheel and each member of the senior staff was a spoke. Each spoke had direct access to the president and each spoke had the same power within the wheel.

By the end of the Truman administration, the White House staff had grown to thirty-two members, a significant increase from the six staff members Roosevelt began with in 1939. What is significant about the Truman administration is not only the increase in the size of the White House staff and the move toward functional assignments, but the activist role that the White House staff undertook. They began to play an active role in designing specific policy proposals, rather than primarily reacting to policy proposals designed by the departments, and in actively dealing outside the White House. Two examples of activist White House staff under Truman are Clark Clifford and John Steelman.

Clark Clifford began his tenure in the White House as the Naval Aide to the President but quickly moved into the position of Special Counsel to the President. As Special Counsel to the President, Clifford was given the role of advising the president on myriad issues. He emerged as one of President Truman's senior advisers and began to move the White House staff from a reactive to a proactive group. Clifford describes this activist role that the White House staff had assumed under Truman:

> The idea was that the six or eight of us (meeting each Monday evening in Jack Ewing's apartment) would try to come to an understanding among ourselves on what direction we would like the president to take on any given issue. And then, quietly, and unobtrusively each in his own way, we would try to steer the president in that direction.[20]

The White House staff became more involved during the Truman years in developing policies for the president than in reacting to and reviewing policies emerging from the departments.

Similarly, John Steelman became an activist member of the White House staff. One of his most significant roles was to serve as the president's negotiator during the steel strike in 1952. When Truman ordered the government seizure of the steel mills to ensure steel production for military hardware during the Korean War, Steelman met with the negotiators for management and for labor throughout the crisis.[21] Steelman was an activist member of the White House staff, not merely an "anonymous" aide recommended by the Brownlow Committee. This marked a significant change in White House staff responsibilities from the Roosevelt years. Only in the waning days of the Roosevelt administration, as Roosevelt's health deteriorated, did White House staff become involved in shaping policy. Under Truman, senior advisers such as Clark Clifford and John Steelman were regularly participating in policy decisions with the president and were actively working as presidential representatives.

During the Truman administration, the White House staff also became more involved in handling press relations. Before each press conference Truman was given a briefing book about issues that were likely to arise during the press conference. White House staff reviewed the briefing book with him and provided ideas about how to handle the press's questions. These press conferences were held in the Indian Treaty Room of the Old Executive Office Building, next door to the White House. Truman relied on his staff briefing books to ensure that he was not caught off guard by questions from the press corps. This process remains in effect today. Presidents routinely are given briefing books before every press conference and discuss probable questions with their staff to make sure that they have the necessary answers. There is nothing more embarrassing for a president than to be caught off guard on a question and to have no immediate answer, especially if the press conference is being carried on live national television.

The Eisenhower Years: 1953–1961

When President Eisenhower entered office in 1953, the White House staff had blossomed into a formal structure for advising the president on policy issues and for servicing the president in managing the executive branch. The concept of servicing the president includes the nonpolicy roles such as press relations, personnel and patronage, and congressional liaison. President Eisenhower continued the expansion of the White House staff with additional positions for both policy and nonpolicy staff. The march toward the institutionalization of the White House staff was well underway.

General Dwight David Eisenhower, elected president on the heels of his victories over Germany and the Nazi army, brought further enlargement and functional assignment to the White House staff. However, one of the most significant changes to the White House staff was the change from the spokes-of-the-wheel structure, in which every member of the senior staff had direct access to the president, to a pyramidal or **hierarchical structure.** In Eisenhower's hierarchical structure, staff cleared appointments and issues to be discussed with Sherman Adams, the president's new chief of staff. Eisenhower had drawn on the recommendations of an advisory commission, chaired by Nelson Rockefeller, to design the White House staff around defined job assignments and around a reporting structure through a chief of staff.[22] This structure not only reduced the somewhat chaotic process of decision making in the White House but greatly appealed to Eisenhower, who had a very formal, military approach to organizations.

The term **chief of staff,** new to the advisory structure lexicon, was taken directly from the military lexicon. Every general had a chief of staff to serve as the gatekeeper to the general's door.[23] Anyone who met with the general first had to be cleared through the chief of staff. This protected the general's time and ensured that only significant issues were addressed by the general. Eisenhower used this format, a format in which he had routinely operated during his professional career, as a pattern for the White House staff structure.

Sherman Adams, a former governor of New Hampshire and one of Eisenhower's key advisers in the 1952 election, quickly became preeminent in the White House structure in his role as chief of staff. Adams determined who would meet with the president, what papers the president saw, and what the president's schedule would consist of. According to Adams, Eisenhower "simply expected me to manage a staff that would boil down, simplify and expedite the urgent business that had to be brought to his personal attention and to keep as much work of secondary importance as possible off his desk."[24] But Adams was more than a gatekeeper. He was also the president's representative to the executive departments. One famous instance of the power that Adams held involved two feuding cabinet officers who argued over the nominee for a major agency appointment. Adams frankly told the two that they could not see the president about this issue. "Either you make up your minds," Adams informed them, "or else tell me and I will do it. We must not bother the president with this. He is trying to keep the world from war."[25]

But Adams was also a representative of the president to the outside world, as John Steelman had been during the steel strike. During the Little Rock integration crisis in 1957, Adams met with southern governors and members of Congress to find a compromise short of sending in federal troops.[26] When Adams tried to move Governor Orval Faubus and Eisenhower to a conciliatory position, Attorney General Herbert Brownell adamantly objected to any decision that would allow Little Rock High School to continue to be segregated. Eisenhower eventually agreed with Brownell and sent in federal troops, but the illustration reinforces the influence that White House staff had in policy decisions. Eisenhower not only added a chief of staff, but added a number of other **functional positions.** In addition to the chief of staff, Eisenhower added positions for a press secretary, congressional liaison, staff secretary, and cabinet affairs secretary. Again, this was in line with Eisenhower's experience in the military, where each member of the staff had a single, focused assignment.[27] Eisenhower preferred the structured, less chaotic staff structure imposed by the hierarchical model than the often free-wheeling collegial structure of the Roosevelt and Truman administrations.

Although Eisenhower continued to expand the White House staff, most of the positions created tended to be managerial, rather than policy-oriented. One of the most important positions that was created under Eisenhower was the press secretary. The press secretary, James Hagerty, helped Eisenhower deal with the new medium of television, which instantly reached a national audience. Another new position created was the congressional liaison, held by Major General Wilton Persons and later by Bryce Harlow. Persons and Harlow actively pushed presidential objectives in legislative initiatives, always ensuring that members of Congress knew where the president stood on pieces of legislation. Other newly created positions included the Cabinet Secretariat and the Staff Secretary. The Cabinet Secretariat, under Max Raab, ensured that all cabinet members were consulted on policy issues and that cabinet-level decisions were always in line with the presidential perspective. The Staff Secretary dutifully ensured that all relevant memos from the cabinet officers to the president were circulated throughout the White House staff and that comments were solicited when appropriate. The Eisenhower staff greatly routinized the management of policy issues with which the White House dealt. Issues brought to the White House by the departments were "staffed out" by a variety of White House staff, a management structure that had been used only haphazardly in the Truman and to some degree the Roosevelt years.

The Kennedy Years: 1961–1963

With the White House staff continuing to grow in size and functional assignments during the Eisenhower years, quite predictably the next phase of White House staff development was a movement toward increased policy roles for the staff. The pendulum was moving back. Where Eisenhower had used his staff primarily to review and refine departmental policy initiatives, John F. Kennedy sought to increase the use of White House staff in the development of policy initiatives. Eisenhower had relied heavily on his cabinet for policy development and had used the cabinet secretariat in the White House to coordinate the cabinet's policy recommendations. Eisenhower's expansion of the White House staff was not intended to rival the advisory role of the cabinet but rather to provide consistent direction to the cabinet and a more orderly discussion of cabinet-originated proposals. The White House staff also enhanced the president's ability to deal with the press, Congress, and his own cabinet and thus performed a strictly management role.

Nevertheless, the expansion of the White House staff under Eisenhower had been significant. In a formal recommendation to John F. Kennedy immediately after his election in 1960, the Brookings Institution recommended that the president consider reducing the size of the White House staff because it duplicated "the machinery" of the departments.[28] But the call by the Brookings Institution fell on deaf ears, for Kennedy's White House continued to expand, as had Eisenhower's. Although members of Kennedy's staff did not create new proposals, they saw their role as encouraging departmental staff to move in certain policy directions. As Patrick Anderson noted, "not since Roosevelt had there been a President so distrustful of the bureaucracy and so willing to let his personal aides prod, double-check and bypass it."[29] Kennedy encouraged the White House staff to act as an advisory mechanism to provide oversight of departmental proposals and to foster discussions on new initiatives. Nelson Polsby described the "inevitable frustration" of the Kennedy White House staff "of trying to move entrenched bureaucracies" in line with presidential priorities.[30] The White House staff became a tool under Kennedy to prod the bureaucracy and to energize the departments in support of presidential proposals.

Members of the Kennedy White House staff not only performed more oversight of the departments than had previous White House staffs, but they also began to initiate policy discussions with the departments. Rather than react to departmental initiatives, Kennedy White House staff became proactive in policy matters, and began to formulate policy.[31] McGeorge Bundy began working with the departments in direct supervision of foreign policy, and Theodore Sorensen similarly began to directly supervise domestic policy. Bundy and Sorensen led the departments toward policy proposals that had been initiated in their White House offices.[32]

The Kennedy White House returned to the Roosevelt–Truman model of a spokes-of-the-wheel structure and abandoned the chief of staff model that Eisenhower had instituted. In Kennedy's view, the hierarchical model stymied creative decision making and reduced the president's ability to discuss wide-ranging possibilities with staff. Arthur Schlesinger, a key Kennedy staffer, quotes a speech that Kennedy made to the National Press Club in 1960 in which he said that "the President must place himself in the very thick of the fight."[33] For Kennedy, having the chief of staff block senior staff from meeting with the president hindered a free flow of ideas within the staff. Kennedy wanted to have a constant dialogue with his staff, both individually and in groups, to explore policy. Kennedy wanted the exchange of ideas, rather than the more formal approach, fostered during the Eisenhower years, of written proposals.

One of the key strategies used by Kennedy to gain greater control over departmental policy making was the use of subcabinet personnel. In past administrations, cabinet officers were given authority by the president to appoint their own subcabinet personnel. Kennedy reversed this trend to some degree, although not totally, and began to directly appoint subcabinet personnel from the White House. Among those appointed directly by Kennedy were Undersecretary of State Chester Bowles and Assistant Secretary of State G. Mennen Williams. Both were appointed before Dean Rusk was offered the position of Secretary of State. Kennedy also endeavored to increase the number of African-Americans in senior federal positions, appointing George Weaver as Assistant Secretary of Labor, Carl Rowan as Deputy Assistant Secretary of State, and Robert C. Weaver as Housing Administrator.[34]

The move toward greater White House control over the policy-making process included one other critical feature: creation of in-house advisory units for policy. Although Eisenhower had created a number of functional units within the White House, such as the press secretary, congressional liaison, and cabinet affairs, these units were primarily administrative in nature. Kennedy became the first president to create an in-house policy unit: the Office of Science and Technology, created in 1962. Built on President Eisenhower's task force called the President's Science Advisory Committee (PSAC) chaired by Massachusetts Institute of Technology president James R. Killian, Kennedy created a staff unit in the White House for science and technology, particularly to advise the president on the space race in the aftermath of the Soviet Union's launch of the *Sputnik* satellite.

The Johnson Years: 1963–1969

Having succeeded to the presidency without an electoral mandate, Johnson made few changes in the Kennedy governing style or in the Kennedy agenda. During his first address to Congress, Johnson said, "Let us continue . . . on our course so that we may fulfill the destiny that history has set for us."[35] The Johnson presidency began with many of the same staff and organizational structures in the White House that President Kennedy had created. "National grief gradually gave way to a national sense of restoration and confidence," noted political scientist Ervin Hargrove, "and

Johnson distinguished himself by his part in the continuing ceremony of passage out of grief."[36]

Lyndon Johnson continued the trend toward White House staff activism in policy making. White House staff emerged as activists in both oversight of departmental policy making and in developing policy recommendations within the White House.[37] Joseph Califano, for example, became Johnson's point person in domestic policy. Califano worked directly with the cabinet officers to ensure that departmental programs were in line with presidential objectives. As the White House increased its staff throughout the Johnson years, in-house coordination of departmental policies became more prevalent. A major point of concern in the White House was in-house co-ordination of civil rights issues. Califano worked closely with Lee White, the White House civil rights coordinator, on solutions, and both Califano and White worked particularly closely with Robert Weaver, the first black cabinet officer and Secretary of Housing and Urban Development. Califano characterized the personnel activism by the White House staff this way: "His [Johnson's] staff system was frenetic, seeking a cure for every ill; his appearance was one of indefatigable perpetual motion, in constant conversation and consultation."[38] It is important to point out here that toward the end of the Johnson administration the Vietnam War had captured the president's time and attention. With thousands of soldiers losing their lives in the Vietnam War month after month, and with anti-war protests regularly dominating the evening news casts, Johnson relied heavily on his White House staff to oversee his active domestic agenda, giving his staff substantial power in overseeing policy issues.

By the end of the Johnson administration in 1969, the White House staff had emerged as the president's primary advisory structure. Policy advisers began to populate the senior White House staff. The tide of change had carried in a new wave of activism in the White House. The Johnson White House staff, in a trend that had started two and a half decades earlier, was now large enough and specialized enough to craft presidential initiatives and to have some degree of oversight of departmental programs. That staff, which had grown in size from 50 in 1944 to 273 in 1968,[39] and had fluctuated to even higher levels during the administration, marked a further escalation of the power and influence of the White House staff.

The Nixon Years: 1969–1974

The Nixon presidency continued the escalation of the power and influence of the White House staff. But the organizational structure of the White House staff that had dominated the Kennedy and Johnson years changed. Nixon abandoned the spokes-of-the-wheel structure that both Kennedy and Johnson had used and returned to the hierarchical staff structure that Eisenhower had started. Nixon's decision to use the Eisenhower model was due to several factors. First, Nixon sought to concentrate his efforts on foreign policy issues and did not want to deal with domestic policy matters. He wanted his chief of staff to sort out any problems that arose in the domestic arena and to protect him from squabbling cabinet officers. Second, Nixon was an intensely private individual. Unlike Kennedy and Johnson, who thrived on the interpersonal contact of staff discussions, Nixon preferred to privately review staff recommendations in the solitude of the Oval Office. Third, Nixon sought to emulate Dwight

Eisenhower, for whom he had enormous admiration. Nixon took great pride in having been chosen as Eisenhower's vice president. Since the chief of staff structure had worked for Eisenhower, it would work for Nixon.

As chief of staff, Nixon chose his campaign manager and close friend, Harry Robbins (H.R.) Haldeman. Haldeman quickly took control of the White House staff and made sure that Nixon was protected from either cabinet or staff trying to get into the Oval Office. Haldeman was the gatekeeper through whom all visitors had to be cleared and with whom all paperwork had to be reviewed. No paperwork and no individual was allowed into the Oval Office without clearance from Haldeman, and this was the way Nixon wanted it. When Haldeman was forced to leave the White House in 1973 as a result of his involvement in the Watergate scandal, General Alexander Haig took over as chief of staff and continued the gatekeeper role. Both Haldeman and Haig saw their jobs as gatekeepers rather than as policy makers. In a symposium at the University of California at San Diego in 1986, Haldeman was asked how he viewed the job of chief of staff. His reply was that the chief of staff had to be "operational" rather than "policy making." "Toward this end," Haldeman noted, "virtually all the staff members must be people with Brownlow's passion for anonymity."[40] At the same conference Haig reiterated Haldeman's view of an operational chief of staff, stating that "the tendency of White House staff to put themselves in a position where they determine policy and act in behalf of the president . . . is a very, very dangerous, pernicious situation."[41] In spite of their belief that they should be primarily gatekeepers, both Haldeman and Haig still had enormous power over issues confronting the president. As presidential gatekeeper, the chief of staff determined what issues the president should deal with and what people the president should talk to. And, just as importantly, the chief of staff had his own staff to help make decisions. The White House chief of staff, as had other positions of the White House staff, was gaining in size and power under each presidency.

Nixon's decision to provide H.R. Haldeman with his own staff was an example of the expanding role of the White House staff. Not only did the number of senior staff expand under Nixon, but so did the number of junior staff. This was due in part to the era in which Nixon took office. He had entered office in a period of enormous social upheaval. The war in Vietnam had aroused national passions to a point where marches against the war became routine occurrences. Civil rights leaders continued to mount public pressure against racial segregation, voting irregularities, and job inequality. And changes in social welfare legislation through Lyndon Johnson's Great Society programs had expanded the safety network for economic security of the nation's poor, elderly, and disabled.

The result of this pressure on presidential leadership was a continued movement by Richard Nixon to build in-house structures for policy advice. White House staff could provide information and advice quickly and with total understanding of the president's political and programmatic goals. Nixon heavily relied on the National Security Council (NSC), created by the National Security Act of 1947, for international policy advice. Deliberations on military tactics were thoroughly debated in the National Security Council throughout the war, and its recommendations were given to Nixon for assessment. Nixon relied on Henry Kissinger, his national security adviser and the staff director of the National Security Council, for both information and evaluations of military strategy in Vietnam. When Nixon sought to rebuild a relationship with China, he turned to Kissinger for advice rather than to Secretary of State William Rogers.

Kissinger provided Nixon a sophisticated in-house advisory structure for foreign policy, using data from the Central Intelligence Agency and Departments of Defense and State. Rather than gather the cabinet officers to discuss foreign policy or military issues, Nixon would meet instead with Kissinger or with Kissinger's NSC staff. The expansion of the National Security Council staff under Kissinger was another major turning point in the evolution of the White House staff. Kissinger had a large, technically competent staff to review data coming in from the foreign policy machinery and to make recommendations on that data. The White House now had not just policy advisers, but large staffs for the president's policy advisers.

The concept of building staff within the White House staff was widespread. Nixon also built staff under his domestic advisers, Arthur Burns and Daniel Patrick Moynihan. Burns was given the assignment by Nixon to make sure that all of the campaign promises of the 1968 election were in tune with departmental policy proposals. Nixon did not want any of the departments moving forward on a policy that was out of line with the campaign agenda, and Burns was assigned to protect the president's interests. Moynihan was given a more specific job assignment on the White House staff—reducing urban tension, which had overflowed during the 1968 Democratic convention and led to rioting across the country. Nixon created the Urban Affairs Council (UAC) by executive order,[42] with Moynihan as executive director of the council, to address mounting racial problems in the cities and to develop strategies for improving the growing housing blight and job abandonment in the inner cities. Creation of the Urban Affairs Council within the White House was the first step toward creating an in-house advisory structure for domestic policy.[43] Previous administrations had used senior staff, such as Samuel Rosenman under Roosevelt, John Steelman under Truman, and Joseph Califano under Johnson, to manage domestic policy. But none had large staffs to assist them or had the official sanction of an executive order to support their activities.

Within a year, however, Nixon realized that the personal and professional conflicts between Burns and Moynihan were providing unnecessary tension within his domestic advisory structure.[44] Burns and Moynihan clashed over their relationships with the departments and in particular over the validity of Moynihan's proposals for welfare reform.[45] Burns and Moynihan were both relieved of their domestic policy roles in 1970, and the next phase in the development of the White House policy structure emerged.[46] The Urban Affairs Council was superceded by another in-house domestic policy unit, the **Domestic Council,** under the auspices of another White House staffer, John Ehrlichman. Ehrlichman vividly described a 1969 conversation between Nixon and Roy Ash in which the decision to create the Domestic Council was formulated. Ash had been the central figure in creating the reorganization plan. According to Ehrlichman,

> Nixon asked Roy Ash, "Why do I have to put up with this on the domestic side. There's got to be a more orderly way of going about the development of domestic policy than this. Henry (Kissinger) never bothers me like this. Henry always brings me nice, neat papers on national security problems and I can check the box. Nobody badgers me and picks on me. But these two wild men on the domestic side are beating me up all the time." So they went off and devised the Domestic Council.[47]

Nixon's Domestic Council was formally created through Reorganization Plan No. 2, submitted to Congress on March 12, 1970. The Reorganization Plan called for creation of the Domestic Council as a parallel to the National Security Council and for the creation of the Office of Management and Budget (OMB) to replace the Bureau of the Budget. As was the National Security Council, the Domestic Council would have the domestic cabinet officers and the postmaster general as members plus the president and vice president and the director of the Office of Economic Opportunity. John Ehrlichman would serve as the Assistant to the President for Domestic Affairs and as staff director of the Domestic Council. In essence, the Domestic Council would be used to gather cabinet members on a regular basis to ensure that they understood the president's domestic goals and objectives. Ehrlichman's White House staff would be used to frame domestic policy initiatives and to oversee departmental programs. Nixon's creation of a formal White House structure for domestic policy was the first step in institutionalizing a process for domestic policy making in the White House. Every successive administration has continued to have an in-house unit for domestic policy making.

The emergence of both large domestic and foreign policy staffs during the Nixon administration was a significant step in the evolution of the White House staff. Nixon not only relied on the advice of his White House staff, but the White House staff itself had large staffs to develop that advice. A **mini-bureaucracy** had grown in the White House during the Nixon years, with staff having job descriptions and specific job assignments. Senior White House staff had junior staff reporting to them and junior White House staff had their own staff reporting to them. Just as cabinet officers had deputy secretaries and assistant deputy secretaries reporting to them, senior White House staff had their own deputies, their own special assistants, and their own clerical staff. The National Security Council had a significant staff, the Domestic Council had a significant staff, and numerous other parts of the White House, such as the speechwriting office, the press secretary's office, the counsel's office, and the personnel office each had significant staffs. Even the chief of staff, H.R. Haldeman, had a staff.

The Ford Years: 1974–1977

The growth of the White House staff continued after Nixon left office. When Gerald Ford entered office in mid-1974 following Nixon's resignation, he faced mounting public pressure to deal with a growing economic crisis, including both rising interest rates and unemployment. When the Military machine that had brought nearly full employment was cut as the Vietnam War wound down, problems with the economy began to mount. Ford's transition advisers recommended that managing the growing economic crisis should be a White House priority. To this end they recommended creating a new advisory structure called the "Economic Policy Board" (EPB). Ford envisioned the Economic Policy Board as an equal partner in the advisory process with the Domestic Council and the National Security Council. The Domestic Council would focus on domestic issues, the National Security Council would focus on foreign-policy issues, and the Economic Policy Board would focus on economic issues.[48] Thus, the Ford administration continued the trend instituted by the Nixon administration of creating a formal policy unit within the White House to manage policy issues.[49] One of the more specialized White House staffing units created by Ford was the Office of Consumer Protection, headed by Virginia Knauer. By the mid-1970s, both broad and more specialized policy issues were being managed in the White House by entire policy units, with staffs regularly increasing in size.

Ford generally continued the White House organization that Nixon had instituted, maintaining a strong chief of staff and strong organizational units, such as the National Security Council and the Domestic Council. However, most of the staff changed, since Ford thought that many had been tainted by Watergate (even though few knew anything about the Watergate affair). He did make one change to the position of chief of staff, choosing to call the position "staff coordinator." Ford saw the phrase chief of staff as being too closely aligned with H.R. Haldeman, who had resigned over his participation in Watergate. In addition, there were many who thought that the White House staff, and Haldeman in particular, had isolated Nixon to the point at which he did not receive adequate advice on how to handle the break-in of the Democratic National Committee headquarters at the Watergate complex during the 1972 elections. Both Donald Rumsfeld and Dick Cheney, Ford's first and second chiefs of staff, were given the official title of staff coordinator.

The Carter Years: 1977–1981

When Jimmy Carter entered the White House in 1977, the White House staff had grown to nearly 500. Carter continued to use the large policy staffs of the Domestic Policy Office and the National Security Council for policy development and departmental oversight. The Economic Policy Board that Ford had created was merged back into the Domestic Policy Office, as it had been under Nixon. And as had each of his predecessors, Carter continued to expand the role of the White House staff as the presidency became more involved in a broad range of policy issues.[50] Carter added more policy units, including individual units for managing the drug crisis, dealing with women's issues, interacting with state and local governments, and handling special interest groups. The legacy of the Carter years is its expansion of the White House staff into single-issue units, rather than the broad policy units encompassed under domestic and foreign affairs.

Carter's expansion of the White House staff into this variety of individual units was done for two reasons. First, it was a means of providing direct political access to groups who had supported Carter during the 1976 campaign. Since Carter had essentially run against the establishment of the Democratic Party, and had publicly reproached the Democratic Party during the 1976 election, he used the White House to nurture special interest groups for the 1980 election. Second, in campaigning against the federal bureaucracy during the 1976 presidential campaign, Carter had pledged to deliver services in a more efficient and effective manner to the public, thereby cutting the cost of doing business in the federal government. By expanding the number of White House staff responsible for policy matters, Carter expanded the access points for policy input from special interests. Policy input was no longer limited to the traditional access points of the departments, whose staff could skew the information in their favor or fail to forward to the message to the White House. The expansion of the White House staff was primarily a tool to protect Carter's political base.

Carter's decision to revise and expand the operational framework of the White House added new layers of senior staff, all of whom sought access to the president. Carter welcomed the senior staff into the Oval Office and used the spokes-of-the-wheel staff structure for decision making. As had Kennedy and Johnson, Carter enjoyed the constant exchange of ideas among his senior staff during discussions in the Oval Office and never sought to keep any of his staff from meeting with him. He chose not to have a chief of staff and believed in an open-door policy. But after two years of this structure, Carter found that his time was being consumed with staff discussions and squabbles among cabinet officers. In the summer of 1979, barely a year and a half after taking office, Carter changed his staff structure and installed Hamilton Jordan as chief of staff. Jordan remained chief of staff for about a year, when allegations of cocaine use arose and he was forced to resign.[51] Jack Watson, the president's senior adviser for intergovernmental affairs, moved to the chief of staff position for the remainder of the administration.

The Reagan Years: 1981–1989

The effort by Jimmy Carter to expand the White House staff to protect his political base proved less than successful, for in 1980 former Governor Ronald Reagan of California captured the Oval Office. The expansion of the White House staff began to moderate under Reagan, who campaigned on a pledge to reduce the federal budget and cut the bureaucracy. Reagan kept the White House staff at existing levels.

Although Reagan did not dramatically change the size of the White House staff, he continued to centralize policy making in the White House (which Richard Nixon and Gerald Ford had formalized) and to work with special interest groups (which Jimmy Carter had formalized). Perhaps the most significant contribution of Ronald Reagan to the development of the White House staff was refinement of the domestic policy process under Martin Anderson, director of the Office of Policy Development, which had oversight of domestic and economic policy.[52] Anderson used the White House staff to oversee the administration's domestic and economic policy agenda, ensuring that departments clearly understood Reagan's priorities and that all departmental policies met those priorities. This entailed frequent and regular interaction with the department secretaries and their policy staff to ensure that departmental programs met presidential objectives. Reagan created cabinet councils, consisting of cabinet officers and White House staff, to frame policy initiatives. This ensured that the White House was involved in every phase of departmental policy development and implementation. According to presidential adviser Edwin Meese, there would be "an orderly process (within the White House) for reviewing departmental issues requiring a decision by the President."[53] Departments were constantly supervised by the White House. All departmental initiatives flowed through the White House to ensure consistency with presidential objectives. The role of the White House staff was to develop broad policy goals for the administration, craft a few specific policy goals and legislative initiatives, and to provide constant programmatic guidance to the departments.

The White House staff under Ronald Reagan was overseen by the triumvirate of James Baker, Edwin Meese, and Michael Deaver. Rather than a single chief of staff,

Reagan divided the responsibilities of the chief of staff into three positions. Baker would have the formal title *chief of staff*, but his responsibilities would focus on foreign policy and on legislative affairs. Meese would have the formal title of *counselor to the president*, but he would function as a co-chief of staff with Baker. Meese's role was to oversee domestic policy and ensure that the cabinet councils operated smoothly. Finally, Michael Deaver would have the formal title of *deputy chief of staff*, but would handle the administrative details of running the White House. Deaver handled such diverse activities as the president's advance team, state dinners, who could play on the White House tennis courts, and how the president travels. In his book, *Behind the Scenes*, Deaver quotes Reagan as he explains to Meese the triumvirate concept. "Ed, I have really thought about this a lot," Reagan says, "and I have decided to divide the White House responsibilities. I plan to make Jim Baker the chief of staff and you my chief counsel. Jim will run the White House and deal with legislation. You will have the policy shop."[54] While this may have been Reagan's initial plan, Deaver ended up with a key portion of the triumvirate responsibilities.

James Baker and Edwin Meese basically split the policy oversight responsibilities, with Baker in charge of foreign policy and Meese in charge of domestic policy. Baker oversaw the National Security Council and Meese oversaw the Domestic Council and the cabinet councils. The White House staff continued to have broad oversight over the departments, reviewing all policy proposals initiated by the departments to ensure that they were in line with Reagan's agenda items. The staff also tried to ensure that the departments were coordinating their activities and did not have programs that duplicated activities.

The triumvirate system worked throughout Reagan's first term but was abandoned in the second term. Deaver left the administration to form a consulting business, Meese moved over to the Justice Department as Attorney General, and Baker traded jobs with Treasury Secretary Donald Regan. But Regan soon fell into disfavor with Reagan, partly for his autocratic handling of the White House staff and partly for his failure to bring closure to the Iran–contra affair, which rocked the Reagan presidency. After only two years in office, Regan resigned and was replaced by Senator Howard Baker (R-Tenn). Baker left after only a year and was replaced by his deputy, Kenneth Duberstein.

The constant turnover in the senior staff during the second term contributed to a lack of direction. The first term had produced significant legislative victories, such as the tax cut, reductions in the federal work force, and significant increases in the defense budget, but the second term was dominated by Iran–contra and implications that Reagan was not in control of his own White House staff. The implication that National Security Adviser John Poindexter and a junior staffer in the National Security Council, Oliver North, had sold arms to Iran in violation of a presidential embargo and had funneled money to the Nicaraguan contras (who were seeking to overthrow the entrenched government) in violation of the Boland Amendments, seriously damaged the Reagan presidency. One presidential commentator, Haynes Johnson, went so far as to describe Reagan as "sleepwalking through history,"[55] partly because of his failure to oversee the policy decisions his own staff was making.

The Reagan White House had a large, specialized, and very technically competent staff, as were all recent White House staffs. But unlike recent White House staffs, President Reagan did not regularly discuss policy decisions with staff. Instead, the staff, who were fiercely loyal to Reagan and to his ideals, believed that they were in tune with Reagan's goals and objectives and often briefed the president on what they believed the decision should be. There were fewer options prepared for Reagan than there had been for Eisenhower under his Cabinet Secretariat process, and fewer discussions with staff than there had been under Kennedy, Johnson and Carter. And unlike Nixon, Reagan did not spend hours reviewing options papers. As a result, staff often presented Reagan with their views on issues and Reagan followed their suggestions. There was little discussion. Secretary of State Alexander Haig described Reagan as operating "in a cloud," with few hard facts at his disposal and little knowledge of major issues, particularly foreign policy issues.[56] Haig blamed the staff for controlling decision making and for developing too few policy options for Reagan.

The Bush Years: 1989–1993

The White House staff of George Bush were less involved in either programmatic oversight or policy development than the staff of Ronald Reagan. Nevertheless, the staffing size and number of staffing units remained approximately the same. The Bush White House was less controlling than the Reagan White House with regard to policy oversight of the departments. There were two reasons for this pullback. First, the Bush administration was driven by the Reagan Revolution's promise to cut the federal budget. Office of Management and Budget Director Richard Darman and Chief of Staff John Sununu became the point persons of the administration.[57] Their goal, with Bush's approval, was to reduce the mounting deficit and cut the federal budget. This meant that new program initiatives would be minimized and existing programs might be cut. The White House domestic and economic policy office under staff director Roger Porter had relatively little reason to work with the departments.[58] Darman's staff at OMB had replaced the White House staff as the overseers of departmental policy. And just as significant in the policy process, Porter seemed to prefer to focus on micromanagement rather than the macro issues that his predecessor, Martin Anderson, had focused on.[59]

Porter shied away from broad management issues with the departments and immersed himself in two pieces of legislation: the Clean Air Act and the Civil Rights Act. Both were reauthorizations of existing legislation that the Republican White House wanted to shape, particularly in light of the Democratically controlled House and Senate. However, Porter continued to have a large staff to handle domestic and economic policy issues. The Bush White House used its staff somewhat differently than did the Reagan White House, but the number and roles remained essentially the same.

The organizational structure of the Bush White House was the dominant Republican pattern: a strong chief of staff in a hierarchical structure. Bush chose New Hampshire Governor John Sununu as his chief of staff, by-passing his vice-presidential chief of staff, Craig Fuller. Fuller, who was offered the job of deputy chief of staff, left during the transition rather than take a second-tier position. Sununu immediately downsized the number of senior White House staff (those with the title *Assistant to the President*) to thirteen from the twenty-two at the end of the Reagan administration. This reduced the number of people seeking access to the president and gave

President	Year	Number of Senior Staff Members
Nixon	1969	14
Ford	1974	13
Carter	1977	10
Reagan	1981	14
Bush	1989	15
Clinton	1993	22

Source: Office of the Federal Register/National Archives and Records Administration. *The United States Government Manual 1969.* Washington, DC: Government Printing Office, 1969; Office of the Federal Register. *U.S. Government Manual 1974,* 1974; Office of the Federal Register. *U.S. Government Manual 1977,* 1977; Office of the Federal Register. *U.S. Government Manual 1981,* 1981; Office of the Federal Register. *U.S. Government Manual 1989,* 1989; Office of the Federal Register. *U.S. Government Manual 1993,* 1993.

FIGURE 5.3   Number of Senior White House Staff: 1969–1993.

Sununu greater control over the staff. Bush, in fact, did not want an activist White House staff, since he planned to rely heavily on his cabinet to manage the government[60] (Figure 5.3).

Sununu was a strong chief of staff, serving both as the president's gatekeeper and as the president's representative in policy negotiations. In the reauthorizations for both the Civil Rights Act and the Clean Air Act, Sununu met with members of Congress to handle the negotiations. He also met with members of Congress on bills concerning Medicare catastrophic coverage, federal funding of abortions, and the savings and loan banking crisis. He became not merely an aide or an anonymous assistant but an active representative of the president. No chief of staff had ever played the activist role that John Sununu did. John Podhoretz, a member of the Bush White House staff, gave a terse description of Sununu in his book, *Hell of a Ride.* "Sununu had control of policy. He negotiated with Congress. He kept track of the status of major administration initiatives, and did so with great efficiency."[61] Sununu dominated the White House staff and became deeply involved in policy issues, making recommendations to the president and urging the president to take his point of view. To a large extent, however, Sununu's activist role as chief of staff was imperative to Bush's presidency, for the campaign of 1988 had produced few policy goals or general themes.

When Kuwait was invaded by Iraq in 1991, the Bush presidency seemed to be saved. In spite of a lackluster domestic agenda, the public surged to support the president when he sent several hundred thousand troops to defend Kuwait and vanquish the Iraqi invaders. Bush gathered Chairman of the Joint Chiefs of Staff Colin Powell, Secretary of State James Baker, Secretary of Defense Dick Cheney, National Security Adviser Brent Scowcroft, and John Sununu to decide the U.S. diplomatic and military offensive. Sununu now ranked among the senior-most members of the president's administration. He was a voting member of the president's foreign policy team. He was no longer an aide, but a member of the decision-making team.

The White House staff had become an integral part of the president's decision team by the end of the Bush administration in 1992. This was a trend largely created by the Reagan triumvirate. Prior White House staffs had seen their roles as providing the president information from which to make a decision and offering options they felt were most politically advantageous. Both Reagan's and Bush's senior staff operated autonomously, often meeting with members of Congress and constituent groups to discuss how the president wanted to proceed. White House staff had moved from policy advisers to the president to representatives of the president and, often, to policy negotiators. Nixon, Ford, and Carter had far greater control over their White House staffs than did Reagan or Bush. But it is important to note that the power of the White House staff is only what the president wants it to be, and clearly Reagan and Bush were comfortable with the White House staff having significant independent power. The White House staff did not overstep the boundaries created by the president. If the president empowers the White House staff to negotiate policy issues, then White House staff have that power. If the president wants to review all policy options, then the structure will be so framed.

By the end of the Bush administration, the White House staff had continued to gain power as policy representatives of the president, capable of negotiating on his behalf. This power was built on the depth of policy information that had been gathered and synthesized by an ever-increasing White House staff—in order for senior staff to have power, they must have information being developed by their own junior staff. Thus, the size of the White House staff grows as more information is needed for policy development and oversight. Bush's White House staff continued to specialize, continued to have functional units, and continued to grow.

The Clinton Years: 1993–Present

The final stage of the transformation of the White House staff from the small, generalized staff of 1939 to the current centralized policy structure began in 1993 with Bill Clinton's presidency. The Clinton White House was characterized by its large senior staff (with forty percent more senior staff than George Bush's White House) and by its singularly large number of political positions on the senior staff. Clinton added numerous White House staff positions that were politically rather than policy oriented.

The focus of the development of the White House staff in the Nixon through Bush administrations had been on the increase in policy-making responsibilities and the increase in staff within those policy-making units. The hallmark of the Clinton White House has been its increase in the number of positions on the senior staff assigned to political oversight of policy making. Clinton created a complex advisory structure with intertwined policy and political staffs that gauged every policy proposal for political acceptability (Figure 5.4).

In the Nixon through Bush administrations, a time frame in which the White House became the center of policy making, policies had been primarily developed during the campaign. Once the campaign staff became the White House staff, their task was to implement the policies generated during the campaign and to ensure that departmental policies met the presidential agenda.

Clinton White House 1993	Nixon White House 1969
1. Chief of Staff	1. Counselor to the President
2. Senior Policy Adviser	2. Assistant to the President
3. Counselor to the President	3. Counsel
4. Assistant to the President/ Deputy Chief of Staff	4. Assistant to the President
5. Assistant to the President/ Deputy Chief of Staff	5. Special Consultant to the President
6. Intergovernmental Affairs	6. Assistant to the President
7. Legislative Affairs	7. Assistant to the President
8. Communications	8. Special Assistant to the President
9. Assistant to the President/ Deputy Director of Communications	9. Assistant to the President for National Security Affairs
10. Assistant to the President/ Senior Adviser	10. Communications
11. Public Liaison	11. Assistant to the President for Urban Affairs
12. Scheduling and Advance	12. Secretary to the Cabinet
13. Office of National Service	13. Special Consultant to the President
14. Staff Secretary	14. Press Secretary
15. Management and Administration	15. Science Adviser
16. Chief of Staff to First Lady	
17. Assistant to the President/ Deputy Director of Political Affairs	
18. Domestic Policy	
19. Economic Policy	
20. National Security Affairs	
21. Science and Technology	
22. Counsel	

Source: Office of the Federal Register/National Archives and Records Administration. *The United States Government Manual 1969.* Washington, DC: Government Printing Office, 1969; Office of the Federal Register. *U.S. Government Manual 1993,* 1993.

FIGURE 5.4   **Expanding White House Staff Roles.**

The Clinton White House operated somewhat differently. Policies were constantly refined by the White House staff even after the election to ensure that they had the broadest possible public support. Policies that had in the past been developed by the domestic and economic policy staff and then moved into the departments were now subjected to an added layer of political staff in the Clinton White House. Of the twenty-two senior staff (defined as those with the title of "Assistant to the President" or its equivalent), only three senior staff were directly involved with policy making (the domestic adviser, the economic adviser, and the national security adviser). The senior staff was dominated by political staff such as the Senior Policy Adviser (George Stephanopoulos), Senior Adviser (Bruce Lindsey), Counselor to the President (David Gergen), Political Affairs Director (Rahm Emanuel), and the

Deputy Chief of Staff for Political Affairs (Harold Ickes). In addition to the blatantly political staff were the covert political staff—Intergovernmental Affairs, Public Liaison, Personnel, Communications, and Press Secretary. On the staffing chart issued by the White House, of the twenty-two senior staff, the three policy offices were ranked numbers eighteen, nineteen, and twenty. This illustrates the importance that the president placed on political decision making in the White House. In comparison, the policy staff of every president from Nixon through Bush had ranked within the top ten staff members, and usually within the top five.

The Clinton White House expanded the number of players in the president's advisory network, particularly the number of *political* players. By 1998 the White House staff was expanding not only its policy structure but also the political framework for making policy decisions.

While the Clinton White House was building new roles within the staff, they were also working on a staff structure that most effectively served the president. At the outset of the administration Clinton did not want a strong chief of staff, preferring instead the spokes-of-the-wheel system used by his Democratic predecessors. Clinton brought his childhood friend, Thomas "Mack" McLarty, to run the White House. But McLarty was not given a gatekeeper role or a policy-making role, rather he was asked by Clinton to bring order to the White House staff and keep it running smoothly. Not surprisingly, in the absence of a gatekeeper, the many White House senior staff sought access to the Oval Office and soon overwhelmed the president with options on policy matters. Clinton was constantly meeting with staff and poring over position papers. It was Clinton's decision, however, to choose one of the options. Staff did not make the decision for him, although they often recommended a particular option among several possibilities.

By August 1994 Clinton realized that his White House staff was in some disarray and that his time was not being wisely managed because of constant interruptions by staff. He asked McLarty to take a new job in the White House as a presidential ambassador to corporate leaders; he was given the title *Counselor to the President.* The move of McLarty to the somewhat amorphous position of Counselor to the President was reminiscent of Daniel Patrick Moynihan's positions in the Nixon White House. McLarty was replaced by Leon Panetta, director of the Office of Management and Budget and former chairman of the House Budget Committee. Panetta moved quickly to assume the gatekeeper role and gain control of the president's time. This entailed ending the spokes-of-the-wheel structure and overseeing the daily schedule. Panetta also reduced the number of staff at senior staff meetings, thereby limiting the information line and reducing the power of many White House staff. Panetta remained as chief of staff until the beginning of the president's second term in 1997, when his deputy, Erskine Bowles, moved into the position. Bowles was replaced in 1999 by his deputy, John Podesta.

Conclusion

The White House staff has undergone a variety of changes since George Washington served as the nation's first president. With only a single aide-de-camp, Washington worked with his department heads to lead the nation. But as the nation grew and the demands on presidential leadership grew, the president began to expand his own staff to help in the decision process. The presidential staff began with a few assistants in the 1800s, often paid out of personal funds by each president, to a small staff of secretaries and clerks authorized by Congress. Not until 1939, however, did the president gain Congressional approval to create a White House office with professional and clerical staff funded by the public treasury. The creation of the Executive Office of the President and the White House staff in 1939 transformed the presidency.

Roosevelt's 1944 staff of fifty-one grew dramatically during the next five decades, both in size and scope of responsibilities. By the time the Clinton administration had taken office, the White House Office numbered over four hundred staff. The fifty years between Roosevelt and Clinton saw the White House staff evolve slowly, from a few generalists under Roosevelt who provided broad advice to the president to a large staff of specialists in functionally specific staffing units.

The most significant change in White House staffing patterns emerged during the Nixon administration, when the White House staff became the center of administration policy making, with both broad oversight of departmental policy making and a limited degree of policy development. Some presidents, such as Ronald Reagan, sought to impose presidential doctrine on the departments through the White House staff. Other presidents, such as Bill Clinton, sought to develop and refine policy proposals through the White House staff. The Clinton White House staff spent considerably more time refining and reframing ideas among the large, often disparate members of the staff than working with the departments. This meant fewer programs moving toward fruition.

There is no ideal model for the White House staff. Presidents need to create a staff that reflects their management style. But presidents today have the ability to mold their policy structure in various ways given the institutionalized structures for domestic, economic, and national security policy. How they choose to use those structures will vary from president to president. Ronald Reagan used the structure quite differently than did Bill Clinton. The structure is in place, however, as a result of fifty years of evolution.

Will the White House staff continue to change? Absolutely. Will the White House staff continue to grow? Probably. Will the president continue to use the White House staff as his (or her) primary advisory structure? Probably. Because this is a constantly changing system, we can only make educated guesses as to how it will evolve. It is a fairly reasonable assumption that in light of the centrifugal forces on cabinet officers, growing federal mandates, divided government, and the failure of Congress to exercise significant policy leadership, the president will continue as the nation's policy leader. This necessitates not only a strong advisory structure within the White House, but a White House staff that will continue to change as presidential needs require. Based on the trends of the four stages in the evolution of the White House staff, the White House will most likely continue to add layers of staff and to increase the number of players. The degree of politicization of the process will vary by president, but the use of White House staff rather than outside political consultants to advise the president on the political wisdom of policy initiatives will undoubtedly continue. In summary, the White House staff will continue to grow both in size and in function in the immediate future.

Key Words

Brownlow Committee

chief of staff

Committee on Administrative Management

Domestic Council

Executive Office of the President

functional positions

hierarchical structure

in-house advisory structure

kitchen cabinet

mini-bureaucracy

Reorganization Act of 1939

spokes-of-the-wheel structure

Notes

1. William Safire. *Before the Fall: An Inside View of the Pre-Watergate White House.* Garden City, NY: Doubleday, 1975, p. 116.
2. Louis W. Koenig. *The Invisible Presidency.* New York: Holt, Rinehart, & Winston, 1960.
3. Alexandar M. Haig, Jr. *Caveat.* New York: MacMillan, 1984, p. 150.
4. David B. Truman. *The Government Process.* 2nd ed. New York: Knopf, 1971, p. 406.
5. James MacGregor Burns. *The Crucible of Leadership.* Boston: Houghton Mifflin, 1973, p. 127.
6. Edward S. Corwin, "Wanted: A New Type of Cabinet." *The New York Times Magazine,* October 10, 1948, p. 14.
7. Harold C. Relyea. "The White House Office." *The Executive Office of the President.* In: Harold C. Relyea, ed. Westport, CT: Greenwood Press, 1997, p. 40.
8. Michael Nelson. *The Presidency from A to Z.* rev. ed. Washington, DC: Congressional Quarterly Press, 1994, p. 395.
9. Quoted in John Hart, *The Presidential Branch: From Washington to Clinton.* 2nd ed. (Chatham, NJ: Chatham House, 1995), p. 17.
10. Alfred D. Sander. *A Staff for the President: The Executive Office 1921–52.* Westport, CT: Greenwood Press, 1989, p. 52.
11. Peri Arnold. *Making the Managerial Presidency: Comprehensive Reorganization Planning 1905–1996.* 2nd ed. rev. Lawrence, KS: University Press of Kansas, 1998, p. 114.
12. Lyn Ragsdale. *Vital Statistics on the Presidency: Washington to Clinton.* Washington, DC: Congressional Quarterly, 1996, pp. 264–267.
13. *U. S. Government Manual, 1939.* Washington, DC: Government Printing Office, 1939.
14. Stephen Hess. *Organizing the Presidency.* 2nd ed. Washington, DC: Brookings Institution, 1988, p. 25.
15. Bradley H. Patterson, Jr. *The Ring of Power: The White House Staff and Its Expanding Role in Government.* New York: Basic, 1988, p. 56.
16. For detailed discussions of the White House staff see Harry S Truman, *Memoirs. 1945: Year of Decision.* Garden City, New York: Doubleday, 1955; and Margaret Truman. *Harry S Truman.* New York: Pocket Books, 1974.
17. Hess. *Organizing the Presidency,* pp. 42, 43.
18. Truman. *Memoirs, 1945:* pp. 12–13.
19. Clark Clifford. *Counsel to the President: A Memoir.* New York: Random House, 1991, p. 77.
20. Cabell Phillips. *The Truman Presidency.* New York: Penguin, 1966, p. 164.
21. Truman. *Memoirs, Years of Trial and Hope 1946–52.* New York: Smithmark 1996 p. 531.
22. Michael Medved. *The Shadow Presidents.* New York: New York Times Book Co., 1979, p. 245.
23. For an excellent discussion of Sherman Adams's early role as chief of staff, see Herbert Brownell and John P. Burke. *Advising Ike: The Memories of Attorney General Herbert Brownell.* Lawrence, KS: University Press of Kansas, 1993.
24. Sherman Adams. *First Hand Report.* New York: Harper, 1961, p. 50.
25. Medved. *The Shadow Presidents,* p. 245.
26. Brownell. *Advising Ike,* pp. 208–209.
27. Stephen E. Ambrose. *Eisenhower, The President.* vol. 2. New York: Simon & Schuster, 1984, p. 77.

28. *Study of the 1960–61 Presidential Transition*. Washington, DC: Brookings Institution, November 11, 1960.

29. Patrick Anderson. *The President's Men*. Garden City, NY: Doubleday, 1969, p. 233.

30. Nelson Polsby. *Congress and the Presidency*. 4th ed. Englewood Cliffs, NJ: Prentice Hall, 1986, p. 35.

31. Charles E. Walcott and Karen M. Hult. *Governing the White House from Hoover through LBJ*. Lawrence, KS: University Press of Kansas, 1995, p. 151.

32. For a detailed discussion of Bundy's role in managing the anti-Diem coup, see Richard Reeves. *President Kennedy: Profile of Power*. New York: Simon & Schuster, 1993, p. 641.

33. Arthur M. Schlesinger, Jr. *A Thousand Days*. Boston: Houghton Mifflin, 1965, p. 120.

34. Ibid., p. 851.

35. *Public Papers of the Presidents of the United States: Lyndon B. Johnson, November 22, 1963 to June 30, 1964* Washington, DC: Government Printing Office, 1965, p. 8.

36. Erwin C. Hargrove. *The President as Leader*. Lawrence, KS: University Press of Kansas, 1998, p. 113.

37. Emmette S. Redford and Richard T. McCulley. *White House Operations: The Johnson Presidency*. Austin, TX: University of Texas Press, 1986, p. 51.

38. Joseph A. Califano, Jr. *A Presidential Nation*. New York: Norton, 1975, p. 242.

39. Lyn Ragsdale. *Vital Statistics on the Presidency: Washington to Clinton*. Washington, DC: Congressional Quarterly, 1996, pp. 258–259.

40. Samuel Kernell and Samuel L. Popkin. *Chief of Staff*. Berkeley, CA: University of California Press, 1986, p. 195.

41. Ibid., p. 110.

42. Executive Order #11452, July 23, 1969: Created through Executive Order as the Council on Urban Affairs, the popular name became the Urban Affairs Council.

43. Richard M. Nixon. *RN: The Memoirs of Richard Nixon*. New York: Grosset & Dunlap, 1978, p. 342.

44. For a discussion of the Moynihan–Burns relationship, see the exit interview of John Whitaker, May 4, 1975, White House Central Files, pp. 8–9, Nixon Presidential Materials, College Park, Maryland.

45. Shirley Anne Warshaw. *The Domestic Presidency: Policy Making in the White House*. Needham Heights, MA: Allyn and Bacon, 1997, pp. 30–34.

46. Arthur Burns was appointed chairman of the Federal Reserve Board and Daniel Patrick Moynihan was moved to another position in the White House as Counselor to the President, with no specific responsibilities other than "advise" the president. He left the White House in 1970 and returned to Harvard University to teach. From 1973 to 1975 Moynihan served as Ambassador to India.

47. Interview with John Ehrlichman, Kenneth W. Thompson., ed. *The Nixon Presidency: Twenty-Two Intimate Perspectives*. Lanham, MD: University Press of America, 1987, p. 124.

48. See Roger B. Porter. *Presidential Decision-Making: The Economic Policy Board*. Cambridge, England: Cambridge University Press, 1980.

49. Shirley Anne Warshaw and John Robert Greene. "Brushfires: The Departments, the Domestic Council, and the Policy Agendas in the Ford White House." *Congress and The Presidency*, vol. 21, no. 2, Autumn 1994, p. 84.

50. Griffin B. Bell. *Taking Care of the Law*. New York: Morrow, 1982, p. 46.

51. Jordan was cleared of all charges by an independent counsel. Jordan was the first person investigated under the Ethics in Government Act of 1978, which required the Justice Department to use an independent counsel when allegations of wrongdoing were directed at cabinet officers and senior administration officials.

52. Martin Anderson. *Revolution: The Reagan Legacy*. Stanford, CA: Hoover Institution, 1988 (updated 1990), p. 202.

53. From a speech made by Edwin Meese on April 23, 1981, to the American Society of Newspaper Editors. Quoted in "White House Decision Making Continuation of California System." *Congressional Quarterly*, May 9, 1981, p. 827.

54. Michael K. Deaver. *Behind the Scenes*. New York: Morrow, 1987, p. 125.

55. Haynes Johnson. *Sleepwalking Through History*. New York: Doubleday, 1991.

56. Haig. *Caveat*, p. 354.

57. For a wide-ranging discussion of the Bush White House staff structure and its role in policy development, see Richard Darman. *Who's in Control? Polar Politics and the Sensible Center.* New York: Simon & Schuster, 1996.

58. See James Pinkerton. "Life in Bush Hell." *The New Republic,* December 14, 1992, p. 22.

59. Michael McQueen. "Presidential Policy Adviser Faces Complaints That His Idea Menu Offers Leftovers and No Punch." *Wall Street Journal,* June 20, 1989, p. A20.

60. Gerald F. Seib. "Bush, in Assembling Staff of His Administration, Takes the Experienced Not the Power-Hungry." *Wall Street Journal,* January 17, 1989, p. A22.

61. John Podhoretz. *Hell of a Ride.* New York: Simon & Schuster, 1993, p. 89.

Chapter 6

❖❖❖

THE EXECUTIVE OFFICE
OF THE PRESIDENT

When we look at the presidency and try to understand the various organizational units that advise and support the president, the two units that immediately come to mind are the cabinet and the White House staff. These are the most examined and the most discussed by scholars, the press, and the public. The role of the cabinet is to manage the executive departments and the role of the White House staff is to develop the president's agenda and work with the departments and Congress to implement the agenda.

Yet another large organizational unit that reports to the president, the Executive Office of the President (EOP), created in 1939, is just as critical to managing the executive branch and moving the president's agenda forward. Unlike the cabinet and the White House staff, however, the role of the Executive Office of the President is to be nonpolitical and to provide coordination of executive branch programs. The Executive Office of the President provides an institutional memory for every new administration, to ensure that the machinery of government continues with minimal interruption. Most of the staff members in the Executive Office of the President are career employees, although some of the senior staff members are political appointees.

The Executive Office of the President has become known as the "presidential branch," because it maintains oversight of the executive branch and guides political policy-making. Without this presidential branch, the president would not be able to manage the enormous bureaucracy within the federal government. In recent administrations, particularly since the Nixon administration, presidents have expanded both the size and the role of the Executive Office of the President. The White House Office and the Office of Management and Budget in particular have grown significantly since the Nixon administration. Even Ronald Reagan, a staunch advocate of reducing the political bureaucracy, increased his own bureaucratic organization in the Executive Office of the President. Reagan's Office of Management and Budget director David Stockman became both the director and the enforcer of administration policies. As James W. Davis points out, "President Reagan utilized a key agency [OMB] in the presidential branch to centralize the direction of the federal government."[1] The Executive Office of the President provides the president an organizational structure that can bring the disparate parts of the federal government together and can ensure that those disparate parts work toward implementing the president's agenda.[2]

The Executive Office of the President contains about a dozen units—the exact number varies from administration to administration. At the time of President Roosevelt's death, the *U.S. Government Manual* (the official guide to governmental offices and their staffs) listed six units of the EOP. That number had grown to eleven units by the end of President Roosevelt's term, and has grown only slightly in recent years.[3] Presidents create new units, move units to an executive department, and disband units throughout their term in office. But the great majority of the units within the Executive Office of the President remain from administration to administration and provide an institutional memory for the executive branch. All the units within the Executive Office of the President are created by executive order or by legislation. The most visible of the units in the Executive Office of the President is the White House Office, with about four hundred fifty staff. In addition, the Executive Office of the President houses the Office of the Vice President, the First Lady's staff, the National Security Council, the Office of Management and Budget, the Office of Policy Development, the Office of the U.S. Trade Representative, the Council of Economic Advisers, the Office of Science and Technology Policy, the Office of Administration, the President's Foreign Intelligence Board, the Council on Environmental Quality, and the Office of National Drug Control Policy.[4]

Some units are disbanded when a new president takes office. For example, Nixon disbanded a unit created by Johnson called the Office of Economic Opportunity and moved many of its functions to the Department of Health, Education, and Welfare. Carter disbanded the Economic Policy Board created by President Ford and moved its responsibilities into the Domestic Policy Office. President Johnson created the National Council on the Arts in 1964 but a year later moved its functions to the National Foundation on the Arts and the Humanities.

Units are generally created either to provide information to the president that the executive departments cannot readily handle or to emphasize an area that has the highest presidential priority. Units often are created to deal with pressing social and economic problems. For example, President Reagan wanted a staff within the Executive Office of the President to focus on the growing drug problem in the nation. The Reagan administration had targeted the drug issue as a priority agenda item. In particular, Mrs. Reagan had been an outspoken advocate of her "Just Say No" program geared to children who were faced with choices about using drugs. As a result, in 1988 President Reagan sought and received congressional approval for creation of the Office of National Drug Control Policy within the Executive Office of the President. In 1974, when the energy crisis overwhelmed the nation, causing lines at gas pumps and wreaking economic havoc in the transportation industry, President Ford received congressional approval for the Energy Resources Council in the Executive Office of the President to oversee energy policy. The responsibilities of the Energy Resources Council were folded into the newly created Department of Energy in 1977.

This chapter will examine the history of the Executive Office of the President, particularly the role that President Roosevelt played in its development, and will look at the units that comprise the Executive Office of the President today. Three units will not be included in this chapter: the White House Office, the Office of the Vice President (covered in separate chapters), and the First Lady's office.

Reorganization Plans and the Brownlow Committee

As the nation moved from an agricultural base to an industrial one in the late nineteenth and early twentieth centuries, the role of the federal government was expanded. The number of civilian employees in the federal government, federal expenditures, and the civilian work force all increased, contributing to growing problems of inefficiency and overlapping programs. There was little oversight of departmental programs from a central staff in the executive branch. In order to deal with these problems, President Taft established a commission in 1911, formally known as the Commission on Economy and Efficiency, although most referred to it as the **Taft Commission.** The Taft Commission was charged with examining the various parts of the federal executive branch and with making recommendations for improved administrative management. Taft appointed Frederick Cleveland, a senior official with the New York Bureau of Municipal Research, a New York City think tank, to chair the commission. Founded during the Progressive era, the New York Bureau of Municipal Research had been created by a small group of urban reformers, mostly from the academic community. Their work had produced volumes of information on municipal reform and proposals for improving urban management.[5]

Cleveland's expertise in management information provided Taft what he needed to evaluate the wide-ranging programs within the executive branch. Cleveland approached his job in a rather novel way for the time, which was to look at the executive departments as interlocking units, with the president as its chief executive officer. Cleveland found that the independence of the cabinet secretaries in managing their departments closely paralleled the independence of department heads in the cities.

In the cities of the early twentieth century, department heads, such as the public works director, ran their departments as independent agencies, with little connection to the mayor or other departments. These urban departments were often self-contained units, much as the federal executive agencies had become. Cleveland sought to translate his experiences at the urban level to finding solutions for the rambling and often disconnected executive branch, whose departments were often more tied to Congress than to the president. As presidential scholar Peri Arnold describes Cleveland's approach to the study,

> An overall picture of the executive branch was to be the framework for data collection. From a modern perspective, it is difficult to appreciate how innovative was Cleveland's model of the organization of the executive branch. No longer were these agencies to be understood as single units tied to Congress by an umbilical cord of statute and appropriation. Rather, they would be seen as part of a whole that had this new conception, the traditional picture of the dominant tie of agency to legislature is an intrusive element—a pathology.[6]

Under Cleveland's leadership, the Taft Commission created 110 separate task forces to review executive programs. But the departments often balked at the idea of increasing their ties to either the president or other executive agencies, preferring to continue their near-autonomy in program management and budgetary discretion. Congress became equally unhappy with the Taft Commission, whose recommendations could potentially threaten their relationships with the departments. In 1912, when President Taft sought additional funding for the commission (from the $100,000 originally allocated to $250,000), Congress acted decisively by cutting the appropriation to $75,000 and directing that only three staff members could be funded under the appropriation. Cleveland was forced to reduce the size of the commission and to cut staff, leaving only himself and two other commission members. The commission received no funding in 1913 and was disbanded.

Before disbanding, the Taft Commission produced a report that criticized the departments for their lack of formal budgets, for bureaus that were unnecessary or had overlapping duties, and for the absence of standardization of policies across departments, along with other recommendations. The commission had to discontinue its activities before it moved on to several other proposals, such as one to have a unified Defense Department rather than a War Department. This proposal was not acted on until 1947, when Congress passed the National Security Act.

The general thrust of the Taft Commission's recommendations was that the president had little capacity for strong managerial control over the executive branch, largely due to the absence of an executive budget and proposals that were managed through the White House. Although the Taft Commission had not improved the president's management capacity over the executive branch, it had sparked significant discussion that would lead to changes in the near future for presidential management. The Progressives took up the cause of changes in the executive branch, which contributed to its continued high profile in discussions on the presidency. Perhaps the most lasting contribution of the Taft Commission was the realization that a major problem existed in presidential management of the executive branch, which could not be dealt with on a piecemeal basis. A significant overhaul of the current structure of the executive branch had to be designed and implemented.

The overhaul of the executive branch was sidelined during the next decade, first by World War I, then by the debate over the League of Nations, and finally by President Wilson's stroke, which left him unable to make far-reaching decisions about government administration. Wilson was succeeded by Warren Harding, who was not particularly interested in changes in presidential management of the executive branch. In his view, the presidency was simply a ceremonial job and Congress was the decision maker. Harding viewed the existing relationship of the departments and Congress as quite acceptable. During the 1920 presidential campaign, Harding promised to return the country to "normalcy," in which the nation depended on Congress for leadership. Harding had a narrow view of his constitutional powers and viewed Wilson's often-expanded view of presidential power as out of line with the Constitution.

In spite of Harding's view of the presidency and its relationship to Congress, he realized the need for improving management in the executive branch—particularly, dealing with overlapping programs in departments and programs that did not fit into departments. As had Taft, Harding viewed the efficiency and economy that could be gained from reorganization of the executive branch as a reason to move forward with reorganization planning. Harding did not view reorganization as an expansion of presidential power or a realignment of the traditional relationship of the departments to Congress, but rather as a necessary part of managing the executive branch. He subsequently created a task force to continue examining government efficiency, whose job was to prepare a report for the Joint Committee on Reorganization in Congress.

The task force recommended that a number of programs be moved from one department to another and recommended the creation of two new departments. Harding supported the recommendations, although he failed to take immediate action when his cabinet balked at them. The Secretary of Agriculture was particularly upset when Harding recommended moving the Forest Service to the Agriculture Department. Finally, in 1923, Harding gained the support of his cabinet for a reorganization plan for the executive branch that created a unified Defense Department, moved the Forest Service to the Interior Department, revamped the Commerce and Labor Departments, and created a Department of Education and Welfare. The reorganization plan ensured that the units within each department were logically housed and that new departments would provide for more effective management of federal programs.

Although Congress had originally supported the task force, once the report was presented that support eroded considerably. The Joint Committee on Reorganization in Congress, after examining the task force report, realized that many of the traditional alignments between Congress and the departments were being threatened by the reorganization plan. In addition, the Joint Committee realized that the executive branch was seeking to manage departmental organization, an area previously controlled by Congress through the authorizing legislation. The executive branch had never sought to challenge that organization or to put forward proposals for new departments; this had always been the prerogative of Congress. Most of the reorganization proposals put forward by Harding died in Congress, but one survived: the creation of a Bureau of the Budget to oversee the development of a unified federal budget. Congress soon passed the Budget and Accounting Act of 1921, which created the Bureau of the Budget within the Treasury Department.

The creation of the Bureau of the Budget was a major step forward for presidential management of the executive branch, because it created for the first time a uniform federal budget rather than a series of departmental submissions to Congress. As the momentum was growing for greater presidential control over the budget and management of the executive branch, one group, the Institute for Government Research, a predecessor to the Brookings Institution, went so far as to recommend that the Bureau of the Budget become a staff agency directly under the president. This recommendation would become a reality when the **Reorganization Act of 1939** allowed President Roosevelt to move the Bureau of the Budget into the newly created **Executive Office of the President.**

When Warren Harding died in 1923 and Calvin Coolidge succeeded to the presidency, the momentum that reorganization had gained was lost. Although Coolidge saw reorganization as beneficial to presidential management of the executive branch, he was unwilling to challenge Congress and to actively support the task force recommendations. When members of his cabinet testified before the Joint Committee on Reorganization that the reorganization plan would not be beneficial, Coolidge let them testify and offered no criticism.

The process of reexamining presidential management of the executive branch finally took a major leap forward after Coolidge left office and Herbert Hoover was inaugurated. Hoover, who had served as President Harding's Secretary of Commerce and as President Wilson's U.S. Food Administrator during World War I, had a clear view of government organization and management practices. For Hoover, reorganization of the departments would improve how the departments delivered their programs and would improve the president's ability to coordinate their programs. However, Congress refused to accept many of the recommendations for reorganization from the past few years or those that were developed under Hoover.

While Congress did not accept most of the reorganization plans put forth during the first three decades of the twentieth century, the debate on how the executive branch should be managed had become a major point of discussion. This discussion alone was important, for it acknowledged the growing responsibilities of the executive branch and the need to centralize management under the president. While no conclusion was reached during this period, the discussion was symbolic of the changing relationship between the president and Congress and the increasing responsibility that the burgeoning federal government was placing on presidential management. The increasing pressure to develop a more manageable structure for the executive branch through reorganization planning was a significant step in the evolution of the presidency.

The New Deal and the Brownlow Committee

By the time of the election of 1932, management of the executive branch had become a central campaign issue. Both Hoover and his challenger, Franklin Delano Roosevelt, sought to include some form of reorganization planning in their campaigns. With Hoover's defeat in the 1932 election, Roosevelt became the new champion of reorganization. Roosevelt's decision to support reorganization planning was largely born of necessity, for when he took office the federal budget was in disarray. Federal revenues were significantly down following the 1929 stock market crash and the entire economy was in decline.

Roosevelt created two advisory groups to help devise ideas to improve presidential management of the executive branch. The first advisory structure focused on creating new programs and the second group focused on improving management of the executive branch. The first group was assembled by Samuel I. Rosenman, a justice of the New York State Supreme Court and a political supporter of Roosevelt.[7] During the 1932 presidential campaign, Rosenman strongly urged Roosevelt to assemble a group made up of university faculty to discuss national problems and to propose solutions. The group that emerged was made up primarily of members of the Columbia University faculty, a logical choice for Roosevelt who was serving as governor of New York during his presidential campaign. They wrote speeches for Roosevelt, developed background memoranda, and hashed out new proposals with him. They became his personal think tank, arguing for new programs and proposing new agenda items. Once elected, Roosevelt took many members of this group to Washington, placing them in various government positions. The group continued to advise Roosevelt regularly once he moved into the White House, as had many presidential kitchen cabinets. Called the **brains trust** by the *New York Times* because of their university affiliations, the group became a key part of the president's advisory circle.

The second advisory structure that Roosevelt created were advisory councils focused on management of the executive branch rather than on programs and initiatives, which the brains trust had concentrated on. As one of his earliest moves toward improving presidential management of the executive branch, Roosevelt created the National Emergency Council in 1933, with the task "to centralize the work of putting the country back on its feet."[8] But little came of the council's activities. While the National Emergency Council failed to spark significant recommendations for change, another planning group did. The National Resources Planning Board, created in 1933 under the original name of the National Resources Committee, was staffed with a small group from the brains trust. The group included the president's uncle, Frederick Delano, who was also a well-known city planner, Wesley Mitchell, a Columbia University economist, and Charles E. Merriam of the University of Chicago. The group was supposed to focus on natural resource and environmental planning, but quickly saw their charge as much larger in a managerial sense. In June 1935 they recommended to the president (using their new name of the National Resources Committee) that he strengthen his own staff, rather than reorganize the executive branch, with six "disinterested" individuals who would oversee various parts of the New Deal programs.

The National Resources Committee turned for advice to Louis Brownlow, who was the director of the Public Administration Clearing House in Chicago, an independent agency that was closely aligned with the University of Chicago. Brownlow urged Roosevelt and the committee to approach natural resource planning using solid management and administration techniques. Merriam supported Brownlow's vision of planning, but urged Roosevelt to go one step further by improving the president's management capabilities throughout the entire federal government. Merriam thought that solid management and administration techniques should be used across the federal government, not merely in natural resources planning. Merriam and Brownlow proposed to Roosevelt during late 1935 that the National Resources Committee should ask the Social Sciences Research Council, a nonprofit think tank, to prepare a management study of the federal government. The council would, according to Merriam, prepare recommendations to help "the Executive Office to be developed on the side of management and administrative supervision." The most important point made by Merriam in this proposal with direct regard to presidential management was the role that the President's staff would have in overall management, the organization of that staff, and their role with regard to the agencies.[9]

Although Roosevelt supported the concept of such a management study, he was not happy that the study would be funded by the Rockefeller Foundation, given the Republican leanings of the Rockefeller family. Instead, rather than a private study committee, Roosevelt chose to create a public study committee in 1936. Roosevelt chose Brownlow to chair the committee. The three-member committee was rounded out with Lewis Merriam of the Brookings Institution and Luther Gulick, director of the Institute of Public Administration.

By November 1936, the committee had developed an overview for presidential management of the executive branch and a proposal for enhancing the president's ability to handle that management. The report prepared by the panel, generally referred to as the **Brownlow Committee,** recommended that:

- the president should be the center of managerial direction and control of all executive branch departments and agencies;
- the president does not presently have adequate legal authority or administrative machinery to centrally manage and control the departments and agencies; and
- the restoration of the president to a position of central management and control of the executive branch will require certain changes in law and administrative practice.

In order to accomplish these goals, the report recommended that the president strengthen his management capabilities by:

- making staff or institutional agencies directly responsible to the president, who would establish a White House secretariat headed by an executive secretary who would maintain communication with all such agencies, except the Bureau of the Budget, which should report directly to the president;
- granting the president continuing executive branch reorganization power, conditioned by congressional veto authority, with reorganization research supported by the Bureau of the Budget, and
- giving the president power to create temporary emergency agencies, when conditions warrant, and authority to transfer the activities of these agencies into the permanent executive branch establishment after an emergency has passed.[10]

Roosevelt accepted all of the recommendations except that of a White House secretariat. Instead he wanted formal presidential assistants. The Brownlow Committee translated this request into an organizational unit called the "Executive Office of the President" and called for six presidential assistants to work directly with the president in the new Executive Office. Roosevelt concurred, and he supported submitting the report to Congress for action, which he did in January 1937.

The panel's report was all but forgotten in Congress as Roosevelt sent a request to increase the membership of the Supreme Court to Congress three weeks later. His "court-packing" proposal dominated congressional discussions and the reorganization plans became lost in congressional politics. According to Donald Stone, director of the Bureau of the Budget under President Truman, Congress "was stunned" by the Brownlow Committee's recommendations. Between the court-packing scheme and the reorganization proposal, Stone noted that "the members of Congress and other opposed groups alleged that the President was trying to become a dictator."[11] Congress was not about to pass the reorganization plan after the court-packing maneuver.

Not surprisingly, Roosevelt's popularity slipped in 1937 but was bolstered in 1938 with proposals for an economic recovery bill. By 1939, Congress was again supporting the president and passed the Brownlow Committee's report, providing the president reorganization authority for the executive branch as a tool to promote efficient presidential management. Following passage of the **Reorganization Act of 1939,** Roosevelt issued Executive Order 8248 on September 28, 1939, creating **The Executive Office of the President** (EOP). Roosevelt finally had a tool for managing the executive branch (Figure 6.1).

The Executive Office of the President that was created had six units:

1. A White House Office with six administrative assistants for the president in addition to the existing personal aides and the clerical offices.
2. The Bureau of the Budget, relocated from the Treasury Department.
3. A National Resources Planning Board.
4. A Liaison Office for Personnel Management.
5. An Office of Government Reports.
6. An Office of Emergency Management.[12]

By the end of President Truman's term, Congress had added several more units to the Executive Office of the President: the Council of Economic Advisers, the Central Intelligence Agency, the National Security Council, and the National Security Resources Board. Throughout the administrations of every successive president, units within the Executive Office of the President have varied, as both the presidents and Congress have made additions and deletions. Since 1939, forty separate units have been added to the Executive Office of the President by various presidents, although most were disbanded by later administrations. There are currently approximately twelve units within the Executive Office of the President. By 1998, the Executive Office of the President totaled approximately 1,800 employees, with budgets totaling over $200 million (Figure 6.2).

Presidents have increasingly relied on the Executive Office of the President as a master key in the tools available for managing the executive branch. Regardless of how many campaign promises are made to cut the federal bureaucracy, the Executive Office of the President is rarely included in the staff reductions once the administration takes office. Several years ago at the Symposium on American Politics held at Boston College, Hugh Heclo observed that in spite of differing political philosophies and personal governing styles, all recent presidents have heavily used and often expanded the role of the Executive Office of the President. Remarking on Reagan's

White House Office	Bureau of the Budget
National Resources Planning Board	Liasion Office for Personnel Management
Emergency Management Office	Office of Government Reports

FIGURE 6.1   Executive Office of the President: 1939.

White House Office	Office of Management and Budget
Office of the Vice President	U.S. Trade Representative
Office of the First Lady	Office of Policy Development
National Security Council	Office of Science and Technology
Council of Economic Advisers	Office of National Drug Control Policy
Council on Environmental Quality	Office of Administration
President's Foreign Intelligence Advisory Board	

FIGURE 6.2   Executive Office of the President: 1998.

heavy use of the EOP, particularly through David Stockman and the Office of Management and Budget, Heclo astutely commented, "If this is what has happened with an antigovernment party in power, the aspirations of the Executive Office of the President founders may not be so archaic after all."[13]

The following section provides an overview of many of the stronger units of the Executive Office of the President that exist today. Many of these units are housed in the Old Executive Office Building, next door to the White House. Their proximity to White House staff allows for constant interaction on matters of departmental budgeting, program management, and legislative clearance issues. Without the information provided by the Executive Office of the President's units, the White House staff would be unable to advise the president in as much detail as they now do. The list that follows includes the three oldest units in the Executive Office of the President (the Office of Management and Budget, the Council of Economic Advisers, and the National Security Council) plus the newer units that are currently operating (the Council on Environmental Quality, the U.S. Trade Representative, the Office of Administration, the Office of Science and Technology, the Office of National Drug Control Policy, the President's Foreign Intelligence Advisory Board, and the Office of Policy Development).

The Office of Management and Budget
(Bureau of the Budget)

The largest unit within the EOP is the **Office of Management and Budget** (OMB), described by Larry Berman as the "most highly developed administrative coordinating and program review unit in the Executive Office of the President."[14] The agency is responsible for preparing the president's budget requests to Congress, advising the president on legislative proposals from the departments, and improving interagency coordination.

Created in 1970, the OMB was built on the foundations of the **Bureau of the Budget.** President Nixon reorganized the Bureau of the Budget, adding numerous responsibilities and renaming it the Office of Management and Budget. The expanded role of the new office involved not only budget preparation but an expanded role in coordinating and managing departmental budgets. Nixon's larger goal of enhancing presidential management of the executive branch was the primary reason for redesigning the role of the Bureau of the Budget, and the management role of the new Office of Management and Budget was central to Nixon's efforts to presidentialize the bureaucracy. As President Taft had found a half century earlier, the executive departments often acted with little coordination in their program or budget planning. The OMB constituted a major step toward effective management of the executive branch. Robert Taft and Frederick Cleveland had started the process moving; Nixon finally made one part of the process a reality.

Prior to 1921, when the Bureau of the Budget was created, the president's budget was assembled by the Department of the Treasury. Treasury requested that every executive department prepare an annual budget, which were then compiled and sent to Congress with little alteration. No attempt was made to ensure that programs did not overlap or duplicate each other, and no attempt was made to bring revenues in line with expenditures. Because revenues generally exceeded expenditures during the nineteenth century, the process of balancing the budget was not of particular concern. The president had little or no discussion with the Treasury Department before the budget was sent to Congress.

When President Taft's Commission on Economy and Efficiency examined the roles of the various executive departments in 1912, they found that the budget was rarely developed as a unified program for national spending. The Taft Commission recommended designing a new budget process that would give the president substantial responsibility for comprehensive budgetary planning. Opposition in Congress during the Taft administration and the First World War during the Wilson administration put the budget issue on the back burner of legislation. When Warren Harding took office, the issue resurfaced, and in 1921 the Budget and Accounting Act was passed by Congress, which provided for the Bureau of the Budget to develop the federal budget. Agencies would submit their budgets to the Bureau of the Budget, but all of the departmental budgets would be evaluated and revised around a single presidential budget. The Bureau of the Budget would continue to be located within the Treasury Department, but it would have a director and an assistant director appointed by the president. The first head of the Bureau of the Budget was General Charles G. Dawes. He viewed himself as an assistant to the president whose job was to bring economy and efficiency to the federal government through the budget process. Dawes saw the Bureau of the Budget as the heart of the move to bring about the economy and efficiency in government that the Taft Commission had so eloquently supported a decade earlier.

When Franklin Delano Roosevelt entered office, he encouraged further efforts to improve presidential management of the executive branch. Roosevelt encouraged the Committee on Administrative Management, chaired by Louis Brownlow, to consider not only White House staffing assistance but also institutional assistance for improving presidential management of the executive branch. When he met with the leaders of Congress to support the recommendations of the Brownlow Committee, Roosevelt sought institutional help from the Bureau of the Budget. He said that,

> I also need managerial agencies to help me in this job on fiscal, personnel and planning. Greater aid should be given to me by the Bureau of the Budget, which now reports to me directly. It should be authorized to improve its staff and to perform certain services on coordination of informational activities.[15]

Roosevelt was successful in enlarging the scope of responsibility of the Bureau of the Budget, for Executive Order 8248 (which created the Executive Office of the President) of September 8, 1939, broadened the role of the Bureau of the Budget to not only develop the federal budget but to advise the president on proposed legislation. The Bureau of the Budget was no longer simply a staffing unit that developed a unified budget; now it was a staffing unit that oversaw how legislative proposals from the departments met the president's budget objectives. In essence, the Bureau of the Budget had become a legislative clearinghouse after 1939 in addition to its traditional budget role (Figure 6.3).

Office	Established
Office of Administration	1977–
National Council on the Arts	1964–1965
Bureau of the Budget	1939–1970
Office of Civil and Defense Mobilization	1958–1961
Committee for Congested Production Areas	1943–1944
Office on Consumer Affairs	1971–1973
Office of Defense and Civilian Mobilization	1958–1958
Office of Defense Mobilization	1950–1953, 1953–1958
Domestic Council	1970–1977
Domestic Policy Staff	1977–
Office of Drug Abuse Policy	1976–1977
Special Action Office for Drug Abuse Prevention	1971–1975
Council of Economic Advisers	1946–
Office of Economic Opportunity	1964–1975
Council on Economic Policy	1973–1974
Office of Emergency Management	1940–
Office of Emergency Planning	1961–1968
Office of Emergency Preparedness	1968–1973
Office of First Lady	N/A
Office of Environmental Policy	N/A
Energy Policy Office	1973–1974
Energy Resources Council	1974–1977
Council on Environmental Quality	1970–
Federal Energy Office	1973–1974; 1976–1976
Federal Property Council	1973–1977
Office of Government Reports	1939–1942. 1946–1948
Office of Intergovernmental Relations	1969–1972
Council on International Economic Policy	1971–1977
Office of Management and Budget	1971–
National Council on Marine Resources and Engineering Development	1966–1971
Mutual Security Agency	1951–1953
National Aeronautics and Space Council	1958–1973
National Critical Materials Council	1984–
Office of National AIDS Policy	N/A
Office of National Drug Control Policy	1988–
National Economic Council	1993–

Continued

FIGURE 6.3   Executive Office of the President Units: 1939–1998.

Office	Established
National Energy Office	1973–1973
National Resources Planning Board	1939–1943
National Security Council	1949–
National Security Resources Board	1949–1953
National Space Council	1988–
Operations Coordinating Board	1953–1957
Liaison Office for Personnel Management	1939–1953
Office of Policy Development	1971–1977; 1981–
Presidential Clemency Board	1974–1975
President's Economic Policy Board	1974–1977
Council for Rural Affairs	1969–1970
Office of Science and Technology	1962–1973
Office of Science and Technology Policy	1976–
Office of the Special Representative for Trade Negotiations	1963–1979
Telecommunications Adviser to the President	1951–1953
Office of Telecommunications Policy	1970–1977
Office of the U.S. Trade Representative	1979–
Council for Urban Affairs	1969–1970
Office of the Vice President	N/A
U.S. Trade Representative	1974–
Council on Wage and Price Stability	1974–1981
War Refugee Board	1944–1945
White House Office	1939–

Source: Harold Relyea. *The Executive Office of the President.* Westport, CT: Greenwood Press, 1997; Richard Pious. *The Presidency.* Boston: Allyn and Bacon, 1996.

FIGURE 6.3   Continued

In 1970 the agency underwent another major change when President Nixon further increased its management responsibilities and renamed the unit the Office of Management and Budget. During the transition following his 1968 election, Nixon created a task force on the organization of the Executive Office of the President. The task force recommended that the most important task for the president was to broaden his management capability for the entire executive branch by expanding the responsibilities of the EOP. On April 15, 1969, Nixon announced the creation of the Advisory Council on Executive Organization, under the direction of Roy Ash, chairman of Litton Industries. The **Ash Council** made its recommendations to Nixon in October 1969 and on March 12, 1970, the president issued Reorganization Plan No. 2 to implement those recommendations. The reorganization plan called for the Bureau of the Budget to gain new responsibilities, and its name changed to the Office of Management and Budget to reflect those responsibilities.

Much as the Taft Commission and the Brownlow Committee had been charged with developing reorganization proposals for the president, the Ash Council had been charged with expanding the president's ability to manage the evergrowing executive branch. The reorganization message that Nixon sent to Congress noted that the main goal of the new Office of Management and Budget would not be preparation of the budget, but to assess "the extent to which programs are actually achieving their intended results, and delivering the intended services to the intended recipients."[16] The new agency would give the president greater control over managing the executive branch, with the ability to both control the departmental budgets but also to conduct program evaluations and recommend improvements in program management.

With the formalization of the enhanced management role of the Office of Management and Budget in 1970, Nixon wanted to establish a closer role between the White House staff and the OMB staff. This new role brought the director of the OMB directly into the White House, where an office was provided in the West Wing. In 1973 the director of the OMB was given the additional title of *assistant to the president*, further tightening the relationship between the president's personal staff and the staff of the OMB. The staff of the OMB are housed in the Old Executive Office Building.

Since 1921, when Charles Dawes first directed the cabinet officers to submit their budget requests to the Bureau of the Budget rather than to Congress, the Bureau of the Budget has developed the federal budget. Each department is now requested by the OMB to develop its budget requests around one of four themes: increasing the departmental budget, decreasing the departmental budget, freezing the budget, or holding the line but allowing for inflationary increases. Departments develop their budget proposals, send them to the Office of Management and Budget, and then begin discussion sessions if the OMB staff do not like the budget numbers that the departments submit. Once the departments and the Office and Management and Budget staff have agreed on budget numbers, the White House staff meets with the Office of Management and Budget staff to ensure that the final budget picture meets the political goals of the president. For example, President Bush's Budget Director, Richard Darman, worked closely with White House chief of staff John Sununu to keep the federal budget from requiring new tax revenues. During the 1988 presidential campaign, Bush had promised not to raise taxes through his famous quip "Read my lips. No new taxes." Darman's job was to ensure that the federal budget did not require new tax dollars in order to go forward.

The original mandate of the Bureau of the Budget to foster economy and efficiency in government remains an essential goal of the expanded agency. Overseeing budget cuts and program reorganization has been easier for the Office of Management and Budget to handle than working on new program initiatives has been. Also, adding to the budget has been harder for OMB staff than cutting the budget has been. As a result, there have been uneasy relationships at times between White House staff, who want the president to create new programs in areas that satisfy campaign goals, and the OMB staff, who want to minimize new expenditures. Even in 1998, when the federal budget saw significant surpluses under the Clinton administration, the Office of Management and Budget continued to resist adding funds to existing programs or supporting new initiatives.

In addition to its role as the budget officer for the president, the OMB prepares the detailed analysis of every enrolled bill sent to the president from Congress and recommends whether the president should sign, veto, or simply allow the bill to become law. Since the Constitution requires that the president make a decision on bills within 10 days (Sundays excepted), OMB prepares its analyses for the president during the first five days and gives the White House staff the second five days for its review. When the OMB recommends that the president sign the bill or allow it to become law without his signature, the president nearly always follows the advice. When the OMB recommends a veto, there is less certainty that the president will follow the advice because White House staff often fear political repercussions.

Yet another role of the Office of Management and Budget is to prepare executive orders and proclamations. The agency works with the affected agencies on the impact of the executive order or proclamation, develops analyses of the cost benefit, and makes a recommendation to the president on whether the executive order or proclamation should be carried out.

Since 1970 the management role of the Office of Management and Budget has become one of its largest responsibilities. The Office of Information and Regulatory Affairs in OMB reviews all regulations proposed by the departments, a process known as regulatory clearance. During the Bush administration Vice President Quayle briefly took over this role, but the OMB resumed the role after the Bush presidency. The Division of Federal Procurement Policy examines departmental programs and recommends methods for purchasing goods at a lower price. For example, because of recommendations made by OMB for reducing purchasing costs, departments were encouraged to use the Internet for purchasing materials and buying in bulk. The cumbersome procedures that had guided departmental purchases for years, and had often led to unnecessary costs, were overhauled by OMB as part of its management operations.

The Office of Management and Budget is the largest of the staff agencies of the EOP, advising the president on the budget, legislative clearance, and departmental management issues. Of all the units of the EOP, the OMB provides the broadest range of advisory functions. As a result, its staff and budget are the largest of any unit.

The Council of Economic Advisers

Soon after EOP began functioning as a staff agency for the president, Congress realized that the president needed not only personal staff but professional staff. This was particularly true in the post-Depression years, as the nation struggled to pull itself out of economic recession. In 1946 Congress passed the Full Employment Act, which included a section creating the **Council of Economic Advisers** within the EOP. The Council was statutorily charged with providing the president economic advice on current and future economic conditions, recommending programs and policies that the federal government could undertake to strengthen the economy, and preparing economic reports for the president. The council has three presidentially appointed members, one of whom is designated the chair, and all are subject to the approval of the Senate. The three members of the Council of Economic Advisers were the first officials within the EOP to be subject to Senate confirmation.[17]

The chair can come from the ranks of the current council or can be appointed from outside the council. In 1993, President Clinton appointed Laura D'Andrea Tyson as chair of the Council of Economic Advisers. Tyson had worked on the 1992 campaign, serving as Clinton's economic adviser while maintaining her position as an economics professor at the University of California, Berkeley. When Tyson moved to the White House later in the administration to head the National Economic

Council, Clinton appointed Alice Rivlin from the Office of Management and Budget to head the council.

More often than not, the chair has been appointed from outside the ranks of the council. The chair usually has a Ph.D. in economics, is a senior faculty member at a major university, and is well connected within political circles. The council has approximately thirty members, all of whom serve at the pleasure of the president. The backgrounds of the staff include international economics and trade, public finance, taxation, macroeconomics, and more specific areas such as energy, transportation, banking, health, and welfare. Usually each president appoints an entirely new staff for the council, which means that the institutional memory of the council is severely limited. The high staff turnover is in contrast to the stability of the career staff that exists in the OMB, although many senior OMB staff are political staff rather than career staff. The OMB therefore brings more of an institutional memory to the presidency.

The chair of the Council of Economic Advisers is one of the president's primary economic advisers, often meeting with the cabinet and with the president's senior staff. The chair is one of the three members of the "triad" (including the Secretary of the Treasury and the director of the Office of Management and Budget) who advise the president on economic issues. The triad meets regularly to discuss fiscal and budgetary issues facing the administration. In addition, the chair of the Federal Reserve Board frequently meets with the triad in what has become known as the "quadriad."

Each January the Council of Economic Advisers is required by Congress to prepare the Annual Economic Report to the President, which is transmitted to Congress with a presidential message as a cover. The economic report provides analyses of federal expenditures and revenues and examines both current economic conditions and those projected for the future. In essence, the role of the Council of Economic Advisers has been to develop short-term analyses that provide the president and administration policy makers advice on current economic issues.

The National Security Council

In 1947, the third major unit to be created within the Executive Office of the President was the **National Security Council.** Following World War II, Congress sought to increase the president's national security apparatus. The National Security Act, which became law on July 26, 1947, created a unified Department of Defense. (first discussed by the Taft Commission on Efficiency and Economy in 1921), the Central Intelligence Agency, and the National Security Council. Each of these components of the national security apparatus was geared to providing information to the president for making decisions on matters of national security.

The National Security Council was charged by Congress with advising the president with respect to the integration of domestic, foreign, and military policies that involved national security. Chaired by the president, the statutory members of the council were the vice president, the secretary of defense, and the secretary of state. In addition to the statutory members of the council, the act provided for the chairman of the Joint Chiefs of Staff and the director of the Central Intelligence Agency to serve as advisers. Presidents can also appoint other advisers to the council, such as members of their White House staff. Most recent presidents have included their chief of staff and their national security adviser as advisers to the National Security Council.

The National Security Council has become the most important source of national security information and advice that the president uses. To the dismay of some cabinet officers, presidents rely on the large staff within the National Security Council for most of their national security policy advice. One famous instance of a cabinet secretary becoming concerned about the power of the National Security Council occurred in its formative years. Secretary of Defense James Forrestal emphasized to President Truman that the National Security Act stated that the "Secretary of Defense shall be the principal assistant to the President in all matters relating to national security."[18] In spite of Forrestal's efforts to keep the national security advisory structure firmly held in the Department of Defense, it has moved to the White House and the National Security Council.

The National Security Council has gained a significant part of its power from the role that its staff director has played as a senior member of the White House staff. Since Robert Cutler was sworn in as the first National Security Adviser in January 1953 by President Eisenhower, the role has changed significantly. Cutler saw his role as a policy coordinator, not as a policy maker.[19] When Henry Kissinger was appointed by President Nixon to the dual roles of staff director of the National Security Council and the newly created role of Assistant to the President for National Security Affairs, the National Security Council became a central player in White House decision making. Kissinger used his staff as a means of building information for dealing with the Vietnam War, building bridges to the Soviet Union, and opening the door to China. Under Walter Rostow during the Johnson Administration, the National Security Council staff had approximately 12 professional members. Under Kissinger, that number grew to 50. By the end of the Bush administration, the number had grown to 70 professional staff and 101 support staff.[20] The Clinton administration reduced the number slightly to a total of 147 professional and support staff. These numbers, it should be noted, are only approximate, since presidents often have more staff members than are officially released due to a process known as "detailing."

Other executive departments often lend the president's advisory units, such as the National Security Council, staff members, or "detailees." These detailees are often not counted in the official staffing size released by the advisory units. All presidents use this process to expand the number of positions within the EOP. Not only the size but the composition of the National Security Council staff has changed since its inception. When the National Security Council was created by Congress in 1947, President Truman asked the executive departments to provide staff for the National Security Council. President Kennedy changed this practice and appointed all of the staff directly from the White House, without working through the departments. Presidents since Kennedy have followed the practice of appointing all of the staff directly through the White House personnel operation.

The composition of the National Security Council staff and the background of the staff director are often reflections of how the president addresses national security policy. President Carter, committed to a foreign policy program focused on international human rights and on reducing military expenditures, chose a Columbia University professor, Zbigniew Brzezinski, to head his national security staff. In contrast, President Reagan, committed to increasing military expenditures and bringing down the Soviet Union, chose career military men Robert McFarlane, John Poindexter, and Colin Powell for national security advisers. Even Reagan's Secretary of State, General Alexander Haig, and his Secretary of Defense, Caspar W. Weinberger, the former director of a military defense industry, had strong ties to the military.

Today presidents rely heavily on the advice of the national security advisers. When President Bush was considering the options in the Persian Gulf situation after Iraq invaded Kuwait, General Brent Scowcroft, his national security adviser, was one of the president's closest confidantes. The national security adviser has an office in the west wing of the White House, with very close proximity to the president. The majority of the staff of the National Security Council are located in the Old Executive Office Building, along with other staffing units within the EOP. When Oliver North became embroiled in the Iran–contra events, he operated from his office in the Old Executive Office Building.

The national security adviser is far more visible than is the National Security Council. Although the council meets when national security is at issue, the staff of the National Security Council have become an institutionalized part of the president's advisory structure. The national security adviser regularly meets with the president, regularly attends senior staff meetings, and represents the president on national security matters before House and Senate committee hearings. Unlike the Council of Economic Advisers, the National Security Council is not required to prepare an annual summary for Congress. The National Security Council rarely discusses its findings in public, instead serving as a confidential adviser to the president.

Some national security advisers have been more outspoken in the media than others. Henry Kissinger was a regular contributor to the morning news shows and was a willing discussant for newspaper reporters. During the Carter administration Zbigniew Brzezinski was also quite accessible to the media. In contrast, Brent Scowcroft in the Bush administration and Anthony Lake in the Clinton administration shied away from the public forum and rarely gave interviews to the media. Ronald Reagan had a series of national security advisers, all of whom were reluctant to be presidential spokesmen for foreign policy or national security issues. Even when one of Reagan's national security advisers, Admiral John Poindexter, became embroiled in a heated debate with chief of staff Donald Regan over the president's role in the Iran–contra affair, Poindexter remained out of the public eye. President Clinton's second national security adviser, Samuel "Sandy" Berger, was less reticent than Anthony Lake in seeking the public limelight and was regularly available to the media.

During the post-Vietnam years, the National Security Council has become the principal forum for gathering foreign policy information and for providing the president advice on both national security issues and foreign policy issues. Most presidents enter office with little knowledge of the nation's foreign policy machinery or the foreign and national security issues facing the nation. The availability of an in-house advisory structure of foreign policy experts has enabled the president to obtain detailed briefings on a regular basis. In addition, the national security staff provides the president a coordinating mechanism for the various parts of the foreign policy agencies, including the Departments of Defense and State, the Central Intelligence Agency, and the intelligence units within the Defense Department.

Council on Environmental Quality

Soon after Richard Nixon took office, the National Environmental Policy Act of 1969 was passed by Congress, which established the **Council on Environmental Quality** (CEQ) within the EOP. The Council on Environmental Quality had been included in 1967 legislation sponsored by Senator Henry Jackson (D-Wash.), who had been a major supporter of environmental programs, but had failed to pass. Although Nixon did not actively support the legislation, he did not oppose it when it was finally passed by Congress in 1969 as part of the National Environmental Policy Act. Additional responsibilities for the CEQ were provided the following year in the Environmental Quality Improvement Act of 1970.

The purpose of the council is to develop a coherent environmental policy and to assess environmental policies that are proposed by other governmental units. Members of the Council routinely work with cabinet officers to ensure that departmental programs are sensitive to environmental issues. This has been particularly true with the Department of Transportation, where the nation's highway proposals are routinely subjected to environmental protection standards.

The Council has three members appointed by the president; one of those members is appointed to serve as chair. A professional staff of economists, environmentalists, and other public policy experts work with the three-member council. This structure is identical to that of the Council of Economic Advisers. The first director of the Council of Environmental Quality was Under Secretary of the Interior Russell E. Train, who had a strong commitment to the environment and a working knowledge of government programs. The other two members of the original council were an environmental reporter for the *Christian Science Monitor*, Robert Cahn, and the vice chancellor of the University of California at Santa Barbara, Gordon MacDonald. By the end of the Nixon administration, the staff of the council had grown to sixty.

During the Carter administration the staff continued to grow, and they actively provided policy reports to the White House staff. One of the most lasting contributions of the Carter years was the effort by the council to have communities routinely consider in their zoning decisions the loss of farmland to development. The council was instrumental in working with the executive departments, particularly the Department of Housing and Urban Development, to ensure that federal funds did not contribute to the loss of farmland. One innovative idea that emerged during this period was to allow communities to have land banks of farmland. Communities would pay farmers not to sell their farms in a process called "transfer of development rights." In another case of the activism of the council under the Carter administration, the council issued a report that urged communities to regularly test their water, noting that some water additives possibly caused cancer.

Ronald Reagan had less interest in the Council on Environmental Quality than had any of his predecessors. He sought to increase the staff of the National Security Council, not the Council on Environmental Quality. Consequently, the Council on Environmental Quality lost significant numbers of staff, dropping to nine during the Reagan years. The number grew to thirty during the Bush administration, but was again reduced under the Clinton administration to less than a dozen. The activism of the council during the Carter years and the significant size of its staff proved to be the exception rather than the rule.

President Clinton attempted to abolish the Council on Environmental Quality during the first year of his administration, but since Congress had created it, only Congress could abolish it. The council became the smallest of the units within the EOP during the Clinton administration, as President Clinton moved much of its work to the Environmental Protection Agency. Clinton saw the Environmental Protection Agency as the more logical agency to coordinate environmental policies. During the 1992 presidential campaign, Clinton pledged to reduce the size of government, including the size of the EOP. He specifically pledged to cut twenty-five percent from the White House staff and the EOP. Cuts to the Environmental Quality Council provided some of the necessary staff reductions, since the Environmental Protection Agency could handle much of the work. Although the council was not disbanded by the Clinton administration because of its statutory mandate, it's staff size and policy responsibility were reduced.

During most of the Clinton administration the Council on Environmental Quality was chaired by Kathleen A. McGinty, a former staff member from Vice President Gore's Senate office. McGinty originally joined the White House staff as director of the National Environmental Council, one of three units in the Office of Policy Development. When the tasks of the National Environmental Council came into conflict with those of the Council of Environmental Quality, President Clinton merged the two and placed McGinty in charge. The Office of Policy Development continued to operate with the National Economic Council and the Domestic Policy Council.

Office of the U.S. Trade Representative

The need to oversee the political debate about protective tariffs and the consequences of both domestic and international policy has brought trade policy under the direct supervision of the president. The **Office of the U.S. Trade Representative** (USTR) is now one of the larger units within the EOP, with a staff of approximately 160 in Washington, D.C., and in Geneva, Switzerland. The staff in Washington, D.C., is housed in the Winder Building, one block from the White House.

The trade representative emerged during the Kennedy administration, when President Kennedy was negotiating a round of multilateral trade talks with the European Economic Community. Members of Congress, most notably Congressman Wilbur Mills (D-Ark.), chair of the House Ways and Means Committee, felt that the trade talks had been handled poorly by the State Department. Some members of Congress were angry with the State Department for failing to consider business interests when trade barriers such as tariffs were imposed. Mills successfully inserted into the congressional authorization for the new round of trade talks that a special trade representative, reporting directly to the president, handle the talks rather than representatives of the State Department. The Office of the U.S. Trade Representative was created by Congress in the Trade Expansion Act of 1962 and implemented by President Kennedy in Executive Order 11075 on January 15, 1963. Kennedy immediately named Christian A. Herter the first special trade representative within the newly created Office of the U.S. Trade Representative in the EOP.

The executive order authorized the trade representative to establish all of the nation's official trade policy and to serve as the nation's chief trade negotiator. This role continues today—President Clinton's trade representative is an integral part of administration decision making on trade policy. One of the changes that has been made since the Kennedy administration is the title. President Carter changed the official title of the trade representative in 1979 from the Special Trade Representative, which Christian A. Herter was given under President Kennedy, to the current title, U.S. Trade Representative.

The trade representatives were so successful in the 1960s and 1970s that Congress expanded the job in the Trade Act of 1974 and expanded their powers and responsibilities for coordinating trade policy. When President Carter entered office, he asked Congress for a larger staff and more authority for the trade office, which was approved in Reorganization Plan No. 3 of 1979. The staff grew from 59 to 131 after the reorganization plan went into effect, and its mandate involved the full range of international trade, policy development, coordination, and negotiation functions. In 1993, the Office of the Trade Representative successfully negotiated the North American Free Trade Agreement (NAFTA), which ended tariffs on trade in North America, and became a centerpiece of the first-term legislative successes for the Clinton administration.

The principal goal of the Office of the U.S. Trade Representative is to increase trade opportunities for U.S. companies, encouraging efforts to liberalize rather than tighten trade policy. Many of the tariffs and other restrictions in trade that were imposed years ago during a period of protectionism have been lifted through the efforts of the Trade Representative. As the leading agency on trade policy, the Trade Representative works closely with other departments such as Commerce, State, Treasury and Agriculture. At times, the Commerce Department has sought to gain a larger position in trade policy. Secretary of Commerce Ron Brown, in the Clinton administration, was particularly active in leading trade delegations, but the role of negotiating trade agreements remains firmly seated in the Office of the U.S. Trade Representative within the EOP.

Office of Science and Technology Policy

Presidential interest in science and technology is deeply rooted in our governmental structure. President Jefferson donated his vast library, including many scientific documents, to the fledgling Library of Congress, and President Abraham Lincoln supported the charter of the National Academy of Sciences to provide scientific advice to the federal government. During the administration of Franklin Delano Roosevelt, a number of scientific advisory panels were created to examine how the federal government could utilize the latest scientific research. Roosevelt used an executive order in World War II to create the Council of National Defense to coordinate the nation's nonmilitary science resources with weapons development programs. In 1949 the Council of National Defense was disbanded and replaced by the Office of Scientific Research and Development in the Office for Emergency Management. The director of the Office of Scientific Research and Development, Vanevar Bush (dean of engineering at the Massachusetts Institute of Technology and president of the Carnegie Institution in Washington, D.C.), became a personal scientific adviser to Roosevelt.

The next major step in the evolution of the Office of Science and Technology Policy was in 1951 when President Truman issued an executive order creating the Scientific Advisory Committee (SAC) in the Office of Defense Mobilization in the EOP. Once Russia launched *Sputnik,* the role of the president's science advisers became significantly enhanced. President Eisenhower formally created a position in the White House to advise on scientific and space policy.[21]

The first formal scientific adviser to the president was appointed during the Eisenhower administration. In 1957 Eisenhower appointed James R. Killian, Jr., to serve as the first director of the Office of Special Assistant to the President for Science and Technology. Killian was an advocate for increasing federal funding in areas of science, particularly space. Not surprisingly, Killian encouraged Eisenhower to support creation of the National Aeronautics and Space Administration (NASA) and increased funding for federal science programs. Killian became a personal adviser to Eisenhower and one of his key staff within the White House. Eisenhower then went a step further by creating the President's Science Advisory Committee (PSAC) in 1957, chaired by his science adviser, and located in the White House Office. However, the office had only part-time staff and no operating budget.

During the Kennedy Administration the science adviser was reorganized under the **Office of Science and Technology** through Reorganization Plan No. 2 of 1962. This enlarged the role of the science adviser, but took the position out of the smaller White House staff and put it in the larger EOP and made the director subject to Senate confirmation. Although the office gained a larger staff and more responsibility for managing federal science programs, the role of the science adviser moved from a personal staff role on the White House staff to an agency staff role in the EOP.

During the Nixon administration, the Office of Science and Technology lost significant influence. Other offices, such as the National Security Council and the Office of Management and Budget became the dominant players in policy issues, including science and technology issues. There has also been some criticism of Lee DuBridge, the director of the Office of Science and Technology under Nixon, saying he did not understand the power relationships in the White House. He was unable to gain access to Nixon and was regularly left out of policy meetings. DuBridge's opposition to positions supported by Nixon, such as the supersonic transport, did not help his cause or that of his agency. On January 27, 1973, President Nixon submitted Reorganization Plan 1 of 1973 to Congress, which abolished the Office of Science and Technology. After the agency was abolished in 1973, many of its scientific functions were absorbed by the National Science Foundation and the national security functions were transferred to the National Security Council.

President Ford took a different view of having a science advisory unit in the EOP and supported legislation in Congress to create a new science advisory unit. The National Science and Technology Policy, Organization, and Priorities Act of 1976 created the Office of Science and Technology Policy within the Executive Office of the President, which remains in effect today. The office has a director, and up to four associate directors, all of whom are appointed by the president and are subject to Senate confirmation. Although the legislation does not mandate it, some directors of the Office of

Science and Technology Policy have also served on the White House staff as the president's science adviser. During the Ford administration, Vice President Nelson Rockefeller worked closely with the science adviser. This was in keeping with Ford's mandate that Rockefeller oversee domestic policy initiatives. During the Carter administration the office lost power and a number of its responsibilities were transferred to other agencies. Under Reagan, the office regained some of its influence in White House decision making for science and technology, largely because of its role in research and development for defense programs such as the Star Wars initiative. But in neither the Carter nor the Reagan administration did the science adviser have a White House role as an adviser or "assistant to" the president. In 1988 President Bush reversed this trend and appointed Allan Bromley director of the Office of Science and Technology and also designated him as an assistant to the president in the White House.

The Office of Science and Technology Policy was reorganized to incorporate the National Space Council in 1993, soon after President Clinton was inaugurated. The National Space Council was created by President Bush by an executive order on February 1, 1989, to be a new unit within the EOP. The Bush White House had become increasingly concerned about the growing militarization of space that had developed between the United States and the Soviet Union during the 1980s. The White House was also responding to the national attention that the space shuttle *Challenger* disaster had drawn to the space program. By tying the space program more closely to the decision-making structure within the EOP, President Bush sent a signal to the nation that space was a national priority and would be overseen from the White House. When President Clinton came into office, he tried to streamline the EOP through the merger of the National Space Council and the Office of Science and Technology Policy, giving the latter more clout within the EOP as the center of scientific advice for the president. The Carnegie Commission on Science, Technology, and Government noted of the merger that, "By strengthening the authority of the science adviser and increasing the policy orientation of scientific and technical advice, the steps taken by the Bush and Clinton administrations inaugurated a new era of presidential science advising."[22]

The current role of the Office of Science and Technology Policy is to coordinate space, science, and technology policies across the departments and work with the departments in strategic planning and evaluation. There has been a concerted effort recently to have the Office of Science and Technology Policy also work more closely with other policy coordinating offices within the Executive Office of the President, such as the Council of Economic Advisers, the National Security Council, and the Office of Management and Budget. As issues regarding science and technology permeate every aspect of policy development, the broad coordination of these policy units within the Executive Office of the President has been essential to an integrated policy process.

Office of National Drug Control Policy

One of the more visible units within the EOP in recent years has been the **Office of National Drug Control Policy,** which has the task of coordinating the federal government's response to illegal drugs. The 1988 law governing the office requires that a National Drug Control Strategy be developed by the office, which includes methods for the federal, state, and local governments to work together in controlling the flow of illegal drugs. This was the only unit in the EOP created during the Reagan administration.

The drive to create a unit within the EOP to oversee the national war on drugs began in the Senate in 1982. When an amendment creating the unit was added to an anti-crime bill, President Reagan vetoed the bill, saying that, "the creation of another layer of bureaucracy within the Executive Office of the President would produce friction, disrupt effective law enforcement, and could threaten the integrity of criminal investigation and prosecutions—the very opposite of what its proponents apparently intend."[23] Reagan, an opponent of big government, saw the creation of a drug unit in the EOP as simply the further proliferation of the bureaucracy. This was especially worrisome to Reagan, who had campaigned in his 1980 presidential election on the platform that his administration would reduce, not increase, the size of government. The 1980 campaign pledge to reduce government had been one of the cornerstones of the Reagan campaign, and creation of a new governmental unit barely a year after taking office would certainly have been damaging to his credibility.

By the end of his administration, Reagan became more interested in dealing with the drug crisis and was willing to add a coordinating mechanism within the EOP to handle the job. The timing of the creation of the Office of National Drug Control Policy in 1988 meant that he was not jeopardizing his reputation by supporting a new unit since his administration was virtually over. It also allowed him to institutionalize Nancy Reagan's commitment to anti-drug programs popularized by her "Just Say No" campaign.

President Bush continued the Office of National Drug Control Policy, adding Reagan's former Secretary of Education, William J. Bennett, to head the program. Bennett saw the position as a way to continue his crusade to enhance the nation's educational system, since too many youths were dropping out of school and many ending up in jail as a result of drugs and drug-related crimes. Bennett, a conservative Republican and political supporter of Ronald Reagan, gained immediate authority within the White House staff and the agencies as the president's representative for drug control policy. As a political insider, Bennett gave the office prestige and was able to marshal support within the agencies for coordinating policy decisions. Since the legislation did not allow Bennett to veto agency decisions on drug-control policy, he needed a comprehensive policy to support the new "War Against Drugs," as President Bush called it. Bennett pushed long prison terms for drug pushers, more police surveillance, and quicker movement against suspected dealers.[24]

Bush also saw interdiction at the nation's borders, particularly with Mexico, as a major goal for controlling the flow of drugs. The focus of the office was moved from an internal to an external structure. During the Bush administration, the coordinating efforts of the Office of National Drug Control Policy became secondary to the Immigration and Naturalization Service and the Coast Guard, which dramatically increased their efforts to stop the flow of drugs into the United States at the borders. In addition, President Bush used military support to aid Columbia and a number of Central American countries in destroying fields of hemp and other products. In one case, American troops arrested President Manuel Noriega of Panama on charges of drug trafficking. Noriega was brought to Florida, put on trial, and placed in prison following his conviction.

The Clinton administration again refocused the way in which the National Office of Drug Control Policy was used, finding a middle ground between the internal and external orientations that the Reagan and Bush administrations had on the drug war. Clinton tapped retired General Barry McCaffrey to head the office and gave McCaffrey his support to boldly deal with the nation's drug problems. McCaffrey was able to tie his military connections into the process and was able to marry the programs already underway throughout the nation with the programs initiated under the Bush administration. President Clinton, who prioritized the drug-control issue as part of his domestic program, encouraged McCaffrey's activities. In June 1998, Clinton addressed the United Nations with a speech urging international cooperation on drug control. In order to show the cooperation within his own country, Clinton brought McCaffrey, Attorney General Janet Reno, White House Latin American envoy Mack McLarty, and Health and Human Services Secretary Donna Shalala.

During the three administrations that the National Office of Drug Control Policy has existed, it has been moderately successful as a coordination mechanism for drug-control policy. Presidents Reagan, Bush, and Clinton all gave the office their support and adequate funding to work, but the office did not become a major player within the EOP. The primary reason that it failed to become a major player appears to be because the White House staff and the domestic policy office control the president's time, his schedule, and his agenda items. Because drug control is too difficult for any president to make a measurable change during the term of his administration, it becomes a low-priority topic to the politically sensitive White House staff. The creation of the National Drug Control Office is typical of the type of unit created within the EOP, for it reflects high-priority issues that the president wants to address.

Office of Policy Development

One of the larger units of the EOP is the **Office of Policy Development,** a name that varies from administration to administration. In 1964, the concept of a domestic policy unit to serve as a counterpart to the National Security Council emerged with a proposal from Richard Goodwin, one of Lyndon Johnson's senior White House staff. Goodwin suggested that the president needed a full-time domestic-policy staff, similar to the one he had with a full-time national security staff. As the Vietnam War began to dominate the president's time, the concept of a domestic-policy staff became lost in the foreign-policy problems confronting the White House. Richard Nixon was presented with the same idea of a domestic-policy staff by the Ash Council, which also proposed the creation of the Office of Management and Budget (see section on "The Office of Management and Budget above). On July 1, 1970, Nixon approved Reorganization Plan No. 2, which created the Domestic Council.

Under the reorganization plan, the Domestic Council included the President, who served as chair, the vice president, the attorney general, and the secretaries of agriculture; interior; commerce; labor; transportation; health, education and welfare; housing and urban development; and treasury. The composition of the Domestic Council paralleled that of the National Security Council, in that the president, vice president, and the pertinent cabinet officers were included. Nixon also included a number of members of the White House staff to serve on the Domestic Council to provide broad White House coordination of departmental programs and policies. By adding White House staff to the Domestic Council, Nixon completely restructured the relationship of the White House to the cabinet in domestic policy making. For the first time, the EOP and the White House staff had a direct role with the department in policy management.

The Domestic Council was charged with coordinating the Nixon administration's domestic policy agenda in an effort to reduce the often scattered approach taken by the departments. In large part, Nixon wanted to use the Domestic Council to oversee the development of a coordinated domestic policy for the administration and to ensure that the domestic policy met the political agenda of the White House. The creation of the Domestic Council was another step toward enhancing presidential management of the executive branch, for it brought under the president's immediate watch the supervision of overall domestic planning.

Throughout most of the Nixon administration, John Ehrlichman served as the staff director of the Domestic Council, and had the dual title of assistant to the president for domestic affairs. This was intended to parallel the role that Henry Kissinger played as the staff director of the National Security Council and assistant to the president for national security affairs. Ehrlichman created a significant staff for the Domestic Council, which included nearly fifty members. The staff was divided into policy units, such as community development, law enforcement, natural resources, and human resources.

When Gerald Ford took over the presidency in August 1974, following the resignation of Richard Nixon, he chose to focus on rebuilding confidence in the presidency with the American public rather than on restructuring his executive office. He continued the Domestic Council, although John Ehrlichman resigned during the Watergate problems and his deputy, Ken Cole, continued to run the Domestic Council staff for about a year until James Cannon took over during the early part of the Ford administration. The Domestic Council continued to be divided into subunits, with White House staff responsible for overseeing large policy areas, such as natural resources and community development. All the issues that arose within these policy areas from the departments were supervised by the Domestic Council staff. The White House staff, and the EOP, were completely involved in the domestic policy-making apparatus of the executive branch following the creation of the Domestic Council.

The Ford administration diverged somewhat from the Nixon administration by dividing domestic and economic policy. On September 30, 1974, President Ford created the Economic Policy Board within the EOP through Executive Order 11808. The Economic Policy Board replaced another economic policy unit that had been created barely a year earlier—Economic Policy Council. The director of both the Economic Policy Board and the Economic Policy Council included the president, the vice president, the secretaries of state, treasury, agriculture, commerce, labor, and transportation, the directors of the Office of Management and Budget and the Council of Economic Advisers, the director of the Cost of Living Council, and the executive director of the Council on International Economic Policy. The Economic Policy Board had a staff, as did both the National Security Council and the Domestic Council, with a staff director with the title *assistant to the president*.

Jimmy Carter continued the management of domestic and economic policy from the EOP, although he merged the domestic and economic units back into one unit called the "Domestic Policy Office." Soon after his inauguration, Carter gained congressional approval to reorganize the executive branch by consolidating programs, simplifying the EOP, and creating a new Energy Department. As Carter was a long-time campaigner for increasing economy and efficiency in government, the merger of the domestic and economic policy units was a logical decision for him. Carter believed that the government could be "well organized, efficient, economical, and purposeful."[25] Putting domestic and economic policy back into one unit was a statement on efficiency that Carter felt was critical to fulfilling his promise of streamlining government. Carter's Domestic Policy staff was under the direction of Stuart Eisenstat, who served both as the staff director and as assistant to the president for domestic and economic affairs. The addition of the words "and economic affairs" to his title symbolized the broad sweep that the office had gained during the Ford and Carter administrations.

The Reagan and Bush administrations followed the Carter model and kept the domestic and economic policy units under the umbrella agency, the Office of Policy Development. Under the direction of Martin Anderson and Edwin Harper in the Reagan administration and Roger Porter in the Bush administration, the White House staff and the EOP continued to hold a tight rein on the administration's domestic and economic policy activities.

As often happens when the opposite party takes control of the White House, the organizational structure of the EOP changed when Bill Clinton took office in January 1993. Clinton returned to the Ford model and separated the domestic and economic policy units, creating the Office of Policy Development with a **Domestic Policy Council** and a **National Economic Council.** In addition, the Office of Policy Development had a third unit called the "Environmental Policy Council," although this unit was small and had relatively few responsibilities. The unit was created in deference to Vice President Al Gore, who had a deep concern for environmental issues and wanted those issues at the forefront of presidential management. Clinton attempted to abolish the Council on Environmental Quality in 1994 and replace it with the Environmental Policy Council, but the Council on Environmental Quality had been created by Congress and could only be disbanded by Congress. Eventually, the Council on Environmental Quality remained and the Environmental Policy Council was collapsed, with its functions split between the Council on Environmental Quality and the Environmental Protection Agency.

The two surviving units of the Office of Policy Development, the Domestic Policy Council and the National Economic Council, were successful at overseeing the Clinton administration's domestic and economic agenda. Both units had cabinet and White House staff membership and a staff, with the staff director having the title *assistant to the president.* During Clinton's first term, Carol Rasco served as staff director of the Domestic Policy Council and Robert Rubin as staff director of the National Economic Council. Both Rasco and Rubin met regularly with Clinton and were charged by him with overseeing the administration's policy development in domestic and economic policy.

The President's Foreign Intelligence Advisory Board

One of the older units in the EOP is the **President's Foreign Intelligence Advisory Board** (PFIAB). The Board was established in 1956 by President Eisenhower and was originally called the President's Board of Consultants in Foreign Affairs. The PFIAB currently has eleven members, all of whom are selected from outside of the national government. Their role is to provide the president with an independent source of advice on the effectiveness of the government's intelligence community.

The PFIAB has operated nearly continuously throughout past administrations, with only a brief lapse during the Carter administration. President Carter dismantled the PFIAB in 1977, preferring to rely on the National Security Council and its staff for intelligence advice. President Reagan reinstated the PFIAB in 1981, and it has operated since then by executive order. One of the higher-profile members of the PFIAB in recent years was Nelson Rockefeller, who served on the Board from 1969 to 1974.[26]

Although the PFIAB is one of the oldest units in the EOP, it is probably the unit with the fewest staff and least interaction with the president. The National Security Council currently dominates the foreign-policy advisory system, including intelligence operations. During the Iran-contra scandal of the Reagan administration, however, the Tower Commission report recommended that the PFIAB play a greater role in the oversight of intelligence operations. The Tower Commission suggested that this might prevent a recurrence of the type of operations in which Oliver North was involved.

Office of Administration

As the president increased the managerial role of the White House staff within the executive branch, it became necessary to manage the White House staff itself. President Carter used the reorganization authority provided by Congress in 1977 to create the Office of Administration within the EOP.[27] The **Office of Administration** provides management support for the entire Executive Office of the President, including payroll and accounting, central purchasing, and law and reference libraries. They also provide a reference center for White House staff with research issues.

The concept of the Office of Administration stemmed from a proposal by the President's Advisory Committee on Government Organization (PACGO) during the Eisenhower administration. PACGO examined, among other areas, how the EOP operated. President Eisenhower was constantly concerned with improving the organizational structure of his immediate staff, including the larger EOP. One of PACGO's recommendations was to create a new Office of Administration and Budget in the EOP, which would encompass the Bureau of the Budget and new units for personnel management, planning, and oversight. Maurice Stans, director of the Bureau of the Budget in the Eisenhower administration, adamantly opposed this plan and instead proposed an expanded role for the Bureau of the Budget with the new name, the Office of Executive Management. Neither the PACGO proposal nor Stans's proposal moved forward during the Eisenhower administration, but both surfaced in future administrations.

Maurice Stans's plan for an Office of Executive Management eventually became the Office of Management and Budget during the Nixon administration. Stans was a close friend of Nixon's. They had served together in the Eisenhower administration, and stans had served as Nixon's 1968 campaign finance director and then as the secretary of commerce. The proposal for the Office of Administration and Budget recommended by PACGO was realized in 1977 when President Carter created the Office of Administration.

The Office of Administration was created as part of the broad reorganization authority granted to Carter by Congress in 1977. The two major actions by Carter under his reorganization authority were the creation of the Office of Administration and the creation of the Department of Energy. The Office of Administration fulfilled one of Carter's major campaign pledges—to improve the efficiency of government. Carter saw the new unit as a tool to improve the management of his own staff in the EOP and to serve as a symbol of his efforts to improve the management of the larger executive branch. Creation of the Office of Administration also provided another political benefit for Carter because it allowed him to cut the White House staff and to move those staff into positions in the Office of Administration. Carter had pledged in the campaign to cut the White House staff, which he did.

Summary

In the years between the Nixon and Clinton presidencies, the process of managing the domestic and economic policy agenda from the Executive Office of the President became institutionalized. Every president had a senior staff who worked closely with the executive departments on every aspect of domestic and economic policy development and implementation. The president had gained significant managerial capability through these two units and continued to fulfill the Brownlow Committee's dictum that "the president needs help."

The EOP has expanded significantly since 1939 to increase the president's ability to oversee and manage the burgeoning executive branch. Every administration adds and removes one or more units from the EOP, either for organizational reasons, as Carter did, or for policy reasons, as Reagan did. No single rule exists as to why presidents reorganize the units within the EOP. Each president makes such additions and deletions for his own purposes. Future presidents will undoubtedly continue this process of molding the staffing units within the EOP to fit their own management styles and their own policy priorities.

Key Words

Ash Council
brains trust
Brownlow Committee
Bureau of the Budget
Council of Economic Advisers
Council on Environmental Quality
Domestic Policy Council
Executive Office of the President
National Economic Council
National Security Council

Office of Administration
Office of Management and Budget
Office of National Drug Control Policy
Office of Policy Development
Office of Science and Technology
Office of the U.S. Trade Representative
President's Foreign Intelligence Advisory Board
Reorganization Act of 1939
Taft Commission

Notes

1. James W. Davis. The *American Presidency*. 2nd ed. Westport, CT: Greenwood Press, 1995, p. 166.
2. John Hart. *The Presidential Branch*. 2nd ed. Chatham, NJ: Chatham House, 1995, p. 5.
3. Harold C. Relyea. "The Executive Office Concept." In: Harold C. Relyea, ed. *The Executive Office of the President: A Historical, Biographical and Bibliographical Guide*. Westport, CT: Greenwood Press, 1997, p. 25.
4. James P. Pfiffner. "Executive Office of the President." In: George T. Kurian, ed. *A Historical Guide to the U.S. Government*. New York: Oxford University Press, 1998, p. 472.
5. Peri Arnold. *Making the Managerial Presidency: Comprehensive Reorganization Planning, 1905–1996*. 2nd rev. ed. Lawrence, KS: University Press of Kansas, 1998, pp. 30–31.
6. Ibid., p. 33.
7. Relyea. "The Executive Office Concept," p. 8.
8. Peri E. Arnold. "Executive Reorganization and the Executive Office of the President." In: Harold C. Relyea, ed. *The Executive Office of the President: A Historical, Biographical and Bibliographical Guide*. Westport, CT: Greenwood Press, 1997, p. 90.
9. Louis Brownlow. *The Autobiography of Louis Brownlow, Volume II: A Passion for Anonymity*. Chicago: University of Chicago Press, 1958, p. 327.
10. Ibid., pp. 376–377.
11. Donald C. Stone. "Administrative Management: Reflections on Origins and Accomplishments." *Public Administration Review*, January/February 1990, p. 5.
12. Hugh Heclo. "The Executive Office of the President." In: Mark Landy, ed. *Modern Presidents and the Presidency*. Lexington, MA: Heath, 1985, p. 68.
13. Ibid., p. 80.
14. Larry Berman. *The Office of Management and Budget and the Presidency: 1921–1979*. Princeton, NJ: Princeton University Press, 1979, p. ix.
15. Herbert Emmerick. *Federal Organization and Administrative Management*. University, Alabama: University of Alabama Press, 1971, p. 207–208.
16. *Public Papers of the Presidents of the United States: Richard Nixon, 1970*. Washington, DC: Government Printing Office, 1970, pp. 260–261.
17. Hart., p. 156.
18. Alfred D. Sander. *A Staff for the President: The Executive Office 1921–1952*. Westport, CT: Greenwood Press, 1989, p. 235.
19. Charles E. Walcott and Karen M. Hult. *Governing the White House from Hoover through LBJ*. Lawrence, KS: University Press of Kansas, 1995, p. 168.
20. John P. Burke. *The Institutional Presidency*. Baltimore: Johns Hopkins University Press, 1992, p. 17.
21. Walcott and Hult., p. 197.

22. Carnegie Commission on Science, Technology, and Government. *Science and Technology and the President: A Report to the Next Administration*. New York: Carnegie Corporation of New York, January 1997.
23. *Public Papers of the Presidents of the United States: Ronald Reagan, 1983*. Washington, DC: Government Printing Office, 1984, p. 49.
24. Mark J. Rozell. *The Press and the Bush Presidency*. Westport, CT: Greenwood Press, 1996, pp. 94–95.
25. Jimmy Carter. *A Government As Good as Its People*. New York: Simon & Schuster, 1977, p. 60.
26. David Barrett and Christopher Ryan. "National Security." In: Relyea, *The Executive Office of the President*, p. 191.
27. Relyea. "The White House Office." In: Relyea, *The Executive Office of the President*, p. 74.

Chapter 7

THE PRESIDENT AND THE BUREAUCRACY

As the nation has grown both in geographic size and in population, the responsibilities of the national government have grown concurrently. The roles and responsibilities of the government have grown to encompass more than fourteen hundred different programs, housed in fourteen executive agencies and numerous independent agencies and regulatory commissions, with a budget of over $1.7 trillion. This explosion in the responsibilities of the national government has led to a proliferation of the bureaucracy. The relationship between the president and the bureaucracy has often been difficult, as presidents endeavor to move their programs forward through an often intransigent federal work force. In the latter half of the twentieth century this has become a significant problem for presidents, who often see the departmental bureaucracies slowing down federal programs or moving programs in directions that are not in line with presidential goals and objectives.

Modern presidents have had to deal with a rapidly burgeoning bureaucracy. During the 1960s and 1970s, a host of new agencies emerged, both large departments and smaller agencies and commissions. In general, the new departments were among the largest in the federal structure. The Department of Housing and Urban Development (established in 1965), the Department of Transportation (1966), the Department of Energy (1977), and the Department of Education (1979) were significant parts of the federal bureaucracy. The environmental movement led to creation by executive order in 1970 of the Environmental Protection Agency and of the Consumer Product Safety Commission in 1972. Only in the past half century have presidents had both the benefits and the problems of a diverse, politically powerful, and extremely large federal bureaucracy (Figure 7.1).

Background of the Federal Bureaucracy

Although the term *bureaucracy* is not mentioned in the Constitution, the framers understood that a rather large work force would be necessary to administer the programs

Executive Department	Year Established	1996 Paid Civilian Employment
Agriculture	1889	105,500
Commerce	1913	35,200
Defense	1947	800,000
Education	1980	4,800
Energy	1977	19,700
Health and Human Services	1980	58,800
Housing and Urban Development	1965	11,900
Interior	1849	70,500
Justice	1870	106,300
Labor	1913	16,700
State	1789	23,700
Transportation	1966	63,900
Treasury	1789	153,300
Veterans Affairs	1989	223,700

Source: Budget of the United States Government, Fiscal Year 1997: Analytical Perspectives. Washington, DC: U.S. Government Printing Office, 1996.

FIGURE 7.1   Federal Civilian Employment in Executive Departments for Selected Years.

mandated by Congress. Article II, Section I, of the Constitution provides strong evidence of the framers' intent that the federal government would have a work force to handle the business of government by directly referring to the existence of the executive departments. Article II specifies that the president should "require the Opinion, in writing, of the principal Officer in each of the executive Departments," providing strong evidence that the department were to fall within the executive branch. In addition, Article II further discusses the existence of different classifications of people who would work within the executive departments, requiring the higher levels of officials to be confirmed by the Senate. This presupposes the existence of a larger work force, or bureaucracy, to carry out the business of government.

The federal **bureaucracy** began in 1789 during the administration of George Washington when Congress created three executive departments (State, Treasury, and War) plus an Attorney General. Three years later, in 1792, Congress created the U.S. Post Office, which soon became the largest government employer. By 1801, the federal government employed three thousand people, most of whom were Post Office employees.

The earliest federal employees were friends of the president or the cabinet officers and were generally from the higher social classes. Family background and family connections to the national office holders were often the criteria for obtaining a federal job. This process for hiring federal employees dominated the early stages of the government's growth, and is bracketed in the years from 1789 to 1829. Most federal employees during this era were highly educated and considered to be America's upper class. Both the Federalist and the Republican parties followed this pattern in hiring federal employees, which was often referred to as "government by gentlemen." The Age of Jackson, as the administration of Andrew Jackson was called, brought a major change to the process of hiring federal employees. As one scholar described the earlier years, "However competent administrators in the early Republic may have been, their emphasis on social status as a qualification was clearly undemocratic and at odds with American ideas about equality."[1] Under Jackson, numerous federal employees were hired as a political reward for their work during Jackson's two presidential campaigns, in 1824, when he was defeated, and in 1828, when he won. Describing Jackson's hiring policy, Senator William Learned Marcy of New York commented, "To the victor belong the spoils," which led to the phrase "the spoils system."

The **spoils system** emerged after Jackson's election to the presidency, a system in which campaign work and loyalty to the president became the ticket to federal employment. Under the spoils system, federal jobs turned over at the beginning of every presidency and supporters of the incoming president gained the government jobs. Appointing political supporters to federal jobs was not a new practice, since even George Washington had done it, but merit had always been the watchword of past administrations. Under the Jacksonian spoils system, merit was placed at less of a premium than political support.

When Andrew Jackson came into office, the federal bureaucracy had approximately 11,000 positions. Less than a year after taking office, Jackson had removed 1981 people from their jobs and placed his own supporters in those jobs.[2] One Supreme Court justice remarked with chagrin that "the President grossly abuses the power of removal."[3] According to some counts, Jackson replaced about one government employee in six during the eight years of his presidency. The politicization of the federal civil service, particularly for those who had actively supported the president, was launched during the presidency of Andrew Jackson. A leading Jackson biographer commented that "though succeeding presidents were to go further and to do much more than Andrew Jackson toward turning the civil service into a political tool, the fact remains that he had opened the door."[4]

Andrew Jackson ushered in a new era of hiring federal employees when he changed the character of the federal bureaucracy through regular turnovers for patronage employees. Succeeding presidents continued to use the federal bureaucracy as a source of patronage for political loyalists. By the latter half of the nineteenth century, it had become common practice for a large part of the federal government to turn over after every election. Following the Civil War, the size of the federal government took a significant turn upward. The Pension Office was established in 1866, for example, to pay benefits to the thousands of northern veterans who had fought in the Civil War. Other federal offices, such as the newly created Department of Agriculture (although it did not become a full cabinet-level department until 1889), added more and more employees to the federal ranks.

By the late 1870s, the issue of whether the federal government should have employment based on merit rather than patronage had become a favorite topic of conversation. President Rutherford B. Hayes supported the idea, and he argued that test scores and ability should replace patronage in federal employment. Hayes put forth legislation for the reform, but Congress failed to pass it. When President Garfield replaced Hayes in the White House, he too supported reform of the federal employment process and promised to complete the efforts that Hayes had begun. As a member of the House of Representatives, Garfield had supported reforms for the civil service; but he did not move immediately on changing the civil service rules, and he worked diligently once in the White House to reward his own supporters with federal jobs. As fast as Garfield appointed people, more applied for jobs. One estimate is that only one in twenty of Garfield's supporters who sought jobs were rewarded with jobs.[5] One of those who applied for a job but did not get one was Charles J. Guiteau; on July 2, 1881, he shot Garfield at a railroad station in Washington, D.C. After lingering near death for eleven weeks, Garfield died on September 19, 1881. The assassination proved to be the push that was required to move civil service reform forward.

In 1883 the Congress passed the **Civil Service Act,** which had been sponsored by Senator George H. Pendleton (D-Ohio). The Pendleton Act, as it became known, provided for federal office seekers to take an examination to qualify for jobs. It established the Civil Service Commission and placed a relatively small number of federal employees under the authority of the commission. Civil Service Commission jobs could only be obtained by taking a competitive test. Commission jobs were referred to as the "classified services." This system gave everyone equal footing in qualifying for certain federal jobs and clearly increased the opportunities to hold federal jobs. However, the president remained a central figure in the new civil service process. First, Congress placed the civil service program within the executive branch under the direction of the president. Second, the law required the president to appoint the three-member Civil Service Commission, with the consent of the Senate, which was to make the rules for governing the civil service. And finally, the law allowed the president to broaden the number of positions covered by civil service. When the Pendleton Act first went into effect, only about 14,000 positions, or 10.5 percent of the federal work force, were included, making its influence on federal hiring minimal.

When Grover Cleveland became president in 1885 and Benjamin Harrison became president in 1889, both continued the former practice of firing numerous federal employees and replacing them with patronage employees. Harrison dismissed more than thirty-five thousand employees in the first year of his presidency.[6] When Cleveland regained the presidency in 1893, he again appointed partisans to federal positions. However, as Cleveland prepared to leave office he extended civil service protection to nearly one third of the work force to protect his appointees. This extension brought the total number of protected civil service workers to 85,000, out of the total workforce of 205,000. President McKinley, not a complete believer in a work force without patronage employees, slowly added more eligible jobs to the civil service lists.

When Theodore Roosevelt entered the presidency in 1901, he was already well versed in the issues of civil service reform. President Harrison had appointed Roosevelt as chairman of the Civil Service Commission in 1889. Roosevelt bolstered the ranks of covered employees under civil service to sixty-four percent from the forty-one percent that had existed during McKinley's presidency. As the Progressive movement began to dominate the political spectrum in the early 1900s, patronage and political appointments became synonymous with corruption. The march continued during the Progressive Era, and by 1924 about eighty percent of federal jobs fell under civil service protection. The process had a slight setback during the administration of Franklin Delano Roosevelt, when the creation of thousands of new jobs under the New Deal programs was handled without consideration of civil service protection. Under Roosevelt, the number of civil service jobs actually decreased to sixty-one percent of the federal work force during the mid-1930s. Although Roosevelt was committed to the concept of civil service, he realized that effective management of the executive branch required some positions to be held by political loyalists. The political activities of those political loyalists, however, were limited by passage of the 1939 **Hatch Act.** The act was formally titled the Act to Prevent Pernicious Political Activities, but took its name from its chief sponsor, Senator Carl Hatch of New Mexico. The Hatch Act prohibited all federal employees from participating in partisan politics and also made it illegal to dismiss non-policy-making federal employees for partisan reasons. An amendment to the Hatch Act in 1993 modified the prohibition by stating that most federal employees could engage in some partisan activities after work hours.

When Roosevelt asked the Brownlow Committee to give him advice on strengthening his overall management of the executive branch, they responded by recommending creation of a personal White House Staff and an increased number of policy-making jobs exempt from civil service. The recommendation for civil service reform involved replacement of the Civil Service Commission by a Civil Service Administration, to be housed in the newly created Executive Office of the President. The first recommendation was followed by Congress, with the creation of the Executive Office of the President and the White House staff, in the Reorganization Act of 1939 which implemented some of the Brownlow Committee's recommendations. The second recommendation was not followed. Fears of losing long-standing allies in the departments through a revamped civil service process and fears of the whole process being housed directly under the president led to strong opposition in Congress and its ultimate rejection. But Roosevelt managed to slightly circumvent the rejection of his second proposal by creating a position on his new White House staff called the Liaison Office for Personnel Management.[7] The office was eventually abolished in 1953 by the Eisenhower administration. Although Roosevelt had tried to curb the growing power of the bureaucracy by increasing the number of non–civil service employees, the number of civil service employees continued to grow. By the end of the Truman administration, the proportion of employees within the civil service had grown to eighty-seven percent of the federal bureaucracy. Truman supported civil service, arguing in his memoirs that it protected against "influence peddlers and favor seekers."[8] But Truman also saw the problems with a federal government completely dominated by a bureaucracy with only civil service employees. As Roosevelt had been, Truman was concerned that the federal government was becoming so bureaucratic that it was at times unresponsive to presidential goals and objectives. Truman was so sensitive to the importance of maintaining the upper levels of the bureaucracy with loyalists that he brought Donald Dawson onto the White House staff with the sole responsibility of ensuring that political loyalists were in the jobs. Commenting on his role in the White House, Dawson said matter of factly, "patronage is essential to governing."[9] Truman was a pragmatist, though, and when faced with a difficult election in 1948 and the possibility of a Republican gaining the presidency, he used the power of the executive order to broaden the number of federal employees covered by civil service. Truman feared that a Republican would dismantle many of the New Deal and Fair Deal programs by bringing in thousands of new federal employees into positions not covered by civil service. Extending civil service protected the policies that had moved forward during the Roosevelt and Truman administrations.

When Dwight Eisenhower entered the presidency in 1953, he took over a federal government that had been run by presidents from the Democratic Party for two decades. The largely civil service bureaucracy had become deeply involved in the administration of the New Deal programs and committed to their success and even their expansion. Eisenhower hinted that there were large numbers of disloyal and even unproductive bureaucrats.[10] Faced with the dilemma of having an unsympathetic bureaucracy administer a new set of programs, President Eisenhower created a commission to examine how the executive branch could become more responsive to presidential goals and objectives. For the first time in history, a president was faced with a very large federal bureaucracy that he could not easily control. He could not replace existing officeholders with appointees of his choice, as Andrew Jackson had done, nor could he expand the number of jobs, as Roosevelt had done. Eisenhower was in the unique position of having a large federal bureaucracy that was not completely sympathetic to the new administration. He had to balance the need for maintaining competency in the bureaucracy, which civil service ensured over the spoils system, with the need for presidential oversight of the executive branch. One of the first moves that Eisenhower made with regard to the bureaucracy was in early 1953, only two months after his inauguration. He created a new section of civil service called Schedule C appointments, which involved fifteen hundred confidential and policy-making positions, generally positions below the deputy and assistant secretary level. The Schedule C appointments were exempt from the civil service merit tests and could be appointed directly by the president. Today, the Schedule C appointments remain a key part of the president's managerial force within the executive branch and the formal list of positions available to presidents is called the **plum book.**

The next major move that President Eisenhower made to gain greater control over the growing bureaucracy and its civil service was to work with a new commission to study the issue. Both the president and Congress saw the need for a reexamination of the executive branch and the difficulty presidents had in managing a largely civil service work force. In early 1953, the Commission on Organization of the Executive Branch of Government was created by Congress and chaired by former President, Republican Herbert Hoover. The Second Hoover Commission followed the 1949 First Hoover Commission in examining the operations and organization of the executive branch. Although Eisenhower did not completely support the creation of the commission, he realized that it might lead to enhancing presidential management of the burgeoning federal bureaucracy.[11]

Congress gave the commission the task of looking at a wide variety of organizational and administrative issues in the executive branch, not merely the civil service issue. With regard to presidential management of the executive branch, the Second Hoover Commission concurred with the idea of a separate Senior Civil Service for policy-making positions, which endorsed the earlier decision of President Eisenhower to create the **Schedule C** positions. By 1998, approximately five thousand positions fell under the category of Schedule C positions, including twenty-three hundred policy-making positions in the departments; the remaining are part-time positions, including board and commission members who often serve without pay. These positions, however, are but a fraction of the nearly three million federal employees who are covered by civil service protection. The bureaucracy is overwhelmingly civil service in the modern age. The last modicum of patronage in the executive branch ended in 1969 when President Nixon placed all 70,000 postmasters and rural letter carriers within the federal merit system.

The concept of the Schedule C appointment has been to ensure that presidents have the ability to hire people at senior levels who support their policies. As one commentator described this process, "A candidate for president who has a clearly articulated policy perspective as to what the role of government should be and, therefore, what the role of the departments and agencies should be, must of necessity choose personnel who understand and support his policy perspective."[12] Presidents view their Schedule C, or political, appointments as the center of their ability to manage the executive branch.

Eisenhower's adoption of Schedule C appointments allowed presidents greater control over the executive branch, but as the size of the federal government continued to increase, the number of Schedule C appointments remained relatively flat. By the time President Carter entered office in 1977, the bureaucracy had swelled from 2,583,000 federal employees during the Eisenhower administration to 2,848,000 federal employees, with no significant increase in the Schedule C appointments.[13] Carter decided to try to restructure the civil service process to further enhance presidential control over the bureaucracy. His solution was not to enlarge the number of Schedule C appointments but to restructure the civil service program to allow some top level civil service employees to remain in the civil service but become eligible for certain financial rewards for supporting presidential initiatives. The **Senior Executive Service (SES)** was created by the **Civil Service Reform Act of 1978** giving presidents the ability to move policy-making civil service employees into a separate class of employees.

This proposal had been originally introduced by the Second Hoover Commission, but had not received significant support from either the president or Congress. Under the Civil Service Reform Act of 1978, eligible federal employees who accepted the senior executive service would remain in the civil service system and would be protected from removal, but were subject to some presidential controls. The law covered employees in the pay classifications of GS 16 to GS 18. If employees in the senior executive service totally supported presidential initiatives and aggressively worked within their departments to move those initiatives forward, they would be rewarded with bonuses of up to twenty percent of their base salary. But if they proved not to be supportive of presidential initiatives once they had moved into the senior executive service, presidents could change their job location and their jobs, although not reduce their salary or their job classification. The threat of being transferred to a desolate (or at least distant) location with an unchallenging job proved to be a powerful incentive for SES staff. To ensure that staff in the SES and other parts of the civil service received fair evaluations by their political supervisors, the Civil Service Reform Act of 1978 established the Merit System Protection Board. The lure of significant salary bonuses for supporting presidential initiatives proved to be exactly the boost President Carter was seeking to move the federal bureaucracy closer to the needs of the presidency.

Power of the Bureaucracy

Bureaucratic power is based on three sources: the power of specialized knowledge and information, the power of the interest groups they represent, and the power of Congress to fund their programs. At the heart of bureaucratic power is the power of specialized knowledge. Departmental staff members often enter their jobs with a high degree of knowledge about the programs with which they work. Many have scientific, technical, and specialized training that stem from years of work in their fields. They are **policy experts.** In contrast, presidents and their White House staffs have only a general knowledge (if any) about each of the numerous programs that the executive branch administers. Presidents need the information and advice that the bureaucracy provides. For example, presidents know little about nuclear waste disposal, hydroelectric power, or supercolliders and rely on the experts in the Department of Energy to develop appropriate policies. Similarly, presidents know little about light rail and other mass-transit systems, federal fees on the inland waterways, or trucking weights on interstate highways. They leave development of these policies to the experts in the Department of Transportation. Specialized knowledge provides bureaucracies enormous power in the policy process, for it allows the departmental staff to set the standards in many programs.

The number of agencies within each department and the number of programs that each agency is responsible for makes it virtually impossible for the political staff to operate without the strong support of the career staff. The sheer size of the departments and the volume of knowledge necessary to run the departments give the career staff substantial leverage in influencing the policy-making process. Cabinet officers and their political appointees generally allow the career staff to make the decisions on how programs should be run. Only when the president is seeking major overhauls to programs, such as in welfare or education, or is seeking to dramatically cut programs do the political appointees become directly involved in program management. Often, when the political appointees are seeking a different course of action than the career staff support, a test of wills develops. The career staff will use every tool available to them, including stalling actions and marshaling support from Congress and from interest groups, to stop the course of action. An old adage is that the career staff can afford to wage the war, knowing full well that the average cabinet officer lasts only eighteen months to two years in the job.

Career staff members also have a significant influence at the beginning of the administration, when the political appointments are being made. Because of the increase in the number of political appointments over the years and the increased clearance time from both the Federal Bureau of Investigation (FBI) and from the Senate, the political appointments are slow to move into the departments. This gives the career staff more time to build a relationship with the cabinet officer and top political staff and to keep policy decisions within their realms. As more and more political staff are appointed and receive clearances, the less responsibility the career staff have for influencing top-level decision making.

Control of information is another power that bureaucrats possess in the policy-making process. Presidents are generalists; their White House staffs are also generalists, although they are growing more specialized as the size of the White House staff increases. The career staff in the departments control the information that the political staff need to make informed decisions. The more specific the information that departmental staff control, such as scientific information at the Centers for Disease Control and Prevention or technical information at the Federal Aviation Administration, the more power the departmental staff has. When political staff members make decisions, they need the information provided by the career staff. In many cases in which such scientific or technical information is provided by the career staff, the information can be so framed as to ensure that the policy makers support the bureaucracy's viewpoint.

In most cases, presidents are eager to allow the career staff to handle the policy decisions. But there are important cases in which the bureaucracy and the White House conflict on how policies should be developed and interpreted. For example, during the early years of the Nixon administration, the Department of Health, Education, and Welfare took the position that federal funds should be cut off to any school district that failed to show progress in eliminating segregation. The Supreme Court had spoken in the 1954 *Brown v. Board of Education* decision that schools had to move "with all deliberate speed" to end segregation.[14] Nearly twenty years later many inner-city schools in the north and most southern schools had made little progress toward desegregation. The staff in the Department of Health, Education, and Welfare had been working for years to push school districts toward compliance with the Supreme Court decision and given schools endless deadlines, which they had missed. The decision to cut off funds was the last tool at their disposal to move the districts toward desegregation.

This decision led to significant political problems for Nixon, who did not want to pursue this policy until after the 1972 presidential election. Many northern states complained because the Department of Health, Education, and Welfare had changed its policy of only going after southern school districts that had segregated schools. Under the new policy, schools with de facto segregation in the north would also be targeted. Nixon tried to have the policy reversed, but in the process somewhat of a war developed with his own Department of Health, Education, and Welfare. Leon Panetta, who eventually became chairman of the House Budget Committee and later became President Clinton's White House chief of staff, was a key member of the department who helped to develop the policy. Nixon fired Panetta for his opposition to White House policy, but Nixon could not fire the majority of staffers who were working on the policy. Eventually the policy was implemented during the Nixon administration, although Nixon was able to stall it long enough to move through the 1972 election without a large outcry from the southern states.

Nixon had another problem with the bureaucracy interpreting policies quite differently from the way the White House interpreted them. In this case, the problem stemmed from a series of programs started by the Department of Housing and Urban Development for improving housing and infrastructure in a small number of inner cities. Nixon wanted to cut the program, called the "Model Cities Program," entirely from the department, but the bureaucracy was deeply vested in the program. Staff from the Department of Housing and Urban Development had created the program, had lobbied President Johnson to support it, and had lobbied members of Congress to support it. They felt that the program was essential to rebuilding the nation's inner cities, for it targeted money directly to improving blighted downtown housing districts. Nixon, whose natural political bases were not the urban areas, opposed the program. He opposed many of the targeted categorical grant programs that had been developed during the Johnson administration, particularly those aimed at urban environments that had a primarily Democratic political base. Nixon wanted to change the way the federal government allocated money and was moving from the categorical grant structure to the general revenue programs, which provided federal funding to communities regardless of poverty indices. The poverty indices for communities had been the primary threshold indicator for many of the categorical grant programs, indices which had effectively eliminated many of the suburban and rural areas that were Nixon's traditional political base. Over the strong objections of the staff in the Department of Housing and Urban Development, Nixon cut the Model Cities Program by $215 million.[15]

One of the problems that presidents face in dealing with the bureaucracy is that departmental staff become deeply invested in their own programs. When presidents want to eliminate a program, such as in the Model Cities Program, or to change the direction of a program, such as cutting off funding for segregated school districts, departmental staff may oppose the presidential action. For a number of reasons, departmental staffers strongly believe in their programs and become protective of their missions. In some cases, the career staff members have worked for many years on the programs, nurturing them through their developmental stages. To have presidents suddenly cut off or curtail the program is very difficult for the career staff to accept. Career staffers often initiate actions to deter the presidential instructions, such as slowing down the process and recruiting support from Congress and interest groups.

In Nixon's case, the career staff was concerned about the direction the administration was taking. The New Federalism of the Nixon administration was directed at decentralizing the policy decisions from the federal level to the state and local levels. Nixon did not oppose the services that the federal government delivered in the same way that Ronald Reagan did in the 1980s, but wanted those services delivered at a different level of government. For Nixon, the best approach would be to hand state and local governments large amounts of money to manage their own programs, with little centralized control at the federal level. Eventually Nixon was successful in implementing a part of this approach through the general revenue-sharing funds for community development activities.

Another reason that bureaucrats become vested in their programs involves job security. If presidents threaten to reduce or eliminate programs, career staffers become concerned that their own jobs may be in jeopardy. Career staff will lobby to keep a program alive if the program is being threatened and their jobs could be elim-inated. Similarly, if programs are being shifted to another department in a reorganiza-tion move, career staff will lobby to stop it. During the Carter administration propos-als were floated by the president to move the food stamp and other nutrition programs housed in the Department of Agriculture to the Department of Health, Ed-ucation, and Welfare, which administered the larger spectrum of social service pro-grams. Career staff in the Department of Agriculture heavily lobbied to stop the transfer and were successful. The career staff in the Agriculture Department feared that their jobs were threatened and feared that the programs that they had carefully built could be revamped in the Department of Health, Education, and Welfare. On one hand, the career staff members were concerned for their own jobs, but on the other hand the career staffers in the Agriculture Department were concerned that their programs would be poorly administered in another department. Bureaucratic power contributed significantly to Carter's failure to move this decision forward.

Members of Congress have also invested a significant amount of time working with the departments to develop these programs. Committee staffers in Congress are extremely knowledgeable about the programs and, as have the career staff, have in-vested a considerable amount of their time in working out the program goals and ob-jectives and finding the appropriate funding level. All these programs have under-gone a lengthy process in Congress in which the committee staff held markups, hearings, and numerous conversations with interested parties. As a result, members of Congress have a stake in departmental programs and do not easily acquiesce to presidents who wish to change the rules or to end programs without having been con-sulted. In Nixon's case, the liberal Democratic Congress conflicted with the conserv-ative president, leading to serious disagreements on the direction of a number of pro-grams. When career staff from the departments sought the assistance of members of Congress in trying to influence presidential policy, they were only too happy to assist.

During the Carter administration, the career staff strongly supported farm orga-nizations that were lobbying to increase federal subsidies for wheat, corn, cotton, soybeans, and rice. Carter opposed the increases since he felt it would be detrimental to his efforts to balance the federal budget. The Secretary of Agriculture, Bob Berg-land, agreed with the career staff and the farm organizations and lobbied Carter to reverse his decision. Bergland even went to Congress and testified on behalf of the subsidy increases.[16] Lobbying Congress directly to reverse a presidential position is a frequent technique of departmental staff, although usually the lobbying is done quite subtly, without the involvement of the cabinet secretary. Bergland was eventually fired by Carter.

The second ally that career staffs seek are the constituent groups. Interest groups have a vested interest in ensuring that departmental programs that affect their con-stituents will succeed. When Nixon sought to dismantle the Model Cities Program, constituent groups such as the League of Cities adamantly opposed the action. Often, constituent groups band together to pressure Congress and the president to stop an action. Constituent groups provide both funding and votes during elections, and elected officials usually try to satisfy constituent demands. Members of Congress are extremely sensitive to the power of constituent disagreement with presidential or congressional action. In 1995 when Speaker of the House Newt Gingrich tried to end funding for the Corporation for Public Broadcasting, the public called, wrote, faxed, and personally visited members of Congress to register their anger at the decision. Gingrich was forced to back down from his position after members of his own party refused to support his decision.

The relationship between the career staff, members of Congress, and the constituent groups is referred to as the **iron triangle.** Presidents have a great deal of difficulty changing programs if any of the parts of the iron triangle oppose the change. If any part of the iron triangle opposes a presidential program, they work with the other two parts to defeat the presidential action. Although career staffers are part of the executive branch and are under the president's jurisdiction, they have at times become powerful opponents of presidential programs. Since Congress provides funding for departmental programs, the career staff seeks support for their positions from members of Congress. Members of Congress support the career staff, since the departments are important in serving their own constituents. If departments are slow to respond to congressional requests to service problems their constituents are having, the member of Congress suffers. Members of Congress who can solve their constituents' problems with the federal government are remembered at election time. To accomplish this, members of Congress need a sympathetic bureaucracy. The iron triangle has proven to be a formidable obstacle for presidents who try to move or cancel programs.

Another powerful tool that the bureaucracy possesses to affect the course of policy making involves their discretionary authority in **rule making.** Congress generally writes laws with broad language, leaving the departments to develop the specific rules for implementing the programs. This discretionary authority is the result of the thousands of bills that Congress has to handle every year. Members do not have the time or the inclination in most cases to become bogged down in addressing every procedural detail needed to make the program operational. The details are left to the departments to craft. This discretionary authority provides the departments a significant role in determining the direction that programs will take. Administrative discretion in writing the regulations is a major part of the independence that the bureaucracy has developed from both Congress and the president. Administrative discretion, or rule administration, is also present in the interpretation of the rules and regulations governing the programs. As career staff change, new interpretations of the law can be drawn, leading to different applications of the same law. The ability to determine whether the administrative rules that govern the program have been broken is also a part of the discretionary authority that the career staff hold. The process known as rule adjudication allows departmental staff to examine whether departmental regulations have been violated. In summary, the bureaucracy has a significant role in shaping departmental policy, and it is often difficult for presidents to shift policy to a different direction when the bureaucracy is opposed.

One of the more difficult decisions that presidents make in managing the bureaucracy is to choose effective cabinet officers. In this case, effective management means the ability of the cabinet officer to work well with the career staff. Cabinet officers who have clear agendas that threaten the traditional role of the department can cause significant rifts between presidential policy and departmental implementation. For example, President Reagan appointed a conservative farmer, James Watt from Wyoming, who had been active in Republican Party politics as his first secretary of interior. Watt directed the department to cut off all communication with environmental groups, particularly those that wanted to expand federal holdings. Watt wanted to reverse the continued expansion of the national park system. Since the vast majority of employees in the Interior Department were deeply committed to the national parks, the career staff began to oppose Watt's policies. In addition, Watt ordered the sale of coal exploration and development rights on public lands and doubled the land available to oil companies for offshore oil exploration. Staff in the Interior Department had built careers on protecting public lands from private encroachment and were against what they considered exploitation of the public lands. Watt lasted only two years in the position, eventually driven out by a coalition of interest groups and career staff that adamantly opposed his policies. President Reagan was forced to replace him when members of Congress, responding to interest group and bureaucratic pressure, in turn pressured the president. The political power of the bureaucracy is significant when it feels its mission is threatened by political leaders. The bureaucracy understands the power of political pressure and does not hesitate to use it.

Such political power came to bear on President Clinton in early 1993 when he tried to change military policy regarding gays and lesbians serving in the armed forces. Through an executive order, President Clinton directed the armed forces not to terminate the service of anyone because of sexual orientation. The military was opposed to this policy and used their political skills to bring broad-based pressure on the president. Members of Congress responded to the career staff in the military and joined the Pentagon's demand that the president modify his order. Senator Sam Nunn (D-Ga.), a powerful senior Senator from the president's own party, led the opposition in Congress. The President was ultimately forced to change his policy to satisfy the demands of the career staff in the Pentagon. The "don't ask, don't tell" policy replaced the no-termination policy originally put in place by President Clinton.

Finally, in the discussion of bureaucracy power is the problem of bureaucratic rivalries. Bureaucratic rivalries have often taken on a life of their own, with the president having little control over territorial battles. Several years ago the Occupational Health and Safety Administration, which has jurisdiction over safety in the workplace, began to develop guidelines for noise standards in the workplace. When the Environmental Protection Agency staff reviewed the proposed regulations, they opposed them on the grounds that they were not strong enough. The ninety-decibel noise level that the Occupational Health and Safety Administration supported was viewed as inadequate by the Environmental Protection Agency.[17] Both agencies had legislative mandates to protect workers from high noise levels, a problem that arises regularly in the federal government. Overlapping jurisdictions cause numerous battles between agencies, and such warfare is difficult for the president to adjudicate, given agency mandates. Peter Woll, one of the nation's leading scholars on bureaucratic politics, noted that "clear-cut legal authority for agency independence helps the bureaucracy to ignore presidential demands."[18] When agencies have the legal authority to proceed, even though that legal authority comes into conflict with other agencies, the president can only use the power of persuasion, as Richard Neustadt argues, to bring the agencies together in a working alliance.[19]

Presidential Strategies for Controlling the Bureaucracy

Managing the federal bureaucracy has become one of the most difficult jobs that presidents face during their tenure in office. Overlapping jurisdictions, conflicts between agencies, and bureaucrats committed to protecting their programs have caused presidents significant problems in achieving the goals and objectives to which they have dedicated themselves during the presidential campaign. Few presidents enter office with the full knowledge of the power of the bureaucracy and the influence the bureaucracy has in controlling departmental programs. But they learn quickly and begin to develop strategies to constrain the bureaucracy.

In order to gain greater control, or management, over the bureaucracy and to make the bureaucracy more responsive to presidential goals and objectives has led presidents to explore new ways of dealing with the career staff. Three strategies have been used by recent presidents to increase their management of the departments and their career staff. The first strategy has been to increase the size of the White House staff, the second has been to increase the size of the presidential bureaucracy, and the third has been to move presidential loyalists into the departments in the a variety of political appointments.

The first strategy of increasing the size of the White House staff grew out of a fear that the bureaucracy was obstructing political plans. Presidents increase the size of their staffs to monitor the actions of the departments and to ensure that the presidential agenda is being implemented. As Francis Rourke observes, "This monitoring is designed to insure that the policies that agency bureaucrats are pursuing on a daily basis are those of the president, and that they have not been altered to conform to the preferences of the bureaucracy or its clients."[20]

The efforts toward **increasing the size of the White House staff** for policy and departmental control began during the Kennedy administration. John F. Kennedy distrusted the bureaucracy and began to centralize policy making in the White House, removing a significant degree of power from the departments. As Patrick Anderson noted, Kennedy was so distrustful of the bureaucracy that he built his own White House staff and encouraged "his personal aides to prod, double-check, and bypass" departmental staff.[21] Kennedy's strategy for dealing with the bureaucracy was to add White House staff to oversee the development and implementation of departmental programs and to ensure that the bureaucracy was following presidential directions. Joseph Califano was among the White House staff added by Johnson to oversee the burgeoning domestic programs, particularly the programs administered by the Department of Health, Education, and Welfare. Califano's expertise with these programs later led President Carter to include Califano in his cabinet as Secretary of Health, Education, and Welfare. President Johnson continued the use of the White House staff for departmental oversight and further increased the size of the staff.

The second wave of strategies to gain control over the departmental bureaucracies began during the Nixon administration. When President Nixon entered office in January 1969, he was confronted with many of the same problems that his mentor, President Eisenhower, had faced with regard to the federal bureaucracy. After eight years of Democratic administrations (Kennedy and Johnson), the Republicans regained power in the Nixon administration. But Nixon was concerned that the federal government was peppered with liberals whose goal was to continue to build the Great Society programs that began during the Johnson administration. Nixon simply did not trust the bureaucracy to move forward on the agenda items established for his administration, many of which included cutbacks to Great Society programs. "The Great Society was created by liberal academics and bureaucrats," Nixon said, continuing that "at the beginning of my second term, Congress, the bureaucracy, and the media were still working in concert to maintain the ideas and ideology of the traditional liberal establishment."[22] For Nixon, the bureaucracy was part of the liberal establishment and therefore was not to be trusted.

Nixon followed Kennedy and Johnson's strategy of enlarging the White House staff to oversee the bureaucracy, but went to almost extreme lengths by building the largest White House staff in history. Nixon created the Domestic Council to give the White House direct control over domestic policy making and expanded the National Security Council for added control over foreign policy making. In addition, Nixon sought and received reorganization authority from Congress, which resulted in the creation of the Office of Management and Budget within the Executive Office of the Presidency. The Office of Management and Budget replaced the Bureau of the Budget, adding departmental oversight and management to the responsibilities of the new agency. Creation of the Office of Management and Budget was the cornerstone of Nixon's efforts to enlarge the presidential bureaucracy. Nixon added numerous roles and responsibilities to the Office of Management and Budget as a tool for reviewing departmental programs, including the responsibility of reviewing every regulation that the departments promulgated and reviewing every legislative proposal that came from the departments.

The strategy of increasing the **presidential bureaucracy** included the addition of several other units within the Executive Office of the President to bypass the departments for policy development. When presidents believe that the departments are unable or unwilling to move quickly on presidential policy proposals, they have created units within the Executive Office of the President to handle the job. For example, President Johnson created the Office of Economic Opportunity to manage the War on Poverty, since he did not trust the career staff in the executive departments to move rapidly on his proposals. Similarly, President Nixon created the Council of Environmental Quality to manage the environmental policies that the administration wanted to move forward. President Ford created the Office of Energy Policy to formulate and coordinate energy policies, and President Carter created the Office of Drug Abuse Policy to coordinate federal drug abuse programs.

All of these units were created within the Executive Office of the President with the primary purpose of ensuring that issues of significant presidential concern were supervised within the presidential bureaucracy. Recent presidents have followed this tradition and used the Executive Office of the President as a tool for addressing specific policy issues. For example, the Space Council in the Executive Office of the President was created at the beginning of President Bush's term in office to ensure greater presidential control over military and nonmilitary uses of space. President Bush wanted a single agency to oversee the often-uncoordinated programs that were using spacecraft and missilry, including the space shuttle programs of the National Aeronautics and Space Administration and the antiaircraft programs of the Defense

Department. In addition, numerous private companies were launching satellites for commercial purposes. The Space Council was created to oversee the vast number of space-related issues. President Clinton later merged the Space Council into the Office of Science and Technology Policy, creating one large unit. Every president has used the Executive Office of the President as a means of enhancing presidential control over the executive departments, using the presidential bureaucracy to oversee the permanent bureaucracy.

The third strategy that presidents employ to deal with the career staff is to fill as many positions in the departments as possible with presidential loyalists. For many years, presidents allowed their cabinet officers to choose their own political staff. By political staff, we mean political appointees who are not covered by civil service. Cabinet officers chose their senior departmental staff, the political appointees, from among their own friends and from a pool of technical experts. Often, the senior departmental staff members were policy experts with little or no relationship to the president. Usually, though not always, the senior staff were of the same political party as the president. But in many cases the policy experts chosen by the cabinet secretaries had little or no knowledge of presidential goals and objectives, had not worked in the president's campaign, and did not personally know the president. These policy experts often had their own goals and objectives for the departments, quite separate from any goals and objectives that the president had. This increased problems that the president had in managing the bureaucracy, since presidential goals and objectives that should have been reinforced by the political staff were not. At times, presidential goals and objectives were openly opposed by the political staff.

When Richard Nixon took office, he pledged to his cabinet officers that they could continue the seasoned tradition of appointing their own political staff. Cabinet officers were free to hire their own staff without White House clearance. As Nixon said, Cabinet officers "were to run their own shows."[23] But within a relatively short period, Nixon became frustrated with the decisions emanating from the departments and reversed his decision. To a large degree, he blamed the political staff for not having gained greater control over the departmental policies. Nixon was particularly critical of the policies coming out of the Department of Housing and Urban Development and the Department of Health, Education, and Welfare, which he believed were perpetuating Great Society programs that he wanted to cut back. Nixon's strategy for dealing with this problem was to put the White House in control of all sub-cabinet political positions through a system of central clearance. Richard Nathan, who worked in the Office of Management and Budget, wrote a book about this process, which he named the "administrative presidency."[24] Nathan described how Nixon directed his White House personnel office to ensure that all political appointees were cleared by the White House for their political views. He did not want political appointees with liberal political views in policy-making positions.

Nixon began changing the profile of his political appointments after the 1972 presidential election. He asked for the resignations of all 2000 political appointees, including the deputy secretaries in each department. Many of the political staffers were fired and others were moved to different positions. With the large number of vacancies that were then available in the political ranks, Nixon appointed numerous people from the campaign staff, the Committee to Re-Elect the President (CREEP), to policy-making positions. This was an attempt to move loyalists into the senior levels of government and thereby reduce the problems of cooption that had occurred in the first term. But Nixon began to lose interest in overseeing the transformation of the subcabinet structure when impeachment hearings related to Watergate began to dominate his time and that of most senior members of the White House staff. The **administrative presidency** did not live up to its full potential because neither Nixon nor the White House staff continued to ensure that the new political staff was gaining control over the career staff.

The concept of moving presidential loyalists, or at least political loyalists, into policy-making positions was not a priority in the Ford administration. In fact, Gerald Ford tried to distance himself from his predecessor and promised an open administration, including returning the selection of subcabinet officials to the cabinet officers. Jimmy Carter followed this path and also promised an open administration, calling on his cabinet officers to choose the most qualified people they could, regardless of political affiliation. In Carter's case, this call for an open administration led to an administration of technocrats at the subcabinet level. Most of the technocrats had prior experience in the program and policy areas they were administering and had clear views on how those policies should move forward. Unfortunately, these views often were in conflict with those of the White House, forcing Carter to change his mind on how the permanent government should be managed. After eighteen months in office, Carter called an end to cabinet officers making their own choices for the subcabinets and required all political appointments to be cleared through the White House. Carter wanted to continue to have staff at the subcabinet level with strong policy expertise, but he wanted to ensure that those appointees supported the goals and objectives of the administration. Unlike Nixon, who was concerned that political liberals were running the departments, Carter was concerned that subcabinet staffers were not aggressively working toward either his program goals or his administrative goals of enhancing efficiency and economy in government.

When Ronald Reagan entered office, he established a new standard for managing the bureaucracy through political appointments. For Reagan, every subcabinet official had to pass a test of loyalty to Ronald Reagan and loyalty to the principles that Reagan espoused. Nominees for subcabinet positions had to meet a five-point test:

1. They had to have a philosophy in tune with the president.
2. They had to have a competency to pursue the philosophy of the president.
3. They had to have personal and professional integrity.
4. They had to be team players.
5. They had to be tough enough to take the abuse from the press, Congress, and the constituent groups.[25]

The result of this test for political appointees, which was managed through the White House personnel office's central clearance program, was to bring many campaign workers into the departments and many conservative Republicans into the departments. Loyalty to the party and to the president were the key requirements for working in the executive branch, not competence in the programs as it had been in the Carter administration. The personnel selection system imposed by Reagan was part of the grand design to minimize the career staff's influence over departmental policy decisions. Some Cabinet officers balked at the directive and tried to bring in their own staff without White House clearance. For example, Caspar Weinberger, Secretary of Defense, tried to bring Frank Carlucci into the department as his principal deputy. The White House personnel operation refused to accept Carlucci, who had been serving as deputy director of the Central Intelligence Agency under President Carter. The very mention of the Carter administration sent shudders up the spines of the Reagan personnel team. Weinberger eventually won and brought Carlucci into the Defense Department, but Carlucci was the exception. In general, cabinet officers in the Reagan administration were given subcabinet personnel approved by the White House. The White House sent the cabinet officers a short list of acceptable personnel from which the cabinet officers could choose. At times, however, only one person was on the list, and the cabinet officer was required to choose that person for the position. Control of personnel selection for subcabinet personnel became an important part of the Reagan strategy for keeping the permanent government in line with presidential goals and objectives.

While these three strategies remain the primary tools that presidents use for managing the bureaucracy, they have also made significant use of the Civil Service Reform Act of 1978 which allows senior staff in the civil service to accept a position in the Senior Executive Service (SES). By moving top levels of career staff into the Senior Executive Service, presidents have been able to add another layer of control over the bureaucracy. When career staff accept a position in the Senior Executive Service, they move into a separate classification that rewards job performance with salary bonuses. The political staff who approve these salary bonuses make judgments based on the success of the president's goals and objectives within each department. The more assistance that staff in the Senior Executive Service provide to the political staff in moving the president's programs forward, the more financial reward they will receive. Today, the SES has more than thirteen thousand positions.[26] The SES has become a powerful tool for presidents, when worked in alliance with presidential appointments.

One of the constraints on political appointments has been the **Ethics in Government Act of 1978.** This act requires senior political appointees to disclose their income, liabilities, and assets; dispose of any holdings or debts that might be affected by their decisions in government; and refrain from having any dealings with a department or agency for at least one year after leaving office. President Clinton went one step further and required all his appointees to sever all relations with their departments for five years after leaving office. The requirements imposed by the Ethics in Government Act of 1978 have limited the number of people who are willing to enter government service and been available to presidents for office. Many of President Reagan's friends declined to disclose their financial holdings and chose instead to remain part of the president's kitchen cabinet. The restriction had been difficult for many possible political appointees to accept, particularly if they are in the Washington community as lobbyists or in similar positions. Not only do political appointees have to disclose their holdings, but they are prohibited from engaging in any lobbying activity with their former department, which could affect their future job. One Reagan staffer, Michael Deaver, left the White House at the beginning of the president's second term but began a lobbying business that built on White House contacts. Deaver was eventually tried by an independent counsel under the Ethics in Government Act of 1978 and convicted of violating the law.

Reorganization as a Tool for Managing the Bureaucracy

Although Nixon saw the bureaucracy as philosophically opposed to his positions and sought reorganization authority from Congress to create the Office of Management and Budget to provide greater departmental oversight, the concept of using reorganization for managing the bureaucracy is deeply rooted in the modern presidency. Franklin Delano Roosevelt used his reorganization authority to improve his management over the executive departments.

The Roosevelt era had been marked by enormous increases in the size of the federal bureaucracy, which had expanded dramatically as a result of the New Deal programs. During Roosevelt's first term in office, Congress passed laws that had been crafted by Roosevelt to rebuild the economy after the Depression. More than sixty new agencies were created to support the New Deal programs, including the Tennessee Valley Authority (TVA), the Social Security Administration (SSA), and the Securities and Exchange Commission (SEC). The defense bureaucracy also grew during the war years, as the United States fought wars on two different fronts against Japan and Germany. The number of federal employees grew from 1,128,000 in 1940 to 2,117,000 a decade later, as the federal government expanded to handle the increased domestic and defense-related responsibilities.[27]

By 1937 Roosevelt realized that as the role of the federal government expanded and the bureaucracy increased, he was losing a significant degree of control over policy making. Agencies were moving on policy decisions with little coordination with each other and with only minimal consultation with the president. As Peri Arnold noted in his examination of reorganization planning, "Coordinating his creations was the President's next task."[28] Toward that next task, Roosevelt established the Brownlow Committee in 1936 to advise him on various techniques to improve his capabilities for monitoring the departments. The Brownlow Committee made a number of recommendations, including seeking reorganization authority from Congress to create a personal staff for the president. Congress approved the ideas generated by the Brownlow Committee and approved reorganization authority for Roosevelt in 1939. Using the authority provided in the Reorganization Act of 1939, Roosevelt created the Executive Office of the President and its chief component, the White House staff.

The White House staff has become one of the president's most important tools in managing the executive branch. Since the Nixon administration, the White House staff has evolved into its own bureaucracy, with large staffs specializing in many policy areas. Today, departmental staff regularly meet with White House staff to discuss policy proposals and to ensure that the proposals meet presidential goals and objectives. In addition, White House staff try to reduce tensions between departments and build bridges between agencies that share responsibilities for large programs; for example, agricultural programs are overseen by the Department of Agriculture but are also overseen by the Departments of Commerce and State when international trade agreements include sales of agricultural products.

Richard Nixon used his reorganization authority to create the Office of Management and Budget as a tool to manage the executive branch, but he also tried to use his reorganization authority to merge executive departments. Nixon's efforts to merge departments of the executive branch into **superdepartments** came through the Advisory Council on Government Reorganization, chaired by Roy Ash. The Ash Council, as it was known, recommended creation of the Executive Office of the President and the Domestic Council in order to give the president increased staff capabilities for managing the executive branch. The Ash Council also recommended the creation of four superdepartments. Under the superdepartment concept, four of the cabinet secretaries (all of whom were loyal Nixon supporters) would be given the additional title of *counselor to the president*. Under this plan, each of the four cabinet secretaries would be given authority for coordinating policy issues across a number of executive departments. Secretary of Agriculture Earl Butz was given the area of natural resources; Secretary of Health, Education, and Welfare Caspar Weinberger was given the area of human resources; Secretary of Housing and Urban Development James Lynn was given the area of community development; and Secretary of the Treasury George Shultz was given the area of economic affairs. The four superdepartments would be reorganized with the following jurisdictions:

> *The Department of Natural Resources:* Land, recreation, water resources, energy, and mineral resources.
>
> *The Department of Human Resources:* Health services, income maintenance and security, education, manpower, and social and rehabilitation services.
>
> *The Department of Economic Development:* Food and commodities, domestic and international commerce, science and technology, labor relations and standards, and statistical economic development.
>
> *The Department of Community Development:* Housing, community development, metropolitan development, and renewal development.

The departmental supersecretaries would work closely with the president's chief White House staff members, John Ehrlichman, H.R. Haldeman, and Henry Kissinger and the director of the Office of Management and Budget, Roy Ash, who was appointed after heading the Ash Council. According to Nixon, these four supersecretaries and the senior members of the White House staff would have the responsibility "to integrate and unify policies and operations throughout the executive branch. . . . And to oversee the activities for which the president is responsible."[29] The plan was initiated in January 1973 but was never fully implemented. Cabinet secretaries balked at having a layer between them and the president, particularly a layer of peers. The plan died when Watergate problems engulfed the president and his staff, leaving the departments to return to their prior structure.

Jimmy Carter also used the tool of reorganization to enhance his management of bureaucracy, beginning the process soon after taking office. During the transition, Carter pledged to begin comprehensive reorganization of the executive branch that would reduce the number of federal agencies from 1900 to 200, including many of the federal advisory commissions. As governor of Georgia, Carter had cut the number of state agencies from 300 to 22 during his four-year tenure in office and he promised to do the same in the nation's capital.[30] For Carter, reorganization would provide the tools to bring economy and efficiency to government, tools that he did not have with the bureaucracy working against him to protect their territory.

Less than a month after his inauguration, Carter sought reorganization authority from Congress. On February 5, 1977, Carter asked Congress for reorganization authority that would provide him the ability to improve the "management, efficiency, and delivery of federal services."[31] In other words, reorganization of the departments would provide greater management of the bureaucracy. Congress approved the reorganization authority and Carter quickly designated a unit in the Office of Management and Budget, called the "Reorganization Project," directed by Harrison Wellford to oversee the reorganization planning. Carter used his reorganization authority to create one new department, the Department of Energy, and to divide another department into two. The Department of Health, Education, and Welfare was split into the new Department of Education and the Department of Health and Human Services.

Creation of the Energy Department was designed to bring myriad energy-related agencies under one umbrella agency, the Energy Department. If Carter were going to achieve major changes in energy policy, he needed to have one clear position on energy policy and one clear voice articulating that position. By reducing the number of voices in energy policy and the number of bureaucracies involved, Carter was able to bring the resources of the presidency into management of energy issues. James Schlesinger, Carter's appointee to head the newly created agency, had spent considerable time in government and was attuned to bureaucratic politics. His strategy was to use the Energy Department to reduce overlapping jurisdictions, coordinate programs, and minimize territorial confrontations by bringing the often disparate bureaucracies under one roof.

Creation of the Education Department in 1979 was supported by Carter primarily for political rather than managerial reasons. During the presidential campaign, Carter had promised the National Education Association (NEA) that if they supported him he would reward that support by creating a separate Department of Education. The NEA had long wanted a department devoted solely to education. The support was far more tepid for the creation of the Department of Education within Congress than it had been for the Department of Energy, but the reorganization bill was approved.

The bureaucracy within the Department of Health and Human Services and other departments proved to be powerful opponents of the White House, as they tried to move programs into the Department of Education. The Head Start program, for example, which was geared to early education for children of poorer families, remained in the Department of Health and Human Services in spite of Carter's efforts to move them. The Indian Schools' programs remained in the Department of the Interior, and the Department of Labor retained control of its education and training programs. The bureaucracy had mobilized its vast network of clientele groups to ensure that these programs remained outside of the new Department of Education, where traditional alliances could have been jeopardized. Carter also tried to create a Department of Natural Resources through a reorganization plan announced on March 1, 1979. The proposal would have transferred the Forest Service from the Department of Agriculture and the National Oceanic and Atmospheric Administration from the Commerce Department. The bureaucracy quickly went to work to ensure that this proposal failed, which it did. On May 15, 1979, the White House pulled the reorganization plan for a Department of Natural Resources.

Carter's use of reorganization authority had not significantly added to his control of the executive branch, except through some consolidation of the energy programs. In fact, Secretary of Health, Education, and Welfare, Joseph Califano argued that creation of the Department of Education actually added to the president's managerial burden by adding another cabinet-level department for the president to deal with. For Califano, the new Education Department "would be adding yet another person reporting directly to him (Carter), further straining his span of control."[32] A strong argument could be made that Carter's attempt at controlling the bureaucracy through reorganization was a dismal failure, since the bureaucracy had significantly grown with the reorganization rather than been reduced.

In retrospect, neither of the departmental reorganization efforts initiated by Presidents Nixon and Carter significantly contributed to the president's ability to manage the federal government. Nixon's efforts ended in total failure when the superdepartment concept fell apart, and Carter's efforts ended in administrative failure when the bureaucracy was actually increased by the two new departments. But their reorganization efforts were not totally in vain. The Nixon reorganization plan had included three parts: creation of the Office of Management and Budget, creation of the Domestic Council, and creation of the superdepartment structure. The first two parts of the plan did contribute to presidential control over the bureaucracy and remain in effect today (although the Domestic Council has been renamed). Carter's plan for reorganization was not particularly successful itself, but another part of Carter's plan for improving management of the bureaucracy was successful. The creation of the Senior Executive Service during Carter's term proved a powerful tool for presidents in their management of the executive branch.

President Clinton had a brief try at reorganization, but it too failed. One proposal that came out of the National Performance Review called for the transfer of the law-enforcement functions of the Drug Enforcement Administration (DEA) from the Treasury Department to the FBI in the Justice Department. Both DEA career staff and Justice Department career staff opposed the move, leading to its withdrawal. Another reorganization proposal recommended by the Clinton administration was to eliminate the Agriculture Department's Food Safety and Inspection Service and to have the Food and Drug Administration within the Department of Health and Human Services handle this role. Not only did the Department of Agriculture's career staff adamantly oppose the program but they enlisted members of the House and Senate Agriculture Committees to their defense. This plan for reorganization also was abandoned.

Personnel Management and Other Tools

Reagan approached the issue of presidential management of the executive branch having learned the lessons of history. Armed with the experiences of recent presidents in departmental management and oversight, Reagan chose not to use the tools of reorganization but rather to focus on various aspects of personnel management, privatization, regulatory review, and the budget process.

Although each of these four techniques was important to the Reagan strategy of enhancing its control over the sprawling federal bureaucracy, personnel management was at the core of the strategy. His first move was to issue an executive order for a hiring freeze. This tactic would effectively reduce the number of career staffers through attrition and be a small but important part of his personnel-management strategy. In addition to the hiring freeze, field offices were cut and positions eliminated. In the Department of Interior, for example, dozens of federal mine inspectors lost their jobs.

Reagan's most important tactic for personnel management was to gain control over political appointments. All presidential appointees were chosen for their partisan politics and loyalty to the president. Although Reagan's two most recent Republican predecessors, Nixon and Ford, sought to populate the senior staff with conservative Republicans, they were far less adamant than Reagan was. Using the Presidential Personnel Office, Reagan used his appointment power to advance the conservative agenda that he had run for office on. All of the 2700 patronage positions were subject to the political tests that the Presidential Personnel Office required of every appointee. Anyone who did not satisfy the test of commitment to the president's agenda was not hired. As the deputy director of Reagan's Office of Presidential Personnel commented, "anyone who is considered for a position in the Administration should have a clearly demonstrated support for this agenda."[33]

One of the tools that Reagan used to highlight the importance of the personnel process in his administration was to place the director of the Office of Presidential Personnel, E. Pendleton James, in the West Wing of the White House. Past personnel directors had been housed in the Old Executive Office Building next to the White House. James was given the title *assistant to the president* and made a member of the senior White House staff. Another tool that the administration used was to have annual meetings of the entire political staff with the president in what was called the **Executive Forum,** which was held in Constitution Hall. During the two-hour session, Reagan would give a short speech to reinforce his agenda and then talk casually with his senior political staff. This gave the political appointees an opportunity to talk directly with the president and to hear directly from the president the administration's goals and objectives.

Reagan's theory on personnel management was that if the senior political staff were loyal to the agenda, there would be less likelihood of cooption. Nixon's domestic policy adviser, John Ehrlichman, had warned that career staff often move the political staff away from presidential positions to positions favored by the career staff. Ehrlichman described this process as the political staff marrying the natives.[34] The Reagan Republicans gave the process another twist by saying, "It is clearly a strategy that calls for an enhanced role for political appointees as operatives of the president within the executive branch"[35] The term *operatives of the president* provides strong evidence that the Reagan strategy for personnel management was to ensure that all political appointments were Reagan loyalists who would move the presidential agenda forward.

While personnel management of the political appointees was a central part of Reagan's efforts to gain control over the bureaucracy, it was only one of several tools. Another tool that Reagan used was to reduce the power of the bureaucracy in decision making by privatizing some of the functions of the federal government. This reduced the authority of career staff to determine where the resources of the federal government were placed.

Yet another tool used by the Reagan administration to control the bureaucracy was to reduce the discretionary authority of the career staff in formulating regulations for legislative mandates. Since Congress writes laws in general language, the departmental staff were responsible for writing the specific language, or regulations, for implementing the law. Departmental staff have "bureaucratic discretion" to shape the broad legislation through regulation. Reagan ordered the departments to reduce the number of regulations for all new legislation and to review all existing regulations. This strategy kept the career staff from having control over developing the programmatic details of how policies would be implemented. With fewer regulations and regulations written with vaguer language, the political staff had a greater opportunity to guide the direction of the programs. All regulations that were written by the departments had to be reviewed by the Office of Management and Budget. Regulations that were too long, too detailed, or too liberal in orientation were disallowed by the Office of Management and Budget and sent back to the departments to be rewritten. Regulatory oversight proved to be an important means of gaining control over the bureaucracy, particularly the oversight of the Office of Management and Budget.

Reagan did not leave any door open for the bureaucracy and sought to use every means available to ensure that the Reagan agenda was not stifled or softened at the administrative level by the career staff. One of the doors that Reagan shut on the bureaucracy was the power of the budget to continue programs that the departments had built up over the years. Again turning to the Office of Management and Budget to enforce the Reagan agenda, the White House gave the director of OMB, David Stockman, cabinet status and complete discretion over departmental budgets. Stockman began to cut funding for programs that did not fit the administration's goals and objectives and rarely changed the decision even after cabinet officers pleaded for the funding to be restored. Since the career staff had successfully protected their programs for years, Stockman believed it was unlikely that even the administrative strategy of peppering the departments with Reagan loyalists would effect significant change. The budget process was considered to be a critical tool for managing bureaucratic power.

Since only, on average, one in one thousand employees was a political appointment, the odds were overwhelmingly against significant change using only the personnel process. For Stockman, the budget would lead to more immediate results in curtailing programs that the administration was unhappy with. Writing in his memoirs, *The Triumph of Politics*, Stockman stated that, "Over the decades the politicians had lured tens of millions of citizens into milking: cows, food stamps, Social Security, the Veterans Hospitals, and much more. They were getting more than they deserved, needed, or were owed. For the Reagan Revolution to add up, they had to be cut off."[36] The budget cuts would enable the Reagan administration to bypass the bureaucracy, which would be slow to make changes or cuts to programs on their own. Even direct orders from cabinet officers did not have the effect on cutting programs that budget cuts did.

Reinventing Government and Bureaucratic Management

Reagan's strategy of containing the bureaucracy through personnel management, regulatory policy, and budget controls had been quite different from the reorganization techniques used by Nixon and Carter. President Clinton's technique for personnel management had little in common with any of his recent predecessors. Clinton's strategy for personnel management focused primarily on cutting the federal bureaucracy and gaining the support of the career staff by reducing the number of political supervisory personnel. The second part of this process was premised on having a career bureaucracy sympathetic to the goals of the administration. Clinton sought to reduce the number of employees within the bureaucracy to reduce the number of points at which his own policies could be thwarted by bureaucratic action. By eliminating positions in the career staff, Clinton hoped to increase the survival rate of his programs. The strategy also called for increasing the discretionary authority of the career staff, a position adamantly opposed by Clinton's immediate predecessors. Clinton thought that giving the career staff more discretionary authority would increase their loyalty to the administration. As a press release by the **National Performance Review** stated, the immediate goal of the reinventing government program was "to focus on the unleashing of the human potential in the workforce to improve operations."[37]

The strategy for managing the federal bureaucracy was laid out during the 1992 presidential campaign when Clinton promised that if elected he "would change the way government does business." Once in office, he launched the National Performance Review, a task force under the direction of Vice President Al Gore. The goals of the National Performance Review were to "reinvent government" by making the bureaucracy more efficient, accountable, and effective. To a large degree, these were the same words used by Jimmy Carter in his 1976 presidential campaign. But Carter approached the process differently, focusing on reorganization as the means to increase bureaucratic efficiency.

Clinton's National Performance Review task force was based on the principles outlined in a book entitled *Reinventing Government*, by David Osborne and Ted Gaebler.[38] Osborne and Gaebler argued that the organizational structure of the federal government does not allow enough flexibility in decision making because of its hierarchical nature. In their view, decision making should be focused at the lower levels of the bureaucracy rather than the higher levels. This would allow a quicker response time to the clientele that the departments service rather than going through layers of clearance. By downsizing the bureaucracy, individual staff members would have more discretionary authority to move on issues and provide the clientele significantly faster service. When Gore's National Performance Review task force wrote its report, entitled "From Red Tape to Results: Creating a Government that Works Better and Costs Less," the principles that Osborne and Gaebler had laid out were firmly incorporated into the report.

The report made more than eight hundred recommendations for streamlining the way the bureaucracy did business. By reducing the size of the bureaucracy and reducing the costs of the federal government, Gore predicted that government efficiency could take over from "old fashioned, outdated government." The report calculated that the federal government could save $108 billion over five years and eliminate more than two hundred and fifty thousands jobs. A report issued by the National Performance Review staff in mid-1998 listed its accomplishments after five years as an overall reduction of 291,000 federal positions and savings of about $118 billion. The National Performance Review had successfully reduced the federal bureaucracy and enhanced the decision-making power of lower-level employees, which was Clinton's primary tool for gaining control over the career staff.

The tool that Nixon and Reagan had used for personnel management (ensuring political consistency in the political appointments) did not seem to be a major factor in the Clinton strategy. Clinton centralized the hiring of all political appointments in the White House, as Nixon and Reagan had done, but used very different criteria for appointments. Where adherence to political goals and objectives was the central theme for the Nixon and Reagan personnel offices, the Clinton personnel office sought to transform the character of the executive branch. For Clinton, the departments should have senior staff "that looked like America." This phrase referred to Clinton's belief that the policy-making levels had been peppered for too long with white males rather than with a broad range of ethnic groups and with women, many of whom lived in Washington, D.C., and were part of the revolving door of government. To rectify this, he directed that all cabinet and subcabinet positions be subject to the test of ethnicity, gender, and geography, or the EGG test. His main goal for the political staff was not personnel management, as it had been for Nixon and Reagan's administrative presidencies, but for increasing the visibility of women and minorities at the highest levels of the federal government.

Having therefore discarded the political appointments as a tool for gaining control over the bureaucracy, Clinton turned to the National Performance Review as the backdrop for his efforts to cut the size and thus the power of the federal bureaucracy. Unlike past presidents, who had publicly scorned the power of the bureaucracy, Clinton constantly praised the bureaucracy and promised to arm it with greater authority by cutting out unwanted layers of personnel and decentralizing decision-making authority. While Clinton was cutting more than two hundred thousand positions, he was carefully praising the bureaucracy and building their trust.

Personnel Management Through White House Control

Every president since Franklin Delano Roosevelt has realized the necessity of gaining greater control over the career staff to ensure that presidential goals and objectives are moved forward. While presidents have utilized a variety of techniques to build their management capabilities, all presidents have used the White House staff as a bridge to the departments and the departmental bureaucracy. The White House staff has been used, particularly since the Nixon administration, to work directly with the subcabinet political staff in the departments. By working directly with the political staff rather than only with the cabinet secretaries, the White House staff can keep the political staff within the presidential rather than the departmental orbit.

In order to keep the political staff in the presidential orbit, White House staff host regular meetings in the White House to discuss policy issues. How a policy should be implemented, legislative strategies, and problems with other agencies are frequent topics of these meetings. By having regular contact with the senior departmental staff, White House staff try to reinforce the administration's agenda and the immediate policy goals. Reinforcement works to keep the departmental staff attuned to presidential goals and to keep the staff from aligning with the career staff. As long as the political staff believe that they are representatives of the president to the department rather than representatives of the department to the president, the White House staff is comfortable. As soon as the political staff become representatives of the department to the president, they become advocates for departmental programs that are often low on the president's priority list or even targeted for elimination. White House staff use all sorts of mechanisms to build strong relationships with the political staff, such as the social tools of inviting them to state dinners at the White House, inviting them to use the White House tennis courts, and letting them use the president's box in the Kennedy Center. There are also the administrative tools of creating working groups of political staff both within a department and across departments to forge bonds of allegiance to presidential programs.

The tools available to the White House for building collegial relations among the senior staff across the departments are an important part of managing the bureaucracy. Political scientist Hugh Heclo referred to the presidential appointments as "a government of strangers."[39] The president rarely knows the second level of government employees, the political appointments, and they rarely know each other. The problem of having a government of strangers is that they can easily become coopted by the bureaucracy to move away from the president and toward the career staff. By aggressively creating opportunities for the political staff to get to know each other and to work together, the White House has reduced the likelihood of the political staff becoming coopted.

Building Bridges to the Bureaucracy

Although presidents have developed a number of ways to exercise control over the bureaucracy, they have also developed a number of ways to build bridges to the bureaucracy. The most important bridge that a president can build is to have a cabinet secretary and subcabinet staff who gain the trust of their departments. Departmental leadership is a critical part of establishing strong relations between the White House and the career staff.

Cabinet secretaries have to believe in the mission of their departments. When Ronald Reagan pledged to dismantle the Department of Education and brought in a cabinet officer who publicly supported the idea, the career staff began a campaign against the political staff. Bureaucrats began working with their allies in the education unions, particularly the National Education Association, which had strongly lobbied for creation of the Department of Education, to prevent Reagan from gaining reorganization authority. Similarly, Reagan's appointment of Anne Gorush Burford was a dismal failure given her open opposition to the mission of the department she headed, the Environmental Protection Agency. Burford saw many of the agency's regulations as too burdensome on business and industry, a view for which career staff in the Environmental Protection Agency had little support.

Departmental leaders must also be able to rally congressional and constituent support for agency programs. If the political leaders are able to rally such support, the career staff will have greater respect for them and will be more eager to work with them. Respect is a powerful tool in building alliances with the career staff. At times, this means that the departmental leader has to carefully tread between presidential goals and objectives and departmental goals and objectives.

The power of the president to manage the bureaucracy depends on the tools that are used. Presidential leadership of the bureaucracy is essential in order to move the administration's goals and objectives forward. The more tools that are used, the more successful the president will be in having a strong working relationship with the career staff. The key to successful leadership of the bureaucracy is for presidents to build bridges to the career staff, not burn them.

Key Words

administrative presidency
bureaucracy
Civil Service Act of 1883
Civil Service Reform Act of 1978
Ethics in Government Act of 1978
Executive Forum
Hatch Act of 1939
increasing the size of the White House staff
iron triangle

National Performance Review
Permanent bureaucracy
Plum book
policy experts
presidential bureaucracy
rule making
Schedule C positions
Senior Executive Service
spoils system
superdepartments

Notes

1. Jack E. Holmes, Michael Engelhardt, Robert E. Elder, Jr., James M. Zoetewey, and David K. Ryden, "The Bureaucracy." In: *American Government, Essentials and Perspectives.* 3rd ed. New York: McGraw-Hill, 1998, pp. 382–383.
2. Marquis James. *The Life of Andrew Jackson.* New York: Bobbs-Merrill, 1938, pp. 215–216.
3. Ibid., p. 216.
4. Ibid., p. 217.
5. Craig Bledsoe. "Executive Branch Pay and Perquisites." In: Michael Nelson, ed. *Guide to the Presidency.* 2nd ed. Washington, DC: Congressional Quarterly, 1996, p. 977.
6. Ibid., p. 980.

7. John Hart. *The Presidential Branch: From Washington to Clinton.* 2nd ed. Chatham, NJ: Chatham House, 1995, p. 35.

8. Harry S Truman. *Memoirs of Harry S Truman.* New York: Smithmark, 1996, p. 43.

9. Hugh Heclo. *A Government of Strangers: Executive Politics in Washington.* Washington, DC: Brookings Institution, 1977, p. 93.

10. Herman Miles Somers. "The Federal Bureaucracy and the Change of Administration." *American Political Science Review,* vol. 48, 1954, p. 131.

11. Peri E. Arnold. *Making the Managerial Presidency: Comprehensive Reorganization Planning 1905–1996.* 2nd rev. ed. Lawrence, KS: University Press of Kansas, 1998, p. 169.

12. Becky Norton Dunlop. "The Role of the Office of Presidential Personnel." In: Robert Rector and Michael Sanera, eds. *Steering the Elephant: How Washington Works.* New York: Universe, 1987, p. 145.

13. George T. Kurian. *Datapedia of the United States, 1790–2000.* Lanham, MD: Bernan, 1994, p. 440.

14. *Brown v. Board of Education* (I), 347 U.S. 438 (1954).

15. Dennis R. Judd. *The Politics of American Cities.* Boston: Little, Brown, 1979, pp. 308ff.

16. Shirley Anne Warshaw. *Powersharing: White House–Cabinet Relations in the Modern Presidency.* Albany, NY: State University of New York Press, 1996, p. 115.

17. Peter Woll. *American Bureaucracy.* 2nd ed. New York: Norton, 1977, p. 105.

18. Ibid., p. 215.

19. Richard E. Neustadt. *Presidential Power and the Modern Presidents.* New York: Free Press, 1990.

20. Francis E. Rourke. "Bureaucracy in the American Constitutional Order." In: James P. Pfiffner and Roger H. Davidson, eds. *Understanding the Presidency.* New York: Longman, 1997, p. 199.

21. Patrick Anderson. *The President's Men.* Garden City, NY: Doubleday, 1969, p. 233.

22. Richard M. Nixon. *RN: The Memoirs of Richard Nixon.* New York: Grosset & Dunlap, 1978, p. 761.

23. Theodore H. White. *The Making of the President 1968.* New York: Atheneum, 1969, p. 504.

24. Richard P. Nathan. *The Plot That Failed: Nixon and the Administrative Presidency.* New York: Wiley, 1975.

25. Author interview with James Watt, Secretary of Interior.

26. *Statistical Abstract of the United States 1997.* Washington, DC: Government Printing Office, 1997, p. 349.

27. Kurian, p. 440.

28. Peri E. Arnold. *Making the Managerial Presidency,* p. 89.

29. Quoted in Nathan. *The Plot that Failed,* p. 69.

30. Joel Havemann. "Reorganization—How Clean Can Carter's Broom Sweep?" *National Journal,* January 1, 1977, p. 6.

31. *Public Papers of the Presidents of the United States: Jimmy Carter, 1977.* vol. 1. "Reorganization Plan Authority." Washington, DC: Government Printing Office, 1978, pp. 82–84.

32. Joseph A. Califano, Jr. *Governing America.* New York: Simon & Schuster, 1981, pp. 277–278.

33. Becky Norton Dunlop. "The Role of the White House Office of Presidential Personnel." In: Rector and Sanera, eds. *Steering the Elephant,* p. 148.

34. John Ehrlichman. *Witness to Power: The Nixon Years.* New York: Simon & Schuster, 1982.

35. Robert Rector and Michael Sanera. "The Reagan Presidency and Policy Change." In: Rector and Sanera, eds. *Steering the Elephant,* p. 333.

36. David Stockman. *The Triumph of Politics: The Inside Story of the Reagan Revolution.* New York: Avon, 1986, p. 12.

37. Quoted in press release on the Internet. Retrieved online at http://www.npr.gov.

38. David Osborne and Ted Gaebler. *Reinventing Government: How the Entrepreneurial Spirit Is Transformed in the Public Sector.* Reading, MA: Addison-Wesley, 1992.

39. Heclo. *A Government of Strangers: Executive Politics in Washington.*

Chapter 8

THE PRESIDENCY AND THE SUPREME COURT

As the power of the presidency has grown throughout the past two hundred years, there have been numerous challenges to the constitutional authority of the president. These challenges, which have originated from Congress as well as from private citizens and private enterprise, have usually been resolved in favor of the president. The Supreme Court has said that although presidential power is not clearly defined at times in the Constitution, it is an expansive power. Rarely does the Supreme Court deny presidents authority to carry out their role as the nation's chief executive.

There are two explanations for the Supreme Court's support of an expansive interpretation of presidential powers. The first is that Article II vests the president with "the executive power." This phrase provides the president broad authority for a multitude of executive actions. The second explanation is that presidents usually have broad public support for their actions and substantial political support. Even the Supreme Court is not immune to the power of public support for a president. This is not to say that the Supreme Court will never rule against presidential action, but it does not usually happen. On issues of great controversy between the president and Congress, a frequently used technique by the Supreme Court is to call the issue a political question and refuse to intervene. Presidential power is a difficult commodity to evaluate, since the Constitution has given only cursory provisions to define that power. The language of the Constitution in Article I is very specific in defining the powers of Congress, yet far less specific in Article II in defining the powers of the president. To some presidents, this lack of specificity in the Constitution provides an open door to extending power as far as possible. To other presidents, this lack of specificity provides few openings and actually shuts the door to extending power.

Every president since Franklin Delano Roosevelt has believed that the Constitution opens the door to extending power. We have been in an era of presidential government since Franklin Delano Roosevelt in which presidents have consistently viewed themselves rather than Congress as the nation's leader. In this battle for leadership between the president and Congress (a battle won by Congress during the nineteenth and early twentieth centuries), the president has taken the lead. The latter half of the twentieth century has seen the move from congressional government to presidential government, as presidents have begun to assert their prerogative powers. Ever since Roosevelt's masterful rebuilding of the nation following the Great Depression and his command of the nation during World War II, the American people have looked to the president to lead the country. This leadership has often required the exploration of authority not expressly granted in the Constitution, and has led to a number of challenges to that authority for the Supreme Court to decide. As the nation moved through a series of continuous crises from the Great Depression through the Cold War, presidents continued to expand their power, almost unchecked by either the Court or the Congress.

The Supreme Court has sought to provide a framework for defining prerogative power without tilting the delicate balance in the checks-and-balances system that the framers intended. While the Supreme Court has recognized the need for the president to be able to act swiftly in times of national crisis and to be the primary voice of the nation in foreign policy, it has also kept the president from exercising power before all legislatively mandated options have been explored. However, the rule of thumb has been that if the Constitution is silent on an issue and the president seeks to gain control over that power, the Supreme Court will support the president. For example, the Constitution is silent on the power of removing cabinet officers from office. Congress demanded that it be consulted to approve all removals, but the president argued that since the Constitution deals with appointments only, removals are not subject to legislative review; the Supreme Court supported the president's position. Similarly, the Constitution is silent on the power of abrogating a treaty. Congress demanded that all treaties that the president seeks to terminate had to be approved by the Senate, as was true in the ratification process of treaties. The Supreme Court again supported the president, arguing that since the architects of the Constitution chose to keep that power from Congress the president must have the power. The expansion of presidential powers over the past two centuries has been routinely challenged in the Supreme Court, usually by Congress but sometimes by others, on the grounds that the president has exceeded the power delineated in the Constitution. The march toward expanding presidential power began with President Washington and continues today. As presidential scholar Edward Corwin noted, "Taken by and large, the history of the presidency is a history of aggrandizement."[1] We remain in an era of presidential government and, in the absence of a major change in precedents established by the Supreme Court, that is not likely to change.

Prerogative Powers of the President

Challenges to presidential authority stem from the fact that the Constitution does not clearly delineate the powers of the president. Article I of the Constitution states that Congress has "all legislative power herein granted" and provides an extended list of legislative powers. In contrast, Article II of the Constitution simply states that the "the executive power" is vested in the president but provides very little in the way of guidance as to what that executive power shall be. Alexander Hamilton described this rather vague delineation of powers in the executive branch as a means to ensure that the president has the ability to carry out his responsibilities with energy, the "energy in the executive" as he phrased it.[2] This energy meant that the president was not constrained by a list of powers that may not deal with every issue that arose. The language of Article II was intended by the framers to be elastic, to be broad enough to expand presidential power to meet the needs of the nation.

The concept of **prerogative power,** or expansive power, is rooted in the English philosopher John Locke's theory of executive power in *Of Civil Government: Second Treatise,* written in 1689. In Chapter 14, "On Prerogative," Locke states that executives must act to protect the general welfare or public good in all cases and under all circumstances. Locke wrote that "in many cases where the municipal law has given no direction . . . those must necessarily be left to the discretion of him that has the executive power in his hands, to be ordered by him as the public good." He continued by arguing that executives can "enlarge their prerogative" as they please as long as their goal was to protect the "public good."[3] For Locke, the use of power not specifically delineated by law or written word was an important part of protecting the **public good.** The executive, Locke said, must have the power "to act according to discretion for the public good, without the prescription of law and sometimes even against it."[4] Prerogative power was the power to protect the citizenry without the specific prescription of law.

Although the ability to use prerogative power is not written into the Constitution, the possibility that presidents would need to act in times of crisis or in times when no other rules exist was of constant concern to the framers. Hamilton's argument that there must be energy in the executive and his argument against a council for reasons of accountability point to the knowledge that presidents would need to act quickly and decisively at times without clear direction from the Constitution or from Congress. To some extent the framers did provide certain prerogative powers in the Constitution by allowing presidents to suspend habeas corpus in times of national emergency, as Abraham Lincoln did during the Civil War. A safeguard was built into the Constitution for presidents who misused their prerogative power by giving Congress the power of impeachment. Congress could use their constitutional powers of impeachment and conviction to remove a president whom they felt had pursued powers that did not satisfy the test of serving the public good.

Doctrine of Necessity

The concept of having prerogative powers that provided extra-constitutional authority to presidential actions was endorsed by Thomas Jefferson in what became known as the **Doctrine of Necessity.** Writing to his friend Robert Colvin in 1810, Jefferson said that "a strict observance of the written law is doubtless one of the higher duties of a good citizen. But it is not the highest. The laws of necessity, of self preservation, of saving our country when in danger, are of a higher obligation."[5] Jefferson's purchase of the Louisiana Territory in 1803 is often cited as an example of his use of prerogative power. The Louisiana Purchase was handled by Jefferson independently of Congress, although Congress later appropriated funds for the purchase and ratified the treaty. Since no rules or guidelines existed on how the federal government could purchase additional lands, Jefferson simply acted on his own authority. On another occasion Jefferson wrote of his broad interpretation of presidential power, "that every good officer must be ready to risk himself in going beyond the strict line of the law, when the public preservation requires it, his motives will be a justification."[6] Jefferson was a firm believer in expanding executive power as far as possible, choosing not to consult Congress when he didn't want to and choosing to give his own definition to the vaguely written Constitutional powers.

Abraham Lincoln followed Jefferson's interpretation of expansive executive power during the Civil War in numerous cases. Without consulting Congress, Lincoln sent troops to protect the beleaguered Fort Sumter. Lincoln argued that the nation was under attack and that his duty was to protect the nation or, as John Locke would describe it, to protect the public good. Lincoln himself referred to his actions throughout the Civil War as a "public necessity."[7] He called out troops, proclaimed martial law, emancipated the slaves, and seized private property, all in the name of protecting the public good.

Stewardship Theory

Theodore Roosevelt continued to build on the Lockean theory of prerogative powers by declaring that it was the right and duty of the president "to do anything that the needs of the nation demanded unless such action was forbidden by the Constitution or by the laws. . . . I acted for the public welfare."[8] For Roosevelt, the president was a steward of the people, based on his belief that the executive power was not limited "only by specific restrictions and prohibitions appearing in the Constitution or imposed by Congress."[9] Roosevelt's **stewardship theory** provided further support for Locke's prerogative powers and Jefferson's doctrine of necessity in which the president had the power to deal with issues that were not specifically addressed in the Constitution. The stewardship theory of executive power provided Roosevelt the foundation for his broad use of executive agreements. When the Senate refused to ratify several treaties, Roosevelt issued executive orders to put the agreements into effect. Roosevelt's predecessor, William McKinley, also had an expansive view of executive power, sending several thousand American troops to China to help suppress the Boxer Rebellion without consulting Congress.

Constructionist Theory

The stewardship theory of executive power was challenged by William Howard Taft, who argued that presidents were limited by the language of the Constitution. If the Constitution did not authorize the power in the executive, the executive did not have that power. For Taft, the language of the Constitution and the construction of the Constitution determined how presidents could conduct their official duties. "The true view of executive functions," Taft said, "is, as I conceive it, that the President can exercise no power which cannot be fairly and reasonably traced to some specific grant of power or justly implied and included within such grant as proper and necessary."[10] The **constructionist theory** said that the president could not exercise a power that could not be traced to a specific act of Congress or to the Constitution. President Taft's view of governance directly opposed Presidents Jefferson, Lincoln, and

Roosevelt. Under the constructionist theory of executive power, presidents were limited to those few powers delineated in the Constitution and the grant of authority that congressional mandates gave to the president. Taft rejected the concept of extra constitutional powers or prerogative powers.

Franklin Delano Roosevelt and Prerogative Powers

When Franklin Delano Roosevelt entered the presidency, he revitalized the stewardship theory of his cousin, Theodore Roosevelt. He tried to expand the size of the Supreme Court, embargo foreign countries, exchange American destroyers for the lease of English military bases, and manage the crippled economy with minimal constitutional authority. One of Roosevelt's boldest moves was to act without the prescription of law behind him when in 1942 he ordered Congress to repeal part of the Emergency Price Control Act or he would refuse to enforce it. Roosevelt argued that in the tradition of Locke, Jefferson, and Lincoln he had the power to act to protect the nation and to protect the general welfare and the public good. Roosevelt also added, as had Lincoln, that war provided further necessity for the executive to move decisively to protect the nation. For Roosevelt, extraordinary times demanded extraordinary measures.

Although many of Roosevelt's actions during his tenure in office fueled debate on prerogative powers, none fueled the fire so much as his removal of Japanese-Americans to protective custody in relocation camps. By an executive order issued on February 19, 1942, Roosevelt restricted the movement of Japanese-Americans living on the West Coast and established curfews. He ordered the Secretary of the Army to create "defense zones" on the West Coast. Over 110,000 Japanese-Americans living in California, Oregon, Washington, and Arizona were moved to relocation camps in interior states between February and March 1942.[11] The order was in effect until January 2, 1945. At the time, the public supported the action, fearing a widespread Japanese conspiracy within the United States. Since the exercise of prerogative power depends on support from the citizenry, Roosevelt was not challenged on his order to take Japanese-Americans to a central location until the war was over. The Supreme Court unanimously upheld the curfew order as a legitimate part of the president's discretionary authority within his war powers. In another case, the Supreme Court upheld the removal of Japanese-Americans from their homes to internment camps since Congress had supported the president's action with the War Relocation Act. The Court ruled that the action was also within the war powers of the president.

The expansion of presidential power since the administration of George Washington has continued unabated to the present. While some presidents, such as Taft, have not used their prerogative powers, most presidents have. In some cases presidents have been brought down by public opinion for exceeding their power either by being voted out of office or through the impeachment and conviction power of Congress. Lyndon Johnson was effectively voted out of office (although he chose not to run since public opinion had turned against him) for his actions in the Vietnam War. Richard Nixon was nearly impeached (but resigned before the impeachment vote) because of his role in the Watergate break-in. Although there are public sanctions on the abuse of prerogative power, these sanctions are rarely enforced. The most common method of sanctioning presidents who abuse or extend their prerogative power beyond acceptable limits has been through the Supreme Court. The Supreme Court has addressed a number of decisions made by presidents, approving some decisions and rebuking others.

Judicial Review

The power of judicial oversight of presidential actions stems in large part from the principle of judicial review, established in 1803 in the case of **Marbury v. Madison.** During the late 1700s, party activism and party animosity had risen to new heights since the start of the republic. President John Adams's Federalist Party had fought bitterly with members of the Republican Party led by Thomas Jefferson. One of the last acts passed by the Federalists in Congress during Adams's presidency was the Judiciary Act of 1801. The act expanded the number of new judges, as well as marshals and justices of the peace, and reduced the number of justices on the Supreme Court from six to five, stating that the next vacancy would not be filled.[12] As the Adams administration drew to a close in 1800, Secretary of State John Marshall appointed William Marbury as a justice of the peace for the District of Columbia. This was one of more than two hundred judicial appointments that Adams made in the waning days of his administration under the terms of the Judiciary Act of 1801. The commission for Marbury was appropriately signed by Marshall, and his seal affixed to the commission, but the commission was not delivered to Marbury before Adams left office. Before leaving office, Adams also named Marshall to the Supreme Court as the chief justice.

As soon as Jefferson was sworn into office, he sought the repeal of the Judiciary Act of 1801. The law was repealed by a sympathetic Congress in March 1802. Anticipating the repeal of the law, Jefferson ordered Secretary of State James Madison to ignore Marbury's commission and not to deliver it. Marbury sued Madison in federal court to have the commission delivered in the case of Marbury v. Madison. The legal argument that Marbury used was that the Judiciary Act of 1801 was legal and binding on the president until repealed. Since the law had not been repealed when Marbury's commission was issued, the commission was binding. In February 1803 the Supreme Court issued a ruling that established two precedents. First, by ruling that the president had acted in violation of the law, the Court established itself as the arbiter of executive–legislative conflicts. Second, by ruling that the law was unconstitutional, the Court established the principle of judicial review.

With regard to the first point, limiting presidential power, the Court ruled that Jefferson should not have denied Marbury his commission, which had been duly signed and sealed by the former administration. Chief Justice Marshall bluntly wrote in his decision that the president had overstepped his authority and in the future should not fail to carry out his "ministerial duties." Although a major constitutional issue had been addressed by the Court, Marbury lost his case. Marbury failed to gain his commission in spite of Marshall's support and in spite of Marshall's rebuke of the president because the Judiciary Act was ruled unconstitutional. Since Marbury no longer had standing since the law was voided, Marshall could not order Jefferson to deliver the commission to Marbury. This averted another showdown between the president and the Supreme Court, since Jefferson might have refused to accede to the command.

With regard to the second point, establishing judicial review, the Court ruled that "it is emphatically the province and duty of the Judicial Department to say what the law is. Those who apply the rule to a particular case, must of necessity expound and interpret the rule."[13] But the principle of judicial review took another twist before the year was out, further strengthening the power of the Supreme Court. Thomas Jefferson was not willing to allow the Court to have the final say on these matters. For Jefferson, the Supreme Court had failed to reach the appropriate decision primarily because it was biased against the Republicans. According to Jefferson, the Court had opposed his position for political rather than constitutional reasons. Jefferson's solution was to seek retribution using the time-honored method of political action. With Jefferson's support, Republicans in Congress began impeachment hearings against Justice Samuel Chase, a Federalist. They successfully impeached Chase and the Senate then held a trial to consider conviction and subsequent removal from office. Vice President Aaron Burr presided over the trial in the Senate. After a turbulent trial, the Republicans failed to gain a two-thirds majority for the conviction, so Chase was not removed from office. To a large degree, the trial of Justice Chase was a trial of the Supreme Court's powers to render judicial review. Had the Senate convicted Chase, the Supreme Court may have become hesitant in future years to render decisions that challenged the authority of either the Congress or the president.

Andrew Jackson and Judicial Review

The issue of judicial review arose again during the Jackson administration, when Andrew Jackson refused to acknowledge that only the Supreme Court had the authority to declare a bill unconstitutional. In Jackson's annual message to Congress in 1830 he supported the constitutionality of the tariff act passed in 1828. This was an early warning to the Supreme Court that he intended to question the constitutionality of bills emerging from Congress. Two years later that warning became a reality. In Jackson's message of July 10, 1832, vetoing the bill to recharter the Second Bank of the United States, he passionately argued that the president must have independent decision-making power with regard to the constitutionality of laws. Both the president and the Supreme Court, Jackson argued, had the power to determine whether a law was unconstitutional. In his veto message Jackson defined the authority of the presidency by stating, "The Congress, the Executive, and the Court must each for itself be guided by its own opinion of the Constitution. Each public officer who takes an oath to support the Constitution swears that he will support it as he understands it, and not as it is understood by others."[14] Jackson was firmly opposed to the power of the Supreme Court as the only arbiter of the Constitution. For Jackson, presidential power also included the power to determine constitutional questions that emanated from lawmaking.

Throughout his presidency, Jackson acted without fear of the Supreme Court constraining his power. When Georgia resisted a Supreme Court decision in 1832 to release a prisoner from jail, Jackson resisted any action to enforce the ruling.[15] Jackson reportedly said of Chief Justice John Marshall's ruling, "John Marshall has made his decision, now let him enforce it!" When the South Carolina legislature later that year adopted the doctrine of nullification to declare null and void federal laws of which it did not approve, Jackson finally stepped in. He firmly declared that the doctrine of nullification was unacceptable and reaffirmed the supremacy of national laws over state laws. Georgia subsequently backed down, as did South Carolina, averting a national crisis. The decision of Jackson not to support the Supreme Court in the Georgia case was no longer an issue, but it had again raised the question of the executive branch enforcing decisions from the judicial branch.

Abraham Lincoln and Judicial Review

The president again came into conflict with the Supreme Court during the Lincoln administration, but the stage for that fight had been set several years earlier. When Lincoln was running against Stephen Douglas for the Senate seat from Illinois in 1858, he participated in a series of debates, known as the Lincoln-Douglas debates. During one debate on the 1857 *Dred Scot* decision[16] in which the Supreme Court had denied the right of slaves to bring suit in federal court, Lincoln argued that the Supreme Court did not have sole power to make these decisions. He asserted that the president had equal authority to deal with such issues.

Once president, Lincoln asserted a strong executive power, particularly after the Civil War began. In his first inaugural address in 1861, Lincoln addressed the power of the Supreme Court and his view that at times the Court could make poor decisions. Lincoln said that "the people will have ceased to be their own rulers" should the Court make an "erroneous decision." Clearly, Lincoln was not averse to taking action that the Court could oppose. The clash between the Court and Lincoln did not occur until after Lincoln's death. Only a few weeks after the attack at Fort Sumter by Confederate troops, Lincoln ordered the suspension of the writ of habeas corpus. Chief Justice Roger Taney, who authored the *Dred Scot* decision, declared that Lincoln had no such authority, but Lincoln responded that in times of national emergency his duty was to protect the nation and the "public safety."[17] Lincoln's view of presidential power was built on the Lockean theory of prerogative power to ensure the public good. In somewhat of a footnote to the constitutional battle that Chief Justice Taney waged with President Lincoln over presidential power was the fact that Taney was the chief defender of Andrew Jackson's view of expansive presidential power when he served as Jackson's Attorney General.

After the Civil War had ended and Andrew Johnson had taken over the government following the assassination of Lincoln, the issue of prerogative power was litigated in the Supreme Court. Had Lincoln gone too far during the Civil War in his expansive view of presidential powers? In the only test case of the use of prerogative power that grew out of Lincoln's presidency, the Supreme Court failed to specifically address the issue. The Supreme Court did not admonish Lincoln for his actions, nor did it demand that such actions not occur in the future. In the major case of the era regarding abuse of power, **Ex parte Milligan** in 1866, the Supreme Court did not challenge Lincoln's authority to suspend the writ of habeas corpus; rather, the Court ruled that the procedures put in place for trying prisoners was unacceptable since the civil courts were still operational. The Court said that "it is essential to the safety of every government that, in a great crisis, like the one we have just passed through, there should be a power somewhere of suspending the writ of habeas corpus."[18] The only rebuke to Lincoln was that the use of military tribunals instead of civil courts was unconstitutional.

The broader questions of prerogative power were also addressed in more specific cases not specifically defined by the Constitution. These cases include the role of the president as chief executive, commander in chief, chief diplomat, and others. What are the limits on the power of the president in appointment and removal, in pardons and in sending troops into hostile situations? The question of prerogative power has extended to the president as chief executive, such as executive privilege, executive orders, and executive agreements.

The President as Chief Executive

As chief executive, the president is vested under the Constitution with the power to execute the laws. The job of chief executive requires the president to create an administrative apparatus to manage the federal government, an apparatus that has burgeoned into an executive branch of more than three million employees today. The task of running the executive branch has led to numerous conflicts between the president and Congress over the extent to which the president can make decisions without legislative approval. In these conflicts, the Supreme Court has been forced to intervene. However, in the vast majority of decisions, the Court has ruled in favor of the president rather than Congress. These decisions have contributed to the expansion of presidential power and the growing use of prerogative power. When the Constitution has failed to provide adequate definition to whether Congress or the president has the controlling interest, the Court has usually supported the president.

Appointment Power

Article II of the Constitution gives the president the authority to "nominate, and by and with the advice and consent of the Senate, shall appoint ambassadors, other public ministers and consuls, judges of the Supreme Court, and all other Officers of the United States, whose Appointments are not herein otherwise provided for, and which shall be established by Law." Although the president has the constitutional authority to make executive appointments, the Civil Service Act of 1883 restricted those to certain high-level appointments. All cabinet-level and subcabinet-level appointments are made directly by the president, although certain lower-level federal court positions are made in concert with Senate delegations as a matter of political courtesy (senatorial courtesy). The Constitution clearly provides the power of appointment to the president, but the power of removal of those appointments has been the subject of considerable controversy.

Removal power was not addressed in the Constitution. Neither Article I defining the powers of Congress nor Article II defining the powers of the president provide for the authority to remove a senior political appointee within the executive branch. The issue first arose in 1866 when Congress passed the Tenure of Office Act over President Andrew Johnson's veto, which required the president to seek the approval of the Senate when removing a cabinet member. Johnson fired Secretary of War Edwin M. Stanton later that year and was impeached in 1868 for violating the law.[19] The Senate, which came within one vote of conviction, allowed Johnson to retain his presidency by refusing to convict following the House impeachment. Congress eventually repealed the Tenure of Office Act in 1887. But in the interim Congress passed another act dealing with presidential removal of one group of presidentially appointed employees, the postmasters. The 1876 act, which governed the removal of postmasters was not affected by the repeal of the Tenure of Office Act and remained in effect. This act was to be the grounds fifty years later for another challenge to the president's removal power.

Since the political process had resolved the removal issue during the administration of Andrew Johnson, the judicial process was not called on for further action. Not until the twentieth century did the removal issue finally come before the Supreme Court. In the 1926 case of **Myers v. United States,** the Supreme Court ruled that President Woodrow Wilson did have the authority to remove a postmaster, Frank S. Myers, in Portland, Oregon. Myers sued to regain his job, but lost his case. The Court ruled that the president did have the power of both appointment and removal. "Our conclusion," wrote Chief Justice William Howard Taft, "is that Article II grants to the President the executive power of the government . . . including the power of appointment and removal." Taft further stated that "the moment that he (the president) loses confidence in the intelligence, ability, judgement, or loyalty of one of them, he must have the power to remove him without delay."[20] For Justice Taft, the Constitution clearly provided the president the authority to appoint and to remove officials of the executive branch. But the issue had not been permanently resolved, because Justice Taft had addressed only removal of appointments with purely executive functions.

The issue of appointment and removal came before the Supreme Court again in 1935 when President Roosevelt tried to remove a commissioner from the Federal Trade Commission. Under the legislation governing the commission, the president could appoint but could not remove without cause. Removal for political reasons, such as differences in political philosophy, was barred by the enabling statute. William E. Humphrey was a conservative Republican appointed to the commission in 1931 by President Herbert Hoover. Roosevelt wanted a more moderate Republican on the commission to move his New Deal programs forward and, as a result, he dismissed Humphrey. Humphrey died shortly after his dismissal, but his executors appealed the decision in federal court in the case of **Humphrey's Executor v. United States.**[21] In this case, the removal issue was somewhat different than it had been a decade earlier in the *Myers* case. When President Wilson tried to remove the postmaster, Frank Myers, the Court ruled that he had the full constitutional authority to do so since the postmaster performed purely executive functions. When President Roosevelt tried to remove William Humphrey from the Federal Trade Commission, the Court ruled that a commissioner's duties were quasi-legislative and quasi-judicial and not purely executive in nature. As a result, the appointment power of the president was subject to the language of the Federal Trade Commission Act, which allowed removal only for "inefficiency, neglect of duty, or malfeasance in office." In its decision the Supreme Court determined that the president's removal power was limited to those positions that were purely executive in function, such as the postmaster, and could be limited by statute for positions with quasijudicial or quasilegislative functions, such as the Federal Trade Commission.

During the Eisenhower administration a similar case arose, **Wiener v. United States,**[22] in which President Eisenhower attempted to remove a member of the War Claims Commission who had been appointed by President Truman. The Supreme Court unanimously stated that Eisenhower had no authority to remove a member of the commission without sufficient cause. The 1958 opinion cited the role of the commission as being quasi-judicial and thus subject to the precedents in **Humphrey's Executor v. United States.** They said the president's removal power was limited to positions that were purely executive in function.

Over two decades passed before the Court was again to address a major challenge to the president's appointment and removal power. In 1976, the Court ruled that a provision in the Federal Election Campaign Act of 1971, as amended, in 1974 was unconstitutional because it vested appointment of some members of the Federal Election Commission in Congress rather than with the president. In **Buckley v. Valeo** the Court held that all appointees within the executive branch had to be made by the president.[23] The composition of the Federal Election Commission under the 1974 Amendments violated both the separation of powers of the Constitution and the appointment power provided to the president. Congress subsequently passed more amendments to the Federal Election Campaign Act in 1976, addressing the points raised by the Court and making all members of the Commission appointees of the president rather than appointees split between the president and Congress.

Ethics in Government Act of 1978

The issue of removal was raised again in the 1970s, concerning whether the president could remove the independent counsel from office. The Ethics in Government Act of 1978 provided for a special prosecutor (the name was changed to the independent counsel in the 1983 reauthorization) for ethics violations committed by the president and senior officials of the executive branch. The law provided that the Attorney General could ask a special three-judge panel to appoint a special prosecutor for the president and senior executive branch officials. The president could only remove the special prosecutor for cause.[24] An appointment of a special prosecutor was challenged in the 1988 case of **Morrison v. Olson** on the grounds that appointment and removal power should be vested in the president, not the court.[25]

The case involved Alexia Morrison, the independent counsel who was investigating Theodore Olson, a Justice Department lawyer charged with withholding from Congress information on the Environmental Protection Agency. Olson filed suit against Morrison, charging that the Ethics in Government Act of 1978 violated the president's removal power for the independent counsel. Olson argued that the president could not directly remove the independent counsel, except for very specific reasons, which violated Article II of the Constitution. Writing for the majority, Chief Justice William Rehnquist stated that the Ethics in Government Act of 1978 did not violate the president's removal power since the appointments clause of Article II allows Congress to "vest the Appointment of such inferior Officers, as they think proper, in the President alone, in the Courts of Law, or in the Heads of Departments." The Court ruled that since the Ethics in Government Act allowed the federal courts to appoint the independent counsel, it was appropriate for them to remove the independent counsel as the law required. As in *Humphrey's Executor,* Rehnquist said, *Morrison v. Olson* involved an appointment of a person who performed quasi-judicial functions and thus the governing legislation was constitutional. Justice Antonia Scalia dissented, arguing that *Myers v. United States* should be the governing case since the role of the independent counsel was executive in nature and removal should be the sole province of the president. During the Whitewater investigation and the perjury investigation in the Monica Lewinsky case, President Clinton was unable to fire independent counsel Kenneth Starr because of the precedents set in the *Morrison v. Olson* case regarding removal of an independent counsel.

Executive Privilege

The concept of **executive privilege** has been regularly used by presidents since George Washington first refused to comply with congressional demands for information. The concept of executive privilege is a prerogative power without constitutional foundation, but it has been widely used by presidents, particularly in the latter half of the twentieth century. Executive privilege, invoked by presidents who do not want to provide documents to Congress, is based on the principle that the national interest requires some material to remain secret. Presidents have long argued that certain material turned over to Congress would jeopardize sensitive negotiations with foreign countries and thus would jeopardize the national security. Protection of the national security fell under the president's "defend and protect" oath of office and was generally considered an acceptable prerogative power.

George Washington first invoked executive privilege when he refused to comply with a request from the House of Representatives.[26] The House demanded to have the orders that Washington gave to John Jay in 1796 when Jay was negotiating with Great Britain over issues that had not been resolved after the United States declared independence in 1776. Washington viewed the demands by the House as an unacceptable intrusion on his constitutional right to negotiate treaties. The House chastised Washington but did little else. Similarly, Thomas Jefferson supported the authority of the president to withhold documents from Congress, writing that "it was the necessary right of the President of the United States to decide, independently, what papers coming to him as President, the public interest permit to be communicated, and to whom."[27]

In most cases presidents used the shield of executive privilege to keep from turning over to Congress sensitive documents relating to treaty negotiations or other foreign policy discussions. At times, however, presidents used executive privilege to prevent the Congress from obtaining documents relating to domestic issues. Franklin Delano Roosevelt refused to allow the Federal Bureau of Investigation to turn over documents that a House committee requested in 1941. In 1944 the Roosevelt administration refused to turn over other documents on the grounds that letters and memoranda between the president and his cabinet officers were privileged information. During the Truman administration the concept that correspondence between the president and his cabinet officers was privileged was expanded to include presidents and their White House staff. President Truman ordered a member of his White House staff to refuse a House committee that had subpoenaed him.

The term *executive privilege* first came into the political lexicon during the Eisenhower administration when Eisenhower invoked the privilege more than forty times. Eisenhower wrote in a memo to United Nations Ambassador Henry Cabot Lodge, who had refused to testify in congressional hearings that, "The position you propose to take is exactly correct. I would be astonished if any of my personal advisors would undertake to give testimony on intimate staff counsel and advice. The result would be to eliminate all such offices from the Presidential staff. In turn, this would mean paralysis."[28] President Kennedy was careful to limit executive privilege from being widely used by presidential appointees who did not want to testify before Congress. In an exchange of correspondence with a senior member of the House of Representatives, Kennedy firmly stated that executive privilege must have the president's specific approval. Lyndon Johnson later gave the same assurances that the president alone would control the use of executive privilege.

The Kennedy and Johnson limitations on executive privilege did not stop cabinet officers and other high-ranking appointees from refusing to testify before Congress or submitting documents that Congress wanted. Both Kennedy and Johnson wanted to be consulted only to approve or disapprove the decision when these officials invoked executive privilege. When President Nixon entered office, he continued the Kennedy–Johnson tradition of allowing broad use of the executive privilege with his cabinet and White House staff. However, Nixon wanted to personally approve all cases in which executive privilege was invoked. Nixon issued a memorandum to the heads of all executive agencies that said "executive privilege can be invoked only by the President and will not be used without specific Presidential approval."[29]

Executive Privilege and National Security

Throughout the eighteenth, nineteenth, and twentieth centuries, the concept of executive privilege allowed presidents to withhold information from Congress on the vague grounds that national security would be jeopardized because of the sensitive nature of the material. Presidents from Truman to the present have argued that certain conversations between the president and his White House staff and between cabinet officers and their senior staff should be part of the executive privilege. Although national security remains a central theme surrounding executive privilege, modern presidents have used executive privilege as a shield for most policy-related conversations that a president has in private or cabinet members have in private with their staffs. All areas of policy, not just national security policy, have fallen under the protective umbrella of executive privilege.

In 1974 the Supreme Court addressed the issue in the first major challenge of executive privilege. During the Watergate scandal, President Nixon refused to surrender to the special prosecutor taped audio conversations in the Oval Office with his senior staff. The special prosecutor believed that these taped conversations had evidence of a White House cover-up of the break-in of the Democratic Party national headquarters during the 1972 presidential election. When Nixon refused to deliver the tapes of the conversations after a subpoena had been issued, special prosecutor Leon Jaworski went to court. The federal district court supported Jaworski and ordered Nixon to turn over the tapes. Nixon appealed to the Supreme Court in the case of **United States v. Nixon,** but was soundly rebuked. On July 24, 1974, Chief Justice Warren E. Burger delivered the opinion of a unanimous court rejecting Nixon's claim of executive privilege. Writing for the Court, Justice Burger said, "the doctrine of confidentiality of high level officials (cannot) sustain an absolute, unqualified presidential privilege of immunity from judicial process." The Court did not deny that the president had a right to use executive privilege under certain circumstances, circumstances that it did not define. The Court added that "a president and those who assist him must be free to explore alternatives in the process of shaping policies and making decisions and to do so in a way many would be unwilling to express except privately. These are the considerations justifying a presumptive privilege for presidential communications. The privilege is fundamental to the operation of government and inextricably rooted in the separation of powers under the Constitution."[30] The Court said only that the judicial process at times required complete disclosure from the president and his aides, but again did not specify when those times were. In the Nixon case, the fact that a criminal case was underway in which the tapes were involved was enough to justify negating executive privilege. In spite of the limitations that the Court placed on executive privilege with regard to criminal proceedings, the Court acknowledged for the first time that executive privilege was an inherent power of the presidency.

The issue of whether or not the president has to release information to Congress was not addressed in the case of *United States v. Nixon*, and it remains unclear. According to constitutional law scholar J.W. Peltason, the Nixon case suggests that the president would not have to release information to Congress unless the issue involved a criminal case, such as an impeachment process.[31] Even then, however, there are no guidelines, and presidents would probably refuse to deliver the material that Congress requested, forcing the Supreme Court to intervene.

During the Clinton administration, the issue of executive privilege was raised again by independent counsel Kenneth Starr. Starr subpoenaed Bruce Lindsey and Sidney Blumenthal, both senior members of the White House staff, to discuss their knowledge of the relationship between Monica Lewinsky and the president. On May 26, 1998, the district court ordered Blumenthal and Lindsey to testify. Blumenthal did testify before the grand jury but Lindsey refused. In July 1998 the Supreme Court ordered Lindsey to testify. The court followed the precedents set in *U.S. v. Nixon* in its decision for Blumenthal and Lindsey, by supporting the concept of executive privilege for the president and his advisers but not when criminal activity could be involved. Perjury and obstruction of justice were cited as overriding considerations in this case, both circumstances involving criminal activity.

Collisions on Expansive Use of Executive Power

As the president became the dominant player in the development of national policy in the Roosevelt era, confrontations began to erupt with both Congress and the courts on the expansive nature of presidential power. One of the most famous of these incidents involved Franklin Delano Roosevelt's 1937 plan for **court packing,** in which he proposed to expand the size of the Supreme Court as a means of circumventing unfavorable decisions for the administration. By adding his own appointees, Roosevelt planned to ensure that future Court decisions would favor the administration.

The court packing proposal emerged after the Supreme Court had rejected a number of administration-sponsored bills for rebuilding the nation's economy after the Depression. Two of the more prominent decisions by the Supreme Court occurred in 1936, in which both the Agricultural Adjustment Act and the Bituminous Coal Preservation Act were ruled unconstitutional violations of states' rights.[32] Again in 1936 the Supreme Court struck down another administration-sponsored bill, the Municipal Bankruptcy Act, on the grounds that states' rights had been violated. In essence, the Court was opposing a shift in power from state governments to the national government. Conservatives on the Court believed this was an unconstitutional shift of power.

In order to counter the attack on New Deal programs being mounted by the Supreme Court, Roosevelt devised a plan to rapidly change the composition of the Court in his favor. In a message to Congress on February 5, 1937, Roosevelt proposed that Congress reorganize the judicial branch. The proposal called for the number of Supreme Court justices to be increased from nine to fifteen, creating one new seat for each justice who, upon reaching the age of 70, declined to retire. The proposal also called for the addition of fifty new judges for all federal courts plus a number of other changes. Roosevelt reasoned that the changes were necessary to relieve the Court's large caseload. In a radio broadcast to the nation in March 1937 to explain his proposal, Roosevelt said that the Supreme Court had "cast doubts on the ability of the elected Congress to protect us against catastrophe by meeting squarely our modern social and economic conditions."[33] Roosevelt had not adequately gauged the level of public opposition to his court packing idea. He was accused by some of destroying judicial independence and of aggrandizing the power of the presidency. Even the Democratic Congress was divided on the merits of expanding the Supreme Court.

The idea never reached full debate in Congress because the Court itself seemed to resolve the issue. In a series of decisions between late March and late May 1937, the Court upheld the constitutionality of New Deal programs. Support for the court-packing proposal melted away in Congress. The conservative orientation of the Court ended over the next four years as seven justices retired, providing Roosevelt ample opportunity to place his appointees on the highest court. As a result of the changes on the Supreme Court, decisions rendered after 1937 largely supported the legislation that Roosevelt had pushed through Congress for economic recovery. Roosevelt's appointees to the Court included Hugo Black in 1937, Stanley Reed in 1938, Felix Frankfurter and William O. Douglas in 1939, Francis Murphy in 1940, and Robert H. Jackson and James F. Byrnes in 1942. Not surprisingly, when Roosevelt tried to gain reorganization authority for the executive branch in January 1937, Congress was still scarred from the battles of the judicial reorganization plan. Not until 1939 did the reorganization plan for the executive branch become law. Although Roosevelt had not directly challenged the Court's authority, he had sought to circumvent that authority by changing the composition of the Supreme Court.

Roosevelt struggled throughout his presidency to change the character of policy-making from a fundamentally state oriented system to a fundamentally nationally oriented system. His legacy is one of success in this arena, for the character of policy-making today is unquestionably centered in the federal government. As policy-making was moved into the national arena, the responsibility for managing and developing those policies fell to the president. This move to a federally based policy-making system enhanced the power of the presidency and allowed a further expansion of presidential powers.

Truman and the Steel Seizure Case

The expansion of presidential powers was again challenged in the Truman administration, as it had been in the Roosevelt administration, by the Supreme Court. In 1952 the Court was called on to decide whether Truman had overstepped his constitutional authority when he issued an executive order to have the Secretary of Commerce operate the nation's steel mills during a strike.[34] During the Korean War the steel workers threatened to go on strike unless the Wage Stabilization Board approved wage increases. The unions believed that the steel industry was being allowed significant price increases without appropriate wage increases to the unions. When the Secretary of Defense told Truman in early April that the war machinery needed continuous steel production, Truman chose to seize the steel mills and asked the workers to return as government employees. Only hours before the steel strike was to begin, Truman issued an executive order for Secretary of Commerce Charles Sawyer to take over the steel mills. Sawyer then ordered the steel owners to continue to run. the mills using the steel workers. The steel workers immediately sought relief through the Supreme Court, seeking to overturn Truman's seizure of the steel mills.[35] The decision was expedited and returned on June 2, 1952, less than two months after the strike began. In the case of *Youngstown Sheet and Tube Co. v. Sawyer,* the Supreme Court ruled six to three against Truman, arguing that the seizure of the steel mills was an unconstitutional exercise of power by the president.[36] The three dissenters, however, supported Truman's actions, emphasizing that the seizure was prompted by a national emergency. The majority decision did not rule against the use of prerogative power to deal with a national emergency, but rather argued that before the president had taken such action other remedies were available. The specific remedy discussed by the Court was the 1947 Labor-Management Act, better known as the Taft–Hartley Act, which required a cooling-off period before the president could intervene. Theoretically, had Truman allowed the cooling-off period mandated by the

Taft–Hartley Act, the Supreme Court would not have ruled against him. The *Youngstown* decision generally supported a broad interpretation of presidential power, since the Court addressed only Truman's failure to first seek remedies established by Congress. Had those legislatively mandated remedies failed, presumably Truman would have been free to seize the mills using his constitutional authority to "protect and defend" the nation.

The President as Commander in Chief

No power of the president is more clearly delineated in the Constitution than the power associated with the commander in chief role. As clear as the language appears to be, challenges to the commander in chief role have arisen throughout the nation's history. In U.S. history there have been only five declared wars (The War of 1812, The Mexican War in 1846, The Spanish–American War in 1898, World War I in 1917, and World War II in 1941). Therefore, in most cases the president has had to use his powers as commander in chief without congressional sanction. This has opened the door to a number of legal challenges to the president's constitutional authority to use military force.

One of the earliest challenges to presidential authority as commander in chief occurred in 1827. In **Martin v. Mott** the Supreme Court ruled that the president had the authority to call out the state militia, an authority that had been exercised during the War of 1812. In a unanimous decision, the Court ruled that "the authority to decide whether the exigency has arisen, belongs exclusively to the President, and this decision is conclusive upon all other persons."[37] The challenge from the states that did not want to give the president absolute control over the deployment of the military, including the state militias, was resolved in favor of the president. Presidents subsequently deployed troops in various locations around the country and around the world.

The next major test of presidential authority as commander in chief came during the administration of Abraham Lincoln. **The Prize Cases** arose as a result of Lincoln's blockade of southern ports in 1861 after the first shots had been fired in the Civil War.[38] The Union navy captured several neutral ships as they entered southern ports. These ships were brought to northern ports as early prizes of the blockade. Under international law, neutral ships could not be captured and used as prizes before a war had been declared. Since Lincoln did not recognize the Confederacy as a sovereign nation, he would not recognize the conflict under the definition of war, which had to involve sovereign nations. For Lincoln, the Confederacy was involved in an insurrection, not a war, and thus he had full authority to seize the neutral ships.

In its 1863 decision in *The Prize Cases*, the Supreme Court upheld Lincoln's power to impose the blockade. The decision effectively supported Lincoln's view that the Confederacy was involved in an insurrection rather than a war and as such the president had the authority to impose the blockade. Any ships captured as prizes were not subject to international law, which would cover an illegal seizure, since two nations were not involved. The ruling reinforced the president's power to use troops in a national emergency. The Court quoted an act of Congress from 1807 that provided authority for the president to suppress insurrection against the government of a state of the United States. *The Prize Cases* solidified the role of the president to use military force in defense of the nation.

With few exceptions, the Supreme Court has supported the president's use of the military as a legitimate exercise of his constitutional role as commander in chief. Since challenges to the president's war powers and commander in chief powers are generally raised by Congress, presidents try to work with Congress rather than risk having the court oppose such actions. Supreme Court intervention in presidential commander in chief activities is minimized when Congress supports presidential actions.

Overextending the Commander in Chief Role

Two cases stand out, however, in which the Supreme Court has rebuked presidents for overextending their authority in their role as commander in chief. In both cases the nation was at war and in both cases the decisions were not handed down for several years. The first case involved President Lincoln's suspension of habeas corpus during the Civil War and his order that some civilian crimes would be tried in military courts. In a declaration of September 24, 1862, Lincoln announced that "all rebels and insurgents, their aiders and abettors, within the United States, and all persons discouraging volunteer enlistments, resisting militia drafts, or guilty of any disloyal practice affording aid and comfort to rebels against the authority of the United States, shall be subject to martial law and liable to trial and punishment of courts-martial or military commissions."[39] Congress had approved many of Lincoln's decisions during the Civil War, but trying civilians in military courts is not one that had the sanction of Congress. In 1864 Lambdin P. Milligan was charged by military authorities with aiding a Confederate raid into Indiana. The following year he was put on trial, found guilty, and sentenced to death. President Andrew Johnson later commuted the sentence to life.

Milligan appealed to the Supreme Court, which ruled that the president had overextended his powers. In *Ex parte Milligan*, decided in 1866, the Court decided that Lincoln could not subject citizens to military courts when the civil courts were open and operating. The decision established that martial law cannot be imposed unless the area is involved directly in the war, which Indiana was not. Justice David Davis, a Lincoln appointee to the Court, wrote that

> the Constitution of the United States is a law for rulers and people, equally in war and in peace, and covers with the shield of its protection all classes of men, at all times and under all circumstances. . . . Martial law cannot arise from a threatened invasion. The necessity must be actual and present; the invasion must be real, such as effectually closes the courts. . . . Martial rule can never exist where the courts are open and in the proper and unobstructed exercise of their jurisdiction.[40]

The Court ordered Milligan released and issued a strong rebuke to Lincoln. The *Milligan* case established a firm legal precedent for limiting presidential action that affects individual liberties, even in times of war.

In a parallel case during World War II, President Roosevelt's executive order of December 7, 1941, following the bombing of Pearl Harbor declared martial law on Hawaii and later ordered the relocation of Japanese-Americans on the West Coast to relocation camps. In **Duncan v. Kahanamoku** the Court ruled in 1946 that, based on the standard set by *Milligan*, martial law was only acceptable when an invasion had taken place. Roosevelt was justified in ordering a state of martial law.[41] This ruling gave formal backing to the president's use of emergency powers during wartime. The same Court also wrote in **Korematsu v. United States** (1944) that Roosevelt had the power to impose a curfew in wartime. The Court was divided, however, on the relocation of Japanese-Americans based purely on racial standards. In a divided six to three ruling, the Court said that the president's commander in chief role allowed him to make decisions, such as the relocation to protect the nation from threatened danger. In a dissenting opinion, Justice Francis Murphy rejected the majority opinion that any threat justified exclusion of one group of people. Murphy wrote in his dissent that "Such exclusion goes 'over the brink' of constitutional power and falls into the abyss of racism."[42]

The history of modern presidents liberally using their commander in chief role is replete with examples. Presidents have carefully sought the approval of both the public and of Congress before taking action, to ensure that challenges to their powers are avoided. No matter how sure presidents are that the commander in chief power of the Constitution provides authority for an action, they do not want to move the issue into litigation in the Supreme Court. During the 1950s President Eisenhower sought and received congressional authorization to block communist aggression in the Middle East. When the Cuban missile crisis broke out in 1962, President Kennedy obtained approval from Congress to "prevent the spread of communism in the Western hemisphere." President Johnson sought and received congressional approval for expanding the war in Vietnam. The Gulf of Tonkin resolution in August 1964 gave Johnson congressional support for using continued military force to prevent further North Vietnamese aggression in South Vietnam. Congress also supported presidential actions by continuing to appropriate funds.

War Powers Resolution of 1973

Although Congress and the president had established a strong relationship with regard to the president's role as commander in chief, this relationship suffered a serious blow during the Nixon administration. The escalation of the war in Vietnam and secret bombing missions in Cambodia led Congress to lose faith in Nixon's leadership, and they urged him to withdraw the troops. When he failed to withdraw the troops, Congress tried to limit the president's commander in chief role. The **War Powers Resolution of 1973,** passed over President Nixon's veto, required consultation with Congress on all deployments in hostile situations and limited the time frame in which presidents could deploy troops. The time frame was for an uncontested sixty-day period with an additional thirty days for troop withdrawal.[43]

The War Powers Resolution has been regularly ignored by presidents, who view the law as an unconstitutional infringement on their commander in chief role. Presidents do not consult with Congress prior to military deployments, especially in secret actions such as during President Ford's attempt to rescue the crew of the *Mayaguez* in 1975. Ford severely criticized the law and defended his refusal to follow the mandates of the war powers legislation. "When a crisis breaks out," Ford said, "it is impossible to draw the Congress in with the decision making process in an effective way." Ford added that the War Powers Resolution was a "serious intrusion on the responsibilities of the president as commander in chief and the person who formulates and ought to execute foreign policy."[44]

The issue has not been brought before the Supreme Court, although during the Persian Gulf War a small group of Democratic members of the House of Representatives argued that President Bush had failed to follow the mandates of the War Powers Resolution. The Court dismissed the challenge on the grounds that it was nonjusticiable since it was a political question. The doctrine involving political questions is based on the Supreme Court's view that the separation of powers theory requires the Court to deal with judicial issues and for the political and policy questions to be worked out directly between the president and Congress. In 1995 the War Powers Resolution again was debated in Congress when the Republicans sought to bring multilateral military actions, such as the peacekeeping role of American troops in Bosnia, under the sanctions of the act. Congress ultimately took no action during the session.

One of the few times that the president has been completely turned down by the Supreme Court in seeking to exercise his commander in chief role was the 1971 **Pentagon Papers** case. President Nixon asked the Court to issue an injunction to stop the *New York Times* from publishing classified material that the Department of Defense had assembled on the Vietnam War. The material, which had been taken by a Pentagon employee, described numerous missions in Vietnam that Nixon had not discussed with either the Congress or the American people. The Supreme Court ruled in *The New York Times Co. v. United States* (1971) that the president did not have the authority to prevent the publication since there was no specific harm to national security.[45] The harm was primarily to Nixon's reputation and to his public approval rating rather than to the broader issue of national security. The Court ruled that freedom of the press could not prevent publication without very compelling reasons.

Commander in Chief Role: Upholding Supreme Court Rulings

Presidents have also used their commander in chief powers to uphold Supreme Court rulings. One of the more famous cases of a president using his commander in chief powers in response to a Supreme Court decision occurred during the Eisenhower administration. Following the Supreme Court's historic decision in 1954 in *Brown v. Board of Education*, which required desegregation to begin "with all deliberate speed," nine black students tried to integrate Central High School in **Little Rock, Arkansas,** during the first week of school in September 1957.[46] Governor Orval Faubus, who opposed desegregation, stood on the steps of Central High School surrounded by the National Guard and refused to admit the black students. The U.S. district court ordered Faubus to allow the students to enter the high school. Faubus, who withdrew the National Guard, allowed mobs to surround the school and prohibit the students from entering. Concerned that Faubus had violated a direct order from the court to allow the students to begin classes, President Eisenhower federalized the National Guard and sent in the 101st Airborne army division to protect the students trying to enter the high school. Eisenhower used his role as commander in chief to enforce the court's ruling and to restore order to the chaos in Little Rock.

The Little Rock incident is one of the more recent cases of presidents exercising the commander in chief role to use military force for domestic affairs. In 1894 President Cleveland sent troops to put down a labor strike against the Pullman Railroad Car Company. Members of the American Railway Union went on strike to protest a reduction in wages. The strike had effectively shut down railway service from Chicago to the western states. When the Pullman Company hired guards to protect company property and the union workers threatened violence, President Cleveland sent federal troops to Chicago. The president then ordered the U.S. Attorney in Chicago to obtain a court order halting the strike, on the grounds that interstate commerce and delivery of the mail were being harmed. Eugene V. Debs, the president of the American Railway Union, challenged the court order and the use of federal troops. The Supreme Court ruled in favor of the president in *En re Debs* in 1895, stating that the president has the authority to send in troops "to brush away all obstructions to the freedom of interstate commerce or the transportation of the mails." The Court also returned to the Lockean principles of prerogative power, stating that the president must discharge his duties to protect the "general welfare."[47] There has been consistent support in the federal courts for the president to exercise his prerogative power to protect the general welfare through the use of military force, as Eisenhower did in Little Rock and as Cleveland did in Chicago.

The President as Chief Diplomat

The architects of the Constitution had no doubts that foreign policy decision making should be lodged in the executive branch rather than the legislative branch. The Constitution gives the president the authority to negotiate treaties and to receive and appoint ambassadors. From these specific grants of authority, presidents have expanded their role into one of the nation's chief diplomat. As Representative John Marshall argued on the floor of the House of Representatives in 1800, during which he was defending a foreign-policy decision by President John Adams, "The president is the sole organ of the nation in its external relations and its sole representative with foreign nations."[48]

Manager of Foreign Policy

The president's role as the chief architect of the nation's foreign policy came into question in 1936 with a lawsuit brought by the Curtiss-Wright Export Corporation, an arms dealer. The lawsuit stemmed from a decision that President Roosevelt made to embargo all weapons sales to the warring nations of Paraguay and Bolivia. Under pressure from isolationists to stay out of the South American war, Congress supported the president's decision and on May 24, 1934, approved a joint resolution that authorized the embargo. Roosevelt then declared the embargo operational and ordered all arms sales halted to Paraguay and Bolivia. The 1936 decision that emerged from the court case, **United States v. Curtiss-Wright Export Corporation,** resulted in a reaffirmation of the president's strong command of the foreign-policy apparatus. Writing for the majority, Justice George Sutherland built on the language of John Marshall in 1800 defending President John Adams. Sutherland said,

The President alone has the power to speak as a representative of the nation. . . . It is important to bear in mind that we are dealing not alone with an authority vested in the President by an exertion of legislative power, but with such an authority plus the very delicate, plenary and exclusive power of the President as the sole organ of the federal government in the field of international relations—a power which does not require as a basis for its exercise an act of Congress.[49]

This decision provided unparalleled judicial support for the president to make decisions for the nation regarding foreign policy. These decisions are, in the words of Justice Sutherland, to be made alone by the president and do not require consultation with Congress. This decision remains the most important Court affirmation of presidential authority in the realm of foreign policy decision-making.

Treaty Negotiations

Treaties are by definition a contract between two nations and thus fall within the realm of foreign-policy decision making. The Constitution clearly delegates authority for treaty making, or treaty negotiations, to the president, although it requires the Senate to consent to the final product. But this broad delegation of power has gone through a number of tortuous twists and turns as Congress has sought to have some role in the treaty process in addition to ratification. Not surprisingly, presidents have sought to keep Congress out of the decision-making process, rarely discussing the treaty negotiations until they are complete. The Supreme Court has never denied the president total authority to manage the treaty negotiation process, nor has it allowed Congress a greater role in that process.

One of the few issues to rise to the Supreme Court with regard to treaties involved the termination of a treaty, a prerogative power that presidents had assumed under their role as foreign policy manager. The Constitution is silent on the issue of termination of treaties and fails to provide explicit directions as to whether Congress must consent to a treaty termination or the action can be unilaterally handled by the president. Absent specific language to the contrary, presidents have assumed that the power belonged in the executive branch and fell within the broad grant of powers to oversee foreign policy.

The treaty-making process is a three-part endeavor. In the first part, the president (or the secretary of state) enters into negotiations with a foreign country to produce the treaty. In the second part, the Senate reviews the treaty and decides whether to approve, reject, or amend it. If amendments are added, the treaty will return to the other country for its approval. Once the treaty is ratified by the Senate, it returns to the president for his signature.

The termination of treaties has no such rules governing the process. The Constitution is silent on treaty termination, and no tradition of cooperation has emerged between the president and Congress. Absent constitutional provisions for treaty termination, presidents have used their prerogative powers to terminate treaties without seeking Senate approval. Relatively few treaties have been terminated, but those that have been terminated did not involve discussions between the executive and legislative branches. The issue never drew any serious attention until the Carter administration terminated a treaty in 1979. The attention paid by Congress to treaty termination was part of a broader effort to rein in presidential powers. Congress was still trying in 1979 to regain powers that it had lost during the Johnson and Nixon administrations. Johnson's Great Society legislation had moved the federal bureaucracy into an institutional powerhouse, transforming the executive branch into the dominant force in domestic policy-making. Nixon's escalation of the war in Vietnam, his impoundment of appropriated funds, and his centralization of power in the Executive Office of the President, had altered the balance in the balance-of-power structure. During the early 1970s Congress took a series of actions to regain some of the power and stature that it had lost during the Johnson and Nixon years. The result was passage of the War Powers Resolution of 1973, the Federal Election Campaign Act of 1972, and the Budget and Impoundment Control Act of 1974. The challenge to presidential power continued to mount even once Jimmy Carter, a Democratic president, took office.

In 1979 a group of Republican Senators, led by Barry Goldwater of Arizona, took the president to court over the termination of the treaty with Taiwan. Carter had terminated the Mutual Defense Treaty of 1954 with The Republic of China (Taiwan) in favor of a treaty with the People's Republic of China (mainland China). Goldwater challenged the president's authority to terminate a treaty without the approval of the Senate. The issue was not directly resolved by the Supreme Court, which decided that the issue was a political question and nonjusticiable. The Court ruled that Goldwater had not acted on behalf of the Congress as an institution but rather on behalf of a small group of Republicans. In his majority opinion, Justice Powell wrote, "In this case, a few Members of Congress claim that the President's action in terminating the treaty with Taiwan has deprived them of their Constitutional role with respect to a change in the supreme law of the land. Congress has taken to no official action. . . . If the Congress chooses not to confront the President, it is not our task to do so." It was clear, however, that the Court would side with the president if the issue became an institutional confrontation, as evidenced by Justice Brennan's opinion in the case which said, "Our cases firmly establish that the Constitution permits to the President alone the power to recognize, and withdraw recognition from foreign regimes. That mandate being clear, our judicial inquiry into the treaty rupture can go no further."[50] Since the Taiwan treaty, no other cases have been brought to the Supreme Court to challenge the termination power of the president or to challenge the power of the president to recognize new governments.

Recognition of Governments of Foreign Countries

During the past two decades presidents have routinely recognized new governments, largely in response to the post–Cold War changes in the Eastern European block of countries. As the Soviet Union crumbled during the mid-1980s, President Reagan recognized a host of new governments, including the Baltic states, such as Estonia and Latvia, and former Soviet states, such as Russia and the Ukraine. President Reagan also recognized the Vatican as an independent nation within Italy. During the Bush administration, East Germany and West Germany were reunited into one nation, Germany, which the President promptly recognized as the official government. Presidents have also recognized exiled governments as the official governmental structure. For example, President Clinton recognized the exiled government of

Bertrand Aristide of Haiti in 1993 rather than the military dictatorship that overthrew him. Aristide eventually was reinstated as the elected head of government and the United States sent troops to Haiti to ensure that he remained in office.

Executive Agreements

Although presidents have the constitutional authority to negotiate treaties, that authority is tempered by the Senate's obligation to ratify treaties. In times of heightened institutional conflict, such as existed during the 1960s and 1970s, and in times of heightened partisan conflict, such as during the 1980s and 1990s, presidents have a more difficult time in gaining Senate support for ratification. Often, the Senate seeks to curb presidential control of the process by demanding amendments, thus requiring the treaty to be returned to the other country for review, or delaying the approval time. To circumvent the Senate, presidents have routinely used the **executive agreement** as a tool for international accords. President McKinley used an executive agreement to end the Spanish–American War, President Theodore Roosevelt signed an executive agreement with Japan that recognized Japan's military protectorate in Japan, and President Franklin Roosevelt widely used executive agreements during World War II.

The constitutionality of the executive agreement was upheld in the case of *United States v. Belmont* in 1937, which supported President Roosevelt's 1933 action that recognized the Soviet Union through executive order. The Supreme Court ruled that "Governmental power over external affairs . . . is vested exclusively in the national government. And in respect of what was done here, the Executive had authority to speak as the sole organ of that government."[51] Justice Sutherland, writing for the Court, was reiterating John Marshall's famous phrase, a phrase the Court was to use in the *Curtiss-Wright* decision. The Court again upheld the right of the president to negotiate executive agreements in the 1942 decision *United States v. Pink*, regarding diplomatic relations with Soviet Union. In the words of Justice William O. Douglas, executive agreements were part of the "modest implied power of the President who is the sole organ of the Federal Government in the field of international relations."[52] The repetition of the phrase "the president is the sole organ of foreign policy" provides a constant affirmation to the principle that the president, not Congress, represents the nation in both military and diplomatic relations with foreign nations.

Presidential Immunity

Since the framers first debated what powers the chief executive would have, the issue of accountability has dominated the discussions. Alexander Hamilton argued, for example, that the executive should be singular rather than plural to ensure accountability of action. The issue of accountability has also dominated the election process and the removal process. Can a president be sued by a private party for actions related to official business? Can a president be sued for actions that occurred prior to his or her presidency? What immunity does the president have for carrying out official functions? What are the differences between ministerial and executive actions?

One of the first major decisions on presidential immunity came after the Civil War in the 1867 decision of *Mississippi v. Johnson*.[53] The case grew out of the internal struggles that the nation was facing in the aftermath of the Civil War. Congress passed a number of laws that became known as the Reconstruction Acts, which imposed military rule over the southern states until new governments could be formed that were loyal to the Union. Andrew Johnson, a southerner from Tennessee, vetoed the bills, but the vetoes were overridden. The state of Mississippi sued Johnson and asked the Supreme Court to prohibit him from carrying out the Reconstruction Acts on the ground that the laws were unconstitutional. The Court responded by denying Mississippi's argument. The Court did not act on the constitutionality of the acts, but rather ruled that Johnson had the constitutional responsibility to execute the law. In essence, the Court said that Johnson had immunity from such state actions since as president he was carrying out his responsibility to execute the law.

The issue remained out of the courts for more than a hundred years until it arose during the Nixon administration. While Nixon was in office, a federal employee named A. Ernest Fitzgerald testified before Congress that the Air Force had $2 billion in cost overruns on the development of the C-5A transport plane. Thirteen months later his employer, the Defense Department, fired him, citing departmental reorganization. Fitzgerald sued a number of federal officials, including Nixon, who had personally approved his firing. In the 1982 case of *Nixon v. Fitzgerald*, the Court ruled that the president had immunity from lawsuits related to his official actions. Writing for the Court in a split decision of five to four, Justice Lewis Powell said that "because of the singular importance of the President's duties, the diversion of his energies by concern from private lawsuits would raise unique risks to the effective functioning of government. . . . In view of this special nature of the President's Constitutional office and functions, we think it appropriate to recognize absolute Presidential immunity from damages liability for acts within the 'outer perimeter' of his official responsibility."[54] The Court effectively gave the president complete protection from lawsuits arising out of any official action. The combined effect of the *Mississippi* decision and the *Fitzgerald* decision was to provide a heavy blanket of immunity for presidents in the official conduct of business.

Although the Supreme Court had provided strong precedent for immunity for nearly all actions carried out during the president's term in office, the Court had not addressed whether the President should be shielded from suit during the presidency for actions prior to the term in office. Could the president be sued while in office for civil actions that occurred prior to taking office? In 1996 the Court addressed this issue of immunity in the lawsuit of *Clinton v. Jones*, which sought to prevent Paula Corbin Jones from bringing suit against President Clinton until after his term was over. President Clinton's attorneys argued that by allowing the suit to go forward, the president would be distracted from carrying out his constitutional responsibilities. They also argued that it would set a dangerous precedent and open all president to a floodgate of meritless lawsuits. Paula Corbin Jones's attorneys argued that the president does not have immunity from actions that occurred prior to the presidency, nor was there any reason to prevent those civil actions from moving forward before the term of office was complete. The Court ruled in favor of Jones and allowed the lawsuit to proceed, stating that the president does not have absolute immunity from civil cases of action arising prior to assuming the office.[55] The Court also ruled that it did not believe a flurry of "frivolous" lawsuits would be filed as a result of this decision and that the president had adequate time to deal with the lawsuit without jeopardizing his constitutional responsibilities.

Overview of Supreme Court Challenges to Presidential Power

There have been relatively few challenges to presidential power that have risen to the level of the Supreme Court. Although presidents have regularly used their prerogative powers to expand their authority, the Court has rarely acted to curb those powers. When President Lincoln suspended habeas corpus and declared martial law, the courts supported his actions on the grounds that in a national emergency the president was empowered to protect and defend the nation. The only rebuke given the president by the Court several years later, when Lincoln was dead and the war over, involved the use of military tribunals. The Court directed that military tribunals could not be used if the civil court system was fully functioning.

This was hardly a negation of Lincoln's emergency or war powers, rather it was an affirmation that Lincoln had the authority to invoke such powers but that certain guidelines (such as using civil courts) had to be followed. The protection of individual liberties has always been paramount in our governmental system. Lincoln's suspension of habeas corpus and the declaration of martial law impinged on individual liberties, which forced the Court to give added scrutiny to the use of prerogative powers. The Court's decision was based on protecting both the national interest by allowing Lincoln's actions and on protecting individual liberties by defining the limits of Lincoln's authority. This principle of executive power was reiterated by the Court during World War II, when President Roosevelt declared martial law in Hawaii. The Court again allowed martial law but curbed the use of military tribunals when civil courts were operational.

When President Truman used his prerogative powers to take over the steel mills in 1952, the Supreme Court did not admonish him for his actions, only for his failure to exhaust the remedies they felt were available. In this case, the remedy was allowing the cooling-off period provided for in the Taft–Hartley Act before presidential action was taken. The Court was acknowledging Truman's authority to prevent a steel strike during a national crisis, in this case the Korean War, but again wanted to ensure that certain guidelines were followed (legislative provisions for dealing with strikes through the Taft–Hartley Act). Had the war been closer to American shores rather than halfway around the world, the Court might not have put such limits on Truman's decision to seize the steel mills to keep the machinery of war in gear.

The only moderate blow to the president's use of prerogative powers came during the Nixon administration, when the Supreme Court ruled that President Nixon had to release to the special prosecutor a number of audio tapes from conversations in the

Oval Office. The tapes involved conversations that the special prosecutor believed had evidence of Nixon's direct involvement in a coverup of the break-in at the Democratic Party National headquarters. Nixon's lawyers argued that the tapes were protected by executive privilege and did not have to be turned over to the special prosecutor. In a strong response to Nixon's argument, the Court ruled that executive privilege was a legitimate exercise of prerogative power. But, the Court pointed out, executive privilege did not protect the president if he was involved in criminal activity, such as a conspiracy to cover up criminal activity. The Court's decision to a large degree reinforced prerogative power in the realm of executive privilege, for it supported the president's authority to use executive privilege but established parameters for such use. Those parameters limited executive privilege to conversations that did not involve criminal conduct. While this threshold of executive privilege appears to give presidents ample latitude in their use of executive privilege, it also opens the door to future special prosecutors or independent counsels (or others) to shielding their challenges to executive privilege through implications of criminal behavior. The legacy of relations between the Supreme Court and the president has generally been one of good will and support. The Supreme Court has in most cases upheld the authority of the president in both the use of implied and inherent powers. When Congress has challenged that authority, the Court has routinely supported the president or ruled the issue a political question. Only once, during Roosevelt's aborted attempt to pack the Supreme Court, has there been significant tension between the executive and judicial branches. Presidents rarely comment on Supreme Court rulings of any kind, and, on rulings that affect presidential power, presidents have been particularly careful not to lash out at the Court. Even when President Nixon was forced to turn over the tapes by the Supreme Court, he refrained from any derogatory or confrontational comment.

Presidential Appointments to the Court

The Constitution provides the president the authority in Article II, Section 2, "to nominate, with the advice and consent of the Senate, . . . judges of the Supreme Court." This is part of the president's larger appointment power given in Article II. But, removal of Supreme Court justices and all federal judges is handled through impeachment and conviction rather than direct removal by the president. By taking away the removal power from the president, the Court is protected from retribution for unfavorable decisions. Presidents cannot remove members of the Court because they rule against the president or disapprove of a presidential action.

The power of appointment, however, allows presidents to move the Court in a philosophical direction that could potentially support presidential actions and policies. As one legal scholar noted, "The Supreme Court has always played an active role in our political life . . . and interpretation of the Constitution is in the highest sense a political matter, a choice among conflicting political values."[56] During the 1960s the Supreme Court, under the leadership of Chief Justice Earl Warren, took positions that declared racial segregation in all forms unconstitutional, allowed Congress to legislate against racial discrimination, expanded protection for speech, and expanded the wall between church and state. The Court was often criticized during this era for reflecting a liberal bias in its decisions.

When Richard Nixon was elected to office in 1968 he promised to change the direction of the Court by filling vacancies on the Supreme Court (and throughout the federal court system) with conservatives and moderates. Nixon appointed Warren Burger to replace the retiring Earl Warren and, as other retirements occurred, appointed Harry A. Blackmun, Lewis Powell, Jr., and William Rehnquist. President Ford appointed John Paul Stevens, giving Nixon and Ford five appointees on the nine-member court. With the exception of Justice Rehnquist, who held conservative views, the Nixon and Ford appointments were predominately moderates. The revolution that Nixon had hoped for when his appointments were placed on the Court never happened. In fact, the Burger Court issued the decision that declared most state laws against abortion unconstitutional and approved many affirmative action programs. Although the Court was not as conservative as Nixon had sought, it was far more conservative than it had been prior to his appointments.

Ronald Reagan was also able to shape the Court, and he successfully moved it to the conservative philosophic orientation that Nixon had intended. Reagan's first appointment to the Court was Sandra Day O'Connor, a moderate jurist from the Arizona Court of Appeals, following the retirement of Potter Stewart. When Chief Justice Burger retired, President Reagan appointed Justice William Rehnquist to the chief justice position and appointed Antonin Scalia from the Court of Appeals in the District of Columbia to the Supreme Court. Soon after, Justice Powell retired, providing another vacancy for Reagan to fill, and he did so with Anthony Kennedy from the Court of Appeals for the Ninth Circuit. The appointments of Rehnquist, Scalia, Kennedy were made to give the Court a solid conservative wing to balance the moderates that had been appointed during the Nixon and Ford years. President Bush also made two appointments to the Court, David Souter from the New Hampshire Supreme Court and Clarence Thomas from the Court of Appeals for the District of Columbia, with Souter being generally moderate and Thomas strongly conservative. Since President Carter did not fill any vacancies on the Supreme Court, all eight vacancies filled between 1969 when Nixon took office and 1993 when Bush left office were made by Republican presidents.

President Clinton has made two appointments to the Supreme Court. Ruth Bader Ginsberg from the Court of Appeals for the District of Columbia replaced Byron White and Stephen Breyer, chief judge of the Third Circuit, replaced Harry Blackmun. Since both White and Blackmun had been moderates, the balance of the court had little change. Clinton chose two moderates for the Court, which reflected his political base. The appointments made to the court are made both to appease the president's strongest supporters and to move the court in a direction more philosophically in tune with the administration.

In addition to the political and philosophical importance of filling vacancies on the Court, recent presidents have utilized the Court as a tool to reinforce their commitment to racial and gender diversity. President Reagan and President Clinton both named women to the Court, and President Bush named an African-American. The symbolism of the appointment of women and African-Americans to the Supreme

Court reflects the significant economic and political base that both groups have within the Democratic and Republican parties. The trend will continue as both groups continue to be active participants in the political process. Without doubt, one of the next appointments to the Supreme Court will be a Hispanic-American, reflecting the growing political base of Hispanic-Americans in the United States.

In addition to appointments to the Supreme Court, presidents are constitutionally empowered to make all appointments to the federal courts. This has enabled presidents to place people in the federal court system who share their political views. Republican presidents tend to nominate Republicans and Democratic presidents tend to nominate Democrats; conservatives tend to nominate conservatives and moderates tend to nominate moderates. As a result, most of President Reagan's nominations to the federal court system were conservative Republicans, most of President Bush's nominations were moderate Republicans and most of President Clinton's nominations were moderate Democrats. The only reason all of the nominations do not fall within the president's own party is the rule of senatorial courtesy. The rule allows the two Senators to nominate the federal judges for openings within their state. When both Senators are of the party opposite to the president's, the president has at most times acquiesced to their choice. When only one Senator is of the president's party, that Senator consults the other Senator but has the final word as to the nominee. Therefore, the more members of the president's party in the Senate, the more likely the opportunity is for filling vacancies with appointments from the president's party.

One major change in the federal court system that significantly altered the balance of power occurred during the Carter administration. The Democratically controlled Congress enlarged the size of the federal court system as a way of reducing the court backlog, creating 117 new District Court judgeships and 35 new Courts of Appeals positions. The appointments made by President Carter for these new positions were overwhelmingly Democratic, but also included the most significant number of women and African-Americans ever appointed to the federal bench. Until the Reagan appointees began to fill vacancies, the lower courts were considerably more liberal than the Supreme Court. The enormous number of cases with which the Supreme Court dealt in the 1980s and 1990s was to some degree the result of appeals to a conservative Supreme Court for decisions rendered by more liberal lower courts. Not surprisingly, the longer presidents remain in office the more influence they have in shaping the entire federal judiciary.

Key Words

Buckley v. Valeo (1976)
constructionist theory
court-packing proposal
Doctrine of Necessity
Duncan v. Kahanamoku (1946)
En re Debs (1895)
executive agreement
executive privilege

Ex parte Milligan (1866)
Humphrey's Executor v. United States (1935)
Korematsu v. United States (1944)
Marbury v. Madison (1803)
Martin v. Mott (1827)
Morrison v. Olson (1988)
Myers v. United States (1926)

The New York Times Co. v. United States
   (1971)
Pentagon Papers
prerogative power
The Prize Cases (1863)
public good
removal power
stewardship theory

United States v. Curtiss-Wright Export
   Corp. (1936)
United States v. Nixon (1974)
War Powers Resolution of 1973
Wiener v. United States (1953)
Youngstown Sheet and Tube Co. v.
   Sawyer (1952)

Notes

1. Edward S. Corwin. *The President: Office and Powers 1787–1984.* 5th rev. ed. New York: New York University Press, 1984, pp. 29–30.
2. Alexander Hamilton, James Madison, and John Jay. *The Federalist Papers.* Number 70. New York: Bantam, 1961, p. 423.
3. John Locke. *Of Civil Government: Second Treatise.* Chicago: Regnery, 1955, seventh printing 1968, p. 140.
4. Ibid., p. 136.
5. Cited in Arthur M. Schlesinger, Jr. *The Imperial Presidency.* Boston: Houghton Mifflin, 1989, pp. 23–24.
6. Ibid., p. 24.
7. Elder Witt, ed. *Congressional Quarterly's Guide to the U.S. Supreme Court.* Washington, DC: Congressional Quarterly, 1979, pp. 238–239.
8. Theodore Roosevelt. *An Autobiography.* New York: MacMillan, 1913, p. 389.
9. Ibid., pp. 388–389.
10. William Howard Taft. *Our Chief Magistrate and His Powers.* New York: Columbia University Press, 1916, p. 144.
11. Lee Epstein and Thomas G. Walker. *Constitutional Law for a Changing America: A Short Course.* Washington, DC: Congressional Quarterly, 1996, pp. 175–176.
12. David M. O'Brien. *Constitutional Law and Politics: Struggle for Power and Governmental Accountability.* vol. 1. 3rd ed. New York: Norton, 1997, p. 182.
13. *Marbury v. Madison,* 5 U.S. 137 (1803).
14. Richard B. Morris. *Encyclopedia of American History.* New York: Harper, 1953, p. 173.
15. *Worcester v. Georgia,* 31 U.S. 515 (1832).
16. *Dred Scot v. Sanford,* 60 U.S. 393 (1857).
17. Witt. *Congressional Quarterly's Guide to the U.S. Supreme Court,* p. 239.
18. *Ex parte Milligan,* 71 U.S. 2 (1866).
19. Lee Epstein and Thomas G. Walker. *Constitutional Law for a Changing America,* pp. 166–167.
20. *Myers v. United States,* 272 U.S. 52 (1926).
21. *Humphrey's Executor v. United States,* 295 U.S. 602 (1935).
22. *Wiener v. United States,* 357 U.S. 349 (1958).
23. *Buckley v. Valeo,* 424 U.S. 1 (1976).
24. Lee Epstein and Thomas G. Walker. *Constitutional Law for a Changing America,* pp. 164–165.
25. *Morrison v. Olson,* 487 U.S. 654 (1988).
26. Corwin. *The President: Office and Powers, 1787–1984,* p. 212.
27. Quoted in Mark J. Rozell. *Executive Privilege: The Dilemma of Secrecy and Democratic Accountability.* Baltimore: Johns Hopkins University Press, 1994, p. 37.
28. Quoted in Fred I. Greenstein. *The Hidden-Hand Presidency.* New York: Basic, 1982, p. 204.
29. U.S. Congress, Senate, Committee on the Judiciary, Subcommittee on the Separation of Powers. *Executive Privilege: The Withholding of Information by the Executive, Hearings,* 92 Cong. 1st session. Washington, DC: Government Printing Office, July 27–29 and August 4–5, 1971, p. 2.
30. *U.S. v. Nixon,* 418 U.S. 683 (1974).

31. J.W. Peltason. *Understanding the Constitution*. The decision was 8–0 with Justice Rehnquist recusing himself. 14th ed. Fort Worth: Harcourt Brace, 1997, p. 134.
32. Lee Epstein and Thomas G. Walker. *Constitutional Law for a Changing America*, pp. 238–239.
33. "Address by the President of the United States," March 9, 1937. In: Henry S. Commager, *Documents of American History*, 9th ed. New York: Appleton-Century-Crofts, 1973, pp. 383–387.
34. Witt. *Congressional Quarterly's Guide to the U.S. Supreme Court*, p. 244.
35. For a detailed discussion of Truman's handling of the steel strike, see Richard E. Neustadt. *Presidential Power and the Modern Presidents: The Politics of Leadership from Roosevelt to Reagan*. New York: Free Press, 1990, pp. 16ff.
36. *Youngstown Sheet and Tube Co. v. Sawyer*, 343 U.S. 579 (1952).
37. *Martin v. Mott*, 12 Wheat (25 U.S.) 19, 30 (1827).
38. *Prize Cases*, 2 Black (69 U.S.) 635, 638 (1863).
39. Quoted in Daniel C. Diller and Stephen H. Wirls. "Commander in Chief." In: Michael Nelson, ed. *Guide to the Presidency*. 2nd ed. Washington, DC: Congressional Quarterly, 1996, p. 668.
40. *Ex parte Milligan*, 71 U.S. 2 (1866).
41. *Duncan v. Kahanamoku*, 327 U.S. 304 (1946).
42. *Korematsu v. United States*, 323 U.S. 214 (1944).
43. Witt. *Congressional Quarterly's Guide to the U.S. Supreme Court*, p. 196.
44. Quoted in Larry Berman. *The New American Presidency*. Boston: Little, Brown, 1997, p. 75.
45. *The New York Times Co. v. United States*, 403 U.S. 713 (1971).
46. *Brown v. Board of Education (I)*, 347 U.S. 483 (1954).
47. *En re Debs*, 158 U.S. 1 at 4, 18–19 (1895).
48. *United States Congress, Debates and Proceedings, First Congress, 1st session, March 3, 1789 to Eighteenth Congress, 1st session, May 27, 1824.* 42 vol. Washington, DC: Gales & Seaton, 1834–1856, pp. X-596, 613–614.
49. *United States v. Curtiss-Wright Export Corp.*, 299 U.S. 304 (1936).
50. *Goldwater v. Carter*, 444 U.S. 996, 100 S.Ct. 533 (1979).
51. *United States v. Belmont*, 301 U.S. 324 at 330 (1937).
52. *United States v. Pink*, 315 U.S. 203 at 229–230 (1942).
53. *Mississippi v. Johnson*, 71 U.S. 475 1867.
54. *Nixon v. Fitzgerald*, 457 U.S. 731 (1982).
55. *Clinton v. Jones*, 117 S.C. 1636 (1997).
56. J.W. Peltason. *Understanding the Constitution*, p. 39.

Chapter 9

THE PRESIDENT AND CONGRESS

Presidential leadership is a multifaceted process, involving the institutional resources of the presidency, the personal skills of the president, and a collaborative relationship with Congress. In order for presidents to move most of their policies forward, Congress must pass the requisite authorization and, in many cases, appropriations. Some policies can be achieved through executive actions, such as executive agreements and executive orders, and others can be achieved through administrative action within the executive departments. Policy development and implementation can also be achieved, to some degree, by fostering a supportive environment in the executive departments by choosing senior political staff who are loyal to presidential objectives. Yet most policies must have congressional authorization and funding in order to move forward. Presidents need to build bridges to Congress.

Building strong bridges to Congress is a critical part of presidential leadership, one that will make or break a president's ability to craft new policies and to set in motion new directions for the country. Some presidents, such as Lyndon Johnson, have been highly skilled at working with Congress and have achieved strong legislative records. Other presidents, such as Jimmy Carter, have been uncomfortable with the personal interaction necessary to gain legislative support for their legislative priorities. Presidents who have been successful at dealing with Congress have had a combination of strong interpersonal skills, an understanding of how Congress works, experienced White House legislative liaison staffs, and clear policy proposals. Whether the president is operating in an era of divided government, in which one or both houses of Congress are of the opposite party, or in an era of unified government, in which both houses of Congress are of the same party as the president, numerous roadblocks are placed in the path of presidential legislation. These roadblocks are largely due to the institutional rivalry between the president and Congress.

A System of Shared Powers

The institutional rivalry between the president and Congress was designed by the framers of the Constitution to ensure that neither branch controlled the nation's governmental structure. The framers carefully structured a government in which both the president and Congress were involved in creating the laws of the land. The formulation of the nation's laws is constitutionally a mandate of the legislative branch, but presidents have always had a significant role in shaping a portion of the laws generated by Congress. Article II of the Constitution requires the president "from time to time to give to the Congress information of the state of the union, and recommend to their consideration, such measures as he shall judge necessary and expedient." Presidents, particularly modern presidents, have interpreted this phrase in the Constitution to mean that they should develop policy initiatives and ask Congress to form legislation around those initiatives.

During the formative years of the nation's history in the eighteenth and nineteenth centuries, Congress had the primary authority to forge the nation's policy agenda and to pass the necessary laws to implement that agenda. This was called the era of **congressional government.** Woodrow Wilson, in a book written with material from his Ph.D. dissertation at Johns Hopkins University, chronicled the dominance of Congress in the policy process. Writing in *Congressional Government*, Wilson said, "The business of the President, occasionally great, is usually not much above routine. Most of the time it is mere administration, mere obedience of the directions from the masters of policy, the Standing Committees."[1] When Wilson wrote this in 1885, Congress was the dominant player, leaving the president to the "mere administration" of the laws.

Congressional dominance of the policy process continued into the mid-twentieth century when Franklin Delano Roosevelt turned the system upside down and began aggressively sending legislative proposals to Congress. Roosevelt's proposals were designed to bring the nation out of the Great Depression in the 1930s by using government programs as a tool for economic recovery. Roosevelt's activism with Congress in the policy process began a new era in executive–legislative relations known as the era of **presidential government.** The opening which the Constitution provided for presidents to forge policy proposals for Congress has opened the door to the current state, in which policy-making is a shared responsibility. Both Congress and the president initiate policy initiatives for deliberation in the legislative process. Although the president technically initiates these policy proposals, only members of Congress can introduce the proposals as bills for legislative consideration. Working with Congress in the development of these policy proposals is one of the President's most effective mechanisms for leading the legislative process. Creating legislation has become, to a significant degree, a shared power in the modern presidency, encouraged by Congress and nurtured by the president.

Veto Power

Another shared power in the legislative process is the veto. The Constitution requires in the **presentment clause** of Article I, Section 7, that before a bill becomes law, the bill must be "presented to the President of the United States; if he approve, he shall sign it, but if not, he shall return it with his Objections to that House in which it shall have originated, who shall enter the Objections at large on their Journal, and proceed to reconsider it." This three-part procedure gives the president the authority to sign the bill, not sign the bill, or veto the bill. The presentment clause allows the president the latitude of signing bills that the administration supports. Bills that the president does not sign still become law after the requisite ten days but do not necessarily have the president's support. The most significant act that the president can perform is to veto the bill, which abruptly ends months if not years of legislative maneuvering on the bill. All vetoes are constitutionally required to be accompanied by a veto message, outlining why the president is opposed to the bill. Veto messages often provide an outline of the steps necessary to transform the bill into an acceptable piece of legislation that would persuade the president to sign it.

Veto power is a particularly strong tool in managing legislative decisions since veto overrides require a two-thirds vote in both houses of Congress. The overwhelming majority of presidential vetoes have not been overridden. Through 1995, only 105, or four percent, of the 2532 regular vetoes have been overridden since the presidency of George Washington.[2] In order to override a presidential veto, both houses of Congress must build bipartisan coalitions to garner the necessary two-thirds vote. In most cases, this means that members of the president's own party must vote against the president and be publicly cited as taking a stand against the president. Few members of Congress are eager or willing to stand against the president of their own party. Presidents have significant means of punishing those who oppose them, including not supporting those members in their reelection campaigns, blocking funding from the national party committees, withholding passes for VIP White House tours, not issuing invitations to White House bill signings or state dinners, and a host of other routine courtesies. Members of the president's party carefully consider the repercussions of a vote to override a presidential veto, which keeps veto overrides at the seven percent level.

Most presidents do not use their veto power often, choosing to use other strategies to work out differences in legislation moving through Congress. When presidents use their veto authority, it is primarily for bills regarding major public policy issues opposed by the administration. In their analysis of vetoes since 1945, David Rhode and Dennis Simon determined that vetoes are generally used when public support is behind the president's position.[3] If public support erodes, members of Congress are more likely to push for a veto override. President Clinton, for example, chose to carefully exercise his veto power and did not issue a veto until June 7, 1995, when he rejected a $16 billion rescission bill from a Republican-controlled Congress. This exercise of the veto by President Clinton occurred two and a half years after he entered office. Not once in the entire first two years of his term when Congress was controlled by Democrats did President Clinton exercise his veto power. In contrast, President Roosevelt regularly used his veto power, with a record 372 vetoes in his tenure in office, of which only 9 were overridden.[4]

If presidents do not support a bill in Congress, they can both personally lobby against the bill and marshal the resources of the White House and departmental lobbying staffs. In addition, presidents can marshal the support of special interest groups to join in their opposition to the bill. If all of these efforts fail and the bill is passed by both houses of Congress, the president can use the veto power. Veto power allows the president to send a bill back to Congress within ten days (Sundays excepted) with a written message detailing why the president opposes the bill. Once the decision has been made to veto a bill, presidents are generally careful to contact congressional leaders and supporters of the bill to notify them that a veto is imminent. Lyndon Johnson, for example, called one Democratic senator in the middle of the night to alert him of a veto the next day. This presidential courtesy helps to bridge the political chasms often caused by vetoes.[5]

Congress can override the veto, as it did in 1973 with President Nixon's veto of the War Powers Resolution, but overrides do not often happen. In the period from 1789 to 1995, only 105 of the 2,532 vetoes were overridden. If the Congress does not act on the president's veto, the bill dies. If two-thirds of the members present in both the House and the Senate pass the bill again, then the bill becomes law.

Presidents have one other alternative when vetoing a bill, known as the pocket veto. The Constitution states in Article I, Section 7, that "if any Bill shall not be returned by the President within ten Days, (Sundays excepted) after it shall have been presented to him, the Same shall be a Law, in like Manner as if he had signed it, unless the Congress by their Adjournment prevents its Return, in which cast it shall not be a Law." If the Congress adjourns without giving the president the full ten days (Sundays excepted) to make a decision on the bill, the bill is effectively vetoed if the president does not sign it. Thus, if Congress sends the president a bill and adjourns seven days later, the president has to sign it within those seven days or it is effectively vetoed. Unlike the veto that presidents issue through a message to Congress, the pocket veto simply occurs if Congress adjourns before the ten days (Sundays excepted) have passed and the bill has not been signed (Figure 9.1).

Appointment Power

While presidents have a significant role in shaping the legislative process through proposing legislation and through the veto, they also are constrained by Congress in other facets of their relationship with Congress. Congress has the constitutional authority to approve all presidential appointments through Senate ratification. **Appointment power** allows presidents to choose individuals to serve at senior levels of the administration, such as judges of the federal court system and as ambassadors. Article II, Section 2, of the Constitution constrains the president from independently choosing these appointments without the advice and consent of the Senate. Even the president's cabinet officers, who are the most senior members of the administration, must be voted on by the Senate. While few cabinet and subcabinet appointments are rejected by the Senate, the process places another check on presidential decision-making by the Congress. The only exception to the Senate's control over the confirmation process involves the nomination of a vice president. According to the twenty-fifth amendment ratified in 1967, both the House and the Senate must approve the nomination of the vice president when there is a vacancy in the office.

President	Regular Votoes	Overrides	Pocket Vetoes
George Washington	2	0	0
John Adams	0	0	0
Thomas Jefferson	0	0	0
James Madison	5	0	2
James Monroe	1	0	0
John Quincy Adams	0	0	0
Andrew Jackson	5	0	7
Martin Van Buren	0	0	1
William Henry Harrison	0	0	0
John Tyler	6	1	4
James K. Polk	2	0	1
Zachary Taylor	0	0	0
Millard Fillmore	0	0	0
Franklin Pierce	9	5	0
James Buchanan	4	0	3
Abraham Lincoln	2	0	5
Andrew Johnson	21	15	8
Ulysses S. Grant	45	4	48
Rutherford B. Hayes	12	1	1
James A. Garfield	0	0	0
Chester A. Arthur	4	1	8
Grover Cleveland (1st term)	304	2	110
Benjamin Harrison	19	1	25
Grover Cleveland (2nd term)	42	5	128
William McKinley	6	0	36
Theodore Roosevelt	42	1	40
William H. Taft	30	1	9
Woodrow Wilson	33	6	11
Warren G. Harding	5	0	1
Calvin Coolidge	20	4	30
Herbert Hoover	21	3	16
Franklin D. Roosevelt	372	9	263
Harry S Truman	180	12	70
Dwight D. Eisenhower	73	2	108
John F. Kennedy	12	0	9
Lyndon B. Johnson	16	0	14
Richard M. Nixon	26	7	17
Gerald R. Ford	48	12	18
Jimmy Carter	13	2	18
Ronald Reagan	39	9	39
George Bush	29	1	17
Bill Clinton	17	1	0
Total	1465	105	1067

Source: Harold W. Stanley, and Richard G. Niemei. *Vital Statistics in American Politics*. 4th ed. Washington, DC: Congressional Quarterly, 1994.

FIGURE 9.1   Presidential Vetoes: 1789–1996.

This has occurred only twice since 1967, when Spiro Agnew resigned in 1973 and Gerald Ford was chosen by President Nixon to serve as vice president, and in 1974 when Gerald Ford became president and chose Nelson Rockefeller as vice president.

The Constitution provides a system not of divided powers but of shared powers, in which both the executive and legislative branches share responsibility for the senior managers of the nation's governmental business. While the president is the chief executive and empowered to execute the laws, the Constitution requires the execution of the laws to be handled by people who are acceptable to both the president and the Congress. This system of shared decision-making for appointments ensures that the president does not employ people who are unacceptable to the majority of American citizens, which the Congress represents as a body. Most of the time that the Senate rejects presidential nominees there is public support for the decision. For example, when President Bush nominated former Senator John Tower of Texas to serve as the secretary of defense, the Senate rejected the nomination. The Senate argued that Senator Tower's current employment as a lobbyist for the defense industry would violate his independence in issuing defense-related contracts. The case was well documented by the Senate, and President Bush had little public support to continue with Senator Tower's nomination. In another Senate confirmation battle, Lani Guinier was nominated by President Clinton to head the Justice Department's Civil Rights Division, but her positions on broadening affirmative action had little public support. The Guinier case was somewhat different from the Tower case, since the former centered on ethics issues and the latter on political differences.

The failure of presidential nominations to gain Senate approval has occurred in several recent nominations to the Supreme Court. Nominations to the Supreme Court are perhaps the most contentious of all presidential nominations, often rising to the top of the congressional calendar and dominating prime-time news. Members of Congress at times object to nominees who appear to have a philosophical orientation that would mitigate unbiased interpretations of the Constitution. For example, soon after Richard Nixon was inaugurated, Justice Abe Fortas, known for his liberal views, resigned his position on the Supreme Court. President Nixon nominated Judge Clement Haynesworth, a southerner who fulfilled Nixon's goals of placing a southern conservative on the Court. The Democratically-controlled Congress opposed adding a conservative to the Court who generally opposed expanding civil rights for minorities. Rather than removing Haynesworth's name from consideration, Nixon allowed the full Senate to vote. Haynesworth was rejected by the Senate in a fifty-five to forty-five vote.

Nixon then nominated Judge Harrold Carswell, a Florida judge who had similar conservative credentials. When the Senate investigators determined that Judge Carswell had worked to keep a golf course segregated and had at one time adamantly supported segregation, the Senate also rejected his nomination. After nearly a year of problems with the Haynesworth and Carswell nominations, President Nixon tried again in the spring of 1970 by nominating Judge Harry Blackmun of Minnesota. Blackmun, a moderate, was quickly confirmed. The Congress had opposed the nominations of Haynesworth and Carswell not simply for their conservative orientation, but for their opposition to what members of Congress viewed as indefensible positions with regard to constitutional law.

President Reagan faced similar concerns in Congress when he nominated Judge Robert Bork to fill the vacancy created by the retiring Justice Lewis Powell. Judge Bork had written legal opinions critical of Supreme Court decisions on the expansion of minority civil rights, privacy, and women's rights. His views were predominantly conservative and often the antithesis of those held by most members of Congress. The trend toward an expansive view of civil rights and liberties had dominated Supreme Court decisions for several decades, a trend that Judge Bork indicated he would try to reverse. In October 1987 Congress rejected Bork's nomination by the widest margin ever delivered against a Supreme Court nominee, fifty-eight to forty-two.

After the failure of Judge Bork's nomination, President Reagan nominated a California law professor, Douglas H. Ginsburg. Ginsburg faced a similar uphill fight to gain approval, since he was considered nearly as conservative as Bork. When the Senate investigations revealed that he had tried marijuana both as a student and as a law professor, Ginsburg withdrew his name. Reagan's third try at filling Justice Powell's position was Anthony M. Kennedy, a moderate California judge. He was confirmed by a unanimous vote.

George Bush filled two openings in the Supreme Court during his one term in office. The first came in 1990 after the retirement of Justice William Joseph Brennan, Jr. Bush chose Judge David H. Souter, a moderate New Hampshire Supreme Court judge who had only weeks earlier been appointed to the federal appeals court in Boston. Bush wanted to avoid a fight in the Senate, as Reagan had encountered with the Bork and Ginsburg nominations, by choosing a noncontroversial nominee. His choice of Souter easily passed through the confirmation process with a ninety to nine vote.[6]

By the middle of his term, however, President Bush was willing to support a conservative nomination to the Court. He chose Clarence Thomas, chair of the U.S. Equal Employment Opportunity Commission, to fill the vacancy created by the retiring Justice Thurgood Marshall. Thomas was an African-American, as was Marshall. Although Congress was eager to fill the vacancy created by Marshall with another African-American, they were hesitant to fill the position with a conservative who was opposed to affirmative action. During the Senate Judiciary Committee hearings, one witness, Anita Hill, adamantly opposed Thomas's appointment on the basis that he had sexually harassed her. When the hearings concluded that the evidence could not support Hill's charges, the Judiciary Committee again returned to the debate over Thomas's confirmation. In a very heated debate, Thomas was finally confirmed in the full Senate by a narrow vote. When President Clinton nominated Judge Ruth Bader Ginsberg from the District of Columbia for the Court in 1993, she had little opposition in the Senate. As only the second woman nominated for the Court, she received broad support in spite of her career as general counsel for the liberal-oriented American Civil Liberties Union (ACLU) from 1973 to 1980.

In general, presidential appointments to the Supreme Court are routinely approved by Congress. Such routinization is largely a result of presidents becoming sensitized to their political environment. It does not serve the interests of the president or of Congress for presidential appointments to be turned down. Presidents do not try to antagonize Congress by nominating very conservative or very liberal jurists to the Court, nor does Congress try to deny the president's constitutional power of appointment. When nominations are rejected, Congress appears to be confrontational with the president and the president appears to be antagonistic with Congress. While many nominations are delayed, few nominations to the Court are turned down, especially if the president has adequately worked with the members of the Judiciary Committee to obtain their support before the nomination is formally made.

Treaty Power

Another province of policy-making shared by the legislative and executive branches is the **treaty power.** As with other areas of foreign policy, treaties remain primarily an executive function. Only after the negotiations on the treaty are concluded does Congress become involved. While Article II of the Constitution requires that presidents have the "advice and consent of the Senate" to make treaties, presidents have traditionally not sought the advice of the Senate in treaty negotiations. George Washington, struggling to build bridges to the legislative branch, met with members of the Senate in August 1789 to discuss a treaty with the Creek Indians. After a brief series of discussions, Washington concluded that the process was counterproductive. Washington quickly pulled away from making the Senate a collaborator in treaty-making and moved all decision-making for treaties to the executive branch. Ever since Washington's experience with Congress in treaty making, treaties have been handled by the executive branch, usually by the Department of State. Recently, commercial treaties have been handled primarily by the Department of Commerce and the U.S. Trade Representative within the Executive Office of the President rather than the Department of State. Former Senator Fred Harris aptly describes the current treaty process as being reactive rather than proactive. According to Harris, the treaty process has become "a reactive one [by Congress], a power of ratification or rejection, not formal prior advice."[7]

Presidents routinely send diplomatic, trade, and military treaties to Congress to confirm. These are usually handled expediently by the Senate. In most cases, there is little debate on the treaties, for any changes demanded by the Senate would require new negotiations with the other nation or nations involved. Since such changes would be time consuming and may jeopardize the entire treaty, treaties are usually ratified as offered by the executive branch. Some very-high-profile treaties have been rejected, such as the second round of nuclear disarmament treaties during the Carter administration known as the Strategic Arms Limitation Talks II (SALT II). Other high-profile treaties have come close to rejection, such as the North American Free Trade Agreement (NAFTA) during the first term of the Clinton administration.

Treaties that are in jeopardy of failing, such as the NAFTA treaty, require the president to use all of the skills of presidential leadership, including arm twisting. When the Democratic House leadership began to oppose the NAFTA treaty, President Clinton was forced to garner votes outside his own party. This process expends considerable political capital that the president has stored and reduces political capital available for future lobbying activities in Congress. Although President Clinton succeeded in gaining ratification of the NAFTA treaty, presidents do not often oppose the leadership of their own party, nor do they risk failure on such high-profile items.

While treaty-making is a shared power between the executive and legislative branches, other aspects of international agreements and foreign-policy management are not shared powers. The absence of specific language in the Constitution for any part of foreign policy except treaties and appointment of ambassadors has provided presidents broad latitude in controlling the process. The Supreme Court has supported this assumption of power by the president in various decisions, including *United States v. Curtiss-Wright Export Corp.* (1936),[8] in which the Court noted, the "exclusive power of the president as the sole organ of the federal government in the field of international relations," and in *Goldwater v. Carter* (1979),[9] in which the Court ruled that only treaty ratification falls within the joint powers of Congress. Other aspects of diplomatic relations such as recognition of foreign governments, treaty termination, and neutrality decisions are determined solely by the president. Since the Constitution is silent on whether these are joint decisions between the executive and legislative branches, presidents have used their prerogative powers and determined that they are not shared decisions. The Court, in the limited rulings that have been made on the issue, has consistently supported the president.

War Powers

One of the most contentious areas of shared powers involves **war powers,** since neither branch is given clear direction for managing war powers for the nation. Article I, Section 8, of the Constitution gives Congress the power to provide for "the common Defense and general welfare of the United States" in addition to the power to "declare War, grant Letters of Marque and Reprisal, and make Rules concerning Captures on Land and Water." But the Constitution provides a balance to its delegation of authority in war powers by giving the president control over the military in Article II, Section 2, as "Commander in Chief of the Army and Navy of the United States, and of the Militia of the Several States, when called into the actual Service of the United States."

This dual delegation of authority to manage the nation's military operations has been dealt with quite amicably during most of the nation's history. Normal troop movement has always been within the province of the commander in chief role of presidents. Only when military action is required against a foreign country do war powers come into question. At what point does the president need to seek a declaration of war from the Congress before moving forward with military action? The answer traditionally has been that when citizens of the United States have been threatened by a foreign nation, either directly or indirectly, presidents use military force to protect them. Presidents have legitimized this interpretation of their authority by citing their constitutional responsibility to "protect and defend" the nation. President Jefferson used this interpretation to send the navy to ward pirates off the Barbary Coast of Spain after a series of attacks on American merchant ships. President Lincoln used this interpretation to send troops to Fort Sumter after the attack by Confederate soldiers. In more modern times, President Ford used his authority to rescue the crew of a merchant marine vessel who had been captured by the Cambodian army and President Carter used his authority in the rescue attempt for the hostages held in the Iranian embassy. Each of these military actions was conducted to "protect and defend" American citizens. The central theme involved was "defense" in each action, a theme that precluded the involvement of Congress and the declaration of war.

The concept of "protect and defend" has taken a number of winding turns in the latter half of the twentieth century, as presidents have expanded "defense" to incorporate defense of democratic principles (Vietnam), defense of American economic interests (Kuwait), protection from chemical and biological weapons (Iraq), and in retaliation of attacks on the U.S. military (Libya). Congress has endeavored to place limitations on how presidents interpret their commander in chief role through legislation. The War Powers Resolution of 1973 requires presidents to consult with Congress before committing troops to "hostile" situations and limits actions to sixty days, or ninety days under certain circumstances, without further approval by Congress. Presidents have ignored this law, arguing that it unconstitutionally infringes on their commander in chief responsibilities.

Gerald Ford argued that the law was not only unconstitutional, but that it was unrealistic to expect the president to consult with Congress in all military and national security matters. "If we, as a Nation, are to be respected by our adversaries," Ford said, "and if we can look forward to . . . cooperation from our allies, our President as Commander in Chief has to have the authority to act. We cannot take the time to have 535 Secretaries of State or Secretaries of Defense."[10]

In contrast to this former president's view is the view of a former Senator, who argues, "Consultation with Congress should be required well in advance of military action by the president, not only because this would be the right and constitutional thing to do, but also because two (or a good many more) heads are, indeed, better than one. Consultation can help prevent mistaken decision and action."[11]

The debate on whether presidents will seek the collective judgment of Congress in determining military action will continue, but presidents are unlikely to yield their commander in chief authority to such collective decision making. Unless the Supreme Court determines that the War Powers Resolution of 1973 is constitutional, presidents will essentially ignore it. A significant case in support of this proposition involves President Clinton and the bombing of Iraq in 1998. On the eve of the impeachment vote in December 1998, President Clinton ordered bombing raids into Iraq to destroy weapons plants and other critical infrastructure. In spite of the House of Representatives being only hours away from considering an impeachment, the president chose to conduct a major military action without consulting Congress. The War Powers Resolution of 1973 has little effective power over presidential actions.

Nondelineated Shared Powers

As government has become increasingly large and increasingly complex, both the president and Congress have tried to improve the way they do business. For Congress, this has meant minimizing the number of mandates placed in legislation. Congress has largely delegated to the executive branch the authority to write the specific language implementing the legislation. By purposely writing legislation in very vague, general language, Congress has allowed the executive branch to prepare the rules and regulations governing the legislation.

But Congress has at times been concerned that the executive branch might write language that it does not support. In order to protect itself from these possibilities, Congress has interwoven a series of statements in some bills that provide for a veto of certain provisions. If the executive branch does not write language that satisfies members of Congress, the **legislative veto** written into the law allows Congress to void specific decisions that are made using the law. For example, the governing statute for the Immigration and Naturalization Service (INS) allows Congress to void decisions made by staff from the INS. In 1983 the Supreme Court ruled in the *Immigration and Naturalization Service v. Chadha*[12] decision that this legislative veto violated the presentment clause. Once a bill has been signed by the president into law, the Court ruled, only the executive branch can execute the law. Congress cannot intervene in the execution of the law.

In spite of the very clear decision in *Immigration and Naturalization Service v. Chadha* that banned Congress from further legislative vetoes written into laws, the practice has continued. The legislative veto, however, serves the needs of both the Congress and the president. The practice of writing vague, general laws allows the executive branch to develop the language implementing the law. This is a powerful tool for managing the executive branch, for it allows the executive branch to create language that supports presidential goals and objectives and reduces duplication of services. Control of the execution of the law is firmly rooted in the executive branch when departmental staff have decision-making power over the language of the rules governing implementation. The legislative branch also prospers using the legislative veto, since it allows Congress to deal with the plethora of laws that they must handle without getting bogged down in detail. The legislative veto allows Congress to write general laws and move on to other matters. In addition, the legislative veto minimizes the expertise that members of Congress have to develop on any one issue. In order to adequately write a law that covers the contingencies that most members of Congress want incorporated, they would have to have more expertise than they have. The legislative veto allows members of Congress to pass a law with minimal expertise and minimal attention to detail, since the enabling legislation allows a veto over the decisions made by the executive branch. Enabling legislation that does not carry a legislative veto does not provide for legislative interaction in the decision process.

The Constitution has created a system of shared powers between the executive and legislative branches in many policy areas. The president shares the appointment power, the treaty power, the war powers, and to some degree the legislative power with Congress. In addition to these constitutionally shared powers, an accommodation has been reached between the two branches with regard to delegation of powers through legislation. Since the president continues to allow legislative vetoes to be incorporated into legislation without a court challenge, there is an implied acquiescence to a role for Congress in the execution of the laws.

This implied acquiescence through the legislative veto has been fortified through the ever-increasing role of Congress in oversight of executive programs. Based on authority granted in the Legislative Reorganization Act of 1946, Congress examines the implementation of the programs created by law to ensure that they are being managed in accordance with the law. Too much deviation from the letter and the spirit of the law will cause Congress to reevaluate continuing authorizations and appropriations for the law. The president and his staff provide Congress information as required in oversight hearings in order to minimize any confrontations that would cause the program to be redesigned or terminated by Congress.

The President as Legislative Leader

The president as legislative leader is perhaps the most important role that the president has in relation to Congress. "In this century," notes congressional scholar Barbara Hinckley, "Congress has looked to the president for legislative initiative."[13] Stephen Wayne refers to the modern presidency as "the legislative presidency," reflecting the strong role that the president plays in the legislative process. As Wayne notes, "Congress' seeming inability to provide comprehensive legislative programming and, until recently, comprehensive budgeting has literally forced the president and his staff to develop mechanisms and processes for legislative policy-making."[14]

The president has become central to the legislative process. But presidents are still only a part of the legislative process; a partnership with the Congress is also required. Developing a partnership is an awkward process in any relationship, for it is one filled with successes and failures. In order for the partnership to flourish, both the president and Congress have to compromise on proposals that they support. In his inaugural address, President Bush extended his hand saying, "We need a new engagement between the President and Congress. . . . We need to compromise. . . . We need harmony."[15] The success of any president in this process depends on knowing when to compromise on a proposal, when to withdraw a proposal, and when to fight for the proposal's survival. During President Clinton's tenure in office, he compromised with Congress to move the welfare reform bill forward, he withdrew his health care bill when support in Congress eroded, and he fought for passage of his free trade zones in the North American Free Trade Agreement (NAFTA).

The partnership that evolved in the mid-twentieth century between the president and Congress in formulating legislation is one that was unheard of during the 1800s. Had Woodrow Wilson been alive today, he would have marveled at the change in the role that Congress plays. The era during which Wilson wrote *Congressional Government* in 1885 was far different from what exists today. No partnership existed in the era of congressional government, only a strong Congress and a weak president to execute the laws passed by Congress. Wilson had such little regard for the power that the president had that he referred to the president as "the titular head of the executive."[16] Wilson clearly had a change of heart, however, when he became president. By 1907, Wilson had substantially changed his view of the presidency. He felt that only the president can, "win the admiration and confidence of the country, and no other single office can withstand him, no combination of forces will easily overpower him."[17] The current era of presidential government has evolved as presidents have gained staffs to assist in policy formulation and as laws have become so complex that presidential guidance is often necessary. Presidential activism in congressional affairs is partly the result of an enhanced White House staffing capability to monitor legislative action.

Presidential Staffing: The Office of Congressional Relations

Monitoring legislative affairs through the White House Office of Congressional Relations (recently renamed the Office of Legislative Affairs) has enabled presidents to become active participants in the legislative process. The availability of a large, technically expert staff in the White House provides the president not only the capability of monitoring legislation but the capability of lobbying on behalf of or in opposition to legislation.

The Office of Congressional Relations (OCR) was created by President Eisenhower in 1953 as part of the larger staff buildup begun in the Roosevelt administration. Following passage of the Reorganization Act of 1939, which established the Executive Office of the President and the White House staff, President Roosevelt instituted a staffing system to assist him in managing the executive branch. Prior to having the staff provided through the Executive Office of the President, presidents relied on kitchen cabinets, commissions, task forces, and cabinet secretaries to advise them on policy and legislative matters. During the Roosevelt and Truman administrations, the White House staff was composed of a number of generalists who advised the president on a wide range of issues, including legislation. During the second term of the Truman administration, the role of monitoring legislation was given to two assistants to the appointments secretary, Charles Maylon and Joseph Feeney. Not until the Eisenhower administration was a job specifically devised to manage the administration's lobbying efforts in Congress and to monitor other legislation moving through Congress. Eisenhower appointed his deputy chief of staff, Major General Wilton B. Persons, to direct a newly established legislative affairs office.

Bradley Patterson, who served in the Eisenhower White House, describes the creation of the congressional liaison as "an ambulatory bridge across a constitutional gulf."[18] The Eisenhower era continued a presidential activism begun under Franklin Delano Roosevelt in which presidents were actively involved in formulating legislation, rather than passively involved in responding to legislative direction. Patterson's "ambulatory bridge" was a necessary product of this presidential activism.

Eisenhower was particularly adept at building relations with Congress both directly and indirectly. Indirectly he often used his cabinet officers, such as Secretary of the Treasury Robert Anderson, to handle behind-the-scenes conversations with members of Congress. Anderson had almost daily contact with Senate Majority Leader Lyndon Johnson.[19] Fred I. Greenstein refers to Anderson as the "political conduit" for Eisenhower to the daily pulse of the Senate. In order to directly build strong relations with Congress, Eisenhower had informal evening meetings at the White House with House Speaker Sam Rayburn and with Lyndon Johnson.[20]

The **Office of Congressional Relations (OCR)** is divided into two units, one responsible for the House and one for the Senate; each has a deputy director. The director of the entire office has the title *assistant to the president*, signifying that the role of congressional liaison is one of the senior members of the White House staff. All senior staff meetings in the white House include the congressional liaison office director, and most larger staff meetings include the two deputy directors of the office. Typically, the congressional liaison office is one of the largest units in the White House, with large staffs for both the House and the Senate units. Although most of the staff is housed across the street from the White House in the Old Executive Office Building, the director is housed in the White House, usually in close proximity to the president. President Johnson placed such value on the role of the congressional liaison office, that its director, Larry O'Brien, was the highest paid person on the White House staff.

One of the anomalies about the congressional liaison staff, and particularly the director, is that most do not come from the campaign. Directors and their staffs tend to be products of Capitol Hill, most having served in some senior capacity for a member of the House or Senate. Such experience with legislative affairs by the congressional liaison staff provides the presidential staff expertise both in the legislative process and with the players in that process. In contrast, most of the other members of the White House staff are products of the campaign and many have long personal associations with the president. Presidential success on Capitol Hill can be measured to some degree by the expertise of the congressional affairs director. For example, one of the reasons that Jimmy Carter failed to achieve more success in Congress was that he chose his friend, Frank Moore, as his congressional affairs director. Moore had served as the director of a planning commission in Georgia, on which Carter had served for several years, near Carter's hometown but he had no experience on Capitol Hill. Moore's complete inexperience in Congress proved to be a disaster to the Carter legislative plan.

Ronald Reagan, on the other hand, chose an experienced director, Max L. Friedersdorf, to head his legislative office. Friedersdorf had worked for many years in Congress for a House member from Indiana and had worked on both the Ford and Nixon White House congressional liaison staffs. Friedersdorf had also served as chairman of the Federal Election Commission, broadening his ties to members of Congress.[21] In spite of the battles between Reagan and the Democratic House leadership, Speaker of the House Thomas P. "Tip" O'Neill praised Friedersdorf and his staff, characterizing them as "an experienced and savvy team."[22] Reagan's choice of Friedersdorf, and his assistant Kenneth Duberstein, to manage the congressional affairs office clearly contributed to the administration's legislative success rate.

Bill Clinton learned the lessons of his predecessors and also chose an experienced Washington insider, Howard Paster, to direct his congressional liaison office. Paster had worked both in the Carter White House and in Congress before moving to the private sector as chairman of Hill and Knowlton, a large public relations firm with national and international clients. But Paster did not fare as well as Friedersdorf had within the White House staff structure. Paster's significant credentials in managing legislative affairs were not enough to overcome his status as an outsider in the White House. "To the close-knit Clinton crew," commented one member of the White House staff, "he was an outsider. He was everything the Clintonites were not. He was eastern, liberal, and a veteran Washington deal maker."[23] Much to his dismay, Paster was often left out of senior staff discussions on major legislation. The failure to include Paster in many of the early discussions on health care reform contributed to its failure in Congress. Paster could not move forward a proposal that he knew little about, including the legislative strategy that was being developed by the health care team in the White House. Haynes Johnson and David Broder, two journalists who covered the Clinton administration, describe a growing alienation between some members of the White House staff, including the congressional liaison staff, and the health care team, managed by Hillary Rodham Clinton. They describe Paster's attitude as becoming increasingly cynical during the first year of the administration. The attitude of Paster, his staff, and others who were left out of the health care legislation planning, according to Johnson and Broder was, "They're so smart. Let them figure out how to pass it."[24]

Paster also failed to work well with Thomas "Mack" McLarty, the chief of staff, causing significant friction between the two in developing legislative strategies for other administration proposals. In retrospect, McLarty noted that "we should have included Paster in more discussions."[25] Although legislative experience is an important part of managing legislative affairs for the White House, clearly it is not the only part of succeeding in the liaison office. There appears to be no clear model for how important insider status is, but there does appear to be ample evidence that legislative experience is critical to a successful congressional liaison.

The role of the congressional affairs staff is quite diverse within the broad scheme of enhancing the president's legislative goals. Charles E. Walcott and Karen M. Hult divide the responsibility of the OCR staff into two broad areas: staffers with policy responsibility and staffers involved in representational activities. Those involved in policy areas work to support or to block legislation in Congress. Those involved in representational areas provide or withhold favors to members of Congress and deal with the routine aspects of presidential dealings with members of Congress.[26] Staff from the OCR must manage the numerous small, informal meetings that the president has with members of Congress, ensuring that the president is briefed not only on the legislation being discussed but on the legislation near and dear to members' hearts. Some of the most intricate wheeling and dealing is accomplished at these informal gatherings. But these apparently spontaneous discussions on legislation between the president and members of Congress demand a substantial amount of staff work in the White House.

One of the daily activities of the congressional liaison staff is to provide the president with names of members of Congress who should be called that day regarding either legislation or personal matters. An important part of building bridges to Congress is personal networking. One way to do this is to call members of Congress to offer sympathy for the death of a spouse or other family member, to offer support in times of personal crisis, and to offer good wishes if a member is hospitalized. This is done without regard to partisan affiliation and has become an expected practice of the president. The president is given a briefing schedule of whom to call, what to say, and details of the reason the call is being placed. Building these personal bridges to Congress is an essential part of the legislative presidency, but a part that requires the time and expertise of a large and experienced White House congressional liaison staff.

The liaison staff is also responsible for overseeing the journey of legislation through Congress, working with members in the House and Senate to support presidentially sponsored legislation or to block presidentially opposed legislation. In many cases, the president will take no position on a bill and will try not to become involved in partisan battles over the legislation. Again, the liaison staff needs to advise the president on those pieces of legislation that no position is being taken. When the president is trying to move a major piece of legislation forward, all of the resources of the executive branch and of the presidency are brought to bear on Congress. This may include the additional lobbying efforts of the congressional liaison staffs of the departments, meetings with the president, and invitations to presidential events. Norman C. Thomas and Joseph A. Pika describe the way the White House staff gathers legislative votes as one of "bargaining, arm-twisting, and confrontation."[27]

But the job of the congressional liaison staff does not end on the Capitol steps. As one former White House staffer noted of the job, "for the legislative affairs staff the end of the day in Congress is only another beginning. Their East Wing offices then become an "elves' factory," producing briefings and bios on who is coming to see the president in the near future, writing up one-pagers for the presidential phone calls, or inquiring in the agencies about the status of an issue or product."[28]

Invitations to presidential events are one of the more innovative tools that a president can use to encourage members to support legislation. Richard Nixon used cruises down the Potomac River on the presidential yacht *Sequoia* to garner support for his policies, then he rewarded that support with invitations to use the presidential box at the Kennedy Center and to attend state dinners. President Clinton used invitations to use the White House tennis court to reward members of Congress, while Presidents Ford and Clinton often used golfing outings as a reward. Some members of Congress who have offered consistently strong support for the president are even offered trips on Air Force One with the president.

Managing congressional relations has become an art in recent years. Simple tasks such as bill signings have become a symbol of how far presidents will go to nurture strong congressional relations. President Carter, who did not see the value of building bridges to Congress, held bill signings in the Rose Garden with little fanfare. When he signed bills, he reached into his pocket and used a felt-tipped pen which he then returned to his pocket. This was in part symbolic of his attitude toward Congress and in part symbolic of his cost-cutting endeavors. In contrast, each of his successors has held very elaborate bill signings in the Rose Garden, symbolic of their efforts to build bridges to the legislative branch. Presidents Reagan, Bush, and Clinton have had a number of pens on the table as they signed the enrolled bill. A different pen was used for each letter of the president's signature and then handed to a key sponsor in the House and Senate. The pens were elaborate ballpoint pens with the seal of the President of the United States on the side. They were elegant and suitable for framing, which was routinely done with a picture of the bill signing, and these could be placed in the member's office.

Breakfast meetings have been another tool to bridge the gulf between the president and Congress. These meetings foster personal relationships and contribute to a sense of shared mission. But breakfast meetings, as any other meetings, must be carefully structured when they involve the president and members of Congress. President Carter started his presidency hosting the congressional leadership with orange juice and pastries in a very simple breakfast. Speaker of the House Thomas P. "Tip" O'Neill mentioned to Carter that this was hardly appropriate for these meetings, but little changed. President Reagan, in contrast, conducted breakfast meetings with full breakfasts of bacon and eggs and an assortment of pastries and muffins using the official White House china and linen tablecloths. While this may seem to be a relatively small matter, members of Congress saw the ritual as an expression of regard for the guests; it contributed to strengthening the bridge between the White House and Capitol Hill.

One of the more recent activities of the legislative affairs office has been to coordinate all of the mail that comes into the White House from members of Congress. Congressional mail is logged into computers, immediately acknowledged, and then forwarded either to the president or to the appropriate cabinet officer for action. A special tracking system follows all correspondence that is forwarded to the cabinet officers to ensure that action has been taken and that the mail does not lay unattended once it reaches the departments.[29] Failure to take action on correspondence from members of Congress could lead to significant repercussions in the legislative process, repercussions that could have been avoided if adequate attention is paid by the staff to legislative correspondence. Presidents have relied heavily on their congressional liaison staffs to coordinate the key pieces of legislation that support their agenda items. But the job is a very difficult one and often impossible to fulfill completely. As one journalist described the job of congressional liaison, "he not only had to satisfy his boss, the President, which was hard enough, but also had to keep happy one of the world's largest group of egoists and chronic malcontents, the 535 members of Congress . . . and no matter how much he did for the lawmaker, it was never enough."[30]

The legislative presidency requires the White House to have a congressional liaison staff with a thorough knowledge of congressional politics, legislative procedures, and presidential goals and objectives. One of the stronger models in recent years for the process of moving legislation through Congress was during the Reagan administration, when chief of staff James Baker worked closely with the liaison staff to determine which legislative initiatives should receive priority in the legislative process. Baker often met with members of Congress to provide further support for presidential positions, especially for pieces of legislation that were central to the president's agenda. This model was also followed in the Bush administration, when chief of staff John Sununu worked closely with congressional liaison Frederick McClure. Sununu often met directly with members of Congress, as Baker had.

In the Clinton administration, chief of staff Mack McLarty continued the lobbying efforts that Baker and Sununu had used, but did so with less coordination with the congressional liaison office than had been used in former administrations. Other members of the White House staff also worked directly with Congress, without the congressional liaison. One example of senior White House staff operating outside of the congressional liaison office during the Clinton administration involved the legislation for the national service bill. The lobbying effort for the national service bill in the first year of the Clinton administration was handled nearly completely by Eli Segal and George Stephanopoulos, rather than Paster and the congressional liaison staff. Both Segal and Stephanopoulos had worked on the campaign and had known Clinton prior to the election. Both had worked on the concept of national service during the campaign and become strong advocates for the proposal as part of the president's priority agenda. Steven Waldman, a writer for *Newsweek*, refers to the "Segal team" [rather than the Paster team] as the "White House strategists" responsible for managing the congressional lobbying effort.[31] Although Paster's experience in dealing with legislative affairs far exceeded that of either Segal or Stephanopoulos, he was not part of many of the strategy sessions to move the bill through Congress. In fact, Waldman later wrote in the book on the Clinton administration's lobbying activities for the national service bill and Paster is rarely mentioned.[32]

Building bridges to Congress is an essential part of the legislative presidency and the position of the congressional liaison is critical to building those bridges. Presidents need an experienced staff in their congressional liaison office who can handle the myriad services requested by members of Congress, can deftly count votes during legislative sessions, and can convince members of Congress to support the president's legislative agenda. The current era of presidential government requires presidents to have sophisticated congressional liaison staffs. Presidential activism in congressional affairs is largely the result of an enhanced staffing capability to monitor legislative affairs.

Central Clearance

Another piece to the puzzle that allows presidents to be activists in the legislative process is the **central clearance** provided by the **Legislative Reference Office** in the OMB. The Legislative Reference Office reviews all enrolled bills (bills that have passed both the House and the Senate) and all legislative submissions from the departments. The office is intended to be nonpartisan and purely objective in its review of enrolled bills, leaving political recommendations to the White House staff. Enrolled bills that are controversial will receive suggestions from both the OMB and the White House staff. Noncontroversial enrolled bills, which the majority of bills are, receive only the OMB recommendation (and at times a recommendation from the counsel's office). The data from the Legislative Reference Office indicates that the president follows their recommendations most of the time (ninety-nine percent) when approval is recommended but less than seventy-six percent of the time when disapproval is recommended.[33] This disparity in percentages can be explained because disapprovals or vetoes are usually politically rather than constitutionally based and require a substantial commitment of political capital. The decision-making process in the Legislative Reference Office is intentionally nonpolitical and is primarily staffed with career civil servants rather than political appointments.

President Truman was the first president to institutionalize the use of central clearance, developing the Office of Legislative Reference in 1947 in the Bureau of the Budget. One of the first major roles that the office performed was to track the Taft–Hartley legislation in 1947 as it wove its way through the House and Senate and to analyze the final bill. The Legislative Reference Office provided substantial data that President Truman used to veto the bill, a bill that Truman disparagingly referred to as the "Slave Labor Act."[34] Truman used the office not only to track legislation, but to provide information to members of Congress on the bills that he was supporting. One staffer described the process as "explanatory," adding that the bureau staffers were "explanatory people. We were not peddlers of doctrine."[35] Their role was to ensure that members of Congress understood what bills the president supported and what bills he opposed. The process not only successfully built new bridges to Congress but also expanded the legislative presidency.

In 1970, President Nixon expanded the oversight role of the Legislative Reference Office to include the review of all departmental legislative proposals. OMB ensured that the departmental proposals did not duplicate other departmental programs, and, perhaps most importantly, were in line with presidential goals and objectives. The expanded role of the Office of Management and Budget has given its staff a major role in the legislative presidency. The director of the OMB has become one of the most powerful members of the White House and is included in all major legislative strategy sessions. In recent administrations, OMB directors have been considered so important to the president that they participate in cabinet meetings and White House staff meetings.

One of the most recent examples of an OMB director becoming a powerful White House insider was David Stockman, President Reagan's director of the **Office of Management and Budget.** During his tenure, Stockman used his authority to deny departments nearly all of the new programs they sought through new legislation as part of the budget-cutting process.[36] The central clearance function of OMB enabled Stockman to review all legislative requests put forth by the departments to screen them for new funding requests, which he quickly denied. During the Bush administration, OMB director Richard Darman[37] used the tools of central clearance for reviewing every legislative program from the departments to ensure that it did not include budget increases or additional program costs. Leon Panetta and Alice Rivlin were equally aggressive in their tenures as OMB directors during the Clinton administration. Central clearance has become a leading tenet of all recent administrations, as presidents attempt to manage the extraordinary amount of legislation generated not only from Congress but also from the executive branch.

Central clearance has also allowed presidents to tighten their control over the legislative process. All legislation sponsored by the executive branch must be cleared through the Office of Management and Budget, reducing direct negotiations between the departments and the Congress and narrowing the access points for special interest groups. The tighter the control the president maintains over executive branch legislation, the more influence the president maintains over the legislative process.

Party Leadership

The success of the legislative presidency involves both the institutional resources of the presidency and the personal skills of the president. These skills are particularly important with regard to building bridges to the party leadership in Congress. Without the active support of the leadership, presidents reduce their ability to gain support within the party. Of all the factors that can influence a member of Congress in deciding whether to support a presidential initiative, party is the most important. Voting in both the House and the Senate is predominantly along party lines. In order to ensure party loyalty, presidents need to work closely with the party leadership (Figure 9.2).

A central role of the **party leadership** in Congress is to inform members what position the party is taking with regard to impending legislation. As the number of bills moving forward in Congress regularly increases, members are unable to keep track of the volume of material on which they must vote. The party leadership provides members with an important, although not the only, guide in their voting behavior. For presidents to ignore the party leadership in designing their legislative packages can only damage those packages. The party leadership can prioritize policy initiatives, ensuring that they will be considered during the current legislative session and can maneuver those initiatives to the most favorable committee. In addition, members of the president's party provide the bulk of legislative support for the president's legislative agenda.[38]

Years	President & Political Party	House Majority Party	Senate Majority Party
1953–55	Eisenhower (R)	(R)	(R)
1955–57	Eisenhower (R)	(D)	(D)
1957–59	Eisenhower (R)	(D)	(D)
1959–61	Eisenhower (R)	(D)	(D)
1961–63	Kennedy (D)	(D)	(D)
1963–65	Kennedy (D)/L. Johnson (D)	(D)	(D)
1965–67	L. Johnson (D)	(D)	(D)
1967–69	L. Johnson (D)	(D)	(D)
1969–71	Nixon (R)	(D)	(D)
1971–73	Nixon (R)	(D)	(D)
1973–75	Nixon(R)/Ford (R)	(D)	(D)
1975–77	Ford (R)	(D)	(D)
1977–79	Carter (D)	(D)	(D)
1979–81	Carter (D)	(D)	(D)
1981–83	Reagan (R)	(D)	(R)
1983–85	Reagan (R)	(D)	(R)
1985–87	Reagan (R)	(D)	(R)
1987–89	Reagan (R)	(D)	(R)
1989–91	Bush (R)	(D)	(D)
1991–93	Bush (R)	(D)	(D)
1993–95	Clinton (D)	(D)	(D)
1995–97	Clinton (D)	(R)	(R)
1997–99	Clinton (D)	(R)	(R)
1999–01	Clinton (D)	(R)	(R)

FIGURE 9.2   Political Parties of Presidents and Congress: 1953–2001.

Most members of the party consider the president the natural party leader. The president is the leader not only of the country, but also of the party. This role provides presidents an unparalleled opportunity, if they use it, to move their legislative agenda through Congress. Some presidents have worked harder than others at building relations within their own party. Jimmy Carter ignored the party leadership, under the assumption that his programs did not need any particular legislative support. Nelson Polsby, writing in *Congress and the Presidency*, depicts Jimmy Carter's failure in Congress as largely self-created. "President Carter worked hard and successfully to master the essential as well as many of the inessentials, of the programs he advocated," noted Polsby. "He acted as though the politics of being President were a branch of nuclear engineering rather than of human relations."[39] Carter failed to nurture the party leadership, using the perks of office such as invitations to state dinners, and to consult with the party leadership on legislative strategy. One of Carter's most visible failings was his submission of several pieces of major legislation to one committee, which overloaded the committee and contributed to significant delays. The party leadership would have offered strategies to spread the legislation around to several committees had they been consulted.

Presidents must provide direction to the party leadership on the administration's priorities but must also be sensitive to the legislative proposals that the party leadership supports. Members of Congress are continually seeking ways to improve their stature in their home districts, which translates into delivering a continuing line of federal money into their home districts. Such money might be sought for a new office building to house federal agencies, upgrades to a mass-transit system, more civilian jobs at a military base, or a new highway. Senator Robert Byrd (D-W.Va.) was famous in the Senate for the plethora of funding that he secured for his home state, such as a large facility to house the Federal Bureau of Investigation and a major four-lane highway across the state. Public works projects, such as dams and levees along the intercoastal waterways, are particularly important to members of Congress to secure for their home districts. Representative "Bud" Schuster (R-Pa.), who chaired the House Transportation Committee, secured millions of dollars for his home district of Altoona, Pennsylvania, and became known as the king of highway money. So much highway money flowed into the Altoona region that one four-lane federal highway was gratefully named by his constituents as the Bud Schuster Highway. At one point in 1998 Schuster even attempted to force the Pennsylvania Turnpike Commission to have no tolls within his district so that his constituents could travel the road for free. This failed to pass. Although these expensive projects are typical of what are known as pork-barrel politics, they are important to members of Congress. Presidents rarely oppose such projects for fear that their own legislative priorities would be endangered.

Another technique for managing legislative action was made available to the president through the Line Item Veto Act of 1996. The **line item veto** allowed the president to choose certain parts of an appropriations bill and veto only the line or lines in the bill that were objectionable. Many states have given their governors this authority, but at the federal level the line item veto was considered unconstitutional because it violated the presentment clause of the Constitution. The presentment clause requires that all bills must be signed or vetoed by the president in their entirety. In spite of this seemingly clear language in the Constitution, the new leadership of the 104th Congress under House Speaker Newt Gingrich pushed through legislation allowing the line item veto. Gingrich and a number of other Republicans had prioritized the line item veto as part of their proposals for the new Congress outlined in the Contract with America. The Contract with America was a platform of ten legislative proposals that a number of Republicans had campaigned for in the 1994 elections.

The Line Item Veto Act of 1996 allowed the president to review all spending and tax legislation and decide what parts should be approved and what parts should be vetoed. The law permitted the president to veto individual items within five days of signing the bill into law. In January 1997 six members of Congress challenged the constitutionality of the Line Item Veto Act in the Supreme Court. The Justices ruled against the challenge, deciding that the six members did not have standing to challenge the law since no vetoes had been delivered by the president at that point. On August 12, 1997, President Clinton became the first president in history to use the line item veto, and over the next nine months he struck eighty-two items from eleven laws, including $1.9 billion in spending over the next five years.[40]

In the process of deciding which items to veto, Clinton worked assiduously not to choose items that were critical to the electoral base of any member of Congress. In each of the line item vetoes, the White House staff carefully analyzed whether or not the failure to move forward on the vetoed project would jeopardize the political health of the member. Only the items that were considered by the White House to be politically dispensable were approved for veto. This strategy was essential to keeping the lines of communication open to Congress and to keep the bridges in executive–legislative relations from collapsing. After the vetoes, which had been so carefully crafted, few voices of discontent were heard, especially from the Republican leadership.

The line item veto allowed Congress to pass legislation that included large public works projects, and other such projects, knowing that the president would veto them for budget reasons. By including these projects in the legislation, members could go back to their districts and argue that they tried to move the project forward but the president vetoed it. Members of Congress succeed with their constituents and the president succeeds with the larger national constituency for his protection of the budget. Both Congress and the President saw the line item veto as a winning process, but on June 25, 1998, the law was declared unconstitutional by the Supreme Court in the case of *Clinton v. City of New York*.[41] The city of New York was given standing by the Court because one line item veto had included medical reimbursements to New York City.[42] New York City had brokered a settlement with Congress to reimburse disputed federal Medicaid payments made to New York hospitals since 1992 which the Clinton administration had refused to pay. A line item veto by President Clinton had taken out the reimbursement that Congress had placed in the federal budget bill. After the successful challenge to the line item veto, New York City received the disputed medicaid payments. The line item veto had only a short life in executive–legislative relations.

Public Support

Another important tool in building support in Congress for presidential initiatives is through broad public support. Public support can be viewed both in terms of specific presidential initiatives and broader public support for the administration in its legislative program. **Public opinion operations,** such as the Gallup Poll, routinely poll voters to assess their overall view of the administration. Presidents who have strong standing in the public opinion polls are more likely to have a strong standing among members of Congress than if they have lower public opinion ratings.

Presidents use various techniques to build public support for their programs. President Roosevelt, whose health did not permit much travel, used radio addresses to discuss his legislative proposals and to extol the virtues of other programs already in place. When television became the primary medium of mass communication, presidents began holding regular press conferences to discuss specific legislative goals. But press conferences soon proved to be a tool for the media more often than for the president, so the use of press conferences has become far less important for presidents to move their message forward.

Several recent presidents have returned to the Roosevelt tradition of using radio addresses. President Clinton gave a radio address every Saturday throughout his administration to explain a specific piece of legislation that he supported or to discuss broader national issues. President Carter preferred using television to address the American people through a series of fireside chats, as he called them. The fireside chats were held in the White House with the president sitting at his desk talking directly to the nation. The fire was always blazing in the fireplace, which led to the phrase fireside chat, and Carter wore a sweater rather than a coat and tie. Behind the desk where Carter sat were an American flag and pictures of his wife, Rosalyn, and his daughter, Amy. This created an informal sense to the speech and invoked a sense of patriotism and family values.

Another technique used by presidents to build broad public support for their programs, and for their presidency in general, are trips around the country to address a specific issue. During the 1993 battle over the North American Free Trade Agreement (NAFTA) in Congress, President Clinton crisscrossed the nation giving speeches in support of the NAFTA treaty. These speeches were given significant advance treatment by the White House, to ensure that they had both local and national media attention. When possible, the speeches were given in outdoor settings with dramatic backgrounds to enhance the visuals on television. For example, after supporting a project that allowed additional water to flow into the Grand Canyon through the Colorado River, President Clinton stood on the edge of the Grand Canyon to praise the importance of federal efforts to improve America's national waterways. Presidents have enormous power to use the "bully pulpit," as Theodore Roosevelt called it, to move their policies forward. Whether presidential speeches are directed at a specific piece of legislation or at general administration policies, the public makes assessments about the administration. The more positive those assessments are, the more positive public opinion will be.

Positive public opinion translates into the power to persuade members of Congress, as Richard Neustadt argues in his classic book, *Presidential Power and the Modern Presidents*.[43] Neustadt explores whether the president is a clerk, simply executing the laws and serving as the chief administrative officer, or leads the nation (and Congress) in its policy decisions. He concludes that the Constitution provides little inherent authority and power for the president to lead the nation. "The presidency is a clerkship that serves to keep government going," he notes.[44] Yet, the potential for leadership is powerful if individuals know how to use their personal skills. Leadership for Neustadt is based on the power of persuasion—persuading the nation that the administration's agenda is sound and by persuading members of Congress that individual pieces of legislation are worth supporting. A successful legislative presidency is based on building broad public support for the administration's policies using, among other tools, the **power of persuasion.**

Building a Legislative Agenda

Building a successful **legislative agenda** is also dependent on having a clearly articulated set of legislative goals from which Congress can act. These goals and objectives are developed from the laundry list of campaign promises from the past election. One of the major tasks of the transition team is to narrow the numerous promises that were made throughout the general election and to determine eight to ten themes that can be translated into legislation. For the Reagan administration, a short list of priorities included tax cuts, increases in defense spending, cutting the deficit, and reducing federal bureaucracy. For the Clinton administration, the list of priorities included a stimulus program to reinvigorate the economy, campaign finance reform, comprehensive reform of health care, and a national service bill.[45]

There has been an effort within the past sixty years to move legislative proposals into Congress as soon as possible after the inauguration, largely to try to replicate the success that Franklin Roosevelt had in his first **one hundred days** in office. Between March 9 and May 17, Roosevelt had eleven major bills passed. On the first day that his proposals were introduced, March 9, 1933, the Emergency Banking Relief Bill was passed by both houses, which included an astoundingly brief forty minutes of debate in the House of Representatives.[46] Other bills introduced during these first three months of the administration also enjoyed relatively brief debates in the House and the Senate and easily gained approval.

Roosevelt's success was due largely to the legislation being ready to introduce as soon as the administration took office. Members of Congress were receptive to the proposals and eager to support any efforts that could bring the nation out of the depths of the Great Depression. Textbooks often referred to Roosevelt's first one hundred days as the honeymoon period, and encouraged presidents to emulate Roosevelt by having legislation ready to act on as soon as possible. "Hitting the ground running" became the watchwords of this philosophy.

But Roosevelt lived in an extraordinary era, in which Congress was grappling for solutions to the economic problems that the nation was facing. Succeeding presidents were not nearly as successful in their first one hundred days as Roosevelt. Roosevelt set the benchmark against which all succeeding presidents are measured.

Richard Nixon had few measurable successes in his first one hundred days. By the end of the summer of 1969, nearly nine months after entering office, Nixon called his senior staff into his office and questioned why one of his major initiatives, the welfare reform package, had not moved off the drawing boards of the White House into the halls of Congress as a piece of legislation. The answer, according to his staff, was that his two senior domestic policy advisers, Daniel Patrick Moynihan and Arthur Burns, could not reach an accord on what the legislation should involve. Other domestic initiatives had also been slow to move into legislative proposals due to conflicts between Moynihan and Burns. Nixon restructured his White House staff soon after, replacing Moynihan and Burns with John Ehrlichman.

Nixon's primary problem in creating initiatives for the first one hundred days was that although he had campaigned against the burgeoning of the federal government created by the Great Society programs, he had never specified what to change. Campaign promises were often thematic rather than specific, as was true in most presidential campaigns. The theme most often repeated in the Nixon campaign was welfare reform. When the administration took office Nixon expected Moynihan and Burns to quickly carve out a new welfare program, but personality clashes between the two kept this from occurring. Similarly, other initiatives failed to move forward because of the Moynihan–Burns clashes.

Gerald Ford faced a similar set of staffing clashes when he entered the White House, which resulted in few measurable legislative successes during his early months in office. When Ford took over the reins of office in August 1974 following Nixon's resignation, he decided to keep many of the Nixon staff in the White House while also keeping many of his staff from the vice president's office.[47] This led to numerous confrontations over policy. Nixon's staff, led by chief of staff Alexander Haig, and Ford's staff, led by speech writer Robert Hartmann, disagreed on almost every possible issue. The problem was exacerbated by Ford's pardon of Richard Nixon, which led members of Congress to oppose almost everything moving out of the White House after that. In addition, Nelson Rockefeller's confirmation hearings during the fall of 1974 dominated Congress and essentially blocked passage of any of Ford's programs during that period. Ford was also faced with a highly charged Democratic Congress that was not eager to support further legislative proposals from a Republican president. The Ford presidency, while somewhat of an anomaly in history, was not that far apart from other presidencies in its first one hundred days. Legislative successes were not strong for any president after Roosevelt's first one hundred days.

One argument could be made that Nixon, by choice, and Ford, by default, did not invest in developing a legislative strategy during the transition to "hit the ground running" as soon as the president was sworn into office. Yet the experience of Jimmy Carter, who did invest heavily in transition planning, indicates that planning is not always the key to success during the first one hundred days. Carter entered office in 1977 following a very close election against Gerald Ford. Unlike Nixon, Carter spent a considerable amount of time during the election process developing a strategy for moving his legislative agenda forward. During the spring of 1976, Carter put Jack Watson in charge of transition planning, which included both personnel for the new administration (the Talent Inventory Program) and legislative proposals for the first one hundred days. Watson, who had been on Carter's staff during his tenure as governor of Georgia, was committed to ensuring a smooth transition and to having a platform of legislative proposals ready to move forward. Carter, however, campaigned on very vague proposals of increasing government efficiency and reducing overlapping and duplicative programs. There were few concrete proposals identified by Carter, due to Carter's preference for campaigning against Ford's record and the Republican Party in general, rather than campaigning for his own agenda. "Whenever our party has fought for legislation that would benefit the average American," Carter said in a typical rejoinder against the Republican Party, "our opponent's party has fought against that progress."[48] One of the few concrete proposals that Carter put forth during the election was to seek authority from Congress to reorganize the executive branch. The reorganization authority created by Congress in the Reorganization Act of 1939 had been allowed to lapse in 1973 in an attempt by Congress to curb the imperial presidency of Richard Nixon.

Once in office, Carter went forward with studies for reorganization to cut the number of federal agencies from 1900 to 200. These changes involved restructuring existing agencies and abolishing nearly 1400 federal advisory commissions. During the transition, Watson and campaign manager Hamilton Jordan focused on reviewing legislation and treaties that would expire when they took office in 1977 and began examining the reorganization proposals.[49] Their efforts during the transition were not aimed at developing new legislative proposals but rather at preparing for a major reorganization effort once in office. The only major piece of legislation that was developed during the transition period was a bill to create a Department of Energy.

James Schlesinger, who had been a senior adviser to Carter on defense policy during the campaign, was in line to become the Secretary of Energy. During the transition period Schlesinger focused on developing the energy legislation while Watson and Jordan focused on the reorganization plan. Not surprisingly, few presidentially sponsored initiatives moved through Congress during the first one hundred days of the Carter administration.

When Ronald Reagan entered office, he had a firmer idea of the policies that he wanted immediately transformed into legislation. At the heart of Reagan's plan for legislative change was a major tax cut to jumpstart the economy, which had deteriorated during the Carter administration. In the October 28, 1980, presidential debates in Cleveland, Reagan posed the question to the nation on live television, "Are you better off than you were four years ago? Is it easier for you to go and buy things in the store than it was four years ago? Is there more or less unemployment in the country than there was four years ago?"[50] The solution that Reagan proposed was to cut the personal income tax rate by thirty percent over the next three years and to scale back federal spending by ten percent. Martin Anderson, an economist from Stanford University who was Reagan's senior domestic policy adviser on the campaign, advised Reagan to focus his energies on attacking the largesse in the economy. The strategy seemed to work, as Haynes Johnson reported as he interviewed voters during the campaign. Johnson quotes a California laborer as saying, "I want to see a change of people advising on economic policy in Washington. I don't believe that the Carter administration understood economics . . . we've got to get our economy back in shape or we're going to lose everything."[51]

In addition to targeting the economy in his campaign themes, Reagan also targeted military readiness. Richard Allen, Reagan's foreign policy adviser, tried to focus campaign speeches on Carter's failure in leadership in national security and foreign policy. Allen focused Reagan's speeches on strengthening the nation's military defense system and building technological superiority over the Soviet Union. Reagan supported a twenty-five percent increase in the navy's shipbuilding program, production of the B-1 bomber (which Carter had opposed), and increased pay for the military. Reagan blasted Carter for "a naive and discredited philosophy that military strength beyond a minimum level is irrelevant."[52] The specter of the American hostages in Iran and the failed rescue mission, while not directly targeted by the Reagan campaign, was always implied in the attacks on the current state of America's military defense system. Carter was never able to mount an offensive campaign, partly because his own staff became mired in defensive maneuverings.

After securing a stunning 489 electoral votes to win the election, Reagan began a transition process that included choosing White House staff, cabinet officers, and the wide range of subcabinet personnel. The personnel process was of great concern to the Reagan campaign staff, who wanted to ensure that the new administration was composed of conservatives and of Reagan loyalists. Development of a legislative program became secondary to the personnel process, due in part to the rather short list of legislative proposals that the administration wanted to move forward immediately and in part to the emphasis on personnel selection. As Martin Anderson noted, "the personnel selection process was the most thorough and comprehensive undertaken in the history of American transitions" to ensure that appointees "did not betray the policies the campaign was fought on."[53]

The legislative program was centered around a very focused list of tax cuts and increased spending for the military and other defense programs. Max Friedersdorf, who directed the congressional liaison team, wanted to capture the momentum of the landslide victory, but targeted nine months rather than one hundred days for his legislative thrust. "We knew we had to get our bills enacted before the Labor Day recess," Friedersdorf said, "and the President was determined not to clutter up the landscape with extraneous legislation."[54] Friedersdorf's immediate efforts were devoted to building bridges to Congress and to using the president as a lobbyist for administration programs. James P. Pfiffner describes Reagan's lobbying efforts during the transition process, "The President-elect held a series of dinners to which he invited members of Congress . . . and Republican members of Congress were invited to advise the transition teams in the departments."[55] Reagan sought the advice of the leadership of both parties, particularly courting Speaker of the House Thomas P. "Tip" O'Neill. The transition and early months of the administration were devoted to courting Congress rather than seeking specific legislative packages.

Reagan's first one hundred days in office were focused on the administrative management of the executive branch. Personnel management under E. Pendleton James, White House personnel director, and budget management under David Stockman, director of the Office of Management and Budget, became the primary concerns of the administration during the early months. Stockman, a former congressman who had worked on the campaign, focused on economic reform through reductions in the federal budget. Every department was ordered by the Office of Management and Budget to reduce their expenditures for the next fiscal year. Using an unparalleled mastery of departmental budget detail, Stockman was able to pressure every cabinet officer into significant program reductions.

While Pendleton James and David Stockman were handling administrative transformations of the executive branch, Max Friedersdorf was working the halls of Congress to manage the legislative changes sought by the administration. By the end of 1981, less than a year after taking office, Reagan and his team had succeeded in a series of major legislative victories:

1. The Economic Recovery Tax Act, projecting $750 billion in multi-year tax reductions,
2. A budget reconciliation act, reducing domestic spending by more than $35 billion,
3. Increased defense spending for 1982 to $200 billion,
4. Reductions in the food stamp program and the Aid to Families with Dependent Children (AFDC),
5. Reductions in the Medicaid and Medicare programs.[56]

The careful attention to building bridges between 1600 Pennsylvania Avenue and Capitol Hill and to maintaining a relatively short list of proposals for the new Congress led to swift adoption of Reagan's legislative agenda.

The Bush transition team had not been as well developed as either the Carter or Reagan teams, largely because the Bush campaign offered few proposals for legislative action. The heart of the Bush campaign was to "continue the Reagan Revolution," which involved reducing federal spending, and to keep the federal tax burden from increasing. Throughout the campaign Bush promised that there would be no new taxes under his administration, and at one point firmly announced to a gathering that they should "Read My Lips. No New Taxes."

George Bush's quest for the presidency began long before the 1988 primary season. A shadow campaign organization called The Fund for America's Future had been created in May 1985 to provide a vehicle for the Bush organization to raise money to dole out to other candidates during the 1986 elections. Presidential candidates frequently used political action committees such as The Fund for America's Future to support candidates who could later become helpful in their presidential campaigns. Bush traveled around the country meeting Republican candidates and Republican voters in anticipation of his run for the presidency, with the political action committee providing the financial momentum.

When the Bush organization transformed itself into a presidential campaign (the "Bush for President" campaign and later the "Bush/Quayle" campaign), the fund-raising base, the Republican state and local committee base, and the Republican voter base, all had been put in place. Bush had built a solid Republican base in 1988 and needed to carry only enough momentum during the campaign to keep from losing the Reagan Democrats. His campaign staff told him to "go out and campaign, . . . issues and substance were less important."[57] The emphasis on continuing the Reagan Revolution overshadowed all other considerations of a legislative agenda that could be discussed in the campaign.

Issues and substance became secondary to simply smiling and extolling the virtues of family values, patriotism, and the smoothly running economy. A typical Bush speech delivered during the campaign occurred in San Antonio, Texas, in September 1988 attacking Governor Michael Dukakis of Massachusetts, the Democratic presidential candidate, for supporting a school child's right to be silent when the Pledge of Allegiance was said. "I believe our school children have the right to say the Pledge of Allegiance to the Flag of the United States. I don't know what his [Dukakis] problem is with the Pledge of Allegiance."[58] Rather than focusing on proposals for new directions for the nation, the Bush campaign used a good deal of negative advertising to attack their opponent for his liberalism, questionable patriotism, and failed leadership at the helm of Massachusetts state government. They succeeded, and in January 1989, George Bush became the first president in sixty years to move into the White House in a friendly takeover. Not since Republican Calvin Coolidge passed the mantle to fellow Republican Herbert Hoover had there been a friendly transition of power from one administration to the next.

The Bush transition team was led by codirectors Craig Fuller and Robert Teeter, whose task was to design the administrative and legislative changes that the administration wanted to move forward. The only planning prior to the transition had been done by Chase Untermeyer, a campaign strategist and senior member of the Bush vice presidential office. Untermeyer had begun gathering names for the multitude of political appointees that the Bush administration would need to make as soon as they took office. Fuller and Teeter set in motion a series of task forces to assess what the department programs consisted of and how their personnel systems and budgets operated. But the legislative agenda for the new administration was primarily developed by the Heritage Foundation, which developed a 900-page volume entitled *Mandate for Leadership III*. This compendium of departmental programs was a continuation, or follow-up, to the volumes prepared for Reagan. *Mandate for Leadership* was prepared for the 1980 Reagan transition and *Mandate for Leadership II* was prepared for the 1984 Reagan transition. *Mandate for Leadership III* recommended continuing the programs in place from the eight years of the Reagan administration and recommended no major new legislative programs.

When reporters started to question the Bush transition team on their legislative plans for the first one hundred days of the new Congress, James Pinkerton (assigned to manage the legislative initiatives for the first one hundred days) announced that they intended to wait until the departmental staff were in place before making any legislative decisions. "When the White House is 5% staffed, [we're not ready] to write a 100-days plan."[59] When word leaked out that the transition staff had no firm ideas for legislative proposals, lobbyists began to inundate them with proposals. Environmental groups, for example, sent in more than seven hundred proposals for the transition team to review. Similarly, the Aircraft Owners and Pilots Association, with 275,000 members, offered to work with the transition team on transportation issues.

As the inauguration drew closer, senior staff in the transition team began to formulate a series of issues that would need legislative attention in the new administration. They reviewed Bush's campaign positions and assembled a series of issues that they thought could be moved into legislative proposals. But, as one staffer noted, their goal was only to move "a discreet number" of proposals forward during the first one hundred days.[60] These proposals were designed not to disrupt the Reagan Revolution but to refocus the revolution around the Bush campaign theme of a "kinder, gentler" nation. Not surprisingly, the legislative proposals were extremely moderate in nature. The major initiatives included seeking reauthorization of the Clean Air Act with several modifications, supporting reductions in the tax rate on capital gains, developing new education programs, and improving the quality of child care programs.[61] Bush's modest domestic agenda was balanced by an equally modest foreign policy agenda. All of the new administration's proposals continued Reagan's policies, such as continuation of the strategic defense initiative (SDI), support for the single-warhead mobile Midgetman missile, and a reduction in missile warheads proposed in the Strategic Arms Reduction Treaty (START).

When Bill Clinton wrested the reins of government from George Bush during the 1992 election, he became the first Democrat in twelve years to move into the White House. The Clinton campaign used the same technique that George Bush had used four years earlier on Michael Dukakis—attacking his opponent's record. Clinton hammered Bush on the sagging economy and on Bush's perceived focus on foreign rather than domestic policy. As Clinton campaign strategist James Carville recommended, the Clinton campaign focused "like a laser beam" on the Bush administration's failure with the economy. Bush, on the other hand, focused on themes of family values and ignored the attacks on his handling of the economy. Unfortunately, polls indicated that only fifteen percent of the public[62] were interested in family values as a matter of public policy but instead were far more interested in economic issues. As the traditionally Republican-oriented *New Republic* commented on the sagging Bush campaign, "We can see no consistency or meaning in George Bush's domestic record, except a fitful effort to appease public opinion to win re-election."[63]

When the final tally was in, Clinton had amassed 357 electoral votes and Bush 168. Although Ross Perot had nineteen percent of the popular vote, he received no electoral votes. The transition process for the Clinton team began as soon as the votes were counted, but little preparation had been made. Unlike his Democratic predecessor, Jimmy Carter, who had quietly developed a transition team during the campaign, Clinton had used all of his campaign resources for getting elected. Having won the election, the campaign staff immediately had to turn their attentions from campaigning to governing. At his first press conference after the election, Clinton announced that he would begin developing legislative proposals to cut the federal deficit and to stimulate the economy. His solution for cutting the deficit was very Carteresque: cutting the size of the federal bureaucracy and reorganizing or cutting numerous boards and commissions. And in a move similar to the Reagan transition, Clinton then promised to build an administration that "shared my vision" for America.[64] But Clinton's vision for the administration was less politically and philosophically oriented than Reagan's vision had been, for at the heart of Clinton's plan for the senior staff was one that had both ethnic and gender diversity.

The challenge to increase diversity in cabinet and subcabinet appointments dominated the transition process, as all appointments became subject to the EGG (ethnicity, gender, and geography) test.[65] Even names submitted for ambassadorial positions were subject to the EGG test. "Walking on EGG shells" became the watchwords of the transition as thousands of names were reviewed for their acceptability on the EGG standards. As one Clinton aide noted, he wanted to make sure that "more than the usual white boys who run Washington" were given jobs in the administration.[66] While part of the transition team was working on the administrative side of personnel decisions to ensure diversity, another part of the transition team was reviewing departmental programs and budgets. A series of task forces reviewed departmental issues, largely as a guidebook for the new staff that would take over the department after the inauguration. Each task force, or "cluster group" as they were called, was required to develop a forty to sixty-page report on the departments they covered.[67] The task force recommendations were very similar to those that were prepared for the new administration by the Progressive Policy Institute (PPI), the political arm of the Democratic Leadership Council (DLC), which both Clinton and vice president-elect Albert Gore had been instrumental in creating. The Progressive Policy Institute prepared a book entitled *Mandate for Change*, modeled on the Heritage Foundation's *Mandate for Leadership* books for the Reagan and Bush transitions.[68]

Very little was actually accomplished during the transition with regard to developing a legislative plan for the first one hundred days. As do most presidential campaigns, the Clinton campaign had developed few specific policy initiatives. The Clinton campaign had combined the narrow theme of economic recovery with attacks on the Bush administration's record in office to successfully win the election.

The transition had been primarily devoted to choosing cabinet and subcabinet staff and to reviewing departmental programs. When the transition staff had completed most of their administrative issues, they turned to legislative matters.

During early December 1992, president-elect Clinton held a two-day conference in Little Rock, Arkansas, with more than 400 economists, business executives, technology experts, and state and local government officials to develop an economic plan. The two-day economic summit focused the transition team on the complexity of the nation's economic problems, resulting in a decision to slowly develop the appropriate legislation. This decision meant that during the first one hundred days the administration would not send any major economic proposals to Congress. They also decided to wait on proposals for health care reform and welfare reform, which had been two campaign themes, in order to adequately study the issues and develop appropriate legislative packages.

In the absence of major economic proposals to move forward, the Clinton White House turned to administrative action to build public support for their programs. Using executive orders, the president lifted the gag rule on abortion counseling in federally funded clinics, lifted the ban on fetal-tissue testing, and approved converting a percentage of the government automotive fleet to natural gas. Since the administration was not prepared to hit the ground running with legislative action, they were prepared to hit the ground running using administrative action. But one administrative action, lifting the ban on gays in the military, caused a significant public backlash. Any gains that had been accomplished by other administrative actions were voided by the outcry against lifting the ban on gays in the military. Members of Congress, including Senator Sam Nunn (D-Ga.), adamantly opposed the president's position. This simple administrative act immediately led to battles with members of Congress that could have been avoided with a stronger transition process.

Conclusion

Presidents who are successful in moving their legislative programs through Congress have diligently worked to build strong bridges in executive–legislative relations. The supports for these bridges include carefully developed legislative programs, skillful party leadership, astute use of the congressional liaison office, and constant attention to establishing strong personal contacts in both houses of Congress.

The legislative presidency involves a coordinated effort in the White House to develop a concise legislative program from the laundry list of campaign promises. Every candidate in a presidential campaign promises more than can be reasonably delivered, especially in the short term. The task of the White House staff is to focus on a short list of key campaign promises and to translate that list into a legislative agenda. Once the legislative agenda is established, the president needs to work in concert with the House and Senate leadership to ensure that the legislation is broadly spread across committees. The president also needs to establish strong relationships within his own party to ensure that the legislation moves forward swiftly and without significant amendments.

In recent administrations presidents have not taken full advantage of the three-month transition period to build their short list of legislative programs. This has reduced the president's ability to hit the ground running and to take advantage of the honeymoon period in the first one hundred days in office. The trend recently has been to use all of the resources of the campaign for winning the election rather than channeling some of the resources toward governance once elected. Transitions have focused more often on the administrative presidency (personnel) than on the legislative presidency (legislation).

One of the advantages that modern presidents have in managing their relationship with Congress is that shared powers provide the upper hand to the president. The presentment clause requires that all legislation must be approved or disapproved by the president. Approval includes actively signing or passively allowing a bill to become law. The power to disapprove, or veto, legislation is a powerful tool for controlling legislation. Legislation that is unacceptable to the administration can be vetoed, and vetoes are rarely overridden in Congress. Statistics show that only seven percent of presidential vetoes have been overrriden since George Washington's administration.

The appointment process is another shared power, but one that Congress does not often seriously exercise. The vast majority of presidential nominees receive Senate approval. This is due primarily to the large number of presidential appointments that Congress has mandated be confirmed by the Senate. The Senate does not have the staff to adequately review every nominee who requires confirmation. Most nominees, therefore, are easily confirmed. In recent years several Supreme Court nominees have been rejected by the Senate, but they were the exception not the rule. Most appointments move through the confirmation process with little difficulty.

The treaty process, also a shared constitutional process, has been largely dominated by the president. The president negotiates treaties without consulting Congress and seeks legislative approval only of the final product. In order to circumvent the approval process because of the often lengthy approval time, presidents have increasingly turned to executive agreements. Congress has not tried to hinder this technique for international agreements, but has insisted (through the Case Act of 1972) that Congress be notified of all executive agreements.

The era of presidential government and the legislative presidency has been significantly enhanced by the reactive rather than proactive nature of the modern Congress. This is due to several factors. Perhaps the most important factor is the constant growth in federal programs since the New Deal. As the size of the federal budget has grown, more and more federal benefits have become available for individuals and for business and industry. Members of Congress have focused their attentions on servicing their constituents and obtaining as many federal dollars as possible for their districts. They are reactive rather than proactive on the major pieces of national legislation, allowing the president to control the direction of the legislative agenda. Another factor is the sheer size of the House and Senate. With 435 members in the House and 100 members in the Senate, consensus is difficult to reach on priority issues. Finally, the absence of strong party leadership and the continuing power that committee chairs maintain to control the legislative agenda reduces the leadership that Congress can provide.

In contrast, the president can provide a clear national agenda and can rally public support around that agenda. Presidents have the advantage in the system of shared powers that the framers created, but that advantage is dependent on the skillful use of the institutional resources of the presidency, the persuasive skills of the president, and building strong bridges to Congress. The keys to power are in the hands of the president, if only the president knows how to use them.

Key Words

appointment power
central clearance
congressional government
legislative agenda
Legislative Reference Office
legislative veto
line item veto
Office of Congressional Relations
Office of Management and Budget

one hundred days
party leadership
power of persuasion
presentment clause
presidential government
public opinion operations
treaty power
veto power
war powers

Notes

1. Woodrow Wilson. *Congressional Government*. Baltimore: Johns Hopkins University Press, 1981 (first published in 1885), p. 170.
2. Richard A. Watson. *Presidential Vetoes and Public Policy*. Lawrence, KS: University Press of Kansas, 1993, p. 110.
3. David W. Rhode and Dennis M. Simon. "President's Vetoes and Congressional Response." *American Journal of Political Science*, August 1985, p. 307.
4. Harold W. Stanley and Richard G. Niemei. "Vetoes from 1789 to 1992." *Vital Statistics in American Politics*. 4th ed. Washington, DC: Congressional Quarterly, 1994, p. 252.
5. Richard A. Watson. *Presidential Vetoes and Public Policy*, p. 110.
6. David G. Savage. *Turning Right: The Making of the Rehnquist Court*. New York: Wiley, 1992, pp. 352–358.
7. Fred R. Harris. *Deadlock or Decision: The U.S. Senate and the Rise of National Politics*. New York: Oxford University Press, 1993, p. 17.
8. *United States v. Curtiss-Wright Export Corp.*, 299 U.S. 304 (1936).
9. *Goldwater v. Carter*, 444 U.S. 996 (1979).
10. Gerald Ford. "Congress, the Presidency, and National Security Policy." *Presidential Studies Quarterly*, Spring 1986, pp. 223–237.
11. Harris. *Deadlock or Decision*, p. 257.
12. *Immigration and Naturalization Service v. Chadha*, 462 U.S. 919 (1983).
13. Barbara Hinckley. *Stability and Change in Congress*. 4th ed. New York: Harper, 1988, p. 234.
14. Stephen J. Wayne. *The Legislative Presidency*. New York: Harper, 1978, p. ix.
15. Richard Darman. *Who's in Control? Polar Politics and the Sensible Center*. New York: Simon & Schuster, 1996, p. 215.
16. Wilson. *Congressional Government*, p. 173.
17. Arthur S. Link. *Woodrow Wilson and the Progressive Era: 1910–1917*. New York: Harper, 1954, p. 34.
18. Bradley H. Patterson, Jr. *The Ring of Power: The White House Staff and Its Expanding Role in Government*. New York: Basic, 1988, p. 151.
19. Kenneth E. Collier. *Between the Branches: The White House Office of Legislative Affairs*. Pittsburgh: University of Pittsburgh Press, 1997, p. 41.

20. Fred I. Greenstein. *The Hidden-Hand Presidency: Eisenhower as Leader.* New York: Basic, 1982, p. 42.
21. Charles O. Jones. "Ronald Reagan and the U.S. Congress: Visible-Hand Politics." In: Charles O. Jones, ed. *The Reagan Legacy: Promise and Performance.* Chatham, NJ: Chatham House, 1988, p. 35.
22. Thomas P. O'Neill, with William Novak. *Man of the House: The Life and Political Memoirs of Speaker Tip O'Neill.* New York: Random House, 1987, p. 345.
23. Jeffrey H. Birnbaum. *Madhouse: The Private Turmoil of Working for the President.* New York: Random House, 1996, p. 25.
24. Haynes Johnson and David S. Broder. *The System.* Boston: Little, Brown, 1996, p. 611.
25. Interview with Thomas McLarty.
26. Charles E. Walcott and Karen M. Hult. *Governing the White House from Hoover through LBJ.* Lawrence, KS: University Press of Kansas, 1995, p. 29.
27. Norman C. Thomas and Joseph A. Pika. *The Politics of the Presidency.* 4th rev. ed. Washington, DC: Congressional Quarterly, 1997, p. 224.
28. Patterson. *The Ring of Power,* p. 156.
29. Ibid., p. 154.
30. Birnbaum. *Madhouse,* p. 24.
31. Steven Waldman. *The Bill.* New York: Viking, 1995, p. 215.
32. Ibid.
33. Wayne. *The Legislative Presidency,* p. 76.
34. Clark Clifford. *Counsel to the President: A Memoir.* New York: Random House, 1991, p. 85.
35. Quoted in Larry Berman. *The Office of Management and Budget and the Presidency: 1921–1979.* Princeton, NJ: Princeton University Press, 1979, p. 42.
36. David Stockman. *The Triumph of Politics: The Inside Story of the Reagan Revolution.* New York: Avon, 1986, p. 123.
37. Richard Darman. *Who's In Control?*
38. Barbara Hinckley. *Stability and Change in Congress,* p. 241.
39. Nelson Polsby. *Congress and the Presidency.* 4th ed. Englewood Cliffs, NJ: Prentice-Hall, 1986, p. 68.
40. Linda Greenhouse. "High Court Takes Hard Look at Line Item Vetos." *New York Times,* April 18, 1998, p. A1.
41. *Clinton v. City of New York,* 524 U.S. 417, 118 S.Ct. 2091. (1998).
42. Linda Greenhouse. "Justices to Hear President's Appeal on Line Item Veto Ruling." *New York Times,* February 28, 1998, p. A7.
43. Richard E. Neustadt. *Presidential Power and the Modern Presidents: The Politics of Leadership from Roosevelt to Reagan.* New York: Free Press, 1990.
44. Ibid., p. xv.
45. Elizabeth Drew. *On the Edge.* New York: Simon & Schuster, 1994, p. 52.
46. Pendleton E. Herring. *Presidential Leadership.* New York: Farar and Rinehart, 1940, p. 44.
47. John Robert Greene. *The Presidency of Gerald R. Ford.* Lawrence, KS: University Press of Kansas, 1995.
48. Patrick Anderson. *Electing Jimmy Carter: The Campaign of 1976.* Baton Rouge: Louisiana State University Press, 1994, p. 107.
49. Shirley Anne Warshaw. *The Domestic Presidency: Policy Making in the White House.* Needham Heights, MA: Allyn and Bacon, 1997, p. 85.
50. Jeff Fisher. *Presidents and Promises: From Campaign Pledge to Presidential Performance.* Washington, DC: Congressional Quarterly, 1985, p. 138.
51. Haynes Johnson. *Sleepwalking Through History: America in the Reagan Years.* New York: Doubleday, 1991, p. 134.
52. Dick Kirschten. "The National Security Issue—A Matter of War and Peace." *National Journal,* October 11, 1980, p. 1690.
53. Martin Anderson. *Revolution: The Reagan Legacy.* rev. ed. Stanford, CA: Hoover Institution, 1990, p. 196.
54. Stephen J. Wayne. "Congressional Liaison in the Reagan White House: A Preliminary Assessment of the First Year." In: Norman Ornstein, ed. *President and Congress: Assessing Reagan's First Year.* Washington, DC. American Enterprise Institute, 1982, pp. 56–57.
55. James P. Pfiffner. "The Carter–Reagan Transition: Hitting the Ground Running." *Presidential Studies Quarterly,* Fall 1983, p. 627.

56. Charles O. Jones. "Ronald Reagan and the U.S. Congress." In: Charles O. Jones, ed. *The Reagan Legacy: Promise and Performance*. Chatham, NJ: Chatham House, 1988, p. 39.

57. David Hoffman and Ann Devroy. "The Complex Machine Behind Bush." *Washington Post*, November 13, 1988, p. A16.

58. Bill Peterson. "Bush Fans Rhetorical Six Guns in Texas." *Washington Post*, August 26, 1988, p. A6.

59. Burt Solomon. "Formulating Policy for Bush in 1989 Is Lagging Behind at Transition Office." *National Journal*, December 17, 1988, p. 3207.

60. Burt Solomon. "Bush Promised New Faces But He's Hiring Old Friends." *National Journal*, January 21, 1989, p. 143.

61. Burt Solomon. "Low Expectations." *National Journal*, November 12, 1988, p. 2841.

62. Laurence I. Barrett. "A New Coalition for the 1990's." *Time*, November 16, 1992, pp. 47–48.

63. "Clinton for President." *The New Republic*, November 9, 1992, p. 7.

64. Gwen Ifill. "Clinton's High Stakes Shuffle to Get the Right Cabinet Mix." *New York Times*, December 21, 1992, pp. A1, D11.

65. Al Kamen. "Administration Still Walking on EGG Shells." *Washington Post*, April 19, 1993, p. A21.

66. Thomas L. Friedman. "Diversity Pledge Slows Clinton on Appointments." *New York Times*, January 12, 1993, p. A18.

67. "Clinton's Cluster Coordinators, Who's Who." *Washington Post*, November 26, 1992, p. A27.

68. Will Marshall and Martin Chram, eds. *Mandate for Change*. New York: Berkley, 1992.

Chapter 10

The President and Public Opinion

Building bridges to the public is perhaps the most important task of any president. Without public support for their programs, presidents will inevitably falter in office and fail to be reelected. There is no substitute for public support, for without it few presidents are able to survive. Their programs languish in Congress and the public seeks new leadership at the next election. Presidents need the support of the American public not just on election day but throughout their terms in office.

Clearly, the process of building public support is a double-edged sword, for it involves both leading and following public opinion. On one hand, presidents need to lead public opinion toward the policies and programs that the administration wants to move forward. Presidents need to be proactive, to convince the public that the policies they propose are important, are necessary, and will benefit the majority of citizens. But presidents also need to be reactive, to follow public opinion, to shape policies around issues that have strong public support. The task of presidential leadership is to ensure that the administration's agenda has a careful mix of policies that address both the presidential agenda and the public agenda.

A successful administration is one that can rally public support behind presidential initiatives, including initiatives that are both proactive and reactive, and can move those initiatives through Congress. Building bridges to the public and rallying public support for legislative initiatives are concepts that most presidents are quite comfortable with. Rallying public support behind presidential initiatives generally comes naturally to modern-day presidents, largely due to the nature of the campaign process.[1] Candidates are used to being both proactive and reactive during the presidential campaign.

Every four years Americans go to the ballot box to cast their votes for president. The candidate who has the strongest public support wins the election. In the same way that candidates rally public support to ensure their election, presidents rally public support once in office to ensure that their programs move forward through the legislative labyrinth. During the campaign, candidates tailor their agendas around themes that have broad public support. The same process continues once the candidates are in office. Presidential agendas are built around agendas created in the campaign. There is virtually no difference between the campaign agenda and the presidential agenda, except that the presidential agenda is more detailed.

The campaign to win public opinion does not end on election day. Presidents continue the constant drive for public support once in office, continuing to ensure that the campaign agenda has successfully translated into a governing agenda. Writer Sidney Blumenthal, who later became a member of the Clinton White House staff, commented that the move from campaign to governance was more of a "permanent campaign."[2] The process of governing, Blumenthal said, was really a continuation of the campaign's drive to build public support. The line where campaigning ended and governance started was not clear, but the continuing nature of campaigning once in office is a peculiarly modern occurrence.

Why have presidents been forced to continue in the campaign mode once in office? A significant part of the explanation is the nature of the modern political structure. As political parties have become less involved in national issues, and have focused instead on state and local issues, national candidates have had to build their own bases of public support. Candidates could not rely on the national parties to deliver votes anymore, as they had in the days of party bosses and machine politics. The coalitions of support that candidates built to win the election often became the coalitions of support that presidents built to win congressional support for programs.

Another part of the explanation for the constant campaign after the election is the complexity of presidential leadership. Although the campaign must by its nature be limited to a few major issues on which the majority of citizens can agree, the process of governance is far more complicated. Governance involves addressing numerous issues that have multifaceted solutions that do not lend themselves to building simple coalitions of support. The task of presidential leadership is to cast these diverse coalitions of support behind policies created by the administration. This process involves convincing citizens that the policies proposed, although not exactly what they want, will in the end serve their interests. Although *campaigning* for public support may seem unpresidential, it is exactly what presidents are doing throughout their administration.

Perhaps the most important explanation for the increasing role of campaigning for public support once in office has been the expanded role that the president has taken in the modern presidency. Congressional government has given way to presidential government. Since the administration of Franklin Delano Roosevelt, presidents have dominated the policy-making process and established broad legislative agendas. In order to move these programs forward, presidents have campaigned for public support throughout their presidencies. The campaign for public support is constant.

Direct and Indirect Impact of Public Opinion on Legislative Action

Members of Congress have grown quite attuned to measuring public opinion, and they generally gauge their votes on the depth of public interest and support for legislative action. Just as the president campaigns for public support, members of Congress track public opinion polls to assess the president's overall political support across the nation. If the public opinion polls indicate strong public support for the president and presidential policies, members of Congress are more likely to support legislative proposals from the White House. Inversely, low public opinion polls will produce less congressional support for presidential proposals.

As we gauge public support for presidential policies, however, it is important to separate the direct and indirect impact of that support. The direct impact of public opinion on legislative action is to warn members of Congress that the president has broad public support for major policy proposals. Members of Congress may not want to jeopardize their own electoral positions by opposing legislation that has broad public support. We define major policy proposals as those that significantly reframe public policy and move the nation in a new and often different direction. Such major policy proposals would include the Civil Rights Act of 1964 during the Johnson administration, the Clean Air Act of 1970 during the Nixon administration, and the Welfare Reform Act of 1995 during the Clinton administration. These three examples exemplify major policy proposals that received broad-based public support. Presidents with broad public support are usually, but clearly not always, successful at moving major legislative programs through Congress.

The indirect impact of public opinion occurs when presidents have high public opinion polls and can move a range of minor programs through Congress on the strength of their public standing. In these cases, the policy proposals may have low public visibility but may succeed on the strength of presidential popularity. Presidents who do not have strength in the public opinion polls often have a more difficult time moving both major and minor programs through Congress.

Presidential strength in the public opinion polls does not ensure success for all programs and policy initiatives. There are clear limits on how far public opinion will move presidential policies in Congress. Political scientist James Anderson places a clear limitation on how far public opinion will influence legislative votes. According to Anderson, while presidents can use the strength of their public standing to move major programs through Congress, minor programs are often less affected by presidential popularity. "The legislator deciding how to vote on a specific tax amendment or public-works bill," notes Anderson, "will probably be unaffected by public opinion in any direct sense."[3] Anderson attributes this voting behavior to a lack of public awareness on how members vote on the floor of the House or Senate. If members of Congress vote against a relatively minor bill supported by a popular president, there will be limited, if any, repercussions from the public. Few people follow the daily voting decisions of their members of Congress, especially on projects that have little direct affect on them.

George Edwards is more direct in his assessment of why there are few repercussions from the public. In his book *The Public Presidency*, Edwards argues that "public opinion is often not crystallized" and is "subject to sharp fluctuations."[4] Both Anderson and Edwards view the problem essentially the same way. They perceive a general lack of public interest in many issues that come before the House and the Senate for a vote. The level of support for the president in the public opinion polls often has little influence on these minor House and Senate votes.

Another explanation for the ability of presidents to build broad public support only for major public policy issues is expressed by political scientist Thomas Patterson, who writes, "public opinion is seldom fixed when it comes to questions of how to resolve policy issues. Political leaders typically have leeway in deciding a course of action."[5] Patterson depicts public opinion as divided into policy issues that directly affect them and issues that have no direct bearing on them. Unless an issue is of direct concern, the public will not become engaged in the policy-making process. This leaves members of Congress to pursue their own course of action in spite of lobbying by the president. Patterson issues a caveat to this picture of public opinion. He argues that if presidents can bring substantial pressure from small interest groups that are affected by the policy, Congress will often respond. Thus, public opinion, albeit limited, can be mobilized by the president to move a presidential policy through the legislative process if there is substantial support among a limited political community. Lobbying by the cable industry and the telephone industry for deregulation under the Telecommunications Act of 1996 is an example of Patterson's thesis, for President Clinton worked with a narrow group of lobbyists to move this bill forward. The majority of the public had little interest in or knowledge of this bill.

In contrast to the level of public support for minor issues, the level of public support has significant influence in House and Senate votes for major issues. Presidents who have significantly high numbers in public opinion polls can translate that support into legislative success. The task of modern presidents, particularly in the age of mass communications, has been to create broad public support for key administration policies. This support is provided by communication through television, radio, and most recently the Internet. Such broad public support inevitably influences the voting behavior of members of Congress and produces victories for the president on his legislative agenda. However, the number of programs that can bridge the public's wide gap in policy orientation are relatively few.

While presidents need public support to move their initiatives through Congress, many presidential actions do not require congressional approval. The most common instance of a president moving with little or no public support is a military engagement. In some cases, presidents do not inform the public of their military actions until after the action has taken place. Public opinion comes into play only after the action. Rarely does the American public oppose military actions, particularly those that involve protecting American citizens or American interests or that save the lives of innocent citizens embroiled in a civil war. The public has given broad latitude to presidents for the use of the military around the world, under the assumption that presidents are better informed about issues of national security and foreign policy. When President Reagan sent troops to Grenada to quell a rebellion and to safely remove American medical students from the university, the public had few debates on the wisdom of the decision. Similarly, when President Bush sent troops to free Kuwait from the Iraqi invasion, the public had few reservations about the decision. Even when President Clinton supported sending American troops to Bosnia to fulfill the peace settlement in the Dayton Accords, he experienced little public disapproval. While public opinion, at times, seems to constrain domestic policy, it generally does not constrain foreign policy. One of the few times that public opinion has constrained military or foreign policy was the Nixon administration's decision to pursue "peace with honor" and withdraw the troops from South Vietnam. Public opinion, through protest marches and boycotts, essentially forced Nixon to end the war in Vietnam.

Although public opinion does not generally restrict a foreign policy, it can play a significant role in encouraging a foreign policy. This creates a paradox in presidential policy-making. For example, public opinion supported President Carter's decision to recognize mainland China in 1979. The decision was widely supported across the United States and encouraged by many corporate entities, who wanted to open lines of trade with China. Without the broad public support for recognizing mainland China, it is doubtful if Carter would have risked his limited political capital on a foreign-policy initiative that had few immediate benefits to the administration. Similarly, President Clinton's decision to approve the drug certification for Mexico (certifying that Mexico was aggressively reducing drug smuggling into the United States) in 1999 was widely supported by public opinion. The American public viewed Mexico as a close ally and did not want to close the lines of communication with one of only two countries with whom we share a border. In general, the public also wanted to keep tourism open, cheap labor markets available, and trade zones in place and did not offer any opposition to the administration's decision. The decision was supported by most Hispanic Americans, who have become a significant voting bloc, and by business and industry, who sought to foster new markets.

Building Public Support for Presidential Programs

How presidents build public support for their programs remains a constant challenge, because it requires both personal skill and the use of institutional resources. To some extent, the ability of presidents to build public support for their programs is a product of the era in which they live. During the 1940s, in an era of economic crisis and international war, the nation looked to Franklin Delano Roosevelt for leadership. Roosevelt was able to create domestic programs and promote military action in both the Atlantic and Pacific wars with relatively little public opposition. Without question, Roosevelt had broad public support for his initiatives. The presidency in this era was looked to as one of leadership and power.

The "heroic presidency," as it was called by scholars, dominated the policy-making process in executive–legislative relations for nearly forty years, from the 1930s to the 1970s. The power of the modern presidency appeared virtually unlimited in this era, according to presidential scholars Thomas Cronin and Michael Genovese.[6] The **heroic presidency** was one in which presidential leadership went virtually unchallenged and presidential proposals were often moved through Congress with little debate. The public viewed the president as the nation's leader and rarely challenged his decisions. Public opinion stood steadfastly behind the president in most major policy issues, until the Vietnam War when Presidents Johnson and Nixon failed to heed public opinion to pull out of the war. The notion of the heroic presidency changed during the 1970s.

During the 1970s the nation rejected the notion of a strong president. Nixon's failure to inform the nation about the escalation of the Vietnam War, his impoundment of funds, and his coverup of the Watergate break-in dramatically reduced public support of presidential leadership. Presidents Ford and Carter paid the price for Nixon's flawed presidency, for the public turned to Congress for policy leadership.

The nation moved from the heroic presidency to the **imperiled presidency.**[7] The public's infatuation with Congress was short-lived, and by 1980, with the election of Ronald Reagan, the nation was again looking to strong presidential leadership. The imperiled presidency gave way to a renewed heroic presidency, in which presidential policies rather than congressional policies dominated the national agenda. Except for the brief flirtation with congressional government in the late 1970s, the presidency has remained at the center of national policy-making since Franklin Delano Roosevelt's administration. The task of presidents throughout the post-Roosevelt years has been to adequately gauge and then build public opinion to ensure broad public support for presidential initiatives.

Public Opinion and Democratic Government

The concept of building public opinion in support of presidential goals and objectives is not a new phenomenon, but it is one directly tied to our democratic traditions. Unless presidents actively court public support for their programs, we could easily move toward an autocratic state. Two political scientists, Robert Shapiro and Lawrence Jacobs, who have studied public opinion argue that efforts by presidents to build public support for their programs is at the heart of our political system. According to Shapiro and Jacobs, creating a strong base of public support for presidential actions is essential to ensuring that government remains a government by the people. "By definition," they contend, "in a democracy (from the Greek word *demos*), the people are supposed to rule. Democratic institutions embody the will of the people in public policy decisions."[8] When presidents reach out to the people to seek their support for programs, they are moving forward programs that have the consent of the governed. As the preamble to the Constitution describes the new national government, it is a government for "we the people." Without broad public support for governmental policies, the government would no longer be legitimate.

In *Federalist 69* Alexander Hamilton listed the qualities of a king and the qualities of a president, carefully showing that the king had unlimited power but that the president had numerous limitations on his power. Hamilton's goal in writing *Federalist 69* was to explain to the citizens of New York (to whom the *Federalist Papers* were directed) that the presidency was an office that could not become an office of tyranny. For Hamilton, the power of the president was constrained by the public will. The public elected the president, the Constitution limited presidential power, and the public will guided the president in national policy-making. Unlike the king, who made policy based on personal preference, the president made policy based on national preference. The public good would define national goals that the president pursued.

The Hamiltonian view of a strong but constitutionally limited presidency was put into practice by George Washington. Although conscious of his official responsibilities, Washington constantly tried throughout his term to ensure that the public good was at the center of the national government's policy-making. In his farewell address, he cautioned against factions taking over the government and urged future presidents to protect this value system for fear of "the ruins of Public Liberty."[9] Recent scholarship on the presidency has reinforced the value in our democratic system of the strong relationship between presidential policies and public opinion. Louis Koenig, one of the nation's leading presidential scholars, writes that, "The hours when the American Presidency has enjoyed its most brilliant effectiveness, when democracy and the strong executive seem in finest congruence, are those when the Chief Executive rallies public sentiment behind policies addressed to the public good."[10] Thus, public opinion is intended in our political structure to be a major source of influence in public policy-making, guiding presidents in their decisions to ensure the public good.

The concept of public opinion guiding public policy-making has not been without its difficulties. In the later eighteenth century there was a constant fear by the majority of the population of tyranny in public policy making. While presidents needed to ensure that the public good was incorporated into public policy decisions, they could not trust public opinion to be the sole determinant of policy decisions. The passions of the majority may not be wise public policy. In order to temper the risk that presidents would be driven by the passions of the majority, the framers developed the electoral college structure to shield the election process from majority rule. In addition, the framers created an indirect election structure for members of the Senate. Senators were to be chosen by the delegates to the state legislatures, who were assumed to be more educated and less subject to charismatic leadership than members of the public at large. Presidents remained ever-vigilant in their response to public opinion throughout this period, a vigilance that did not moderate until the beginning of the twentieth century when Theodore Roosevelt actively recruited public support for his programs. All modern presidents, from Franklin Delano Roosevelt to the present, have actively sought to lead public opinion in support of their programs.

By reaching out to build public opinion for programs, presidents have ensured that government will continue to act as a democratic institution. When presidents no longer reach out to build public opinion for their programs they are likely to be viewed as despots or tyrants, and their programs are more likely to fall. Arthur M. Schlesinger, Jr., captured this sense of tyranny when he referred to the Nixon presidency as *The Imperial Presidency*.[11] Nixon had impounded funds appropriated by Congress for a number of programs, misused governmental agencies, and had engaged in a secret war in Vietnam. Eventually, the public lost confidence in Nixon, and he was forced to resign in the aftermath of the Watergate scandal. Nixon's case exemplifies the public's intolerance for presidents who operate without public support for their policies. Programs that presidents want to move forward must have broad public support or presidents risk losing the legitimacy of their office.

In contrast, public opinion can also provide great support for the president in times of crisis. For example, during his administration President Reagan significantly reduced taxes, cut government programs, and added funding to the defense structure. These were Reagan's policies, but each had broad public support. His public opinion polls were consistently high (except for a brief period at the beginning of the administration) throughout his first term.

By 1985, when the Iran–contra scandal broke, Reagan was at the height of his popularity and had easily won a second term by defeating Walter Mondale in the 1984 election. Not surprisingly, the strength of his high public opinion polls kept Reagan from being impeached or from suffering any significant damage to his presidency as a result of the Iran–contra scandal. His public opinion ratings remained strong even throughout the House and Senate hearings. When Colonel Oliver North said that he was only following orders, presumably from President Reagan, public opinion did not waver in its support for the president.

Similarly, public opinion largely saved President Clinton from conviction in the Senate in the aftermath of the Monica Lewinsky scandal. Although President Clinton was impeached by the House in late 1998, the Senate did not convict him, largely due to his significant standing in the public opinion polls. The economic policies that President Clinton had moved forward throughout his administration created low unemployment, low interest rates, and a boom economy for the nation. Public opinion so strongly supported presidential policies that Clinton's presidency was saved, despite allegations of personal misconduct and perjury in a civil lawsuit.

Having strong ratings in the public opinion polls can provide numerous benefits for presidents. It can provide support for major legislative policies. It can provide a reserve of good will in times of scandal. And it can generate support for a host of other policies the administration wants to move forward. The key to maintaining public support is to narrow the agenda around policies with broad public appeal (which polling can often identify), to build personal relationships with the press corps, and to use the institutional resources of the White House press office to lead the press. The following section explores each of these keys to power in maintaining public support for presidential policies and for the presidency as a whole.

Building Public Opinion Through the Media

Throughout the early years of the nation, public opinion often framed presidential action. Newspapers in particular would support or oppose a policy, urging the president to follow public opinion as the newspapers defined it. Only in more recent times have presidents themselves tried to mobilize public opinion through the media, because more resources have been made available to them. Building public opinion for policy-making goals through the media is a time-honored tradition in the American governmental structure. Pamphlets such as Thomas Paine's *Common Sense* sought to arouse public sentiment in favor of the Revolution, and newspapers that published *The Federalist Papers* sought to win public support for the new Constitution. Both state constitutions and the new federal Constitution were ever-vigilant in their protection of freedom of the press, protecting political debate through the media.

The first amendment to the Constitution specifically provided for a free press, with no governmental controls or censorship. Unlike the press in Great Britain, which often was subject to governmental oversight, the American press was given complete freedom from governmental oversight or intervention. Not surprisingly, the press quickly became a vehicle for citizens to support or oppose governmental policies. However, it was not a widely used vehicle until the late 1700s. Benjamin Franklin, a printer by trade, launched one of the nation's earliest newspapers, the *Pennsylvania Gazette*, in 1729. Only a few newspapers existed as late as the 1750s, with most being weekly newspapers in larger cities. Not until 1783 did the first daily newspaper emerge.[12] During this latter era, newspapers often were the voice of dissent against British rule. Their role was to chronicle governmental actions of which they disapproved and rally public support to oppose those actions. When the colonies gained independence, the role of the newspapers did not significantly change. They continued to agitate for governmental change or certain governmental actions. After the Constitution was signed in 1787, newspapers began playing a major role in supporting or opposing the ratification of the Constitution.

One of the major changes that occurred in the government's relationship with the press came during the ratification process, when political parties began to take an active role in nurturing public opinion. Newspapers, which were often organs of the political parties, presented arguments for and against the Constitution's ratification depending on which political party financed them.

Newspapers Target Presidents for Their Policies

Newspapers in the late 1700s and early 1800s were often controlled by the political parties that supported or opposed positions taken by presidents and leading members of Congress. In 1789, Alexander Hamilton started *The Gazette of the United States* to serve as an outlet for the Federalist Party's perspective. The Republican Party countered with its own newspaper, *The National Gazette*. In a letter to Washington several months after the administration had taken office, Hamilton complained that *The National Gazette* was too partisan, for "the leading object of [the paper] has been to render me, and all the measures connected with my department, as odious as possible."[13] The printed word, particularly through both partisan and nonpartisan newspapers, was used extensively across the nation to influence the discourse on public policy.

Presidents were often the targets of this discourse, for newspapers during the Federal period were prone to attacking policies of the fledgling administration and particularly to attacking Washington himself. In 1794, for example, the newspaper *Aurora* in Philadelphia attacked Washington as a "tyrant" for sending federal troops to suppress the Whiskey Rebellion.[14] Other newspapers referred to Washington as a dictator for his decision not to support the Jay Treaty and to declare neutrality in the war between England and France. Writing in his biography of Washington, Woodrow Wilson described the newspaper attacks thus: "harder things had never been said of king and parliament than were now said of Washington and his advisers."[15] By the end of his second term, Washington had reached a low in his popularity, in large part due to the vitriolic attacks by some newspapers. Unlike modern presidents, however, Washington did not have the institutional resources of a press secretary or a communications staff to monitor the press, nor did he have the ability to reach the public and counter the attacks through another medium, such as radio or television. Washington was largely at the mercy of the press, as were other presidents of this period.

During the administration of Andrew Jackson, the press became equally intense in their attacks. To some extent the attacks were due to the partisan nature of the press throughout the early decades of the nineteenth century. Newspapers continued to be funded by political parties and regularly took partisan positions on issues. Jackson himself contributed to the intense partisanship of the press by providing government printing jobs to newspapers favorable to the administration. The **partisan press** lasted into the administration of Abraham Lincoln, when Lincoln created the Government Printing Office in 1860.

One of Jackson's major battles with the press came during the summer and fall of 1832, while he was running for reelection. During the campaign many of the nation's leading newspapers denounced him for supporting changes in the way federal deposits were made at the Bank of the United States. Leading newspapers such as the *Washington Globe* and the nation's largest magazine, the *Saturday Evening Post*, denounced Jackson's decision in the bank issue.[16] Nicholas Biddle, who ran the Bank of the United States, so strongly opposed Jackson's decision that he hired several national magazines, such as *The American Quarterly Review*, to print pro-Bank stories.

Abraham Lincoln did not fare much better than had Washington or Jackson in managing the influence of the press on public opinion. During the 1864 election, the editor of the New York *Tribune*, Horace Greeley, attacked the decisions made by Lincoln during the Civil War and urged voters to support Salmon P. Chase, the Secretary of the Treasury, for president. Greeley felt that Lincoln was "not one of those rare men who mold their age into the similitude of their own high character, massive abilities and lofty aims."[17] Although Washington was essentially defeated by the press in his last years as president, since he chose not to run for a third term, Lincoln was not defeated. He was able to capture the election and continue into a new term. The press continued to be a powerful tool throughout the nineteenth century in moving public opinion for or against presidential policies.

Little had changed by the turn of the century when Theodore Roosevelt took over the reins of government. In 1904 when Roosevelt was campaigning for his first elected term, Joseph Pulitzer, a New York newspaper publisher, began a series of attacks on Roosevelt's domestic policies. Pulitzer suggested in his *New York World* that Roosevelt had accepted large corporate contributions for his campaign chest and in return protected big business from government regulation. Although Roosevelt won the election, his battles with the press may have led to his decision not to seek a full second term.

The problem that presidents faced with the press during the period prior to the advent of the mass media was that they could not easily counter the attacks by newspapers. Public opinion was often molded by the newspapers, which frequently had very one-sided views of presidential decision making. This left presidents in the untenable position of having few outlets to counter the criticisms hurled by the newspapers. This was particularly true during the mid-1800s to early 1900s, when newspapers were owned by **newspaper barons,** such as Joseph Pulitzer and William Randolph Hearst. Their primary goal was to sell newspapers, not engage in political discourse. Sensationalism became the central theme of newspaper reporting. For example, in February 1898, when the American battleship *Maine* sunk in Havana harbor, both Pulitzer and Hearst's newspapers ran sensational stories that the ship had been sabotaged. The front page of Pulitzer's New York *World* said "*Maine* Explosion Caused by Bomb or Torpedo," which purposely fueled public opinion to move toward war with Spain. There was in fact little evidence that the *Maine* had been the victim of any bomb or torpedo.[18]

Most of the serious reporting in this era involved a group of reporters known as **muckrakers,** who sought to expose corruption in government and business. Many of the reporters who delved into government policy worked for magazines, such as *Harper's*, rather than the large newspaper organizations. This type of reporting, also referred to as **yellow journalism,** embodied the Progressive era's agenda for reform. Not until the national news services, such as the Associated Press and United Press International, entered the news business were readers given less biased reporting and less sensationalism in their daily newspapers. The invention of the telegraph allowed news services to wire their stories to newspapers that joined the syndicate. The **wire services,** as the Associated Press and the United Press International were frequently called, produced simple, fact-based stories that were appropriate to every newspaper. Wire service reporting provided the first even-handed stories that most newspapers had printed. This proved to be a significant benefit to presidents, for the American public was given a more even-handed picture of presidential actions.

Newspapers Become Less Partisan in Their Reporting

By the early 1900s the newspaper publishing business underwent another significant change as many individual owners sold out to corporate holding companies. When the great newspaper barons began to sell their businesses to these holding companies, the news business also became more open. As the twentieth century began to dawn presidents were not as likely to be attacked in the press. Newspapers began to take on an air of more impartiality in their reporting, which was a welcome change for the White House.

The changing nature of the newspaper business and the emergence of mass media in the form of radio in the 1920s were the first steps in dramatically altering the president's ability to influence public opinion. Presidents were no longer at the mercy of political opponents who owned newspapers. They were no longer subject to the one-sided view of a disenchanted newspaper. Radio allowed presidents to reach out to the public and explain themselves, bypassing the newspapers. Presidents could now directly explain to the public their positions on policy issues. Television would later prove to be the greatest of all communication media, for presidents could talk directly to the public and have the public see their every move. The transformation of the presidency during the administration of Franklin Delano Roosevelt can be attributed to many factors, one of which was clearly the ability of the president to directly influence public opinion through the mass media.

Newspapers Measure Public Opinion Through Polling

As presidents and other political leaders sought to gauge public opinion through coverage from newspapers, newspapers in turn began to calculate presidential strength through polling data. The first foray by newspapers into calculating presidential performance came with early attempts at polling. During the 1800s newspapers began to measure the strength of public opinion with regard to presidential elections. These were not attempts to measure public support for presidential policies, only attempts to determine whether polling could predict presidential strength at the ballot box. As early as 1824, a newspaper in Harrisburg, Pennsylvania, the *Pennsylvanian*, began to forecast presidential elections by asking small groups of people how they were going to vote. Because the sample was so limited, the process was called "straw" polls. During the late 1800s the process was enlarged from the **straw polls** to very large samples.

In 1892 the editors of the *New York Herald* asked newspaper editors from around the country to conduct their own polls. The *Herald* then tabulated these results to form the first national sample to predict a presidential election. The next step was when the literary magazine *Literary Digest* created the first mass sample from their own mailing lists and in 1916 began to poll for presidential elections. In general, the *Literary Digest* proved accurate in its predictions, accurately predicting the winner of every presidential race from 1920 through 1932.[19] But in 1936 the *Digest* predicted that Alfred Landon would win over incumbent Franklin Delano Roosevelt.[20] The polling technique that the *Digest* had used in previous elections was to rely on its own membership lists, a membership that was more affluent than the public at large. But in the 1936 election the *Digest* decided to broaden its sample, and it used a compilation of names from telephone directories around the country and a list of people who had registered automobiles. The combined lists totaled ten million people, each of whom received mock ballots for the 1936 election. At the end of October, 2,376,523 ballots had been returned to the *Digest*, from which they determined that Landon would beat Roosevelt.[21] When Roosevelt won by sixty-three percent of the popular vote, the *Digest* was forced to examine its polling techniques. The problem that led to the sampling error was because, according to one analysis, "only the rich had telephones [the telephone directory used] and automobiles [the automobile registration list]."[22] As a result, the sample used by the *Digest* was not representative of the national population, for its lists were dominated by richer voters, who supported Landon.

In order to remedy the problems that the *Digest* faced, new polling techniques began to emerge in the 1930s based on the concept of **random sampling.** George **Gallup** correctly predicted the 1936 presidential election using respondents who were selected randomly using scientific polling techniques. Gallup enjoyed only short-term success, however, as he suffered a major setback in the 1948 election when he predicted that Thomas E. Dewey would unseat the incumbent president, Harry S Truman. Gallup predicted that Truman would receive only forty-five percent of the popular vote, but Truman actually won forty-nine percent of the popular vote. The predictions by Gallup and other pollsters led one newspaper, the Chicago *Tribune*, to publish an election-night edition with the headline "Dewey Defeats Truman."

Gallup's prediction was based on polling results that ended ten days before the election and failed to detect significant support that Truman had built in the final days of the campaign. Gallup subsequently refined his polling technique and has been very successful at predicting presidential elections in the past fifty years.[23] Since his 1948 miscalculation, Gallup has also heavily relied on computers and telephones for his polling operation.[24] Both have dramatically increased the accuracy of polling. We will examine polling in more detail later in this chapter.

Early Presidential Efforts to Influence Public Opinion

While newspapers often attacked presidents and presidential decisions throughout the eighteenth and nineteenth centuries, they did so with relative impunity. Presidents had few avenues of recourse to challenge the newspaper attacks or to ensure that their actions were fully understood by the public. Public opinion was often molded by the press rather than by presidential action or reaction. Perhaps the most frequently used tool that presidents employed during this era was to take the "grand tour," a long trip, often taking weeks or even months, in which the president tried to marshall public support for the administration. President Washington began the tradition of a grand tour in 1791, when he traveled across the south to rally support for his new administration.[25] Throughout his two months of travel he met with elected officials, had dinners with leading members of the community, and gave speeches on the state of the nation. For Washington the trip proved to be moderately successful, for he was able to personally blunt some attacks against his administration and, more importantly, to build support for his administration. This was particularly important as the Republicans in Congress, and even Thomas Jefferson in his own administration, were leading attacks against his policies.

Andrew Jackson was equally adept at using travel to blunt some attacks against his administration. Jackson's trips were not as long as Washington's grand tour, but were effective at building public support for the administration. Having widely traveled the country throughout his losing campaign in 1824, and having again widely traveled the country throughout his winning campaign in 1828, Jackson was masterful on the road throughout his presidency. His oratory was famous, having been honed during his terms in both the House of Representatives and the Senate.

Presidential activism in building public support for presidential policies was halted after Jackson left office, when political parties underwent a realignment and the Whigs gained control of the executive branch. The Whig theory of legislative supremacy essentially dismantled the powers of the chief executive. During the administrations of Taylor, Fillmore, Pierce, and Buchanan, the political philosophy of legislative supremacy kept presidents confined to the White House. Since Congress dominated the policy-making process, presidents were neither required nor inclined to use the presidential office as a tool for building public support.

Abraham Lincoln, whose Republican Party captured the White House in 1860, took a new view of executive–legislative relations. For Lincoln, the presidency was an office of leadership and policy-making. Unlike his predecessors, however, Lincoln chose not to use public speeches or grand tours as a means of building public support. This was partly due to his personal desire to stay close to his young family who lived in the White House and partly due to the demands on his time from the Civil War that arose soon after he took office.

Lincoln's choice for building public support for his wartime policies was to use the newspapers themselves to send messages across the country. He met frequently with newspaper editors and reporters at the White House, answering questions often leading questions. He was always willing to give interviews and anxious to discuss administration policies. His success with the press proved largely personal, for he was always cordial and quite personal in his one-on-one interviews at the White House. Writing in their book, *The Press and the Presidency*, John Tebbel and Sarah Miles Watts state that,

> In assessing Lincoln's long relationship with the press, somehow one always comes back to the human side of it, as is so often the case with this president. The contentious editors, the imperious generals, the large questions of policy seem less meaningful than the kind of intimacy Lincoln was able to establish because of the humanity for which he is revered today, alone among all the others who have occupied the White House.[26]

Lincoln was able to move his message forward in the press, essentially without leaving the White House. Although they were hardly universally supportive of him, Lincoln was able to use the press to build public support for his views on slavery, on the secessionist states, and for his use of emergency powers during the Civil War. Lincoln's strategy for presidentializing the press extended even further, however, than the intermittent meetings in the White House. Lincoln appointed several influential journalists to his administration, including Gideon Welles as his Secretary of Navy.[27] More then half a dozen prominent journalists were placed in high-level positions throughout the administration. One can assume that the press was more supportive of the Lincoln presidency because of these appointments, since they indicated a certain respect for the press as a competent, fair group. Lincoln's actions were a classic example of cooption—the president coopted the press by bringing key members into his own administration.

After Lincoln's death, the adversarial relationship between the press and the president resumed. With the exception of Ulysses S. Grant, presidents during the latter half of the nineteenth century viewed themselves as policy implementers rather than policy leaders. Presidents had little need to build public support for policies they were not in charge of. This changed at the turn of the century, however, when Theodore Roosevelt moved into the presidency after the assassination of William McKinley in 1901. Roosevelt's view of the presidency was different from that of his immediate predecessors.

Roosevelt believed that the president should have broad powers to protect the public welfare. He wanted to expand the use of executive power without usurping it. Roosevelt explained his view of executive power in his autobiography, writing, "I acted for the common well-being of all our people, whenever and in whatever manner was necessary, unless prevented by direct constitutional or legislative prohibition."[28] He referred to himself as the "steward of the people," leading current scholars to refer to Roosevelt's interpretation of executive power as the **stewardship theory.**

Roosevelt was eager to go directly to the public to carry his message. One of his earliest tools was the campaign speech from the back of a train. He mastered this technique during the campaign of 1900 with McKinley and then in 1904 for his own campaign. Presidents of the nineteenth century utilized these **whistle-stop tours** on trains to tour the country and tout their message. At every town in which the train stopped, irreverently called the whistle stop, the presidential candidate would stand on the platform at the end of the train and give a speech to rally voters for his campaign. Speeches tended to be the same from train stop to train stop, extolling the virtues of the candidate and generally condemning the opponent. However, once the candidate captured the election, trips outside of Washington, D.C., were relatively few. Presidents remained at work in the White House and rarely traveled outside of the city except for vacations. Not until the next election cycle did presidents venture out to travel and give speeches. The only nineteenth-century president to venture out of the nation's capital was Andrew Johnson, who made speeches in the southern and midwestern states to build support for his Reconstruction policies.[29]

Not surprisingly, the twentieth century brought major changes to the way presidents operate and in particular to the way presidents engage the public. Theodore Roosevelt campaigned the way every recent president had, standing on the back of trains, giving speeches at each whistle stop. But Roosevelt did not return to the White House and remain there for the next four years of his presidency as other past presidents had. He chose to continue to travel across the country on trains, building public support for his presidential policies. Roosevelt, as had George Washington, saw the grand tour as a vehicle for taking his message directly to the public. At one point in 1907 Roosevelt went on a river boat down the Mississippi River with members of the Inland Waterways Commission.[30]

Roosevelt's unconventional behavior began in 1901, soon after McKinley's death. He began making speeches for his programs, using what he referred to as the "bully good pulpit" of the presidency.[31] Roosevelt's oratory capabilities were legendary, and he frequently left the White House to build public support for his programs. But Roosevelt put limits on the rallying effects of presidential speeches. He believed that Congress should be free from public pressure and able to consider proposals without the passions of public sentiment. For Roosevelt, the **bully pulpit,** as it became known, was an important tool for moving presidential programs to the forefront of public debate and for building public support. However, once Congress had engaged in formal discussions on those programs, Roosevelt refrained from further action. He did not try to build public support once Congress had begun their deliberations.

Roosevelt's success at building public support to, as historian Arthur Link describes it, "bludgeon Congress into action," led Woodrow Wilson to continue an activist approach to managing the presidency.[32] Writing in 1913 on the eve of his inauguration, Wilson described his view of the presidency,

> [The President] is expected by the Nation to be the leader of his party as well as the Chief Executive officer of the government, and the country will take no excuses from him. He must play the part and play it successfully or lose the country's confidence. He must be prime minister, as much concerned with the guidance of legislation as with the just and orderly execution of law . . . .[33]

For Wilson, an activist presidency meant serving as the nation's "political spokesman."[34] Wilson sought to build political support among members of Congress of his own party. Unlike Roosevelt, who stopped at the door of Congress in rallying public support, Wilson worked at building party support for his programs and then maneuvering them through Congress. He worked closely with House and Senate leaders on legislation and became the first president since Thomas Jefferson to give an annual State of the Union address to Congress in person. Presidents for the past one hundred years had sent written messages to Congress, choosing not to lobby Congress in favor of their proposals.

Wilson approached the relationship with Congress in a new light. Wilson saw himself as the party leader, and with that role came the responsibility of working with the party in Congress to move presidential proposals forward. While Roosevelt stopped at the door of Congress, Wilson continued through the door. Wilson believed that a "president's power was greatest," state political scientists Raymond Tatalovich and Byron Daynes, "when he exerted leadership over both his party and public opinion."[35] Wilson worked closely with the Democratic caucus in the House of Representatives to move the platform of the Progressives forward. For Wilson, the role of party leader included building national public support for the party's programs in general and for presidential policies in particular. Although Wilson's party lost control of both houses of Congress in 1918, he continued to seek public support for his policies. He became especially active in making speeches as he sought to build a national consensus for his internationalist policies and his intervention in the European war, later referred to as World War I. His activist approach to building public support for his policies came to an abrupt end in 1919 when he was felled by a stroke. Although he remained in office, his wife and a small cadre of White House advisers essentially ran the executive office.

When Wilson's term ended, there were a series of presidents who followed a constructionist rather than activist theory of presidential power. Warren Harding, Calvin Coolidge, and Herbert Hoover each viewed the office of president as one limited by constitutional mandates. As their Whig predecessors had allowed congressional government to prosper in the mid-1800s, the three presidents who followed Wilson allowed Congress to dominate the policy-making process. They saw little need to mobilize public opinion for policies and thus did not participate in active campaigns to build public opinion for administration policies. They saw their role as not to create policy but to execute it.

With the 1932 election a new era of presidential leadership emerged in which presidents actively sought to manage the news about presidential actions and policies. Managing the news became a natural outgrowth of Roosevelt's presidential activism. Roosevelt followed the precedents set by Washington, Lincoln, Theodore Roosevelt, and Wilson, each of whom viewed the executive office as one of active leadership. Franklin Delano Roosevelt, who was a fifth cousin of Theodore Roosevelt, courted public opinion as a means of moving presidential programs through Congress. While Wilson had used the party as the primary source of building public support, Roosevelt went directly to the public through the media.

His ability to attract a broad media following was largely a product of the times, for two reasons. The first was that Roosevelt had made the presidency the dominant force in American politics, eclipsing both Congress and the political parties as the center of political decision-making. The failing economy had provided Roosevelt a platform for restructuring the role of the national government from one of reaction to one of action, from a secondary player to the primary player in the federal system. The **New Deal programs** changed the way the national government interacted with its citizens, suddenly playing the role of provider and protector. Roosevelt's view of using the federal government to provide a safety net of economic stability for America's citizens dramatically reframed the way the nation viewed the president and the federal government. Suddenly the news media wanted access to Roosevelt, to talk directly with him about his policies and programs.

The elevation of Franklin Delano Roosevelt to the most powerful political player in the country brought the news media to the steps of the White House. State and local government, Congress, and all other government entities were now in a secondary role in the policy structure. The president dominated policy-making and the media wanted to talk to him directly. Richard Brody writes in his study, *Assessing the President,* that, "as the president has evolved as the **focus of national politics,** he has also become the attention of news media coverage and, unquestionably, the most prominent political figure to the American public."[36]

The second reason that allowed Roosevelt to capture the attention of the media was the **advent of radio** in the 1920s. Radio brought Roosevelt directly to the people and opened the door to wide-ranging policy discussions by the print media. Radio also provided Roosevelt the opportunity to directly address attacks on his programs and gain public support. Mary Stuckey refers to this period when radio changed the way presidents molded public opinion as "the presidency goes public."[37] Roosevelt's use of radio provided the opportunity to speak directly to the people, without intermediaries in the press changing or commenting on the message. The president could go public anytime he wanted, without intermediaries.

Managing the News: Press Conferences

With changing communications technologies and the move from congressional to presidential government in the 1930s, presidents began to actively seek ways to manage the news. Efforts at managing the news were the first direct attempts to control the information the public received about governmental actions. The White House was beginning to find avenues for channeling information to the public that would build public support for their programs. Presidents wanted to transmit their messages directly to the public without interpretation so that they could control the messages.[38] Since the 1940s the press conference has been one of the primary tools that presidents use to communicate directly with the public. As presidential scholar Clinton Rossiter noted in 1956, "the most influential channel of public opinion to and from the president that has been opened up in recent years is the press conference."[39]

The presidential **press conference** was first formalized in the Wilson White House, but rarely used again until Franklin Roosevelt took office. Theodore Roosevelt had set the process in motion for press conferences by setting aside space in the White House for press offices. Although Theodore Roosevelt did not hold formal press conferences, he knew many of the reporters on a first-name basis and had extremely cordial relations with them. He would often give reporters detailed information about his priorities for the administration. Wilson built on the idea that the White House could be used to nurture the press and created a formal process, the press conference, for meeting with the press.

Presidents Taft, Harding, Hoover, and Coolidge did not share Roosevelt or Wilson's view that the press should be nurtured and did not try to establish either formal relations (as did Wilson) or informal relations (as did Roosevelt) with the press. Harding, Coolidge, and Hoover held intermittent press conferences, but required written questions submitted in advance. Each selected a few of the written questions to answer but gave only short, noncommittal answers. Not until Franklin Delano Roosevelt took office was there an active attempt to work with the press again. Press conferences were reestablished in 1933 and have been used throughout every administration since that time.

Wilson began the process for formally dealing with the press by naming his personal secretary, Joseph Tumulty, to serve as a liaison between the press and the president. Although Tumulty was not a press secretary, and did not answer questions or meet directly with the press, he became the first White House staff member to act as a direct link between the press and the president. The foundations for later White House press staff were laid by Tumulty's rudimentary role in managing press relations. Wilson's concept of a press conference was quite different from the current press conference; he simply gathered the press in the Oval Office for a question and answer session. At his first press conference, eleven days after the inauguration, 125 reporters met with Wilson in the Oval Office. Wilson was not particularly comfortable with the press and offered answers in as few words as possible. A week later, Wilson tried again. Two hundred reporters came to the second press conference, and they were moved into the East Room of the White House. The meeting again went poorly, for Wilson was not open with the reporters and again offered little information for them. As one reporter noted of the meeting, "[Wilson] came into the room suspicious, reserved, a little resentful—no thought of frankness and open door and cordiality and that sort of thing."[40]

In general, reporters often found their meetings with Wilson to be oriented less toward discussion and more toward professorial lecture, with Wilson lecturing to them as he would one of his students at his previous job as president of Princeton University. Although the sessions were not always as productive as either Wilson or the press corps would have liked, Wilson continued to hold press conferences throughout the next twenty-one months, meeting twice a week in the Oval Office, usually Monday and Thursday mornings at 10:00 a.m.[41] When the war broke out, Wilson found a convenient reason to reduce the frequency of press conferences, particularly after the sinking of the *Lusitania* in May 1915. Throughout the remainder of his presidency, he held only three more press conferences because the war dominated his time and, in the last two years of his presidency, because of his failing health.

When Franklin Delano Roosevelt took the reins of office in 1933, a new era of activist government began. It was the perfect time to reinstate the press conference strategy for building public support, for Roosevelt needed the press to explain his policies to the public and the press needed Roosevelt to fill their newspapers. Government was changing during the 1930s, as the locus of attention for the news was no longer the expansion of business and industry, such as Standard Oil and Gulf Oil and the big steel and railroad companies, but the expansion of government. The press was eager to cover the president and to tell the story of what the government was doing to change the lives of ordinary Americans. The news of government action sold papers.

Roosevelt's relations with the press were very different from Wilson's. Where Wilson was distant and withdrawn, Roosevelt was warm and affable. Some have even referred to Wilson's relations with the press as "glacial reserve."[42] In contrast, Roosevelt would sit at his desk with the press corps surrounding him in the Oval Office, often telling jokes and smiling. At the end of the first press conference the tone was so affable that the press corps gave Roosevelt a standing ovation. Although the relationship was cordial, Roosevelt insisted on firm rules for the sessions. There would be no written questions and many of the answers would be given off the record. Roosevelt named a liaison with the press, Stephen T. Early, who was often referred to as the press secretary. Early was a former Associated Press reporter who had known the president since his days as assistant secretary of the navy. Early was popular not only with Roosevelt but with the press corps in general.

The press conferences throughout the Roosevelt administration proved to be extremely beneficial to both the president and the press. The president was able to have a constant dialogue with the American public through the press, explaining his programs and focusing their attention on the programs of highest priority to him. Similarly, the press benefitted from the press conferences by having a steady stream of information for their newspapers, much of which made the front pages. The success that Roosevelt had with the press was a combination of the events of the time and his own personality. Unquestionably the press needed Roosevelt to explain the tumultuous change that government was undergoing. Without the access that the press had to Roosevelt, they would have had great difficulty in explaining to their readership the reasons that programs were being put forward to the Congress. But there appears to be another reason for the success of the press conferences—Roosevelt's own personality. He seemed to genuinely enjoy the sessions, and he bantered back and forth on a personal level. He knew most of the press corps' names and engaged in many unrelated conversations for what appeared to be the sheer enjoyment of their company. The personal chemistry that Roosevelt had with the press ensured that they told the public what Roosevelt wanted them to.[43] They rarely attacked his programs and never attacked him personally. They developed an unwritten rule never to mention Roosevelt's inability to walk as a result of damage suffered in his legs from polio.[44] Nor did the press mention Roosevelt's close relationship with his personal secretary, Missy Lehand, or with Lucy Mercer Rutherford, who was with him when he died in 1945 in Warm Springs, Georgia. To some extent the code of ethics that the press established to protect Roosevelt's personal life was a product of the time, but to some extent it was due to the close bond that he had established on a personal level with members of the White House press corps through the press conferences.

Truman continued the press conferences that Roosevelt had built up over his twelve years in office. Press conferences had become institutionalized under Roosevelt and, although future presidents would experiment with format, none dared refuse to meet on a regular basis with the press. The twice-weekly press conferences continued under President Harry Truman, but they were briefer and had less give-and-take on a personal level. They were regularly held in the Indian Treaty Room of the Old Executive Office Building, which was more formal than the Oval Office had been. Press conferences often focused on the war and on reconstruction efforts in Europe, allowing Truman the opportunity to explain directly to the public the implications of the North America Treaty Alliance (NATO) and the Marshall Plan.

When Dwight Eisenhower entered the presidency, he brought a new dimension to press relations. He appointed the first official press secretary, James Hagerty, who was given full responsibility for regularly dealing with the press and was given authority to directly answer their questions. Hagerty, a former *New York Times* reporter and press secretary to Governor Thomas E. Dewey, would meet with Eisenhower before the press conference to brief him on issues about which there would likely be questions from the reporters. Although Eisenhower was quite comfortable in the press conferences, his military background ensured that he was always prepared for the questions that might be asked.

Eisenhower continued the Roosevelt and Truman tradition of holding regular weekly press conferences, meeting on Wednesday mornings at 10:30. He continued

Truman's tradition of holding the press conferences in the Indian Treaty Room of Old Executive Office Building. Eisenhower's delivery style at the press conferences was folksy at times, commander in chief at other times. For Eisenhower, the press conferences provided an unparalleled opportunity to talk directly with the American people to explain presidential decisions and to highlight issues of particular concern to Eisenhower. Historian Stephen Ambrose, who worked with Eisenhower on his memoirs and then wrote a biography of Eisenhower, described the press conferences as a way for the president to stay in control of press coverage. According to Ambrose,

> [Eisenhower] used the reporters, and later the TV cameras, to reach out to the nation. One of his basic principles of leadership was that a man cannot lead without communicating with the people. Through the conferences, he could educate, inform, or confuse if that suited his purpose.[45]

The press conference provided Eisenhower a national platform to explain policies and positions, but also to confuse the audience if necessary. When Eisenhower did not want to take a position on an issue or to criticize a member of his own party in Congress, he could manipulate his answer in such a way as to provide no information. The press would quote his answer, he would appear to be forthright with the public, but in reality had carefully chosen his words and provided little new information.

In one notable press conference in 1953, Eisenhower was asked to comment on Senator Robert Taft's statement that the United States should consider pulling out of Korea and let England and other allies continue with the truce negotiations. Rather than criticizing a leading member of his own party, Eisenhower chose to answer the question with an evasive answer, suggesting that Taft's comments had been misinterpreted. Eisenhower's answer deflected attention away from Taft's proposal, which in fact had been accurately quoted, and allowed the truce negotiations to continue.[46] Eisenhower had used the press to move public attention away from Taft's proposal and had turned their attention to other issues. One of the great successes of Eisenhower's press conferences was his ability to talk about issues that he wanted on the front pages and to ignore issues he wanted to move to the back pages. Eisenhower remained loyal to the press throughout his two terms in office, conducting 193 press conferences.[47] He maintained fairly regular press conferences, meeting every two or three weeks, even calling the press to his home in Gettysburg, Pennsylvania, following his heart attack in 1955.

Two changes occurred in the way press conferences were conducted during the Eisenhower administration, both of which served the president's interests by providing channels of direct communication with the public without censorship or comment by the reporters. The first change involved the preparation of transcripts. Hagerty hired a transcription service to attend every press conference. The transcripts were then released to the press, having been subject to some editing by the White House, to ensure that the president was correctly quoted. In many cases, newspapers ran large excerpts from the transcripts, which further ensured that the president's words were not changed or mischaracterized. The ability to go directly to the public with a message significantly enhanced the president's ability to mold public opinion.

The second major change that occurred in press conferences during the Eisenhower administration was the introduction of television cameras. In 1955 Eisenhower supported Hagerty's request to allow television cameras to cover the press conferences. Hagerty correctly determined that through the unedited and direct communication that television provided to the public, Eisenhower could sell his message more directly than through other news outlets. Approximately sixteen news cameras, with sixteen-millimeter film rather than a live broadcast, were set up at the back of the Indian Treaty Room. The evening news programs showed parts of the news conference, allowing Eisenhower to talk directly to the public without editing by reporters.

Eisenhower's attention to the way the public perceived his decisions and his interest in building public support for his policies led to yet another innovation in managing the press. Building on the way that Franklin Delano Roosevelt had courted the press in his low-key, informal press conferences in the Oval Office, Eisenhower established a series of informal dinners at the White House for approximately fifteen reporters who regularly covered the president. After dinner, Eisenhower and the reporters would sit with drinks in a very informal setting. "We would have drinks," stated NBC correspondent Robert Scherer who attended many of the dinners, "and he [Eisenhower] would sit next to the piano and hold forth at further length."[48] Eisenhower's nurturing of the press and his expansion of outlets for coverage of his own press conferences paint a picture of a shrewd manager of the news throughout his entire term of office.

John F. Kennedy was equally astute at managing the news. He cultivated relationships with the press, holding small informal chats in the Oval Office with selected reporters and entertaining members of the press corps at White House luncheons. Kennedy ended the practice of editing the press conference transcripts as a means of gaining favor with reporters and moved the press conferences to the auditorium in the State Department, since the press corps had grown to over three hundred. The press conferences tended to be low-key, fast-paced sessions, in which Kennedy largely charmed his audience. His mastery of detail for policy issues and his affability provided a backdrop of casual, easy-going relations with the press. Not surprisingly, Kennedy's popularity rating averaged a remarkable seventy-one percent.[49]

Kennedy, as Eisenhower, never entered a press conference unprepared. Before every press conference, Pierre Salinger, White House Press Secretary, and other senior members of the White House staff would meet for breakfast with the president to brief him and to anticipate questions. Salinger also met regularly with the press officers from the executive departments to ensure that the president was knowledgeable about issues across the administration. The result of this intense preparation for the press conferences was that when Kennedy went before the press, he appeared comfortable, knowledgeable, and in command of the policy process. One political analyst, Arthur Krock, described the Kennedy team as using the "utmost subtlely and imagination" in their practice of the art of news management.[50] The reward for this mastery of the press was an endless stream of positive news coverage and a guilded age for the presidency.

Lyndon Johnson, who continued the process of regular press conferences, was less comfortable with the press than Kennedy had been. Although he was well prepared for the meetings, engaging in the same intense staffing sessions before each press conference, Johnson tended to answer questions more slowly and thoughtfully than Kennedy had. Johnson was not as at ease with the press as Kennedy, largely due to a difference in style and personality. Some have even suggested that Johnson's discomfort in press conferences was partly due to his fear that he would slip into using profane words or incorrect grammar on national television, as he often did in private.

News management was focused on highlighting the issues that the president wanted on the front page, but at times during the 1950s and 1960s "news management" meant protecting presidential interests. Three cases of presidents distorting the facts for their own interest come to mind. In the first case, Eisenhower misled the press in the U-2 spy incident. In 1961, the Soviets shot down a U-2 spy plane that was taking high-resolution pictures of Russia. Eisenhower had been advised by the director of the Central Intelligence Agency (CIA) and by the Defense Department that the pilots of these planes were unlikely to survive a crash since they were flying at such a high altitude. Pilots also carried cyanide pills, and they were under orders to ingest them if by any chance they did survive a crash. When the Soviet army shot down and captured a pilot on a secret reconnaissance mission in a U-2 spy plane, Eisenhower denied we were engaging in any spy activities or were flying over Soviet territory. The Soviets produced the pilot and forced Eisenhower to change his story and admit that the United States was spying.

In a second case of news management, Attorney General Robert Kennedy had emphatically denied to the press that any Americans had been killed in the 1961 Bay of Pigs invasion. When Senate Republican leader Everett Dirksen of Illinois revealed that four Americans had been killed in the invasion, President Kennedy was forced to admit that Dirksen was correct. The Kennedy administration had fabricated the original story as part of its insistence that Cuban nationals had masterminded and carried out the invasion without U.S. assistance. In fact, the CIA had trained the Cubans and been deeply involved in the invasion.

A third example of deception of the press as part of news management occurred during the Johnson administration. As the war in Vietnam escalated in the late 1960s, an increasing number of U.S. soldiers were sent to Vietnam. The war intensified as the U.S. military presence increased and there is some evidence that China began to provide support for the North Vietnamese. The Johnson administration was not forthcoming with the actual numbers of U.S. soldiers that were being sent to Vietnam or the number of casualties in the war. The management of information released to the news media by the president and the Defense Department was carefully planned to reduce public opposition to the war. These efforts ultimately failed; President Johnson did not seek the 1968 Democratic nomination because of mounting opposition to his conduct of the war.

Two presidents in recent times who have had contrasting relations with the press are Richard Nixon and Ronald Reagan. Nixon disliked the press, assuming that they had a liberal bias and were generally inclined against his more conservative policies. He simply did not have the personality to handle the rapid-fire question and answer session that was the modern press conference. He often became flustered at the questions and defensive about his answers. There was little personal chemistry between Nixon and members of the national press corps. Nixon also had a low tolerance level for reporters who attacked any aspect of his policies. His anger at some reporters for their coverage of administration policies became so intense that he directed his press secretary, Ronald Ziegler, to take away the press passes of some reporters. They were, in essence, "blackballed" by the administration and were not allowed to attend any of the formal briefings by the president at the White House. This decision proved to have broad repercussions, for Nixon continued to receive harsh treatment from the banned reporters. Once other reporters heard about the banishment, they too began to highlight the problems rather than the successes of the administration. Nixon's mishandling of individual reporters eventually led to serious repercussions for the administration in the way the press covered the administration's activities.

Nixon was a classic example of how not to deal with the press, but Ronald Reagan was the perfect example of strong press relations. Reagan entered the White House without fear of the press or of meeting with them. This may be due in part to his former career in acting. From the moment Reagan entered office, he was being hailed as "the great communicator." He handled press conferences with the same ease that John F. Kennedy had brought to them, although Reagan never had the mastery of detail that Kennedy had. Reagan often handled the press with humor. During the 1984 election the seventy-three-year old Reagan debated younger Democratic challenger Walter Mondale in Kansas City. When asked during the discourse whether age was going to be a factor he simply replied, "I am not going to exploit for political purposes my opponent's youth and inexperience." The crowd roared while Mondale laughed, but the press wrote favorably about Reagan that night.[51] One journalist commented that Reagan had "the entire Washington political community under the magic of his charm."[52] Reagan often entertained the press at the White House and built the type of network of personal relationships that Eisenhower and Kennedy had.

Both George Bush and Bill Clinton were adequate at dealing with the press, although neither was quite as at ease in press conferences as Reagan. Reagan, Bush, and Clinton all assiduously nurtured personal relationships with the press, inviting them to travel on Air Force One in small groups for background information, hosting informal events at the White House, and even allowing them to meet during presidential vacations. Ronald Reagan took small groups of reporters on horseback trips through the hills of his ranch near Santa Barbara, California. George Bush would take reporters on his speedboat for rides in the ocean around his summer home in Kennebunkport, Maine. Bill Clinton was more protective of his vacation time, largely because it involved his teenage daughter, Chelsea, whom the family tried to protect from the press. But Clinton was very attentive to the press in Washington, D.C., where he held luncheons for the press, regularly attended the annual Gridiron Dinner, and allowed small news teams to interview him in a one-on-one format in the Oval Office. Martha Kumar and Michael Grossman conclude in their research that coverage of presidents increases in its criticism when presidents are inattentive.[53] Reagan, Bush, and Clinton all tried to be very attentive to the press.

Managing the News: The White House Press Office

As presidents strive to influence the course of public opinion, they create new mechanisms for building that support. One of the more recent mechanisms that presidents have created is the White House Press Office and the White House Office of Communications. Both of these in-house advisory structures provide the president additional staff to advise him on techniques for nurturing the press, mastering difficult questions, and dealing with the ever-expanding press corps.

The **press secretary** has the task of working with the president to champion administration policies, but also must protect the president from an overzealous press. President Eisenhower was the first president to create a formal office, with staff, to manage press relations. James Hagerty was formally known as the president's press secretary, a job that every president since Eisenhower has maintained. Since Hagerty, the position of press secretary has been given such weight in the White House that it generally is given senior status with the title *assistant to the president and press secretary*. Senior staff meetings in the White House tend to include the press secretary. Since the Nixon administration, the office of the press secretary has burgeoned, with numerous positions, such as deputy press secretary, emerging. In recent years, the press office has divided itself into functional groups, with some members of the press office assigned, for example, to the national news magazines, some to the larger dailies, and some to national television. A segment of the press office also covers the foreign press corps.

When Nixon changed the structure of the White House press corps, moving them back to the White House and requiring official press credentials to attend White House press conferences, he also limited the size of the White House press corps. In general, the configuration of the press corps today includes only the national media, including the large newspaper chains, the major dailies such as the *Washington Post*, the *New York Times*, and the *Wall Street Journal*, major television and radio outlets, and the predominant members of the foreign press. The size of the press corps is limited by the size of the room in the White House in which the president gives press conferences.

The job of the White House press office is to provide a constant flow of news to the press on the president's daily activities and policy issues for which the president wants to create public support. Every morning the president's press secretary gives out a schedule of the president's activities and briefly reviews these activities. Some activities will allow time with the press, such as when a visiting head of state is meeting with the president or when a cabinet officer has a major policy to discuss. Most meetings are not available to the press and are listed only to advance the concept of an open administration. In the post-Watergate era, presidents have tried to give the public a detailed picture of their official day. The availability of the daily schedule is intended by the White House press office to reduce any suspicion by the public that the president is engaged in any kind of secret negotiations and to assure the nation that the president is deeply involved in discussions with his staff and cabinet on policy issues. Presidents who appear to be engaged in decision-making receive higher marks in public opinion rankings.

Another role of the press secretary in the daily briefing is to hand out press releases on various policy issues in which the president is directly engaged. For example, Larry Speakes, Reagan's press secretary, routinely provided the press detailed information on proposed changes in the tax laws that would reduce individual tax rates. By doing so, Reagan sought to move into the public arena the benefits of the tax cuts rather than allowing the opposition to put forward questions about raising the deficit with the tax cuts. Reagan's strategy ultimately proved successful, for public opinion overwhelmingly supported the tax cuts and Congress passed the requisite legislation. While the press secretary's actions in the daily briefings certainly did not control how the public viewed the tax cuts, they were important in moving the president's perspective to the front pages of the news. Equally as important, by dominating the news with Reagan's perspective on the tax cuts and influencing public opinion at an early stage in the process, opponents of the tax cut entered the debate at a disadvantage.

The more informed the press secretary is on issues, the more informed the public will believe the president is on issues. Having a well-informed, articulate, and easygoing press secretary is essential to the White House. Most press secretaries have operated with the full confidence of both the president and the press. Several press secretaries, however, have not been particularly successful, causing the president's level of popular support to drop.

Ronald Ziegler, Richard Nixon's press secretary came to the job with no experience in dealing directly with the press. His only previous job had been in public relations for a large corporation. Ziegler often had only a general knowledge of presidential policies, leading the press to seek other sources of expertise in the White House. Members of the White House staff, most notably Henry Kissinger, often provided the press background information because Ziegler was ill-prepared. Ziegler often deferred to agency press offices, such as the Department of Defense, for specific material. The press corps generally bypassed Ziegler, but when he called the Watergate scandal only a "third-rate burglary" and nothing to be concerned about, he lost a good deal of his already tarnished credibility. The ineptitude of Ziegler may have contributed to Nixon's declining popularity and to his inability to bolster public confidence in his programs.

Gerald Ford faced a somewhat different problem with his press secretary, Gerald terHorst. When terHorst did not believe that he was part of the president's inner circle, he quit. The specific issue that drove terHorst out was his deep opposition to Ford's pardon of Nixon. Ford did not include him in the decision-making and merely called terHorst into the Oval Office to inform him of the decision and to tell him to prepare a public statement. Had Ford worked more closely with terHorst on a strategy to blunt public opposition to the pardon, perhaps terHorst would not have quit and perhaps public-approval ratings for Ford may have been higher.

Bill Clinton's first press secretary, DeeDee Myers, faced a similar problem in that she was not included in the White House senior staff. Her title was reduced to deputy assistant to the president and press secretary, placing her in the second tier of White House staff. Often she was called on during the daily briefings to explain issues she knew little about. The failure to bring Myers into the inner circle and her subsequent failure to adequately defend administration policies most likely contributed to low public opinion ratings during the first two years of Clinton's administration. In 1994, when Leon Panetta took over as chief of staff, he insisted that Myers be replaced by a new press secretary. When Michael McCurry took over in January 1995 as press secretary, he insisted that he be given the title *assistant to the president* and be included in senior staff meetings. Both demands were agreed to by Panetta, and Clinton's relationship with the public and the press rose.

The press secretary provides the president with one of the most important tools for managing the press. Effective press secretaries can explain presidential policies and focus attention on the policies that the administration wants to prioritize. They become, to a large extent, extensions of the president, serving as a surrogate to the press. The job of the press secretary is to constantly ensure that the message that the White House wants to deliver to the public is effectively delivered.

Managing the News:
Photo Opportunities and Staged Events

Presidents have a wide range of opportunities available to place themselves in the best possible public light and a position that enhances their public standing. Press conferences and press coverage of presidential policies are an conspicuous means for presidents to get their message to the public, but other means are also available to the White House. These are less direct and more subtle ways of showing the president as building public support for the president. While press conferences serve to provide the public with specific policy information, more subtle avenues of dealing with the public may prove equally as valuable for building public support.

Among these more subtle avenues are the many photo opportunities of the president made available to the press. Typical **photo opportunities** are Rose Garden bill signings, in which the president signs a major bill surrounded by key members of Congress and often people affected by the bill. For example, when President Bush signed the Americans with Disabilities Act, he had not only members of Congress but also a host of disabled citizens, including many in wheelchairs. The indelible picture in the public mind was that Bush was a national leader, capable of moving major pieces of legislation through Congress, and that he was a champion of all people, not just a small group of political and economic elites. The pictures of a president in the White House with a foreign head of state provide a similar image of leadership and strength. Even when presidents host the winners of the World Series for a photo opportunity, the press office is sending a message to the public. Two powerful messages are sent in this case: first that the president is the nation's highest representative and in that capacity is congratulating the winning team, and second that the president associates with winners. Although subtle, the messages are effective. For the press office, the phrase "a picture is worth a thousand words" provides incalculable benefits to the image of the president.

Many photo opportunities are created outside of the White House. When presidents travel on state business, they ensure that the press sees them working with other world leaders on crucial international issues. President Carter called the press together to witness the handshake between middle-eastern leaders following the Camp David Accords; similarly, President Clinton ensured that the press captured the handshake following the interim peace accords between the Israelis and the Palestinians, known as the Wye River Agreement. Presidents use their prestige as an international leader to build their prestige in domestic affairs and therefore frequently travel outside the United States and frequently create photo opportunities during these travels.

In a very similar vein to the photo opportunities for official functions are **staged events.** The press office often works to create events that will draw media attention and show a favorable side of the president. These are part of the broad attempt to show the president as a leader and as a popular president. President Clinton, for example, went to Buffalo, New York, during the impeachment process to speak before a packed crowd in an auditorium of nearly twenty thousand cheering people. The message that the White House wanted to send the American people was that the public supported the president in spite of the events in Washington, D.C. This proved to be a powerful message, for the news shows led their broadcasts with the story of a still-popular president being wildly applauded in Buffalo.

Staged events can include less dramatic events than the one in Buffalo. President Bush was frequently seen jogging through the streets of Washington. The press office viewed the jogging as an indication that the president was in vigorous health and by implication was vigorously engaged in his job. The jogging scenario also reinforced Bush as an ordinary citizen, seeking exercise on the streets of the city. In reality, the White House has a full-scale gymnasium and jogging course.

All of the efforts to create photo opportunities and staged events are done to portray the president as an engaged leader, constantly in touch with the people, but also a leader of world-standing who deals with major national and international issues. Very subtle ways of drawing attention to the president can also be handled through staged events. For example, President Carter always wore a sweater in his fireside chats to reinforce his humanism and to show that the energy crisis had touched the White House. White House thermometers were turned down to sixty-eight degrees and the lights on the outside of the White House were turned off. President Reagan always wore a small flag on his lapel and President Bush had family pictures on his desk. Each of these small details were consciously created by the White House staff to create a picture of a strong but caring president. Each of these staged events contributed to building public support for the president. Public appearances, national addresses, and ceremonial appearances all fall into the category of staged events, but events that reinforce presidential leadership and tend to build public opinion ratings.

Presidential Polling

Another tactic that presidents use to manage public opinion is to gauge how the public views policy issues and how the public views presidential responses to those issues. Since the Kennedy administration, presidents have engaged in widespread polling operations to assess public opinion on numerous issues. Polling provides the White House information to both reframe their own policies within acceptable public standards and to focus on policies that have broad public support. Do the polls allow public opinion to lead presidential actions? Certainly, the polls provide significant weight in guiding presidents toward positions that have broad political support. Presidents are unlikely to tackle issues for which little public support exists. For example, if the president believed that reducing the number of ships in the navy would reduce defense costs, but found in polling data that the public was strongly opposed to the position, the president would probably find other means of cutting defense costs. Frequently, polling data is used to refine a broad position that the president wants to take to ensure public support.

Polling has become a critical part of every recent administration's efforts to gauge public opinion. White House polling operations have become so essential to policy decisions that they have become an institutionalized part of White House activity.[54] No longer are pollsters hired by the White House to conduct public opinion polls. The Clinton administration brought the polling operation directly into the White House, using it to regularly track presidential standing and support for various administration policies.

Presidents today not only collect polling data from newspapers, magazines, and television, but they also conduct their own sampling data. Regular polling began during the Kennedy administration and has continued throughout each successive administration. Kennedy used polling during his 1960 presidential campaign and brought the technique into the White House. Both Kennedy and Johnson employed private pollsters but had their White House staffs analyze the data and determine how the data would be used in making decisions. Nixon continued to use private pollsters but became deeply involved in the process. His memoranda to aides indicate a president eager to use polling data to find out what policies are of concern "to the average guy."[55] As an indication of the interest placed on polls by the Nixon White House was the sheer number of polls that were conducted. While Kennedy commissioned 16 private polls throughout his administration, the number ballooned to 233 under Nixon.[56] The number of polls conducted since Nixon has unquestionably increased, with indications of almost daily polling by the White House during the Clinton administration.

Leading Public Opinion

Presidents use their institutional resources, such as press conferences and their own press offices, to lead public opinion. Polling has become one of the key new institutional resources to assess the level of public support for presidential positions and for the president personally. When the public is dissatisfied with the president or presidential positions, public opinion polls reflect relatively low satisfaction. During 1994 when the administration's health care reform proposals were being heavily attacked by lobbying interests through a series of television advertisements (the Harry and Louise ads), Clinton's public opinion rating fell into the thirty percent range. This dismal success rating translated into massive dissatisfaction at the ballot box in the midterm congressional elections. Republicans were able to retake both the House and the Senate in the 1994 elections, largely due to widespread public dissatisfaction with the health care proposals.

Once Clinton moved away from health care and toward economic issues, on which he had focused his 1992 election, he was again given a vote of confidence by the public and returned to office in 1996. Throughout his second term, Clinton continued to have high public opinion ratings, averaging in the sixty percent range, largely due to his focus on economic issues. Polling had indicated during the election that the economy was the primary concern of the American public, and those polls allowed Clinton to narrow his message to meet those concerns. His electoral victory in 1992 and 1996 was the product of a carefully honed message to the voters based on detailed polling data.

The question at the heart of this discussion is whether presidents use polling data to focus their own positions or whether presidents use polling data to create acceptable positions within the spectrum of the majority of the public. The answer seems to lie somewhere in between. As presidential scholar George Edwards argues, "Whatever the reasons given, presidents have generally not been content only to follow public opinion on issues. . . . Instead, they usually have engaged in substantial efforts to lead the public."[57] Presidents do not move forward on positions that lack substantial public support. The nature of our democratic system, as discussed earlier, requires presidents to move forward on positions that have broad-based public support. The test of great presidents, however, is to move positions forward that are in the public good but may not have the support of a majority of citizens. Whether the issue is taxation or desegregation, presidents must move forward on policies that serve the public good but may raise the ire of numerous citizens.

Leading public opinion is often difficult. When President Eisenhower insisted that Governor Faubus enforce the desegregation order of a federal judge for Little Rock High School in 1957, he had to lead public opinion, which largely opposed an integrated school system. His means of leading public opinion was not to argue on moral grounds but to argue on legal grounds. The Supreme Court had mandated the decision, he contended, and as president he had to enforce the ruling. This allowed Eisenhower to maintain strong public opinion ratings in spite of a policy position with limited support.

Similarly, President Clinton urged the public not to acquiesce to the tax cuts that the Republicans were supporting in spite of massive budget surpluses. Clinton successfully argued that the surpluses should not be wasted on small individual tax cuts but should go to the larger issues of reducing the federal deficit, enhancing the solvency of the Social Security system, and providing additional funding for educational programs. The argument met the test of serving the public good, an argument that satisfies our sense of presidential leadership on behalf of the broad public interest.

The problem with presidents trying to lead public opinion is that too often the public has narrow and often short-term goals and objectives. It is difficult for many citizens to think globally or to understand the value of programs that do not affect them. How do presidents lead public opinion for policies that are global and long-term? Clearly, this is a difficult question and one that does not easily lend itself to a solution. The most plausible solution is for presidents to develop policies that address the immediate needs of the electorate and then use their institutional resources to build public opinion in favor of smaller, often long-term programs that would address the needs of smaller constituencies. Leading public opinion is the most difficult task that presidents face in office, yet one that provides the greatest rewards for presidents.

Conclusion

The need to build bridges to the public is clear, for without public support presidents have little chance of moving their programs through Congress. But public support is equally as important as presidents engage in policies that do not need direct congressional approval. Although direct approval is not necessary, Congress often seems to be involved in indirect but substantial ways. For example, military and foreign policy decisions made by the president must have broad public support or Congress will end funding. Presidential actions backed by executive order are often in danger of being revoked by legislative action. And laws that had strong presidential backing can fail to have both reauthorizations or appropriations provided by Congress. Congress can reduce funding for presidential programs, cut departmental budgets, or add to programs that the president opposes.

During the years since the administration of Franklin Delano Roosevelt presidents have appealed to the press to take their message forward. During the nineteenth century, the press often attacked presidents for their policies but published few responses from presidents. The process was very one-sided, with the press in total control of the message given to the public. Roosevelt changed the process, using radio and building personal relations with the press through a series of informal press conferences in the Oval Office. Eisenhower built on the Roosevelt model and continued building personal relations with the press, but used the new medium of television to talk directly to the public.

Television opened a major channel of communication to the public. Presidents no longer needed to rely on the newspapers and magazines to get their message out. Television allowed them to get the message out themselves. Presidents began to devise numerous opportunities for direct television coverage, including staged events, photo opportunities, formal press conferences, and speeches. During the latter half of the twentieth century, television became the dominant means of moving the president's message directly to the public. Samuel Kernell refers to this process as "going public," in which presidents talk directly to the public through these venues to define and explain presidential policies.[58] These venues, however, had some degree of filtering since the news programs that covered the president could decide whether or not to include the president and could edit the clips.

Since the 1992 election, the process of going public has taken another turn. Bill Clinton bypassed the traditional media, in which his message was subject to some degree of filtering, and found outlets for talking directly to the public. These outlets included talk shows, such as *Larry King Live* on the CNN network, morning talk shows such as the *Today* show and *Good Morning America*, and the youth-oriented network, MTV. During the 1996 election, President Clinton often invited individual reporters to the Oval Office for informal television conversations and included reporters on Air Force One for interviews. Many of the president's White House staff, cabinet officers, and political supporters have followed the president's lead and now are regular members of the talk show circuit. They can take the president's message directly to the public without being filtered by reporters. The process of going public has been a significant tool in the president's constant efforts to build public support.

This chapter has focused on the reasons that presidents need to build public support for their programs and the means that presidents employ to build that support. Building bridges to the public remains one of the most important tasks of any administration. The degree to which presidents can lead public opinion depends on the degree to which presidents respond to public opinion. Presidential leadership requires a careful mix of reactive and proactive policy development. Leading public opinion (proactive policies) also requires responding to public opinion (reactive policies). The strength of any administration is finding the right mix of proactive and reactive policies and finding the right mix of media strategies to garner public support for the policies. Maintaining public support for the administration's policies is one of the most important keys to successfully managing the presidency.

Key Words

advent of radio

bully pulpit

direct impact of public opinion

Federalist 69

Gallup Poll

heroic presidency

imperiled presidency

muckrakers

New Deal programs

newspaper barons

partisan press

photo opportunities

press conference

press secretary

random sampling

staged events

stewardship theory

straw polls

whistle-stop tour

wire services

yellow journalism

Notes

1. Significant works on presidential leadership of public opinion are by Jeffrey K. Tulis. *The Rhetorical Presidency*. Princeton, NJ: Princeton University Press, 1987; and Samuel Kernell. *Going Public: New Strategies of Presidential Leadership*. 3rd ed. Washington, DC: Congressional Quarterly, 1997.
2. Sidney Blumenthal. *The Permanent Campaign*. New York: Touchstone, 1980.
3. James Anderson. *Public Policy Making*. 3rd ed. Boston: Houghton Mifflin, 1997, p. 147.
4. George C. Edwards III. *The Public Presidency: The Pursuit of Popular Support*. New York: St. Martin's, 1983, p. 10.
5. Thomas Patterson. *We The People*. New York: Norton, 1997, p. 172.
6. Thomas E. Cronin and Michael A. Genovese. *The Paradoxes of the Modern Presidency*. New York: Oxford University Press, 1998, p. 73.
7. Byron Daynes, Raymond Tatalovich, and Dennis Soden. *To Govern A Nation: Presidential Power and Politics*. New York: St. Martin's, 1998, p. 16.
8. Robert Y. Shapiro and Lawrence R. Jacobs, "Public Opinion and Policy Making." In: Caroll J. Glynn, Susan Herbst, Garrett J. O'Keefe, and Robert Y. Shapiro, eds. *Public Opinion*. Boulder, CO: Westview, 1999, p. 299.
9. Washington's Farewell Address, quoted in Malcolm Townsend. *Handbook of United States Political History*. rev. ed. Boston: Lothrop, Lee and Shepard, 1910, p. 121.
10. Louis W. Koenig. *The Chief Executive*. rev. ed. New York: Harcourt Brace, 1968, p. 182.
11. Arthur M. Schlesinger, Jr. *The Imperial Presidency*. Boston: Houghton Mifflin, 1989.
12. Paul C. Light. *A Delicate Balance*. New York: St. Martin's, 1997, p. 70.

13. John Tebbel and Sarah Miles Watts. *The Press and the Presidency: From George Washington to Ronald Reagan*. New York: Oxford University Press, 1985, p. 11.

14. Stefan Lorant. *The Presidency from Washington to Truman*. New York: MacMillan, 1952, p. 38.

15. Woodrow Wilson. *George Washington*. New York: Schocken, 1969 (first published in 1896), p. 305.

16. Arthur M. Scheslinger, Jr. *The Age of Jackson*. New York: Book Find Club, 1945, p. 93.

17. Ibid., p. 260.

18. Alan Brinkley. *American History, A Survey*. 9th ed. New York: McGraw-Hill, 1995, p. 559.

19. Charles Kenney. "They've Got Your Number." In: Allan J. Cigler and Burdett A. Loomis, eds. *American Politics: Classic and Contemporary Readings*. Boston: Houghton Mifflin, 1995, p. 114.

20. Barbara A. Bardes, Mack C. Shelley II, and Steffen W. Schmidt. *American Government and Politics Today: The Essentials*. Belmont, CA: West/Wadsworth, 1998, p. 201.

21. Kenney. "They've Got Your Number," p. 115.

22. Ibid., p. 115.

23. Stephen J. Wayne, G. Calvin Mackenzie, David M. O'Brien, and Richard L. Cole. *The Politics of American Government*. 2nd ed. New York: St. Martin's, 1997, p. 203.

24. Kenney. "They've Got Your Number," p. 117.

25. Koenig. *The Chief Executive*, p. 188.

26. Tebbel and Miles Watts. *The Press and the Presidency*, p. 198.

27. Koenig. *The Chief Executive*, p. 201.

28. Theodore Roosevelt. *An Autobiography*. New York: MacMillan, 1913, p. 389.

29. Richard Pious. *The Presidency*. Needham Heights, MA: Allyn and Bacon, 1996, p. 191.

30. Raymond Tatalovich and Byron W. Daynes. *Presidential Power in the United States*. Monterey, CA: Brooks/Cole, 1984, p. 111.

31. Pious. *The Presidency*, p. 191.

32. Arthur S. Link. *Woodrow Wilson and the Progressive Era 1910–1917*. New York: Harper, 1954, p. 34.

33. Arthur S. Link. *Wilson: The New Freedom*. Princeton, NJ: Princeton University Press, 1956, p. 147.

34. Ibid., p. 34.

35. Tatalovich and Daynes. *Presidential Power in the United States*, p. 86.

36. Richard A. Brody. *Assessing the President*. Stanford, CA: Stanford University Press, 1991, p. 116.

37. Mary E. Stuckey. *The President as Interpreter in Chief*. Chatham, NJ: Chatham House, 1991, p. 29.

38. Stephanie Greco Larson. "The President and Congress in the Media." *Annals AAPSS*, vol. 499, September 1988, p. 66.

39. Clinton Rossiter. *The American Presidency*. 2nd ed. New York: Time, 1960, p. 11.

40. Quoted in Tebbel and Miles Watts. *The Press and the Presidency*, p. 371.

41. Ibid., p. 374.

42. Koenig. *The Chief Executive*, p. 196.

43. See Theodore J. Lowi. *The Personal President: Power Invested, Promise Unfulfilled*. Ithaca, NY: Cornell University Press, 1985, p. 20. Lowi is cautious about the degree of personal charisma that a president can use to move an agenda forward. For example, he argues that Reagan had enormous charisma and a strong bond with the American people, yet was unable to deliver on more than a few programs.

44. Daynes, Tatalovich, and Soden. *To Govern a Nation*, p. 120.

45. Stephen E. Ambrose. *Eisenhower: The President, Volume II*. New York: Simon & Schuster, 1984, p. 53.

46. Fred I. Greenstein. *The Hidden-Hand Presidency: Eisenhower as Leader*. New York: Basic, 1982, p. 75.

47. Ambrose. *Eisenhower*, p. 52.

48. Tebbel and Miles Watts. *The Press and the Presidency*, p. 468.

49. Lyn Ragsdale. "Disconnected Politics: Public Opinion and Presidents." In: Barbara Norrander and Clyde Wilcox, eds. *Understanding Public Opinion*. Washington, DC: Congressional Quarterly, 1997, p. 234.

50. Arthur Krock. "Mr. Kennedy's Management of the News." *Fortune*, vol. 67, March 1963, p. 82.

51. Ronald Reagan. *An American Life: Ronald Reagan: The Autobiography*. New York: Simon & Schuster, 1990, pp. 328–329.

52. Quoted in Eliot King and Michael Schudson, "The Press and the Illusion of Public Opinion: The Strange Case of Ronald Reagan's Popularity." In: Theodore L. Glasser and Charles T. Salmon, eds. *Public Opinion and the Communication of Consent*. New York: Guilford, 1995, p. 133.

53. Martha Joynt Kumar and Michael Baruch Grossman, "The White House and the News Media: The Phases in Their Relationship." *Political Science Quarterly*, vol. 94, Spring 1979, pp. 37–53.

54. Lawrence R. Jacobs and Robert Y. Shapiro. "The Rise of Presidential Polling: The Nixon White House in Perspective." *Public Opinion Quarterly,* vol. 59, Summer 1995, p. 164.

55. Ibid., p. 165.

56. Ibid., p. 168.

57. George C. Edwards III. *The Public Presidency: The Pursuit of Popular Support.* New York: St. Martin's, 1983, p. 39.

58. Samuel Kernell. *Going Public: New Strategies of Presidential Leadership.* 3rd ed. Washington, DC: Congressional Quarterly, 1997.

THE CONSTITUTION OF THE UNITED STATES

We the People of the United States, in Order to form a more perfect Union, establish Justice, insure domestic Tranquility, provide for the common defence, promote the general Welfare, and secure the Blessings of Liberty to ourselves and our Posterity, do ordain and establish this CONSTITUTION for the United States of America.

Article I

Section 1. All legislative Powers herein granted shall be vested in a Congress of the United States, which shall consist of a Senate and House of Representatives.

Section 2. (1) The House of Representatives shall be composed of Members chosen every second Year by the People of the several States, and the Electors in each State shall have the Qualifications requisite for Electors of the most numerous Branch of the State Legislature.

(2) No Person shall be a Representative who shall not have attained to the Age of twenty-five Years, and been seven Years a Citizen of the United States, and who shall not, when elected, be an Inhabitant of that State in which he shall be chosen.

(3) [Representatives and direct Taxes[1] shall be apportioned among the several States which may be included within this Union, according to their respective Numbers, which shall be determined by adding to the whole Number of free Persons, including those bound to Service for a Term of Years, and excluding Indians not taxed, three fifths of all other Persons.][2] The actual Enumeration shall be made within three Years after the first Meeting of the Congress of the United States, and within every subsequent Term of ten Years, in such Manner as they shall by Law direct. The Number of Representatives shall not exceed one for every thirty Thousand, but each State shall have at Least one Representative; and until such enumeration shall be made, the State of New Hampshire shall be entitled to choose three, Massachusetts eight, Rhode-Island and Providence Plantations one, Connecticut five, New York six, New Jersey four, Pennsylvania eight, Delaware one, Maryland six, Virginia ten, North Carolina five, South Carolina five, and Georgia three.

[1]The Sixteenth Amendment replaced this with respect to income taxes.
[2]Repealed by the Fourteenth Amendment.

(4) When vacancies happen in the Representation from any State, the Executive Authority thereof shall issue Writs of Election to fill such Vacancies.

(5) The House of Representatives shall choose their Speaker and other Officers; and shall have the sole Power of Impeachment.

Section 3. (1) The Senate of the United States shall be composed of two Senators from each State, [chosen by the Legislature][3] thereof, for six Years; and each Senator shall have one Vote.

(2) Immediately after they shall be assembled in Consequence of the first Election, they shall be divided as equally as may be into three Classes. The Seats of the Senators of the first Class shall be vacated at the Expiration of the second Year, of the second Class at the Expiration of the fourth Year, and of the third Class at the Expiration of the sixth Year, so that one-third may be chosen every second year; [and if Vacancies happen by Resignation, or otherwise, during the Recess of the Legislature of any State, the Executive thereof may make temporary Appointments until the next Meeting of the Legislature, which shall then fill such Vacancies].[4]

(3) No person shall be a Senator who shall not have attained to the Age of thirty Years, and been nine Years a Citizen of the United States, and who shall not, when elected, be an Inhabitant of that State for which he shall be chosen.

(4) The Vice President of the United States shall be President of the Senate, but shall have no Vote, unless they be equally divided.

(5) The Senate shall choose their other Officers, and also a President pro tempore, in the Absence of the Vice President, or when he shall exercise the Office of President of the United States.

(6) The Senate shall have the sole Power to try all Impeachments. When sitting for that Purpose, they shall be on Oath or Affirmation. When the President of the United States is tried, the Chief Justice shall preside: And no Person shall be convicted without the Concurrence of two thirds of the Members present.

(7) Judgment in Cases of Impeachment shall not extend further than to removal from Office, and disqualification to hold and enjoy any Office of honor, Trust or Profit under the United States: but the Party convicted shall nevertheless be liable and subject to Indictment, Trial, Judgment and Punishment according to Law.

Section 4. (1) The Times, Places and Manner of holding Elections for Senators and Representatives, shall be prescribed in each State by the Legislature thereof; but the Congress may at any time by Law make or alter such Regulations, except as to the Places of choosing Senators.

(2) The Congress shall assemble at least once in every Year, and such Meeting shall [be on the first Monday in December,][5] unless they shall by Law appoint a different Day.

Section 5. (1) Each House shall be the Judge of the Elections, Returns and Qualifications of its own Members, and a Majority of each shall constitute a Quorum to do Business; but a smaller Number may adjourn from day to day, and may be

[3]Repealed by the Seventeenth Amendment.
[4]Changed by the Seventeenth Amendment.
[5]Changed by the Twentieth Amendment, Section 2.

authorized to compel the Attendance of absent Members, in such Manner, and under such Penalties as each House may provide.

(2) Each House may determine the Rules of its Proceedings, punish its Members for disorderly Behavior, and, with the Concurrence of two thirds, expel a Member.

(3) Each House shall keep a Journal of its Proceedings, and from time to time publish the same, excepting such Parts as may in their Judgment require Secrecy; and the Yeas and Nays of the Members of either House on any question shall, at the Desire of one fifth of those Present, be entered on the Journal.

(4) Neither House, during the Session of Congress, shall, without the Consent of the other, adjourn for more than three days, nor to any other Place than that in which the two Houses shall be sitting.

Section 6. (1) The Senators and Representatives shall receive a Compensation for their Services, to be ascertained by Law, and paid out of the Treasury of the United States. They shall in all Cases, except Treason, Felony and Breach of the Peace, be privileged from Arrest during their Attendance at the Session of their respective Houses, and in going to and returning from the same; and for any Speech or Debate in either House, they shall not be questioned in any other Place.

(2) No Senator or Representative shall, during the Time for which he was elected, be appointed to any civil Office under the Authority of the United States, which shall have been created, or the Emoluments whereof have been increased during such time; and no Person holding any Office under the United States, shall be a Member of either House during his Continuance in Office.

Section 7. (1) All Bills for raising Revenue shall originate in the House of Representatives; but the Senate may propose or concur with Amendments as on other Bills.

(2) Every Bill which shall have passed the House of Representatives and the Senate, shall, before it becomes a Law, be presented to the President of the United States; If he approve he shall sign it, but if not he shall return it, with his Objections to that House in which it shall have originated, who shall enter the Objections at large on their Journal, and proceed to reconsider it. If after such Reconsideration two thirds of that House shall agree to pass the Bill, it shall be sent, together with the Objections, to the other House, by which it shall likewise be reconsidered, and if approved by two thirds of that House, it shall become a Law. But in all such Cases the Votes of both Houses shall be determined by Yeas and Nays, and the Names of the Persons voting for and against the Bill shall be entered on the Journal of each House respectively. If any Bill shall not be returned by the President within ten Days (Sundays excepted) after it shall have been presented to him, the Same shall be a Law, in like Manner as if he had signed it, unless the Congress by their Adjournment prevent its Return, in which Case it shall not be a Law.

(3) Every Order, Resolution, or Vote to which the Concurrence of the Senate and House of Representatives may be necessary (except on a question of Adjournment) shall be presented to the President of the United States; and before the Same shall take Effect, shall be approved by him, or being disapproved by him, shall be repassed by two thirds of the Senate and House of Representatives, according to the Rules and Limitations prescribed in the Case of a Bill.

Section 8. (1) The Congress shall have Power To lay and collect Taxes, Duties, Imposts and Excises, to pay the Debts and provide for the common Defense and general Welfare of the United States; but all Duties, Imposts and Excises shall be uniform throughout the United States;

(2) To borrow money on the credit of the United States;

(3) To regulate Commerce with foreign Nations, and among the several States, and with the Indian Tribes;

(4) To establish an uniform Rule of Naturalization, and uniform Laws on the subject of Bankruptcies throughout the United States;

(5) To coin Money, regulate the Value thereof, and of foreign Coin, and fix the Standard of Weights and Measures;

(6) To provide for the Punishment of counterfeiting the Securities and current Coin of the United States;

(7) To establish Post Offices and post Roads;

(8) To promote the Progress of Science and useful Arts, by securing for limited Times to Authors and Inventors the exclusive Right to their respective Writings and Discoveries;

(9) To constitute Tribunals inferior to the supreme Court;

(10) To define and punish Piracies and Felonies committed on the high Seas, and Offenses against the Law of Nations;

(11) To declare War, grant Letters of Marque and Reprisal, and make Rules concerning Captures on Land and Water;

(12) To raise and support Armies, but no Appropriation of Money to that Use shall be for a longer Term than two Years;

(13) To provide and maintain a Navy;

(14) To make Rules for the Government and Regulation of the land and naval Forces;

(15) To provide for calling forth the Militia to execute the Laws of the Union, suppress Insurrections and repel Invasions;

(16) To provide for organizing, arming, and disciplining the Militia, and for governing such Part of them as may be employed in the Service of the United States, reserving to the States respectively, the Appointment of the Officers, and the Authority of training the Militia according to the discipline prescribed by Congress;

(17) To exercise exclusive Legislation in all Cases whatsoever, over such District (not exceeding ten Miles square) as may, by Cession of particular States, and the Acceptance of Congress, become the Seat of the Government of the United States, and to exercise like Authority over all Places purchased by the Consent of the Legislature of the State in which the Same shall be, for the Erection of Forts, Magazines, Arsenals, dock-Yards, and other needful Buildings;—And

(18) To make all Laws which shall be necessary and proper for carrying into Execution the foregoing Powers, and all other Powers vested by this Constitution in the Government of the United States, or in any Department or Officer thereof.

Section 9. (1) The Migration or Importation of such Persons as any of the States now existing shall think proper to admit, shall not be prohibited by the Congress prior to the Year one thousand eight hundred and eight, but a tax or duty may be imposed on such Importation, not exceeding ten dollars for each Person.

(2) The Privilege of the Writ of Habeas Corpus shall not be suspended, unless when in Cases of Rebellion or Invasion the public Safety may require it.

(3) No Bill of Attainder or ex post facto Law shall be passed.

(4) No Capitation, or other direct, Tax shall be laid, unless in Proportion to the Census or Enumeration herein before directed to be taken.[6]

(5) No Tax or Duty shall be laid on Articles exported from any State.

(6) No Preference shall be given by any Regulation of Commerce or Revenue to the Ports of one State over those of another; nor shall Vessels bound to, or from, one State, be obliged to enter, clear, or pay Duties in another.

(7) No Money shall be drawn from the Treasury, but in Consequence of Appropriations made by Law; and a regular Statement and Account of the Receipts and Expenditures of all public Money shall be published from time to time.

(8) No Title of Nobility shall be granted by the United States: And no Person holding any Office of Profit or Trust under them, shall, without the Consent of the Congress, accept of any present, Emolument, Office, or Title, of any kind whatever, from any King, Prince, or foreign State.

Section 10. (1) No State shall enter into any Treaty, Alliance, or Confederation; grant Letters of Marque and Reprisal; coin Money; emit Bills of Credit; make any Thing but gold and silver Coin a Tender in Payment of Debts; pass any Bill of Attainder, ex post facto Law, or Law impairing the Obligation of Contracts, or grant any Title of Nobility.

(2) No State shall, without the Consent of the Congress, lay any Imposts or Duties on Imports or Exports, except what may be absolutely necessary for executing its inspection Laws: and the net Produce of all Duties and Imposts, laid by any State on Imports or Exports, shall be for the Use of the Treasury of the United States; and all such laws shall be subject to the Revision and Control of the Congress.

(3) No State shall, without the Consent of Congress, lay any duty of Tonnage, keep Troops, or Ships of War in time of Peace, enter into any Agreement or Compact with another State, or with a foreign Power, or engage in War, unless actually invaded, or in such imminent Danger as will not admit of delay.

Article II

Section 1. (1) The executive Power shall be vested in a President of the United States of America. He shall hold his Office during the Term of four Years, and, together with the Vice-President, chosen for the same Term, be elected, as follows:

(2) Each State shall appoint, in such Manner as the Legislature thereof may direct, a Number of Electors, equal to the whole Number of Senators and Representatives to which the State may be entitled in the Congress; but no Senator or Repre-

---

[6]Changed by the Sixteenth Amendment.

sentative, or Person holding an Office of Trust or Profit under the United States, shall be appointed an Elector.

[The Electors shall meet in their respective States, and vote by Ballot for two persons, of whom one at least shall not be an Inhabitant of the same State with themselves. And they shall make a List of all the Persons voted for, and of the Number of Votes for each; which List they shall sign and certify, and transmit sealed to the Seat of the Government of the United States, directed to the President of the Senate. The President of the Senate shall, in the Presence of the Senate and House of Representatives, open all the Certificates, and the Votes shall then be counted. The Person having the greatest Number of Votes shall be the President, if such Number be a Majority of the whole Number of Electors appointed; and if there be more than one who have such Majority, and have an equal Number of Votes, then the House of Representatives shall immediately choose by Ballot one of them for President; and if no Person have a Majority, then from the five highest on the List the said House shall in like Manner choose the President. But in choosing the President, the Votes shall be taken by States, the Representation from each State having one Vote; A quorum for this purpose shall consist of a Member or Members from two-thirds of the States, and a Majority of all the States shall be necessary to a Choice. In every Case, after the Choice of the President, the Person having the greatest Number of Votes of the Electors shall be the Vice-President. But if there should remain two or more who have equal Votes, the Senate shall choose from them by Ballot the Vice-President.][7]

(3) The Congress may determine the Time of choosing the Electors, and the Day on which they shall give their Votes; which Day shall be the same throughout the United States.

(4) No person except a natural born Citizen, or a Citizen of the United States, at the time of the Adoption of this Constitution, shall be eligible to the Office of President; neither shall any Person be eligible to that Office who shall not have attained to the Age of thirty-five Years, and been fourteen Years a Resident within the United States.

(5) In case of the Removal of the President from Office, or of his Death, Resignation, or Inability to discharge the Powers and Duties of the said Office, the same shall devolve on the Vice-President, and the Congress may by Law provide for the Case of Removal, Death, Resignation or Inability, both of the President and Vice-President, declaring what Officer shall then act as President, and such Officer shall act accordingly, until the Disability be removed, or a President shall be elected.[8]

(6) The President shall, at stated Times, receive for his Services, a Compensation, which shall neither be increased nor diminished during the Period for which he shall have been elected, and he shall not receive within that Period any other Emolument from the United States, or any of them.

(7) Before he enter on the Execution of his Office, he shall take the following Oath or Affirmation:—"I do solemnly swear (or affirm) that I will faithfully execute

[7]This paragraph was superseded in 1804 by the Twelfth Amendment.
[8]Changed by the Twenty-fifth Amendment.

the Office of President of the United States, and will to the best of my Ability, preserve, protect and defend the Constitution of the United States."

Section 2. (1) The President shall be Commander in Chief of the Army and Navy of the United States, and of the Militia of the several States, when called into the actual Service of the United States; he may require the Opinion in writing, of the principal Officer in each of the executive Departments, upon any subject relating to the Duties of their respective Offices, and he shall have Power to Grant Reprieves and Pardons for Offenses against the United States, except in Cases of Impeachment.

(2) He shall have Power, by and with the Advice and Consent of the Senate, to make Treaties, provided two-thirds of the Senators present concur; and he shall nominate, and by and with the Advice and Consent of the Senate, shall appoint Ambassadors, other public Ministers and Consuls, Judges of the supreme Court, and all other Officers of the United States, whose Appointments are not herein otherwise provided for, and which shall be established by Law: but the Congress may by Law vest the Appointment of such inferior Officers, as they think proper, in the President alone, in the Court of Law, or in the Heads of Departments.

(3) The President shall have Power to fill up all Vacancies that may happen during the Recess of the Senate, by granting Commissions which shall expire at the End of their next Session.

Section 3. He shall from time to time give to the Congress Information of the State of the Union, and recommend to their Consideration such Measures as he shall judge necessary and expedient; he may, on extraordinary Occasions, convene both Houses, or either of them, and in Case of Disagreement between them, with Respect to the Time of Adjournment, he may adjourn them to such Time as he shall think proper; he shall receive Ambassadors and other public Ministers; he shall take Care that the Laws be faithfully executed, and shall Commission all the Officers of the United States.

Section 4. The President, Vice President and all civil Officers of the United States, shall be removed from Office on Impeachment for, and Conviction of, Treason, Bribery, or other high Crimes and Misdemeanors.

Article III

Section 1. The judicial Power of the United States, shall be vested in one supreme Court, and in such inferior Courts as the Congress may from time to time ordain and establish. The Judges, both of the supreme and inferior Courts, shall hold their Offices during good Behavior, and shall, at stated Times, receive for their Services a Compensation which shall not be diminished during their Continuance in Office.

Section 2. (1) The judicial Power shall extend to all Cases, in Law and Equity, arising under this Constitution, the Laws of the United States, and Treaties made, or which shall be made, under their Authority;—to all Cases affecting Ambassadors, other public Ministers and Consuls;—to all Cases of admiralty and maritime Jurisdiction;—to Controversies to which the United States shall be a Party;—to Controversies between two or more states;—[between a State and Citizens of another State];[9]—between Citizens of different States;—between Citizens of the same State claiming Lands under Grants of different States, and [between a State, or the Citizens thereof, and foreign States, Citizens or Subjects].[10]

(2) In all Cases affecting Ambassadors, other public Ministers and Consuls, and those in which a State shall be Party, the supreme Court shall have original Jurisdiction. In all the other Cases before mentioned, the supreme Court shall have appellate Jurisdiction, both as to Law and Fact, with such Exceptions, and under such Regulations as the Congress shall make.

(3) The trial of all Crimes, except in Cases of Impeachment, shall be by Jury; and such Trial shall be held in the State where the said Crimes shall have been committed: but when not committed within any State, the Trial shall be at such Place or Places as the Congress may by Law have directed.

Section 3. (1) Treason against the United States, shall consist only in levying War against them, or in adhering to their Enemies, giving them Aid and Comfort. No Person shall be convicted of Treason unless on the Testimony of two Witnesses to the same overt Act, or on Confession in open Court.

(2) The Congress shall have Power to declare the Punishment of Treason, but no Attainder of Treason shall work Corruption of Blood, or Forfeiture except during the Life of the Person attained.

Article IV

Section 1. Full Faith and Credit shall be given in each State to the public Acts, Records, and judicial Proceedings of every other State. And the Congress may by general Laws prescribe the Manner in which such Acts, Records and Proceedings shall be proved, and the Effect thereof.

Section 2. (1) The Citizens of each State shall be entitled to all Privileges and Immunities of Citizens in the several States.

(2) A Person charged in any State with Treason, Felony, or other Crime, who shall flee from Justice, and be found in another State, shall on demand of the executive Authority of the State from which he fled, be delivered up, to be removed to the State having Jurisdiction of the Crime.

(3) [No Person held to Service or Labor in one State, under the Laws thereof, escaping into another, shall, in Consequence of any Law or Regulation therein, be discharged from such Service or Labor, but shall be delivered up on Claim of the Party to whom such Service or Labor may be due.][11]

Section 3. (1) New States may be admitted by the Congress into this Union; but no new State shall be formed or erected within the Jurisdiction of any other State; nor any State be formed by the Junction of two or more States, or Parts of States,

---

[9]Restricted by the Eleventh Amendment.
[10]Restricted by the Eleventh Amendment.
[11]This paragraph was superseded by the Thirteenth Amendment.

without the Consent of the Legislatures of the States concerned as well as of the Congress.

(2) The Congress shall have Power to dispose of and make all needful Rules and Regulations respecting the Territory or other Property belonging to the United States; and nothing in this Constitution shall be so construed as to Prejudice any Claims of the United States, or of any particular State.

Section 4. The United States shall guarantee to every State in this Union a Republican Form of Government, and shall protect each of them against Invasion; and on Application of the Legislature, or of the Executive (when the Legislature cannot be convened) against domestic Violence.

Article V

The Congress, whenever two-thirds of both Houses shall deem it necessary, shall propose Amendments to this Constitution, or, on the Application of the Legislatures of two-thirds of the several States, shall call a Convention for proposing Amendments, which, in either Case, shall be valid to all Intents and Purposes, as part of this Constitution, when ratified by the Legislature of three-fourths of the several States, or by Conventions in three-fourths thereof, as the one or the other Mode of Ratification may be proposed by the Congress; Provided that no Amendment which may be made prior to the Year One thousand eight hundred and eight shall in any Manner affect the first and fourth Clauses in the Ninth Section of the first Article; and that no State, without its Consent, shall be deprived of its equal Suffrage in the Senate.

Article VI

(1) All Debts contracted and Engagements entered into, before the Adoption of this Constitution, shall be as valid against the United States under this Constitution, as under the Confederation.

(2) This Constitution, and the Laws of the United States which shall be made in Pursuance thereof; and all Treaties made, or which shall be made, under the Authority of the United States, shall be the supreme Law of the Land; and the Judges in every State shall be bound thereby, any Thing in the Constitution or Laws of any State to the Contrary notwithstanding.

(3) The Senators and Representatives before mentioned, and the Members of the several State Legislatures, and all executive and judicial Officers, both of the United States and of the several States, shall be bound by Oath or Affirmation, to support this Constitution; but no religious Test shall ever be required as a Qualification to any Office or public Trust under the United States.

Article VII

The Ratification of the Conventions of nine States, shall be sufficient for the Establishment of this Constitution between the States so ratifying the Same.

DONE in Convention by the Unanimous Consent of the States present the Seventeenth Day of September in the Year of our Lord one thousand seven hundred and Eighty seven and the Independence of the United States of America the Twelfth. In Witness whereof We have hereunto subscribed our Names.

Go. WASHINGTON
President and deputy from Virginia

ARTICLES IN ADDITION TO, AND AMENDMENT OF, THE CONSTITUTION OF THE UNITED STATES OF AMERICA, PROPOSED BY CONGRESS, AND RATIFIED BY THE LEGISLATURES OF THE SEVERAL STATES, PURSUANT TO THE FIFTH ARTICLE OF THE ORIGINAL CONSTITUTION.

Amendment I[12]

Congress shall make no law respecting an establishment of religion, or prohibiting the free exercise thereof; or abridging the freedom of speech, or of the press; or the right of the people peaceably to assemble, and to petition the Government for a redress of grievances.

Amendment II

A well regulated Militia, being necessary to the security of a free State, the right of the people to keep and bear Arms, shall not be infringed.

Amendment III

No Soldier shall, in time of peace be quartered in any house, without the consent of the Owner, nor in time of war, but in a manner to be prescribed by law.

Amendment IV

The right of the people to be secure in their persons, houses, papers, and effects, against unreasonable searches and seizures, shall not be violated, and no Warrants shall issue, but upon probable cause, supported by Oath or affirmation, and particularly describing the place to be searched, and the persons or things to be seized.

Amendment V

No person shall be held to answer for a capital, or otherwise infamous crime, unless on a presentment or indictment of a Grand Jury, except in cases arising in the land or naval forces, or in the Militia, when in actual service in time of War or public danger; nor shall any person be subject for the same offense to be twice put in jeop-

[12] The first ten amendments were adopted in 1791.

ardy of life or limb; nor shall be compelled in any criminal case to be witness against himself, nor be deprived of life, liberty, or property, without due process of law; nor shall private property be taken for public use without just compensation.

Amendment VI

In all criminal prosecutions, the accused shall enjoy the right to a speedy and public trial, by an impartial jury of the State and district wherein the crime shall have been committed, which district shall have been previously ascertained by law, and to be informed of the nature and cause of the accusation, to be confronted with the witnesses against him; to have compulsory process for obtaining witnesses in his favor, and to have the Assistance of Counsel for his defense.

Amendment VII

In Suits at common law, where the value in controversy shall exceed twenty dollars, the right of trial by jury shall be preserved, and no fact tried by a jury, shall be otherwise reexamined in any Court of the United States, than according to the rules of the common law.

Amendment VIII

Excessive bail shall not be required, nor excessive fines imposed, nor cruel and unusual punishments inflicted.

Amendment IX

The enumeration in the Constitution, of certain rights, shall not be construed to deny or disparage others retained by the people.

Amendment X

The powers not delegated to the United States by the Constitution, nor prohibited by it to the States, are reserved to the States respectively, or to the people.

Amendment XI[13]

The Judicial power of the United States shall not be construed to extend to any suit in law or equity, commenced or prosecuted against one of the United States by Citizens of another State, or by Citizens or Subjects of any Foreign State.

[13]Adopted in 1798.

Amendment XII[14]

The Electors shall meet in their respective states and vote by ballot for President and Vice-President, one of whom, at least, shall not be an inhabitant of the same state with themselves; they shall name in their ballots the person voted for as President, and in distinct ballots the person voted for as Vice-President, and they shall make distinct lists of all persons voted for as President, and of all persons voted for as Vice-President, and of the number of votes for each, which lists they shall sign and certify, and transmit sealed to the seat of the government of the United States, directed to the President of the Senate;—The President of the Senate shall, in presence of the Senate and House of Representatives, open all the certificates and the votes shall then be counted;—The person having the greatest number of votes for President, shall be the President, if such number be a majority of the whole number of Electors appointed; and if no person have such majority, then from the persons having the highest numbers not exceeding three on the list of those voted for as President, the House of Representatives shall choose immediately, by ballot, the President. But in choosing the President, the votes shall be taken by states, the representation from each state having one vote; a quorum for this purpose shall consist of a member or members from two-thirds of the states, and a majority of all the states shall be necessary to a choice. [And if the House of Representatives shall not choose a President whenever the right of choice shall devolve upon them, before the fourth day of March next following, then the Vice-President shall act as President, as in the case of the death or other constitutional disability of the President.][15]—The person having the greatest number of votes as Vice-President, shall be the Vice-President, if such number be a majority of the whole number of Electors appointed, and if no person have a majority, then from the two highest numbers on the list, the Senate shall choose the Vice-President; a quorum for the purpose shall consist of two-thirds of the whole number of Senators, and a majority of the whole number shall be necessary to a choice. But no person constitutionally ineligible to the office of President shall be eligible to that of Vice-President of the United States.

Amendment XIII[16]

Section 1. Neither slavery nor involuntary servitude, except as a punishment for crime whereof the party shall have been duly convicted, shall exist within the United States, or any place subject to their jurisdiction.

Section 2. Congress shall have power to enforce this article by appropriate legislation.

---

[14]Adopted in 1804.
[15]Superseded by the Twentieth Amendment, Section 3.
[16]Adopted in 1865.

Amendment XIV[17]

Section 1. All persons born or naturalized in the United States, and subject to the jurisdiction thereof, are citizens of the United States and of the State wherein they reside. No state shall make or enforce any law which shall abridge the privileges or immunities of citizens of the United States; nor shall any State deprive any person of life, liberty, or property, without due process of law; nor deny to any person within its jurisdiction the equal protection of the laws.

Section 2. Representatives shall be apportioned among the several States according to their respective numbers, counting the whole number of persons in each State, excluding Indians not taxed. But when the right to vote at any election for the choice of electors for President and Vice-President of the United States, Representatives in Congress, the Executive and Judicial officers of a State, or the members of the Legislature thereof, is denied to any of the male inhabitants of such State, being twenty-one years of age, and citizens of the United States, or in any way abridged, except for participation in rebellion, or other crime, the basis of representation therein shall be reduced in the proportion which the number of such male citizens shall bear to the whole number of male citizens twenty-one years of age in such State.

Section 3. No person shall be a Senator or Representative in Congress, or elector of President and Vice-President, or hold any office, civil or military, under the United States, or under any State, who, having previously taken an oath, as a member of Congress, or as an officer of the United States, or as a member of any State legislature, or as an executive or judicial officer of any State, to support the Constitution of the United States, shall have engaged in insurrection or rebellion against the same, or given aid or comfort to the enemies thereof. But Congress may by a vote of two-thirds of each House, remove such disability.

Section 4. The validity of the public debt of the United States, authorized by law, including debts incurred for payment of pensions and bounties for services in suppressing insurrection or rebellion, shall not be questioned. But neither the United States nor any State shall assume or pay any debt or obligation incurred in aid of insurrection or rebellion against the United States, or any claim for the loss or emancipation of any slave; but all such debts, obligations and claims shall be held illegal and void.

Section 5. The Congress shall have power to enforce, by appropriate legislation, the provisions of this article.

Amendment XV[18]

Section 1. The right of citizens of the United States to vote shall not be denied or abridged by the United States or by any State on account of race, color, or previous condition of servitude.

---

[17]Adopted in 1868.
[18]Adopted in 1870.

Section 2. The Congress shall have power to enforce this article by appropriate legislation.

Amendment XVI[19]

The Congress shall have power to lay and collect taxes on incomes, from whatever source derived, without apportionment among the several States, and without regard to any census or enumeration.

Amendment XVII[20]

The Senate of the United States shall be composed of two Senators from each State, elected by the people thereof, for six years; and each Senator shall have one vote. The electors in each State shall have the qualifications requisite for electors of the most numerous branch of the State legislatures.

When vacancies happen in the representation of any State in the Senate, the executive authority of such State shall issue writs of election to fill such vacancies: *Provided,* That the legislature of any State may empower the executive thereof to make temporary appointments until the people fill the vacancies by election as the legislature may direct.

This amendment shall not be so construed as to affect the election or term of any Senator chosen before it becomes valid as part of the Constitution.

Amendment XVIII[21]

Section 1. After one year from the ratification of this article the manufacture, sale, or transportation of intoxicating liquors within, the importation thereof into, or the exportation thereof from the United States and all territory subject to the jurisdiction thereof for beverage purposes is hereby prohibited.

Section 2. The Congress and the several States shall have concurrent power to enforce this article by appropriate legislation.

Section 3. This article shall be inoperative unless it shall have been ratified as an amendment to the Constitution by the legislatures of the several States, as provided in the Constitution, within seven years from the date of the submission hereof to the States by the Congress.

Amendment XIX[22]

The right of citizens of the United States to vote shall not be denied or abridged by the United States or by any State on account of sex.

Congress shall have power to enforce this article by appropriate legislation.

[19]Adopted in 1913.
[20]Adopted in 1913.
[21]Adopted in 1919. Repealed by Section 1 of the Twenty-first Amendment.
[22]Adopted in 1920.

Amendment XX[23]

Section 1. The terms of the President and Vice-President shall end at noon on the 20th day of January, and the terms of Senators and Representatives at noon on the 3rd day of January, of the years in which such terms would have ended if this article had not been ratified; and the terms of their successors shall then begin.

Section 2. The Congress shall assemble at least once in every year, and such meeting shall begin at noon on the 3rd day of January, unless they shall by law appoint a different day.

Section 3. If, at the time fixed for the beginning of the term of the President, the President elect shall have died, the Vice-President elect shall become President. If a President shall not have been chosen before the time fixed for the beginning of his term, or if the President elect shall have failed to qualify, then the Vice-President elect shall act as President until a President shall have qualified; and the Congress may by law provide for the case wherein neither a President elect nor a Vice-President elect shall have qualified, declaring who shall then act as President, or the manner in which one who is to act shall be selected, and such person shall act accordingly until a President or Vice-President shall have qualified.

Section 4. The Congress may by law provide for the case of the death of any of the persons from whom the House of Representatives may choose a President whenever the right of choice shall have devolved upon them, and for the case of the death of any of the persons from whom the Senate may choose a Vice-President whenever the right of choice shall have devolved upon them.

Section 5. Sections 1 and 2 shall take effect on the 15th day of October following the ratification of this article.

Section 6. This article shall be inoperative unless it shall have been ratified as an amendment to the Constitution by the legislatures of three-fourths of the several States within seven years from the date of its submission.

Amendment XXI[24]

Section 1. The eighteenth article of amendment to the Constitution of the United States is hereby repealed.

Section 2. The transportation or importation into any State, Territory, or possession of the United States for delivery or use therein of intoxicating liquors, in violation of the laws thereof, is hereby prohibited.

Section 3. This article shall be inoperative unless it shall have been ratified as an amendment to the Constitution by conventions in the several States, as provided in

[23]Adopted in 1933.
[24]Adopted in 1933.

the Constitution, within seven years from the date of the submission hereof to the States by the Congress.

Amendment XXII[25]

Section 1. No person shall be elected to the office of the President more than twice, and no person who has held the office of President, or acted as President, for more than two years of a term to which some other person was elected President shall be elected to the office of the President more than once. But this Article shall not apply to any person holding the office of President when this Article was proposed by the Congress, and shall not prevent any person who may be holding the office of President, or acting as President, during the term within which this Article becomes operative from holding the office of President or acting as President during the remainder of such term.

Section 2. This article shall be inoperative unless it shall have been ratified as an amendment to the Constitution by the legislatures of three-fourths of the several States within seven years from the date of its submission to the States by the Congress.

Amendment XXIII[26]

Section 1. The District constituting the seat of Government of the United States shall appoint in such manner as the Congress may direct:

A number of electors of President and Vice-President equal to the whole number of Senators and Representatives in Congress to which the District would be entitled if it were a State, but in no event more than the least populous State; they shall be in addition to those appointed by the States, but they shall be considered, for the purposes of the election of President and Vice-President, to be electors appointed by a State, and they shall meet in the District and perform such duties as provided by the twelfth article of amendment.

Section 2. The Congress shall have power to enforce this article by appropriate legislation.

Amendment XXIV[27]

Section 1. The right of citizens of the United States to vote in any primary or other election for President or Vice-President, for electors for President or Vice-President, or for Senator or Representative in Congress, shall not be denied or abridged by the United States or any state by reasons of failure to pay any poll tax or other tax.

[25]Adopted in 1951.
[26]Adopted in 1961.
[27]Adopted in 1964.

Section 2. The Congress shall have power to enforce this article by appropriate legislation.

Amendment XXV[28]

Section 1. In case of the removal of the President from office or of his death or resignation, the Vice-President shall become President.

Section 2. Whenever there is a vacancy in the office of the Vice-President, the President shall nominate a Vice-President who shall take office upon confirmation by a majority vote of both Houses of Congress.

Section 3. Whenever the President transmits to the President pro tempore of the Senate and the Speaker of the House of Representatives his written declaration that he is unable to discharge the powers and duties of his office, and until he transmits to them a written declaration to the contrary, such powers and duties shall be discharged by the Vice-President as Acting President.

Section 4. Whenever the Vice-President and a majority of either the principal officers of the Executive departments or of such other body as Congress may by law provide, transmit to the President pro tempore of the Senate and the Speaker of the House of Representatives their written declaration that the President is unable to discharge the powers and duties of his office, The Vice-President shall immediately assume the powers and duties of the office as Acting President.

Thereafter, when the President transmits to the President pro tempore of the Senate and the Speaker of the House of Representatives his written declaration that no inability exists, he shall resume the powers and duties of his office unless the Vice-President and a majority of either the principal officers of the executive departments or of such other body as Congress may by law provide, transmit within four days to the President pro tempore of the Senate and the Speaker of the House of Representatives their written declaration that the President is unable to discharge the powers and duties of his office. Thereupon Congress shall decide the issue, assembling within forty-eight hours for that purpose if not in session. If the Congress, within twenty-one days after receipt of the latter written declaration, or, if Congress is not in session, within twenty-one days after Congress is required to assemble, determines by two-thirds vote of both houses that the President is unable to discharge the powers and duties of his office, the Vice-President shall continue to discharge the same as Acting President; otherwise, the President shall resume the powers and duties of his office.

Amendment XXVI[29]

Section 1. The right of citizens of the United States, who are 18 years of age or older, to vote shall not be denied or abridged by the United States or any state on account of age.

[28]Adopted in 1967.
[29]Adopted in 1971.

Section 2. The Congress shall have power to enforce this article by appropriate legislation.

Amendment XXVII

No law, varying the compensation for the services of the Senators and Representatives, shall take effect, until an election of Representatives shall have intervened.

BIBLIOGRAPHY

A Discussion with Gerald R. Ford. *The American Presidency*. Held on March 25, 1977, at the American Enterprise Institute for Public Policy Research, Washington, D.C. Washington, DC: American Enterprise Institute, 1977.

Abernathy, M. Glenn. *The Carter Years: The President and Policymaking*. New York: St. Martin's, 1984.

Adams, Bruce, and Kavanagh-Baran, Kathryn. *Promise and Performance*. New York: Heath, 1979.

Adams, Sherman. *First Hand Report*. New York: Harper, 1961.

Aitken, Jonathan. *Nixon—A Life*. Washington, DC: Regnery (Distributed to the trade by National Book Network, Lanham, MD.), 1993.

Albertson, Dean, ed. *Eisenhower as President*. New York: Hill and Wang, 1963.

Alexander, Herbert E., and Anthony Corrado. *Financing the 1992 Election*. Armonk, NY: M.E. Sharpe, 1995.

Allison, Graham T. *Essence of Decision, Explaining the Cuban Missile Crisis*. Boston: Little, Brown, 1971.

Ambrose, Stephen E. *Nixon*. New York: Simon & Schuster, 1987.

Ambrose, Stephen E. *Nixon, The Triumph of a Politician 1962–1972*. New York: Simon & Schuster, 1989.

Ambrose, Stephen E. *Eisenhower, The President*. New York: Simon & Schuster, 1984.

Amlund, Curtis Arthur. *New Perspectives on the Presidency*. New York: Philosophical Library, 1969.

Anderson, James. *Public Policy Making*. 3rd ed. Boston: Houghton Mifflin, 1997.

Anderson, Martin. *Revolution: The Reagan Legacy*. Stanford, CA: Hoover Institution, 1988 (updated 1990).

Anderson, Martin. *Welfare: The Political Economy of Welfare Reform in the United States*. Stanford, CA: Hoover Institution, 1978.

Anderson, Patrick. *Electing Jimmy Carter: The Campaign of 1976*. Baton Rouge: Louisiana State University Press, 1994.

Anderson, Patrick. *The President's Men*. Garden City, NY: Doubleday, 1969.

Arnold, James R. *Presidents Under Fire: Commanders in Chief in Victory and Defeat.* New York: Orion, 1994.

Arnold, Peri E. *Making the Managerial Presidency: Comprehensive Reorganization Planning, 1905–1996.* 2nd ed. rev. Lawrence, KS: University Press of Kansas, 1998.

Bagehot, Walter. *The English Constitution.* rev. ed. Ithaca, NY: Cornell University Press, 1963.

Barber, James David. *The Presidential Character: Predicting Performance in the White House.* 4th ed. Englewood Cliffs, NJ: Prentice-Hall, 1992.

Bardes, Barbara A., Mack C. Shelley II, and Steffen W. Schmidt. *American Government and Politics Today: The Essentials.* Belmont, CA: West/Wadsworth, 1998.

Barnes, James A., and Peter H. Stone. "Shameless in San Diego." *National Journal Convention Special,* August 17, 1996, p. 1756.

Bell, Griffin B. *Taking Care of the Law.* New York: Morrow, 1982.

Bell, Terrel. *The Thirteenth Man: A Reagan Cabinet Memoir.* New York: Free Press, 1988.

Berman, Larry, ed. *Looking Back on the Reagan Presidency.* Baltimore: Johns Hopkins University Press, 1990.

Berman, Larry. *The New American Presidency.* Boston: Little, Brown, 1987.

Berman, Larry. *The Office of Management and Budget and The Presidency, 1921–1979.* Princeton, NJ: Princeton University Press, 1979.

Berns, Walter, ed. *After the People Vote: A Guide to the Electoral College.* Washington, DC: AEI Press, 1992.

Bernstein, Carl, and Bob Woodward. *All the President's Men.* New York: Warner Paperback, 1974.

Binkley, Wilfred E. *President and Congress.* 3rd rev. ed. New York: Vintage, 1962.

Birnbaum, Jeffrey H. *Madhouse: The Private Turmoil of Working for the President.* New York: Random House, 1996.

Blumenthal, Sidney. *The Permanent Campaign.* New York: Touchstone, 1980.

Boaz, David. *Assessing the Reagan Years.* Washington, DC: Cato Institute, 1988.

Brauer, Carl M. *Presidential Transitions: Eisenhower Through Reagan.* New York: Oxford University Press, 1986.

Brinkley, Alan. *American History, A Survey.* 9th ed. New York: McGraw-Hill, 1995.

Brody, Richard A. *Assessing the President.* Stanford, CA: Stanford University Press, 1991.

Brownell, Herbert, and John P. Burke. *Advising Ike: The Memoirs of Attorney General Herbert Brownell.* Lawrence, KS: University Press of Kansas, 1993.

Brownlow, Louis. *The Autobiography of Louis Brownlow, Volume II: A Passion for Anonymity.* Chicago: University of Chicago Press, 1958.

Brzezinski, Zbigniew. *Power and Principle.* New York: Farrar, Straus, Giroux, 1983.

Burke, John P. *The Institutional Presidency.* Baltimore: Johns Hopkins University Press, 1992.

Burke, John P., and Fred I. Greenstein. *How Presidents Test Reality.* New York: Russell Sage, 1989.

Burns, James MacGregor. *The Crucible of Leadership.* Boston: Houghton Mifflin, 1973.

Burns, James MacGregor. *The Deadlock of Democracy.* Englewood Cliffs, NJ: Prentice-Hall, 1967.

Bush, George. *Looking Forward: An Autobiography of George Bush.* Garden City, NY: Doubleday, 1987.

Butler, Stuart, Michael Sanera, and Bruce W. Weinrod. *Mandate for Leadership II.* Washington, DC: Heritage Foundation, 1984.

Califano, Joseph, A., Jr. *Governing America.* New York: Simon & Schuster, 1981.

Califano, Joseph A., Jr. *A Presidential Nation.* New York: Norton., 1975.

Campbell, Colin, S.J. *Managing the Presidency: Carter, Reagan, and the Search for Executive Harmony.* Pittsburgh: University of Pittsburgh Press, 1986.

Campbell, Colin, S.J., and Bert A. Rockman, eds. *The Bush Presidency: First Appraisals.* Chatham, NJ: Chatham House, 1991.

Cannon, Lou. *President Reagan: The Role of a Lifetime.* New York: Simon & Schuster, 1991.

Cannon, Lou. *Reagan.* New York: Putnam, 1982.

Cannon, James. *Time and Chance.* New York: Harper, Collins, 1994.

Carnegie Commission on Science, Technology, and Government. *Science and Technology and the President: A Report to the Next Administration.* New York: Carnegie Corporation of New York, January 1997.

Carter, Jimmy. *A Government as Good as its People.* New York: Simon & Schuster, 1977.

Carter, Jimmy. *Keeping Faith.* New York: Bantam, 1982.

Carter, Jimmy. *Why Not the Best?* New York: Bantam, 1976.

Casper, Dale E. *Richard M. Nixon.* New York: Garland, 1988.

Casserly, John T. *The Ford White House.* Boulder, CO: Colorado Associated University Press, 1977.

Channing, Edward. *A History of the United States.* vol. 2. New York: MacMillan, 1938.

Clifford, Clark. *Counsel to the President: A Memoir.* New York: Random House, 1991.

Cohen, Jeffrey. *The Politics of the U.S. Cabinet: Representation in the Executive Branch 1789–1984.* Pittsburgh: University of Pittsburgh Press, 1988.

Collier, Kenneth E. *Between the Branches: The White House Office of Legislative Affairs.* Pittsburgh: University of Pittsburgh Press, 1997.

Combs, James E. *The Reagan Range: The Nostalgic Myth in American Politics.* Bowling Green, OH: Bowling Green State University, 1993.

Commager, Henry S. *Documents of American History.* 9th edition. New York: Appleton-Century-Crofts, 1973.

Congressional Quarterly. *President Carter.* Washington: Congressional Quarterly Inc., 1977.

Corwin, Edward S. *The President: Office and Powers 1787–1984.* 5th rev. ed. New York: New York University Press, 1984.

Corwin, Edward S. "Wanted: A New Type of Cabinet." *The New York Times Magazine,* October 10, 1948, p. 14.

Crabb, Cecil V., Jr., and Pat M. Holt, *Invitation to Struggle: Congress, the President and Foreign Policy.* Washington, DC: Congressional Quarterly, 1980.

Crabb, Cecil V., Jr., and Kevin V. Mulcahy. *American National Security*. Pacific Grove, CA: Brooks/Cole, 1991.

Cramer, Richard Ben. *What It Takes*. New York: Random House, 1992.

Cronin, Thomas E., ed. *Rethinking the Presidency*. Boston: Little, Brown, 1982.

Cronin, Thomas E. *The State of the Presidency*. 2nd ed. Boston: Little, Brown, 1980.

Cronin, Thomas E., and Michael A. Genovese. *The Paradoxes of the Modern Presidency*. New York: Oxford University Press, 1998.

Cronin, Thomas E., and Sanford D. Greenberg, ed. *The Presidential Advisory System*. New York: Harper, 1969.

Dahl, Robert A. *Democracy in the United States: Promise and Performance*. 2nd ed. Chicago: Rand McNally, 1972.

Daniels, Jospehus. *The Life of Woodrow Wilson 1856–1924*. City unknown: Will H. Johnson, 1924.

Darman, Richard. *Who's in Control? Polar Politics and the Sensible Center*. New York: Simon & Schuster, 1996.

Davidson, Roger H., and Walter J. Oleszek. *Congress and Its Members*. 2nd ed. Washington, DC: Congressional Quarterly, 1985.

Davis, James W. *The American Presidency*. 2nd ed. Westport, CT: Greenwood Press, 1995.

Daynes Byron, Raymond Tatalovich and Dennis Soden. *To Govern a Nation: Presidential Power and Politics*. New York: St. Martin's, 1998.

Dean, John. *Blind Ambition*. New York: Simon & Schuster, 1976.

Deaver, Michael K. *Behind the Scenes*. New York: Morrow, 1987.

Derbyshire, Ian. *Politics in the United States: From Carter to Reagan*. Edinburgh: Chambers, 1987.

Diamond, Robert A., ed. *Origins and Development of Congress*. 2nd ed. Washington, DC: Congressional Quarterly, 1982.

DiClerico, Robert E., ed. *Analyzing the Presidency*. Guildford, CT: Dushkin Group, 1985.

Dodd, Lawrence C., and Bruce I. Oppenheimer, ed. *Congress Reconsidered*. 6th ed. Washington, DC: Congressional Quarterly, 1997.

Downs, Anthony. *Inside Bureaucracy*. Boston: Little, Brown and Company, 1967.

Drew, Elizabeth. *On the Edge*. New York: Simon & Schuster, 1994.

Drury, Allen. *Courage and Hesitation*. New York: Doubleday, 1971.

Dugger, Ronnie. *On Reagan: The Man and His Presidency*. New York: McGraw-Hill, 1983.

Dumbrell, John. *The Carter Presidency: A Re-Evaluation*. New York: St. Martin's, 1993.

Durant, Robert F. *The Administrative Presidency Revisited: Public Lands, The BLM, and the Reagan Revolution*. Albany, NY: State University of New York Press, 1992.

Dye, Thomas R. *Who's Running America? The Clinton Years*. Englewood Cliffs, NJ: Prentice Hall, 1995.

Edel, Wilbur. *The Reagan Presidency: An Actor's Finest Performance*. New York: Hippocrene, 1992.

Edwards, George C., III. *At the Margins*. New Haven, CT: Yale University Press, 1989.

Edwards, George C., III. *Implementing Public Policy*. Washington, DC: Congressional Quarterly, 1980.

Edwards, George C., III. *The Public Presidency: The Pursuit of Popular Support*. New York: St. Martin's, 1983.

Edwards, George C. III, Martin P. Wattenberg, and Robert L. Lineberry. *Government in America: People Politics, and Policy*. 3rd ed. New York: Longman, 1997.

Edwards, George C., III, and Stephen Wayne. *Presidential Leadership: Politics and Policymaking*. 4th ed. New York: St. Martin's, 1997.

Ehrlichman, John. *Witness to Power: The Nixon Years*. New York: Simon & Schuster, 1982.

Emmerick, Herbert. *Federal Organization and Administrative Management*. University, Alabama: University of Alabama Press, 1971.

Epstein, Lee, and Thomas G. Walker. *Constitutional Law for a Changing America: A Short Course*. Washington, DC: Congressional Quarterly, 1996.

Evans, Rowland, Jr., and Robert D. Novak. *Nixon in the White House*. New York: Random House, 1971.

Farrand, Max. *The Records of the Federal Convention of 1787*. vol. 2. New Haven, CT: Yale University Press, 1966.

Feerick, John D. *The Twenty-Fifth Amendment: Its Complete History and Early Applications*. New York: Fordham University Press, 1976.

Fenno, Richard F., Jr. *The President's Cabinet*. New York: Vintage, 1959.

Finer, Herman. *The Presidency: Crisis and Regeneration*. Chicago: University of Chicago Press, 1960.

Finletter, Thomas K. *Can Representative Government Do the Job?* New York: Reynal and Hitchcock, 1945.

Firestone, Bernard J. *Gerald R. Ford and the Politics of Post-Watergate America*. Westport, CT: Greenwood Press, 1993.

Fisher, Jeff. *Presidents and Promises: From Campaign Pledge to Presidential Performance*. Washington, DC: Congressional Quarterly, 1985.

Fisher, Louis. *Constitutional Conflicts Between Congress and the President*. 4th ed. rev. Lawrence, KS: University Press of Kansas, 1997.

Fisher, Louis. *The Politics of Shared Power—Congress and the Executive*. 2nd ed. Washington, DC: Congressional Quarterly, 1987.

Fisher, Louis. *President and Congress: Power and Policy*. New York: Free Press, 1972.

Fisher, Louis. *Presidential Spending Power*. Princeton, NJ: Princeton University Press, 1975.

Fitch, Nancy Elizabeth. *The Management Style of Ronald Reagan, Chairman of the Board of the United States of America: An Annotated Bibliography*. Monticello, IL: Vance Bibliographies, 1982.

Ford, Betty. *The Times of My Life*. New York: Harper, 1978.

Ford, Gerald R. "Congress, the Presidency, and National Security Policy." *Presidential Studies Quarterly*, Spring 1986; pp. 223–237.

Ford, Gerald R. *A Time to Heal*. New York: Harper, 1979.

Franklin, Daniel P. *Extraordinary Measures: The Exercise of Prerogative Powers in the United States*. Pittsburgh: University of Pittsburgh Press, 1991.

Frendreis, John P., and Raymond Tatalovich. *The Modern Presidency and Economic Policy*. Itasca, IL: Peacock, 1994.

Genovese, Michael A. *The Nixon Presidency: Power and Politics in Turbulent Times*. New York: Greenwood Press, 1990.

Germond, Jack. *Blue Smoke and Mirrors: How Reagan Won and Why Carter Lost the Election of 1980*. New York: Viking, 1980.

Gilmour, Robert S., and Alexis A. Halley. *Who Makes Public Policy?: The Struggle Between Congress and the Executive*. Chatham, NJ: Chatham House, 1994.

Gimlin, Hoyt, ed. *President Bush—The Challenge Ahead*. Washington, DC: Congressional Quarterly, 1989.

Glad, Betty. *Jimmy Carter, In Search of the Great White House*. New York: Norton, 1980.

Goodsell, Charles T. *The Case for Bureaucracy*, 3rd ed. Chatham, New Jersey: Chatham House, 1994.

Greene, Jack P. *Encyclopedia of American Political History: Studies of the Principal Movements and Ideas*. New York: Scribner, 1984.

Greene, John Robert. *The Limits of Power: The Nixon and Ford Administrations*. Bloomington: Indiana University Press, 1992.

Greene, John Robert. *The Presidency of Gerald R. Ford*. Lawrence, KS: University Press of Kansas, 1995.

Greenstein, Fred I. *The Hidden-Hand Presidency: Eisenhower as Leader*. New York: Basic, 1982.

Greenstein, Fred I. *Leadership in the Modern Presidency*. Cambridge, MA: Harvard University Press, 1988.

Grover, William F. *The President as Prisoner: A Structural Critique of the Carter and Reagan Years*. Albany, NY: State University of New York Press, 1989.

Haas, Lawrence J. *Running on Empty: Bush, Congress, and the Politics of a Bankrupt Government*. Homewood, IL: Business One Irwin, 1990.

Haas, Garland. *Jimmy Carter and the Politics of Frustration*. Jefferson, NC: McFarland, 1992.

Haftendorn, Helga, and Jakob Schlissler, eds. *The Reagan Administration: A Reconstruction of American Strength?* New York: W. de Gruyter, 1988.

Haig, Alexander, M., Jr. *Caveat*. New York: MacMillan, 1984.

Haig, Alexander M., Jr. *Inner Circles*. New York: Warner, 1992.

Haldeman, H.R. *Ends of Power*. New York: Dell, 1979.

Haldeman, H. R. *The Haldeman Diaries: Inside the Nixon White House*. New York: Putnam, 1994.

Hall, David Locke. *The Reagan Wars: A Constitutional Perspective on War Powers and the Presidency*. Boulder, CO: Westview, 1991.

Halperin, Morton H. *Bureaucratic Politics and Foreign Policy*. Washington, DC: Brookings Institution, 1974.

Hamilton, Alexander, James Madison, and John Jay. *The Federalist Papers*. New York: Bantam, 1961.

Hargrove, Erwin C. *Jimmy Carter as President: Leadership and the Politics of the Public Good*. Baton Rouge: Louisiana State University Press, 1988.

Hargrove, Erwin C. *The Power of the Modern Presidency*. New York: Knopf, 1974.

Hargrove, Erwin C. *The President as Leader*. Lawrence, KS: University Press of Kansas, 1998.

Harris, Fred R. *Deadlock or Decision: The U.S. Senate and the Rise of National Politics.* New York: Oxford University Press, 1993.

Hart, John. *The Presidential Branch: From Washington to Clinton.* 2nd ed. Chatham, NJ: Chatham House, 1995.

Hartmann, Robert. *Palace Politics, An Inside Account of the Ford Years.* New York: McGraw-Hill, 1980.

Hazlitt, Henry. *A New Constitution Now.* New York: McGraw-Hill, 1942.

Heatherly, Charles L., ed. *Mandate for Leadership: Policy Management in a Conservative Administration.* Washington, DC: Heritage Foundation, 1981.

Heatherly, Charles L., and Burton Yale Pines, eds. *Mandate for Leadership III: Policy Strategies for the 1990s.* Washington, DC: Heritage Foundation, 1989.

Heclo, Hugh. *A Government of Strangers: Executive Politics in Washington.* Washington, DC: Brookings Institution, 1977.

Heineman, Ben W., Jr., and Curtis A. Hessler. *Memorandum for the President.* New York: Random House, 1980.

Henderson, Philip. *Managing the Presidency.* Boulder, CO: Westview, 1988.

Herring, E. Pendleton. *Presidential Leadership.* Westport, CT: Greenwood Press, 1972 (first published in 1940).

Hersh, Seymour M. *The Price of Power, Kissinger in the White House.* New York: Summit, 1983.

Hess, Stephen. *Organizing the Presidency.* 2nd ed. Washington, DC: Brookings Institution, 1988.

Hickel, Walter J. *Who Owns America?* Englewood Cliffs, NJ: Prentice-Hall, 1971.

Hinckley, Barbara. *Stability and Change in Congress.* 4th ed. New York: Harper, 1988.

Hill, Dilys, and Phil Williams, eds. *The Bush Presidency: Triumphs and Adversities.* New York: St. Martin's, 1994.

Hilleary, John T. *My Thousand Days at the President's House.* New York: Carlton, 1988.

Hobbs, Edward H. *Behind the President.* Washington, DC: Public Affairs Press, 1954.

Hodgson, Godfrey. *All Things to All Men.* New York: Simon & Schuster, 1980.

Hoff-Wilson, Joan. *Nixon Reconsidered.* New York: Basic, 1994.

Hogan, Joseph. *The Reagan Years: The Record in Presidential Leadership.* New York: Manchester University Press, 1990.

Holmes, Jack E., Michael Engelhardt, Robert E. Elder, Jr., James M. Zoetewey, and David K. Ryden, *American Government Essentials and Perspectives.* 3rd ed. New York: McGraw-Hill, 1998.

Horn, Stephen. *The Cabinet and Congress.* New York: Columbia University Press, 1960.

Hoxie, R. Gordon, ed. *The Presidency of the 1970's.* New York: Center for the Study of the Presidency, 1973.

Hoxie, R. Gordon, ed. *The White House: Organization and Operations.* New York: Center for the Study of the Presidency, 1971.

Hughes, Emmet John. *The Living Presidency.* New York: Coward, McCann, and Geoghegan, 1972

Hughes, Emmet John. *The Ordeal of Power.* New York: Atheneum, 1963.

Hummel, Ralph P. *The Bureaucratic Experience*. 2nd ed. New York: St. Martin's, 1982.

Hyman, Sidney. *The American President*. 3rd ed. Englewood Cliffs, NJ: Prentice-Hall, 1990.

Inouye, Daniel D., and Lee H. Hamilton, eds. *Report of the Congressional Committees Investigating the Iran-Contra Affair*. New York: Times, 1988.

James, Dorothy Buckton. *The Contemporary Presidency*. 2nd ed. Indianapolis: Pegasus, 1974.

James, Marquis. *The Life of Andrew Jackson*. New York: Bobbs-Merrill, 1938.

Jamieson, Kathleen H., and David S. Birdsell. *Presidential Debates*. New York: Oxford University Press, 1988.

Jaworski, Leon. *The Right and the Power: The Prosecution of Watergate*. New York: Reader's Digest Press, 1976.

Johnson, Haynes. *In the Absence of Power*. New York: Viking, 1980.

Johnson, Haynes. *Sleepwalking Through History: America in the Reagan Years*. New York: Doubleday, 1991.

Johnson, Haynes, and David S. Broder. *The System*. Boston: Little, Brown, 1996.

Johnson, Lyndon Baines. *The Vantage Point: Perspectives of the Presidency, 1963–1969*. New York: Holt, Rinehart, and Winston, 1971.

Johnson, Richard Tanner. *Managing the White House: An Intimate Study of the Presidency*. New York: Harper & Row, 1974.

Jones, Charles O. *The Trusteeship Presidency: Jimmy Carter and the U.S. Congress*. Baton Rouge: Louisiana State University Press, 1988.

Jones, Charles O., ed. *The Reagan Legacy: Promise and Performance*. Chatham, NJ: Chatham House, 1988.

Jones, Robert. "George Washington and the Establishment of a Tradition." In: Philip C. Dolce and George H. Skau, eds. *Power and the Presidency*. New York: Scribner's, 1976.

Jordan, Hamilton. *Crisis*. Berkeley, CA: Berkeley Press, 1983.

Judd, Dennis R. *The Politics of American Cities*. Boston: Little, Brown, 1979.

Kaufman, Burton I. *The Presidency of James Earl Carter*. Lawrence, KS: University Press of Kansas, 1993.

Kaufman, Herbert. *The Administrative Behavior of Federal Bureau Chiefs*. Washington, DC: Brookings Institution, 1981.

Kearns, Doris. *Lyndon Johnson and the American Dream*. New York: Harper & Row, 1976.

Kellerman, Barbara. *The President As World Leader*. New York: St. Martin's, 1991.

Kenney, Charles. "They've Got Your Number." In: Allan J. Cioler and Burdett A. Loomis, Eds.: *American Politics: Classic and Contemporary Readings*. Boston: Houghton Mifflin, 1995.

Kennedy, John F. *Profiles in Courage*. New York: Pocket Books, 1955.

Kerbel, Matthew Robert. *Beyond Persuasion: Organizational Efficiency and Presidential Power*. Albany, NY: State University of New York Press, 1991.

Kernell, Samuel. *Going Public: New Strategies of Presidential Leadership*. 3rd ed. Washington, DC: Congressional Quarterly, 1997.

Kernell, Samuel, and Samuel L. Popkin. *Chief of Staff*. Berkeley, CA: University of California Press, 1986.

Kessel, John H. *The Domestic Presidency: Decision-Making in the White House*. North Scituate, MA: Duxbury, 1973.

King, Anthony, ed. *Both Ends of the Avenue*. Washington, DC: American Enterprise Institute, 1983.

King, Anthony, ed. *The New American Political System*. Washington, DC: American Enterprise Institute, 1978.

King, Eliot, "The Press and the Illusion of Public Opinion: The Strange Case of Ronald Reagan's Popularity." In Theodore L. Glasser and Charles T. Salmon, eds. *Public Opinion and the Communication of Consent*. New York: Guilford, 1995.

Kissinger, Henry. *White House Years*. Boston: Little, Brown, 1979.

Klein, Herbert. *Making It Perfectly Clear*. Garden City, NY: Doubleday, 1980.

Koenig, Louis W. *The Chief Executive*. rev. ed. New York: Harcourt, Brace, 1968.

Koenig, Louis W. *The Invisible Presidency*. New York: Holt, Rinehart and Winston, 1960.

Kolb, Charles. *The White House Dazed: The Unmaking of Domestic Policy in the Bush Years*. New York: Free Press, 1984.

Kramer, Fred A. *Perspectives on Public Bureaucracy*. Cambridge, MA: Winthrop, 1973.

Kucharsky, David. *The Man From Plains*. New York: Harper, 1976.

Kurian, George T., ed. *A Historical Guide to the U.S. Government*. New York: Oxford University Press, 1998.

Kurian, George T. *Datapedia of the United States*. Lanham, MD: Bernan, 1994.

Kymlicka, B.B., and Jean V. Matthews, eds. *The Reagan Revolution?* Chicago: Dorsey, 1988.

Lance, Bert. *The Truth of the Matter: My Life In and Out of Politics*. New York: Summit, 1991.

Landau, David. *Kissinger*. Boston: Houghton Mifflin, 1972.

Landy, Mark, ed. *Modern Presidents and the Presidency*. Lexington, MA: Heath, 1985.

Langston, Thomas S. *Ideologues and Presidents: From the New Deal to the Reagan Revolution*. Baltimore: Johns Hopkins University Press, 1992.

Lankevich, George J. *James E. Carter, 1924–: Chronology*. Dobbs Ferry, NY: Oceana, 1981.

Laski, Harold J. *The American Presidency*. New York: Grosset & Dunlap, 1940, 1968.

Lasky, Victor. *Jimmy Carter: The Man and the Myth*. New York: Marek, 1979.

Lawler, Thomas Bonaventure. *Essentials of American History*. rev. ed. Boston: Lothrop, Lee, and Shepard, 1910.

Learned, Henry Barrett. *The President's Cabinet: Studies in the Origin, Formation, and Structure of an American Institution*. New York: Franklin, 1912, reprinted 1972.

Leech, Margaret. *In the Days of McKinley*. New York: Harper, 1959.

Light, Paul C. *A Delicate Balance*. New York: St. Martin's, 1997.

Light, Paul C. *The President's Agenda: Domestic Policy Choice From Kennedy to Carter*. Baltimore: Johns Hopkins University Press, 1982.

Light, Paul C. *Still Artful Work: The Continuing Politics of Social Security Reform*. New York: McGraw-Hill, 1995.

Light, Paul C. *Vice Presidential Power*. Baltimore: Johns Hopkins University Press, 1984.

Link, Arthur S. *Wilson: The New Freedom*. Princeton, NJ: Princeton University Press, 1956.

Link, Arthur S., ed. *The Papers of Woodrow Wilson*. vol. 2. Princeton, NJ: Princeton University Press, 1967.

Link, Arthur S. *Woodrow Wilson and the Progressive Era, 1910–1917*. New York: Harper, 1954.

Livingston, William S., Lawrence C., Dodd, and Richard L. Schot, eds. *The Presidency and the Congress—A Shifting Balance of Power?* Austin: University of Texas, 1979.

Locke, John. *Of Civil Government: Second Treatise*. Chicago: Regnery, 1955; seventh printing, 1968.

Loevy, Robert D. *The Flawed Path to the Presidency 1992: Unfairness and Inequality in the Presidential Selection Process*. Albany: State University of New York Press, 1995.

Loewenstein, Karl. *British Cabinet Government*. New York: Oxford University Press, 1967.

Lorant, Stefan. *The Presidency from Washington to Truman*. New York: MacMillan, 1952.

Lowi, Theodore J. *The Personal President: Power Invested, Promise Unfulfilled*. Ithaca, New York: Cornell University Press, 1985.

Lowi, Theodore J., and Benjamin Ginsberg. *Democrats Return to Power*. New York: Norton, 1994.

Lynn, Lawrence E., Jr., and David deF. Whitman. *The President as Policymaker—Jimmy Carter and Welfare Reform*. Philadelphia: Temple University Press, 1981.

Macintosh, John P. *The British Cabinet*. 2nd ed. London: Stevens, 1968.

Mackenzie, G. Calvin, ed. *The Insiders and Outsiders*. Baltimore: Johns Hopkins University Press, 1987.

Mackenzie, G. Calvin. *The Politics of Presidential Appointments*. New York: Free Press, 1981.

Magruder, Jeb Stuart. *An American Life*. New York: Atheneum, 1974.

Maisel, L. Sandy. *Parties and Elections in America: The Electoral Process*. New York: Random House, 1987.

Malek, Frederic V. *Washington's Hidden Tragedy*. New York: Free Press 1978.

Mann, Thomas E., ed. *A Question of Balance: The President, the Congress and Foreign Policy*. Washington, DC: Brookings Institution, 1990

Mansfield, Harvey C. Jr. *Taming the Prince: The Ambivalence of Modern Executive Power*. Baltimore: Johns Hopkins University Press, 1993.

Marshall, Will, and Martin Chram, eds. *Mandate for Change*. New York: Berkley Books, 1992.

Mayer, William G., ed. *In Pursuit of the White House: How We Choose Our Presidential Nominees*. Chatham, NJ: Chatham House Publishers, 1996.

Mayhew, David R. *Congress, The Electoral Connection*. New Haven, CT: Yale University Press, 1974.

Mazlich, Bruce. *Jimmy Carter: A Character Portrait*. New York: Simon & Schuster, 1979.

Mazo, Earl, and Stephen Hess. *Nixon. A Political Portrait*. New York: Harper, 1967.

Mazo, Earl. *Richard Nixon: A Political and Personal Portrait.* New York: Harper, 1959.

McConnell, Grant. *The Modern Presidency.* New York: St. Martin's, 1967.

McConnell, Grant. *Private Power and American Democracy.* New York: Vintage, 1966.

McDonald, Forrest. *Alexander Hamilton: A Biography.* New York: Norton, 1979.

McDonald, Forrest. *The American Presidency: An Intellectual History.* Lawrence, KS: University Press of Kansas, 1994.

McFarlane, Robert C. *Special Trust.* New York: Cadell and Davies, 1994.

McGinniss, Joe. *The Selling of the President 1968.* New York: Pocket Books, 1969.

Medved, Michael. *The Shadow Presidents.* New York: New York Times Book Co., 1979.

Meese, Edwin, III. *With Reagan: The Inside Story.* Washington, DC: Regnery Gateway, 1992.

Meltsner, Arnold J., ed. *Politics in the Oval Office.* San Francisco: Institute for Contemporary Studies, 1981.

Merry, Henry J. *Five Branch Government.* Urbana: University of Illinois Press, 1980.

Mervin, David. *Ronald Reagan and the American Presidency.* New York: Longman, 1990.

Michaels, Judith E. *The President's Call: Executive Leadership from FDR to George Bush.* Pittsburgh, PA: University of Pittsburgh Press, 1997.

Milkis, Sidney, and Michael Nelson. *The American Presidency: Origins and Development, 1776–1993.* 2nd ed. Washington, DC: Congressional Quarterly, 1994.

Mollenhoff, Clark. *The President Who Failed.* New York: MacMillan, 1980.

Mollenhoff, Clark. *Game Plan for Disaster.* New York: Norton, 1976.

Monsen, R. Joseph, Jr., and Mark W. Cannon. *The Makers of Public Policy: American Power Groups and Their Ideologies.* New York: McGraw-Hill, 1965.

Morris, Richard B., ed. *Encyclopedia of American History.* New York: Harper, 1953.

Morris, Roger. *Richard Milhouse Nixon.* New York: Holt, 1990.

Moynihan, Daniel Patrick. *The Politics of a Guaranteed Income.* New York: Vintage, 1973.

Moynihan, Daniel Patrick. *Maximum Feasible Misunderstanding.* New York: Free Press, 1970.

Muir, William K. *The Bully Pulpit: The Presidential Leadership of Ronald Reagan.* San Francisco: Institute for Contemporary Studies, 1992.

Nachmias, David, ed. *The Practice of Policy Evaluation.* New York: St. Martin's, 1980.

Nachmias, David, and David H. Rosenbloom. *Bureaucratic Government USA.* New York: St. Martin's, 1980.

Nadel, Laurie: *The Great Stream of History: A Biography of Richard M. Nixon.* New York: Maxwell McMillan, 1991.

Nakamura, Robert T., and Frank Smallwood. *The Politics of Policy Implementation.* New York: St. Martin's, 1980.

Nash, Bradley D., ed. *Organizing and Staffing the Presidency.* New York: Center for the Study of the Presidency, 1980.

Nathan, Richard P. *The Administrative Presidency.* New York: Wiley, 1983.

Nathan, Richard P. *The Plot That Failed: Nixon and the Administrative Presidency.* New York: Wiley, 1975.

Nelson, Michael, ed. *Guide to the Presidency*. 2nd ed. Washington, DC: Congressional Quarterly, 1996.

Nelson, Michael, ed. *The Presidency and the Political System*. 4th ed. Washington, DC: Congressional Quarterly, 1995.

Nelson, Michael, ed. *The Presidency from A to Z*. rev. ed. Washington, DC: Congressional Quarterly, 1994.

Nessen, Ron. *It Sure Looks Different from the Inside*. New York: Simon & Schuster, 1978.

Neustadt, Richard E. *Presidential Power and the Modern Presidents: The Politics of Leadership from Roosevelt to Reagan*. New York: Free Press, 1990.

Nixon, Richard M. *In the Arena: A Memoir of Victory, Defeat and Renewal*. New York: Simon & Schuster, 1990.

Nixon, Richard M. *Leaders*. New York: Simon & Schuster, 1990.

Nixon, Richard M. *RN: The Memoirs of Richard Nixon*. New York: Grosset & Dunlap, 1978.

Nixon, Richard M. *Six Crises*. Garden City, NY: Doubleday, 1962.

O'Brien, David M. *Constitutional Law and Politics: Struggle for Power and Governmental Accountability*. vol. 1. 3rd ed. New York: Norton, 1997.

O'Neill, Thomas P., with William Novak. *Man of the House: The Life and Political Memoirs of Speaker Tip O'Neill*. New York: Random House, 1987.

Orman, John. *Comparing Presidential Behavior: Carter, Reagan and the Macho Presidential Style*. New York: Greenwood Press, 1987.

Ornstein, Norman, ed. *President and Congress: Assessing Reagan's First Year*. Washington, DC: American Enterprise Institute, 1982.

Osborne, David, and Ted Gaebler. *Reinventing Government: How the Entrepreneurial Spirit is Transformed in the Public Sector*. Reading, MA: Addison-Wesley, 1992.

Osborne, John. *The Nixon Watch*. New York: Liveright, 1970.

Osborne, John. *The First Two Years of the Nixon Watch*. New York: Liveright, 1971.

Osborne, John. *The Second Year of the Nixon Watch*. New York: Liveright, 1971.

Osborne, John. *The Third Year of the Nixon Watch*. New York: Liveright, 1972.

Osborne, John. *The Fourth Year of the Nixon Watch*. New York: Liveright, 1973.

Osborne, John. *The Fifth Year of the Nixon Watch*. New York: Liveright, 1974.

Osborne, John. *The Last Nixon Watch*. Washington: Republic Books, 1975.

Owen, Henry, and Charles L. Schultzer, ed. *Setting National Priorities: The Next Ten Years*. Washington, DC: Brookings Institution, 1976.

Parmet, Herbert S. *Richard Nixon and His America*. Boston: Little, Brown, 1990.

Patterson, Bradley H., Jr. *The President's Cabinet*. Washington, DC: American Society for Public Administration, 1976.

Patterson, Bradley H., Jr. *The Ring of Power: The White House Staff and Its Expanding Role in Government*. New York: Basic, 1988.

Patterson, Thomas. *We The People*. New York: Norton, 1997.

Peabody, Robert L. *Leadership in Congress*. Boston: Little, Brown, 1976.

Peltason, J.W. *Understanding the Constitution*. 14th ed. Fort Worth, TX: Harcourt Brace, 1997.

Peterson, Mark A. *Legislating Together: The White House and Capitol Hill from Eisenhower to Reagan*. Cambridge, MA: Harvard University Press, 1990.

Pfiffner, James P. *The Modern Presidency*. New York: St. Martin's, 1994.

Pfiffner, James P. *The Strategic Presidency*. Chicago, IL: Dorsey, 1988.

Pfiffner, James P. and Roger H. Davidson, eds. *Understanding the Presidency*. New York: Longman, 1997.

Phillips, Cabell. *The Truman Presidency*. New York: Penguin, 1966.

Pious, Richard. *The Presidency*. Needham Heights, MA: Allyn and Bacon, 1996.

Podhoretz, John. *Hell of a Ride*. New York: Simon & Schuster, 1993.

Polsby, Nelson. *Congress and the Presidency*. 4th ed. Englewood Cliffs, NJ: Prentice-Hall, 1986.

Polsby, Nelson, and Wildavsky, Aaron. *Presidential Elections*. 8th ed. New York: Free Press, 1991.

Pomper, Gerald M. *The Election of 1996*. Chatham, NJ: Chatham House, 1997.

Porter, Roger B. *Presidential Decision-Making: The Economic Policy Board*. Cambridge, England: Cambridge University Press, 1980.

Powell, Jody. *The Other Side of the Story*. New York: Morrow, 1984.

Powers of the Presidency. 2nd ed. Washington, DC: Congressional Quarterly, 1997.

President Bush: The Challenge Ahead. Washington, DC: Congressional Quarterly, 1989.

Price, Don K., and Rocco C. Siciliano. *A Presidency for the 1980's*. Washington, DC: National Academy for Public Administration, 1980.

Price, Raymond. *With Nixon*. New York: Viking, 1977.

Purcell, Edward, ed. *The Vice Presidents*. New York: Facts on File, 1998.

Ragsdale, Lyn. "Disconnected Politics: Public Opinion And Presidents. In: Barbara Norrander and Clyde Wilcox, eds. *Understanding Public Opinion*. Washington, DC: Congressional Quarterly, 1997.

Ragsdale, Lyn. *Vital Statistics on the Presidency: Washington to Clinton*. Washington, DC: Congressional Quarterly, 1996.

Rather, Dan, and Gary Paul Gates. *The Palace Guard*. New York: Warner Paperback, 1975.

Reagan, Nancy. *My Turn: The Memoirs of Nancy Reagan*. New York: Random House, 1989.

Reagan, Ronald. *An American Life: Ronald Reagan: An Autobiography*. New York: Simon & Schuster, 1990.

Rector, Robert, and Michael Sanera, eds. *Steering the Elephant: How Washington Works*. New York: Universe, 1987.

Redford, Emmette S., and Richard T. McCulley. *White House Operations: The Johnson Presidency*. Austin, TX: University of Texas Press, 1986.

Reedy, George E. *The Twilight of the Presidency*. New York: World Publishing, 1970.

Reeves, Richard. *A Ford, Not a Lincoln*. New York: Harcourt Brace Jovanovich, 1975.

Reeves, Richard. *President Kennedy: Profile of Power*. New York: Simon & Schuster, 1993.

Regan, Donald. *For the Record*. New York: Harcourt Brace Jovanovich, 1988.

Reichley, A. James. *Conservatives in An Age of Change: The Nixon and Ford Administrations*. Washington, DC: Brookings Institution, 1981.

Relyea, Harold C. *The Presidency and Information Policy*. New York: Center for the Study of the Presidency, 1981.

Relyea, Harold C. *The Executive Office of the President: A Historical, Biographical, and Bibliographical Guide*. Westport, CT: Greenwood Press, 1997.

Renshon, Stanley A., ed. *The Clinton Presidency: Campaigning, Governing, and the Psychology of Leadership*. Boulder, CO: Westview, 1995.

Riccards, Michael P., ed. *The Ferocious Engine of Democracy*. vols. 1 and 2. Lanham, MD: Madison, 1995.

Richardson, Elliot. *The Creative Balance*. New York: Holt, Rinehart and Winston, 1976.

Roberts, Charles, ed. *Has the President Too Much Power?* New York: Harpers Magazine Press, 1973.

Rockman, Bert A. *The Leadership Question: The Presidency and the Political System*. New York: Praeger, 1984.

Roosevelt, Theodore. *An Autobiography*. New York: MacMillan, 1913.

Rose, Richard. *Managing Presidential Objectives*. New York: Free Press, 1976.

Rose, Richard. *The Postmodern President: The White House Meets the World*. 2nd ed. Chatham, NJ: Chatham House, 1991.

Rosenbaum, Herbert D. *The Presidency and Domestic Policies of Jimmy Carter*. Westport, CT: Greenwood Press, 1994.

Rossiter, Clinton. *The American Presidency*. 2nd ed. New York: Time, 1960.

Rourke, Francis E. *Bureaucracy, Politics, and Public Policy*. 3rd ed. Boston: Little, Brown, 1984.

Rozell, Mark J. *Executive Privilege: The Dilemma of Secrecy and Democratic Accountability*. Baltimore: Johns Hopkins University Press, 1994.

Rozell, Mark J. *The Press and the Bush Presidency*. Westport, CT: Greenwood Press, 1996.

Sabine, George H. *A History of Political Theory*. 3rd ed. New York: Holt, Rinehart and Winston, 1961.

Safire, William. *Before the Fall: An Inside View of the Pre-Watergate White House*. Garden City, NY: Doubleday, 1975.

Salaman, Lester M., and Michael L. Lund, ed. *The Reagan Presidency and the Governing of America*. Washington, DC: Urban Institute Press, 1986.

Sander, Alfred D. *A Staff for the President: The Executive Office 1921–1952*. Westport, CT: Greenwood Press, 1989.

Sarkesian, Sam. *Defense Policy and the Presidency: Carter's First Years*. Boulder, CO: Westview, 1979.

Savage, David G. *Turning Right: The Making of the Rehnquist Court*. New York: Wiley, 1992.

Schaller, Michael. *Reckoning with Reagan: America and Its President in the 1980s*. New York: Oxford University Press, 1992.

Schapsmeier, Edward L. *Gerald R. Ford's Date with Destiny: A Political Biography*. New York: Lang, 1989.

Schick, Allen. *The Capacity to Budget*. Washington, DC: Urban Institute Press, 1990.

Schlesinger, Arthur M., Jr. *A Thousand Days*. Boston: Houghton Mifflin, 1965.

Schlesinger, Arthur M., Jr. *The Age of Jackson*. New York: Book Find Club, 1945.

Schlesinger, Arthur M., Jr. *The Imperial Presidency*. Boston: Houghton Mifflin, 1973, revised 1989.

Schoenebaum, Eleanora W. *Profiles of an Era: The Nixon/Ford Years*. New York: Harcourt Brace Jovanovich, 1979.

Seidman, Harold. *Politics, Position, and Power*. New York: Oxford University Press, 1970.

Seligman, Lester, and Cary R. Covington. *The Coalitional Presidency*. Pacific Grove, CA: Brooks/Cole, 1989.

Shapiro, Robert Y. "Public Opinion and Policy Making." In: Robert Shapiro and Lawrence R. Jacobs, eds. *Public Opinion*. Boulder, CO: Westview, 1999.

Sheehan, Neil. *The Pentagon Papers*. New York: Bantam, 1971.

Sheffer, Martin S. *Presidential Power: Case Studies in the Use of the Opinions of the Attorney General*. Lanham, MD: University Press of America, 1991.

Shogan, Robert. *Promises to Keep*. New York: Crowell, 1977.

Shull, Steven A., ed. *The Two Presidencies: A Quarter Century Assessment*. Chicago: Nelson-Hall, 1991.

Shultz, George. *Turmoil and Triumph*. New York: MacMillan, 1993.

Smallwood, Frank. *The Other Candidates: Third Parties in Presidential Elections*. Hanover, NH: published for Dartmouth College by the University Press of New England, 1983.

Sorensen, Theodore C. *Decision-Making in the White House*. New York: Columbia University Press, 1963.

Speakes, Larry. *Speaking Out: The Reagan Presidency from Inside the White House*. New York: Scribner, 1988.

Stanley, David T., Dean E. Mann, and Jameson W. Doig. *Men Who Govern*. Washington, DC: Brookings Institution, 1967.

Stanley, Harold W., and Richard G. Niemei. *Vital Statistics in American Politics*. 4th ed. Washington, DC: Congressional Quarterly, 1994.

Statistical Abstract of the United States 1997. Washington, DC: Government Printing Office, 1997.

Stockman, David. *The Triumph of Politics: The Inside Story of the Reagan Revolution*. New York: Avon, 1986.

Strober, Deborah Hart, and Gerald S. Strober. *Nixon as President: An Oral History*. New York: HarperCollins, 1994.

Stroup, Lawrence. *The Carter Presidency and Beyond*. Palo Alto, CA: Ramparts Press, 1980.

Stuckey, Mary E. *The President as Interpreter in Chief*. Chatham, NJ: Chatham House, 1991.

Study of the 1960–61 Presidential Transition. Washington, DC: Brookings Institution, November 11, 1960.

Sundquist, James L. *Politics and Policy: The Eisenhower, Kennedy and Johnson Years*. Washington, DC: Brookings Institution, 1968.

Swerdlow, Joel L., ed. *Presidential Debates 1988 and Beyond*. Washington, DC: Congressional Quarterly, 1987.

Szanton, Peter, ed. *Federal Reorganization*. Chatham, NJ: Chatham House, 1981.

Taft, William Howard. *Our Chief Magistrate and His Powers*. New York: Columbia University Press, 1916.

Tatolovich, Raymond, and Byron W. Daynes. *Presidential Power in the United States*. Monterey, CA: Brooks/Cole, 1984.

Tatolovich, Raymond, Byron W. Daynes, and Dennis L. Soden. *To Govern a Nation: Presidential Power and Politics.* New York: St. Martin's, 1998

Tebbel, John, and Sarah Miles Watts. *The Press and the Presidency: From George Washington to Ronald Reagan.* New York: Oxford University Press, 1985.

TerHorst, Jerald F. *Gerald Ford and the Future of the Presidency.* New York: Third Press, 1974.

Thomas, Norman C., and Joseph A. Pika. *The Politics of the Presidency.* 4th rev. ed. Washington, DC: Congressional Quarterly, 1997.

Thompson, Kenneth. *Choosing and Using Vice Presidents: A Report of the Sixth Miller Center Commission,* chaired by Senator Edmund S. Muskie and Senator Charles Mathias, Jr. No date listed.

Thompson, Kenneth W., ed. *The Ford Presidency: Twenty-Two Intimate Perspectives of Gerald Ford.* Lanham, MD: University Press of America, 1988.

Thompson, Kenneth W., ed. *The Carter Presidency: 14 Intimate Perspectives of Jimmy Carter.* Lanham, MD: University Press of America, 1990.

Thompson, Kenneth W., ed. *The Nixon Presidency: Twenty-Two Intimate Perspectives of Richard M. Nixon.* Lanham, MD: University Press of America, 1987.

Thompson, Kenneth W., ed. *Leadership in the Reagan Presidency: Seven Intimate Perspectives.* Lanham, MD: University Press of America, 1992.

Tourtellot, Arthur Bernon. *The Presidents on the Presidency.* Garden City, NY: Doubleday, 1964.

Tower, John, Edmund Muskie, and Brent Scowcroft. *The Tower Commission Report: The Full Text of the President's Special Review Board.* New York: Random House, 1987.

Townsend, Malcolm. *Handbook of United States Political History.* rev. ed. Boston: Lothrop, Lee and Shepard, 1905, 1910.

Tramell, Jeffrey, and Gary P. Oscifchin. *The Clinton 500: The New Team Running America 1994.* Washington, DC: Almanac, 1994.

Travis, Walter Earl, ed. *Congress and the President.* New York: Teachers College Press, Columbia University, 1967.

Truman, David B. *The Governmental Process.* 2nd ed. New York: Knopf, 1971.

Truman, Harry S *Memoirs. 1945: Year of Decision.* Garden City, NY: Doubleday, 1955.

Truman, Harry S. *Memoirs: Years of Trial and Hope 1946–52.* New York: Time 1755: Republished by Smithmark 1991.

Truman, Margaret. *Harry S Truman.* New York: Pocket Books, 1974.

Tugwell, Rexford G. and Thomas E. Cronin, ed. *The Presidency Reappraised.* New York: Preger, 1974.

Tugwell, Rexford G. *How They Became President.* New York: Simon & Schuster, 1964.

Tulis, Jeffrey K. *The Rhetorical Presidency.* Princeton, NJ: Princeton University Press, 1987.

Turner, Michael. *The Vice President as Policy Maker.* Westport, CT: Greenwood Press, 1982.

Twentieth Century Fund Task Force on the Vice Presidency. *A Heartbeat Away: Report of the Twentieth Century Task Force on the Vice Presidency.* New York: Priority, 1988.

United States Congress, Debates and Proceedings, First Congress, 1st session, March 3, 1789 to Eighteenth Congress, 1st session, May 27, 1824. 42 vols. Washington, DC: Gales & Seaton, 1834–1856.

United States Congress, Senate, Committee on the Judiciary, Subcommittee on the Separation of Powers. *Executive Privilege: The Withholding of Information by the Executive, Hearings*, 92 Congress 1st session. Washington, DC: Government Printing Office, July 27–29 and August 4–5, 1971.

United States Government Manual, 1939. Washington, DC: Government Printing Office, 1939.

U. S. Bureau of the Census. Statistical abstracts of the United States: 1997. Washington, DC: Government Printing Office, 1997.

Valenti, Jack. *A Very Human President.* New York: Norton, 1975.

Vance, Cyrus. *Hard Choices.* New York: Simon & Schuster, 1983.

Walcott, Charles E., and Karen M. Hult. *Governing the White House from Hoover through LBJ.* Lawrence, KS: University Press of Kansas, 1995.

Waldman, Steven. *The Bill.* New York: Viking, 1995.

Warshaw, Shirley Anne. *The Domestic Presidency: Policy Making in the White House.* Needham Heights, MA: Allyn and Bacon, 1997.

Warshaw, Shirley Anne. ed. *The Eisenhower Legacy.* Silver Spring, MD: Bartleby, 1992.

Warshaw, Shirley Anne. *Powersharing: White House–Cabinet Relations in the Modern Presidency.* Albany, NY: State University of New York Press, 1996.

Warshaw, Shirley Anne, ed. *Reexamining the Eisenhower Presidency.* Westport, CT: Greenwood, 1994.

Waterman, Richard W., ed. *The Presidency Reconsidered.* Itasca, IL: Peacock, 1993.

Watson, Robert A. *Presidential Vetoes and Public Policy.* Lawrence, KS: University Press of Kansas, 1993.

Wayne, Stephen J. *The Legislative Presidency.* New York: Harper, 1978.

Wayne, Stephen J. *The Road to the White House: The Politics of Presidential Elections.* 3rd ed. New York: St. Martin's, 1988.

Wayne, Stephen J. *The Road to the White House 1996.* New York: St Martin's, 1997.

Weinberger, Caspar W. *Fighting for Peace.* New York: Warner, 1990.

Weisbord, Marvin R. *Campaigning for President.* New York: Washington Square Press, 1966.

Weiss, Carol H., and Allen H. Barton, eds. *Making Bureaucracies Work.* Beverly Hills, CA: Sage, 1979.

Wetterau, Bruce. *The Presidential Medal of Freedom: Winners and Their Accomplishments.* Washington, DC: Congressional Quarterly, 1996.

Wheeler, Leslie. *Jimmy Who?* Woodbury, NY: Barrons, 1976.

White, Joseph, and Aaron Wildavsky. *The Deficit and the Public Interest.* Berkeley, CA: University of California Press and Russell Sage Foundation, 1989.

White, Theodore H. *America in Search of Itself.* New York: Harper, 1982.

White, Theodore H. *Breach of Faith.* New York: Dell, 1975.

White, Theodore H. *The Making of the President 1960.* New York: Atheneum, 1961.

White, Theodore H. *The Making of the President 1968.* New York: Atheneum, 1969.

Wills, Garry. *Inventing America: Jefferson's Declaration of Independence.* Garden City, NJ: Doubleday, 1978.

Wills, Garry. *Nixon Antagonists*. New York: New American Library, 1969.

Wills, Garry. *Reagan's America*. New York: Penguin, 1988.

Wilson, James Q., and John J. DiIulio, Jr. *American Government*. 7th ed. New York: Houghton Mifflin, 1998.

Wilson, Woodrow. *Congressional Government*. Baltimore: Johns Hopkins University Press, 1981 (first published in 1885).

Wilson, Woodrow. *George Washington*. New York: Schocken, 1969 (first published in 1896).

Winter-Berger, Robert N. *The Gerald Ford Letters*. Seacaucus, NJ: Stuart, 1974.

Wise, Sidney, and Richard F. Schier. *The Presidential Office*. New York: Crowell, 1968.

Witcover, Jules. *Marathon: The Pursuit of the Presidency. 1972–1976*. New York: Viking, 1977.

Witherspoon, Patricia Dennis. *Within These Walls: A Study of Communication Between Presidents and Their Senior Staffs*. New York: Praeger, 1991.

Witt, Elder, ed. *Congressional Quarterly's Guide to the U.S. Supreme Court*. Washington, DC: Congressional Quarterly, 1979.

Wolanin, Thomas R. *Presidential Advisory Commissions: Truman to Nixon*. Madison: University of Wisconsin Press, 1975.

Woll, Peter. *American Bureaucracy*. 2nd ed. New York: Norton, 1977.

Woodward, Bob. *The Commanders*. New York: Simon & Schuster, 1991.

Woodward, Bob. *The Agenda: Inside the Clinton White House*. New York: Simon & Schuster, 1994.

Wooten, James. *Dasher*. New York: Summit, 1978.

Young, Donald. *American Roulette: The History and Dilemma of the Vice Presidency*. New York: Holt, Rinehart and Winston, 1965.

INDEX